1978

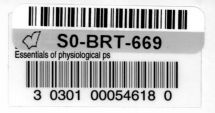

Essentials of
physiological psychology

Essentials of
physiological psychology

Francis Leukel, Ph.D.

Professor of Psychology, San Diego State University,
San Diego, California

with 99 illustrations

The C. V. Mosby Company

Saint Louis   1978

Printed in the United States of America

Distributed in Great Britain by Henry Kimpton, London

The C. V. Mosby Company
11830 Westline Industrial Drive, St. Louis, Missouri   63141

Library of Congress Cataloging in Publication Data

Leukel, Francis.
  Essentials of physiological psychology.

  Based on the author's Introduction to physiological
psychology.
  Bibliography: p.
  Includes index.
  1. Psychology, Physiological.   I.   Title.
[DNLM: 1. Psychophysiology. WL102 L652i]
QP360.L47   152   77-13153
ISBN 0-8016-2994-2

VT/CB/CB   9   8   7   6   5   4   3   2   1

Preface

On a recent sabbatical leave, I spent a year traveling the United States and Canada visiting colleges and universities. My purposes were to acquaint myself with the research in progress in the field of physiological psychology and to talk with professors who use my book, *Introduction to Physiological Psychology*. In soliciting comments on how the book could be improved, a common complaint was that the book contained too much information. I pointed out that many of the chapters were independent of one another, selected chapters could be omitted in a briefer course, and the readings at the end of each chapter could be used to expand other chapters. Many professors who do not specialize in physiological psychology responded that they did not feel knowledgeable enough to make such a selection and asked me to help them in this regard. They also expressed a desire to cover each major topic in the book but to use only the most important material. I finally concluded that the best way to help them was to write a briefer version of the book.

Since I received few complaints about how understandable the text was for the student, I decided that much of the task could be an editing job. As it turned out, a great deal of the text material in *Essentials of Physiological Psychology* was taken from *Introduction to Physiological Psychology*, coming primarily from chapters on the senses and consciousness, motivation, emotion,

learning, and stress. The background material on physiology, the endocrine glands, and the nervous system was condensed and largely rewritten in that process. Condensing and selecting all of this material forced an improvement in the organization of the book. Specifically, the most essential topics from a chapter on the endocrine glands were included in Chapter 2 on the internal environment. Material from a chapter on brain dynamics was integrated with Chapter 3 on the nervous system. Finally, chapters on motor organization and nerve and muscle tissue were condensed to form Chapter 4 on organizing movement. New terms were added to the glossary.

Putting together a briefer text between revisions of the larger book gave me an unusual opportunity to include new research findings that have appeared since publication of the third edition of *Introduction to Physiological Psychology*. I have also included still unpublished material gleaned from travels during my sabbatical leave. Samples of new material include the relation of brain endorphins to pain and schizophrenia, a new theory of brain functions in "dreaming" sleep (McCarley and Hobson), the Stanford clinic studies of sleep disorders, a sleep "hormone" in the cerebrospinal fluid of animals (Pappenheimer), brain-wave studies of biofeedback and the "alpha experience" in meditation, more discoveries concerning hemispheric specialization, stomach versus intestinal cues in food motivation, retro-active amnesia in memory over periods of years, studies of the "poisoned bait response," and the neotropic drugs that seem to improve verbal learning in humans.

It was decided to publish the book in a paperback format to reduce its cost to the student, and an instructor's test manual will be supplied to professors to accompany the text. Besides reducing the demands on the overworked professor's time, the students can blame me rather than their professor if they don't like the questions!

Finally, I would like to thank many professors who took time from their busy schedules to welcome me to their laboratories and to make many helpful suggestions that were incorporated in this book. I must thank them en masse—if my memory were equal to the task, listing them all would make this preface far too long. Perhaps it is already too lengthy!

Francis Leukel

Contents

**Essentials of
physiological psychology**

CHAPTER 1

Physiological psychology: its scope

This chapter will define the topic of physiological psychology and explain how it will be treated in the chapters that follow. Like each of the other chapters, this one will begin with an overview to orient the student to the chapter's content and end with a summary so that the main ideas discussed will not be lost in the details of the subject.

OVERVIEW

The topic of physiological psychology will be defined in terms of what a physiological psychologist does in his role as scientist. His approach to the study of behavior emphasizes that behavior is under the control of the brain as it is influenced by stimulus events inside and outside of the body. The methods used in discovering how the brain goes about its business will be summarized, along with the contributions of other sciences to these methods. Broader discussions of the mind-body problem and the implications of discoveries in physiological psychology conclude the chapter.

DEFINITIONAL PROBLEMS

What is a physiological psychologist? This introduction will take the rather hard-headed approach that a physiological psychologist *is* what he *does*, at least in his scientific and professional role. To find out what physiological psychology is, therefore, we should look at the scientific behavior of physiological psychologists and

also find out what assumptions are behind the behavior of most of them. Then, perhaps, we will have some idea of what physiological psychology can teach us and what it cannot teach us. What is the subject matter and what do we know about it? This chapter will try to define the subject matter, and the rest of the book will sample some of the most important things we know. At the same time, the rest of the book will point out a lot of things we do not know. It turns out that we know many interesting things, but they are few in number as compared with the things we do not know.

SCIENTIFIC APPROACH TO BEHAVIOR

In the first place, a physiological psychologist is a psychologist, and psychology is usually defined as the scientific study of behavior. This means that the psychologist is more interested in behavior than anything else he could study. But isn't this also true of many other occupations? Salesmen, policemen, lawyers, politicians, and many others concern themselves most of the time with human behavior—from buying to law breaking to voting to other human actions. For that matter, we are all interested in human behavior—ours and that of other people.

The catch comes in the word "scientific." Science is an approach to observation and explanation—in this case behavior is the subject—that differs in some important ways from nonscientific observation and explanation. Salesmen, policemen, lawyers, and politicians are interested in understanding enough about why people act as they do in order to accomplish *purpose*—whether that goal is effecting law-abiding behavior or voting for a particular candidate. Once the desired end is accomplished, the limits of their interest have been reached. Psychologists (in their scientific role) seek to understand behavior in order to understand behavior rather than to change people's actions to suit their personal desires. They change stimulus situations and observe changes in responses in order to relate behavioral events to one another so they can predict what will happen next time. A psychologist interested in learning responses might change the length of a list of words to be memorized by his subjects to see if adding each word added an equal amount of study time for his subjects. He wants to find out for the sake of finding out. This is an approach in which the stimulus situation (length of list) is varied to observe the effect on behavioral response (learning time). (The length of list is called the independent variable because it is changed in a way that is independent of whatever else is going on; the learning time is the dependent variable because response change depends on stimulus change.)

PHYSIOLOGICAL APPROACH TO BEHAVIOR

The physiological psychologist introduces a new set of elements into the scheme just given. He wants to know what events inside the body have to do with changes in behavior. His is, therefore, an approach that emphasizes the events occurring in the body, particularly the nervous system. In this sense, the independent variable may be an outside stimulus like changing a learning task or a change inside of the body—the effect of the increase in "blood sugar" that results from an injection of glucose on later eating behavior.

All of this is an oversimplification, of course. If a physiological psychologist

studies changes with age in the electrical activity of the brain, for example, the "variable" of age includes an infinite variety of experiences, the events in the body include at least as many related and unrelated changes in the brain over time, and the electrical symptoms of brain activity include millions of events going on in the brain, many of which are unrelated to age.

The complex nature of the topic does not, however, alter the fundamental assumption that the physiological psychologist makes: *behavior is under the control of events in the brain as they are affected by stimulus events that occur both inside and outside of the body.*

Methods

There are a number of ways to classify the techniques used by physiological psychologists. Regardless of the classification scheme used, it is important to realize that the information gathered is limited by the sophistication of methods for studying the brain and the accuracy of the measurements used. In comparison with the awesome complexity of a brain that may contain 10 billion living cells (in humans) our tools for manipulation and measurement are crude, indeed. We can categorize them under five headings: (1) **stimulation,** (2) **recording,** (3) **ablation,** (4) **anatomical methods,** and (5) **clinical methods.**

Stimulation. Stimulation includes any method of activating the nervous system, whether or not a change in behavior results. In studying the sense organs, their "normal" stimuli may be used to send sensory information to the brain—light for the eye or sound for the ear, for example. In testing the way the sensory information is "coded" for transmission to the brain it is often useful to stimulate the nerves going from the sense organs to the brain or even stimulate the brain itself. Small electrical currents are used because they resemble the electrical activity that can be detected in the sensory nerve cells and brain during their normal activity. Because nerve cells signal each other by releasing small amounts of chemicals, chemical stimuli are often used when the nature is known (tiny tubes are used to deliver the stimulus). Sometimes electrical stimuli are used in an anesthetized animal when much of the brain must be surgically exposed to detect where the nerve impulses go. (Human subjects seldom volunteer for this procedure!) In other cases, stimulating electrodes are precisely placed in different parts of the brain and led to a "plug" cemented to the animal's skull. After recovery, these animals can be "plugged in" and the brain can be stimulated in a known way while they are behaving normally. There are even techniques for attaching the electrodes to an FM radio receiver in the animal's skull and stimulating the brain with an FM transmitter from a distance.

Recording. In general, the term recording means any means of detecting and making a record of behavior or brain activity. Most frequently in physiological psychology, it means detecting and making a record of the electrical activity of the sense organs, nervous system, or responding muscles and glands. The electrodes referred to in the preceding paragraph may be used to detect the electrical activity going on at their locations in the brain. In the normal human subject, electrodes are frequently "pasted" on the skull for crude detection of brain activity conducted through the skull (the EEG or "brain waves") or on the skin over muscles to detect the electrical symptoms of their activity. Sometimes the chemical changes that accompany activity in different parts of the brain can be "sampled" through small tubes implanted at those locations. For electrical signal detection the electrodes can be "plugged in" during normal behavior as previously noted, or broadcast from a radio transmitter (telemetry) attached to the animal's skull to a receiver at a remote location.

Ablation. A part of the brain or a gland (Chapter 2) can be surgically removed and the animal's behavior systematically observed after he recovers. Any change in behavior such as sensory impairment, emotionality, and so on can be attributed to loss of the functions of the part removed. There are many chances for error in this kind of inference because of the way parts of the brain (and glands) interact. These errors will be discussed as the occasion arises.

Anatomical methods. To confirm where a stimulating or recording electrode was placed in the brain or to find out exactly what brain tissue was ablated, the animal's brain must be studied after the experiment is over. The animal is killed, the brain hardened and removed by special techniques, and then cut into thin slices for study under the microscope.

Clinical methods. It should be evident from the methods described so far that most of them cannot be used with normal human subjects! The techniques described have taught us much about the control of behavior by the sense organs, glands, and brain in typical laboratory animals such as the rat, the cat, and the monkey. The brain of man and, therefore, the behavior of man is much more complex, and results obtained from laboratory animals cannot be applied with certainty to man. Man's brain must be studied on a case-by-case basis as it becomes damaged in auto accidents or war injuries, or if it is exposed for necessary surgery (to remove a brain tumor, for example). Subjects suffering accidental brain damage can be given a number of tests to study changes in their behavior—coordination, intelligence, emotionality, and so on. The exposed brain of a surgical patient must be systematically stimulated to "map" sensory, motor, and other areas to plan surgical strategy. The patient is conscious so he can report his sensations and thoughts, and motor responses can be observed. However, the exact site of the stimulation is unknown and so is the extent of the brain damage unless the patient dies and his brain can be studied by anatomical methods (see above). When persons with brain damage die at some later time and their brains become available for study, the lesions are seldom exactly where we would like them to be for the most profitable study, and changes occur between the time of injury and the time of death (often years later).

Scope. The methodology section should not be concluded without pointing out the number of scientific fields with which the physiological psychologist must have some acquaintance. He must know something of the *anatomy* of the nervous system, glands, and muscles. *Biochemistry,* or the chemical reactions of living cells, must be mastered to some degree in order to understand how the brain functions. *Physiology* teaches him how the cells, organs, and systems of the body function for application to behavior. Some knowledge of *electronics* is needed, because the tiny electrical signals of brain activity are amplified and transmitted by electronic means in recording brain activity. Specialists in these fields study them for their own sake. The physiological psychologist masters only those aspects of the other areas that aid him in his attempt to understand behavior in physiological terms.

MIND-BODY PROBLEM

One of the oldest questions in philosophy is the relationship between thought and action—the subjective "mental events" we all experience and the overt behavior we can observe in ourselves and others. This is an oversimplified statement of the mind-body problem. The problem arises in physiological psychology because we depend on the subjective reports of our human subjects as well as on observations of human and animal behavior and the record of electrical and chemical events in the sense organs and brain for our information. Subjective reports are used, for example, when we are trying to establish the response limits of the human eye. What is the least intense light that can be detected by the human subject? is a sample question. The simplest way to find out is to ask the human subject while we vary the light intensity in a systematic and controlled fashion. However, only the subject can directly observe his own perception of

the light. The experimenter cannot "look inside the subject's head" and confirm the information. Yet scientific information is supposed to be "public" rather than "private," that is, subject to direct observation by a number of observers. This approach —the method of **introspection**—is therefore less reliable than direct observation or than electronic recording of the electrical responses of the sense organ, sensory nerves, or brain—the method of **evoked potentials.** All we can do is to dodge the issue, while recognizing that it exists. If the introspective reports of our human subjects agree with one another reasonably well, we assume they are reliable. However, the sense organs and brain go about their business using an electrochemical code, and we can understand that code only by electrochemical means that are not revealed by subjective reports.

The relationship between thought and actions have another aspect. We find that damage to the human brain or electrical stimulation of that immensely complex organ causes profound and largely unpredictable changes in the individual's reported subjective experience as well as in his intellectual and emotional behavior. A number of mood-altering drugs have equally extensive effects. Treatments of these kinds have been given to pschotic patients and to persons with homicidal mania and severe anxiety (see Chapter 15). What are the relationships between chemical and electrical activity in various parts of the brain and subjective experience? We are just beginning to answer these kinds of questions, but many think that study of the way in which the brain governs experience and behavior is our last great scientific frontier. Compared to what we know about matter, what we know about mind is miniscule indeed! To quote Dr. Robert W. Doty,* "Study of the brain is unique in its direct relation to the nature of human ex-

---

*Doty, R. W.: The brain. In Brittanica yearbook of science and the future, Chicago, 1970, Encyclopedia Brittanica, Inc.

perience. Nuclear physicists and cosmologists probe the universe for meaning but the constructs which they achieve can never extend beyond those possible in the processes intrinsic to the brain. In this respect study of the brain is the ultimate science."

IMPLICATIONS FOR THE FUTURE OF HUMANITY

Granting that the structure and function of the brain sets limits on the extent of human knowledge, what implications do our findings in physiological psychology have for society? This is not the kind of question a physiological psychologist asks in his role as a scientist where his only "purpose" is supposed to be discovering how the brain governs behavior. Some tentative answers to the question, however, may motivate the student to study the subject just as they motivate the scientist to continue his complex task.

It has been suggested that the last scientific century was the century of the physical sciences and that we are now entering the century of the biological sciences. The work of many physicists on the nature of matter and energy has culminated in atomic fission and fusion with implications ranging from an unlimited source of energy to the explosive extinction of the human race. The biological century can be said to have opened with the discoveries of Watson and Crick on the physical basis of inheritance and the metabolic control of life; the work of Hess on implanting electrodes in the brain; the discovery of Olds of brain centers whose stimulation leads to "pleasure" and "anxiety"; remote control (radio) stimulation (Delgado); the effects of environment on brain biochemistry and behavior; the transfer of learning by biochemical means; and altered brain biochemistry in psychosis. The list of important discoveries during the last 20 years is a long one, and these are only selected examples. The social implications include engineering or altering our inheritance for desired human characteristics, improving

our ability to learn, increasing our intelligence, controlling the behavior of others against their "will," altering personality and temperament by surgical or biochemical methods, curing psychosis, and increasing or decreasing human aggressiveness and motivations that can lead to war or to scientific discovery. It is early in the biological century, and the applications of these and other discoveries are only beginning to emerge. Many believe, however, that human curiosity will lead to the realization of these and other changes in society if the race survives.

Understanding these and other exciting scientific discoveries requires first an understanding of some of the sciences upon which physiological psychology rests. Accordingly, the book begins with the study of the basic physiology and biochemistry of the body and the anatomy of the nervous system. Then the senses through which the brain processes its information are considered. After mastery of these fundamentals (of interest to many for their own sake), the larger questions of consciousness, motivation, emotion, learning, and stress can be considered. Like the scientist, the student must begin at the beginning.

SUMMARY

The field of physiological psychology can be defined in terms of what a physiological psychologist does in his scientific role. As psychologist and therefore as a scientist, he is interested in the objective study of behavior for its own sake rather than in understanding only enough to influence the behavior of others as the nonscientist intends. As a physiological psychologist he assumes that behavior is under the control of the brain as it is influenced by stimulus events inside and outside of the body. In studying the brain, he uses the methods of stimulation, recording, ablation, anatomical methods, and clinical methods. As a result, he borrows from other fields of knowledge: anatomy, biochemistry, physiology, and electronics, for example.

His study involves him in the mind-body problem—the philosophical question of the relationship between subjective "mental events" and objective observations of behavior, and electrical events in the sense organs and brain because he often uses the method of introspection. He is aware, however, that the method of evoked potentials is more productive because it involves study of the brain on its own electrical and biochemical terms.

Study of the brain may be the ultimate science because all human understanding is limited to intrinsic brain processes. The social implications of the biological discoveries of recent years range from genetic engineering to altering intelligence, personality, or temperament. Before these topics can be understood, however, basic anatomy, physiology, and sensory processes must be studied.

READINGS

Delgado, J. M. R.: Physical control of the mind, New York, 1969, Harper & Row, Publishers.

Fletcher, J.: The ethics of genetic control: ending reproductive roulette, Garden City, N.Y., 1974, Doubleday & Company, Inc.

Fuller, W., editor: The biological revolution: social good or social evil, Garden City, N.Y., 1972, Doubleday & Company, Inc.

Goldsmith, M., and McKay, A., editors: Science and society, New York, 1964, Simon & Schuster, Inc.

McCain, G., and Segal, M.: The game of science, Belmont, Calif., 1969, Brooks/Cole Publishing Company.

Singh, D., and Avery, D.: Physiological techniques in behavioral research, Monterey, Calif., 1974, Brooks/Cole Publishing Company.

Skinner, J. E.: Neuroscience: a laboratory manual, Philadelphia, 1971, W. B. Saunders Company.

CHAPTER 2

The internal environment: the sea within us

OVERVIEW

To begin at the beginning we must understand what life *is* before we can understand how life processes lead to behavior. The most universal functions of life are illustrated by the single cell, followed by the organization of cells into tissues, organs, and systems. This organization is furthered by the nervous system and endocrine glands as they function in maintaining the consistency of the liquid internal environment required by specialized cells. The chemical reactions that maintain life (metabolism) will be explored—from the dietary essentials to energy exchange. The genetic code, by means of which cells reproduce themselves and carry on metabolism, will be explained. The chapter closes with a section on the endocrine glands.

THE CELL AS THE UNIT OF LIFE

What is life, and what constitutes the simplest living organism? Life can be viewed as a complex of chemical reactions and the defining feature of a living organism as the ability to reproduce itself. Viewed in this way, a virus cannot be defined as the simplest form of life. A virus is a complex molecule of **DNA** (deoxyribonucleic acid) or **RNA** (ribonucleic acid) with a protein coat. However, the virus must "borrow" the apparatus of the **cell** to reproduce itself by entering the cell to reproduce its DNA or RNA molecules, destroying the cell in the process (and causing many human diseases thereby!). The cell, however, is the simplest form of life that can independently reproduce itself without depending on other cells, and therefore the cell qualifies as the simplest form of life.

Parts of the cell and their functions

Fig. 2-1 is a simplified diagram of an independent living cell and includes labels of its major parts. Each part of the cell has some role or roles in carrying out the self-perpetrating series of chemical reactions that constitute life.

Cell membrane. The *cell membrane* separates the cell from its fluid environment—usually fresh water (lakes) or salt water (oceans) in single-celled organisms. The cell membrane is responsible for two properties of living organisms: **irritability** and **conduction.** If you were to prod the single cell with a tiny glass rod (the cell is microscopic in size), it would change shape to avoid the stimulus. The cell is therefore irritable (responds to stimuli), and it conducts excitation from the stimulus site to other parts, since the whole cell changes shape. Both of these properties are characteristics of the cell membrane; the chemical reactions underlying irritability and conduction have elec-

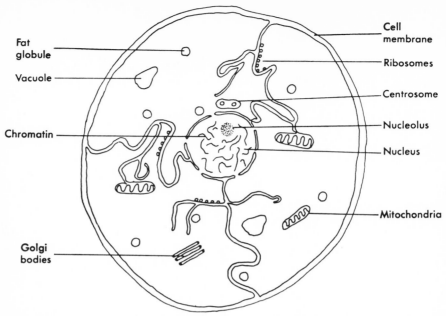

Fig. 2-1. Single cell. Semidiagrammatic sketch of a single-celled organism, showing some of its major features.

trical symptoms that can be detected at the surface of the membrane. In animals (including humans) the cells that have specialized most in irritability are found in the sense organs; cells that specialize in conduction make up the nervous system.

Inclusions. Several complex parts of the cell lie outside the nucleus but inside the cell membrane. Examples in Fig. 2-1 are mitochondria, Golgi bodies, and ribosomes. These and other specialized structures lie in the **cytoplasm,** the liquid of the cell outside of the nucleus. Some of these **inclusions** are responsible for **contraction** and others for **secretion,** the only two responses possible for the cell (or for humans, for that matter). Contraction is seen when the cell changes shape in response to prodding with a glass rod in the example given above. The muscles of the human body are made up, in part, of cells that are specialized in this way: we contract muscles by changing the shape of muscle cells. Secretion occurs when other inclusions manufacture chemicals needed by the cell and release them into the cytoplasm. Cells spe-

cialized for this function in humans form the secreting cells of glands and produce secretions that affect other cells.

Nucleus. Parts of the nucleus of the cell direct its metabolism (see below) and **reproduction.** The DNA molecules of the nucleus of the cell direct (in a way to be described later) every chemical reaction that goes on in the cell; the sum of these reactions falls under the rubric of **metabolism.** Reproduction occurs when the cell reaches a limiting size and divides to form two cells. Each part of the cell divides, including the nucleus. Within the cell nucleus, each DNA molecule divides, the half-molecules forming a pattern on which the missing components are reassembled in the nucleus of the new cell. Reproduction in humans is a much more complex process; however, it is based in part on this same sort of cell division. Reproduction in humans will be discussed in a later section.

How cells specialize

The independent living cell we have just discussed must carry out all of the functions of life on its own, including irritability, conduction, contraction, secretion, and reproduction. In a many-celled or multicellular organism like a human being, each cell *specializes* in performing one life function at the expense of its ability to carry on the other functions of life. The specialized cell depends on other cells for support in those life functions it has given up to some degree. A muscle cell, for example, has become specialized for contraction or changing shape. It has elongated, and the inclusions responsible for changing the shape of the cell (the myofibrils) have become more prominent. As a result, the cell cannot carry on the other life functions as well as the independent all-purpose cell. The muscle cell cannot break down basic foodstuffs from its fluid environment and must be "fed" blood glucose, predigested from food by other cells and delivered to the muscles by the circulatory system. As another example, heart and nerve cells have become so specialized that they cannot reproduce themselves, and the damage from heart attacks and brain injuries is permanent as a result.

Tissues. A **tissue** is a group of cells that are specialized in a similar way to perform a common function. All of the cells of muscle tissue are specialized in the same general way for contraction—they look alike and contract in the same fashion. (There are some differences in the muscle tissue of body muscles, heart muscles, and visceral muscles—further specializations that will be discussed in Chapter 4.) Cells that specialize for irritability form receptor tissue and further specialize according to the form of energy they react to best. Examples are the reaction of receptor tissue of the eye to light and of the ear to sound. Nerve tissue is specialized for conduction, and glandular tissue for secretion. The sperm and ova of men and women are reproductive tissue. There are other kinds of specialized cells that form tissue to perform functions we have not mentioned—connective tissue that holds parts of the body together, vascular tissue in the blood

vessels, and so on. Name a function necessary to life in the complex many-celled human, and a group of specialized cells have formed tissue to support that function.

Organs. An organ is a collection of differently specialized tissues that are organized for the performance of a common general function. It represents an increase in the specialization of each tissue and an increase in the dependence of the differently specialized tissues on each other. For example, the stomach is a digestive organ. It is made up of connective tissue to hold it together, vascular (blood vessel) tissue to nourish it, glandular tissue for digestive secretions, muscle tissue to mix food and move it to the rest of the digestive tract, and so on. As an organ, the stomach has a role in the digestion of food, and each of its tissues contributes in a different way to the performance of that role. Other examples of organs in the body include the brain (nervous), heart (circulatory), kidney (elimination), eye (receptor), and gonads (reproductive). In each case, differently specialized tissues are integrated to perform a function more efficiently than could a single kind of tissue.

Systems. The highest level of integration in the body for the performance of still more general functions is a system. A system consists of several organs, each having a limited role in the overall performance of the system. For example, the digestive system includes the following organs: salivary glands, esophagus, stomach, intestines, liver, and kidneys. The general function of the system is to assimilate food, transform it to a state the specialized cells of the body can use, store it, and eliminate waste products of the whole process. Each organ has a role in that general function. The esophagus specializes in ingestion, the salivary glands, stomach, and intestines in digestion of different kinds, the liver in storage (of blood sugar), and the kidneys in elimination. The nervous system has nerves to carry excitation to and from receptors and effectors (muscles and glands), brain centers to make "connections" between incoming and outgoing excitation, and so forth. All serve the general function of carrying excitation from one part of the body to another so that response to internal and external events can occur. The circulatory system supplies the cells with nourishment and oxygen and removes waste and carbon dioxide with the heart as a pumping organ, the arteries carrying blood to the cells, the capillaries for local exchange, and veins to return blood to the heart.

HOMEOSTASIS

As cells specialize to carry out one function of life at the expense of their ability to carry out other life functions, two consequences ensue: (1) the cells become more *interdependent,* each kind of tissue depending on other cells, organs, and systems to carry out functions for them that they can no longer perform, and (2) the cells become less able to tolerate changes in their fluid environment—the independent all-purpose cell can tolerate changes in temperature, salinity (saltiness), food and oxygen content, and fluid pressure that would kill the specialized cell. The interdependent cells of the human body survive in the tissue fluid that fills the body only if that **internal environment** is kept within narrow limits of physical and chemical change. Both the interdependence of cells in one part of the body on cells in other parts of the body and the need for a constant internal environment require a high degree of coordination of the activities going on in different parts of the body. That coordination is supplied in three ways: (1) the organization of cells into tissues, organs, and systems coordinates body activities that range from digestion to arranging the nervous system to respond to stimuli; (2) the endocrine glands, as explained in a later section, secrete substances carried by the circulatory system to all parts of the body to regulate the metabolism of widely scattered tissues; and (3) the nervous system itself is capable of or-

ganizing internal and external responses to coordinate widespread cell activity and maintain the consistency of the internal environment.

When cells are organized into tissues, organs, and systems, the many events required to carry out a complex process like digestion occur in proper sequence. Salivary glands in the mouth begin breaking down food into usable form, the stomach mixes, stores, and further digests the result, and the small intestine completes the process and transfers the results in a form the cells can use to the circulatory system. The circulatory system is structured to transport digested food (e.g., blood glucose) to the liver and muscles for storage and to the other cells for use. It also removes waste products secreted by the cells and delivers them to the kidney for disposal. The sequence of events supports the interdependence of cells and maintains the consistency of the internal environment.

The endocrine glands of the body secrete their output directly into the tissue fluid as **hormones,** or chemical "messengers." The "code" contained in the chemical structure of the secretion determines what kind of specialized cells it will affect, as shown in more detail in a later section. The hormones are carried all over the body by the circulatory system and affect the kinds of cells that are its "target" tissue in the same ways wherever they are encountered. Hormones are often released in response to a change in the internal environment that could threaten homeostasis. For example, if the body temperature falls, hormones are released that raise the metabolic rate of all of the cells of the body because a by-product of increased metabolism is heat.

The nervous system is, however, the master coordinator of all bodily activity in maintaining the consistency of the internal environment. It controls the activity of many of the systems of the body and directly regulates about half of the endocrine glands. The receptors that stimulate the nervous system respond to internal and external events that threaten the consistency of the internal environment. A fall in blood pressure may reduce circulation of food and oxygen to the cells, but receptors respond and the nervous system speeds up the heart rate. An increase in outside temperature is sensed by receptors in the skin and affects the brain. The reactions include an increase in sweating to cool the body. Finally the nervous system *learns*. In addition to the "built-in" reactions or reflexes noted above, human beings learn to build fires and wear clothes to preserve a constant body temperature. It may be said that the most complex of human reactions are taken to preserve life, and that means preserving the consistency of the internal environment.

All of the metabolic reactions of the body that coordinate cell activity and maintain a consistent internal environment are homeostatic reactions, and their outcome is **homeostasis.** These reactions vary from the simple chemical "buffers" in the tissue fluid that react with acids or bases to prevent an excess of either, to the most complex of human behavior. Homeostasis is the constantly changing balance (dynamic equilibrium) of internal conditions that allows the cells to survive by keeping the internal environment within narrow chemical and physical limits.

Metabolism

Metabolism has already been defined as including every chemical reaction that goes on in a living cell. It also includes all of the chemical reactions that go on in the tissue fluid surrounding the cells. Metabolism therefore includes all of the chemical reactions of life that eventually transform food and oxygen into waste, carbon dioxide, and the energy that supports life.

Organic reactions. Organic reactions are chemical reactions that involve **organic compounds.** Organic compounds all have molecules with a "backbone" or basic structure that consists of a long chain of carbon (C) molecules that are linked together by chemical bonds. Most of the chemical reac-

tions of life involve organic compounds of one kind or another (not *all* organic compounds are involved in the chemical reactions of life). In general, energy is given off when these bonds are broken to make smaller molecules out of large ones (catabolism); energy is required to bond molecules together to make a longer carbon chain (anabolism). The result is a "balanced economy" of energy exchange where catabolic reactions supply the energy for anabolic reactions.

Oxidation. Millions of metabolic reactions occur in support of life. However, if we consider the living organism as an input-output system, all animal life consumes oxygen (O_2) and food and gives off carbon dioxide (CO_2), water (H_2O), waste products, heat, and the energy that supports life. This form of reaction is one of a class of reactions that the chemist calls **oxidation.** A simplified form of the basic equation looks like this: Food $+ O_2 \rightarrow$ Energy $+$ heat $+$ waste $+ CO_2 + H_2O$.

This sequence of events would occur if we burned the food in a fire, except that all of the energy would be lost as heat. (The human body utilizes about 20% of the potential energy of a food and uses some of the heat to maintain body temperature.) This is why the energy value of food is measured in terms of the **calorie,** which is a unit of heat. As every dieter knows, if we consume more calories of food than the energy requirements of the body dictate, the balance winds up as fat deposits! In the human body, the food we eat is broken down into a simpler form by digestion and is combined by the cells with oxygen transported from the lungs by the circulatory system. The waste products (chiefly lactic acid) and carbon dioxide are carried by the circulation to the kidneys and lungs respectively for disposal.

Cell metabolism versus intermediary metabolism (Fig. 2-2). It is convenient to divide the chemical reactions of life into those going on inside the cells themselves, and those taking place in the tissue fluid surrounding the cells. The cellular reactions are **cell metabolism** and the tissue fluid reactions are **intermediary metabolism.** As examples, intermediary metabolism includes digestive reactions that turn food into a form the specialized cells can use (e.g., glucose), and cell metabolism includes reactions inside of the cell, transforming the glucose into waste (lactic acid) with the release of energy to support other chemical reactions in the cell.

Expanding the equation. The three basic classes of animal foods are **fats, proteins,** and **carbohydrates.** They cannot be absorbed or utilized in these forms by the specialized cells of the body, and must be broken down in intermediary metabolism by the digestion into *fatty acids, amino acids,*

and sugars, respectively. In cell metabolism, the cells break down the sugars (chiefly **glucose**) into lactic acid (waste), which releases energy to be stored by the cell and used in other reactions of cell metabolism that require energy. Such energy-requiring reactions include rebuilding the fatty acids into fats and the amino acids into proteins, both materials required for the structure of the cells. Alternatively, the cells can turn the fatty acids or amino acids into glucose and break the glucose down into lactic acid as an additional form of energy. Finally, glucose that is not immediately needed by the cells can be turned into **glycogen** by the liver and stored there and in the muscles for future use by the cells. Some of these reactions are shown in Fig. 2-3, where the bottom line shows the oxidation of carbohydrate into waste products as in the "basic equation" previously given. The middle line shows the process of glucose storage as glycogen. (The double arrows mean that the reaction can proceed in either direction.) The upper line demonstrates the way in which the cells themselves store energy, the next subject of discussion.

The energy released by oxidizing glucose can be "packaged" in a form that is readily available inside the cell. It can be used to make longer carbon chain molecules out of short ones; reversing the process could release energy whenever the cell needed it. The bonds between carbon

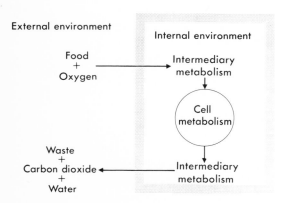

Fig. 2-2. Intermediary metabolism and cell metabolism.

$$AA \rightleftharpoons ADP \rightleftharpoons ATP \rightleftharpoons CP \text{ (energy storage—cells)}$$
$$\Updownarrow$$
$$O_2 + Carbohydrate \rightleftharpoons Glucose \rightleftharpoons Glycogen \text{ (food storage—liver)}$$
$$\Updownarrow$$
$$\left.\begin{array}{l} O_2 + Fat \rightleftharpoons Fatty\ acid \\ O_2 + Protein \rightleftharpoons Amino\ acid \end{array}\right\} \rightleftharpoons Pyruvic\ acid \rightleftharpoons Lactic\ acid + CO_2 + H_2O \text{ (oxidation)}$$

Fig. 2-3. Simplified diagram of reactions involved in carbohydrate metabolism. (Double arrows refer to chemical reactions or energy exchange.) Glucose can be manufactured from carbohydrate, fat, or protein in intermediary metabolism and stored in the liver as glycogen. When used by the cells as food, it is broken down into pyruvic acid and lactic acid before it is eliminated. These reactions release energy that the cell uses to form energy-rich phosphate bonds to store energy. *AA,* Adenylic acid (one bond); *ADP,* adenosine diphosphate (two bonds); *ATP,* adenosine triphosphate (three bonds); *CP,* creatine phosphate.

chain molecules that are used by the cell are energy-rich phosphate bonds. These bonds require a great deal of energy to form (20,000 calories per gram-molecular equivalent) and release as much energy when they are broken. The phosphate bonds are therefore an efficient way for the cell to store immediately available energy.

Dietary essentials

The fats, proteins, and carbohydrates we have just discussed are essential to the animal's diet. To these we must add essential fatty acids, essential amino acids, vitamins, and minerals.

Proteins and fats form the "building blocks" of cell structure, which must be continuously repaired. Proteins are found in meats, some vegetables, and grains of various sorts. Fats are found in animal fats, milk, and butter (saturated fats), or come from grains of various kinds (unsaturated fats) and other vegetable sources. Carbohydrates come from starches and sugars, largely of plant origin. The average American diet is said to consist of 15% protein, 35% fat, and 50% carbohydrate.

The other dietary essentials are needed in smaller amounts. As stated above, proteins are broken down into amino acids and fats into fatty acids for absorption and use by the cells. Although most of the 22 amino acids the body uses can be formed from proteins in intermediary metabolism, there are ten essential amino acids that must be part of the diet because the body cannot manufacture them. There are also three essential fatty acids that the body cannot make from fats in the diet. Vita-

Table 1. Summary of the vitamins: functions, deficiency conditions, and food sources*

Vitamin	Function	Deficiency condition	Food sources
Fat soluble			
Vitamin A (retinal) and provitamin A (α,β,γ-carotene, cryptoxanthin)	Adapts vision to dim light Promotes growth Prevents keratinization of skin and eye Facilitates resistance to bacterial infection	Night blindness Xerophthalmia Hyperkeratosis Poor growth	Vitamin A Liver Egg yolk Milk, butter Provitamin A Sweet potatoes Winter squash Greens Carrots Cantaloupe
Vitamin D (calciferol)	Facilitates absorption of calcium and phosphorus Maintains alkaline phosphatase for optimum calcification	Rickets Osteomalacia	Vitamin D–fortified milk Eggs Cheese, butter Fish
Vitamin E (tocopherols)	Antioxidant (protects vitamins A and C and unsaturated fatty acids)		Vegetable oils Greens
Vitamin K (phylloquinone and farnoquinone)	Blood clotting (formation of prothrombin and proconvertin)	Hemorrhage	Greens Liver Egg yolks

*Modified from Stare, F. J., and McWilliams, M.: Living nutrition, New York, 1973, John Wiley & Sons, Inc.

Continued.

Table 1. Summary of the vitamins: functions, deficiency conditions, and food sources—cont'd

Vitamin	Function	Deficiency condition	Food sources
Water soluble			
Thiamin	Coenzyme TPP (energy from carbohydrate and fat) Formation of ribose for DNA and RNA (transketolase) Conversion of tryptophan to niacin	Beriberi	Meat Whole grain and enriched cereals Milk Legumes
Riboflavin	FMN and FAD for releasing energy Conversion of tryptophan to niacin	Ariboflavinosis	Milk Green vegetables Fish, meat, eggs
Niacin	NAD and NADP to release energy Glycolysis Fatty acid synthesis	Pellagra	Meat, poultry, fish Peanut butter Whole grain and enriched cereals Greens
Vitamin B_6 (pyridoxine)	Transamination and deamination of amino acid Porphyrin synthesis (for hemoglobin) Conversion of tryptophan to niacin Energy from glycogen Formation of histamine, serotonin, norepinephrine		Meats Bananas Whole grain cereals Lima beans Cabbage Potatoes Spinach
Pantothenic acid	CoA component (transfer 2 carbon fragments to release energy) Porphyrin synthesis (hemoglobin formation) Cholesterol and steroid formation		Organ meats Whole grain cereal
Biotin	Releases energy from carbohydrate Fatty acid metabolism Deamination of protein		Egg yolks Milk Organ meats Cereals Legumes Nuts
Folacin (folic acid, pteroyl-glutamic acid)	Transfer of single carbon units Coenzyme in synthesis of: guanine and adenine; thymine; choline; amino acids; porphyrin	Macrocytic anemia	Greens Mushrooms Liver Kidney
Vitamin B_{12} (cobalamin)	Maturation of red blood cells Carbohydrate metabolism for energy for central nervous system Formation of single carbon radicals Conversion of folinic acid to folacin	Pernicious anemia	Animal foods
Ascorbic acid (vitamin C)	Formation of collagen Utlization of calcium in bones and teeth Elasticity and strength of capillaries Conversion of folinic acid to folacin	Scurvy	Citrus fruits Strawberries Papayas Broccoli Cabbage Tomatoes Potatoes

mins are needed in small amounts to form parts of the enzymes that speed up some of the essential chemical reactions of life. Table 1 lists the more well-known vitamins, their food sources, and some of the severe human maladies that result from vitamin deficiencies. The average diet includes sufficient vitamins; supplementary vitamins are rarely needed, no matter how widely they are advertised.

Certain minerals in minute amounts are also vital to normal body function. Table 2 lists them, their function, and food sources. Except in certain parts of the world where the soil is deficient in minerals for vegetables and in grain for poultry and meat production, the average diet includes them all.

Enzymes

Enzymes were mentioned above as chemicals that speed up essential chemical

Table 2. Summary of minerals: functions and food sources*

Mineral	Functions	Food sources
Calcium	Bone formation, maintenance, and growth Tooth formation Blood clot formation Activation of pancreatic lipase Absorption of vitamin B_{12} Contraction of muscle	Milk, cheese, puddings, custards, chocolate beverages Fish with bones, including salmon Greens Broccoli
Chloride	Component of hydrochloric acid Maintenance of proper osmotic pressure Acid-base balance	Table salt Meats Milk Eggs
Cobalt	Part of vitamin B_{12} molecule	Organ meats Meats
Copper	Catalyst for hemoglobin formation Formation of elastin (connective tissue) Release of energy (in cytochrome oxidase and catalase) Formation of melanin (pigment) Formation of phospholipids for myelin sheath of nerves	Cereals Nuts Legumes Liver Shellfish Grapes Meats
Fluoride	Strengthen bones and teeth	Fluoridated water
Iodine	Component of thyroxine and triiodothyronine	Iodized salt Fish (salt water and anadromous)
Iron	Component of hemoglobin Component of myoglobin Component of cytochromes, cytochrome oxidase, catalase, peroxidase Component of myeloperoxidase	Meats Heart, liver Clams Oysters Lima beans Spinach Dates, dried fruits Nuts Enriched and whole grain cereals

*From Stare, F. J., and McWilliams, M.: Living nutrition, New York, 1973, John Wiley & Sons, Inc.

Continued.

Table 2. Summary of minerals: functions and food sources—cont'd

Mineral	Functions	Food sources
Magnesium	Catalyze ATP ↔ ADP Conduct nerve impulses Retention of calcium in teeth Adjust to cold environment	Milk Green vegetables Nuts Breads and cereals
Manganese	Bone development Component of arginase Promotes thiamin storage	Cereals Legumes
Molybdenum	Component of xanthine oxidase Component of aldehyde oxidase	

Phosphorus	Bone formation, maintenance, and growth
	Tooth formation
	Component of DNA and RNA
	Component of ADP and ATP
	Fatty acid transport
	Acid-base balance
	Component of TPP
		Organic
		  Meats, poultry, and fish
		Inorganic
		  Milk, fruits and
		    vegetables

Potassium	Maintenance of osmotic pressure Acid-base balance Transmission of nerve impulses Catalyst in energy metabolism Formation of proteins Formation of glycogen	Orange juice Dried fruits Bananas Potatoes Coffee
Selenium	Antioxidant	
Sodium	Maintenance of osmotic pressure Acid-base balance Relaxation of muscles Absorption of glucose Transmission of nerve impulses	Table salt Salted meats Milk
Sulfur	Component of thiamin Component of some proteins (hair, nails, skin)	Meats Milk and cheese Eggs Legumes Nuts
Zinc	Component of carboxypeptidase Component of carbonic anhydrase	Whole grain cereals Meats Legumes

reactions in metabolism, because vitamins are required to form some of them. (Others are manufactured by cells without using vitamins.) Every chemical reaction in the body must proceed at a minimum rate to provide the necessary energy, structure, and food for the cells. Many metabolic reactions cannot proceed rapidly enough to be effective without the help of enzymes. Enzymes are organic catalysts that act to speed up specific chemical reactions without being destroyed in the process. Therefore only minute amounts are needed because they can be used over and over. Each enzyme is specific to a given chemical reaction, so that which enzymes are present determines which chemical reactions occur—presumably the ones needed by the cell when it manufactures the enzymes it needs. Furthermore, many chemical reactions are reversible (see the double arrows in Fig. 2-3); whether the reaction proceeds in an anabolic or catabolic direction may depend on which enzymes are present. So the presence or absence of selected enzymes can determine which reactions occur in intermediate or cell metabolism and in which direction the reactions proceed. The way the cell manufactures enzymes will form a part of the next topic.

GENETICS AND CELL METABOLISM
The genetic code

The nucleus of each cell in the human body contains 23 pairs of **chromosomes** (colored bodies), 46 in all. One of each pair of chromosomes is inherited from one parent, the other chromosome coming from the other parent. Each chromosome contains **genes,** an abstract term for a chemical structure that determines a unitary human characteristic such as eye color. Individual structures that are genes in the chromosomes also determine the way each cell specializes and control each chemical reaction that goes on in the cell. As a result, each cell in the human body contains the "blueprint" for determining each of the physical characteristics of the individual as well as all information needed to become any kind of specialized cell that exists in the body and carry out any metabolic reaction of which that cell is capable. An awesome blueprint, indeed!

The physical basis for this blueprint is contained in DNA (deoxyribonucleic acid) molecules. Each chromosome contains perhaps 3,000 segments of DNA molecules that act as genes. Each DNA molecule looks like a twisted ladder (Fig. 2-4), with chemical bases forming the steps of the ladder. When a cell divides to reproduce itself, the chromosomes and DNA molecules also divide, leaving two spiral "half-ladders" for the DNA molecules of each daughter cell in each half chromosome. The chromosomes and DNA molecules reassemble their missing halves from raw materials available in the new cell. Thus the segments of DNA molecules that are the genes are reconstituted in the new cells. Therefore, the specialized characteristics of the two new cells become the same as those of the old cell.

The specialized features of a cell depend on the types of protein and fat molecules that are the "building blocks" of the cell's structure—molecules the cell itself manufactures. The synthesis of these molecules of cell structure is controlled by the sequence of the rungs of the stepladder (base sequence) in the DNA molecule. This sequence forms the "genetic code" for directing all of the metabolic reactions in the cell. Some cells use one part of this sequence to specialize as skin cells; others use another part to specialize as liver cells. The DNA molecule synthesizes a messenger RNA (mRNA) molecule on part of its structure (Fig. 2-4). The messenger RNA moves out of the nucleus of the cell to inclusions in the cytoplasm called ribosomes. Here the messenger RNA acts as a pattern to form a second kind of RNA called transfer RNA (tRNA). The transfer RNA then acts as a pattern to assemble amino acids in the proper sequence to form a protein needed as part of the structure of the cell, or to form an enzyme. The enzyme acts to speed up chemical reactions typical of skin cell or a liver cell, depending on the chemical reactions called for by the specific enzyme.

Parts of the DNA molecule direct each metabolic reaction of the cell. Life is basically an involved set of chemical reactions directed in a little-known fashion by different segments of the DNA molecule. For example, a gene, or segment of the DNA molecule, is activated to form messenger RNA (see above) by an "operator" segment that lies next to it on the DNA ladder. The operator segment has a repressor chemically bound to it so that it cannot activate the gene. An enzyme (RNA polymerase) for the needed reaction attaches to the operator, displacing the repressor, and spinning off the necessary messenger RNA that is required as directed by the DNA segment. This is an oversimplified descrip-

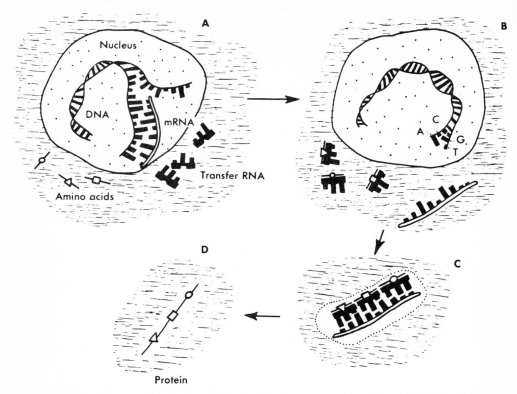

Fig. 2-4. Sequence of events in the manufacture of an enzyme by the cell. **A,** DNA molecule "divides" to form a messenger RNA (mRNA) molecule on part of its structure. The sequence of bases on the DNA molecule (labeled *A, C, G,* and *T* in **B**) determines the shape of the RNA molecule that is assembled. **B,** mRNA has left the cell nucleus. **C,** mRNA is assembling transfer RNA (tRNA) in a cell inclusion, called a ribosome, by serving as a template for the amino acid sequence of the transfer RNA molecule. The transfer RNA in turn is assembling three bases (represented by the *triangle, square,* and *circle*) into a protein or enzyme. **D,** protein or enzyme has left the ribosome to catalyze a chemical reaction in another part of the cell.

tion of a complex process, but it may serve to illustrate how the DNA molecule directs metabolism.

In trying to understand the sequence of bases in the DNA molecule (rungs of the "ladder") that direct each chemical reaction of life, scientists face a formidable task. In attempts to "break the code" of base sequences, they have turned to the DNA of simpler organisms. A bacillus (germ) common to the human digestive system and called *Escherichia coli* has been the favorite subject. *E. coli* is a single-celled organism whose nucleus contains many DNA molecules but far fewer than human

cell nuclei do. As described at the beginning of the chapter, a virus is a DNA molecule with a protein coat that attracts single-celled organisms like *E. coli* as readily as it infects the specialized cells of man. The virus releases its DNA into the cell, leaving its protein coat outside. Inside the cell, the virus DNA uses the substance of the cell to multiply in a parasitic fashion with each new virus DNA acquiring a protein coat. The host cell then bursts, releasing virus DNA that infects other cells. By studying components of this reaction, scientists have learned much about how DNA works.

Two newer approaches have led to a more complete understanding of the DNA mechanisms that are common to all life. One is recombinant DNA technique. and the other is DNA synthesis. The recombinant DNA technique involves injecting genes from other simple organisms into the nucleus of *E. coli* where they combine with the host DNA to form a cell with new genetic instructions—a hitherto unknown bacteria. This has obvious dangers for man; a new and virulent plague of infectious disease to which man has developed no immunity could be unleashed. (A recent international conference has set strict standards to prevent this possibility in laboratories where such research might be undertaken.) Most recently, Dr. Har Gorbind Khorana and his colleagues at the Massachusetts Institute of Technology have culminated a nine-year effort by synthesizing a gene naturally found in *E. coli* from commercially available chemicals (nucleotides), introduced it into *E. coli,* and showed that the gene actually functioned in the manufacture of a cell protein! This involved not only the synthesis of a segment of DNA, but synthesis of the "operator" mentioned earlier that initiates the reaction and a "terminator" molecule that stops it—in addition to a gene that is 207 base pairs long! Although human DNA is 1,000 to 3,000 base pairs per gene, the implications of this research are profound because the same principles are involved. This research brings us closer to understanding DNA mechanisms in man. Many human disorders involve defective genes that may be impaired by virus attachment (this is suspected in diabetes) or by faulty heredity (as sickle-cell anemia or Tay-Sachs disease). By understanding DNA synthesis, genetic "repair" may someday become possible!

Arithmetic of heredity

A gene is the part of a DNA molecule that determines an inherited characteristic that can be identified, such as brown hair or blue eyes. Inheritance and cell specialization depend on the DNA of genes, but genes are packaged in chromosomes, and chromosomes occur in pairs—only half of the chromosomes (23) are inherited from each parent; therefore, only half of the genes and inherited characteristics come from each parent. The chromosomes come in pairs because the half received from one parent must concern the same structures as the half the other parent contributes. If the 46 chromosomes were composed of two unpaired groups of 23 from each parent, some characteristics would be repeated and some would be missing.

Some of the cells of the body are specialized for reproduction; these cells contain the same chromosomes and genes as other cells of the body but are isolated from them by being contained in the reproductive tissue of the male (**testes**) and female (**ovaries).** The reproductive cells of the male and female **gonads** (reproductive organs) multiply in the same fashion as other cells in the body as long as they are in an immature state; that is, each cell splits each of its 46 chromosomes and each of the DNA molecules they contain in forming two new cells by cellular mitosis, or **mitotic division.** In the final division save one, called a *reduction division,* the chromosomes line up by pairs instead of splitting. Each cell receives only one of each pair of chromosomes, ending up with two cells of 23 chromosomes each instead of two cells of 46. Which one of each pair each new cell receives is apparently determined by chance. One of a single pair might wind up in either of the two new cells. In the male a final mitotic division produces four **sperm cells.** In the female one cell of the reduction division and one cell of the final mitotic division are discarded, so that only one **ovum** (egg cell) remains. In fertilization one of the sperm cells penetrates the ovum to contribute its 23 chromosomes to the 23 of the ovum, so that a single cell of 46 chromosomes results. It is from this cell that the mature and complex multicellular organism develops by mitotic division; half of the chromosomes, and therefore half of the genes of each subsequent cell, originate with the female and half with the male.

The single cell that is to form the complete individual begins with 23 pairs of chromosomes and therefore 23 pairs of gene assemblies, with one member of each pair having been contributed by the mother and one by the father. Each chromosome pair contains many pairs of genes, with each gene of a pair of genes regulating the same inherited characteristics in the future offspring. To simplify, consider only one gene pair from a single pair of chromosomes that determines a given characteristic, such as eye color. Assume for the moment that the male contributed a gene for brown eyes (Br) and the female contributed a matching gene for blue eyes (bl). Further assume that the Br gene is **dominant** and the bl gene is **recessive.** This means that an individual having only Br in both members of a gene pair (BrBr) will have brown eyes, and an individual with only bl genes (blbl) will be blue-eyed, and an individual with one of each gene (Brbl) will be brown-eyed, since the brown-eyed (Br) gene is dominant over the recessive blue-eyed (bl) gene. However, the Brbl individual may contribute a bl gene to this offspring. This is true because if either parent carries Brbl in his or her genes, the reduction division will mean that half the cells will carry Br and half will carry bl. Since it is a matter of chance in the reduction division which sperm or ovum gets which of the gene-chromosome groups, the odds are 50-50 that a Brbl individual will contribute a Br gene and 50-50 that he will contribute a bl gene to his offspring. To illustrate further consequences, let us consider two generations:

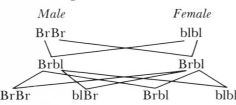

Male   *Female*

BrBr   blbl

Brbl   Brbl

BrBr   blBr   Brbl   blbl

Mating a BrBr with a blbl can only result in Brbl individuals, brown-eyed but **car-**riers of the recessive genes for blue eyes. If two carriers are mated, there are four possible crosses. BrBr, blBr, Brbl, blbl. One in four (on the average) will be brown-eyed and carry only that gene, one in four will be blue-eyed and carry only that gene, and two will be brown-eyed (Br) but carriers of the recessive gene (bl) for blue eyes.

The genes of the inherited DNA molecules determine physical characteristics by the way they control the manufacture of enzymes in the cell. Enzymes that control hair and eye color are examples. In the inheritance of human characteristics some genes act as simple dominants and recessives, such as brown eye color over blue, curly hair over straight, dark hair over light. Some abnormalities may be inherited as dominants, such as short digits or hereditary cataracts, and others as recessives, such as albinism or epilepsy. In the human, however, the DNA molecules are so complex that most inherited characteristics follow these laws only on an *average* basis with many individual exceptions.

Implications for humans. When we combine our knowledge of the arithmetic of heredity, DNA mechanisms, and recent work on human chromosomes, some profound implications for the future emerge. Living human sperm and ova can be sorted under a microscope, and the chromosomes containing the genes for sex determination can be identified. So can chromosomes that contain faulty genes for certain genetic disorders like mongolism (a cause of mental retardation) or sickle-cell anemia (a blood disorder). Understanding of the genetic locus of hereditary characteristics and knowledge of DNA mechanisms may make "genetic engineering" possible. Altering the hereditary characteristics of germ tissue and artificial fertilization of the female with the altered cells could eliminate genetic disease carried by the male. One could determine the sex of offspring by sorting germ cells of both male and female, fertilizing them outside of the body, and reimplanting the germ tissue for an otherwise normal pregnancy. Sorting of germ cells could also be used to select a desirable characteristic when its chromosome locus is known.

ENDOCRINE GLANDS AND THEIR HORMONES

In a previous section (homeostasis), the interdependence of the specialized cells of the body and their need for a consistent internal environment were shown to depend upon (1) organization of tissues, organs, and systems, (2) the endocrine glands, and (3) the nervous system. The endocrine glands are the subject of this section of the chapter (the nervous system is discussed in Chapter 3).

All glands are organs made up in part of cells that are specialized for the secretion of substances needed by the body. Exocrine or duct glands discharge their secretions into a "pipeline" that carries them to where they are needed. Examples are the salivary glands of the mouth and the sweat glands of the skin. Such glands are not the subject of this section. **Endocrine glands,** or ductless glands, have no "pipelines" for their secretions. Endocrine glands discharge their secretions directly into the blood vessels (capillaries) that pass through them. The endocrine gland secretions, called **hormones,** are carried throughout the body by the circulatory system. Depending on the nature of the hormone produced and the characteristics of the cells it encounters, an endocrine gland may affect the functioning of cells, tissues, and organs in many locations throughout the body. Therefore a gland is endocrine if it produces a hormone that (1) is specific to that gland, (2) is distributed by the circulation throughout the body, and (3) has a specific influence on some other part of the body—a **target tissue.**

Hormone characteristics

Hormones are composed of a variety of compounds (for example, steroids, polypeptides, and amino acids) that have specific effects on different kinds of specialized tissue. Some hormones affect most of the cells of the body, irrespective of their specialized structure and functioning. Other hormones affect only cells that are specialized in certain ways—for example, a hormone that affects the ability of kidney tubule cells to reabsorb water from the urine. In this instance the target tissue of the hormone is found only in a single organ, the kidney. However, a given endocrine gland may produce several different hormones if it has several different kinds of secreting cells or if its cells produce more than one kind of secretion. In this case the hormones would act on a variety of target tissues, with different effects on each tissue. To fully understand the function of an endocrine gland, one would have to isolate each of its hormones and test its effects. The problem is further complicated by the fact that endocrine glands affect each other. Hormones from one endocrine gland may excite or inhibit the production of hormones by another endocrine gland—that is, *interactions* occur between endocrine glands.

Some methods and their difficulties

For ethical reasons, animals rather than humans are used as subjects in the research done on the endocrine glands. The early techniques used included removal of the gland for deficiency studies (hyposecretion), injection of excess hormones (hypersecretion studies), or removal of the gland and injection of its hormones when they were known (replacement therapy). These procedures have profound effects on the whole metabolism of the animal and risk death or deformity. More sophisticated newer procedures involve breeding hormone-deficient strains of animals, chemically stimulating or blocking hormone secretion or its effects, or maintaining the gland outside of the body but still a part of the body's circulation (in vitro). The errors in these methods are chiefly caused by interactions between glands. If one gland is removed and an animal develops a symptom—for example, low blood calcium and resulting irritability of the nervous system—the investigator may assume that the gland maintains the calcium level of the blood. However, the gland may produce a hormone that stimulates another gland to perform this function. Even when the hormone has been isolated or synthesized, the effect of a hormone on other glands must be understood.

Once the major role of a hormone in metabolism is established in animal research, however, the results can be applied to human physiology with confidence. There seem to be no major differences in endocrine function between the usual laboratory animals and humans. (This is not true for experiments on the nervous system, as will be seen in Chapter 3.) Of course the secondary consequences of endocrine malfunction on man's personality, intelligence, and other complex behavior are much more profound.

How hormones function

Chemical studies of the molecular structure of hormones show a variety of complex chemical structures: steroids, polypeptides, proteins, and so on. The chemical makeup of a given hormone seems to be "keyed" to the specialized structure of the tissue it is to affect. A few hormones affect all cells—those of the thyroid, pancreas, and gonads are examples (see Table 3). Others, however, affect only one specialized kind of tissue (glucose for the liver, for instance) or a limited number of kinds of tissue (intestines, bone, and liver for parathormone from the parathyroid glands). Some hormones are involved in organized responses to external stimuli, such as the reaction of the adrenal medulla in nervous arousal in an emergency. Others are concerned with consistency of the internal environment, such as the parathyroids and calcium level or the pancreas and blood glucose level. Some endocrine glands of the latter group are stimulated directly to produce a hormone that corrects a lack of balance in internal conditions whenever the imbalance occurs; for example, the pancreas produces more insulin when the blood glucose is too high and less insulin when the blood glucose is too low. (The effect of insulin is to help cells use up blood glucose.) As would be expected from the variety of hormone effects on so many kinds of target tissue, several modes of hormone action are found, with some hormones acting in more than one of the following ways: (1) some hormones form part of *enzymes* and therefore aid in activating chemical reactions in the cells of their target tissue, for example, the thyroxin of the thyroid gland; (2) some hormones modify the membranes of the cells they encounter, adhering to the membrane to make it more or less permeable to specific substances, for example, insulin from the pancreas, which enhances the permeability of cell membranes to blood glucose; (3) some hormones act directly on structures within the cell, for example, adrenal norepinephrine, which acts on the smooth muscle cells of the arteries; and (4) some hormones act on cells by regulating the genetic apparatus, by which they repair and reproduce themselves, for example, the androgens and estrogens of the gonads. These examples serve to illustrate the varied ways in which hormones function.

Endocrine control by the nervous system

There seem to be two fashions in which the nervous system—the major integrating system of the body—exerts control over the endocrine glands: (1) direct excitation from the brain by nerves leading to the gland (the adrenal medulla, pancreas, posterior pituitary, and pineal are examples) and (2) control by the anterior pituitary gland, which is in turn influenced by a part of the brain (the hypothalamus). The first mechanism seems straightforward, but the second requires a little explanation. The anterior pituitary produces three hormones that control, respectively, the outputs of the adrenal cortex, thyroid, and gonads (testes or ovaries). The anterior pituitary is a gland that "hangs" from the bottom of the brain from a "stalk" that emerges from a part of the brain called the

Table 3. Synopsis of endocrine gland functions

Gland	Hormone(s)	Target tissue	Major function	Hyposecretion	Hypersecretion
Thyroid	Thyroxin	All cells	Raises metabolic rate	Lethargy, retardation	Hyperactivity
Parathyroids	Parathormone (vitamin D)	Intestines, bone, kidney	Increases blood calcium, lowers blood phosphate, prevents loss of Ca and P	Hyperactivity, Seizures, Bone deficiencies	Lethargy
Adrenal cortex	Corticoids (steroids)	All cell membranes, liver, gonads	Sodium retention, potassium loss, increased carbohydrate metabolism, glycogen formation, sex hormone effects	Lethargy, fluid retention, weight loss, salt loss	Sexual precocity
Adrenal medulla	Norepinephrine	Heart	Increases heart rate, constricts visceral and peripheral arteries, releases blood glucose, releases ACTH	Unknown	Under stress only
Pancreas	Glucagon	Liver	Increases blood glucose (constr.)	Unknown	Unknown
	Insulin	All cells	Lowers blood glucose	Diabetes mellitus	Hypoglycemia and lethargy
Posterior pituitary	Vasopressin (includes ADH)	Arteries, Kidney	Raises blood pressure (constr.), Water reabsorption	Diabetes insipidus	Unknown (hypertension?)
	Oxytocin	Uterus, Mammary glands	Contraction, Milk secretion		
Anterior pituitary	Somatotrophic	Bone	Body growth	Dwarfism, acromegaly	Giantism
	Thyrotrophic	Thyroid	Thyroxin secretion	See thyroid gland	
	Adrenocorticotrophic	Adrenal cortex	Corticoid secretion	See adrenal cortex	
	Follicle-stimulating	Gonads	Ova and sperm production	Sterility	Unknown
	Luteinizing	Gonads	Sex hormone production	Sexual vigor increases	Decreases vigor
	Lactogenic	Gonads, mammary glands	Corpus luteus development and milk production	Sterility	Known
Testes	Androgens	All tissues	Sexual arousal, primary and secondary sex characteristics	Sexual vigor increases	Decreases vigor
Ovaries	Estrogens	All tissues	Sexual arousal, primary and secondary sex characteristics	Sexual vigor	Decreases vigor
	Progesterone	Uterus	Prepares for embryo, Maintains pregnancy	Sterility	Unknown
Placenta	Chorionic	Uterus	Maintains pregnancy	Miscarriage	Unknown
Pineal	Melatonin	Gonads	Suppress hormone output	Increased sexual vigor	Decreases vigor

hypothalamus. As will be explained in Chapter 3, nerve cells stimulate each other by the release of chemicals called transmitters. A few of these transmitters in the hypothalamus act like hormones because they stimulate the anterior pituitary gland to release hormones that stimulate *other* endocrine glands to release their hormones. The transmitters in questions are therefore called "releasing factors." (Two examples are TRF, or thyrotrophin releasing factor, for thyroid control and LRF, or luteinizing hormone releasing factor, for gonad control.)

Hormone effects (Table 3)

Most of endocrine function is concerned with maintaining homeostasis, normal metabolism, and growth. Human consequences are therefore not noted except when endocrine glands malfunction and hyposecretion or hypersecretion occur. Then the effects on intelligence and personality can be profound, indeed. Hyposecretion of thyroxin by the thyroid gland, especially in childhood, can lead to mental retardation. Parathyroid insufficiency causes seizures resembling epilepsy. Hypersecretion of certain corticords re-

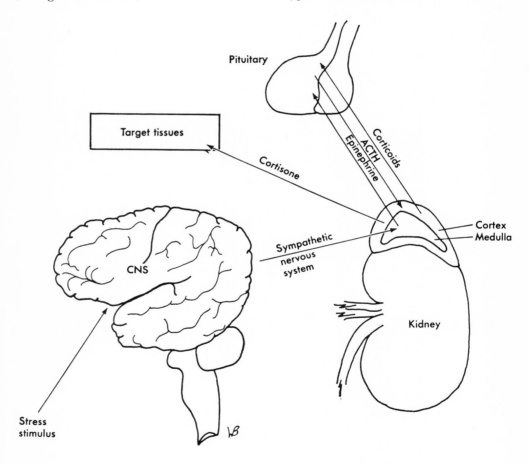

Fig. 2-5. Interaction of adrenal cortex and medulla in stress and alarm reactions. Perception of a stress stimulus results in sympathetic nervous system response, including increased epinephrine secretion by the adrenal medulla. Epinephrine stimulates ACTH output by the anterior pituitary gland. ACTH stimulates the adrenal cortex to increase corticoid output. Corticoids improve nerve tissue excitability and raise the metabolic rate, both adaptive reactions to stress.

sults in premature adolescence and sexual precocity. Oversecretion or undersecretion of STH by the anterior pituitary results in giantism or dwarfism, respectively, with major consequences for the personality of the sufferer. Sexual vigor is affected by the sex hormones and also by the pineal glands. Fortunately, most of these disorders are rare and usually can be treated by surgical or chemical (replacement therapy) means.

Stress and alarm reactions

One set of hormone interactions is of importance to everyday behavior, however. These are the reactions of the two otherwise unrelated parts of the adrenal glands and the anterior pituitary (Fig. 2-5). A sudden or alarming stimulus of any kind arouses a part of the nervous system called the sympathetic nervous system that prepares the body for exertion (Chapter 3). As a part of that reaction, the adrenal medulla is stimulated by sympathetic nerves. It releases a hormone (epinephrine) that assists in readying the body for action (increased heart rate, faster breathing, and so on). The hormone also stimulates the anterior pituitary gland to release ACTH, which stimulates the adrenal cortex. The adrenal cortex output results in further body adaptations to stress.

SUMMARY

The simplest form of life is the single cell that exhibits irritability and conduction as properties of its membrane, contraction and secretion as properties of its inclusions, and metabolism and reproduction controlled by its nucleus. Multicellular organisms are composed of cells specialized for one of these or other life functions at the expense of their ability to carry out the other functions of life. These cells are organized into tissues of similarly specialized cells, organs made up of several kinds of tissues, and systems of a variety of organs with similar overall function. Specialized cells require a more consistent internal environment than independent cells and are

more interdependent. Both requirements are served by the nature of system organization, the endocrine glands, and the nervous system. Homeostasis, or internal consistency, results.

Metabolism includes all of the chemical reactions of life. The reactions concern organic molecules made up of long carbon chains. Breaking these chains releases energy, and building them consumes energy. The overall intake of food and oxygen and output of energy, heat, carbon dioxide, waste, and water is an oxidation reaction. The energy value of a food is related to the heat it gives off in burning, measured as calories. Subsumed under this reaction are many others that go on in the tissue fluid as intermediary metabolism and in the cells as cell metabolism. Food is transformed into glucose or stored as glycogen in intermediary metabolism; the cells store energy in phosphate bonds.

Fats, proteins, carbohydrates, essential amino and fatty acids, vitamins, and minerals are all dietary essentials. Enzymes control metabolism by speeding up needed chemical reactions.

DNA molecules in the chromosomes of the nucleus control metabolism and reproduction. The code lies in the nucleotide sequence of the "rungs" of their "stepladder" form. This sequence controls assembly of messenger RNA (mRNA), which forms transfer RNA (tRNA) that in turn forms amino acids and enzymes. The mechanism has been studied by observing virus attacks on cells. Recombinant DNA research and DNA synthesis have perfected this understanding. Cell reproduction involves cell division including the chromosomes and their DNA molecules.

Genes are nucleotide sequences that determine unitary human characteristics. They are contained in 46 chromosomes, 23 inherited from each parent. Dominant and recessive genes are involved in some pairs, the dominant gene determining the characteristic shown in a mixed pair.

The endocrine glands secrete their hormones directly into the circulation to affect target tissue of a given specialized kind wherever encountered by the hormone. The determination depends on the chemical structure of the hormones and specialized cells, but difficulties are encountered in studying them because glands interact to stimulate each other. Endocrine glands are affected by the nervous system by either direct stimulation or brain (hypothalamus) stimulation of the anterior pituitary that controls some other glands. Hormone action is largely concerned with homeostasis, but malfunction can have serious effects on human intelligence and personality. Stress and alarm reactions involve interactions between the adrenal medulla, anterior pituitary, and adrenal cortex.

READINGS

Arehart-Treichel, J.: Putting human genes on the map, Science News **108**:234-235, Oct. 1975.

Asimov, I.: The genetic code, New York, 1962, Signet Science Library. (New American Library of World Literature, Inc., New York; also Clarkson N. Potter, Inc., N.Y.)

Asimov, I.: The human body, Boston, 1964, Houghton Mifflin Company.

Cavalli-Sforza, L.: The genetics of human populations, Sci. Am. **231**:81-89, Sept. 1974.

Cohen, S. N.: The manipulation of genes, Sci. Am. **233**:24-33, July 1975.

Crick, F. H. C.: The genetic code III, Sci. Am. **215**:55-62, Oct. 1966 (W. H. Freeman Reprint No. 1052).

Crick, F. H. C.: Of molecules and men, Seattle, 1967, University of Washington Press.

Fischberg, M., and Blackler, A. W.: How cells specialize, Sci. Am. **205**:124-140, Sept. 1961 (W. H. Freeman Reprint No. 94).

German, J.: Studying human chromosomes today, Am. Sci. **58**:182-201, 1970.

Goulian, M.: Synthesis of viral DNA, Sci. J. **5**:35-42, March 1969.

Guillermin, R., and Burgus, R.: The hormones of the hypothalamus, Sci. Am. **227**:24-33, Nov. 1972.

Kirshner, N., and Smith, W. J.: Metabolic requirements for secretion from the adrenal medulla, Life Sci. **8**:799-803, 1969.

Lee, J., and Knowles, F. G. W.: Animal hormones, London, 1965, Hutchinson & Co., Ltd.

Lewin, R.: Hormones: chemical communication, Garden City, N.Y., 1973, Doubleday Publishing Company.

Luce, G.: Trust your body rhythms, Psychology Today **5**:52-65, April 1975.

Malvin, P. V.: Interaction between endocrine and nervous systems, BioScience **20**:595-601, 1970.

Matis, T., and Ptashne, M: A DNA operator-repressor system, Sci. Am. **234**:64-76, Jan. 1976.

McEwen, B.: Interactions between hormones and nerve tissues, Sci. Am. **235**:48-58, July 1976.

Ptashne, M., and Gilbert, W.: Genetic repressors, Sci. Am. **222**:36-44, June 1970.

Ruddle, F., and Kueherlapati, R.: Hybrid cells and human genes, Sci. Am. **231**:36-44, July 1974.

Satir, B.: The final steps in secretion, Sci. Am. **233**:29-37, Oct. 1975.

Scrimshaw, N., and Young, V.: The requirements of human nutrition, Sci. Am. **235**:51-64, Sept. 1976.

Sinsheimer, R. L.: Genetic engineering: The modification of man, Impact of Science on Society **20**:279-291, 1970. Reprinted in Leukel, F., editor: Issues in physiological psychology, St. Louis, 1974, The C. V. Mosby Co.

Stein, G. S., Stein, J. S., and Kleinsmith, L. J.: Chromosomal proteins and gene regulation, Sci. Am. **232**:46-57, 1975.

Walker, K.: Human physiology, Baltimore, 1956, Penguin Books, Inc.

Whalen, R. E., editor: Hormones and behavior, Princeton, N.J., 1967, D. Van Nostrand Co., Inc.

Yanofsky, C.: Gene structure and protein structure, Sci. Am. **216**:80-94, May 1967 (W. H. Freeman Reprint No. 1074).

CHAPTER 3

The nervous system: elements and organization

OVERVIEW

Our study of the nervous system begins with the anatomy and functions of its elements: the neurons. The electrical symptoms of nerve cell function will be explained in terms of ion movements, as will the way they excite each other at synapses. Organizing the billions of nerve cells into a nervous system requires their initial grouping in central and peripheral nervous systems with subcategories and an explanation on reflex function. Parts of the brain and their functions follow. Then the organization of these functions completes the chapter.

THE NEURON: ANATOMY AND FUNCTION
Anatomy

A simplified sketch of a "typical" **neuron** is presented in Fig. 3-1. Nerve cells in man are too small to be seen except under a microscope and vary widely in their characteristics, but all nerve cells feature the parts labeled in Fig. 3-1, with the exception of the neurolemma and myelin sheath. **Synapses** between two neurons are shown so that the role of certain parts of the cell may be appreciated. The nerve cell shown is a long, slender one, obviously designed to carry excitation from one part of the body to another. In life the neuron receives excitation at synapses from the terminal arborization of another neuron. At

this point each end foot "contacts" the **dendrites** and **cell body** of the neuron, with each contact being a synapse (actually, there is a small gap between the end foot and the dendrite or cell body). The transferred excitation is focused by the axon hillock on the **axon** and carried down the axon to its terminal arborization at the next set of synapses. Excitation continues to be passed from cell to cell in this manner.

The axon of a neuron may or may not have a **myelin sheath,** which is a fatty covering interrupted at the **nodes of Ranvier.** Nerve cells with myelin sheaths conduct faster than nerve cells without myelin sheaths. The **neurolemma,** a covering for some neurons, is made up of a separate cell (the Schwann cell). It is believed that this cell secretes the fatty myelin sheath. The main function of the neurolemma seems to be supportive—it holds the long, thin axon together.

Axons and long sensory dendrites that resemble axons are often called fibers. The **nerves** of the body are bundles of fibers connecting the brain and spinal cord to the sense organs and muscles. The nerves make up the peripheral nervous system. Their fibers each have a neurolemma but may or may not have a myelin sheath. The axons that lie inside the brain and spinal cord are in the central nervous system and have no neurolemma; they may or may not

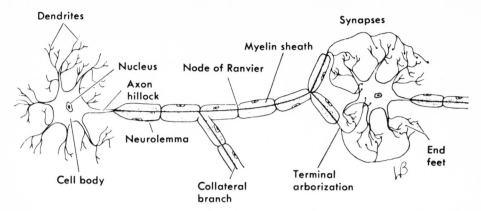

Fig. 3-1. Sketch of a "typical" neuron, showing its major parts. Synapses with a second neuron are also shown.

have a myelin sheath. Their myelin sheaths are believed to be secreted by glial cells, a kind of supporting cell. In any case, bundles of individually conducting fibers held together by connective tissue constitute the nerves of the peripheral nervous system. Bundles of individually conducting axons running from one part of the brain and spinal cord to another, inside the central nervous system, are called **tracts,** instead of nerves.

Anatomical methods

To appreciate what nerve cells look like and what mistakes the anatomist can make in studying their connections with one another, a simplified form of the methods used by the anatomist should be understood. It is difficult to study neurons because of their small size and still more difficult to trace their many connections with one another at synapses. To overcome these difficulties, the anatomist uses two procedures: light microscope observations and electron microscope observations.

Light microscope observations. The largest neurons vary from 50 micrometers (μm) (millionths of a meter) thick at the cell body to 20 μm (about one thousandth of an inch) thick at the axon. Cells of this size can be seen only through a microscope. The tissue must be sliced thin enough so that light will pass through it

(about 40 μm) and placed on a glass slide for observation under the microscope. Before a section of brain or spinal cord can be sliced so thin, it must be hardened with formaldehyde solution (formalin). When the animal is killed, a tube from a formalin bottle is inserted into the heart, which pumps the solution throughout the circulatory system, replacing the blood. Formalin reaches the tissue fluid through the capillary walls and hardens all the body tissues, including the nervous tissue of the brain and spinal cord. The nervous tissue is thereby hardened from the "inside out." The tissue is then removed from the animal and further hardened by freezing or embedding in paraffin, and thin cross sections are sliced from the desired portion with a microtome, a precision slicing instrument. The thin sections are placed in alcohol to remove water and are stained or dyed with solutions that react chemically with one part or another of the nerve cells to color them for clear observation under the microscope. For example, some stains react with the myelin sheath of axons, enabling the anatomist to trace the axons from section to section in the tracts of the brain and spinal cord. Other stains color only cells without a myelin sheath or the cell bodies and terminal arborizations of neurons, permitting study of synapses. Many different specialized types of stains can be used. Stained sections are placed on glass slides and covered for protection. They are then ready for observation.

Electron microscope observations. The **electron microscope** allows a magnification of 10 to 100 times that of the light microscope. Through its use in anatomy, physiology, and physiological psychology, much has been learned regarding the physical and chemical characteristics of synapses.

To oversimplify, the tissue is bombarded with a stream of **electrons,** or negative particles, in a vacuum. The stream of electrons can be focused by magnetic means, just as light can be focused by a lens. The resulting magnification reveals the smallest structures at the synapses. The magnified image is projected on a fluorescent screen at the end of an evacuated tube in the same manner as an image on television.

Electrical methods

Electrical currents. The flow of current through most conductors (such as electrical wires) is the movement of electrons, or negative particles, from a site where there are many of them to a site where there are fewer of them. A conductor is a material that allows this flow to a greater or lesser degree (an insulator is a material that prevents the flow of current). The difference in the number of electrons at two points constitutes the *voltage* (number of **volts**) difference between them. The greater the voltage difference between two points joined by a conductor, the more rapid the current flow will be, that is, the greater the *amperage* (number of **amperes**). Conversely, the greater the *resistance* (in **ohms**) to current flow offered by the conductor, the slower the current flow will be. In measuring currents in living tissue, electrical change is small so that the terms millivolt (1/1000 of a volt), microvolt (1 millionth of a volt), milliampere (1/1000 of an ampere), microampere, milliohms and micro-ohms are often used.

Instruments. The functioning of neurons in carrying nerve impulses along the length of an axon and in exciting other neurons at synapses is usually studied through the electrical activity that constitutes the nerve impulse. In the past the major obstacles to studying the electrical activity of neurons were (1) the small size of the neurons, (2) the minuteness of the electrical change (10/1000 to 70/1000 of a volt), and (3) recording instruments that could not follow electrical events that last only a thousandth of a second. The first problem has been solved by the development of the **microelectrode,** which is small enough to penetrate a single nerve cell, so that the difference in electrical potential between the inside and outside of the single cell can be measured. The second problem has yielded to the vacuum-tube or transistor **amplifier,** which can magnify voltage differences by as much as a million times. The third problem has been overcome by the **cathode-ray oscilloscope,** which measures voltage change as the movement of a stream of electrons, an event that has almost no inertia or lag. The cathode-ray oscilloscope is a simplified version of your television set. A glowing spot caused by a moving beam of electrons moves across the face of the tube in 1/1000 to 1/100 of a second, leaving a glowing line behind it. Changes in the electrical activity of nerve cells when they conduct impulses are recorded by vertical movements of the glowing line. In this fashion, the nerve cell impulse "draws its own picture," which can be photographed for a permanent record.

Bioelectrical currents

Electrolytes. An **electrolyte** is a substance that breaks up into positive and negative **ions** in a water solution. Salt (NaCl) is an electrolyte; in solution it breaks up into a positively charged sodium ion (Na^+) and a negatively charged chlorine ion (Cl^-). The sodium ion is positive because it lacks an electron, and the chlorine ion is negative because it has a surplus electron. Suppose that wires connected to a battery are placed in a solution of salt water. The wires serve as **electrodes** (Fig. 3-2). One wire, the

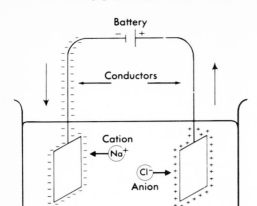

Fig. 3-2. Flow of current through a wire as electron movement and through a salt solution (electrolyte) as ion movement.

cathode, will have more electrons than the other wire, the **anode.** Na^+ ions will be attracted to the cathode to pick up the electron each one lacks. The Na^+ ion is therefore a **cation.** The Cl^- ions will be attracted to the anode to give up the surplus electron that each one possesses. The Cl^- ions are therefore **anions.** A flow of current through the solution results from the movement of both positive and negative ions. Bioelectrical currents, or currents in living tissue, are the result of ion movements of this nature, rather than the movement of electrons through wires.

Resting potential. For reasons to be explained later, the fluid outside the nerve cell has more positive ions than does the fluid on the inside. The positively charged outside of the nerve cell and the negatively charged inside are separated by the nerve (cell) membrane. This state of affairs existing across the nerve membrane is termed a **polarized condition.** The difference in voltage between the positive outside and the negative inside of the membrane of all living cells is called the **resting potential.**

Spike potential. If two electrodes leading to a battery are placed near the axon of a nerve cell (in its fluid medium), the polarized condition of the nerve membrane positive outside will be changed. The polarized condition across the membrane will be increased at the anode, since the few negative anions will give up their surplus electrons to the anode at this point. The polarized condition of the membrane at the cathode will be decreased, since many positive cations will acquire electrons from the cathode. When a critical amount of partial depolarization is reached, an explosive ion exchange occurs across the membrane. The polarized condition of the membrane will be reversed. The membrane becomes negative on the outside and positive on the inside. This polarization reversal will sweep along the length of the axon as the **spike potential.** Behind this moving polarization reversal, the nerve cell will recover its original polarized condition.

All-or-none law. The nerve impulse consists of a rapid exchange of positive and negative ions across the nerve cell membrane when the degree of depolarization reaches a critical value at the cathode. That is, when the polarized condition of the nerve membrane is reduced by a certain amount, the membrane "takes over" and continues the depolarization past the neutral point, so that the outside of the nerve cell membrane becomes negative with respect to the inside. The impulse is self-propagating; that is, the energy for the polarization reversal is supplied by the nerve cell itself, and not by the stimulus that triggers it. Once initiated, the impulse spreads along the axon by ion exchanges through the membrane down the whole length of the axon; the energy for the spread comes from the nerve cell membrane. The **all-or-none-law** states that a nerve cell responds with the total voltage change that its polarized condition permits if, and only if, the stimulus intensity reaches a critical threshold value. Stronger stimuli will not result in a larger or faster nerve impulse since the nerve cell itself, and not the stimulus, provides the energy for the nerve impulse.

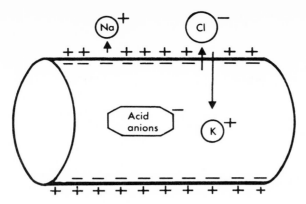

Fig. 3-3. Chemical basis of the resting potential. Negatively charged acid anions are trapped inside the cell membrane because of their size, and positive sodium cations (Na^+) are actively excluded by the membrane ("sodium pump"), whereas positive potassium ions (K^+) are actively included by the membrane. Concentration gradients of chlorine ions (Cl^-) are the result, the Cl^- ions being attracted by the Na^+ ions. Cl^- ions tend to diffuse back inside the membrane. As a net result the membrane is polarized, being positive on the outside with respect to the inside of the cell.

Ion exchanges

Resting potential. The polarized condition of the nerve cell axon is caused by certain properties of the nerve cell membrane with respect to ions—charged chemical elements and molecules. As a result of the characteristics of the nerve cell membrane, there are more positive than negative ions outside the membrane and more negative than positive ions inside the membrane. The imbalance in ions results in a positive charge outside the membrane and a negative charge inside the membrane. The ion imbalance and the consequent resting potential between the inside and outside of the cell membrane are the result of four factors (Fig. 3-3):

1. *Sodium pump.* For reasons that are still not understood, the nerve cell membrane actively *excludes* sodium ions (Na^+) from the cell. Sodium ions carry a positive charge; thus there are more positively charged sodium ions outside the membrane than inside the membrane.

2. *Potassium pump.* Theorists believe that the membrane actively *includes* potassium ions (K^+). That is, it takes any potassium ions encountered in the fluid environment and actively transports them into the cell.

Potassium ions are positively charged, but there are not enough of them inside the cell to offset other ion differences between the inside and outside of the cell. The cell remains, on balance, more positively charged outside than inside.

3. *Ion size.* The cell contains many negatively charged acid molecules (acid anions) that are too large to pass through the pores of the cell membrane. This contributes to making the inside of the cell negative with respect to the outside.

4. *Principle of diffusion.* Chlorine ions (Cl^-) carry a negative charge and are free to move back and forth through the membrane. Substances tend to move from a region of high concentration to a region of low concentration, according to the principle of diffusion. To demonstrate this phenomenon, one need only place a drop of ink into a glass of water; in minutes the ink particles will diffuse throughout the water. According to the principle of diffusion, one would expect to find the same number of chlorine ions inside as there are outside the nerve cell membrane. But chlorine ions carry a negative charge and therefore are attracted by positively charged ions and repelled by negatively charged ions. As

shown earlier, there are more negative acid anions inside the membrane than outside, and more positive sodium ions outside the membrane than positive ions inside the membrane. Therefore, there is an imbalance in favor of positive ions outside the membrane and negative ions inside the membrane. Negative chlorine ions are repelled by the negative ions inside the membrane and attracted by the positive ions outside the membrane; a **concentration gradient** of chlorine ions is built up, with more chlorine ions outside than inside the membrane. For reasons explained above, there is a similar concentration gradient of sodium ions (more outside) and an opposite concentration gradient of potassium ions (more inside). The measured size of these gradients of charged particles is enough to account for the size of the

resting potential, which is about 40 millivolts (mV). The resting potential is accounted for by the imbalance of known positive ions outside the nerve cell membrane and known negative ions inside the nerve cell membrane. These principles are not confined to nerve cells—all living cells seem to be polarized and for the same reasons. However, the specialized feature of nerve cells is their greater ability to alter their polarized condition to produce the nerve impulse.

Nerve impulse. Since a single axon rather than a bundle of axons in a nerve is being discussed, the term should be spike potential, or neuron impulse. The term nerve impulse comes from earlier experiments in which the electrical activity of nerve trunks, rather than of a single axon, was all the experimenters could measure. To

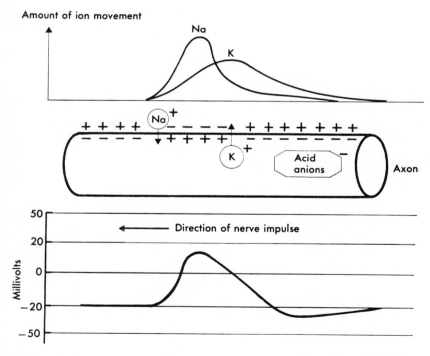

Fig. 3-4. Chemical basis of the nerve impulse. Polarization reversal is caused by an influx of sodium ions (Na^+) when the membrane ceases to exclude them. Recovery of polarization occurs when potassium ions (K^+) move outside the membrane to replace sodium ions. Ion movements are shown as the top graph, events in the axon are sketched in the middle, and electrical changes (millivolts of polarization) are at the bottom, with a common time axis for the three sets of events reading from left to right.

simplify, the nerve impulse in an axon occurs when its polarized condition is reduced enough to "turn off" the sodium and potassium "pumps" (Fig. 3-4). The initial result is a rapid movement of positive sodium ions (Na^+) into the negatively charged interior of the axon. This event reverses the polarized condition of the membrane, so that it becomes positive inside and negative outside—the spike potential. Recovery is initiated by the movement of positive potassium ions (K^+) out of the axon to replace the sodium ions. Potassium ion movement causes the recovery of the normal polarized condition of the axon, that is, the downward limb of the spike potential and parts of the negative and positive after-potentials. The cell is depolarized by sodium ion movement and repolarized by potassium ion movement through its membrane. Negative chlorine ions move first inside and then back outside the membrane in response to changes in its polarized condition. After the action potential is over, the sodium and potassium "pumps" become active again—the sodium is transferred back out of the cell and the potassium is transferred back inside the cell while the resting potential is maintained.

THE SYNAPSE
Transmitters

Refer again to Fig. 3-1. Note that nerve cells contact one another when the terminal arborization of one cell "contacts" the cell body and dendrites of a second cell. Every such contact is a **synapse.** Although there are several kinds of synapses, the variety sketched here is most typical. Each branch of the terminal arborization of the first cell ends in a knoblike structure called an axon terminal, or synaptic knob. The synaptic knobs do not touch the surface of the dendrites or cell bodies but come very close to them, leaving a uniform gap of about 10 nanometers (nm). In Fig. 3-5 a junction between a synaptic knob and dendrite or cell body is shown as it can be seen under the electron microscope. Notice the small globules that concentrate inside the synaptic knobs near the synaptic cleft, the gap between knob and cell body or dendrites. These are the **synaptic vesicles,** which are believed to contain the specific chemical substances by which one

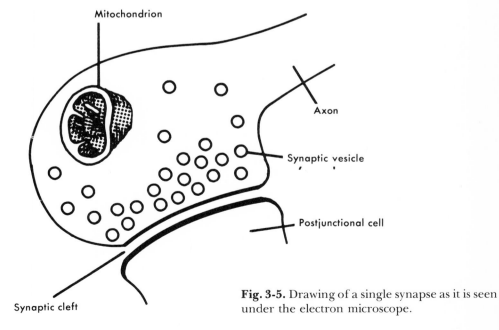

Fig. 3-5. Drawing of a single synapse as it is seen under the electron microscope.

Mitochondrion

Axon

Synaptic vesicle

Postjunctional cell

Synaptic cleft

Table 4. Some known and probable synaptic transmitters*

Probable transmitter substance	Location	Hypothesized effect
Acetylcholine (ACh)	Brain, spinal cord, autonomic ganglia, target organs of the parasympathetic nervous system	Excitation in brain and autonomic ganglia, excitation or inhibition in target organs
Norepinephrine (NE)	Brain, target organs of sympathetic nervous system	Inhibition in brain, excitation or inhibition in target organs
Dopamine (DA)	Brain	Inhibition
Serotonin (5-hydroxy-tryptamine, or 5-HT)	Brain	Inhibition
Gamma-aminobutyric acid (GABA)	Brain (especially cerebral and cerebellar cortex)	Inhibition
Glycine	Spinal cord interneurons	Inhibition
Glutamic acid	Brain, spinal sensory neurons	Excitation
Aspartic acid	Spinal cord interneurons, brain (?)	Excitation
Taurine, serine, substance P	Unknown	Unknown

*From Carlson, N. R.: Physiology of behavior, Boston, 1977, Allyn & Bacon, Inc.

nerve cell excites another at synapses. Two of these *chemical transmitters* are known to be norepinephrine and acetylcholine (ACh), but there are others (Table 4). There are also neurons whose end-feet probably release inhibitory chemical transmitters, such as gamma-aminobutyric acid (GABA), that increase the polarization of dendrites and cell bodies at synapses. Increased polarization can prevent excitation at nearby synapses from excitatory neurons that end on the same cell.

Postsynaptic potentials

When an excitatory neuron releases ACh onto another neuron at its synapses, the chemical transmitter acts to partly depolarize the second cell. The resulting depolarization is called an **excitatory postsynaptic potential,** or **EPSP.** The vesicles in the synaptic knob probably release ACh molecules through the membrane of the synaptic knobs. The ACh molecules drift rapidly across the synaptic cleft to act on receptor sites in the membranes of the cell body and dendrites of the second cell. They appear to make the cell body and dendrites of the second cell more perme-

able to positively charged sodium and potassium ions. The result is the partial depolarization, or graded potential. The cell body and dendrites do not reverse polarization immediately, as an axon does. Ions shift from the area of the axon hillock (Fig. 3-1) to replace those that move into the cell body. Depolarization of the axon hillock causes a nerve impulse in the axon. The nerve impulse sweeps down the axon to the next set of synapses. As long as a large enough negative EPSP is maintained by synapses on the dendrites and cell body, the axon will continue to fire. When fresh ACh is no longer being released at the synapses, the neuron does not continue to fire, because the remaining ACh is rapidly broken down by an enzyme, acetylcholine esterase (AChE).

There are types of neurons that are excited in the normal way but act to prevent the depolarization of neurons on which they have synapses. One type of inhibitory cell known to be important in reflexes is a neuron called a Renshaw cell. Its synaptic knobs have vesicles that probably contain gamma-aminobutyric acid (GABA). Such transmitters *hyperpolarize,* or increase the polarized condition of, the cell body and dendrites on which they are released. The change in potential is called an **inhibitory postsynaptic potential (IPSP).** A hyperpolarized cell is harder to excite with the EPSP produced at excitatory synapses. The cell body and dendrites of a cell may have both excitatory and inhibitory synapses on it; whether it fires depends on the algebraic sum of the EPSP and IPSP influences, which are called **facilitation** and **inhibition,** respectively.

The IPSP is believed to be caused by the effect of the inhibitory transmitter on the membrane. The transmitter probably makes the membrane permeable to potassium ions (K^+) and chlorine ions (Cl^-) encountered in the fluid environment. However, the membrane is not permeable to the slightly larger sodium ions (Na^+), which are outside the membrane. The outflow of positive potassium ions and the inflow of negative chlorine ions increase the polarized condition of the membrane, as there is no corresponding inflow of positive sodium ions. These events make the cell body and dendrites more positive outside and more negative inside. The hyperpolarized cell is more difficult to depolarize, or excite. Potassium salts have been used to hyperpolarize and therefore inhibit parts of the brain in animal learning experiments (spreading depression, Chapter 14).

THE NERVOUS SYSTEM
Some classifications

The nervous system consists of the **brain, spinal cord,** and **nerves.** The nerves connect the brain and spinal cord to the **effectors** (muscles and glands) and **receptors** (sense organs). The brain and spinal cord constitute the **central nervous system,** studied in detail in a later section.

The nerves, made up of bundles of individually conducting parts of nerve cells, or fibers, make up the **peripheral nervous system.** The **sensory nerves** carry excitation from receptors to the central nervous system. The **motor nerves** carry excitation from the central nervous system to the glands and muscles. Sensory and motor nerves branch repeatedly as they reach receptors and effectors over the entire body, and their final branches may contain only sensory or only motor fibers and can be called sensory nerves or motor nerves, respectively. Near their origin in the brain or spinal cord, however, most nerves are *mixed* and contain both sensory and motor fibers.

A further distinction can be made among the independently conducting fibers of the peripheral nervous system. Those sensory fibers coming from the receptors and those motor fibers that reach the somatic or striated, muscles, which move the body about, form the **peripheral somatic nervous system (PSNS).** The PSNS is the part of the peripheral nervous system that is concerned with overt reactions to internal and external stimuli. As treated here, the motor fibers to the smooth muscles and glands form the **autonomic nervous system (ANS),** a different part of the peripheral nervous system. So classified, the ANS is a *motor system only* and will be treated separately because of certain unique features of structure and function. The fibers of the PSNS and of the ANS may be mixed in nerve trunks near their origin at the brain and spinal cord. Certain features of the origin of the ANS are unique, however, as will be explained later.

Peripheral somatic nervous system. The motor nerves going to the body muscles and the sensory nerves coming from the receptors form the PSNS. The PSNS originates in the **spinal nerves** that leave the spinal cord and the **cranial nerves** that leave the brain. Branches of the spinal and cranial nerves spread over the entire body to reach the receptors and somatic muscles. There are 12 pairs of cranial nerves (their functions will be discussed later). Both cranial and spinal nerves occur in pairs because the nervous system is bilaterally symmetrical. Just as you have pairs of identical arms, legs, ribs, eyes, ears, and so on, your brain and spinal cord are made up of identical halves joined at the

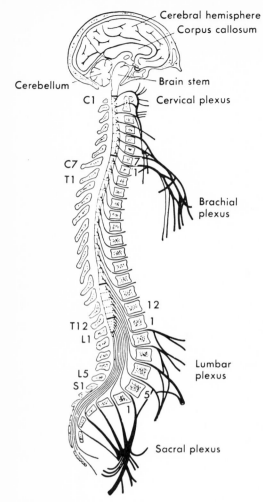

Cerebral hemisphere
Corpus callosum
Cerebellum
Brain stem
C1
Cervical plexus
C7
T1
Brachial plexus
12
1
T12
L1
Lumbar plexus
L5
S1
5
1
Sacral plexus

Fig. 3-6. Drawing of the brain and spinal cord from a midline view. The brain is shown in the median plane (a midline section); the external aspect of the spinal cord is seen from the side. The vertebrae are cut away to show the cord. Note that the cord is shorter than the vertebral column ("backbone"), and the lower spinal nerves must descend before emerging between the vertebrae for which they are named. (From Gardner, E. O.: Fundamentals of neurology, ed. 6, Philadelphia, 1975, W. B. Saunders Company.)

"center." The spinal cord lies within the vertebral column, or backbone, of jointed vertebrae (Fig. 3-6). There are 31 pairs of spinal nerves connecting the spinal cord with receptors and effectors.

Autonomic nervous system

Anatomy. The ANS has been defined as a *visceral motor system,* consisting of those motor nerve fibers of the peripheral nervous system that supply the smooth muscles and glands of the viscera. The ANS motor fibers differ from the motor fibers to the striated muscles in both structural and functional respects (Fig. 3-7):

1. *Dual innervation.* There is only one system of motor fibers to the striated muscles, but each smooth muscle or gland receives two sets of fibers from the ANS (there are exceptions). One set of fibers is from the sympathetic division of the ANS, also called the **sympathetic nervous system (SNS).** The SNS originates in fibers leaving the spinal cord in the central regions. The other division of the ANS is the parasympathetic division, also called the **parasympathetic nervous system (PNS).** The PNS originates in fibers from the cranial nerves and from the lower segment of the spinal cord. As can be seen in Fig. 3-7, each smooth muscle or gland receives both SNS and PNS fibers in a system of dual innervation.

2. *Peripheral ANS inhibition.* The PNS and SNS have opposite effects on the smooth muscles and glands they innervate. If the SNS excites the visceral effector or speeds up its functioning, the PNS inhibits it or slows it down, and vice versa. For example, the SNS increases the heart rate and inhibits the digestive glands, whereas the PNS slows the heart rate and excites the digestive glands. These opposed influences act peripherally, where the nerve fibers reach the effector. By contrast, motor fibers to the striated muscles are excited or inhibited centrally, inside the brain and spinal cord. Somatic nerve fibers fire when excited and do not fire when inhibited. When they fire, a muscle contracts. Thus excitation of a somatic nerve cannot inhibit an effector.

3. *Two fibers in the ANS motor pathway.* Somatic motor axons have their cell bodies in the brain or spinal cord, and their fibers

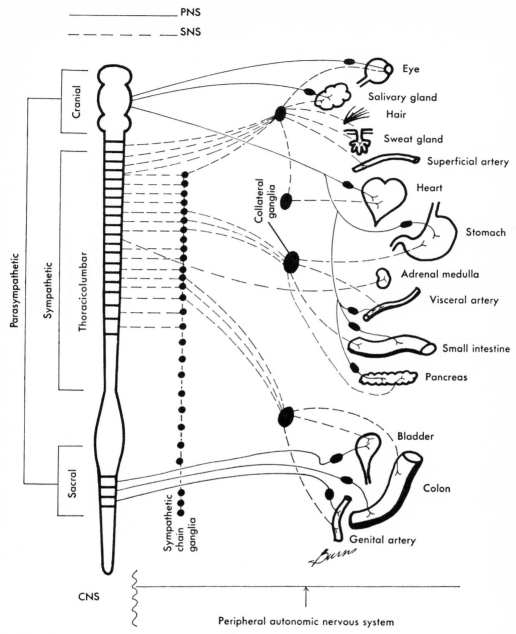

Fig. 3-7. Diagram of the autonomic nervous system, showing sympathetic and parasympathetic divisions.

take an uninterrupted course through cranial and spinal nerves to the somatic muscles. In both divisions of the ANS there are two cells in the motor pathway. The **preganglionic** cells have their cell bodies in the spinal cord and brain, whereas their fibers terminate in **ganglia** (plural of ganglion), which lie outside the CNS. Here they synapse with **postganglionic** fibers, which innervate the smooth muscles and glands. (A ganglion is a collection of nerve cell bodies lying outside the CNS.) The ganglia of the sympathetic division lie along the outside of the vertebrae in an interconnected chain (**sympathetic chain ganglia**) or else among the viscera (**collateral ganglia**) in a nerve network, or **plexus.** The **parasympathetic ganglia** are found near the organs that are innervated by parasympathetic fibers.

4. *Automaticity of effectors.* As will be noted in Chapter 4, the heart and some of the smooth muscles show automatic contractions, with their *rate* controlled by the ANS. Striated muscles do not normally contract unless they are excited by their motor nerves.

Physiology of the ANS. The SNS and PNS differ in function by having opposed effects on the visceral organs, as previously explained—speeding or slowing the heart or digestion, causing opposed contractions in the visceral smooth muscles, and inhibiting or exciting glands. The SNS and PNS also *interact* in the complex responses involved in digestion, respiration, and other internal functions. As explained above, the SNS is organized in a diffuse manner and tends to be aroused as a whole system. The SNS sets off the widespread visceral responses characteristic of arousal and emotion—increased heart rate and rate of breathing and widespread changes in the blood vessels to prepare for exertion. The PNS is discretely organized to influence only a few visceral structures at a time. The PNS provides for the sequence of visceral reactions involved in digestion, food metabolism, and other metabolic responses. Widespread SNS excitation does, however, stimulate more widespread PNS reactions, so that there is a continually changing balance in the influence of the two systems on the viscera.

Secretions. In both the SNS and PNS there are synapses between preganglionic neurons and postganglionic neurons in peripheral ganglia. These are the only synapses between neurons that lie outside the brain and spinal cord in the peripheral nervous system. Like many synapses in the central nervous system, the preganglionic neurons stimulate the postganglionic neurons by the release of acetylcholine (ACh) from synaptic vesicles. After exciting the postganglionic neurons ACh is rapidly broken down under the influence of the enzyme acetylcholine esterase (AChE), which is always present in the tissue fluid surrounding the cells. However, at the junction between the postganglionic neurons and their effectors, the transmitter secretions of the SNS and PNS differ; thus they have opposite effects on the viscera. The PNS releases ACh to stimulate the effector. In the case of the heart the influence is inhibitory, but ACh selectively stimulates certain other smooth muscles, such as those that constrict arteries going to somatic muscle, and dilates arteries going to the digestive system. ACh also stimulates the digestive glands. Since the postganglionic fibers of the PNS excite visceral effectors by the release of acetylcholine, postganglionic PNS fibers are called **cholinergic** fibers.

By contrast the SNS acts on the effector by the release of **epinephrine** or **norepinephrine,** depending on the postganglionic neurons and the organs they innervate. Epinephrine excites the heart to increase the heart rate, excites constricting fibers in the arteries to the digestive system, and excites dilating fibers in the arteries to the muscles to prepare the body for exertion. Norepinephrine, at other endings, inhibits the digestive glands. Since no substance such as AChE is present in the blood to speed the removal of either, *diffuse* reactions result from the spread of these transmitters to nearby effectors. Epinephrine is chemically the same as adrenaline (see below), and thus the postganglionic fibers of the SNS are often called adrenergic.

In addition to the digestive glands, the PNS sends fibers to the islets of Langerhans (beta cells) of the pancreas by way of the vagus nerve. The PNS stimulates the pancreas to release insulin into the bloodstream. Insulin is necessary for blood glucose utilization by all the cells of the body. Insulin appears to aid PNS reactions in a poorly understood fashion. Hence the PNS is sometimes called a vago-insulin system. The SNS, on the other hand, stimulates another gland, the adrenal medulla, which secretes the substances norepinephrine and epinephrine. The SNS is often called, therefore, a sympathetico-adrenal system. (It is interesting to note that no postganglionic fibers are involved. Since the adrenal medulla secretes epinephrine and norepinephrine, many believe it to have developed from postganglionic neurons.) The hormones secreted by the adrenal medulla circulate in the bloodstream and have widespread sympathetic effects on many visceral effectors, which, along with the diffuse anatomic arrangement of the SNS and its lack of an enzyme to destroy the hormones, increase the diffuse effects of the SNS on the viscera.

To the extent that the SNS and PNS could be said to have a purpose, the function of the SNS would be to organize widespread mobilization of the resources of an animal for vigorous physical activity in an "emergency," whereas the PNS functions to conserve the resources of the animal by means of a series of discrete reflex reactions involved in digestion, food storage, and other metabolic reactions. The interactions of the SNS andPNS are involved in complex responses of motivation and emotion.

Emergency theory. The emergency theory of Cannon was proposed as an explanation for the reactions of the SNS. He stated that the SNS mobilized the resources of the animal for "fight or flight" in an emergency. Although the SNS patterns found in rage are somewhat different from those found in fear (Chapter 13), the theory predicts most SNS effects on visceral structures. The Cannon theory is therefore a useful mnemonic device for the student. Arteries contract and relax in different locations, diverting blood from

the digestive system to the somatic muscles to "fuel" their exertions. Heart rate and blood pressure rise for the same reason. Breathing rate increases to provide more oxygen, and the bronchial tubes to the lungs dilate. Sweating increases to cool the body, sphincters contract to "shut off" digestion, digestive contractions of stomach and intestine cease, and epinephrine and norepinephrine are released into the bloodstream by the adrenal glands to make these and other SNS reactions more widespread. To predict the SNS effect on a visceral structure, merely ask what effect "should" be to prepare the body for exertion. PNS effects can be predicted from the emergency theory; PNS effects would be the opposite of the emergency SNS effects.

Central nervous system

Despite the complexity of the responses mediated by the ANS and by the peripheral somatic nervous system, the organization of behavior must be sought in the central nervous system (CNS). The way in which neurons interconnect at synapses in the brain and spinal cord determines organized motor output in response to sensory input. Stimuli in the environment activate receptors, which leads to sensory nerve excitation and eventual motor nerve and muscle or gland response. Which stimulus leads to what response is governed by the "connections" between sensory neurons and motoneurons that are made in the CNS.

The spinal cord: reflexes. One of the simplest stimulus-response, or S-R, relationships that can be observed in behavior is the reflex. Even the most oversimplified diagram of reflex anatomy involves parts of both the CNS and the peripheral nervous system. A reflex mediated by the spinal cord is shown in Fig. 3-8. Five sets of component parts are involved: (1) **receptors,** (2) **sensory neurons,** (3) **association neurons (interneurons),** (4) **motoneurons,** and (5) **effectors.** Stimulation of receptors leads to sensory, or **afferent,** neuron impulses, which excite **association neurons** in

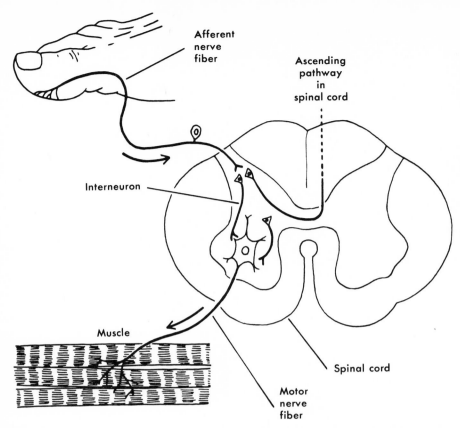

Fig. 3-8. Diagram of the elements in a reflex. (From Vander, A. J., Sherman, J. H., and Luciano, D. S.: Human physiology: the mechanisms of body function, New York, 1970, McGraw-Hill Book Company. Used with permission of McGraw-Hill Book Company.)

the CNS. Association neurons, in turn, fire motor, or **efferent,** neurons, which excite **effectors,** which are muscles or glands. The synaptic connections between neurons are relatively fixed and invariable, so that the response to the stimulus is always the same. Examples of reflexes include jerking the hand off a painfully hot surface, blinking the eyes in response to a puff of air striking the face, and sneezing when the nasal passages are irritated. Once a given set of receptors is stimulated, the response is determined by the "fixed" synaptic connections in the pathway between stimulus and response. The reflex is then "stimulus-bound"—it is determined by the receptors stimulated. For example, stimulating pain receptors in the foot will

cause an animal to reflexly withdraw his leg. Stimulating pressure receptors in the same foot will cause the animal to extend the same leg to support his weight. The pressure and pain receptors lead to different reflex pathways, so that different responses result.

Reflex plan of higher centers. Sensory input from the receptors involved in reflexes, and from many other receptors as well, reaches higher centers in the brain by way of ascending tracts in the spinal cord. Depending on the complexity of the brain centers involved, many thousands of association neurons may be excited. Finally, excitation will return to the spinal cord through descending tracts. The fibers of the descending spi-

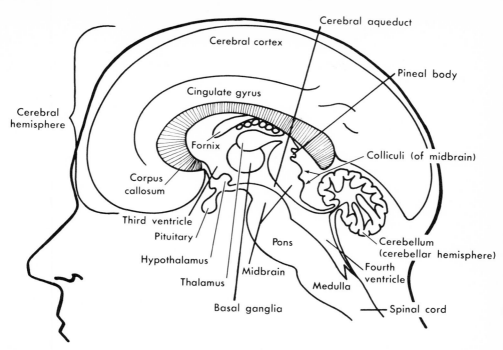

Fig. 3-9. Diagram of a human brain seen from medial plane (split down the middle). Some major features described in the text are seen in the figure.

nal cord tracts will reach the motoneurons to excite response. Considered from this oversimplified point of view, the most complex stimulus-response relations are modeled after the reflex with three major differences: (1) many more association neurons are involved at all levels of the brain and spinal cord; (2) the response is not fixed but varies according to which association neurons intervene between stimulus and response on a given occasion; that is, the S-R pathways vary and are not fixed as in the case of a reflex; and (3) **correlation** of input and **coordination** of output are greater than in the reflex. Excitation must be focused (correlation) from many widespread receptors and tracts on a single brain **center** (collection of synapses) vital to the response. In addition, from such a single brain center, tracts lead to many motoneurons at all levels of the brain and cord. These events happen many times because many centers are involved. The widespread pattern of

motoneuron excitation is such that many muscles are excited in a smooth reaction made possible by coordination of output on the motor side.

PARTS OF THE BRAIN

The brain develops from a hollow tubular structure, as does the spinal cord. The brain is much more extensively developed than the spinal cord, however, and the hollow (tubular) parts are distorted into the **ventricles** and the **cerebral aqueduct** (Figs. 3-9 and 3-10). The parts of the brain that remain as a linear and sequential series of structures are included in the **brain stem** (like the stem of a tree). The brain stem is organized like the spinal cord only in having a central "core" of gray matter (synapses, centers, etc.) surrounded by the white matter of tracts—nerve fibers ascending and descending the brain stem to carry excitation to various levels of the brain and spinal cord. Two pairs of outgrowths from the brain stem overlie it as

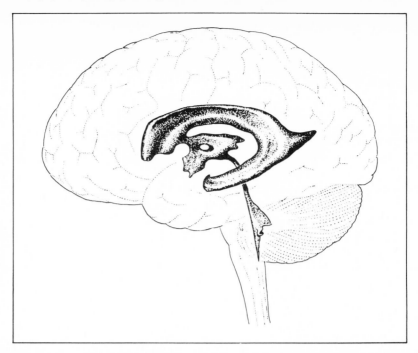

Fig. 3-10. Lateral view of ventricles of brain, surrounded by outline of brain. (From Vander, A. J., Sherman, J. H., and Luciano, D. S.: Human physiology: the mechanism of body function, New York, 1970, McGraw-Hill Book Company. Used with permission of McGraw-Hill Book Company.)

two **cerebral hemispheres** and two **cerebellar hemispheres.** The hemispheres are organized in an opposite fashion to the brain stem so far as gray matter and white matter are concerned. The hemispheres have surface gray matter (called **cortex**). The interior consists of the white matter of fibers reaching the surface gray matter from the brain stem that is beneath the hemispheres.

Important brain structures (Fig. 3-9)

It is helpful to locate the major parts of the brain as "landmarks" before discussing the functions of these and related brain structures. The simplest segment of the brain stem is the **medulla,** which is continuous with the spinal cord. Next in line is the **pons.** Overlying both the medulla and pons are the cerebellar hemispheres (see above). Between the cerebellar hemispheres above and pons and medulla below is the **fourth ventricle,** one of the "hollow" parts of the brain discussed previously. The fourth ventricle is continuous with the cerebral **aqueduct,** the hollow part of the **midbrain.** The cerebral aqueduct opens into the **third ventricle,** a tall and narrow opening surrounded by several other brain stem structures. The floor and part of the walls of the third ventricle form the **hypothalamus.** On both sides of the ventricles lie the egg-shaped thalami (sing., **thalamus**). Lying farther to either side of the midline and embedded in the walls of the cerebral hemispheres, the **basal ganglia (corpus striatum)** are found. The **corpus callosum** is a band of white matter that interconnects corresponding parts of the surface cortex of the cerebral hemispheres. The cerebral hemispheres and cerebellar hemispheres have developed to such an extent that they "surround" most of the brain stem at the top and sides (Fig.

3-10). This is why Fig. 3-9 is a midline or "split-down-the-middle" view, so that the parts of the brain stem may be seen. The ventricles of the cerebral hemispheres are the **lateral ventricles.**

Brain functions

The **medulla** contains many centers for the vital reflexes of the body, which regulate, for instance, heart rate, breathing, and vomiting.

The **cerebellum** regulates balance and coordination of movement. It receives input from the muscles (tension receptors) and inner ear (balance and motion receptors). Output from the cerebellum regulates muscle tone and adjustments in posture.

The cerebellum is connected to the brain stem by the **pons,** a great mass of fibers that surround the brain stem and "grasp" it.

The **midbrain** surrounds the cerebral aqueduct. Above the aqueduct are found the pea-shaped **colliculi** (sing., colliculus), which are visual and auditory reflex centers. The "floor" of the midbrain contains tracts of conducting fibers and a few synaptic centers.

The **hypothalamus** contains many centers that are sensitive to conditions in the fluid **internal environment** of the blood and **cerebrospinal fluid,** the extracellular tissue fluid of the brain and spinal cord. The neurons of these centers act as receptors and are stimulated by changes in fluid salt content and osmotic pressure, chemical composition, and other conditions. Such changes represent **need-conditions** of the tissue or disturbances in internal consistency and homeostasis (Chapter 2). The centers arouse and sustain internal and external responses until the need-condition is corrected and are therefore the basis of **drives.** The response adjustments that result may be as simple as a change in heart rate or may include complex learned behavior such as putting on a coat when one is cold.

The **thalamus** likewise serves as an integrating center. It also serves as a correlating relay center for incoming sensory input to the cerebral cortex. In addition, many impulses going from one area of the cerebral cortex to another travel by way of synapses in the thalamus.

The **corpus striatum,** located in the walls of the cerebral hemispheres, is an earlier development of a set of master correlation and coordination centers in lower animals without a cerebral cortex or without a well-developed cortex. In these animals, particularly birds, the neural connections between stimulus and response for many patterns of instinctive behavior are found in the corpus striatum (basal ganglia and tracts). In man the corpus striatum regulates the sequence and timing of movements, processes certain facial expressions in emotion, and controls "sequential acts" such as swinging the arms for balance when one walks.

The **cerebral cortex** is the highest set of integrating centers of the human brain. Through millions of synaptic connections in the gray matter of the cerebral cortex, any stimulus input can result in any response output. Excitation originating in the receptors and carried to the cerebral cortex through cranial and spinal nerves and tracts is processed by lower centers but may eventually reach the cortex. The cerebral cortex can "connect" any part of the brain with any other part, at least indirectly.

The cerebral cortex undergoes greater development in humans than in any lower animal. The cerebral hemispheres and covering cortex have expanded in size and area until the brain stem is almost completely covered except for the base of the brain. The increase in size of the cortex has resulted in a thickening that forms several *layers* of cells and synaptic connections. There is a great increase in area as well— about 195 cm² (2½ ft.²) in humans. The expansion of the cortex has occurred in the face of a limited cranial capacity, the size of the bony "box" of the skull. As a result the cortex has developed folds to in-

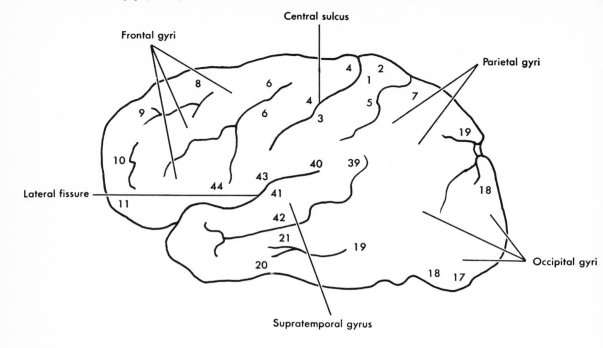

Fig. 3-11. Cerebral cortex, showing some of the major sulci and gyri and some of the principal numbered Brodmann areas.

crease its area within the limited cranial volume, and much of the cortex is buried in the folds, or sulci (sing., **sulcus**), of the brain (Fig. 3-11). The surface areas between the sulci are called gyri (sing., **gyrus**).

Each sulcus and gyrus is named, but only the major ones are important here. The **longitudinal fissure** divides the **cerebrum** into two **cerebral hemispheres** (a fissure is a large sulcus). The **central sulcus** divides each hemisphere into an anterior one-third and a posterior two-thirds of cortical area. The central sulcus lies between the **precentral gyrus** (area 4 in Fig. 3-11) and the **postcentral gyrus** (areas 3, 1, and 2). The **lateral fissure** lies between area 41 and areas 44, 43, and 40.

The cortex is also divided into lobes. The **frontal lobe** is anterior to the central sulcus and includes about one-third of each hemisphere. The **temporal lobe** lies below the lateral fissure—the cerebral hemispheres are shaped somewhat in the form of boxing gloves, and the temporal lobe is like the thumb of a boxing glove.

The **occipital lobe** is the posterior part of the hemisphere, and the **parietal lobe** lies between the occipital lobe and the central sulcus. There is no major sulcus to mark the dividing line between occipital and parietal lobes—the parietal lobe includes area 7, and the occipital lobe, area 19.

The thickness of the cortex is caused by six well-defined cortical layers (in most areas). Functionally, the cortex is *vertically organized,* with excitation carried from cell to cell, largely in a vertical direction. Excitation reaches sensory and motor areas via the white matter of **projection fibers.** Excitation is carried to other cortical areas by way of both lower centers and **commissural fibers** that "loop" down into the white matter and back up again. Various parts of the cortex differ in the relative thickness of the six cell layers. The **Brodmann system** of cortical areas depends on the relative thickness of the cell layers; it is a useful way to refer to a specific part of the cortex. In the Brodmann system, a cross section of the cortex was taken in the postcentral gyrus. The first arrangement

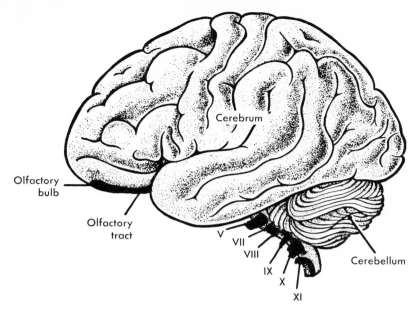

Fig. 3-12. Lateral (from the side) view of the brain.

of cell layers encountered was arbitrarily called area 1. With further cross sections, the first change in the relative thickness of the layers was called area 2, and so on, until the entire cortex had been classified. Sometimes these anatomical differences correspond with known functional differences in the cortex, and sometimes they do not. In any case the Brodmann system is a useful way to refer to specific parts of the cortex.

More functionally, the cortex has also been classified into sensory projection areas, motor projection areas, and association areas. **Sensory projection areas** are those parts of the cortex in which pathways from the receptors, or sense organs, terminate. Thus area 17 is the **visual projection area;** area 41, the **auditory projection area;** areas 3, 1, and 2, the **somesthetic** (skin senses) **projection area;** and so on. The **motor projection area** is the origin of fibers descending in the brain stem and spinal cord to the motor neurons of the cranial and spinal nerves that control the somatic muscles. It occupies area 4. The **association areas** are those which are not directly sensory or motor in function. Classically, they were presumed to "associate"

incoming impulses to the sensory projection areas with outgoing impulses from the motor projection areas to permit responses to stimuli. Association areas are found in the cortex of all four lobes.

Cranial nerves (Fig. 3-12)

Just as the spinal cord is connected to the receptors and effectors of the body by the spinal nerves, the brain is connected to the receptors and effectors of the head and upper body by the 12 **cranial nerves** that emerge from the brain stem in pairs. The first two (olfactory and optic) are not a true part of the peripheral nervous system but are extensions of the brain itself, carrying sensory pathways, or tracts. The cranial nerves are numbered in the order in which they emerge from the brain stem from anterior to posterior (Table 5).

Blood-brain barrier

The brain and spinal cord are surrounded with cerebrospinal fluid, as are the ventricles and spinal canal. The fluid cushions the brain and spinal cord, keeping them away from the surrounding skull and vertebrae so as to minimize damage that could occur from blows to the head or

Table 5. Summary of the cranial nerves*

No.	Name	Origin	Primary functions
I	Olfactory	Olfactory bulb	Afferent for smell
II	Optic	Diencephalon	Afferent for vision
III	Oculomotor	Midbrain	Afferent and efferent to all eye muscles except two
IV	Trochlear	Midbrain	Afferent and efferent to one eye muscle
V	Trigeminal	Pons	Afferent from skin and mucous membranes of head and from chewing muscles Efferent to chewing muscles
VI	Abducent	Pons	Afferent and efferent to one eye muscle
VII	Facial	Medulla	Afferent from taste buds of anterior two-thirds of tongue Efferent to muscles of face and salivary glands
VIII	Statoacoustic	Medulla	Afferent from the inner ear (hearing and balance)
IX	Glosso- pharyngeal	Medulla	Afferent from throat, rear of tongue, and taste buds of posterior one-third of tongue Efferent to throat and one salivary gland
X	Vagus	Medulla	Afferent from throat, viscera, and larynx Efferent to viscera
XI	Spinal accessory	Medulla	Efferent to viscera (via vagus), throat, larynx, neck, and shoulder muscles
XII	Hypoglossal	Medulla	Afferent and efferent to tongue muscles

*Adapted from Wenger, M. A., Jones, F. N., and Jones, M. H.: Physiological psychology, New York, 1956, Holt, Rinehart & Winston, Inc.

spine. It is not known whether the cerebrospinal fluid participates in the exchange of nutrition, oxygen, and waste between the blood and the nerve cells in the same fashion as the other extracellular fluids of the CNS. However, the cerebrospinal fluid is similar to the other extracellular fluids of the nerve cells in that certain substances will not pass from the blood to either fluid. Glutamic acid and other substances that pass readily from the capillaries to extracellular fluid elsewhere in the body do not do so in the brain. Thus physiologists speak of a **blood-brain barrier,** a concept that is important in the study of the effects of various chemicals on the CNS and on behavior. If these chemicals do not pass the blood-brain barrier when they are injected into the bloodstream, they cannot affect the CNS.

FUNCTIONAL ORGANIZATION OF THE BRAIN
Neocortex

The neocortex is the site of intricate, vertical organizations between subsystems of subcortical nuclei. The parietal, occipital, and temporal lobes (POT areas) receive sensory input and seem involved, along with subcortical centers, in learning and memory. The frontal lobes, on the other hand, include the origins of the motor projection systems. In a very general way the POT areas could be regarded as receptive and integrative in function, whereas the frontal cortex organization is expressive and related to brain output. The more anterior parts of the frontal lobes, the so-called **prefrontal lobes,** seem to function in more complex expressive ways. Animal experiments show that they affect the ability to delay response to a stimulus and distractibility. Human brain damage to these areas results in subtle personality disturbances, including increased impulsiveness. The frontal lobes show the greatest increase in size of all the cortical areas as one moves up the mammalian scale from rat to man. This has led some writers to speak of frontalization instead of encephalization. Not enough is known of the role of the frontal lobes in behavior to make such a distinction here.

Reticular and projection systems

The inputs to the cortex from lower brain centers involve conscious states of arousal, attention, and sleep, as well as the inputs governing simple sensation. The brain stem reticular formation (BSRF) is involved as an ascending reticular activating system (ARAS).

Specific thalamic projection system (Fig. 3-13). The classic sensory pathways form a **specific thalamic projection system (STPS)** that results in topographically organized sensory input for vision, hearing, and the skin senses (somesthesia). There are secondary sensory areas for all three senses, but they are phylogenetically older and are not a part of the STPS.

Diffuse thalamic projection system. There are secondary sensory areas for somesthesia, vision, and audition. These secondary areas are supplied partly by the **diffuse thalamic projection system (DTPS)** (Fig. 3-13). The DTPS has a more widespread distribution than does the STPS, represents an earlier form of sensory input, and is less "modality specific." Its arousal by auditory stimulation, for example, may result in a change in nerve impulses reaching widespread areas of the brain. The reaction of the cortex to the DTPS is brief compared to its reaction to the ascending reticular activating system (see below). The cortical responses observed have been called "recruiting responses" because the neural activity in areas supplied by the DTPS becomes more regular and synchronized and has a larger

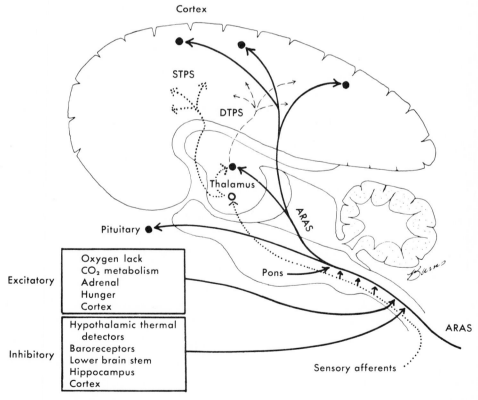

Fig. 3-13. Schematic diagram showing sensory projection to cortex through specific thalamic projection system (STPS), diffuse thalamic projection system (DTPS), and ascending reticular activating system (ARAS).

amplitude. Recruiting responses are probably caused by excitation reverberating back and forth between the thalamus and cortex. The sensory pathways involved begin with the STPS, which has collaterals to diffuse nuclei of the thalamus. These nuclei in turn send fibers to the basal ganglia and to widespread cortical areas. The effect of the DTPS on the secondary sensory areas in particular may serve as a mechanism for *selective attention.* Certain cells in the secondary areas may be active only when the animal is attending to that specific sensory input. This would form a modality-specific mechanism for attention.

Ascending reticular activating system. The **ascending reticular activating system (ARAS)** serves the whole cerebral cortex. The ARAS originates in the central parts of the medulla, midbrain, and diencephalon, as compared to the thalamic projection of the STPS and DTPS. The medulla, midbrain, and diencephalon are like the spinal cord in that the gray matter of nuclei and short interneurons lie in the central core, surrounded by the white matter of myelinated tracts. Much of this central gray matter is composed of short, many-branched, interconnecting cells, called the **brain stem reticular formation (BSRF).** Part of the BSRF forms the inhibitory and excitatory reticular activating systems for motor control, as discussed in Chapter 4. The role of this descending reticular activating system (DRAS) in cortical arousal by reflexes will be further discussed. Part of the BSRF makes up the ARAS (Fig. 3-13). The cells of the ARAS, like those of the DTPS, are fired by collaterals from the incoming sensory pathways of the STPS. The cells of the ARAS fire through many synapses; the relayed excitation being passed from cell to cell up through the central core of the brain stem reaches all areas of the cerebral cortex. The ARAS excites the cells of the cerebral cortex and lowers their threshold to incoming stimuli from other sources. The main function of the ARAS is to "keep the brain awake." The more active the ARAS, the more aroused and alert is the animal. Quiescence of the ARAS results in a low level of cortical activity, a state of sleep, and a higher threshold for the cortex to incoming sensory stimulation.

Descending reticular activating system. As will be described in Chapter 4 on motor organization, the cells of the BSRF can regulate muscle tone by exciting or inhibiting extensor stretch reflexes. To coin a term, this can be called a **descending reticular activating system** (DRAS) because of the role of *sensory feedback* in maintaining states of wakefulness and attention. Perhaps you have noted that your neck muscles ache or your leg muscles are tired after a period of alert, concentrated study, although you have been sitting in a chair the entire time. When the BSRF is active and the cerebral cortex is stimulated by the ARAS, the DRAS increases extensor muscle tone. The more the extensor muscles are contracted in maintaining this tone, the greater is the stimulation of kinesthetic receptors—the receptors in muscles that are sensitive to muscle contraction. Excitation from some of these receptors reaches the cerebral cortex and gives rise to sensations of muscle contraction. In states of alert attention, then, the BSRF activates the cortex via the ARAS and also increases muscle tone. Increased muscle tone fires kinesthetic receptors that feed back excitation to the cerebral cortex, further increasing cortical excitation. Thus the BSRF has both an ascending and a descending activating system.

Limbic system (Fig. 3-14)

The cerebral cortex began in evolution as a correlating center for smell. Some cortex is still closely related to smell, but the piriform lobe and hippocampus are not. Nevertheless, all these related centers are sometimes called the rhinencephalon ("nose brain"). Those parts of the rhinencephalon that are no longer directly involved in smell have formed close connections with some of the cortex to form the

limbic system. The limbic system was so named by Papez because it forms a ring (*limbus,* or "border") in the medial part of each cerebral hemisphere (Fig. 3-14). The limbic system includes the **hypothalamus, septal area** (septum), **cingulate gyrus, hippocampus** and **entorhinal cortex,** most of the **amygdala** (amygdaloid nuclei), and the anterior thalamus. The limbic system receives input from (1) parts of the rhinencephalon still concerned with smell (olfactory bulb and lobe, prepiriform area), (2) sensory areas of the neocortex, (3) the BSRF, and (4) the hypothalamus. The limbic system sends excitation to (1) many areas of the neocortex, (2) the BSRF, and (3) the hypothalamus. In Fig. 3-14, the original circuit of Papez is shown by the black arrows. The Papez circuit involves excitation in a closed reverberating loop, from the hippocampus to the mammillary

bodies of the hypothalamus, from there to the anterior thalamus, thence to the cingulate gyrus and entorhinal cortex, and finally back to the hypothalamus via the hippocampus. Papez suggested that this circuit provides a neural basis for emotional behavior and experience. The suggestion has been a fruitful one. The limbic system has recently been involved in learning research. The hypothalamus governs the autonomic nervous system in emotional states, and two of the most important tracts connecting it with other parts of the brain are found in the limbic system.

The limbic system communicates with the frontal lobes of the neocortex via the anterior thalamus. The frontal lobes play an important role in human personality, and damage to them often causes impulsivity and reduced affect (lack of emotionality). Limbic connections with the parietal,

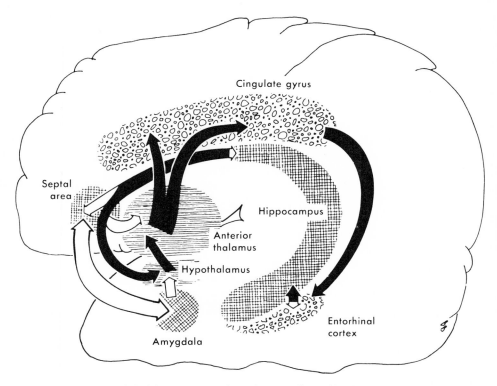

Fig. 3-14. Diagram of limbic system, projected on outline of brain. *Black arrows* are neural connections referred to by Papez (1929) as the limbic pathways. *White arrows* are pathways discovered since then. (Modified from McCleary, R. A., and Moore, R. Y.: Subcortical mechanisms of behavior, New York, 1965, Basic Books, Inc., Publishers.)

occipital, and temporal neocortex (POT "association areas") involve the limbic system in research on learning and memory.

Hypothalamus

The **hypothalamus** consists of a continuous group of nuclei occupying the walls and floor of the third ventricle. Research on the hypothalamus has shown that it plays a dominant role in (1) regulation of the motor activity of the autonomic nervous system, (2) homeostatic response to changes in the internal environment, either by sensitivity of its own cells to these changes or through input from internal receptors, (3) regulation of endocrine output through connections to the pituitary gland and hypothalamic releasing factors (Chapter 2), (4) drives, or the arousal and maintenance of behavior in states of hunger, thirst, sexual input, and so on, and (5) emotional responses in states of rage and fear. The hypothalamus seems to be the pivotal point between somatic and visceral sensory input and somatic and visceral motor output in the responses of the body to internal and external stress. The anterior hypothalamus has been called a **trophotropic** area by Hess because when it is stimulated it causes parasympathetic responses—slowed heart rate, dilation of blood vessels in the stomach and intestines, and drowsiness, as if the animal were digesting a big meal. Responses of the parasympathetic nervous system are also dominant. He referred to the posterior hypothalamus as **ergotropic,** because stimulation there raised the heart rate and blood pressure, made the animal alert and aroused, and often caused him to attack nearby objects or the experimenter. Responses of the sympathetic nervous system were dominant. It is evident that the anterior (and medial) hypothalamus is trophotropic because it stimulates parasympathetic responses. The posterior (and lateral) hypothalamus is ergotropic because it stimulates the sympathetic nervous system.

SUMMARY

The chapter began by identifying the major parts of the neuron: cell body, dendrites, axon, and terminal arborization. A myelin sheath is often secreted by the neurolemma in the PSNS or the glial cells of the CNA. Major features can be observed under the light or electron microscope after slides of the tissue are prepared. To study the function of nerve cells using their electrical characteristics, electricity was reviewed as electron flow in terms of volts, amperes, and ohms, with the microelectrode, the amplifier, and the cathode-ray oscilloscope solving the three major problems involved. Bioelectric currents require the movement of anions and cations to anodes and cathodes respectively—the polarized, positive outside of the cell membrane (resting potential) is reversed (spike potential) during conduction. The nerve cell provides the necessary energy (all or none law). The resting potential is maintained by sodium and potassium pumps as well as large anions inside the cell and a concentration gradient of chlorine ions. During the spike potential Na^+ ions shift inside the cell and K^+ ions replace them during recovery. Chemical transmitters like acetylcholine, norepinephrine, and epinephrine transfer excitation between cells at the synapse (EPSP); GABA creates inhibition (IPSP).

The nervous system consists of the brain and spinal cord (CNS) and the sensory and motor nerves (peripheral nervous system). The latter divide into PSNS and ANS, the (motor) ANS having SNS and PNS divisions with opposing effects on the viscera. Their presynaptic and postsynaptic neuron organizations are similar, but the SNS is diffuse in both anatomy and transmitter action, whereas the PNS is discrete. The SNS prepares the body for emergency action and stimulates the adrenal medulla to secrete norepinephrine and epinephrine.

The spinal reflex is the simplest stimulus-response organization of the CNS with only five "elements." Higher centers add correlation of input and coordination of output. As a hollow structure, the brain includes four ventricles and the cerebral aqueduct; its structure can be divided into the brain stem as compared to the cerebral and cerebellar hemispheres. The medulla, pons, cerebellum, midbrain, hypothalamus, thalamus, corpus striatum, and cerebral cortex were located and their functions briefly explained. The anatomy of the cerebral cortex can be divided into four lobes using two fissures and a sulcus. Sensory and motor projection areas and association areas are defined. The Brodmann system refers to more specific cortical areas. The brain is connected to receptors and effectors by cranial nerves. A blood-brain barrier prevents large molecules from reaching the tissue fluid of the brain.

Some parts of the functional organization of the brain involve the neocortex, reticular and projection systems, the limbic system, and the hypothalamus. The neocortex is involved in the most complex behavior, the STPS carries sensory information, the DTPS plays a role in attention, and the ARAS of the BSRF arouses the whole brain, aided by DRAS feedback effects from the muscles. The limbic system is involved in emotion and learning. The hypothalamus monitors the internal state of the tissue fluid and is involved in drives.

READINGS

Asimov, I.: The human brain, Boston, 1964, Houghton Mifflin Company.

Axelron, J.: Neurotransmitters, Sci. Am. **230:**59-71, June 1974. (W. H. Freeman Reprint No. 1297).

Chauchard, P.: The brain, New York, 1962, Grove Press, Inc.

Eccles, J.: The synapse, Sci. Am. **212:**56-66, Jan. 1965 (W. H. Freeman Reprint No. 1001).

Gardner, E. D.: Fundamentals of neurology, ed. Philadelphia, 1975, W. B. Saunders Company.

Kandel, E. R.: Nerve cells and behavior, Sci. Am. **223:**57-67, July 1970 (W. H. Freeman Reprint No. 1182).

Katz, B.: The nerve impulse, Sci. Am. **187:**55-64, Nov. 1952 (W. H. Freeman Reprint No. 20).

Lewin, R.: The nervous system, Garden City, N.Y., 1972, Doubleday Publishing Company.

Smith, C.: The brain: towards an understanding, New York, 1972, Capricorn books, G. P. Putnam's Sons.

Wilson, J. V.: Inhibition in the central nervous system, Sci. Am. **214:**102-110, May 1966.

CHAPTER 4

Organizing movement: muscles and nervous control systems

OVERVIEW

This chapter treats the organization of movement. It begins with the way different kinds of muscles specialize to carry out different functions, proceeds to the way they are excited by motor nerves, and goes on to show how the motor nerves are controlled by reflexes and by higher levels of the nervous system. Inhibition as well as excitation is treated. There are separate but interacting systems of the brain controlling precise movement, "background" movement, and balance and coordination. The anatomy and function of these three systems is considered in detail.

CLASSIFICATION OF MUSCLE TISSUE

Muscle tissue is made up of cells that are specialized for changing shape, which they accomplish by shortening their elongated form. When muscle cells are attached to one another and to other tissues of the body, they are organized into muscles. Muscles are made up of muscle cells (for contraction), connective tissue (to hold the cells together), vascular, or blood vessel, tissue (to nourish the other cells), and so on. Muscles are therefore *organs* made up of several kinds of specialized tissue.

The way in which muscle cells and other muscle tissue have specialized hinges largely on the rate of contraction required of a given type of muscle and how dependent it is on stimulation from the nervous system. *Contraction rate* and *automaticity* (degree of independence from stimulation by the nervous system) determine the structure and function of muscle cells as organized into muscles. Three types of muscle tissue have resulted: **smooth, striated,** and **cardiac.** Smooth and cardiac (heart) muscles contract slowly and are relatively automatic, contracting without nervous stimulation. Smooth and cardiac muscle tissues are found in the *viscera* (internal organs) and therefore form **visceral muscles.** Striated muscles react rapidly and depend on the nervous system for excitation. Striated muscles move the body (Gr. *soma*) about by pulling on the bony "levers" of the skeleton and are therefore called **somatic muscles.** Visceral muscle has often been called involuntary, since its contractions are largely automatic and one is not aware of them; the contractions involved in the beating of the heart and the digestion of food are examples. Somatic muscle has been called voluntary because one is often aware of the muscle contractions that control movements, and body movements are said to be under the control of the "will." The distinction fails in several ways. Humans and animals learn voluntary control of certain visceral smooth muscles—for example, those involved in the control of the bowel and bladder in becoming housebroken or toilet trained. Somatic (striated, or skeletal) muscles, on the other hand, often react without awareness in reflexes such as those of breathing or in more complex automatic movements such as walking.

STRUCTURE AND FUNCTION OF MUSCLES
Smooth muscle

As previously explained, smooth muscle is specialized for slow, sustained, and often automatic contraction and relaxation and is the type of muscle that forms much of the viscera, or internal organs. When smooth muscle takes a tubular form, as in the arteries and intestines, the tubular structure is often made up of opposed groups of muscle fibers (Fig. 4-1). One set of fibers may be oriented in a circular fashion around the tube. Contraction of these

fibers *constricts* the lumen (the "bore") of the tube to reduce the flow of blood through an artery, to reduce the flow of air through the trachea, or windpipe, or to move food along the intestine. The opposed set of fibers is oriented in a longitudinal direction. Contraction of these fibers tends to shorten the tube and, more importantly, to *increase* its lumen. Despite their automatic contractions, smooth muscles of the arteries, intestines, and so on are supplied with nerve fibers (axons) from the brain and spinal cord by the nerves of the peripheral nervous system. These motor nerves form a special subdivision of the peripheral nervous system called the **autonomic nervous system (ANS,** Chapter 3), which has two divisions, the **parasympathetic division** and the **sympathetic division.** Both divisions supply the tubular type of muscle described here, but in many cases the sympathetic division supplies one set of fibers (for example, the circular fibers), whereas the parasym-

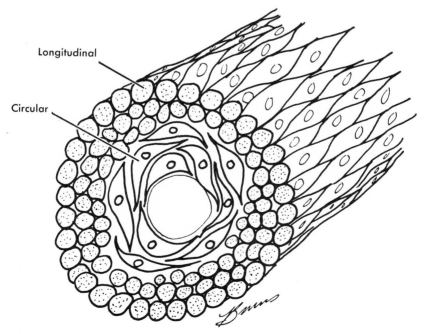

Fig. 4-1. Diagram of how muscle cells are organized in tubular smooth muscle tissue, as in arteries or intestines. Contraction of circular fibers constricts the lumen of the tube, whereas contraction of longitudinal fibers has the opposite effect.

pathetic division supplies the other set of fibers (for example, the longitudinal fibers). In the arteries, excitation by one division of the ANS can restrict the flow of blood to an organ by constricting the artery, whereas excitation by the other division dilates the artery to increase the flow of blood to the organ. The iris, or colored portion of the eye that surrounds the pupil, is made up of circular and radial fibers that are opposed, and the opposed fibers are supplied by the opposed divisions of the ANS. Sympathetic stimulation contracts the radial fibers, which enlarge the pupil and admit more light to the eye, whereas parasympathetic stimulation contracts the circular fibers, which constrict the pupil and admit less light to the eye.

In the case of the intestine, as previously noted, the contractions of the circular and longitudinal fibers are largely automatic, like those of the heart, although stimulated by local factors such as the presence of wastes. In this case stimulation by the parasympathetic division increases the rate of regular contractions, whereas sympathetic stimulation inhibits regular contractions.

In gross appearance, smooth muscles sometimes take a form such as that of striated muscles, with all the fibers oriented in the same direction. This is true of the piloerector muscles, which erect the body hair, and of the sphincters (all circular fibers), whose contraction closes the bowel and bladder openings. In these two cases sympathetic stimulation contracts the muscle to raise the body hair or close the sphincter opening, whereas parasympathetic stimulation inhibits contraction by these muscles. The reasons for these effects will be studied later.

Cardiac muscle

Cardiac muscle is intermediate in functional characteristics between smooth and striated muscle; the heart contracts rapidly like striated muscle, but automatically like many smooth muscles. The membranes of the muscle cells are so closely interwoven that excitation spreads from cell to cell, so that the whole heart muscle contracts almost as a unit, although some parts contract before others. The heart is regularly excited by intrinsic (built-in) nerve tissue and will continue to beat if its nerve supply from the central nervous system fails. This has obvious survival value for the organism. Like smooth muscle, the heart is supplied by the ANS; sympathetic stimulation serves to increase its rate of automatic beating (pumping), whereas parasympathetic stimulation slows its rate of beat, all in response to the circulatory needs of the body.

Striated muscle

Striated, or somatic, muscle contracts most rapidly of the three types of muscle. However, it cannot maintain a strong contraction or series of contractions for as long as smooth or cardiac muscle can. Neither is it automatic in action, as is most visceral muscle; somatic muscle must receive excitation from the central nervous system, by the motor nerves of the peripheral nervous system, to contract under normal circumstances.

The way in which the cells, or fibers, are organized in striated muscle becomes important in understanding its function (Fig. 4-2). All muscle cells are oriented in the long axis of nearly all striated muscles. Connective tissue plays a major role in the structural organization of the muscle. All the cells are linked together by connective tissue, which ultimately connects to tendons on both ends of the muscle; thus shortening of the individual cells ultimately exerts a pull on the tendons and acts so as to shorten the muscle. The tendons are attached to bone at both ends, which enables one to flex or extend the arms, legs, and so forth.

Flexors and extensors. Somatic muscles occur in opposed pairs, called flexors and extensors. Flexors act to bend the digits (fingers and toes), limbs, and body; they react more rapidly than extensors. Extensors act to extend the digits, limbs, and body; they react more slowly than flexors (but can maintain contraction longer). Extensors are also called antigravity muscles, as their action in extending the limbs and body opposes the pull of gravity and maintains the upright position. An exception in man is the flexors of the arms; flexing the arm and fingers opposes the pull of gravity.

Reciprocal innervation. The muscles involved in any given body movement, whether flexors or extensors, are called the **agonist muscles** for that movement. If a flexor is the agonist muscle for a given movement (for example, bending the leg), the extensor muscle that would perform the opposite movement (straightening the leg) is the **antagonist muscle** for that movement. Since agonist and antagonist muscles occur in opposed pairs, an antagonist muscle must relax for an agonist muscle to perform a movement. Both agonist and antagonist muscles are **innervated** (receive nerve fibers) from the central nervous system (CNS) by the motor nerves of the peripheral nervous system.

The CNS is so arranged that when an agonist muscle is excited, its antagonist is inhibited. This is called **reciprocal innervation.**

INNERVATION OF STRIATED MUSCLE
Motor unit

Striated muscle contraction is organized by the way it is innervated (receives nerve fibers for excitation). Each axon of the motor nerve supplying a muscle breaks up into a number of branches (Fig. 4-2). Each branch makes "contact" with a single muscle cell. If the axon of a neuron has 50 branches, that neuron contacts and excites 50 muscle cells at once, whenever it fires. The single nerve cell and all the muscle cells it contacts are a **motor unit,** and this is the unit of contraction for the muscle. If on the average each axon in the motor nerve to a muscle contacts 50 muscle cells to excite them, 50 is the size of the motor unit. The smallest contraction the muscle can make would involve firing one

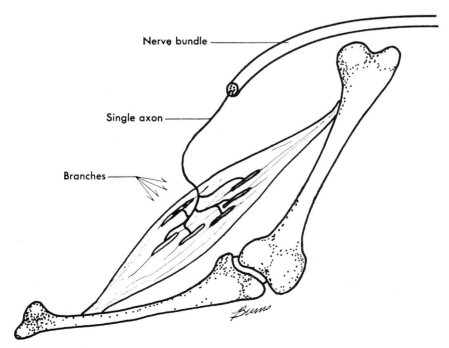

Fig. 4-2. Sketch of motor unit, consisting of single motoneuron (whose axon is shown) and individual muscle cells innervated by branches of that motoneuron.

motoneuron, which would excite 50 cells. Exciting a second neuron to increase the response would involve adding another "set" of 50 muscle cells to the muscle contraction, for a total of 100. Further increases in contraction would involve stepwise increments in motor unit involvement, 50 muscle cells at a time. This does not imply that all active motor units fire simultaneously.

The size of the motor unit for a given muscle depends on the kind of response that muscle will be called on to perform. Muscles involved in gross movements that require only a few different strengths of contraction have large motor units. For example, in extensors such as those of the thighs and back, the motor unit may include 150 cells. When only a few different strengths of contraction are needed for gross movements controlled by the muscle, the motor unit can be large. On the other hand, flexor muscles that control precise movements are called on to contract in many small increments. The motor unit must therefore be small, permitting the muscle to increase its contraction a few cells at a time. The flexors controlling the fingers may have motor units of ten cells, and the muscles controlling eye movements may have units as small as three.

Muscle tone

A few of the motor units of any healthy muscle are always contracting, especially in extensor muscles. This resting contraction is called **muscle tone** and gives healthy muscles their rubbery, "hard" feel to the touch. Muscle tone is increased when the muscle is stretched by body position. As an example, lay your arm on the table, relax it with the elbow bent, and feel he biceps with the other hand. Now straighten your arm out on the table, relax it again, and again feel the biceps. The stretched, or lengthened, muscle will feel firmer to the touch—its tone has increased.

Muscle tone is the partial resting contraction of a muscle in response to a reflex called the **stretch reflex.** Receptors in the muscle respond to stretching of the muscle; sensory neurons are excited and in turn fire some of the motoneurons going to motor units in the same muscle. The more the muscle is stretched, the more stretch receptors will be stimulated and the more motor units will be excited. On the other hand, if the tendon attaching a muscle is cut, the muscle will shorten by one-fourth to one-third of its length and will become completely "limp." None of the stretch receptors will be firing, and therefore none of the motor units of the muscle are active.

Myoneural junction

The **myoneural junction** is the region of contact between branches of the motor nerve cell and each muscle cell in striated muscles. Recall that the axon breaks up into branches, whose number depends on the average size of the motor unit. Each branch reaches a muscle cell to establish a myoneural junction. Myoneural junctions are diagrammed in Fig. 4-3 as they are seen under the high magnification of the electron microscope. Note that the nerve branch forming the myoneual junction loses its myelin sheath covering before spreading out into a nerve ending that appears to be buried in the junctional folds of the membrane of the muscle cell at the **end plate,** or subsynaptic region. A 10 nm gap is evident between the nerve ending and the muscle end plate, and the end plate is extensively folded to increase the area exposed to the fluid of the gap. When the nerve impulse arrives and travels along the axon branch, it is unable to provide enough current to depolarize the muscle cell membrane because the membrane of the muscle cell has an area at least 1,000 times larger than the nerve cell ending; therefore, a chemical event must intervene. As seen under an electron microscope, the nerve ending contains many vesicles (globules). Chemical studies show that the vesicles probably contain acetylcholine (ACh), which acts as a chemical

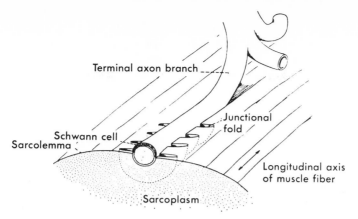

Fig. 4-3. Myoneural junction, drawn as seen under electron microscope. Axon branch loses its myelin sheath and runs in the longitudinal axis of the muscle fiber. Neurolemma (Schwann cell) forms a folded structure near the thickened part of the sarcolemma that forms the end plate. (After Birks, R., Huxley, H. E., and Katz, B.: J. Physiol. [London] **150:**134-144, 1960.)

transmitter over the gap between nerve ending and muscle end plate. As in the case of synapses between nerve cells, arrival of the nerve impulse at the nerve ending is believed to release ACh from the vesicles into the gap between nerve ending and muscle cell end plate. Like nerve cells, the muscle cell has a polarized membrane—positive outside and negative inside—with a concentration of sodium (Na) outside the cell and potassium (K) inside the cell. The ACh *depolarizes* the end plate by making it more permeable to both of these ions; the action of ACh is the same at nerve cell synapses ("short-circuit" theory). This depolarization results in a change in potential across the end-plate region of the muscle cell membrane, called the **end-plate potential** (epp). The epp does not completely depolarize the membrane at the end plate because of the influx of ions from other regions of the membrane. Other regions, however, are depolarized enough by ion movement to initiate a **muscle action potential**—a polarization reversal that sweeps over the entire muscle cell and has the same electrical and chemical basis in excitation and recovery as was described for the nerve cell in Chapter 3. The muscle action potential activates the con-

traction mechanism of the cell. The sequence of events at the myoneural junction is as follows: nerve impulse → ACh transmitter release → end-plate potential → muscle action potential → muscle cell contraction. After it has acted to stimulate the end plate, ACh is destroyed by hydrolysis. The reaction is speeded by the enzyme acetylcholine esterase (AChE), which is present in the tissue fluids.

REFLEXES
Stimulus control

As explained in Chapter 3 the usual reflex has five categories of "elements": (1) receptors, (2) afferent, or sensory, neurons, (3) interneurons, or association neurons, (4) efferent, or motor, neurons, and (5) effectors (muscles or glands). These are categories rather than single elements. In the simplest reflex, such as withdrawing the hand from a painful stimulus, many receptors, neurons, and effectors are involved. The pathways are relatively fixed from receptors to afferent neurons, interneurons, efferent neurons, and effectors and produce an automatic withdrawal response. The stimulation of pain receptors always leads to withdrawal; therefore the reflex response is under *stimulus control.*

However, the exact movement involved in withdrawal will vary to some extent, depending on posture and on the position of the limb relative to the body. For example, the withdrawal movement will involve some different muscle groups when a person burns the back of the hand on a stove as compared to burning the palm. Some different movements will follow, depending on whether one is leaning on that arm. The reflex reactions are *modified* by both spinal and higher centers in such a way as to withdraw the hand efficiently while balance and posture are maintained. Some different interneurons and therefore some different motor neurons and muscles are used, but the *form* of the reaction is determined by "fixed" pathways from the pain receptors through the central nervous system. To paraphrase Sherrington, the nervous system "thinks" in terms of movements rather than muscle contractions.

The kind of stimulus that is used will determine the kind of reflex response that will occur. Different receptors are specialized to respond to different kinds of energy and activate specific kinds of reflexes. For example, the **flexion reflex,** already mentioned, involves contraction of the flexors of a limb in response to pain stimulation of the limb. The nervous "connections" between pain-specialized receptors and flexor muscles are "built into" the central nervous system. For this reason a person will always withdraw his hand from a painful stimulus, and a dog with an injured paw will hold that limb in a flexed (withdrawn) position, even if he has to walk on three legs. On the other hand, the **extensor thrust reflex,** the opposite movement to flexion, will result from the stimulation of pressure and proprioceptive receptors in the limb. Different afferent neurons are fired, and therefore different interneurons, motor neurons, and effectors are activated. Pressure instead of pain stimuli to the sole of the foot, or spreading of the toes, increases contraction of extensor instead of flexor muscles in the limb. In standing or walking, the onset of foot pressure from the weight of the body extends the limb to support the body. The two reflexes are opposed, and if the stimuli for both are used at once, which response will occur? If both pain and pressure receptors in an animal's paw are stimulated, will he flex or extend the limb? This depends to some extent on the intensity of the pain stimulus as compared to that of the pressure stimulus, that is, on the number of receptors and therefore the number of other elements activated. In general, however, the flexion reflex will predominate. It overrides extension because it is a reflex of survival value to the animal.

One of the most important reflexes in posture and movement is the **stretch reflex.** The muscles of the body include some muscle cells that have sensory receptors (annulospiral receptors). The receptors respond to stretch of the whole muscle to stimulate a reflex to contract some of the motor units of the muscle to prevent lengthening of the muscle. Since muscles are stretched to some degree all of the time, the reflex causes a constant partial contraction called *muscle tone* (see discussion of spinal shock on p. 59). The stretch reflex is especially sensitive in extensor muscles like those of the legs that are antigravity muscles; that is, they resist gravity by keeping the legs straight, for example. As weight is shifted from one leg to the other, the corresponding extensors are stretched and react by contracting to support the added load. Finally, the stretch reflexes can be excited by contracting those muscle fibers that have stretch reflex receptors. In this fashion, muscle tone can be increased and movements initiated. (This is one extrapyramidal mechanism for the control of "background movement" that will be discussed later in the chapter.)

Reflex preparations

As already explained, the exact form of a "fixed" reflex response, such as the flexion reflex, will depend on higher centers in the brain that respond to the posture and movements of the animal. Other movements may be set off by the reflex stimuli to higher centers. To keep the reflex as constant as possible while studying it and to prevent most other responses, one cuts the central nervous system above the level of the neurons involved in the reflex. An animal surgically prepared in this way is called a **reflex preparation.** For example, if a flexion reflex of the hind limb is being studied, the spinal cord may be cut above the level of the sensory and motor roots involved in the reflex. This isolates the interneurons from higher centers. Input from the stimulus cannot cause widespread body movements via higher brain centers, and the reflex response will no longer be affected by higher centers that respond to position and movement. As a result the flexion response will be more consistent from one stimulation to the next. The effect of other variables on the reflex can be best studied when the response is consistent.

Spinal preparation. In the spinal preparation just described the spinal cord is severed above the level of the spinal cord involved in the reflex. Reflexes of the limbs are isolated from higher centers in this way. However, spinal preparations have severe practical disadvantages. It is more convenient for the physiologist to study acute preparations, that is, anesthetized animals kept alive only for the duration of the experiment (a day or two). Spinal animals cannot be studied as acute preparations because **spinal shock** ensues when the cord is severed, and the shock lasts for some time. All muscles supplied by motor neurons below the level of the lesion become flaccid (lose tone) and will not react to reflex stimulation. The recovery time involved depends on the development of the brain in the species being studied. Cat and dog—the usual subjects—require about 48 hours for all reflexes to recover, most monkeys about a week, and spinal **(paraplegic)** humans about two to three weeks. Spinal shock is caused by the dependence of the motoneurons on constant

excitation from the brain stem reticular formation (BSRF) and vestibular nuclei of the brain stem (Fig. 4-4). The vestibular nuclei normally bombard the spinal motoneurons with excitation through the vestibulospinal tract. This makes the motoneurons more excitable when incoming reflex stimuli are added. The brain stem reticular formation (BSRF) excites motoneurons by a different mechanism. The BSRF sends excitation to the stretch reflexes. (Contraction of muscle spindles by their motor fibers excites their annulospiral receptors, which in turn send reflex stimulation to the muscles.) The latter mechanism maintains the *tone,* or constant partial contraction, of healthy muscle. When spinal transection interrupts excitation of the muscle spindles, tone is lost and the muscles become flaccid. If the experimenter waits for the animal to recover from spinal shock, the wait is long enough for infection to develop (two to three days). The original operation must therefore be carried out under troublesome aseptic, or sterile, conditions, the incisions carefully closed, and the animal allowed to recover. Such a chronic preparation can be maintained for a long time with careful nursing, but it is troublesome to keep and the animal must be operated on a second time to expose the nervous system for experimental manipulations.

Decerebrate preparation. Spinal shock can be avoided so that acute preparations can be studied if the neuraxis is cut at the level of the midbrain. This procedure does not isolate the cord from all higher centers, but it does cut off most of the brain. The cut lies above the vestibular nuclei and most of the BSRF, leaving them functionally "connected" to the motoneurons. The motoneurons continue to receive excitation from these centers to maintain reflex excitability (Fig. 4-4). The animal will, however, display **decerebrate rigidity,** a state of *exaggerated* extensor tone in which all four limbs are rigidly extended. Extensor tone is caused by stretch reflexes (see above), which depend on excitation

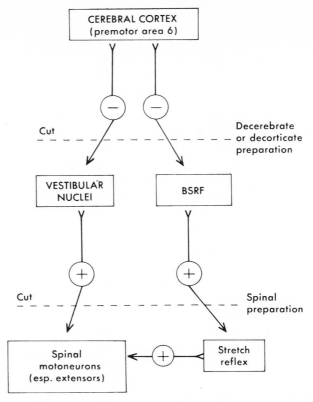

Fig. 4-4. Diagram showing the types of reflex preparation and the excitatory (+) and inhibitory (−) influences of various centers on each other and on the extensor motoneurons.

from the vestibular nuclei and BSRF, particularly the latter. These two centers receive some constant inhibition from the cerebral cortex and basal ganglia. A midbrain transection cuts off inhibition to the vestibular nuclei and BSRF. When the vestibular nuclei and BSRF are released from inhibition by higher centers, their excitatory effect on motoneurons is increased. The effect on extensor motoneurons is the most pronounced, and the limbs are rigidly extended. The **spastic** condition of the extensors is permanent and provides an abnormal background of muscle tension in the study of reflexes.

Final common path

A given muscle response may be excited in several ways. No matter what the input, however, the motoneurons controlling the responding muscles constitute the **final common path** taken by any excitation that elicits the movement. These motoneurons receive excitatory and inhibitory influences from all levels of the CNS. The algebraic sum of the excitation and inhibition that reach the motoneurons of the final common path will determine whether the response will occur and what its extent will be. The extent of the response will also be determined by the manner in which interneurons from several inputs converge and "overlap" as they reach the motoneuron pool for a reflex response.

Inhibition

Phenomena. Two reflexes may be opposed. This was true of the flexion and crossed-extension reflexes in the examples already given. If flexion in a limb is stimulated by a standard stimulus to pain fibers, a certain strength of flexion will occur. If, at the same time, extension is stimulated by spreading the toes of the same limb, flexion will still occur, but the strength or amount of flexor contraction may be reduced by the stimulus to extension. The amount by which flexion is reduced is the amount of **inhibition** of the flexor response caused by the extensor thrust stimulus. A more common example involves crossed extension. If flexion is stimulated in the right hind limb, the left hind limb will extend to support the weight of the animal **(crossed-extension reflex).** If pain fibers in both limbs are stimulated strongly, both hind limbs will flex and the animal will fall, showing that flexion overrides crossed extension just as it overrides the extensor thrust reflex. However, a weak pain stimulus to the right hind limb will cause enough crossed extension to reduce left flexor reaction to pain stimulation of the left limb. Again, the amount by which left hind limb flexion is reduced is the amount of inhibition.

Central mechanisms. At all levels of the central nervous system, inhibition is just as important as excitation. Theoretically, any one of the billions of nerve cells in the CNS could excite any other cell by some indirect pathway of intervening neurons. This would logically mean that the first stimulus the CNS received would cause a spread of excitation from cell to cell until all the cells of the brain were firing in a complete and incapacitating seizure of all the muscles of the body. For the CNS to function in an organized and selective way, some groups of synaptic pathways must be excited while others are inhibited.

At the reflex level of the spinal cord, where inhibition is most easily studied, inhibition occurs when reflex response of the motoneurons is directly prevented via interneurons that are excited by an opposed reflex response. Inhibition may be **presynaptic** or **postsynaptic inhibition.** Postsynaptic inhibition occurs when the collaterals of interneurons for a reflex

stimulate **Renshaw cells,** which in turn inhibit the motoneurons for the *opposed* reflex response. Renshaw cells release gamma-aminobutyric acid (GABA) to hyperpolarize the neurons and make them harder to excite (Chapter 3). The inhibitory influence occurs after the synapses and is therefore postsynaptic. Presynaptic inhibition occurs when the inhibitory neurons or their collaterals contact some of the *axon terminals* of cells that would otherwise excite the motoneurons. They may keep the axon terminals partly depolarized and the transmitter substance of these filaments exhausted so that they cannot participate in depolarizing postsynaptic motoneurons. Such synapses are called **axoaxonic synapses,** in contrast to the normal **axodendritic synapses** (synapses between axon filament endings and dendrites or cell bodies). Inhibition occurs at centers, or groups of synapses, in all parts of the CNS.

Higher-level reflexes

Not all reflexes are mediated by the interneurons of the spinal cord alone. Many reflexes are organized by the interneurons of the brain stem or even the cerebral cortex. The sensory or the motor side of these reflexes, or both, may involve the cranial nerves. Most of the reflex centers are found in the medulla of the brain, since most of the cranial nerves originate in the medulla, but reflexes with centers at higher levels of the brain also occur. The higher level reflexes are usually concerned with two kinds of adaptive behavior:

1. The "vital reflexes" maintain automatic adjustments of the visceral muscles and glands of the body in response to changes in internal states, such as changes in blood pressure and blood chemistry. The motor adjustments are largely accomplished by the autonomic nervous system; the reflexes maintain the consistency of the internal environment necessary for life.

2. Other higher-level reflexes involve postural adjustments and are superimposed on some of the postural spinal reflexes already mentioned. Reflexes of

this kind adjust the whole posture of the body in response to movements of the head and limbs. Complex adjustments of this kind are controlled by the extrapyramidal and cerebellar systems to be discussed in the next section.

ORGANIZATION OF MOVEMENT

The brain integrates behavior in a very complex manner that is constantly modified by input from many sensory receptors. As behavior moves the animal about, the sensory input changes. This is a *feedback* situation—input modifies behavior and behavior modifies input. To consider all the sensory inputs that initiate or modify movement at the same time would unduly complicate this discussion. To simplify matters, all input save that from the "movement receptors" will be ignored. (The movement receptors, or proprioreceptors, will be studied in Chapter 7.) These inputs come from the inner ear (vestibular receptor) to report on position and movements of the head and from joints and muscles to report position and movement of the limbs (kinesthesis). These inputs are the most integral part of the feedback modifying movement. Such inputs must therefore be considered in motor organization. Appropriate change in response to visual, auditory, tactile, and other sensory input will be assumed rather than discussed. To further make the section manageable, a more or less arbitrary distinction will be made between the following three "motor systems" of the body: (1) **pyramidal,** (2) **extrapyramidal,** and (3) **cerebellar.** Modern research shows that these categories are artificial ones, since no one system can operate normally without the others and their major functions overlap so much. However, each system can be said to make a major contribution to behavior, and it is less confusing to discuss them one at a time. Considered in this light, the major contribution of the pyramidal system is the initiation of precise movement, whereas the extrapyramidal system provides for gross "background

movements," and the cerebellar system supports balance and coordination.

Before detail on the anatomy and function of the three systems is given, a broad look at how each contributes to the control of movement and how they interact is a useful approach. A block diagram that extends Fig. 4-4 is given in Fig. 4-5. Fig. 4-4 explained decerebrate rigidity and spinal shock in terms of damage to the extrapyramidal system, although it was not called that at the time. A comparison of the two figures will show that Fig. 4-5 merely adds the pyramidal and cerebellar systems to the extrapyramidal system.

The ultimate aim in control of movement is to make changes in muscle contractions. The pyramidal system does this *directly,* with pathways to the motoneurons of the limbs that excite muscles of precise control—the fingers and toes that execute "target" movements in such precise acts as picking up a pencil. These are movements of the *extremities*—the parts of the limbs most distant from the body trunk. The pathways originate primarily in area 4, the motor area of the cerebral cortex. The extrapyramidal system originates primarily in area 6, the premotor area of the cerebral cortex. It controls the more "axial" muscles of the body that adjust our posture—chiefly gross movements of the arms, legs, and body trunk—shifting our position in such a way as to adjust the body position. These movements form a background to the precise acts controlled by the pyramidal system. Adjustments in posture are primarily made by extensor or antigravity muscles that oppose limb and body flexion that would otherwise result from the force of gravity. Control over motoneurons for these muscles is largely *indirect* and consists of releasing excitatory pathways to the motoneurons from inhibition by area 6 in a patterned way. The vestibular nuclei receive a continuous flow of excitation from the receptors for head position and movement (vestibular senses) and send constant excitation to the extensor motoneurons. The excitation is suppressed

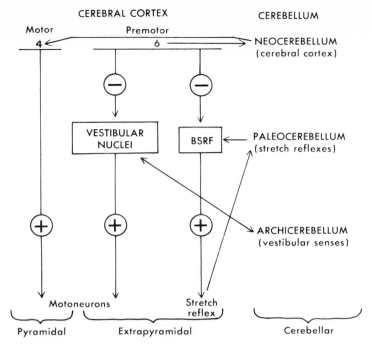

Fig. 4-5. Diagram of interactions between pyramidal, extrapyramidal, and cerebellar systems. *Arrows,* Direction of flow of excitation (+) or inhibition (−). Precise pathways are not given.

in a patterned way by area 6. Body posture is shifted by the release of inhibition from area 6 to vestibular nuclei. The vestibular neurons that are released excite the appropriate extensor motoneurons for an adjustment in posture. A second mechanism for postural adjustment results from releasing motor areas of the brain stem reticular formation (BSRF) from inhibition by area 6. The BSRF receives input from the stretch reflex receptors. The BSRF sends excitation to the stretch reflexes to increase muscle tone. By releasing BSRF fibers that increase muscle tone in the appropriate extensor muscles, body position can be changed.

The cerebellum coordinates movement by (1) integrating input from the vestibular senses for head position, (2) integrating input from the stretch reflexes for limb position, and (3) coordinating background movements controlled by area 6 with the precise movements of area 4. Each part of

the cerebellum is cross connected with every other part, so that all three functions are continuously integrated. The part of the cerebellum that is oldest in evolutionary history was developed in fish that lacked a cortex and were not subject to gravity. The archicerebellum deals with vestibular information on position and movement and is in two-way communication with the extrapyramidal system by the vestibular nuclei. As land-dwelling species developed, stretch reflexes became necessary, and their receptor input developed the paleocerebellum to deal with information about gravitation influence on movement. The paleocerebellum sends its integrated information to the BSRF to make further adjustments in posture by use of the stretch reflex. Finally, when the cerebral cortex developed, the neocerebellum appeared to provide communication between the extrapyramidal and pyramidal systems so that precise movement

Pyramidal system

The pyramidal system contains most of the fibers that run directly from the motor projection areas of the cerebral cortex to excite the motoneurons of the cranial and spinal nerves. These fibers are found chiefly in the **pyramidal tract.** Pyramidal tract fibers that originate in the cerebral cortex pass to the brain stem and spinal cord via the medullary pyramids. The pyramids can be seen on the ventral side of the brain stem, emerging from under the temporal lobes as prominent ropelike strands, diving beneath the pons, and emerging on the ventral side of the medulla to either side of the midline. The *single* cortical area that supplies most fibers to the system is the motor projection area of the brain, area 4 in the Brodmann system (Fig. 3-12). However, all other cortical lobes but the occipital, prefrontal, and temporal contribute fibers to the pyramidal tract.

Topographical organization. The motor projection area of the brain, area 4, is topographically organized. Stimulation of the exposed brain in an anesthetized animal shows that each part of area 4 controls a selected set of the muscles controlling

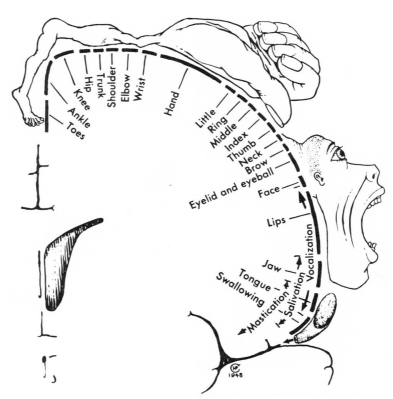

Fig. 4-6. Motor homunculus. Diagrammatic section of precentral gyrus. *Dark lines* represent relative proportion of cortical tissue controlling muscles of parts of the body on the labels. Surrounding the section is a caricature of the body in the same relative proportions. (From Penfield, W., and Rasmussen, T.: The cerebral cortex of man, New York, 1950, Macmillan Publishing Co., Inc.)

body movement. Starting from within the longitudinal fissure that divides the hemispheres in man, one can find movements of the toes, then ankles, and then knees when the cortex is stimulated (Fig. 4-6). Continuing downward in Fig. 4-6, the precentral gyrus elicits movements in a toes-to-head direction, except that the direction is reversed from the tongue upward. The illustration also shows that muscle groups requiring the most precise control, such as the lips and fingers, have a disproportionately large cortical area devoted to them. By contrast, the large muscles of the body trunk are represented by a rather small cortical area. To understand this phenomenon, one must realize that pyramidal neurons control spinal motoneurons rather directly and that each spinal motoneuron controls a *motor unit.* Earlier, it was shown that muscles requiring precise control of movement had fewer muscle cells supplied by each nerve cell than muscles controlling gross body movement. Precise control involves many degrees of contraction, and therefore only a few muscle cells are brought into contraction as each motor nerve cell is excited—a small motor unit. Such muscles require more motoneurons for their size than do muscles controlling gross movements. The motoneurons are stimulated via pyramidal neurons that originate in the cortex. Therefore more pyramidal neurons are found controlling the movement of muscles of precise movement than controlling muscles of gross movement. As a result a greater area of cortex is devoted to precisely controlled muscles, such as those of the lips and fingers, in comparison with muscles of the body trunk.

Anatomy. The pyramidal tracts are largely *crossed,* that is, the left hemisphere of the brain controls the right side of the body and vice versa. Three tracts are involved: (1) the **corticobulbar tract,** which supplies motor fibers of the cranial nerves, (2) the **lateral corticospinal tract,** a crossed tract of the lateral funiculus of the cord, and (3) the **ventral corticospinal tract,** an uncrossed tract of the ventral funiculus of the cord. In each case the fibers run from the cortex to the level of the motoneurons and excite them via interneurons, much like a reflex. All three tracts are shown in Fig. 4-7. The corticobulbar tract contains fibers that originate in the face area of the precentral gyrus. The fibers descend the brain stem of the same side (with few exceptions) and cross at the level of the cranial motoneurons they supply. The lateral corticospinal tract is formed by approximately 75% of the pyramidal fibers that cross at the decussation of the pyramids in the lower medulla. The remaining uncrossed fibers form the ventral corticospinal tract. Most of these fibers cross in the ventral white commissure of the spinal cord at the level of the motoneurons they excite via interneurons.

Symptoms of damage. If area 4 is selectively damaged by surgery, without damage to other areas, a **flaccid paralysis** results in the muscles represented by the damaged area. The muscles retain normal tone, but they are poorly controlled. The paralysis is severe only in the muscles of precise movement (digits, lower limbs, lips, and so forth); the animal is still capable of gross movements. The nervous system is capable of considerable retraining, and some control of the affected muscles can be learned by remaining brain areas. (The younger the animal, the more complete the retraining can be.) Some loss of precise control of muscles, such as those of the fingers or lips, is permanent, however. Accidental brain damage is seldom restricted to area 4, so that flaccid paralysis is rarely seen without symptoms of extrapyramidal damage as well.

Extrapyramidal system

The extrapyramidal system seems largely organized for "background movement," the postural adjustments that accompany more precise movements. For example, when one picks up a pencil from a table, gross adjustments in the position of the body trunk, shoulder, and upper arm

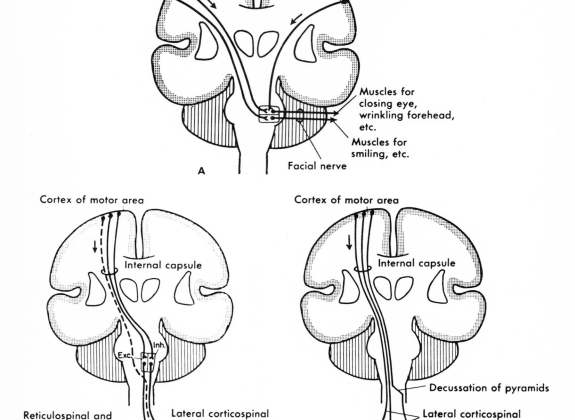

Fig. 4-7. Major motor tracts of brain in diagrammatic form. **A,** Corticobulbar tract. **B,** Reticulospinal and vestibulospinal tracts. **C,** Lateral and ventral (anterior) corticospinal tracts. (From Gardner, E. O.: Fundamentals of neurology, ed. 6, Philadelphia, 1975, W. B. Saunders Company.)

accompany the precise, pyramidally controlled movements of the lower arm and fingers. Many of the cortical fibers of the extrapyramidal system originate in area 6, the **premotor area,** although fibers are supplied by many other areas of the cor-

tex. Intense stimulation of area 6 will lead to gross body movements, although the threshold is higher than that for area 4. Body areas nearer the midline seem to be represented by area 6 as compared to area 4—muscles of the trunk, hip, and shoul-

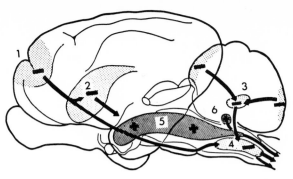

Fig. 4-8. Reconstruction of cat brain showing inhibitory and facilitatory interactions that relate to spasticity and decerebrate rigidity. Inhibitory pathways: *1,* Corticobulboreticular. *2,* Caudatospinal. *3,* Cerebelloreticular. *4,* Reticulospinal. Facilitatory pathways: *5,* Reticulospinal. *6,* Vestibulospinal. (From Lindsley, D. B., Schreiner, L. H., and Magoun, H. W.: J. Neurophysiol. **12:**197-205, 1949.)

der. Topographically, moving from area 4 into area 6 is like moving from areas with more control of the extremities to areas with more control of the body trunk, shoulders, and thighs. However, the mechanisms of extrapyramidal control over the muscles are quite different from the mechanisms of pyramidal control.

Anatomy. The extrapyramidal system consists of an array of relatively short and branching neurons that descend through the brain stem to excite subcortical nuclei; it includes much of the brain stem reticular formation. Some of the pathways—those leading from the cortex to the thalamus, from the cortex to the corpus striatum, from the cortex to the red nucleus (an important motor center in four-legged animals), and from the cortex to the cerebellum—are anatomically distinct. Others can be followed only by the technique of stimulating the cortex and following the course of the resulting nerve impulses with implanted electrodes. All the extrapyramidal pathways that originate in the cortex form part of the **cortically originating extrapyramidal system (COEPS).** Other descending pathways of the extrapyramidal system originate in the nuclei named above as well as in other nuclei of the brain stem. Some of the pathways involved are shown in Figs. 4-7 and 4-8. These path-

ways control "background movements" by adjustment of extensor muscle tone, although this is an entirely different mechanism from the direct control of motoneurons exerted by the pyramidal system. The cortex and the caudate nucleus selectively inhibit a large excitatory area and a smaller inhibitory area in the brain stem reticular formation (BSRF). These two areas give rise to the **reticulospinal tract,** which excites stretch reflexes in the extensors. The BSRF inhibitory area has an inhibitory effect on the motoneurons that stimulate stretch reflexes. The cortex and caudate nucleus selectively suppress these influences to cause a *pattern* of background movement. The BSRF inhibitory area also receives a pattern of inhibition from the cerebellum. In this general way the cortex, caudate nucleus, and cerebellum control the BSRF, which in turn regulates the extensor stretch reflexes. By the mechanism of reciprocal innervation, the contraction of extensor muscles is accompanied by the relaxation of their opposed flexor muscles and vice versa. As a result, the area of the BSRF that is labeled excitatory for extensors inhibits flexors, and the inhibitory BSRF excites the flexors while it inhibits extensors. However, the main influence of the BSRF is to excite extensor muscles via the reticulospinal tract. This is why a decerebrate animal shows decerebrate rigidity, or spastic paralysis. The large excitatory BSRF area is released from the inhibitory influence of the premotor cortex and caudate nucleus when these centers are cut away. Excitation to the extensor stretch reflexes through the reticulospinal tract is thereby increased. The extensors react with strong stretch reflex contractions, and the animal assumes a posture in which all four limbs are rigidly extended.

The extensor motoneurons are subject to direct rather than to indirect excitation by another pathway of the extrapyramidal system. The **vestibular nuclei** of the eighth nerve send excitation directly to the extensor motoneurons by the **vestibulospinal tract** to report on head position and movement (Fig. 4-8). The vestibular nuclei are normally subject to inhibition by the cerebral cortex and caudate nucleus. Their direct excitation of extensor motoneurons is therefore increased when these structures are cut away in decerebration. This adds to the decerebrate rigidity caused by the BSRF. In the normal animal the vestibular nuclei receive a pattern of input reporting on the position and movements of the head. In response the vestibular nuclei send a pattern of excitation to the extensor

motoneurons by the vestibulospinal tract. The extensor muscles respond to adjust the posture of the animal to the position and movements of the head.

Some of the pathways of the extrapyramidal system are involved in a cortical feedback mechanism. Cortical feedback coordinates events in the premotor area and basal ganglia with initiation of movements from pyramidal area 4. Neurons leaving premotor area 6 relay in subcortical nuclei and feed back to area 4. In this manner the "background movements" initiated by the extrapyramidal system are coordinated with the more precise movements initiated by the pyramidal system. The circuit involved is shown in Fig. 4-9 and part of Fig. 4-5. Excitation from premotor area 6 goes to the **basal ganglia** (striatum or putamen, caudate nucleus, and globus pallidus). The basal ganglia send excitation to the thalamus (ventrolateral nucleus), and the thalamus feeds back to both area 6 and area 4. This is a case of *negative feedback* since area 6 and the basal ganglia largely *inhibit* area 4. However, selective inhibition can coordinate the pyramidal and extrapyramidal systems just as well as selective excitation could.

Symptoms of damage. Damage to premotor area 6 or other parts of the COEPS

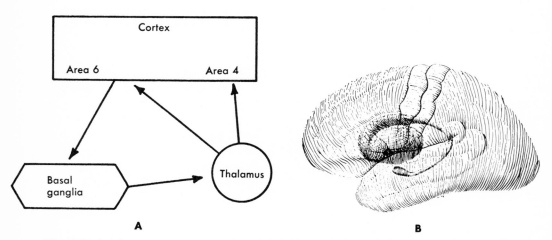

A   **B**

Fig. 4-9. A, Diagram showing some of the relationships between cortical and subcortical motor centers. **B,** Phantom of basal ganglia within cerebral hemisphere. (From Kreig, W. J. S.: Functional neuroanatomy, Evanston, Ill., 1972, Brain Books.)

results in **spastic paralysis** of the affected extensor muscles. This is similar in principle to the decerebrate rigidity already discussed. The excitatory BSRF and vestibular nuclei are released from cortical and subcortical inhibition. As a result, extensor muscle tone is increased, and the affected limbs are rigidly extended in four-legged animals. Extensor muscles are antigravity muscles, as they bear the weight of the animal in reflex standing and prevent the limbs from flexing against the force of gravity. In two-legged primates (including man) the flexors of the arms and hands, rather than the extensors, resist gravity; bending the arm and fingers is done against the force of gravity. As a result the flexors of the arm and hand take on the antigravity role of extensors and are connected to the extrapyramidal system accordingly. Spastic paralysis of the arm and hand in man, therefore, involves a rigidly *flexed* arm, wrist, and hand. This position of arm, wrist, and hand is frequently seen in spastics when damage to the appropriate brain areas has occurred.

Damage to the cortical feedback loop or to its connections with extrapyramidal centers has a more complex and variable outcome. It is now believed that such pathways can be classified by chemical transmitter substances that the nerve cells release to excite other nerve cells of the pathway at synapses. Damage to pathways using acetylcholine as a transmitter ("cholinergic" pathways) are believed responsible for **chorea** (St. Vitus' dance), a disorder (in its most common form) characterized by spasmodic involuntary movements of the limbs or facial muscles. The cholinergic pathways appear to oppose, in a balancing way, pathways that use dopamine as a chemical transmitter. One of these "dopaminergic" pathways involves the *substantia nigra* (black body), a deeply pigmented nucleus of the midbrain. When this nucleus loses its ability to produce dopamine, the nucleus turns pale and **Parkinson's disease** results. Parkinsonianism involves tremor at rest (when movement is not attempted), a disabling limitation of voluntary movement (poverty of movement), and impaired facial expression (masklike face).

Minor damage to the extrapyramidal system from circulatory disorders often occurs in elderly persons, and continuous fine tremors, especially of the hand, are often seen. These tremors usually disappear when a voluntary movement is made. Thus tremors at rest can be suffered by an elderly watchmaker, for example, without unduly affecting the precise movements necessary to his work. Some believe that the feedback loop and connections to other subcortical motor centers suppress continued activity of centers that cause the alternating muscle contractions of tremor.

In the case of chorea, increasing the supply of acetylcholine for the cholinergic pathways is impractical because cholinergic pathways are so widespread in the brain that widespread and debilitating excitation would result. Muscle relaxants, sedatives, hypnotics, and tranquilizers all are drugs that give some symptomatic relief from the continuous movements of chorea. Increasing the dopamine output of the substantia nigra to treat parkinsonianism has been successful, however. The obvious treatment would be to supply the nuclei with dopamine by injecting it into the bloodstream. However, dopamine is too large a molecule to pass the blood-brain barrier (Chapter 3) that exists between the capillaries and the tissue fluid of the brain. The brain can make dopamine from a smaller molecule, called **L-dopa** (3,4-dihydroxyphenylalanine) or levodopa, that *will* pass the blood-brain barrier. Treatment of parkinsonian patients with large doses of L-dopa has resulted in a dramatic relief of the symptoms described above, in many instances. However, there are problems of dosage management and some interesting side effects. The drug often has mood-elevating effects that have relieved some elderly patients from depression and have relieved others from mania (a type of psychosis—see Chapter 15). (This may be the case because the brain can make epinephrine as well as dopamine from

L-dopa. Epinephrine is a mood-elevating drug as well as a transmitter in the sympathetic nervous system.) Less frequently, an increase in the sex drive has been reported—perhaps the first true aphrodisiac has been discovered! The large doses of L-dopa required for successful treatment have been reduced in recent experiments by heating the brain slightly with radio-frequency waves or giving enzyme inhibitors that slow the metabolic destruction of L-dopa.

Cerebellum

The cerebellum regulates the postural adjustments of the extrapyramidal system and governs certain interactions between extrapyramidal and pyramidal systems. The cerebellum brings kinesthetic and vestibular inputs to bear on both systems and plays an integral role in motor organization. It is treated separately in this chapter only for the sake of taking up topics one at a time; in the end, pyramidal, extrapyramidal, and cerebellar influences are part of one motor organization system. The cerebellar contribution to motor organization includes all proprioceptive (movement) and cortical input to the cerebellum and all cerebellar output to cortical and subcortical centers involved in movement. The cerebellum aids in the regulation of balance and coordination.

Anatomy. The cerebellar pathways involve three sets of inputs to the cerebellum and three sets of outputs. All inputs and outputs interconnect by neurons that crisscross the cortex of the cerebellum in both directions; therefore all inputs to the cerebellum affect all outputs from the cerebellum. However, one input and one output form a negative feedback loop from the premotor areas of the cerebral cortex to the cerebellum and back to the motor cortex. From the standpoint of evolution this feedback loop interconnects the newest part of the cerebrum with the newest part of the cerebellum (neocerebellum). A second input from the stretch receptors in the extensor muscles (muscle spindles) stimulates an older part of the cerebellum, the paleocerebellum. This part of the cerebellum regulates extensor tone by its output to the BSRF and other nuclei of the brain stem. The oldest part of the cerebellum (archicerebellum) receives input from the position and movement receptors of the inner ear. Its output also regulates extensor tone but by way of the vestibular nuclei instead of the BSRF. The subdivisions of the cerebellum are given in Table 6 in terms of cerebellar anatomy and evolutionary age (phylogenetic divisions). In Fig. 4-10 are shown some of the parts of the cerebellum in relation to parts of the brain stem.

The **archicerebellum** is the oldest part of the cerebellum and is found in fish, who have no gravity receptors or cerebral cortex. The input to the archicerebellum deals with head position and movement (plus the lateral-line canals that register changes in water pressure). The archicerebellum receives excitation from the inner ear, the semicircular canals signal head movement, and the maculae signal head position (Chapter 7). This input reaches the cerebellum from the eighth

Table 6. Organization of the cerebellum

Phylogenetic division	Anatomical division	Input	Output
Archicerebellum	Flocculonodular lobe	Vestibule, vestibular nuclei	Vestibular nuclei
Paleocerebellum	Vermal areas, anterior and posterior lobes	Vestibular nuclei, kinesthesis	BSRF, vestibular nuclei midbrain thalamus
Neocerebellum	Cerebellar hemispheres	Premotor cortex, olive	Red nucleus (to area 4), thalamus, BSRF

nerve, both directly and as relayed by the vestibular nuclei. The output of the archicerebellum feeds back to the vestibular nuclei. The archicerebellum regulates the excitatory output of the vestibular nuclei to extensor motoneurons (vestibulospinal tract). The resulting pattern of background postural movement depends on the position of the head. The archicerebellum helps to regulate these adjustments (of course the other two lobes of the cerebellum affect the vestibular nuclei through their interconnections with the archicerebellum). Anatomically, the archicerebellum consists of two small paired structures that overhang the brain stem beneath the main mass of the anterior cerebellum, the flocculi (sing., **flocculus**), and a medially placed structure that hangs down in the posterior part of the fourth ventricle, the **nodule.** The archicerebellum is identified with the **flocculonodular lobe.**

The **paleocerebellum** includes the medially placed anterior and posterior lobes of the **cerebellum** and the narrow central vermis that connects them. The paleocerebellum developed when animals left the sea to live on land. Living on land subjected their muscles to the pull of gravity in the absence of the supporting effect of the water. Antigravity muscles, the extensors,

developed receptors that were sensitive to stretching in their intrafusal fibers. Reflexes aroused by stretching resulted to extend the limbs against the pull of gravity. (The stretch reflex has already been discussed.) The sense organs that respond to muscle stretching also connect with tracts of the spinal cord that ascend to the cerebellum. These tracts are the **spinocerebellar tracts,** which carry excitation to the paleocerebellum. After integration with activity in other lobes of the cerebellum, the paleocerebellum acts on the BSRF inhibitory areas with a pattern of suppression from the anterior and posterior lobes (Figs. 4-5 and 4-8). As previously explained, the BSRF regulates the excitability of extensor stretch reflexes, and stretch reflexes are responsible for postural adjustment. The paleocerebellum responds to muscle stretching and other inputs by regulating stretch reflex excitability through the BSRF. The paleocerebellum suppresses inhibitory areas of the BSRF in a patterned fashion so that the extensor tone is regulated in an organized way. Changes in posture result. The whole "circuit" is a patterned mechanism of positive feedback; the excitation of extensor stretch reflexes also arouses centers in the paleocerebellum that act to sensitize

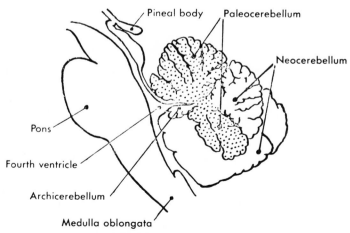

Fig. 4-10. Sketch of major phylogenetic divisions of cerebellum seen from midline. (From Gardner, E. O.: Fundamentals of neurology, ed. 6, Philadelphia, 1975, W. B. Saunders Company.)

stretch receptors. In developing a pattern of stretch reflex excitability, the paleocerebellum also receives input from the vestibular nuclei and other lobes of the cerebellum; it acts on them, and on the midbrain and thalamus as well (Table 6).

The **neocerebellum** is the most recently developed part of the cerebellum in evolution. The development of the neocerebellum parallels the development of the motor areas of the cerebral cortex. As the great cerebral hemispheres began to cover most of the brain, the paired cerebellar hemispheres began to overlie the older areas of the cerebellum, forming the neocerebellum (Fig. 4-10). As the motor and premotor cortex assumed the task of integrating complex movements, interaction with the activity of the paleocerebellum and archicerebellum became necessary. The neocerebellum developed to provide this interaction, and two-way connections were established between cortical motor areas and the neocerebellum. The names of these tracts describe their connections. The **corticopontocerebellar tract** runs from the premotor cortex (area 6) to the cerebellar hemispheres via nuclei in the pons. Fibers leaving area 6 descend in the cerebral peduncles to the pons, where they synapse in nuclei of that area. Neurons from these nuclei cross to the opposite side of the brain stem and ascend to the opposite cerebellar hemisphere. The tract that returns from the neocerebellum to the motor cortex is also crossed, so that the left cerebral hemisphere has two-way connections to the right cerebellar hemisphere and vice versa. The returning tract is called the **dentatorubrothalamic tract** for nuclei where it relays. It originates in the output nucleus of the cerebellar hemispheres, the **dentate nucleus.** The fibers cross, and the tract relays in the red nucleus and the thalamus before projecting to the motor area of the cortex (area 4). The two-way connections between cerebrum and cerebellum form a feedback loop that originates in the premotor cortex (area 6) and ends in the motor cortex (area 4). The

premotor cortex is a major origin for the extrapyramidal system (COEPS), and the motor cortex is a major origin for the pyramidal system. The feedback loop takes "information" about the background movements initiated from area 6 of the COEPS, adds cerebellar inputs from the movement senses, and feeds back the result to area 4. By means of these pathways precise movements initiated by area 4 can be "programmed" by the cerebellum to agree with background movement from area 6 and with input reaching the neocerebellum from other parts of the cerebellum. As Table 6 shows, the neocerebellum also receives inputs from the olive and sends outputs to the BSRF.

Symptoms of damage. Knowing the functions of the three major subdivisions of the cerebellum enables one to predict the consequences of damage to various parts of the cerebellum. The archicerebellum regulates postural extensor tone in response to the vestibular inputs that are governed by head position and movement. Damage to the flocculi or nodule, therefore, results in disturbances of balance. When the paleocerebellum is impaired by damage to the anterior or posterior cerebellar lobes, postural adjustments suffer with the lack of proprioceptive coordination, and a particular uncoordinated (ataxic) gait results, with exaggerated extensor muscle tone. Neocerebellar damage to the hemispheres causes **intention tremor** (tremor when a movement is begun) and overreaching or underreaching when grasping for an object. Some coordination between background movements and precise voluntary movements has been lost. The patient's hand may be steady until he makes a voluntary motion. Tremor then results, and he is unable to coordinate the position of his body in space with the precise motion needed to reach and grasp an object; he therefore overshoots or undershoots.

SUMMARY

Muscles are classified as smooth, striated, or cardiac depending on their function as visceral, limb, and heart muscle, respectively. Smooth muscles are innervated by the opposing sympathetic and parasympathetic divisions of the autonomic nervous system and are usually tubular in form (intestines and arteries, for example). If one division constricts the bore of the tube, the other will increase it. Heart (cardiac) muscle is intermediate in function between long-contracting smooth and rapidly contracting striated muscles. Striated muscles occur as opposed flexors and extensors and are reciprocally innervated. The number of degrees of contraction shown by a striated muscle depends on the average size of its motor units, which are larger for postural extensor muscles than precisely controlled flexor muscles. Striated muscles, especially extensors, show continuous partial contraction (muscle tone) due to their stretch reflexes. Each striated muscle cell is stimulated by a nerve cell branch at the myoneural junction. The axon branch releases ACh to partially depolarize the end plate; the muscle cell membrane reverses polarization like a nerve cell to stimulate the contraction mechanism.

Reflexes have five categories of elements and are under stimulus control. Spinal reflexes can be isolated from higher centers by cutting the spinal cord or upper brain stem. In the former case, spinal shock results when the reflexes are cut off from background excitation by brain stem areas (vestibular nuclei and BSRF). In the latter case, these areas are released from inhibition by the cortex and basal ganglia; decerebrate rigidity ensues. All these influences are focused on the motoneurons, which are the final common path for response. The final common path is subject to inhibition as well; this can be demonstrated by pitting opposed reflexes against one another. Inhibition may be of the presynaptic or postsynaptic variety. Complex vital and postural reflexes are organized at higher brain levels.

The organization of movement results from the interaction of the pyramidal, extrapyramidal, and cerebellar systems. These systems govern, respectively, precise movement, background movement, and balance and coordination. The pyramidal pathways go directly from the motor areas of the cerebral cortex to the motoneurons, while the extrapyramidal and cerebellar systems act indirectly via the vestibular nuclei and BSRF. The vestibular pathways excite extensor motoneurons and are under the inhibitory control of the premotor cortex. So is the BSRF, but the reticulospinal pathways excite stretch reflexes. The pyramidal system is topographically organized at the cortical level and acts via the corticobulbar and the lateral and ventral corticospinal tracts. The extrapyramidal system originates in the premotor cortex (COEPS), vestibular nuclei (vestibulospinal tract), and BSRF (reticulospinal tract). A feedback pathway between the premotor and motor cortex via the basal ganglia and thalamus integrates extrapyramidal and pyramidal functions. Pyramidal damage results in spastic paralysis; extrapyramidal damage involves spastic paralysis if the premotor area is involved (COEPS) and Parkinson's disease or chorea from subcortical damage.

The cerebellum may be classified by its inputs and phylogenetic age. The oldest part (archicerebellum) receives input from receptors for head position and movement. The paleocerebellum has input from the stretch reflex receptors. The newest part (neocerebellum) is in two-way interaction with the cerebral cortex. The input is via the cortico-pontocerebellar tract from area 6; the output is via the dentatorubrothalamic tract to area 4. Archicerebellar damage causes disturbed balance, paleocerebellar damage impairs coordination, and neocerebellar damage results in intention tremor.

READINGS

Evarts, E. V.: Brain mechanisms in movement, Sci. Am. **229**:96-103, July 1973 (W. H. Freeman Reprint No. 1277).

Galambos, R.: Nerves and muscles, Garden City, N.Y., 1962, Doubleday Publishing Company.

Gardner, E. D.: Fundamentals of neurology, ed. Philadelphia, 1975, W. B. Saunders Company.

Hayashi, T.: How cells move, Sci. Am. **205**:184-204, Sept. 1961 (W. H. Freeman Reprint No. 97).

Hoyle, G.: How is muscle turned on and off? Sci. Am. **222**:84-93, April 1970.

Huxley, H. E.: The contraction of muscle, Sci. Am. **199**:67-82, Nov. 1958 (W. H. Freeman Reprint No. 19).

Huxley, H. E.: The mechanism of muscular contraction, Sci. Am. **213**:18-27, Dec. 1965 (W. H. Freeman Reprint No. 1026).

Lippold, O.: Physiological tremor, Sci. Am. **224**:65-73, March 1971.

Llinas, R. A.: The cortex of the cerebellum, Sci. Am. **232**:56-71, Jan. 1975 (W. H. Freeman Reprint No. 1312).

McGeer, P. L.: The chemistry of mind, Am. Scientist **59**:221-229, 1971. Also in Leukel, F.: Issues in physiological psychology, St. Louis, 1974, The C. V. Mosby Co.

Merton, P. A.: How we control the contraction of our muscles, Sci. Am. **226**:30-37, May 1972 (W. H. Freeman Reprint No. 1249).

Ochs, S.: Reflexes and reflex mechanism. In Selkurt, E. E., editor: Physiology, Boston, 1963, Little, Brown and Company.

Ochs, S.: Upper somatic and visceral control. In Selkurt, E. E., editor: Physiology, Boston, 1963, Little, Brown and Company.

Porter, R. E., and Franzini-Armstrong, C.: The sarcoplasmic reticulum, Sci. Am. **212**:72-80, March 1965 (W. H. Freeman Reprint No. 1007).

Sherrington, C.: The integrative action of the nervous system, New Haven, Conn., 1961, Yale University Press.

CHAPTER 5

Introduction to the senses

OVERVIEW

This is the first of six chapters that will be devoted to the human senses. Before discussing specific sensory inputs, certain concepts that apply to all of the senses and measurement of their properties should be understood. A chapter introducing the senses seems an appropriate place for these concepts.

STIMULUS

A **stimulus** is any physical energy that excites a receptor. This statement ends, by definition, the old argument over whether a tree falling in the forest makes a noise if there is no one there to hear it. The falling tree creates an energy change that is not a stimulus because it does not excite an animal receptor. (If a "noise" is a stimulus, the tree made no noise.)

Receptors

Receptors consist of tissues or organs that are specialized to respond to a specific *form* of energy. The sensory tissue involved is not only specialized for irritability; it is specialized to be more irritable to energy change of a specific variety and range of intensity. The tissue is said to have a low **threshold** to the energy change for which it is specialized. The threshold for a receptor is the minimum energy that will stimulate that receptor. Receptors are specialized in humans for five types of stimulus energy: mechanical, thermal, chemical, acoustical, and photic. Receptors specialized for mechanical stimulation include the skin receptors for pressure and pain, proprioceptive receptors in the muscles and joints that report limb position and movement, and receptors in the viscera that give sensations accompanying hunger (stomach contractions, for example). Thermal receptors in the skin report the temperature of the environment. Taste and smell are chemical receptors; that is, they respond best to substances in solution. For taste the substances are dissolved in saliva; for smell, airborne particles dissolve in the moist mucous surfaces of the nasal passages. Acoustical receptors are modified pressure receptors in the ear that respond to rapid variations in air pressure, called sound. Audition (hearing) shares with vision the function of reporting events that occur at a distance from the subject. Visual receptors are photic receptors and respond to light, a part of the spectrum of electromagnetic energy. Receptors specialize in different ways in different parts of the body, but the examples given survey most of the sensory mechanisms of the body that give rise to sensations.

Some specialized receptors in the body do not cause sensations when stimulated. These receptors stimulate reflexes and brain activity without exciting parts of the brain where activity leads to conscious awareness. (We may become aware of the responses that occur.) Some of the reflexes involved include "automatic" responses to receptors in the inner ear that help us maintain balance and coordination. Other receptors initiate reactions that regulate the consistency of the internal environment—receptors that respond to an increase in blood pressure by reflexly slowing the heart rate, for example. Still other receptors in the hypothalamus are sensitive to the internal changes that result from need states like hunger or thirst. These and other receptors may arouse the brain and change behavior without direct awareness like receptors that respond to an increase in blood pressure by reflexly slowing the heart rate.

Adequate and inadequate stimuli

When a receptor is activated by the form of energy for which it is specialized, that receptor has received an **adequate stimulus.** This is true even if it is not the kind of receptor that can give rise to conscious sensations. For example, light is the adequate stimulus for the eye. When the receptor responds to a form of energy for which it is not specialized, it receives an **inadequate stimulus.** Pressure on the eyeball from a finger can cause a sensation of light, even though the eye is specialized to respond to light rather than to pressure. The eye has a low threshold to light and a high threshold to pressure, but the pressure threshold can be exceeded and thereby stimulate the retina (sensory tissue of the eye).

Law of specific nerve energies

A receptor may be a separate group of specialized cells or a specialized ending on a nerve cell. Adequate stimulation of a receptor results in a **generator potential** in the specialized tissue or ending. A generator potential is a change in electrical potential by the receptor. The generator potential, in turn, fires a **nerve impulse** in the sensory nerve fibers leading to the CNS. The nerve impulses result in a sensation. The form that the sensation takes—light, sound, taste, and so forth—depends on the receptor or neuron stimulated. This statement is the **law of specific nerve energies.** The law holds because the neurons from different receptors go to different *places* in the brain. One sees light because the optic nerves lead to the visual areas of the brain, not because their nerve impulses are different from the nerve impulses reaching a different part of the brain from the ear. Electrical stimulation of the eye, the optic nerves, or the visual area of the brain causes a sensation of light. Stimulation of nerves leading to the auditory area causes a sensation of sound, even though the auditory impulses and visual impulses look the same on an oscilloscope. As Sherrington once stated, the nerve impulse is the "universal currency" of the nervous system.

Attributes of sensation

What characteristics of sensation are measurable and common to all sensory modalities? What happens in the sensory neurons, according to the law of specific nerve energies, when these attributes are varied? These are the questions attacked in this section, beginning with the four measurable attributes that all the senses have in common: (1) **quality,** (2) **intensity,** (3) **extent,** and (4) **duration.**

Quality. Sensory quality is the attribute that distinguishes one sensory modality from another. It also distinguishes *qualitatively* different attributes within a sensation, such as hues for vision and tastes for gustation. For senses that have more than one quality, there are **primary qualities** and **secondary qualities.** Primary qualities are the basic differential responses of the receptor. Their combination produces all the other qualitative differences, or secondary qualities, of sensation. Whether these basic responses (sensations) depend on a single receptor or a combination of receptors, they cannot be analyzed further by the subject. To take a visual example, the color red is primary and appears only red. The color orange is secondary, and primary yellow and primary red can be detected in orange just by looking at it.

The difference between primary and secondary qualities can be most clearly seen in further examples from various sensory modalities. Somesthesia (organic and skin sensitivity) has four primary qualities that appear to be four kinds of sensory modality: pressure, warmth, cold, and pain. Secondary somesthetic qualities such as tickle or itch are produced by combinations of these four primary qualities. The kinesthetic and vestibular senses are difficult to analyze in terms of sensory quality because they do not result in conscious sensations. Taste has four primary qualities: sweet, sour, bitter, and salt; all other tastes are combinations. Smell appears to have seven primary qualities: camphoraceous, musky, floral, pepperminty, ethereal, pungent, and putrid. Audition has but one quality—pitch—so that secondary qualities do not result. Vision has the four hue qualities of red, blue, yellow, and green; all other hues result from combinations of two or more of these qualities.

Quality indicates *what* sensory system or what *part* of a sensory system is functioning, whereas the other three attributes (intensity, extent, and duration) show only *how* it is functioning. Thus one speaks of the loudness of a pitch rather than the pitch of a loudness, or the brightness of a hue rather than the hue of a brightness. Intensity, extent, and duration modify quality, but quality does not usually modify the other three attributes in a systematic way.

Intensity. The sensed intensity of a stimulus increases with the intensity of the physical energy that is stimulating the receptor. However, the relationship is not a linear one. That is, equal increases in physical energy do not lead to equal increases in sensation intensity. At low intensities a small increase in stimulus energy makes as much *difference* in the intensity sensed as a large increase in the stimulus at high intensities—a whisper can be heard in a quiet room, but one shouts to be heard over the roar of a jet engine. Furthermore, quality and intensity interact. In hearing, for example, the ear is most sensitive to tones in the middle of the musical scale of pitch (a quality), and the eye is more sensitive to some hue qualities than it is to others. Pressure, pain, warmth, and cold all vary in sensed intensity, as do taste and smell. Auditory intensity is loudness and visual intensity is brightness. The attribute of intensity, then, is important for all the senses.

Extent. Extent is the "area" of the perceptual field covered by the stimulus. This means the *size* of the area of pressure, pain, warmth, or cold on the skin, or in the viscera for somesthesia. The extent of the tongue occupied by a taste is another example. Extent has not been investigated for smell. There is, however, a dimension of auditory volume that is separated from loudness, although it interacts with both loudness and pitch. Visual extent is the proportion of the visual field occupied by a stimulus.

Duration. Duration is merely the period of time over which a sensation lasts in any of the sensory modalities.

Sensory attributes and the law of specific nerve energies

The statement has been made that all nerve impulses "look alike," whether in somesthesia, proprioception, taste, smell, audition, or vision. Sensory modalities differ according to the *place* in the brain reached by sensory neurons serving different sensory modalities—the brain has visual projection areas, auditory projection areas, and so forth. Stimulating the eye with light or even pressure leads to a visual sensation because the sensory nerves lead to the visual area of the brain. Differences in modality are also differences in sensory quality; thus these variations in quality may depend on the *place* in the brain reached by the fibers serving each modality. Somesthetic pressure and some proprioception reaches the somesthetic projection area; there is reason to believe that most pain and perhaps temperature excitation terminate in lower centers. Sensory modality seems to depend on the part of the brain stimulated.

Whether different qualities *within* a sense modality depend on the stimulation of different parts of their projection areas in the brain is not known. The taste receptors appear to send various *patterns* of excitation to the brain to signal salt, sweet, bitter, or sour. There seem to be seven different kinds of smell receptors for the seven olfactory qualities, but it is not known if the excitation of these receptors reaches different places in the olfactory projection areas. There appear to be three receptors serving the four primary hue qualities for vision, but the reaction of the visual projection area to these receptors is unknown. Auditory fibers excited by different pitches do reach systematically different places in the auditory area of the brain, however. There is some evidence for a "place theory" for sensory quality, but it is far from complete.

Intensity of the stimulus affects each sensory modality in the same way. As intensity is increased, more receptors and therefore more sensory neurons fire. Furthermore, each neuron fires more frequently.

Extent, logically, has a single cue—the *area,* or extent, of the receptor field stimulated, and therefore the extent, or proportion, of the projection area in the brain being excited.

Duration depends on the duration of excitation of the receptor and therefore on the duration of excitation to a projection area of the brain.

METHODS OF MEASUREMENT
Introspection

As pointed out in Chapter 1 in the discussion of the mind-body problem, the simplest way to study the response characteristics of a human sense organ is to stimulate it in an appropriate (adequate) way and ask the subject about his sensations. Much of the earlier work on sensory mechanisms was done in this way, and we have a lot of useful information about the sensitivity, qualities, intensity range, and other characteristics of the human senses as a result. The problem is that the human brain does not receive its information as sensations but rather as nerve impulses governed by the law of specific nerve energies. If we are ever to learn how the brain deals with this information to produce conscious attributes of quality, intensity, extent, and duration, we must study the information the brain receives as nerve impulses (and the chemical events underlying them). This is only the first step toward learning how the brain integrates nervous activity so as to lead to a response.

Evoked potentials

In animal studies the method of evoked potentials is most commonly used. Electrodes are placed in the sense organs, sensory nerve cells, and/or the brain, and the electrical responses to sensory stimulation are recorded. (There are very few human volunteers for this sort of thing!) This has the advantage of telling us what kind of "signals" the sense organs send to the brain in response to various kinds of stimulus change. It has the promise of telling us how the brain deals with the information. It does not, of course, tell us whether the animal senses the stimulus change, unless we train the animal to respond in a specified way to the stimulus if he senses it.

Thresholds

A threshold is a limiting (minimum or maximum) energy change measured in terms of physiological recordings of receptors or nerve cells or in terms of reported sensation (in humans). The questions to be asked include the following: (1) What is the minimum energy sensed (**absolute threshold**)? (2) What is the least *difference* in energy sensed (**difference threshold**)? (3) What is the maximum energy sensed; that is, when does increasing the stimulus energy not increase the sensation intensity (**terminal threshold**)? There are, then, three types of thresholds, each a measurement of physical energy as it affects sensation or receptor response. In visual intensity, for example, the absolute threshold for brightness is the dimmest light the subject can detect. The difference threshold is the smallest difference in brightness the subject can detect. The terminal threshold is the brightest light and the most intense sensation that the subject can experience; further increases in intensity do not make the light appear brighter to the subject. All three of these receptor and sensation responses have absolute and fixed values at a given moment. However, the sensitivity of the visual receptors varies from moment to moment. This will cause the absolute, difference, and terminal threshold values to vary from one measurement to the next. In addition, the subject makes *errors* in reporting his sensations, the experimenter makes errors in varying the stimulus and recording the results, and the stimulus light is not perfect. Fluctuations in receptor sensitivity and measurement error are involved. Some kind of average measurement is needed for the absolute, difference, and terminal thresholds. This means that any threshold is a derived *statistical* value rather than an absolute value for receptor sensitivity.

Absolute threshold. Frequently the absolute threshold is called "threshold," with the prefix absolute implied. The absolute threshold is most precisely defined as the minimum energy that results in a sensation (that stimulates a receptor) 50% of the time. As noted above, the 50% "average" value is used because the sensitivity of the receptor, the attention of the subject, and measurement errors fluctuate. Obviously, the more intense the energy, the greater will be the percentage of occasions that it will stimulate the subject—a more intense light will be detected more often, for example.

Difference threshold. The difference threshold is defined as the least difference between two stimuli in a given direction that can be detected 50% of the time. The same considerations requiring an average value for the absolute threshold are doubly involved for the difference threshold, since two stimuli, rather than one, are used.

Terminal threshold. At the other end of the scale from the absolute threshold is the terminal threshold. It is applied most readily to differences in the intensity and quality of stimuli. In terms of intensity it would be the stimulus whose increase in intensity leads to no increase in sensation intensity half the time. As an example from quality thresholds, when increases in the frequency of a sound pass the range where the subject can hear them 50% of the time, the terminal threshold for pitch has been reached. However, there are two difficulties with the terminal threshold: (1) as the terminal threshold for intensity is approached, pain is sensed, and damage to the receptors may result; thus for practical reasons the terminal intensity threshold is often measured in terms of the onset of pain and (2) quality and intensity interact. For example, the sensory *range* for pitch increases with increased intensity, so that both the absolute and terminal threshold values change—the subject can hear both lower and higher pitches at increased intensity.

Psychophysics and sensory attributes

Psychophysical methods can be used to determine thresholds for quality, intensity, extent, or duration in any sensory modality. Absolute, difference, and terminal thresholds can be determined for each attribute. In studying sensory quality, which stimulus value represents the absolute threshold and which represents the terminal threshold is rather arbitrary; together they represent the *range* of qualities responded to by the receptor. In vision the hue quality is represented by a range of electromagnetic wave lengths from 400 to 750 nm (4000 to 7500 Å); beyond those limits the eye does not respond. Pitch, in hearing, corresponds to sound frequencies ranging from about 20 to 20,000 cycles per second (or hertz); other frequencies do not stimulate the auditory receptors, regardless of their intensity. Qualitative thresholds for somesthesia, proprioception, and the chemical senses have received little study, but measurement is at least theoretically possible.

Intensity thresholds have been studied in most sensory modalities. In vision, absolute, difference, and terminal thresholds for brightness have been established. These thresholds have also been measured for auditory loudness, intensity of each quality of taste, warmth, and pain, as well as for weight lifting (proprioception). The dimension of extent has been given the most attention in studies of visual size discrimination. Absolute thresholds of visual extent are the basis of the tests of visual *acuity* necessary in fitting eyeglasses. Difference thresholds for visual extent have been published as size judgments, but a terminal threshold merely means that the visual field is filled. The dimension of auditory extent (volume) has been scaled as it relates to pitch and loudness. Difference thresholds for extent of pressure sensations have been investigated. Absolute and difference thresholds for kinesthesis have been studied by measuring the smallest angle of arm movement detected by the subject and the smallest difference between two anges sensed.

The measurement of duration is much the same for each modality and requires little attention here. Absolute and difference thresholds are the only ones studied; logically there can be no terminal threshold for duration of a stimulus as long as the subject is awake.

SENSORY PHENOMENA
Adaptation versus habituation

Adaptation. Energy of specific physical nature and amount was defined as the adequate stimulus for a given receptor—light of a specified intensity and wavelength range for the eye, air pressure changes of a specified frequency and amplitude for the ear, and so on. Increases in energy within these limits result in increases in the perceived intensity of the stimulus. In some receptors *constant* energy input over a period of time results in a *decrease* in perceived intensity. If the decrease in perceived intensity results from a decrease in receptor sensitivity, the phenomenon is called **adaptation.** For example, the smell of flowers is quite noticeable on entering a florist's shop, but it nearly disappears after remaining in the shop for 20 minutes or so. The reason is that the receptors have become insensitive to the flower odor. The extent to which receptors adapt differs from one sensory modality to another. Adaptation to a constant stimulus is nearly complete for smell under most conditions, resulting in no stimulation after a period of time. Taste adaptation is usually about half complete. Adaptation to moderate stimulus intensities is complete for temperature. Some adaptation occurs in vision and hearing. Very little adaptation occurs for pressure, pain, kinesthesis, or the vestibular senses. If the pressure receptors adapted, one would "lose touch" with his environment. If pain receptors adapted, one would become unaware of injurious stimuli. If kinesthetic receptors adapted, one would lose sensations of position and movement. If the vestibular receptors adapted, one would lose his balance. On the other hand, vision and hearing receptors must change sensitivity in order to increase their intensity range so that they can respond to intense lights and sounds without suffering damage from overstimulation; yet they must respond to faint lights and sounds when not adapted. Once smell or taste receptors have signaled the new stimuli they encounter, they can become insensitive to them without depriving the brain of useful information. Temperature receptors adapt after the body has made the adjustments to temperature change that keep the internal environment constant. If the body cannot cope with cold or warm stimuli in this manner, the receptors continue to signal this fact to the brain.

Habituation. Despite the fact that some

receptors are always adapted, the brain receives more information from the remaining receptors than it can cope with at any one time. Of course, some receptors act only to set off coordinated reflexes of various kinds, and one is not aware of these inputs as such. However, the responses to them stimulate other receptors that "feed back" to contribute to the brain's information load. This load of inputs is more than the higher centers of the brain can cope with all at once. Consequently, one is not *aware* of many inputs until he turns his attention to them. This phenomenon is called **habituation.** For example, the reader is unaware of the pressure of the clothes on his back or the background noises in the room until his attention is called to them. The receptors have not adapted, because he is aware of the pressure and sound stimuli when he turns his attention to them. Habituation therefore depends on the function of higher brain centers. These centers deal with only a limited number of the inputs bombarding the brain at any given time.

Consequences of adaptation: contrast and afterimages

When a sense organ adapts to a stimulus of a given *sensory quality,* its sensitivity to other sensory qualities may be unimpaired or even enhanced. Continued stimulation of the eye with red light, for example, decreases sensitivity to red but *increases* sensitivity to green. A continuous sweet stimulus raises the taste threshold to sweet but *lowers* the threshold to sour. This phenomenon is called **contrast.** When both stimuli are present at once, **simultaneous contrast** occurs. For instance, if the subject looks at a card painted half red and half green, the red area next to the green will look redder than the remainder of the red area, and the green area next to the red will look greener than the remainder of the green. Devotees of Chinese sweet and sour spareribs are enjoying simultaneous contrast—the sweet taste is accentuated by

the presence of the sour taste and vice versa.

If stimuli that mutually enhance one another are presented in succession rather than simultaneously, **successive contrast** will occur. If you look at a red card until your visual receptors have partially adapted and *then* look at a green card, the green card will look greener than it otherwise would because the eye has increased sensitivity to green. In a similar way a lemon tastes more sour after eating a candy bar.

Afterimages occur when the receptors continue to respond after the stimulus ceases acting on them. **Positive afterimages** usually result from *brief, intense* stimulation. The receptor continues to respond for a time just as it did during stimulation. For example, if you stare briefly at an unshaded light bulb and then look at a blank wall, you will continue to see the filament of the bulb for a time.

Negative afterimages result from *prolonged, moderate* stimulation of a given quality. The receptors adapt to that quality, and the threshold of another quality is lowered so that the second quality is perceived when the first is no longer sensed. When the stimulus is removed, the receptors continue to respond, not with the same quality, but with an *opposite* quality. Thus, if you stare at a green card for a minute or two and then look at a gray wall, you will perceive the image of a red card on the wall.

Compensation and fusion

If two stimuli of different quality are presented to the same receptor, either **compensation** or **fusion** may occur. Compensation occurs when the two stimuli interact to neutralize the response of the receptor. For example, the odors of balsam and beeswax are quite distinct when smelled one at a time. If both stimuli are presented at once, the subject smells nothing. Fusion occurs when the two stimuli interact so as to cause a *qualitatively* different sensation. For example, a mixture of red and yellow stimuli can result in sensation of orange.

RECEPTOR CLASSIFICATION
General and special senses

Receptors are classified as **general** if they are found throughout the body and as **special** if they are found only in the head. The general receptors serve as a sense that is often called **somesthesia** (Gr., body perception); it includes **pressure, pain, warmth, cold,** and **kinesthesis** (sense of body position and movement from the muscles and joints). Pressure, pain, warmth, and cold receptors are found just below the surface of the skin over the entire body. A less extensive distribution of poorly specialized receptors that serve these four senses are found in parts of the viscera. The special senses in the head are more highly evolved and have more complex sensory mechanisms. In the course of evolution they probably developed in the head because that end of the animal encountered the environment first as the animal moved about. (It has also been suggested that this is the reason the brain is in the head.) The special senses include **olfaction** (smell), **vision, gustation** (taste), **audition** (hearing), and **vestibular sensitivity** (head position and movement).

Internal and external senses

Receptors are also classified as **exteroceptors, interoceptors,** and **proprioceptors** by the origin of their stimuli. Exteroceptors are located at or near the body surface and signal events going on in the external environment. They serve the **cutaneous general senses** of pressure, pain, warmth, and cold. The *cutaneous,* or skin, senses are the general senses located just beneath the surface of the skin; they do not include the same general senses when they are located in the viscera. The special senses of vision, audition, olfaction, and gustation are also exteroceptors when they function to detect external events. Vision and audition are primarily extero-

ceptors. Olfaction is an exteroceptor when the subject smells a stimulus in the external environment, and gustation is an exteroceptor when taste is used to explore the outside world.

Interoceptors are receptors that detect events going on inside the body. Olfaction and gustation are interoceptors when one smells and tastes during eating and digestion. Other interoceptors are located inside the viscera, chiefly in the walls of the digestive and urogenital tracts. They are **organic** rather than cutaneous receptors. The special senses of olfaction and gustation are therefore organic only when the stimulus comes from within the digestive tract, as in eating. The **organic general senses** of pressure, pain, warmth, and cold are included; receptors for these senses are found in the viscera.

Proprioceptors include the *general* **kinesthetic receptors** located in the muscles, tendons, and joints, as well as the *special* **vestibular receptors** found in the nonauditory inner ear. As previously explained, the kinesthetic receptors are included in the general classification because they are found throughout the body, whereas the vestibular receptors fall into the special category because they are found only in the head. Proprioceptors signal body position and movement.

SUMMARY

A stimulus is any physical energy change that activates a receptor. Receptors are specialized to respond to specific forms of energy change, whether they cause a sensation or a reflex response. The appropriate stimulus for a receptor is an adequate stimulus; other stimuli are termed inadequate. However stimulated, a nerve impulse to the CNS results, and the sensation or reflex depends on where the impulse reaches the CNS according to the law of specific nerve energies. All nerve impulses are similar in other respects.

The attributes of sensation are quality, intensity, extent, and duration. Sensory modalities differ in primary quality, but some senses also have more than one primary quality; secondary qualities result from "mixtures" of primary qualities. The relationship between stimulus intensity and sensory response is not linear; at higher intensities, stimulus intensity must be increased more and more for a detectable increase in receptor response. Some senses differ in response extent according to the size of the receptor area stimulated and duration is merely the period of time the input lasts. In some modalities primary qualities each have their own receptors; in others an input pattern determines quality. Intensity is signaled by the number of active receptors and the rate of firing in sensory neurons. Although introspection is the simplest way to measure the characteristics of sensory input, the method of evoked potentials measures the kind of information the brain receives. Absolute, difference, and terminal thresholds are used in measuring the characteristics of a sensory modality by psychophysical methods.

Adaptation and habituation are characteristics of sensory inputs. Adaptation can result in sensory contrast and afterimages. An afterimage will be positive or negative depending on the intensity and duration of the original stimulus. Either compensation of fusion can result from a mixture of sensory qualities.

Receptors are classified as general or special senses according to their body location. They are also classed as interoceptors, proprioceptors, or exteroceptors, depending on the stimulus source.

READINGS

Blough, D. S.: Experiments in animal psychophysics, Sci. Am. **205:**113-122, July 1961 (W. H. Freeman Reprint No. 458).

Boring, E. G.: The physical dimensions of consciousness, New York, 1963, Dover Publications, Inc.

Boring, E. G., Langfeld, H. S., and Weld, H. P.: Foundations of psychology, New York, 1948, John Wiley & Sons, Inc.

Case, J.: Sensory mechanisms, New York, 1966, Macmillan Publishing Co., Inc.

Crombie, A. C.: Early concepts of the senses and the mind, Sci. Am. **210:**108-116, May 1964 (W. H. Freeman Reprint No. 184).

Green, R. T., and Stacey, B. G.: Misapplication of the misapplied constancy hypothesis, Life Sci. **5:**1871-1880, 1966.

Held, R.: Placticity in sensory-motor systems, Sci. Am. **213:**84-94, Nov. 1965 (W. H. Freeman Reprint No. 494).

Mueller, C. G.: Sensory psychology, Englewood Cliffs, N.J., 1965, Prentice-Hall, Inc.

Murch, G. M.: Visual and auditory perception, New York, 1973, Bobbs-Merrill Co., Inc.

Stevens, S. S.: On the psychophysical law, Psychol. Rev. **64:**153-188, 1957 (Bobbs-Merrill Reprint No. P-336).

von Békésy, G.: Similarities of inhibition in the different sense organs, Am. Psychol. **24:**707-719, 1969.

von Buddenbrock, W.: The senses, Ann Arbor, 1958, University of Michigan Press.

CHAPTER 6

Somesthesia: the body condition senses

OVERVIEW

This chapter deals with senses that inform us of the *condition* of the skin, muscles, and viscera regarding sensations of pressure, warm, cold, and pain. In each case, what we know and do not know about the receptor mechanisms for these four inputs will be taken up in turn. The chapter closes by tracing the somesthetic pathways in the central nervous system.

The sensations that seem to come from the body are of two general kinds: (1) those of *condition*, such as pressure, pain, or temperature sensations in some part of the body, and (2) those of *position* and *movement* of some part of the body. The sensations of *condition* are the subject of this chapter.

SOMESTHESIA

Somesthesia (Gr., body perception) includes sensations of pressure, pain, and temperature and their complex combinations that come from all over the body. Somesthetic sensations are further classified according to which of the three layers of body tissue is stimulated. Sensations from the skin are called **cutaneous** somesthetic sensations, sensations from the muscles are **muscular** somesthetic sensations, and sensations from the viscera are **visceral** somesthetic sensations. In each case sensations of pressure, warmth, cold, and pain are involved.

The cutaneous sensations originate from

receptors located just beneath the surface of the skin. These receptors have received the most study because they are most accessible to the investigator and because they relate to conditions at the surface of the body, where the outside world is encountered. Somesthetic receptors stimulate reflex responses from pressure receptors that affect posture; warm and cold receptors stimulate homeostatic reflexes that maintain body temperature; and pain receptors initiate protective reflexes that prevent injury. Along with other exteroceptors such as those serving vision and hearing, these receptors initiate complex adjustments to changes in the environment that are often accompanied by awareness of that environment—"touch" (pressure) sensations used in finding the way past obstacles in a dark room, temperature changes that lead one to put on or take off a coat, pain sensations that prevent one from stepping into a shower when the water is too hot, and so on.

Somesthetic sensations from the muscles also initiate reflexes. Pressure sensations in joints set off complex coordinated reflexes that make a movement depend on the initial position of a limb. Input from temperature receptors changes the blood flow to a muscle as needed. Pain reflexes in muscles can cause contractions (cramps). These simpler adjustments are usually accompanied by awareness and are followed by more complex responses to the conditions signaled by the receptors.

Visceral somesthetic sensations come from the gut (digestive organs) and the blood vessels. Pressure sensations are often felt in digestion, and they initiate reflexes necessary for that process. Pressure receptors initiate the reflexes that empty the bladder and bowels. Temperature stimulation seems to be restricted to the mouth and esophagus, but in combination with pain, it can prevent swallowing or cause vomiting of a dangerously hot or cold substance. Visceral pain is poorly localized, but it still serves a warning function, particularly in the case of headache or stomach pain. All these sensations are interoceptive.

Somesthetic sensations—cutaneous, muscular, or visceral—can serve to arouse and sustain behavior when adverse or uncomfortable sensations are involved. This is particularly true of pain. Some somesthetic sensations can therefore act as drives since a drive is any mechanism that arouses and sustains behavior. Pressure, warmth, cold, and pain sensations are included therein. Pressure sensations from the bowel and bladder arouse and sustain behavior until evacuation reflexes are permitted to act. Our adjustments to pain and to excessive heat or cold also act as drives. Internal or external warmth, cold, or pain will sustain a high level of response activity until a comfortable temperature is found or until pain is relieved.

METHODS OF STUDY

What is known of somesthetic input comes from three study approaches: introspective, anatomical, and physiological.

Introspective study involves the familiar approach of stimulating a human subject under controlled conditions and asking him to report his sensations. The sensations of warmth, cold, pressure, and pain from the surface of the skin have been studied in this way. Sometimes the introspective technique has been combined with the anatomical technique, as when points on the skin sensitive to these four stimuli are mapped, after which the skin of that area is removed, stained, and sectioned for study of skin receptors under the microscope.

Anatomical study involves the tracing of tracts and centers in the brain served by sensory nerves coming from somesthetic and proprioceptive receptors. Introspective studies are subject to error because they involve only those receptor mechanisms concerned in conscious sensations and because subject reports cannot be confirmed except by other subject reports—there is no way of comparing the conscious sensations of two subjects. Anatomical studies can tell us only what receptors and tracts look like—not how they work in organizing responses. Furthermore, tracing anatomical tracts in the brain that serve sensation reveals only the most direct input pathways.

Pathways involving many synapses and diffuse inputs cannot be traced by anatomical means because they are so diffuse that they show only the many *possibilities* for input. The ones which are actually involved in receptor input can be detected only by physiological means. The favorite physiological method for this purpose is the *method of evoked potentials*. The receptors are stimulated electrically or, by use of their adequate stimuli, in an anesthetized animal. Electrodes are placed in various tracts, brain areas, and brain nuclei to detect where the input *actually* goes. New anesthetics have been developed that do not depress the excitability of the brain, yet they paralyze response on the part of the animal so that reactions of the brain to sensory input can be studied with the brain in a more or less normal condition. It is assumed that if the adequate stimuli for pressure, temperature, and so on are used, the appropriate inputs are being stimulated. Unfortunately, the animal cannot be asked to report on what other inputs are stimulated at the same time. To that extent our data are uncertain.

The physiological methods remain,

however, the ones least subject to error. The newest and most promising of these methods involves implanting electrodes in the brain of an anesthetized animal that is allowed to recover and then can be "plugged in" to record electrical activity of specific parts of the brain while the animal is responding normally to stimuli controlled by the experimenter. This is the most "true-to-life" situation; ultimately it will probably give us the most information on the way the sensory systems of the brain transact their business and control the behavior of the normal animal. Unfortunately, there is not yet as much information based on the newer methods as we would like.

SOMESTHETIC QUALITIES

The primary qualities of somesthesia are pressure, cold, warmth, and pain. Introspectively, these are the irreducible qualities of somesthetic sensation, although combinations of these sensations, as well as intermittent stimulation, can produce more complex sensations. The bulk of the evidence suggests that each of the four primary qualities represents a separate sensory *modality*, that is, a pressure sense, warmth sense, cold sense, or pain sense. However, some hold that one or the other of these inputs, particularly that of pain, may represent a pattern of inputs rather than a separate modality. In any case it is evident that each of the four modalities, except pain, is served by several kinds of receptors.

Secondary qualities can result from either intermittent stimulation of one primary quality or the combination of two or more primary qualities. Examples of intermittent stimulation are the tickle sensation, which results from intermittent pressure stimulation, and the itch, which is caused by intermittent pain stimulation. A combination of primary pressure and cold sensations results in a secondary sensation of wetness from dry stimuli; weak pressure and warmth produce an oily sensation. Hardness has been produced by cold pressure with a good boundary, and softness, by an uneven warm pressure with a poor boundary. Stickiness is a variable moving pressure and clamminess can be sensed from a cold softness that is reported to be unpleasant.

PROOF FOR FOUR MODALITIES OF SKIN SENSITIVITY

Visceral and muscle somesthesia are not ordinarily accessible to stimulation in human subjects who can report on their sensations while being stimulated. Most of the evidence was derived from experiments involving cutaneous sensitivity, and the evidence emphasizes the *punctate,* or point-to-point, distribution of spots on the skin that are most sensitive to pressure, cold, warmth, or pain. Reliable distribution of spots that are sensitive to each primary quality have been found, despite the many kinds of receptors found in the skin.

Skin mapping

The skin on different parts of the body may be marked off in tiny (1 mm) squares by use of a stamp pad and ink. This produces a small area marked like graph paper. Each square is then stimulated with a hair (for pressure), a warm or cold rod (for temperature), and a needle (for pain). By grading the intensity of each stimulus, absolute thresholds can be established for each square. Although nearly all spots will respond to pressure, some will have a higher threshold than others. Different spots will be *differentially sensitive* to cold, warmth, and pain as well. One spot may have a high threshold to cold and a low threshold to warmth, whereas another may show the opposite effect. This suggests that one spot is closer to a warm receptor and the other closer to a cold receptor. Furthermore, those parts of the body that are most sensitive to cold stimulation may not be the same parts that are most sensitive to pressure or pain. For example, the face is exquisitely sensitive to cold but relatively insensitive to pain. A simple demonstration of punctate sensitivity may be made by drawing a pencil point lightly across the skin; pressure, warmth, cold, and various secondary qualities such as tickle and itch will be aroused in turn as the stimulus passes over different points of the skin. As the pencil is drawn over the fingertip, more pressure sensations will be felt; drawing it across the cheek results in more cold sensations. Again, this demonstration provides an indication of the different distribution of receptors for the four cutaneous sensations.

Spark gaps

The stimuli used so far arouse pressure sensations because they distort the skin surface. In another method of stimulation, sparks from a high-voltage source may be "jumped" to the skin in order to electrically stimulate receptors there. If the amperage (rate of current flow) is kept small, the subject does not sense a shock. Instead, from different points on the skin he will sense pressure, warmth, cold, or pain, as well as combinations of these sensations; warmth, cold, or pain can therefore be stimulated independently of pressure sensations.

Excitation and conduction time

If different kinds of receptors serve the four primary qualities, then the receptors should also differ in the rapidity with which they respond, and the sensory neurons should differ in the rapidity with which they conduct impulses to the central nervous system. Reaction time to the four kinds of stimuli should differ as a result, and this seems to be the case. Adaptation time also differs for the four stimuli, indicating receptors that adapt at different rates. Most of the nerve fibers serving pressure are large fibers of the A group with myelin sheaths that conduct rapidly, and reaction time is therefore faster in response to pressure stimuli than in response to warm, cold, or some pain stimuli. The pressure receptors adapt more rapidly than the others. Reaction time for cold is slightly faster than that for warmth—many of the fibers for both seem to be of the

smaller and slower conducting B group, but the cold-sensitive receptors are closer to the surface of the skin than are the warm receptors and may therefore be affected sooner by the adequate stimulus. Both adapt, but not as rapidly as pressure receptors. Cold receptors adapt more slowly than those for warmth. Pain may be served by both A and C fibers. The small C fibers predominate, however, and conduction speed and reaction time for pain are usually slowest of all. Pain receptors also adapt less and more slowly than those for the other three qualities.

Different effects of cocaine and asphyxia

Cocaine affects fibers without myelin sheaths more than myelinated fibers. C fibers are anesthetized first, then B, and then A. The drug abolishes dull pain (C fibers) first, then temperature change (B fibers), then touch (pressure from A fibers), and finally sharp, or prick, pain (smaller A fibers). **Hypoxia,** or lack of oxygen, has the opposite effect. It affects myelinated fibers first. Sensations from a limb can be asphyxiated (abolished through lack of oxygen) by cutting off blood flow with a tourniquet. Hypoxia abolishes pressure (touch) first, then temperature change, and then pain. As circulation is restored, pain returns while the limb is still numb (no pressure sensations). Anyone who has had a limb "go to sleep" from poor circulation caused by an awkward position can testify that "pins and needles" (pain) sensations return before the limb senses touch.

Nerve pathways. The cutaneous somesthetic modalities are carried in different parts of the tracts of the spinal cord. The anatomy will be considered in detail near the end of this chapter. As further proof for four modalities, however, tract location differentiates between two groups of sensory modalities. Nerve impulses resulting from pressure stimulation are carried in tracts of the dorsal and ventral funiculi of the cord; nerve impulses serving temperature and pain are carried in tracts in the lateral funiculi. Cranial nerve input for pressure goes to one nucleus, and pain and temperature go to another.

PROBLEMS OF FURTHER MODALITY SPECIFICATION

Despite the proofs for four somesthetic modalities, problems are involved in further specification of the receptor and neural mechanisms underlying the four primary somesthetic qualities. These problems include identifying projection areas in the brain and receptor specificity.

Projection areas

Separate sensory projection areas in the cerebral cortex have been identified for the sensory modalities of audition and vision. If pressure, warmth, cold, and pain are separate sensory modalities, their pathways should end on separate projection areas in the cerebral cortex. As far as is known, impulses for pressure arrive at areas 3, 1, and 2 on the postcentral gyrus of the cortex—the somesthetic projection area. Fibers that are carried in the dorsal columns of the spinal cord serve pressure and kinesthesis and end on different parts of the somesthetic sensory projection area. The somesthetic projection area is topographically organized, with inputs from different parts of the body surface ending on different parts of the projection area in a systematic way. Input from single fibers serving joint sensibility appears to end posterior to input serving pressure from the same body area, however. Single-fiber studies do not reveal direct pain input extending beyond the thalamus. The evidence for temperature projection is uncertain. The pain pathways have many collateral fibers to the brain stem reticular formation, which serves to arouse the cortex and other parts of the brain. Similar collateral fibers have not been found for the more discriminative pressure and kinesthetic inputs. Finally, there are indirect inputs through the thalamus for all four modalities that can arouse the sec-

ondary somesthetic sensory areas (SII and SIII).

Receptors

If pressure, cold, warmth, and pain are separate senses, then their receptors should have specialized in different ways so that each is sensitive to a specific kind of physical energy. Differences in specialization would be likely to cause differences in the appearance of the various receptors. Are there four or more different kinds of sensory transducers beneath the skin that correspond to the four somesthetic modalities? Anatomical studies show that there are many different looking receptors beneath the skin. The functions of some are understood, but the functions of others are in doubt. The most common receptor ending, an **anastomosis,** or network, of free nerve endings is the least specialized, however. It is difficult to prove four classes of specialized receptors in some areas of the body that are sensitive to the four somesthetic qualities, because *only* free nerve endings are found in these areas. For example, the pinna (external ear) is sensitive to pressure, cold, warmth, and pain; yet it contains only free nerve endings. Perhaps there are four kinds of free nerve endings that differ biochemically or in some other way that is not apparent under the microscope. Perhaps these endings differ in their "connections" to different parts of the brain and are not otherwise specialized at all. Evidence is lacking on these points. There are more specialized receptors in the more sensitive areas of the skin, and the specialized nature of some of them is understood. It may be that these specialized receptors have evolved from different kinds of free nerve endings. Others feel that some specialized endings are merely tangled "rejects" from among free nerve endings that never reached their destination near the skin surface.

STRUCTURE OF THE SKIN

The structure of the skin must be considered to see how receptors have specialized for pressure, cold, warmth, and pain (Fig. 6-1). The skin consists of two layers, the tough outer **epidermis** and the thick fibrous inner **dermis.** Beneath these two layers is an insulating layer of **subcutaneous fat,** a layer that is thicker (and therefore softer) in women than in men. The top layer of the epidermis (corneum) is made up of dead cells because living cells cannot survive exposure to air, water, or the temperatures and pressures of the external environment. These dead cells are continually flaking off—you can see a white streak made up of these cells by raking a fingernail across your arm. The outer, dead layer of epidermis is continually replaced by living cells from the inner layer of epidermis (malpighian layer).

Some of the more superficial receptors (believed to serve light pressure or touch) are found in the inner layer of epidermis, principally **free nerve endings** and **tactile discs.** Most of the cutaneous receptors are found in the dermis, whose ridged surface accounts for fingerprints and palm prints of the hand. **Meissner's corpuscles** and **basket endings** are believed to serve touch, whereas **Krause's end bulbs** may be cold receptors and **Ruffini's endings** may serve warmth. **Pacinian corpuscles** (deep pressure receptors) are found at the surface of the subcutaneous fat layer. The form of the receptors shown in Fig. 6-1 is an idealized one in each case; many mixed and unidentifiable forms of **encapsulated** nerve endings are found, and some areas

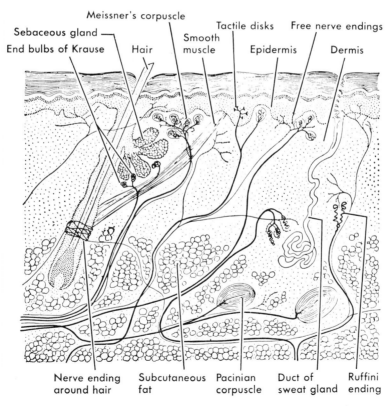

Fig. 6-1. Composite diagram of skin and its receptors. Epidermis, dermis, and subcutaneous fat layers are shown, with receptors to be found in each layer. Not all endings shown are found in any one skin area. (From Gardner, E. O.: Fundamentals of neurology, ed. 6, Philadelphia, 1975, W. B. Saunders Company. Modified from Woolard, H. H., Weddel, G., and Harpman, J. A.: J. Anat. **74:**413-440, 1940.)

of the body have only free nerve endings. Finally, specialized endings are constantly dying or being destroyed by direct damage or lack of an adequate local blood supply. They are replaced, however, as regenerating fibers reach peripheral tissue.

PRESSURE
Receptors

Several kinds of specialized endings appear to serve pressure sensitivity. Most of them are located near the surface of the skin, although some are located deeper beneath the skin and in the viscera, joints, and connective tissue of muscle. The adequate stimulus for each receptor seems to be a kind of mechanical deformation. Basket endings encircle the base of each body hair and are sensitive to movement of the hair, as you can discover by bending a single hair on your arm with the point of a pencil.

Meissner's corpuscles are found in hairless regions that are particularly sensitive to touch (light pressure), such as the fingertips. This distribution suggests that they are specialized pressure-sensitive receptors. They are dermal layer receptors. Free nerve endings are found in the epidermis over the entire body. In slightly more touch-sensitive regions they become more or less specialized tactile discs. These superficially located free endings and tactile discs do not serve pain, because the superficial epidermis can be peeled off without pain sensations; their superficial location suggests that they are pressure receptors. They are found in the less pressure-sensitive areas of the skin, where more specialized looking receptors appear to be absent.

Pacinian corpuscles are deep pressure receptors. They are located beneath the dermis, respond to skin deformation, and are especially sensitive to vibration. These receptors are also found in the mesenteries, sheets of transparent connective tissue from which the intestines hang beneath the stomach. Here they are sensitive to the movements of the stomach and in-

testines in digestion. Pacinian corpuscles are found in the walls of hollow viscera, such as the bladder and colon, and give rise to the sensations accompanying the need to urinate or defecate. They are also found near joints, where they signal position and movement of the limbs.

Most modern writers assume that there are two principal sets of cutaneous pressure receptors: (1) basket nerve ends around hair follicles and (2) Meissner's corpuscles in hairless areas. The belief is based on the distribution of pressure-sensitive "spots" on the skin, with the most sensitive spots to "windward" of the way hair leans, so that the basket ending beneath that spot is stimulated. Another reason is the greater frequency of Meissner's corpuscles in the most pressure-sensitive hairless areas. Free nerve ends in the epidermis are believed to give less discriminative pressure sensations and pacinian corpuscles can react to rapid pressure change in a brief fashion. Mechanical experiments with skin stimulation have established that the true adequate stimulus for pressure at the skin is tension or "stretch" of the skin (force per linear extent of skin contacted). A hair glued to the skin and pulled will give the same pressure sensation as pushing an equal-sized hair into the skin.

In animal studies, recording from single sensory nerve fibers serving the skin has revealed two types of response to pressure stimulation and therefore two kinds of receptors with different functions: (1) One type of receptor causes a rapid burst of firing in its neurons, after which the receptor adapts; sometimes a second burst of firing results when the stimulus is removed. (2) The second type of receptor reacts to stimulus onset by causing a high-frequency transient burst of firing that depends on the rate of stimulus onset; this burst of firing declines to a steady rate of discharge. Functionally, the first type of receptor acts as a movement detector. The second type reacts to both movement and the intensity of continuous skin deformity.

Movement detection alerts us to pressure change on the skin, whereas a steady rate of neuron firing keeps us "in touch" with the environment.

Sensitivity

The pressure sensitivity of different points on the surface of the body can be tested by using weighted rods on different contact areas. A rod (esthesiometer) is placed lightly on the skin, and weights are added until the subject reports a pressure sensation. In an older method, bristles of increasing thickness are pressed against the skin until they bend. The thinnest bristle the subject can sense under this much pressure gives a rough guide to the threshold. Some parts of the body are found to be much more sensitive than others. The tongue probably has the lowest absolute threshold, and the fingertips are also sensitive. These parts have more specialized receptors than parts of the body with higher thresholds, such as the back of the forearm or the loin.

Two-point threshold

Sensitivity to pressure can also be tested by using the **two-point threshold.** This is the smallest distance between two points that can be recognized as distinct by the subject. It is therefore a difference threshold rather than an absolute threshold. However, it should indicate sensitivity because it is closely related to pressure receptor *density* in the area tested, that is, to the number of receptors there are per square centimeter of skin surface. If two adjacent receptors are stimulated by the two points, the sensation will be that of a single point. For recognition of two distinct points, stimulated receptors must be separated by unstimulated receptors. The more pressure receptors there are in a given skin area, the closer together they will lie—and the closer together will be two points that are recognizable by the subject as separate. The results obtained by using the two-point threshold agree closely with those from absolute threshold measurements ob-

tained in testing the relative sensitivity of various parts of the body to pressure.

Localization

The ease with which one can locate a pressure stimulus on the skin surface (localization) should also indicate receptor density. The closer together the receptors are in an area of the skin, such as the fingertip, the more nerve fibers there are to reach the central nervous system from pressure receptors in that area; consequently, the larger is the cortical projection area devoted to that part of the body. To simplify, the brain has more separate receptor inputs in that area and is therefore more able to locate precisely the point stimulated. Experiments on localization show that where the absolute and two-point pressure thresholds are lowest, localization is most accurate.

In contrast with the fairly accurate localization of pressure sensations on the body surface, visceral localization is very poor. Visceral sensations are felt as diffuse, partly because there are fewer pressure receptors in the viscera. On the other hand, localization of bladder pressure, for example, is quite accurate. One reason suggested for poor visceral localization is the lack of confirmation by other senses. Pressure stimuli on the skin can be confirmed by sight or touch often enough so that the subject learns to relate small differences in skin stimulation to small differences in the point stimulated. Obviously one cannot see pressure stimulations being applied to the stomach or intestines. One can, however, sense the pressure relief in the bladder that results from urination.

Adaptation

Adaptation is partly a function of the receptor and partly a function of the stimulus. Continuous pressure stimulation of a part of the body will result in a gradual decrease in sensation, and sometimes the adaptation will be so complete that no pressure is sensed. This is true of light pressure sensations such as those commonly resulting from wearing eyeglasses or rings, the presence of which can no longer be felt after a time. It also takes a long time after a pressure stimulus is removed before the skin recovers its original shape; thus the distortion of the pressure endings continues to change after the stimulus is removed. The receptors continue to fire neurons, giving a pressure sensation that is similar to a positive aftersensation. As a result, removal of a ring or a wristwatch may leave the sensation that one is still wearing it because the skin is still distorted for a time. This may be one reason why rings and watches are so often mislaid.

TEMPERATURE

Cold and warmth appear to be separate sensory modalities, although experiments on one of these senses commonly involve the other. When cutaneous temperature sensitivity is studied, for example, local reactions in the blood vessels of the skin to a warm stimulus will change the threshold to cold, and vice versa. In response to a warm stimulus, blood vessels near the surface will dilate to cool the area; the threshold for subsequent warm stimuli will be raised and the threshold for cold stimuli lowered. In response to a cold stimulus the same vessels will constrict to preserve body heat, thereby raising the threshold to subsequent cold stimuli and lowering the threshold to warm stimuli. The skin temperature at which neither warm nor cold sensations are experienced is called **physiological zero;** physiological zero shifts as a result of blood vessel reactions in the skin and also as a result of adaptation in the receptors themselves. The adequate stimulus for cold is a temperature at the skin surface of 35° to 39° C or below; the adequate stimulus for warmth is a temperature of 34° to 35° C or above. These temperatures overlap because of changes in physiological zero. The adequate stimulus temperature depends on the skin temperature itself. The sensation of *heat* is a secondary quality composed of warmth and

pain stimulation; the "stinging cold" occasionally experienced in cold climates is a combination of cold and pain.

Skin mapping

Cold and warm spots on the skin can be mapped with small cold and warm stimulus points, as with the punctate stimuli used for pressure. They show a fairly reliable distribution (70% to 80%) but are not as fixed as are pressure-sensitive points. The receptors for warmth and cold are farther beneath the skin than the more superficial pressure receptors, and localization may suffer as a result. In addition, temperature changes are more diffusely spread throughout the skin than are the mechanical distortions of pressure. The skin is more sensitive to cold than to warmth in terms of the number of sensitive spots per square centimeter. The areas of the body most sensitive to cold, however, are usually also those most sensitive to warmth, although there are reliable exceptions to this rule. In general, the face is one of the most sensitive areas to both kinds of stimuli.

Receptor location

Cold and warm "pulses" can be applied to the outside of the prepuce (foreskin) of the penis, and their arrival at the underside of the prepuce can be measured with appropriate instruments. This procedure can be used to calculate the rate at which the change in temperature moves through the thickness of the prepuce. By timing the report of a cold or warm sensation by the subject, the depth of the cold and warm receptors can be estimated. The results suggest that the cold receptors lie about 0.1 mm below the surface and that the warm receptors are more diffusely spread about 0.3 mm below the surface. The experiment also shows that each type of receptor responds to the *absolute temperature* at its depth rather than to a gradient of temperature change from "outside" to "inside." The pulse may be sent through the prepuce from either the "outside" skin surface or the "inside" mucous surface without a change in threshold. The data on the depth of receptors thus obtained agree with the data from experiments with the dog and cat; in the latter experiments a cold or a warm pulse is used as a stimulus to the tongue, and the time required for nerve impulses to begin is computed.

Receptors

There appear to be both specialized and unspecialized receptors for cold and warm stimuli. Krause's end bulbs (Fig. 6-1) are found at the proper depth (0.1 mm) to serve as cold receptors, judging by the experiments on the prepuce that were just described. These receptors are found in mucous membrane regions and in other areas sensitive to cold, such as the face. In one experiment, tissue was removed and studied under the microscope after having been mapped and the cold spots marked. Krause's end bulbs were found nearer cold spots than spots less sensitive to cold. The experiment has been repeated on the prepuce of the penis, where the depth of the receptors has been more precisely determined. In a more daring experiment the transparent cornea of the subject's eye was stained (with methylene blue) and studied under a microscope while it was being stimulated. Only Krause's end bulbs and free nerve endings are found at the edge of the cornea. In the areas most sensitive to cold, Krause's end bulbs could be seen.

Ruffini's endings are at the proper depth (0.3 mm) to serve as warm receptors. They are found most profusely in warmth-sensitive parts of the body. Mapping warm spots and then studying the skin under them with a microscope has been done in the same way as that described for cold. The prepuce and other warmth-sensitive parts of the skin have been studied in this manner. The results are not as clear-cut as those for cold spots. However, when Ruffini's endings are found, they usually lie near spots on the skin that are the most sensitive to warm stimuli.

If Krause's end bulbs are cold receptors and Ruffini's cylinders are warm receptors, they are not the only endings serving warm and cold. In some nonmucous areas such as the palm of the hand, there are many encapsulated endings. In these areas, however, the encapsulated endings are too varied for classification. Other areas such as the pinna (external ear) have only free nerve endings. These areas *are* sensitive to cold and warmth but less so than areas with specialized receptors. In areas supplied only by free nerve endings, perhaps the free endings near the surface are cold receptors and those deeper beneath the skin are warm receptors. Free nerve endings may be arranged in layers—the most superficial ones for pressure, deeper ones for cold, still deeper ones serving warm, and the deepest endings serving pain. However, there are theorists who believe that the *pattern* of input from nerve endings determines all four somesthetic qualities.

Adaptation

All the temperature figures given for cold and warm responses are subject to change because of adaptation in the receptors and because of blood vessel constriction or dilation. As previously pointed out, continuous warm stimulation causes the warm receptors to adapt and causes the blood vessels to dilate, raising the threshold for warmth and lowering the threshold for cold. Continuous cold stimulation will cause the cold receptors to adapt and will constrict the blood vessels under the skin, thus raising the threshold for cold and lowering the threshold for warmth. These adjustments in response to temperature change can cause physiological zero to vary from 20° to 40° C. The change in physiological zero can be a general one involving the whole body, as when one adapts to a temperature change in passing from an air-conditioned room into the outdoor heat or as when one adapts in passing from a heated house to the winter cold outdoors. On the other hand, the change in physiological zero may be restricted largely to the part of the body exposed to a temperature that necessitates adaptation. For example, the right hand can be temperature-adapted in a bowl of 40° C water and the left hand temperature-adapted in a bowl of 20° C water at the same time. Then if *both* hands are plunged into 30° C water, the right hand will feel cold and the left hand will feel warm.

Viscera and muscles

There appear to be no temperature-sensitive receptors in the muscles or their blood vessels. Visceral sensitivity seems confined to the esophagus and stomach. Hot or cold food seems to "disappear" on swallowing only to "reappear" in the stomach. The esophagus is sensitive to temperature throughout its length, but localization there is poor except at the upper and lower ends. Sensations from the middle area are sensed as coming from the upper or lower part, or both.

PAIN

Pain is one of the most difficult sensory modalities to study as a sensation because the affective perceptual reactions to it are so overpowering. Pain "hurts" so much that the subject has difficulty in responding to it as a sensation. Yet pain has received much study because of the importance of the topic to the practice of medicine. Pain is useful as a diagnostic tool since it usually is set off by tissue damage. At the same time an understanding of pain is necessary to the control of pain during surgery and dental procedures. Pain, furthermore, is the most potent stimulus known to arouse and sustain behavior; it is therefore important to the study of *drives*. Pain stimuli set off somatic and visceral reflexes. The body's first "line of defense" against injury is the somatic withdrawal reflexes; the visceral, glandular, and autonomic "emergency responses" of the sympathetic nervous system form a second line of defense. The third is sensation, which leads to drives and the perception of pain.

Sensation or perception

Using brave human subjects for introspection studies and anesthetized animals for evoked potential experiments, pain can be studied as a simple sensory modality. In the human experiments, absolute, difference, and terminal thresholds can be established and these facts will be briefly noted. Other phenomena like adaptation and habituation can be studied in humans. Evoked potential studies in anesthetized animals have helped to establish the nerve pathways for pain—the pathways are so diffuse that they are difficult to trace by simple anatomical methods. However, the perception of pain is what counts as far as human beings are concerned. Careful experiments at McGill University and elsewhere have established that pain is the result of a competition between two or more sensory inputs, even at the level of the spinal cord and cranial nerve nuclei. A questionnaire has been devised for human subjects that differentiates different "kinds" of pain and the perceptual reactions to them. A theory results that explains the Chinese practice of acupuncture and leads to more precise alleviation of chronic pain. A more recent explanation for acupuncture involves secretions of "natural" morphinelike substances by the pituitary gland to block the pain pathways. These topics will be taken up after a brief survey of what has been learned by treating pain as a simple sensation.

Pain as sensation

Pain appears to be a sensory modality, and not just a change in quality that results from overstimulation of pressure or temperature receptors. There are several lines of evidence for this point of view. Extreme pressure, warmth, or cold can produce pain, but the pain sensations will "coexist" with pressure, warmth, or cold. Furthermore, pain can be aroused by sparks "jumping" from a voltage generator to the skin without arousing sensations of pressure, cold, or warmth. Pain impulses are carried in the lateral funiculi of the spinal cord. Cutting these tracts relieves pain without disturbing touch sensations that are carried in the dorsal and ventral funiculi of the cord. As shown earlier, drugs such as cocaine affect unmyelinated pain fibers before they anesthetize the myelinated fibers carrying touch sensations, yet cutting off circulation to a limb will affect pressure sensations more than pain because this action affects myelinated fibers first.

Receptors

Some free nerve endings are known to be pain receptors. Areas of the skin having only free nerve endings are also sensitive to temperature and pressure. It is probable that the anastomoses of free nerve endings that serve pain lie deeper beneath the skin than those serving pressure. As evidence, the superficial epidermis can be peeled off without causing pain—only pressure endings seem affected. Also, a light touch to the cornea results in sensations of pressure rather than pain; the cornea contains only free nerve endings. The difference between the free endings serving pressure or temperature and those serving pain is not clear; perhaps the pain endings lie deeper beneath the skin surface than either pressure or temperature, or they differ biochemically.

There has been some debate over the possibility of two pain receptor systems. Recalling the sensations experienced the last time you "barked" a shin will reveal a "bright" first pain, followed by a "raw," burning second pain. It has been suggested that the first pain comes from lightly myelinated A-delta fibers that supply free nerve endings in the dermis near the epidermis. These fibers conduct impulses more rapidly than do the C fibers that supply deeper free endings in the dermis. Pain stimulation without mechanical distortion of the skin in animals gives both A-delta and C action potentials in the nerve serving that area of skin, which suggests that two pain systems have been stimulated. Other investigators believe that the first pain is merely a mixture of pressure and pain sensations, the pressure being carried by A-delta and the pain by C fibers. In one experiment square-wave electrical stimuli and fine needles were used to stimulate skin pain without skin distortion (pressure), and the subjects reported only second pain. In another experiment an investigator bared a nerve in his own finger and stimulated it electrically, only to fire the lower threshold A-delta fibers. A stinging pain resulted. But when the stimulus was altered to fire C fibers as well, a severe, long-lasting, aching pain resulted. Cutting off the circulation to a limb affects myelinated fibers first and blocks "first pain," leaving only the "burning" second pain sensation. Thus the bulk of the evidence suggests two pain systems.

Pain sensitivity and localization

The distribution of pain endings and therefore the distribution of pain sensitivity varies widely from one part of the body to another. Pain sensibility is found in the hollow viscera, joints (aches), and muscles (cramping, pains), although more is known of cutaneous pain because it is the most accessible to stimulation. Cutaneous pain sensitivity varies from **analgesic** (insensitive) areas, such as Kiesow's area on the inner cheek opposite the second lower molar, to exquisitely sensitive areas, such as the "hollows" (fossae) of the body (armpit, back of knee joint, etc.). Cutaneous pain localization is excellent; it is better than pressure localization. Muscular pain localization is accurate, as the experience of cramping pain in muscles shows. Visceral pain localization is poor, except for the pain receptors on the covering of bones. "Bone bruises" are quite accurately localized, for example. Visceral pain is often confused with skin or muscle pain, as will be seen later (referred pains). It is not known whether visceral pain localization is poor because of a sparse supply of pain endings in the hollow viscera, or whether pain is poorly localized because the location of the injury producing pain cannot be confirmed by the other senses. When one has a "stomachache," he cannot look to see whether the stomach or the intestine is inflamed. The location of a "bone bruise" or of pain from a cut finger can be confirmed by both touch and sight.

Adequate stimulus

The adequate stimulus for pain is unknown, despite over 40 years of diligent research. Some scientists believe that the pain endings are so unspecialized that the whole concept of an adequate stimulus for pain is meaningless. In other words, the endings respond as well to one kind of stimulus as they do to another, but their threshold is so high and they lie so deep beneath the skin that tissue damage usually occurs in the course of stimulating them. Perhaps mechanical distortion of the spray of free nerve endings is one adequate stimulus. The viscera may be cut or burned without pain to a patient undergoing surgery under local anesthesia, but stretching, twisting, and especially distention cause extreme pain from visceral pain endings. One promising theory holds that injured tissue releases a substance called **neurokinin,** which is the adequate stimulus for pain endings. The substance is also believed to be responsible for the local vasodilation (reddening and swelling) that accompanies pain. Chemical analysis of the fluid of blisters, as well as other tissue fluid from injured areas, has revealed higher amounts of polypeptides of this sort than can be found in normal tissue. Pain is highly sensitive to the H^+ (hydrogen) ion of acids, but this is not the only ion stimulating pain—excess K^+ (potassium) causes exquisite pain, whereas lack of K^+ is analgesic (stops pain). This has led to the idea that the release of K^+ by injured cells causes pain, but we know that lack of K^+ affects nerve impulses of any kind (see Chapter 3).

Pain thresholds

Pain thresholds can be measured by the algesimeter, an instrument similar to the esthesiometer used for pressure thresholds. A sharp needle is substituted for a dull point. The needle can be loaded with varying weights until pain is sensed. Sensitivity measurements, as absolute thresholds for various parts of the body, agree well with the distribution of pain "points" plotted on the skin by mapping. The instrument of choice for measuring the effects of drugs, adaptation, and so on is the Hardy-Wolff-Gooddell apparatus. This device uses the inadequate stimulus of heat, radiated from a lamp to a black spot on the subject's forehead. The black spot absorbs all the radiant energy, and a shutter times the exposure (three seconds). Brave subjects have established absolute and terminal (skin burn) thresholds. Difference thresholds have been established, and an equal-unit dol scale of just noticeable differences (JNDs) per unit has been established. (Dol is from Latin *dolor,* meaning pain.)

Adaptation. Whether pain results in adaptation depends on the stimulus and the definition one uses for adaptation. When it is defined as loss of sensitivity in the receptors and an increasing pain threshold, pain does not appear to result in adaptation, as measured by the Hardy-Wolff-Gooddell apparatus when the subject adjusts the stimulus himself to keep the pain level constant over as much as a half hour. Pain sensitivity may increase slightly under these conditions. Later experiments, using hot water as a stimulus, show two kinds of pain as far as adaptation is concerned. "Phasic" (weak) pain adapts and "static" (strong) pain that nears the intensity causing tissue damage does not adapt. Pain intensity may increase more than slightly under conditions of tissue injury. The difficulty here involves a "vicious circle" of self-stimulation that increases the pain input: pain causes reflex muscle contraction; the rigid muscle contraction reduces the blood flow to the area (ischemia), acting as a tourniquet; this causes more pain, more reflex contraction, and so on.

Habituation. Despite its insistent quality,

humans can learn to ignore long-continued pain. However habituated one becomes, the pain intensity is just as great when attention is paid to it. Individuals differ widely in their ability to ignore pain. Habituation is most common under conditions of excitement and distraction—football players have been known to play almost an entire game with a broken ankle without being aware of it, only to feel intense pain when the game was over. Other motivation variables are important. For example, soldiers being evacuated from battle have been reported to deny pain from severe wounds, presumably because they were overjoyed at having escaped alive from the battlefield.

Referred pain

Referred pain occurs whenever pain sensations that originate in one part of the body are perceived as coming from another part of the body. Usually, visceral pain is referred to skin or muscle. A common example is the pain of heart disease, which is referred to the shoulder muscles (hence this condition, *angina pectoris,* is named for pectoral muscles). In most cases the sensory neurons from the area originating the impulses and those from the area of referred pain enter the same dorsal spinal root or cranial nerve. This fact has led to speculation that a "short circuit" of the nerve impulses occurs; for example, impulses from the heart may stimulate the same area of the brain as impulses from the shoulder. Others have speculated that poor visceral localization leads the subject to locate the pain in an area more frequently stimulated and therefore more accurately localized.

Headaches

Headaches are obviously caused by stimulation of pain receptors in the head, but there are as many kinds of headaches as there are receptor locations. For example, "tension" headaches may be caused by overcontraction of muscles, particularly in the forehead. Sinus headaches may result from pressure attributable to lack of drainage of the hollows or sinuses in the bones of the head, especially the face. Migraine headaches are believed to be caused by dilation of blood vessels in the head that may make pain receptors in the walls of blood vessels accessible to chemicals that would otherwise not reach them—histamine, bradykinin, or neurokinin, depending on the theorist. The problem of what is the adequate stimulus for headache is as complex as the problem of the adequate stimulus for any variety of pain.

Analgesics

Analgesics are drugs that relieve pain without causing unconsciousness. Aspirin, opiates (in small doses), and various synthetic drugs are included. Experiments have shown that analgesics raise the pain threshold, as measured with the Hardy-Wolff-Gooddell apparatus.

Pain as perception

Attention is a factor that changes the response to pain in many situations. Under hypnosis, pain sensations can be completely blocked—even reflex response to pain is impaired. On good subjects, hypnosis can be used rather than anesthetics for major surgery. Many reactions to pain seem to be learned ones—dogs raised in isolation show only reflex reactions to pain and do not learn to avoid painful stimuli. On a higher level, injuries that relieved soldiers of combat were perceived as less painful than similar injuries in civilian surgery. Pain thresholds, as tested on the Hardy-Wolff-Gooddell apparatus, vary considerably from day to day in normal subjects and are still more variable in psychotic persons. In one study, opiates appeared effective in 75% of the cases by relieving anxiety and producing a "bemused state" (whatever that is). In 35% of the cases a placebo (inactive drug) was successful in relieving pain reactions.

The diffuse nature of the pain pathways results in several perceptual phenomena. Cutting the pain pathways in the spinal cord (anterolateral cordotomy) relieves intractable pain; yet the pain may return, in whole or in part, after a period of years. Amputees who have lost a limb report pain referred to the absent limb—phantom limb pain—at intervals for many years. There are rare cases of congenital insensitivity to pain—people born without the ability to sense physical pain. These individuals must always be on guard to avoid seriously injuring themselves on hot or sharp objects. Some of them lack reflexes to pain. All show apparently normal nerve endings when sections of their skin are studied under a microscope. Other subjects have been found who lack only the subjective response to pain—they sense and react to pain as they do pressure or temperature, as a simple sensation. These subjects are like the isolated dogs mentioned above. They can, however, be taught to fear pain.

Pain as a sensation seems to be organized on lower levels of the brain than other somesthetic sensations, yet the perceptual reactions to it include the highest parts of the brain. Removing the cortex of one cerebral hemisphere does not interfere with the perception of pain, although it may raise the threshold. The pain pathways end on a part of the thalamus different from that of pressure pathways; pain stimulation does not result in evoked potentials of the cerebral cortex as pressure stimulation does. Pain caused by cortical stimulation or damage is rare, but pain is common when the thalamus is stimulated or damaged. Severe intractable pain may be relieved by a **prefrontal lobotomy,** a surgical procedure that severs the nerve fibers going from lower centers of the brain to the frontal lobes. The operation does not change pain thresholds, but the subject shows little subjective response to pain unless his attention is directed to it. He reports that he senses the pain but that it "doesn't bother him." When he attends to the pain sensations, his subjective response is increased, however.

The McGill questionnaire. Owing to their interest in the relief of pain by electrical stimulation of the nervous system (gate control theory to be discussed later), Melzack and his colleagues at McGill University have devised a questionnaire to see if qualitatively different types of pain can be isolated. The questionnaire is primarily based on verbal descriptions of pain qualities. In one test of the questionnaire, eight known pain syndromes proved to be discriminably different, the instrument making a correct classification in 77% of the cases. The value of the questionnaire lies in its use as a diagnostic technique, of course. But it can also be useful in testing analgesics for various types of pain as well as electrical stimulation for the relief of pain based on the gate control approach.

Gate control theory. The gate control theory proposes a mutually inhibitory relationship between small-diameter and large-diameter sensory fibers. The small C fibers signal pain, and the large A fibers signal other sensory events. As shown in Fig. 6-2, both A and C fibers have branches going to the first input cells (substantia gelatinosa). A fibers excite the first input cells, which block the effect of A fibers on the dorsal horn cells by presynaptic inhibition. Thus the A fibers act to inhibit themselves by a feedback mechanism after a brief burst of excitation to the sensory pathways. They also act to block C fiber input by way of the first input neurons. C fibers, on the other hand, inhibit the first input neurons so that they can excite the dorsal horn cells of the sensory pathway. At low levels of stimulation, bursts of A fiber input and a little C fiber input will reach the sensory pathways. At the high levels of sensory input that accompany injury, the C fibers will fire the sensory pathways at a high rate, recognized by a central decoder mechanism as pain. Central control over this input is recognized in the scheme, as early A fiber input can reach the brain, and the brain can respond by blocking the sensory input through a central control mechanism, preventing the frequency of input firing recognized as

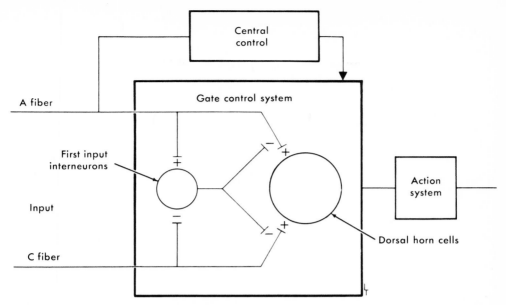

Fig. 6-2. Gate control theory of pain: − at a synapse means inhibition; + indicates excitation. (Redrawn from Melzack, R., and Wall, P. D.: Science **150:**971-979. Copyright 1965 by the American Association for the Advancement of Science.)

pain. This ingenious theory has also been used to explain the Chinese practice of acupuncture. An ancient therapy, acupuncture has been used for centuries to relieve pain, even during major surgery, by the placement of fine needles at charted locations of the skin and vibrating or twisting them. According to gate-control theory, the treatment would be more likely to stimulate large A fibers than small C fibers, thereby blocking the C fiber pain perception with additional A fiber input. Electrical stimulation that affects low-threshold A fibers but not high-threshold C fibers is a new therapy for intractable pain and is now being used with initial reports of success in controlling pain.

Stimulation to relieve pain. If pain can be relieved by a level of nerve cell stimulation that fixes more A fibers without increasing their competition from C fibers, electrical stimulation would be a more precise method of control than fine needles. Accordingly, stimulators have been devised to accomplish this end. The stimulation may be delivered to the skin of the injured area

(to stimulate underlying nerves) or by implanted electrodes in the dorsal column of the spinal cord (which contains large-fiber pathways) or in selected areas of the brain stem that activate a "pain suppressor system." (The latter appears to activate a pain-suppressing pathway that descends the spinal cord to block pain inputs.) The varieties of pain treated include phantom limb pain, low back pain, arthritis, injury due to accidents, and pain due to terminal cancer. Relief is achieved in a majority of cases according to the McGill questionnaire and other tests; the effects of a single treatment frequently last for hours. In some cases, patients have been given small portable stimulators connected to their electrodes so that they can stimulate themselves for relief when they sense pain. In the case of skin stimulation, the effects seem no greater than those for acupuncture. In cases of terminal cancer with its perceptual attributes of anxiety and dread that accompany pain, antianxiety drugs are often used as well with either electrical stimulation or an opiate for pain. The pain-suppressing pathway mentioned above is ineffective when a morphine antogonist (naloxone) is administered. This suggests that some morphinelike pain inhibitor is released by the pathway at its pain-blocking synapses.

Endorphins. Recently, a class of chemicals (peptides) called **endorphins** have been found in the hypothalamus, third ventricle, and pituitary gland. These chemicals are isolated in such small quantities (e.g., $10^{-10\text{ mole}}$) that they could be transmitters at synapses. One of them is over 200 times as effective in blocking pain as morphine but is rendered ineffective by the same drug (naloxone) that prevents morphine analgesia. Naloxone can also prevent the pain relief due to brain stimulation, as previously described. Perhaps the brain and or pituitary gland produces its own morphine! As an alternative to the gate control theory of pain, Dr. Bruce Pomeranz of the University of Toronto suggests that the needle treatment stimulates receptors (in the muscles) whose sensory pathways stimulate the pituitary to release endorphins. In his scheme. the endorphins would be carried by the circulation to pain pathways in the brain where they would block pain perception at synapses.

SOMESTHETIC PATHWAYS
Dermatomes (Fig. 6-3)

Each dorsal root in the spinal cord contains sensory neurons serving pressure, temperature, and pain receptors from the surface of the skin. The area served by a single dorsal spinal root is called a **dermatome** and is named for the spinal root. For example, L-1 would be the dermatome on either side of the body, served by the first lumbar spinal root. Since there are 31 pairs of dorsal spinal roots, there should be 31 pairs of dermatomes for the body and neck (except for the lack of a first cervical dorsal root). The face and most of the head are served by the fifth cranial nerve (the trigeminal nerve). Somesthetic, visceral, and muscular in-

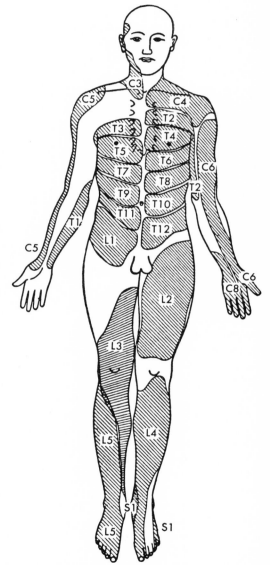

Fig. 6-3. Human dermatomes. Successive dermatomes, labeled by spinal segment, are shown on alternate sides of the body to display the extent to which they overlap. (Based on data from Foerster, O.: Brain **56:**1-39, 1933; redrawn by Lewis, T.: Pain, New York, 1942, Macmillan Publishing Co., Inc.)

put is also serially arranged, according to the dorsal spinal roots and cranial nerves.

Further understanding of somesthetic sensibility depends on knowing the anatomy of the sensory pathways involved. As an aid to the understanding of these pathways, their common features will be presented first, together with some notes on terminology. Then three major tracts in the spinal cord that differ by modality will be described, together with three nuclei that serve the same purpose for cranial nerves. Finally, the centers that serve these pathways in the thalamus and cortex will be described. The sizes of the dermatomes for pressure sensibility shown in Fig. 6-3 are larger than those for temperature and show more overlap; the dermatomes for pain are still smaller.

"Three-neuron" plan

Typically, a somesthetic **first-order neuron** runs from the somesthetic receptor to the spinal cord, where it enters the dorsal root, ascends, and synapses within two or three segments of the cord with **second-order neurons** in the gray matter of the dorsal horn. (Kinesthesis and some pressure inputs are exceptions.) The second-order neuron crosses to the opposite side of the cord, enters the white matter, and ascends to join with other neurons in the **medial lemniscus** of the brain stem. It

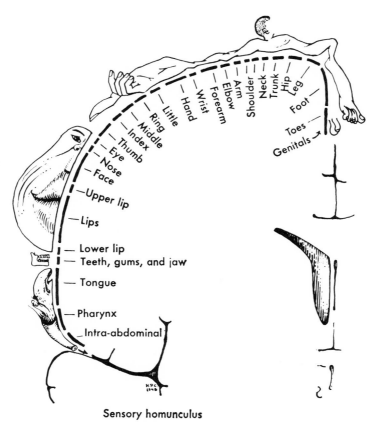

Sensory homunculus

Fig. 6-4. Sensory homunculus laid out on a cross section of one cerebral hemisphere. Length of each black line represents the proportion of sensory cortex devoted to part of body shown by labels; caricature of head and body above the lines is in about the same proportion. (From Penfield, W., and Rasmussen, T.: The cerebral cortex of man, New York, 1950, Macmillan Publishing Co., Inc.)

ends on the **posteroventral nucleus** of the thalamus, synapsing with **third-order neurons.** Third-order neurons run from the thalamus to the somesthetic sensory projection area on the postcentral gyrus of the cerebral cortex (areas 3, 1, and 2—Chapter 3). In the trigeminal nerve serving the face, first-order neurons carry impulses to the sensory nuclei of the fifth nerve; second-order neurons cross the brain stem to join the medial lemniscus; and third-order neurons run from the thalamus to the cortex.

Fiber grouping

The second-order neurons, ascending the cord as tracts, are grouped by *modality*. Kinesthesis (such as joint sensibility) and fibers from specialized pressure receptors are carried in the dorsal funiculus. Fibers from less specialized (higher threshold) pressure receptors send impulses up the ventral funiculus. Pain and temperature tracts are found in the lateral funiculus. In the medial lemniscus the fibers are rearranged according to their dermatomes of origin as well, so that in the thalamus and

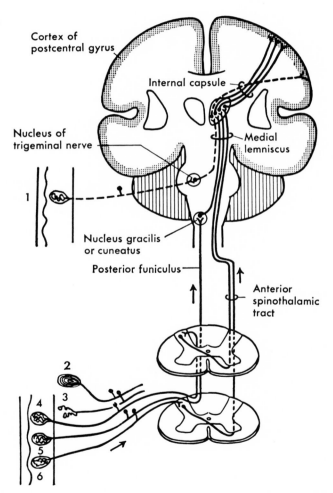

Fig. 6-5. Afferent pathways for kinesthesis and pressure sensations. Although not shown separately, the mesencephalic nucleus of trigeminal nerve is anterior part of nucleus shown, whereas main sensory nucleus is posterior part. In spinal tracts anterior is equivalent to ventral in the text, and posterior to dorsal. (From Gardner, E. O.: Fundamentals of neurology, ed. 6, Philadelphia, 1975, W. B. Saunders Company.)

cortex, fibers project in a **topographical organization** (Fig. 6-4). On the postcentral gyrus of the cortex the most caudal parts of the body are found at the beginning of the gyrus (in the longitudinal fissures); first the genitals and buttocks, next the feet and legs, then the body, the arms, and finally the face (compare Fig. 6-4 with Fig. 6-3).

Spinal tracts

Spinal tracts are typically named for their origin, their destination, and sometimes the funiculus of the cord in which they lie. Thus the lateral spinothalamic tract begins in the spinal cord, ends in the thalamus, and lies in the lateral funiculus of the cord. We are concerned with three somesthetic tracts; two of them are named in this fashion.

Dorsal columns (Fig. 6-5). First-order neurons carrying kinesthetic impulses from the joints that signal limb position, from the more sensitive cutaneous pressure receptors, and from the pacinian corpuscles (deep pressure) are carried in the **dorsal columns.** These neurons enter the cord and ascend the dorsal funiculus without crossing, to end on the **gracile** and **cuneate nuclei** of the medulla. Second-order fibers from these nuclei cross and take up a ventral position in the medulla to form the **medial lemniscus.**

Ventral spinothalamic tract (Fig. 6-5). First-order neurons from more crude pressure receptors synapse with second-order neurons in the dorsal gray columns of the cord. The second-order neurons cross and ascend the ventral funiculus of the cord in the **ventral spinothalamic tract,** which joins the medial lemniscus in the midbrain.

Lateral spinothalamic tract (Fig. 6-6). First-order neurons from pain and temperature receptors synapse with second-order fibers in the dorsal gray columns of the spinal cord. The second-order neurons cross to the opposite side of the cord and ascend the lateral funiculus as the **lateral spinothalamic tract.** Thus, in an operation to relieve intractable pain in the left leg,

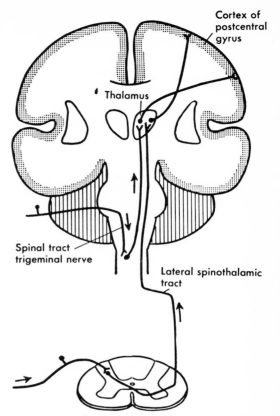

Fig. 6-6. Afferent pathways for pain and temperature. The uncrossed pathway for pain is not shown. (From Gardner, E. O.: Fundamentals of neurology, ed. 6, Philadelphia, 1975, W. B. Saunders Company.)

part of the right lateral funiculus of the cord could be cut above the level of entrance of these neurons. This would cut off pain and temperature sensation without disturbing kinesthetic and pressure pathways, which are carried in the dorsal and ventral cord. The lateral and ventral spinothalamic tracts join in the medulla, and both join the medial lemniscus in the midbrain.

Cranial nerve nuclei

In the spinal cord the modalities are separated into three different spinal tracts. In the brain stem the modalities are separated into three different cranial nerve nuclei, and the separation is a little more complete. Only kinesthetic input reaches one nucleus, only pressure input the second, and only temperature and pain input the third.

Mesencephalic nucleus of fifth nerve (Fig. 6-5). First-order neurons of the fifth nerve from kinesthetic receptors end in the mesencephalic (midbrain) nucleus of the fifth nerve. Second-order neurons that originate here cross the brain stem to join the medial lemniscus.

Main sensory nucleus of fifth nerve. First-order neurons in the fifth nerve from pressure receptors reach the main sensory nucleus of that nerve. Second-order neurons originating here cross the brain stem to join the medial lemniscus.

Spinal nucleus of fifth nerve (Fig. 6-6). First-order neurons from pain and temperature receptors enter the brain stem and descend in the medulla as the spinal tract of the fifth nerve. These neurons end on the **spinal nucleus** of that nerve in the lower medulla. The second-order neurons that originate here cross to join the medial lemniscus in the midbrain.

Thalamic and cortical projection

As described in the beginning of this section, the fibers from all the somesthetic inputs are rearranged in the medial lemniscus according to origin as well as modality. The thalamic nuclei are therefore arranged topographically, and the third-order neurons and cortical projection area are also topographically ordered. There is evidence, however, that pain and temperature *sensations* are largely organized at the thalamic level, and pressure and kinesthetic sensations are organized at the cortical level.

SUMMARY

Somesthesia consists of the condition senses of pressure, pain, and temperature from the skin, muscles, and viscera. These senses have been studied by introspective, anatomical, and physiological (evoked potential) methods. Introspectively, there are primary and secondary somesthetic qualities. Proofs for four modalities of skin sensitivity come from skin mapping, spark gap stimulation, excitation and conduction time, the effects of cocaine and asphyxia, and different nerve pathways. Difficulties in further modality specification result from studies of their receptors and projection areas in the brain. A variety of specialized pressure receptors are found in the most sensitive skin areas, but other areas have only unspecialized free nerve endings. Studies of the two-point threshold, localization, and adaptation have also been made. Temperature sensitivity includes separate cold and warm modalities, revealed by skin mapping and receptor location; both specialized and "unspecialized" receptors are involved. The two senses interact in the adaptation that sets physiological zero in the skin; visceral and muscular sensitivity is poor. Pain may be studied as a sensation or a perception, the latter because of intense affective reactions. The cutaneous receptors are two sets of free nerve endings with different conduction times. Skin pain sensitivity varies widely by body area, and the adequate stimulus is unknown. There is no true adaptation, but habituation occurs. Thresholds, referred pain, headaches, and analgesics were discussed. As perception, pain is affected by prefrontal lobotomies and the McGill questionnaire reveals a variety of different kinds of pain. The gate control theory asserts that pain occurs when C fibers gain ascendency over A fibers in controlling the central sensory pathways. Both acupuncture and electrical stimulation may relieve pain by stimulating A fibers or releasing a morphinelike neural transmitter at pain-blocking synapses. Pituitary endorphins carried by the bloodstream may be responsible for the effect.

The somesthetic nerve pathways begin, in part, with the skin dermatomes. A "three-neuron plan" is involved in carrying the excitation to the brain, where a topographical organization is seen in the cerebral cortex. The modalities are somewhat separate in the dorsal columns, ventral and lateral spinothalamic tracts, and three nuclei of the fifth cranial nerve. The topographical reorganization begins in the medial lemniscus.

READINGS

Gardner, E. D.: Fundamentals of neurology, ed. 6, Philadelphia, 1975, W. B. Saunders Company.

Livingston, W. K.: What is pain? Sci. Am. **188:**59-66, March 1953 (W. H. Freeman Reprint No. 407).

Loewenstein, W. R.: Biological transducers, Sci. Am. **203:**98-108, Aug. 1960 (W. H. Freeman Reprint No. 70).

Melzack, R.: The perception of pain, Sci. Am. **201:**41-49, Feb. 1961 (W. H. Freeman Reprint No. 457).

Melzack, R.: How acupuncture works: A sophisticated Western theory takes the mysteries out, Psychol. Today **7:**28-38, 1973.

Melzack, R.: Phantom limbs, Psychol. Today **4:**63-68, Oct. 1970.

Melzack, R.: The puzzle of pain, New York, 1973, Basic Books, Inc.

Montagna, W.: The skin, Sci. Am. **212:**56-66, Feb. 1965 (W. H. Freeman Reprint No. 1003).

Mountcastle, V. B., and Powell, T. P. S.: Neural mechanisms subserving cutaneous sensibility. In Gross, C. G., and Zeigler, H. P., editors: Readings in physiological psychology, New York, 1969, Harper & Row Publishers.

Reigel, M. G.: Pain control through hypnosis, Science News **110:**283-285, Oct. 30, 1976.

von Buddenbrock, W.: The senses, Ann Arbor, 1958, University of Michigan Press.

Weisenberg, M.: Pain: clinical and experimental perspectives, St. Louis, 1975, The C. V. Mosby Co.

CHAPTER 7

Proprioception: the movement senses

OVERVIEW

The two sets of receptor inputs that are sensitive to the *position* and *movement* of different parts of the body are the subjects of this chapter. Collectively, such input is known as proprioception. One set of proprioceptive receptors is found in the muscles, tendons, and joints, where they respond to muscle tension and the position and movement of the limbs. These receptors serve the sense classed as kinesthesis (Gr., motion perception). The other set of receptors is in the inner ear, or vestibule. The vestibular senses respond to the position and movement of the head. Conscious sensations are not a direct result of most proprioceptive inputs. Reflex *responses to* proprioception *result* in sensory input that *is* vital to orientation. Furthermore, the reflexes set off by proprioceptors are very important to normal behavior—literally, a coordinated movement cannot be made without them.

The kinesthetic input will be considered first. Joint sensitivity results in conscious sensations of limb position because the input reaches the highest levels of the brain. The reflex input that is the basis for coordinated movement will be discussed next; this input goes primarily to the cerebellum and is not consciously sensed. The tendon jerk and stretch reflexes are used to show how posture and coordination depend on sensory input from the stretching of muscles.

The vestibular senses are discussed next. The semicircular canals respond to head rotation, and the sacs respond to linear (straight-line) movements of the head. The nerve pathways for reflex response to these two inputs are summarized. First, the semicircular canal receptors and their adequate stimuli are explained, and then the reflex responses to them are examined. The receptor mechanisms of the sacs and their reflex responses follow. The chapter closes with some practical applications of knowledge about the vestibular senses.

KINESTHESIS
Joint sensibility

The receptors that give conscious sensations of limb position and movement are found mainly in the joints. Some sensations of limb position and movement come from the connective tissue covering tendons and muscles and from the pull on the skin as a limb is moved or placed in an extreme position. However, if you close your eyes, rest your right arm on the table, and grasp the index finger with your left hand and flex it back and forth, the resulting sensations of movement will come primarily from the joints of the right index finger. Local anesthetics that paralyze receptors in the skin and muscles impair position sense very little, as the joint receptors are not involved. The joint receptors, as well as all the other receptors contributing to sensations of limb position and movement, appear to be pressure receptors of one kind or another. Unlike pressure receptors in other parts of the body, they adapt very little under continuous stimulation, as when the body is maintained in one position for a long time. This fact is important because constant sensory input must keep us aware of body position at all times so that movement can begin from a known posture. In the joints, most of the pressure receptors involved are pacinian corpuscles. The pathway by which their excitation reaches the cerebral cortex was discussed in Chapter 6. This pathway shares the dorsal columns of the spinal cord with pathways going to the cerebellum for reflex control of movement. The importance of the dorsal column kinesthetic pathways can be seen in victims of tabes dorsalis (destruction of the kinesthetic input by syphilis). The victim lacks knowledge of the position of his limbs because he lacks joint sensitivity; he must watch his feet in order to walk. Even then, his walk is poorly coordinated; he "throws" his legs out and his feet slap the ground at every step because kinesthetic input is not available.

The pathways from the joint receptors to the cerebral cortex are long; the input involves long conduction and synaptic delay times. Such an input can guide and direct slow and voluntary movements such as those involved in a sorting task. The input can also report on body position before, during, and after a more rapid movement. However, the pathways are too slow for rapid correction of a movement, once it is initiated. In a golfer's swing, for example, the golfer may be aware when the movement is initiated that he is going to hit the ball incorrectly, but any attempt to consciously correct his swing will only make matters worse. It appears that the movement is "programmed" by higher centers that set off a series of *reflex* reactions in lower centers. These reflex reactions automatically control a rapid sequence of movements once they are initiated. The feedback from conscious sensations in limb position and movement before, during, and after the swing may be used to correct the reflex "program" for the next try. The input cannot be used to correct the swing while it is in progress. The sensory mechanisms for reflex programs of rapid movements and for automatic postural adjustment are the topic of the remainder of the section on kinesthesis.

Tendon jerks

If the tendon of a muscle is struck with a rubber hammer or with a chopping movement of the heel of the hand, the muscle will react with a rapid and brief contraction—a **tendon jerk.** If a subject is seated with his legs dangling, striking the patellar tendon (just below the kneecap) causes a rapid contraction of the quadriceps (thigh) muscle and a kicking motion of the leg—the so-called knee jerk reflex. The quick contraction is a response to stretching of the muscle caused by hitting the tendon to which it is attached. Similar tendon jerks can be stimulated in both flexor and extensor muscles over the entire body by striking their tendons. The tendon jerk is a reflex that is stimulated by receptors in the muscles that are sensitive to the *stretch* of the muscle. Striking the tendon results in rapid stretching of the muscle to which it is attached. The same muscle responds by contracting in a reflex fashion.

The tendon jerk is, then, a reflex. Reflexes (studied in Chapter 4) are made of five elements: (1) receptors, (2) sensory neurons, (3) association neurons, (4) motoneurons, and (5) effectors. Tendon jerks require less time between stimulus and response than other reflexes because fewer synapses are involved. Measurements of the time required show that no association neurons are involved in the tendon jerk. It is a **monosynaptic** reflex, having only one set of synapses between the sensory neurons and motoneurons. The sensory neurons make direct functional connections with the motoneurons; thus only four reflex elements are involved.

Stretch reflex

The stretch reflex involves exactly the same elements as the tendon jerk—the same receptors, sensory neurons, motoneurons, and effectors. The **stretch reflex** is the reflex contraction of extensor muscles in response to a more gradual stretching from the pull of gravity (for example, when shifting body weight bends the knee), rather than the abnormally rapid stretching of tendon jerks. Extensor muscles are stretched when a limb is flexed by either the force of gravity or antagonist flexors. When stretched by the force of gravity as it bends a limb, the extensor muscles react by contraction and straighten the limb. Since the onset of the stretching is more gradual, stretch receptors begin to fire a few at a time as their thresholds are reached. The contraction response that straightens the limb is therefore smooth and gradual as more and more groups of muscle fibers respond. For example, as the knees bend under the weight of the body, the tendon of the quadriceps (thigh) muscle is stretched over the kneecap. The muscle reacts to stretch by contraction, which straightens the leg. With normal shifts in posture, the amount of stretching of various extensor, or antigravity, muscles changes. Their reflex contraction varies in proportion to the amount of load imposed on them, enabling the body to remain upright. If you shift your weight from your right leg to your left, the extensors of the left leg will be stretched more and will increase their contraction to compensate for the change in posture. Stretch reflexes are therefore important to normal postural adjustments.

As pointed out in Chapter 4, muscles are always stretched to some degree and are therefore always partly contracted in response, giving rise to **muscle tone,** the partial contraction of healthy muscle that varies with position (stretch). The postural changes in stretch reflex adjustment are simply increases or decreases in muscle tone. Flexor muscles are not needed for upright posture since they bend rather than extend the limbs. They have a higher response threshold to stretching than do extensor muscles, have less tone as a result, and do not show reflex contractions to gradual stretching, although they will react to the more rapid stimulus of tendon jerks. In humans the flexors of the arms and hands oppose gravity rather than the extensors; for example, bending the elbow opposes gravity. The arm and hand flexors show all the characteristics of extensor muscles in the rest of the body, including postural stretch reflexes.

Input to the cerebellum

The stretch reflex inputs set off spinal reflexes. These inputs also reach higher centers. Such centers are responsible for overall coordination of the body through their influence on the excitatory and inhibitory reflexes involved in muscle tone and the stretch reflex. These are the centers whose activity is "programmed" by the highest parts of the brain, as when a rapid coordinated movement such as swinging a golf club at a ball is executed. As explained at the beginning of this section, the movement is set once it is programmed and initiated by the highest parts of the brain. The movement is nevertheless dependent on the flow of input from the stretch receptors.

VESTIBULAR SENSES
Labyrinth

The **vestibular senses** respond to head position and movement and set off many reflexes that enable us to maintain an upright posture. The receptors are located in the nonauditory part of the **labyrinth** of the inner ear, the part of the structure shown in Fig. 7-1 that is not involved in hearing. The labyrinths are located in the temporal bones, internal to the pinna, or external ear, on each side of the skull. Each

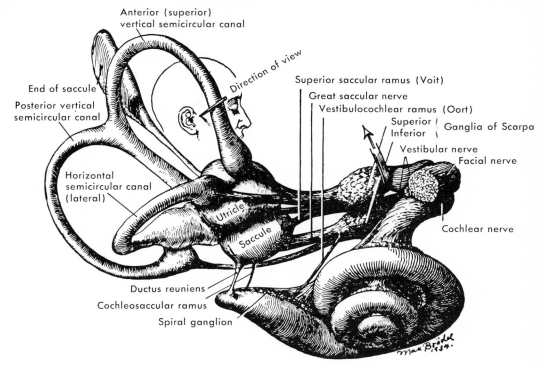

Fig. 7-1. Membranous labyrinth and its nerve supply. (*Utr.,* utriculus.) The saccular ramus and the saccular and vestibular nerves are parts of the vestibular nerve supply. The ampulla is the bulblike swelling on one end of each semicircular canal. Other structures are auditory in function. (Modified from Hardy, M.: Anat. Rec. **59:**404, 1934.)

labyrinth is surrounded by fluid **peri-lymph,** and the nonauditory parts are filled with fluid **endolymph;** thus the whole structure is cushioned by fluid. The labyrinth walls are a membranous (membrane) structure. The nonauditory part of this structure can be classified into two sets of receptor structures on both structural and functional grounds: (1) the **semicircular canals,** which respond primarily to rotation of the head, and (2) the **sacculus** and **utriculus** (collectively called **sacs**), which respond primarily to head position and linear motions of the head. The three semicircular canals have a common opening near their ampullae (sing., ampulla)—the bulge on each canal at one end. There they communicate with the utriculus, which in turn opens into the sacculus. The ampullae, the sacculus, and the utriculus

are individually served by branches of the statoacoustic, or eighth, nerve.

Nerve pathways

Nerve fibers that respond to stimulation of the semicircular canals and sacs pass in the eighth nerve to the four **vestibular nuclei** of the medulla. Here they initiate *reflex* responses to head position and movement. The **medial longitudinal fasciculus** carries excitation from the vestibular nuclei to nuclei serving cranial nerves III, IV, and VI for reflex eye movements and to XI for reflex head movements. The **vestibulospinal** tract carries excitation down the spinal cord to the extensor motoneurons to vary posture as a function of head position. Other pathways reach the cerebellum for more general balancing reactions. Excitation can also reach vomiting centers in the medulla (to cause motion sickness or sea-sickness).

Sensations

Conscious sensations do not result directly from stimulation of the nonauditory labyrinth by head position and movement. Most of the strong sensations that result from changing head position are caused by reflex *responses* to the change. For example, sensations of dizziness from spinning around and around, as children often do, come from reflex responses. The eyes move reflexly back and forth, so that the visual field seems to "swim" by. Reflex changes in extensor muscle tone cause the subject to feel that he is falling.

Semicircular canals

The semicircular canals lie in three planes of space at right angles to each other. There is a horizontal, anterior vertical, and posterior vertical canal in each labyrinth (Fig. 7-1). The horizontal canal inclines at about 30 degrees; the anterior and posterior vertical canals are at right angles to it and to each other. As a result, the anterior vertical canal on one side of the head is parallel with the posterior vertical canal on the other side of the head, and vice versa.

Ampulla. The bulblike swelling at one end of each semicircular canal where it joins the utriculus is called the **ampulla** (Fig. 7-1). Inside the ampulla a ridge of sensory cells, the **crista,** is found (Fig. 7-2, *A*). These sensory cells have hair-cell endings that thrust into an overlying gelatinous (jellylike) mass called the **cupula.** Together, the cupula and crista occupy most of the internal space of the ampulla. This means that any circulation of fluid through the semicircular canals will push against the cupula, bend the hair cells, and stimulate the fibers of the eighth nerve.

Rotational stimulation. Rotation of the head in any plane of motion will stimulate one semicircular canal more than the others because they are at right angles to one another; each canal is stimulated most by rotation parallel to it. The pattern of input from the three canals on both sides

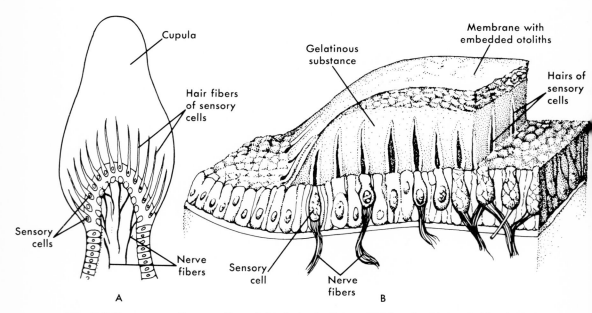

Fig. 7-2. Receptors of nonauditory labyrinth. **A,** Crista. **B,** Macula. (From Geldard, F. A.: The human senses, ed. 2, New York, 1972, John Wiley & Sons, Inc.)

of the head can be used to detect the direction of the rotation. For example, consider stimulation of the horizontal canal by spinning around in a rotating chair. During *acceleration,* from rest to a maximum rate of spin, sudden rotation of the canal will "move the canal around its fluid" because of the inertia of the rest of the fluid (Fig. 7-3, *A*). This will cause fluid pressure against the cupula, bending the hair cells and stimulating the nerve fibers in the crista. When the rotating chair reaches a constant speed, stimulation will cease because the canal and the fluid will be rotating at the same speed and not in motion relative to each other. If the speed of rotation is too low for centrifugal force to be felt, no reflex reactions or sensations will result. When the rotation is suddenly *stopped* (decelerated), the horizontal semicircular canal will again be stimulated. The fluid will tend to keep moving in the direction in which the subject was rotating because of inertia of motion (Fig. 7-3, *B*). Fluid will press against the cupula from the opposite direction, as compared to acceleration. Deceleration will give the same reflexes and sensations as if the subject had *begun* rotating in the opposite direction. Excitation from the semicircular canals depends on rotational *acceleration* and *deceleration* rather than on constant motion

and occurs in relatively brief periods against a resting discharge level. Nerve fibers from the crista of the ampulla show a resting discharge level of about five impulses per second, a rate that is increased by ampulla-trailing acceleration and decreased by ampulla-leading acceleration.

Sacs

The **utriculus** communicates with the semicircular canals, and the **sacculus** communicates with the utriculus. The sacs are thus filled with the same fluid endolymph as the semicircular canals. However, their sensory structures are primarily specialized to respond to *head position* and to *linear acceleration* and *deceleration* rather than to rotary movements. The utriculus seems to be more important to behavior than the sacculus; destruction of the utriculus disturbs equilibrium and locomotion, but destruction of the sacculus does not lead to these symptoms. The input of the sacs seems more important in lower animals such as fish, amphibians, reptiles, and birds than it is to man and other mammals. Humans can maintain equilibrium with vision when the sacs are destroyed, but they cannot stand erect on one foot with eyes closed, and they lose orientation without a horizon—when swimming under water, for example.

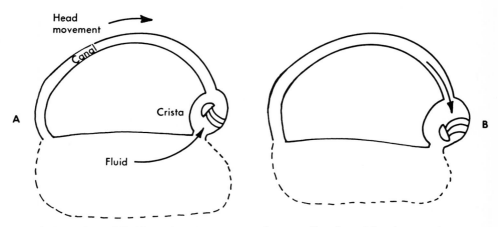

Fig. 7-3. Action of fluid motion on receptors in ampulla of semicircular canal.

Macula. The patch of sensory tissue on the inner surface of each of the sacs is called the **macula.** Its structure is shown in Fig. 7-2, *B*. The sensory cells extend hairlike processes into the cavity of the sac; the hairs are enveloped with a thick jellylike substance. On the free surface of the jelly rest many tiny particles of calcium carbonate (limestone "rocks"), the **otoliths.** The bases of the sensory cells are enveloped by basketlike endings of vestibular nerve fibers. These fibers are stimulated by the sensory cells when the hairlike processes are bent or pulled by movement of the "top-heavy" mass of jellylike material. Stimulation should occur whenever the hair cells are not upright or when the head is moved suddenly. The structure is like molded gelatin, with weights on top and hairs thrust into it from the bottom; movement "jiggles" the structure, and anything but an upright position displaces it to one side.

Hair cells. The hair cells are stimulated on being bent or pulled when the "top-heavy" mass of jelly that envelops them is shifted from an upright position. Motion affects the gelatinous mass in the same way that shaking or tilting a gelatin mold af-fects gelatin. The stimulation results from linear acceleration or deceleration of the head or from head positions that tilt the hair cells and their enveloping jelly from an upright position.

Head position. Since the postural muscles must continuously be informed of head position, the hair cells maintain a continuous or "resting" rate of neural firing, even when they are in an upright position. The **macula utriculi** in each inner ear have their hair cells upright when the head is erect. Tilting the head will result in a different direction of movement of the ge-latinous mass for every different head movement. The pattern of stimulation that results depends on the fine structure of the hairs (Fig. 7-4). Each hair cell has hairs of graduated length. When head movement tilts the top-heavy gelatinous mass in the direction of the longest hair, the firing rate in nerve fibers from that receptor is *in-creased;* movement in the opposite fashion *decreases* the rate of firing. Since the longest cilia of hair cells in different parts of the utriculus are oriented in different direc-tions, a different *pattern* of increases and decreases in the firing of sensory fibers will result from each different head move-

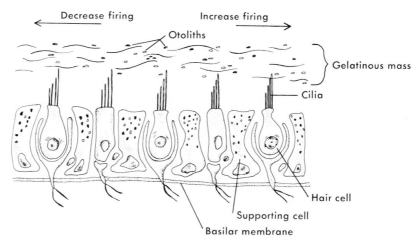

Fig. 7-4. Sketch of fine structure of macula, showing arrangement of hair cells (cilia) for each receptor. The longer hairs are responsible for sensitivity to direction of tilt. (From Flock, A., and Duvall, A. J.: The ultrastructure of the kinocilium of the sensory cells in the inner ear and lateral line organs, J. Cell Biol. **25:**1-8, 1965.)

ment. The sensory code is probably *topographic,* with a different spatial pattern of input reaching the vestibular nuclei for each position and movement of the head. The macula sacculi in each inner ear functions in the same fashion, save that its hair cells are oriented laterally (point out toward the sides) when the head is in an upright position. As previously noted, the utriculus is much more important to orientation than the sacculus.

Acceleration and deceleration. Sudden linear movement of the head stimulates the maculae, especially the macula utriculi. This can distort sensations of the upright position when visual cues are not a help. For example, in flying, sudden acceleration makes the pilot feel that he is climbing and sudden deceleration that he is diving, even though he is in straight and level flight.

Eye reflexes and head position. Changes in head position result in elevation of the eyes when the head is lowered, depression of the eyes when the head is raised, and rotation of the eyes when the head is tilted. All these reflexes aid the eyes in becoming oriented toward a level horizon. The eye reflexes originate in visual input as well as in the maculae. They are mediated by the medial longitudinal fasciculus pathways to the nuclei serving cranial nerves III, IV, and VI for the eye muscles. (These pathways were described earlier in the chapter.) At the same time, change from the normal erect head position stimulates the maculae to send excitation to the neck muscles in order to return the head to the erect position. Here the medial longitudinal fasciculus carries excitation to cranial nerve XI for excitation of the neck muscles.

Righting reflexes

In four-legged animals, when the neck muscles react so as to restore the upright position of the head, the neck is "twisted" if the body is not erect. This twisted position stimulates proprioceptors in the neck muscles, and the input of these proprioceptors reaches descending tracts in the spinal cord going to the motor nerve supply of the body trunk. The body muscles are then stimulated to restore the upright position of the body. The sequence involved in neck and body righting reflexes is most clearly observed by holding a cat upside down and dropping it from a position 4 or 5 feet off the floor. First the head turns toward the upright position, next the forelimbs, and then the hind limbs. Twisting of the neck has stimulated the upper body trunk, and twisting of the upper trunk has stimulated the lower trunk, all in sequence. At the same time, extensor tone has been increased, and the animal will land with all four limbs stiffly extended to cushion the shock.

Postural reflexes. The head also "leads" (caused by visual and macular input) in regulating posture. In animals the forelimb and hind limb extensor tone will vary with head position. If a cat lowers its head in looking under an object, forelimb extensors will relax and hind limb extensors contract—the forepart of the body will be reflexly lowered and the hindpart elevated. If the head is raised above the normal position, preparatory to jumping up on an object, forelimb extensors will contact and hind limb extensors relax. The forequarters will be raised and the hindquarters lowered in position for the jump. These reflexes can be demonstrated in cats with the higher parts of the brain removed as long as the connections between the sacs, medulla, and spinal cord motoneurons are intact.

Vestibular senses: practical implications

In general the vestibular senses depend on normal conditions of gravity and acceleration to furnish accurate input for normal responses. They evolved in fish, which are thus able to orient themselves in a three-dimensional environment with little gravitational effect and little visual orientation. Evolution has adapted mammalian vestibular senses to gravity, subordinated them to accurate visual input, and developed them to respond to the amount and kind of acceleration and deceleration found in normal body movement. When their normal stimulation pattern is changed, the resulting input can cause extreme disorientation and nausea, especially when accurate visual input does not correct for their misinformation. As pointed out previously, the extreme acceleration or deceleration encountered in flying an airplane can cause a pilot in level flight to believe that he is climbing or diving if he is flying "blind," that is, without a natural visual horizon. Centrifugal forces change stimulation to the sacs in a climb, a dive, or a turn, although the semicircular canals seem little affected. A pilot who is flying upside down in a "loop" may be experiencing suffiicient centrifugal force to feel that he is upright. One of the most difficult problems in learning to fly is the necessity of disregarding vestibular input and depending strictly on vision—either a view of the horizon or, still more difficult, instrument reading when flying "blind." Research on the vestibular apparatus and the effects of weightlessness received a great deal of attention with the advent of space flight. In early experiments a weightless environment could be maintained for as long as 15 seconds by flying an aircraft with a large empty cabin in a parabolic curve—first a climb and then a dive. This method is still used in training for space flight. Orientation under conditions of weightlessness can also be taught through scuba diving; underwater the subject has the same specific gravity as the water. Neither method provides any sensations of up or down and there is no visual horizon. Space flights have resulted in initial symptoms of nausea and dizziness among some astronauts, but these seem to abate in a day or two and can be minimized by practice with the training methods described above. Given enough visual and tactual cues, space flights of over a month have produced no lasting disorders of the vestibular apparatus, although a period of some hours is required to readapt completely to normal gravity.

Finally, regular rhythmic motions that differ enough from those of walking can cause carsickness, airsickness, or seasickness, because of the nausea centers in the medulla. The primary component causing the disturbance seems to be vertical motion rather than pitch (fore and aft motion) or yaw (side-to-side motion). The frequency and amplitude of the vertical motion seem to be the important variables—frequencies near 20 per minute and amplitudes of about 7 feet being most disturbing. Drugs have proved to be of some help, and fortunately most people adapt, as when a sailor gets his "sea legs." A combination of scopolamine and dextroamphetamine has been found recently to prevent motion sickness by action on the autonomic nervous system.

SUMMARY

Proprioception is sensory input for body position and movement. It includes kinesthesis from the general receptors in joints and muscles and vestibular sensitivity from the nonauditory labyrinth. Kinesthesis in the limbs gives rise to conscious sensations of position and movement when receptors in the joints (mostly pacinian corpuscles) are stimulated. These receptors adapt little, so that one is always aware of limb position. Their pathways upward in the dorsal columns of the cord reach the cerebral cortex. Because many synapses are involved, cortically originated "voluntary" response to joint receptors is slow. This input can regulate slow "voluntary" reactions, but it is too slow to correct a rapid movement in progress. Rapid movements are regulated by reflexes in lower centers of the brain and spinal cord that are "programmed" by the cortex, cerebellum, and other higher centers.

Kinesthesis also includes sensory input from the muscles and tendons that does not cause conscious sensation. This input participates in the reflex "programs" mentioned above and is important to posture and coordination. One such reflex that can be shown in exaggerated form is the tendon jerk. Striking the tendon of a muscle causes a quick contraction of the muscle. This reflex is stimulated by receptors in the muscle that are sensitive to the stretching of the muscle when the tendon is struck. The reflex is rapid because it is monosynaptic.

More gradual stretching of extensor muscles elicits a more gradual extensor contraction in the stretch reflex. The stretch reflex is elicited in extensor muscles when limbs are flexed by the pull of gravity; it straightens those limbs and thus is an antigravity reflex. Shifts in posture change the pattern of stretch reflexes in extensors in normal postural adjustment. All muscles are anatomically stretched to some degree, and their stretch reflex response causes the muscle tone that varies with position (amount of stretching). Arm and hand flexors in humans are antigravity muscles that react like extensors.

The vestibular senses are special senses located in the nonauditory part of the membranous labyrinth. The nonauditory labyrinth is surrounded by perilymph and contains endolymph. Its semicircular canals respond to head rotation, and its sacculus and utriculus to position and linear motion of the head; both are served by part of the eighth nerve that goes to the four vestibular nuclei of the medulla. The vestibular nuclei mediate reflexes rather than conscious sensations. The medial longitudinal fasciculus carries excitation to nerves III, IV, and VI for reflex eye movements and to XI for reflex head movements. The vestibulospinal tract carries excitation to spinal extensor motoneurons for postural adjustment, and other pathways reach the cerebellum for complex coordination. The anterior vertical, posterior vertical, and horizontal semicircular canals in each temporal bone are at right angles to one another, and each canal responds most to movement in its own plane. Three-dimensional movement detection is thus provided.

The ampulla of each canal contains a crista of sensory cells, with hair endings thrust into an overlying gelatinous cupula. Fluid circulation in the semicircular canals pushes against the cupula to stimulate the hair cells. Rotary acceleration or decelera-tion of a canal, rather than a constant rotation, is the adequate stimulus.

The sacs include the sacculus and utriculus, the latter being the more important. The sensory structure in each is the macula, consisting of hair cells surrounded by a jellylike material with otoliths on its free surface. Hair cells provide continuous postural information by a resting rate of firing in their sensory fibers. Displacement of the jelly by linear acceleration and deceleration and head positions in which the hair cells are not upright stimulate or inhibit the hair cells for a topographically patterned input. In the utriculus the hair cells are oriented vertically and in the sacculus they are oriented laterally, so that each head position or movement has a different pattern of stimulus input. Departures from the vertical head position cause compensating eye movements that maintain the horizon and reflex reactions of the neck muscles that return the head to the erect position. Proprioceptors in the neck muscles stimulate reflex reactions of the body muscles to restore the upright position in the righting reflexes. Forelimb and hind limb extensors in animals adjust to head position in postural reflexes.

In general, the vestibular senses depend on normal gravity and body movements. The extreme accelerations, decelerations, and centrifugal forces that occur in flying can cause disorientation unless there are visual cues. Lack of graviation in outer space can cause lack of orientation. Large and regular vertical movement can cause carsickness, seasickness, and airsickness through nausea reflex centers in the medulla.

READINGS

Merton, P. A.: How we control the contraction of our muscles, Sci. Am. **226:**30-37, May 1972 (W. H. Freeman Co. Reprint No. 1249).

Mueller, C. G.: Sensory psychology, Englewood Cliffs, N.J., 1965, Prentice-Hall, Inc.

Wilson, V. J.: The labyrinth, the brain, and posture, Am. Scientist **63:**325-332, May-June 1975.

von Buddenbrock, W.: The senses, Ann Arbor, 1958, University of Michigan Press.

CHAPTER 8

The chemical senses: taste and smell

OVERVIEW

The chemical senses are so named because they are normally and adequately stimulated by substances in solution. They include gustation (taste), olfaction (smell), and the common chemical sense. The common chemical sense is the simplest and will be disposed of first; it is stimulated by dissolved irritants in the eyes, nose, throat, and other mucous areas. The sensory mechanism seems identical with pain; however, the "stinging" quality of ammonia in the eyes and nose or pepper in the mouth seems different from other kinds of pain to the subject.

Gustation will be taken up next. Most of the taste receptors are confined to the tongue. Their primary qualities are sweet, salt, sour, and bitter. What is known of the adequate stimuli for these four taste qualities will be summarized. The nerve pathways for taste will be described. When receptors and nerve pathways are understood, experiments on the physiology of taste can be discussed. Phenomena of taste thresholds, adaptation, contrast, compensation, fusion, and so on conclude the section on gustation.

Olfaction is the final topic of the chapter. After some introductory remarks, the receptors and their nervous connections will be described. Olfactory qualities and the sensory mechanisms underlying them will

be discussed. Theories of olfactory sensory mechanisms will be summarized. Remarks on olfactory phenomena such as adaptation, compensation, and anosmia (smell "blindness") conclude the chapter.

COMMON CHEMICAL SENSE
Quality

The **common chemical sense** refers to the sensitivity of the mucous membranes of the body to dissolved irritants. The term is most frequently used in referring to the "stinging" quality that is aroused in the mouth by "hot" foods such as chili peppers. However, vaporizing substances such as ammonia cause stinging sensations in the eyes and nose, and these sensations are also caused by the common chemical sense. In the eyes and nose the irritants cause tears and nasal secretions, respectively, as anyone who has smelled ammonia or peeled an onion can testify. Nasal sensitivity seems the greatest (a few thousandths of 1% for some gases), eye sensitivity is intermediate, and sensations from the mouth may require a solution of 3% to 5% of some of the most irritating substances. Common chemical sensitivity is not confined to the nose, eyes, and mouth. Any mucous membrane, such as those of the anus and genitals, has common chemical sensitivity.

Common chemical sensations may be related to pain by the subject, but they seem subjectively different from pain in quality, being described as "stinging" or "burning" sensations. Common chemical sensations in the mouth may be pleasant in mild arousal—when one "tastes" peppermint or a dry martini, common chemical stimulation is the "stinging" part of the "flavor." It has been argued that the common chemical sense differs from pain because the sensory quality seems different to the subject and because drugs affect these sensations in a different way (for example, cocaine anesthetizes skin pain much more readily than the common chemical sense). The change in sensory quality can probably be explained by differences in the stimuli causing common chemical sensation from those causing skin pain; dissolved mucous irritants *should* cause a different sensation from that of skin pain stimuli, just as skin pain from a burn differs from that caused by a cut. Drugs can "deaden" skin pain more readily than they can deaden the common chemical sense. However, drugs may be less effective when the nerve endings are more directly stimulated by irritants on sensitive mucous surfaces. Finally, the anatomy of the receptors for pain and of the common chemical sense are identical, as are their pathways to the brain. It may be concluded that the common chemical sense is pain sensitivity in the mucous membranes, that is, pain stimulated by irritants dissolved in the mucus covering the mucous membranes.

Receptors

The receptors are free nerve endings distributed to the tongue, nasopharynx, orbit, and other mucous surfaces. Like other pain endings their threshold is relatively high, but the central nervous system response fatigues slowly, and the receptors adapt little under most conditions of chemical stimulation. In part, receptor adaptation is rare because the dissolved irritant is not a "constant" stimulus; the chemical changes it initiates in the tissue are a process of active change. The "bite" of a pep-

permint stick will not change greatly, then, no matter how long you chew on it—and your eyes will not adapt to peeling onions.

Nerve pathways

The fibers from the mouth, tongue, orbit, and nasal passages that serve pain reach the brain stem in cranial nerves V, VII, IX, and X. They are distributed with other pain fibers to the spinal tract and nucleus of the fifth nerve. The spinal nucleus relays excitation to the thalamus and, unlike other pain inputs, to the postcentral gyrus of the cerebral cortex (somesthetic projection area). As with other pain fibers, there are many collaterals to the reticular formation of the brain stem that arouse the brain to greater activity and contribute descending output to muscles. Pain input of any kind stimulates the nervous system to much activity.

GUSTATION

Taste sensitivity is caused largely by receptors on the tongue in adults (children sometimes have taste receptors in the cheeks; these receptors later disappear). Sensitivity is also found in the palate or roof of the mouth (for sour and bitter) and the larynx. Strictly speaking, taste receptors give rise only to sensations of sweet, salt, sour, and bitter; the complex of the subtle sensations called "taste" in everyday speech includes smell, common chemical sensitivity, and somesthesia. A food is said to taste bland when "stinging" common chemical sensations are not present. Foods taste flat when one has a head cold because it is then impossible to smell food. Hold your nose and you cannot *taste* the difference between a slice of apple and a slice of raw potato—they can be distinguished only by their texture (somesthesia). Coffee tastes hot as well as bitter and corn bread tastes "coarse"—both warmth and texture are somesthetic sensations. This shows that gourmets depend more on smell than taste. As used here, however, gustation refers only to sensations of sweet, sour, bitter, and salt.

Methods and definitions

As usual, the four primary taste qualities have been distinguished by the reports of human subjects. In the usual experiment of this kind, various solutions are applied to the tongue of the subject, and he reports on what he tastes. (The tongue is washed with water between tests to avoid interference among successive stimuli.) Agreement among subjects is the criterion for naming taste qualities, and subjects largely agree on sweet, salt, sour, and bitter, or mixtures of these, as being all they taste under such circumstances. Animal experiments often involve washing the tongue of an anesthetized animal with the same solutions while recording from the seventh or ninth cranial nerve. As will be seen later, individual receptors for each of the qualities do *not* seem indicated by the data that result from nerve cell recording. However, the *patterns* of nerve cell firing are such that the central nervous system could detect four kinds of signals corresponding to four taste qualities (three in the case of the cat, which does not respond to sweet).

Development

The development of taste sensitivity begins before birth, when sensory branches of nerves VII and IX invade the epithelial cells of the mucous membranes of the tongue. Under this influence (called **sensory appropriation**) the epithelial cells de-

Surface of tongue

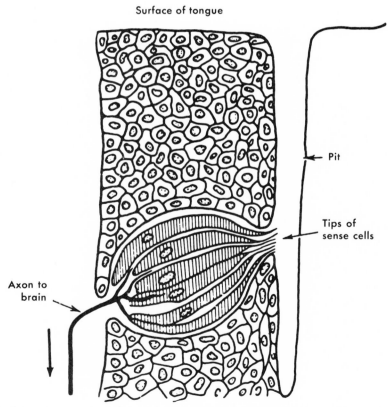

Pit

Tips of sense cells

Axon to brain

Fig. 8-1. Sensory structures for taste. Circumvallate papilla seen in diagrammatic cross section, with taste buds lining the walls and their tips opening to the "moat" surrounding the papilla. (From Geldard, F. A.: The human senses, New York, 1953, John Wiley & Sons, Inc.)

velop into specialized receptors. Development is complete at puberty, but the receptors begin to atrophy after about 45 years of age. These changes are related to the gonadal hormones; taste receptors atrophy after castration in animals, but they can be reestablished by injections of the missing sex hormones. Apparently taste matures at puberty and atrophies as the output of gonadal hormones falls off in middle and old age. This has important consequences for nutrition in older people, who frequently lose interest in food and do not eat enough.

Receptors

The taste receptors are spindle-shaped cells, each of which has a single hair. They occur in clusters of 2 to 12, surrounded by supporting cells (Fig. 8-1). The whole structure is called a **taste bud** because of the resemblance to a flower bud. The taste buds are most frequently found in the pa-

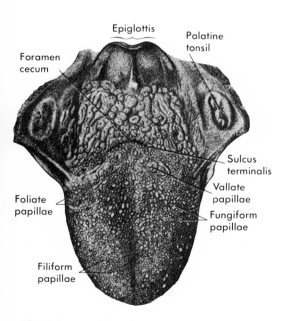

Fig. 8-2. Location of papillae on tongue. (After Kahn: Das Leben des Menschen, W. Keller & Co.; from Neal, H. V., and Rand, H. W.: Comparative anatomy. Copyright 1936 by McGraw-Hill Book Company, Inc. Used by permission of McGraw-Hill Book Company.)

pillae of the tongue (Fig. 8-2). The papillae are structures in the tongue, made up of a "moat" surrounding an "island." The taste buds thrust their hairs into the moat from the sides of the island and the walls of the moat. The moat serves to contain the solution to be tasted so that it can affect the hair cells; these receptors in turn set off nerve impulses in the taste nerve fibers. There are four types of papillae on the tongue (Fig. 8-2), but those in the center of the tongue do not contain taste buds. Only the tip, sides, and back of the tongue are taste-sensitive.

Qualities. Stimulation of the tongue with various solutions identifies four primary taste qualities when smell, temperature, somesthesia, and common chemical sensitivity are ruled out. The four primary qualities are sweet, salt, sour, and bitter. The adequate stimulus for sweet is sucrose (sugar). The best salt response comes from NaCl (common table salt) solutions. Weak solutions of hydrochloric acid (HCl) provide the most adequate stimulus for sour. Bitter sensations result from stimulation with quinine solutions. In humans the order of increasing sensitivity to the four primary qualities is sweet, salt, sour, and bitter when the test solutions named above are used. This order of sensitivity is at body temperature—all tastes except sour change sensitivity with temperature change. (If saccharin is used to stimulate sweet, this quality has the lowest threshold except for bitter.) All the more complex tastes are compounds of these four primary qualities; an experienced taster can detect which of the four are present and which are absent in a complex taste.

Detection is aided because the tongue is not equally sensitive to the four primary qualities at the tip, sides, and back. The tongue is most sensitive to sweet at the tip, bitter at the back, and sour at the sides. Salt sensitivity is widespread, but somewhat greater at the tip. Common reactions to three of the four tastes confirm the different sensitivity of parts of the tongue. In tasting a pleasantly sweet substance, a person "purses" his lips to concentrate the solution near the tip of the tongue. In response to a very bitter substance, a person gags, which acts to remove the substance from the back of the tongue and palate. Very sour solutions cause an open-mouthed frowning expression, which removes the solution from the sides of the tongue and palate. In addition to the subjective primary nature of the four qualities and the different sensitivity of various parts of the tongue, narcotizing the tongue with cocaine gives evidence for four primary qualities. As the drug takes effect, taste sensations disappear in the following order: bitter, sweet, salt, and sour. This is not the same as their order of sensitivity—the drug is affecting the four qualities differently, and the tongue is not just losing sensitivity.

Stimuli

The nature of the adequate stimulus for two of the primary qualities is clearer than for the other two. Sour and salt are stimulated by **ions,** or electrically charged atoms or molecules, in solution. Less is known about what affects the sweet and bitter tastes. The biggest mystery is how the receptors react to solutions to cause nerve impulses.

The sour taste is stimulated by the positively charged hydrogen ion (H^+), an ion that dissociates well from weak acids in solution. The effectiveness of the H^+ ion is modified by the **buffer** action of the saliva. Saliva contains substances that neutralize either acid H^+ ions or basic OH^- ions. The more readily an acid gives off H^+ ions in solution, the more sour it tastes. However, organic ions are more sour than inorganic ions that dissociate to give off an equal number of H^+ ions. Furthermore, not all acids are sour; for example, amino acids are sweet, and picric acid is bitter. The H^+ ion may be the most important agent in a sour stimulus, but other factors are involved.

Both the positive and negative ions of salts are important to their salty taste. (A positive ion is called a cation and a negative ion an anion; see Chapter 2.) In table salt (NaCl) the cation (Na^+) seems more important than the anion (Cl^-). Other anions joined with Na^+—for example, $NaSO_4$—taste salty, and other cations joined with Cl^-, such as KCl, taste salty, although the taste varies in quality and intensity. NaCl is the most effective stimulus; the other salts taste less salty, and some have a mixed salt and bitter taste. Salts often taste bitter at threshold concentrations as well. The size of the salt molecule (its molecular weight) seems related to whether a salt will taste salty or bitter; the larger salts, such as sodium acetate, often taste bitter. As with sour, ions are the most important part of the salt stimulus, but other factors are involved.

Less is known about what makes a stimulus taste sweet. The sweetest substances are organic compounds that do not break up into ions. Most of the sugars taste sweet if the carbon chain of their molecule is not too long; sucrose is the sweetest. There are exceptions to these rules, however. Some of the inorganic lead and beryllium salts taste sweet, and a slight change in the molecular geometry of a sugar that does not change its carbon chain can change its sweetness. Increases in molecular size (molecular weight) can cause a compound to change from sweet to bitter. An increase in concentration of some sweet solutions can also change their taste; saccharin is the sweetest substance known when diluted, but it tastes bitter in concentrated solutions. Many bitter and sweet compounds have similar chemical and physical properties. About all that can be said is that the geometry of the molecule is the most important factor known to determine sweetness.

Of all the primary tastes the least is known about bitter. Although quinine solutions are the stimuli generally used for bitter in the laboratory, alkaloids and some complex inorganic salts are also bitter. The bitter taste does not depend on ionization, but some ionizing metals are bitter in solution. As previously noted, some salts taste bitter at threshold concentrations, some salts with large molecules taste bitter, some sugars with large molecules taste bitter, and concentrated sweet stimuli can change to bitter. Molecular size and shape are important, but that was what was said about sweet. Little is really known about either stimulus.

Nerve pathways

The nerve pathways serving taste are partly unique to taste and partly shared with somesthesia. Taste fibers from the tongue go to their own primary nucleus in the brain stem. However, the second-order fibers that arise here join second-order somesthetic fibers en route to the thalamus. The third-order fibers from the thalamus to the cortex are also anatomically mixed with somesthetic fibers. Most of the first-order taste fibers are carried in the seventh (anterior tongue) and ninth (posterior tongue) cranial nerves. Upon reaching the brain stem, they form a tract, the **tractus solitarius;** the excitation is passed on by the nucleus of that tract. The second-order fibers join the medial lemniscus and end on the **arcuate** (face) **nucleus** of the thalamus, along with second-order somesthetic fibers representing the face. The third-order fibers project with somesthesia from the face on area 2 of the postcentral gyrus. They are adjacent to the part of the precentral motor area (area 4) controlling the chewing muscles. Sensory input from somesthetic sensations of the mouth, taste, and motor control of chewing are as close anatomically as they are functionally.

Physiology of taste

The physiology of the taste receptor is largely a mystery. Substances must be in solution to stimulate the hair cells—one cannot taste a piece of stainless steel because it does not dissolve in saliva—but little else is known about how the hair cells respond. Experimenters have stimulated individual hair cells with micropipettes,

and recordings have been made of the electrical responses of individual hair cells and individual afferent neurons. These experiments will be briefly described. What is confusing is that some single receptors fire neurons in response to more than one of the primary qualities. Anatomical studies using the electron microscope explain this by showing that each neuron innervates several receptor cells—the receptor cells may differ in which stimuli they respond to, but each could fire the nerve cell. Individual receptor cells of a taste bud (papilla) have been stimulated with solutions from a micropipette and stimulated electrically with a microelectrode. Individual receptor cells respond to a single quality only, although a single papilla may contain cells responding to different qualities. Cells responding to different qualities differ in appearance as seen through a microscope and differ in sensitivity to different electrical stimulus frequencies. What is puzzling about all this is that a single sensory nerve fiber may be stimulated by several receptor cells, each responding to a different quality. Some more complex *pattern* of input must signal each quality. Furthermore some receptors respond to temperature as well as to taste. Some chemical event in the receptor initiates nerve impulses in response to solutions at a specific location on the receptor cell. In the end perhaps a match can be found between the shape and charge of the molecules or ions that stimulate taste and the physical shape or charge of the receptor sites. This has been done for smell but not for taste.

Generator potential. Microelectrodes have been used to penetrate single taste receptor cells and record their generator potential in response to taste stimuli. As in other types of receptors it is the generator potential that fires the nerve impulses for taste by depolarizing the nerve cell. What is unusual about the generator potential for taste receptors is its duration—the potential requires 10 to 15 seconds to reach its maximum.

Nerve fiber recording. Single fibers from the ninth nerve of the cat respond to more than one stimulus solution washed over the tongue. Of course only the smaller fibers go to a single receptor—the larger ones go to two or more receptors. However, the only information the brain receives is nerve impulses; it cannot distinguish between two receptors served by the same fiber. The pattern of fiber response is shown in Table 7. Four classes of fibers were found: those responding to salt or acid (salt fiber); acid alone (acid fiber); quinine alone (quinine fiber); or acid, quinine, and water (water fiber). (Other studies show two different kinds of response to salt.) The code to the central nervous system would involve detecting salt when the salt fibers fired, sour when both salt and acid fibers fired, and bitter when the quinine fiber fired. (The cat does not sense sweet, but fibers responding to sweet have been found in the dog and rat.) Doubt has been cast on the water fiber because the saliva is a little salty, and the response of the water fiber to salt may depend on the state of adaptation of the tongue. Nerve recordings in humans show no response to distilled water. It is evident in any case that the primary qualities depend on *patterns* of input rather than on single-receptor stimulation.

Temperature response. Single afferent neurons in the cat respond to temperature as well as to taste. One investigator found that only 2 of 28 units that he studied responded to taste alone. Some responded to taste and to cooling, others to taste, warming, and cooling, and still others to temperature changes only. Perhaps this is why taste thresholds are so intimately dependent on temperature.

Taste phenomena

Taste receptors are affected by temperature and prior adaptation. Temperature affects the sensitivity of the receptors and therefore their input pattern and the taste that is peceived. Furthermore, some receptors respond to both temperature and taste. Adaptation to one taste can enhance or depress sensitivity to another taste, giving contrast or compensation effects. Unlike some of the other senses, the primary qualities do not fuse to give a "new" taste. There is so little fusion in taste that an experienced observer can always detect which of the four primary qualities are present and which are absent.

Taste thresholds. The threshold for taste varies according to the area of the tongue stimulated, as previously described. The tip of the tongue is most sensitive to sweet and salt, the sides to sour, and the back to bitter. For any of these areas, reliable absolute thresholds can be established for each of the four primary tastes, provided that the tongue is rinsed between stimuli to prevent adaptation effects. The temperature of the stimulus solution must also be held constant. Absolute thresholds vary with the duration of stimulation as well. Difference thresholds have also been reliably measured, and an equal-interval scale

Table 7. Response of single fibers of taste nerves in the cat*†

Stimulus	Water fiber	Salt fiber	Acid fiber	Quinine fiber		Theoretical sensation
H_2O (salt 0.03 M)	+	0	0	0	→	Water
NaCl (0.05M)	0	+	0	0	→	Salt
HCl (pH 2.5)	+	+	+	0	→	Sour
Quinine	+	0	0	+	→	Bitter

*From Cohen, M. J., Hagiwara, S., and Zotterman, Y.: Acta Physiol. Scand. **33:**316, 1955.
†Single fibers of nerve IX either do respond (+) or do not respond (0) to solutions washed over the tongue, showing *patterns* of response to primary qualities (see text).

of taste units called "gusts" has been established. The absolute threshold for taste is much higher than the threshold for smell, but their difference thresholds are much the same.

Temperature. Extreme hot or cold temperatures decrease sensitivity to all the primary taste qualities except sour. If sugar is added to a very cold glass of iced tea, the tea will be too sweet when it reaches room temperature; the same is true of a very hot cup of coffee. Taste is most sensitive in a range of temperatures (17° to 42° C, or 62° to 107° F) that is near body temperature (37° C, or 98.6° F).

Adaptation. Taste, like most other senses, shows loss of sensitivity with continuous stimulation. Taste adaptation can be made complete for a given stimulus and area of the tongue under laboratory conditions. Adaptation is most rapid at stimulus temperatures where the receptors are most sensitive. The threshold is lower and adaptation is faster for warmer solutions (32° versus 17° C). Thus we can be reasonably sure that it is the receptor and not the central nervous system that is adapting, because stimulus temperature affects the receptor, not the central nervous system. It has also been found, as expected, that the stronger the stimulus for any quality, the longer is the adaptation time and the longer is the perod required to recover normal sensitivity. However, complete adaptation occurs only in the laboratory. A substance being tasted under normal conditions is shifted over different areas of the tongue—new receptors are continually being stimulated. Presumably, even an all-day sucker would remain somewhat sweet at the end of the day. Partial adaptation is common, however. Experts have estimated that a person is 25% to 40% adapted most of the time to the various taste qualities encountered. Of course, taste adaptation can be prevented by taste **contrast,** or mutual taste enhancement, when "opposite" qualities are involved. Under normal conditions taste contrast is usually the rule. Adaptation to one complex of taste qualities is prevented by contrast with another complex of different taste qualities. For this reason, gourmets drink wine with food; the taste of the wine prevents adaptation to the taste of the food, and the taste of the food prevents adaptation to the taste of the wine, permitting maximum enjoyment of both. The wine is selected to match the intensity of the food stimulation so that one taste does not mask the other taste. For example, mild white wine goes with the bland taste of fish, and stronger-tasting red wine is chosen to match the more intense flavor of beefsteak. Temperature effects are also involved: the taste intensity of the white wine is reduced by chilling it, whereas red wine is served at room tempeature for greater taste intensity.

Compensation. Certain tastes raise one another's threshold, especially salt and sour. Salted grapefruit or salted beer tastes neither as salt nor as sour as expected, for example. Compensations of this kind require stimulus intensities well above the normal threshold.

Fusion. As previously pointed out, there is little fusion in taste. In hearing, notes can blend in a chord; in vision, hues can blend to form a new color. In taste, a trained observer can usually detect which of the four primary qualities are present because they do not blend to produce novel tastes (secondary qualities).

OLFACTION

Smell is much more difficult to study than is taste, but it is probably a more important sense, even in humans. As previously explained, odor forms a large part of the "flavor" of food, which tastes "flat" when the olfactory passages are blocked, as when one has a head cold. There would be no gourmets if it were not for smell! Smell probably accounts for as much as two-fifths of the "taste" of food. This seems reasonable; smell has been estimated to be 10,000 times more sensitive than taste, as measured by stimulus concentrations, although the difference thresholds are about the same. (However, the technical difficulties of studying odor thresholds can generate threshold differences of 150 times, depending on the methods used.)

Olfaction is important in another way. It acts independently of taste, as an exteroceptor. As an exteroceptor, or distance receptor, smell joins vision, audition, and somesthesia in exploring the environment. Smell is not so important in this sense to humans as it is to four-legged animals; in humans the nose is not so close to the ground, from whence most odors emanate. However, human reactions to odor may be subjectively as important to man as to animals. The perfume industry spends millions of dollars on odor research, and men as well as women spend more millions on preparations that either add smell to their bodies or remove it. Humans subject the air to substances in spray cans that cover unpleasant odors or, in some cases, that make us anosmic, so that we can smell neither pleasant nor unpleasant odors. The wine industry is as interested in the smell of their product as in its taste and devotes as much energy to that end. Even used-car dealers have found that they can raise their prices and more readily sell cars when the interiors have been sprayed to give that "new-car smell."

In the face of all this activity it is only recently that two useful theories of olfaction have been possible and a list of seven primary olfactory qualities has been developed. Earlier efforts were blocked by difficulties of stimulus presentation and receptor study. The olfactory receptors are so sensitive (as little as 0.00004 mg of mercaptan per cubic meter of air is detectable) and so inaccessible (above the nasal passages) that control of stimulus concentrations is very poor. Recording from receptors or nerve tracts is equally difficult. In animal research it is difficult surgically to "get at" the receptor or nerve tracts serving olfaction because of their location. As a result, less is known of the electrical characteristics of receptor or afferent neuron response to smell than is the case for taste.

Earlier studies of smell resorted to cataloging the thresholds of various substances in an attempt to find odor groups whose thresholds were alike. It was assumed that these groups would form the primary odor qualities. Stimulus-control difficulties impeded this approach. A theory based on examination of the physical shapes of odorous molecules has generated an acceptable list of primary qualities and some knowledge of how these molecules must affect the olfactory receptor. Other useful theories are based on temporal and spatial patterns of stimulation of the receptors.

Receptors

The olfactory receptors are located high in the nasal cavities (Fig. 8-3). They are specialized hairlike endings (cilia) on bipolar nerve cells (olfactory receptor, Fig. 8-4). The bipolar cells, or olfactory receptors, are surrounded by yellow-brown supporting cells, with the whole being called the **olfactory epithelium.** The olfactory epithelium is located on both sides of the **nasal septum,** which completely separates two olfactory passages, one for each nostril. The two smell-sensitive areas are also called the **olfactory clefts.** Each covers about 2.5 cm² (1 square inch) on either side of the nasal septum. The olfactory cleft is located in the "roof" of the nasal passages, high above the baffle-shaped **turbinate bones** (Fig. 8-3). Inspired air reaches this olfactory epithelium by eddy currents created by the turbinate bones, especially with vigorous sniffing. Expired air stimulates the olfactory epithelium by the rear access to the **nasopharynx** (for interoception). The olfactory epithelium is covered with mucus that bathes the odor-sensing hair endings (cilia) of the bipolar nerve cells. Presumably, odorous vapor must dissolve in mucus to reach the hairlike endings of the olfactory receptors because the hairs barely reach the surface of the mucus covering them.

Nervous system

The axonlike dendrites of smell-sensitive bipolar receptor cells pass through tiny holes in the bone that forms the roof of the

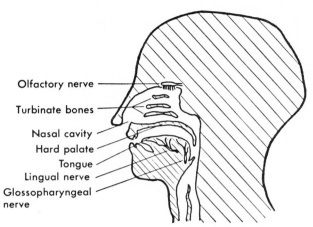

Fig. 8-3. Nasal passages. (From Pfaffman, C.: Studying the senses of taste and smell. In Andrews, R. C., editor: Methods of psychology, New York, 1948, John Wiley & Sons, Inc.)

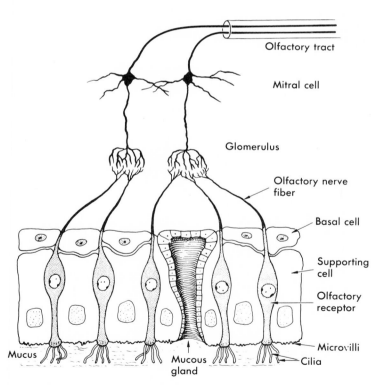

Fig. 8-4. Olfactory epithelium and neural connections to CNS. Orientation is similar to that of Fig. 8-3. (Modified by E. O. Gardner from Moulton, D. G., and Beidler, L. M.: Physiol. Rev. **47:**1-52, 1967, and from Schneider, R. A.: N. Engl. J. Med. **277:**299-303, 1967. In Gardner, E. O.: Fundamentals of neurology, ed. 6, Philadelphia, 1975, W. B. Saunders Company.)

nasal cavity and the floor of the braincase (Fig. 8-3). The fibers end in the **olfactory bulbs,** which are the swellings on the ends of the **olfactory tracts,** located on the base of the brain. The short bipolar nerve cells are the true olfactory nerves that form cranial nerve I (the olfactory bulbs and tracts are part of the brain). The bipolar cells end in complex synapses in the olfactory bulbs, called **glomeruli** (Fig. 8-4). Pathways in the olfactory tracts lead from here to the **prepiriform area** of the ventral surface of the cerebral cortex. This projection area is the oldest part of the cortex, phylogenetically, since the cerebral hemispheres originated as a correlating center for smell. Olfaction also shows its antiquity in that it is the only sensory input that does not relay excitation in the thalamus or related centers.

One fruitful approach to odor investigation is the study of the interaction of odors with one another. This approach uses the **mixing olfactometer.** Air is bubbled through several odorous substances into different tubes. The tubes are led to a mixer that can select any combination of them. The result is diluted by a known flow of outside air and led to a nose cone for smelling. Proportions of odorous mixes can be rather precisely controlled in this manner.

Thresholds. The findings for absolute and difference thresholds for odor vary according to the method used; thus olfactory data are not usually very reliable. An absolute threshold as low as 0.0004 mg/M^3 of air has been obtained for mercaptan, one of the most odorous substances known. This is about one molecule in 50 trillion. However, a 20 cc sniff would contain 10 trillion molecules of the substance. Calculations involving models of the nasal passages indicate that roughly 2% of inhaled molecules stimulate the receptors. Further calculations involving odor intensity and response probability suggest that only 40 cells must respond to the inhaled molecules to be detected by the subject! However, odor sensitivity does not com-

pare with visual or auditory sensitivity for the amount of molecular energy involved in the absolute threshold, but the threshold is lower than that for taste or somesthesia. Unlike other senses with low absolute thresholds, there is a rather high difference threshold for the sense of smell. Although the absolute threshold for odor is much less than that for taste, the difference thresholds are comparable.

Sensory mechanisms

To some extent an odorous substance must be (1) volatile, (2) soluble in water, and (3) soluble in fat. A *volatile* substance evaporates molecules into the air so that they may reach the olfactory receptors. Some powerful odors such as musk are not very volatile, but since sensitivity to them is high, relatively few molecules need to reach the receptors for detection. Volatility is a necessary but not sufficient condition for odor; pure water, for example, is highly volatile, but odorless. Most of the organic compounds are both odorous and volatile, whereas most inorganic compounds are neither. *Water solubility* is also related to odor. Presumably, odorous molecules must dissolve in the mucus covering the receptors in order to reach them, and mucus has a high water content. Exceptions can be found among the alcohols, however. *Fat solubility* may be related to odor because the cell membranes of the receptors contain fat and would be most sensitive to compounds that dissolve in cellular fat. Most fat-soluble compounds are odorous if they are also water-soluble. Yet exceptions can also be found to this rule: acetone, for example, is odorous but has low fat solubility. Fat and water solubility may, like volatility, be a necessary but not sufficient condition for odor. Very odorous compounds may require less water or fat solubility because relatively few molecules need to reach the receptors.

Recording

Recordings have been taken from the olfactory epithelium. Rabbits, fish, hedgehogs, and frogs are favorite subjects, because of the (relative) accessibility of the receptors. Records have been taken from the cat and even humans. Gross electrical responses of the receptor surface (the **electroolfactogram,** or EOG) are somewhat unreliable, single-cell recordings are difficult because of the size of the cells (about 1 μm in diameter), and tracing evoked potentials in the sensory pathways is a losing battle against background "noise." The potentials are also very sensitive to elimination by most anesthetics.

The EOG from the receptor surface is not a true generator potential for single-cell evoked potential response but serves as a rough indicator of receptor activity. There is some evidence for a primitive spatial patterning of different odors on the receptor surface (olfactory epithelium) from degeneration studies—lesions in the olfactory bulb affect this pattern—and from single-cell evoked potentials to different odors.

Theories of olfactory receptor mechanisms

There are several theories of how the olfactory receptor works, but only the most recent versions predict odors with reasonable accuracy.

The two most promising efforts at theorizing are comparatively recent. One attacks the code for smell from the point of view of the spatial and temporal (timing) characteristics of the receptor surface. The other theory rationalizes the shape and charge of the stimulating molecules. The two theories are not in conflict because they concern different aspects of the sensory code.

The first of these theories (Mozell) holds that the spatial and temporal characteristics of the receptor surface respond to different molecules in different ways, providing the brain with a "pattern" in space and time of the reaction of the surface for odor detection. This is the **gas chromatograph theory.** (Chemistry students will detect the resemblance of the pattern to a gas chro-

matograph.) Patterning of this sort has been recorded from branches of the olfactory nerves in the frog, and the idea is a promising one.

A later version of an old chemical theory is equally promising because it concerns the question of how the odor stimulus acts on the individual receptor cells. It is based on the *physical shape* or *electrical charge* of odorous molecules and is called the **stereochemical theory.** The theory does not specify the chemical event that is initiated in the receptor by the odorous molecule. The theory does state that the molecule must physically "fit" one or more of five *receptor sites,* or "holes," on the receptor hair endings or else be attracted by *positively* or *negatively charged* sites on the receptors. The seven sites, when individually stimulated, give rise to seven primary odor qualities. Stimulation of combinations of the primary sites gives rises to secondary, or mixed, odors. This occurs when a molecule will fit more than one site, depending on how it is oriented, or when a molecule is flexible enough to adapt itself to more than one site. More recently, the author of this theory (Amoore) has abandoned the "classical site-fitting concept" of his theory, but not the idea that the psychophysical basis for odor depends on molecular size and shape. The theory has also been modified to take into account the orientation of the molecule when it reaches the receptor surface—it might arrive "upside down," and probability modifications are thereby needed. Variations in stimulus volatility (vaporization) and adsorption of receptor surfaces further improve the predictive value of the theory.

Olfactory qualities: stereochemical theory. The idea that odorous substances give off molecules that must fit variously shaped "pores" in the receptors is an old one. In modern form it began with the observation that the molecules of most odorous substances had carbon chains four to eight carbons long. It was noted that a slight change in molecular geometry made a big difference in odor. The organic chemistry

Table 8. Primary odors and familiar stimuli that resemble them*

Primary quality	Familiar stimulus
Camphoraceous	Mothballs, camphor
Musky	Angelica root oil
Floral	Roses
Minty	Peppermint candy
Ethereal	Dry-cleaning fluid
Pungent	Vinegar
Putrid	Rotten egg

*Based on data from Amoore, J. E.: Ann. New York Acad. Sci. **116:**457-476, 1964.

literature was searched for data on odors. The seven primary qualities that resulted and familiar stimulus examples are given in Table 8. Information was then collected on the physical shapes of molecules stimulating the seven primary odors. In five cases, odors that smelled alike had molecules that were shaped alike. In the other two cases they had a similar charge. Pungent molecules had a deficiency of electrons and a positive charge and would be attracted to a negatively charged (excess electrons) site. Putrid molecules had excess electrons, were negatively charged, and presumably would be attracted to a positively charged (deficient electrons) site. Models were made of the molecules stimulating primary odors, and the shape of the receptor sites that would fit such molecules was predicted and modeled (Fig. 8-5). The ethereal site is a narrow slot, the camphoraceous a hemispherical basin, the musky a larger elliptical flat-bottomed pan, the floral keyhole-shaped, and the minty wedge-shaped. Tests of the theory have been made in which the primary or mixed odors were predicted from the shape or charge of over 200 compounds; only one prediction seemed incorrect. When a mixing olfactometer is used to compare odors, subjects cannot tell the difference between substances whose molecules fit the same receptor site. New organic molecules have been synthesized to fit receptor site models, and the resulting odors have been correctly predicted. Complex odors have been synthesized by mixing primary odors, and the odors of the mixtures have been predicted. The theory has an impressive amount of evidence in its support. The stereochemical theory is incomplete because it does not specify the chemical event that occurs at the receptor site. However, it has produced a list of seven very promising primary olfactory qualities and has accurately described the nature of their stimuli.

Olfactory phenomena

Adaptation. In common with most other senses, olfaction adapts rather readily. Adaptation is complete for most single odors; the time required depends on the intensity of the odor (usually varying from 1 to 10 minutes under laboratory conditions). This fact reduces the effect of the most expensive perfume to an initial impression! On the other hand, even the odor of a fertilizer factory is unnoticeable after 20 to 30 minutes. Adaptation to single odors can be dangerous, as when miners do not detect a gradual increase in methane gas, or a leak in a household gas line allows gas to permeate the air too gradually, so that the receptors adapt before it is noticed. Absence of smell stimuli for a time results in an increased sensitivity to various odors amounting to 10% to 40%, depending on the test odor. Apparently one is partially adapted to odors most of the time, including one's own body odor, when "even our best friends won't tell us." It is difficult to predict, however, what effect adaptation to one odor will have on another odor. Adaptation to one odor may raise or lower the threshold to another odor. It may also result in a change in quality for the second odor. For example, adaptation to camphor raises the odor threshold to eau de cologne, but it does not affect the threshold for benzaldehyde. **Compensation** between odors also occurs; for example, the odors of balsam and beeswax cancel one another. Odor often changes quality with changes in stimulus intensity. Ionone, a substance used in perfume, changes its odor from cedar-wood to violets with decreasing in-

Receptor   Odorant   Site plus
site   molecule   molecule

Ethereal

Camphoraceous

Musky

Floral

Minty

Fig. 8-5. Models of olfactory receptor sites and of molecules that "fit" them in the stereochemical theory of odor. (From Amoore, J. E.: Ann. N. Y. Acad. Sci. **116:**457-476, 1964.)

tensity. Perhaps adaptation effects in complex odors can be rationalized in terms of the stereochemical theory, but the attempt has not yet been made.

Anosmia. Complete lack of smell sensitivity is rare, but cases are known. It seems to be an inherited defect. **Anosmia** may also result from long-standing nasal irritation or from blocking of the nasal passages, as in a head cold. The anosmic individual can still "smell" substances in-

jected into the bloodstream, which shows that some functions of the receptors are intact. The chemical nature of the receptor process is supported by this observation and by the fact that certain odor thresholds (for example, macrocyclic lactone [Exaltolide]) vary with the estrogen level of the blood and therefore with the menstrual cycle in women. Temporary, partial, or complete anosmia can result from water in the nose, anesthesia, and other conditions.

SUMMARY

The senses that are normally and adequately stimulated by substances in solution are the chemical senses. They include the common chemical sense, gustation, and olfaction. The common chemical sense is pain sensitivity to dissolved irritants in the mucous membranes. It is most frequently stimulated by spicy foods in the mouth, but irritating vapors can also stimulate the eyes, which are more sensitive, and the nasal passages, which are still more sensitive. The nerve pathways are identical with those for skin pain, but the sensory quality seems different because the usual stimulus is different from that for skin pain. Adaptation is seldom complete because chemical stimulation is a process that is seldom constant; thus the receptor has no chance to adapt.

Gustation is limited to receptors on the tongue, palate, and larynx. The sensations commonly called "taste" include common chemical sensitivity, somesthesia from the mouth, and olfaction as well. The tongue receptors give rise to primary sensations of sweet, salt, sour, and bitter, in an ascending order of sensitivity that depends on temperature, when they are stimulated by solutions of sucrose, sodium chloride, hydrochloric acid, and quinine, respectively. The taste receptors on the tongue are in papillae, which are "moatlike" and "island-like" structures with taste buds lining their walls. The receptors developed from ordinary epithelial cells under the influence of sensory appropriation from nerves VII (anterior tongue) and IX (posterior tongue) and under the influence of the gonadal hormones. The tongue is most sensitive to salt and sweet at the tip, sour at the sides, and bitter at the back; the center is insensitive. These four primary qualities do not fuse to give novel secondary sensations.

Sour is primarily stimulated by the H^+ ion. Salt sensations are usually caused by Na^+ cations or Cl^- anions, or both. Sweet substances are organic molecules with short carbon chains, and bitter substances include quinine, alkaloids, and complex inorganic salts. Salts often taste bitter at threshold, and concentrated sweet stimuli can taste bitter. Molecular size and shape are important in sweet and bitter stimuli. The nerve pathways for taste have their own primary nucleus—the nucleus of the tractus solitarius—but the second- and third-order neurons follow the somesthetic pathways to the cortex via the thalamus.

Experiments with microelectrode recording in the nerve pathway and with the stimulation of individual taste receptors by micropipettes show that gustation has unusually long generator potentials and that there are different types of taste receptors in response characteristics. Some complex *pattern* of input signals each quality, because individual taste nerve cells respond to more than one quality. In addition, taste neurons serve two or more receptors, as shown in single-fiber experiments with cats. Other neurons respond to both temperature and taste.

Taste sensitivity is also dependent on stimulus temperature, with thresholds for all four qualities except sour being lowest in a range near body temperature. Within this range, difference thresholds vary as intensity is increased. Taste adaptation is most rapid in the same temperature range where the receptors are most sensitive, indicating that the adaptation is caused by the receptor rather than by the central nervous system. Complete adaptation is not found outside the laboratory because, under ordinary circumstances, the substance being tasted is moved about the mouth from one receptor to another.

For complex tastes, adaptation is usually prevented by mixing tastes, as in drinking wine with food. The primary qualities, however, interact to enhance or depress one another. Fusion does not occur.

Olfaction is important as an exteroceptor in exploring the environment and important as an interoceptor because it forms part of "taste." Although olfaction as an exteroceptor is not as useful for humans as for other animals, human reactions to smell are equally important. However, research on smell has been hampered by the sensitivity of the receptor and its inaccessibility. Thus little is known of the physiology of smell. The receptors are hairlike endings on bipolar nerve cells that are bathed in mucus. They are located on both sides of the nasal septum on the roof of the nasal cavity above the turbinate bones. The two smell-sensitive areas are each called an olfactory cleft, or olfactory epithelium. Eddy currents of air created by the turbinate bones reach the receptor from the nostrils or the nasopharynx. Vaporized substances in the air stimulate the bipolar cell receptors. The axonlike dendrites of the bipolar cells reach the olfactory bulbs through holes in the bony roof of the nasal cavity and constitute cranial nerve I. Synapses, called glomeruli, transfer the excitation to second-order neurons going to the prepiriform area of the cortex.

For controlled stimulation of the receptor, the newest techniques involve the use of a mixing olfactometer. Threshold data vary widely according to the method used as well as the stimulus odor. Despite the sensitivity of the receptor, the difference thresholds are comparable to those for taste. Volatility, water solubility, and fat solubility seem necessary conditions for smell stimuli. The stimulus must reach the receptors as vapor, dissolve in watery mucus, and affect receptors whose membrane includes fat. Most organic compounds meet these conditions; most inorganic compounds do not. Recordings have been taken from the olfactory epithelium in animals (EOG) and from the nerve cells in animals and humans.

The gas chromatograph theory asserts that the sensory code has a spatiotemporal character. The stereochemical theory states that an odorous molecule must physically "fit" one of five receptor sites or be attracted to a negatively charged or a positively charged site. The seven primary odor qualities that result are ethereal, camphoraceous, musky, floral, minty, pungent, and putrid. The shapes of the receptor sites have been predicted from the shapes of the molecules. Subjects cannot tell the difference between odors whose molecules would fit the same receptor sites, and the odors of synthesized molecules have been predicted. Flexible molecules that would fit more than one site have mixed odors that are equally predictable. The theory is incomplete because it does not specify the chemical event that occurs at the receptor site.

In other olfactory phenomena, adaptation to single odors is complete in less than a half hour, usually in one to ten minutes. An individual is usually 10% to 40% odor adapted under normal conditions. Adaptation to one odor may lower the threshold to another odor (compensation), raise the threshold to another odor (compensation), or change the quality of another odor. These effects have been unpredictable so far. Complete anosmia occurs, but this is rare. It may be inherited or caused by damage to, or blocking of, the nasal passages. Since even anosmic people can "smell" substances in the bloodstream, the receptor events are probably chemical in nature.

READINGS

Amoore, J. E., Johnston, J. W., and Rubin, M.: The stereochemical theory of odor, Sci. Am. **210:**42-49, Feb. 1964 (W. H. Freeman Reprint No. 297).

Haagen-Smit, A. J.: Smell and taste, Sci. Am. **186:**28-32, March 1952 (W. H. Freeman Reprint No. 404).

Mueller, C. G.: Sensory psychology, Englewood Cliffs, N.J., 1965, Prentice-Hall, Inc.

Pfaffman, C.: The afferent code for sensory quality, Am. Psychol. **14:**226-232, May 1959 (Bobbs-Merrill Reprint No. P-275).

von Békésy, G.: Taste theories and the chemical stimulation of single papillae. In Gross, C. G., and Zeigler, H. P., editors: Readings in physiological psychology, New York, 1969, Harper & Row, Publishers.

von Buddenbrock, W.: The senses, Ann Arbor, 1958, University of Michigan Press.

CHAPTER 9

Audition: how we hear

OVERVIEW

The sense of hearing, called audition, is the subject of this chapter. Audition is the most complex sensory input thus far explained. (Vision is equally complex, if not more so.) To understand audition requires some knowledge of (1) the nature of the *physical energy* that provides the sensory stimulus and (2) the anatomy of the auditory mechanism. With this background, (3) the *physiology* and (4) *psychophysics* of hearing can be understood. These are the topics of the chapter in their order of presentation.

The stimulus energy will be explained first in its simplest form, a sine wave of periodic changes in air pressure. A sine wave "tone" has simple characteristics of amplitude, frequency, and phase. More complex tones are also periodic waves of sound energy. Complex periodic waves are subject to a frequency analysis that reduces them to sine waves; aperiodic waves ("noise") cannot be consistently reduced to sine waves. The anatomy of the receptor mechanism that responds to sound energy is the next topic. The parts of the outer, middle, and inner ears change air pressure waves into vibrations of receptor cells in the organ of Corti. The nerve impulses that result are carried to the brain along the pathways described next. The organization of the input is further improved by output pathways from the brain back to sensory nuclei and receptors.

The physiology and psychophysics of hearing involve the study of the manner in which these sensory and nervous mechanisms permit the brain to analyze pitch and loudness. Pitch is analyzed by the location of stimulus effects on hair cells along the length of the organ of Corti. A different set of hair cells responds to increased vibrations of the organ of Corti in detecting loudness. Both sets of hair cells set up the "generator potential" (which can be detected as a cochlear microphonic potential), and this potential probably causes sensory nerve impulses. Disturbance of any part of the auditory mechanism can cause auditory defects. Different kinds of auditory defects result from impairment of outer, middle, or inner ear mechanisms. The psychophysics of hearing involves absolute and difference thresholds for intensity and frequency as well as sound localization.

PHYSICS OF SOUND

Any solid body will vibrate when struck, however brief its motion. The vibrations of some solid objects are regular, consistent, or periodic. This is true of a tuning fork, for example (Fig. 9-1). The regular movements of the tuning fork have a characteristic frequency or rate as well as a characteristic amplitude or extent. The motions of the tines of the tuning fork cause it to strike molecules of air. The air molecules collide with one another to transmit energy from molecule to molecule as the molecules vibrate back and

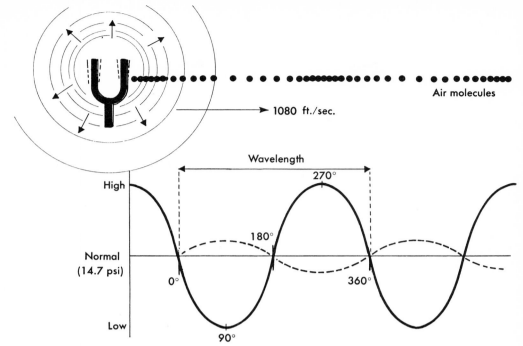

Fig. 9-1. Characteristics of sound energy. Vibrations of a tuning fork cause collisions of air molecules that radiate air pressure variations in all directions. Variations can be plotted as a simple sine wave. The sine wave has characteristics of amplitude, wavelength, frequency, and phase.

forth. The energy radiates in all directions from the vibrating source. Since the vibrating source has a consistent frequency and amplitude of vibration, so do the air molecules. Air pressure is determined by how close together the molecules are. Since the air molecules are colliding with one another and then moving apart in a regular fashion, waves of air pressure *change* constitute sound. Pressure changes of consistent frequency and amplitude *are* the sound that radiates outward from the sound source.

Sine wave

Certain uniform bodies vibrate with a simple motion. The sound waves they produce—alternatively compressed and rarefied air molecules—have a simple pattern of air pressure change. The molecules alternately strike one another in a compressed area and are driven apart in a rar-

efied area. Since air pressure is merely the density of air molecules, pressure at a given point will be first above, then below, normal pressure. A graph of the pressure changes of air with the distance from the vibrating source gives a simple sine wave of air pressure change at any given instant (Fig. 9-1).

Amplitude. The amount of compression and rarefaction of the air molecules will depend on how hard the tuning fork is struck and therefore on how far the tines of the fork vibrate back and forth to condense and rarefy the air. **Amplitude** is the total amount of air pressure change from condensation to rarefaction (higher to lower air pressure). Changes in amplitude are detected by the ear as changes in **loudness.** (The intensity of the stimulus is proportional to the square of the amplitude of the pressure change.)

Frequency. Different tuning forks will

vibrate at different rates, each having a characteristic **frequency** of vibration. Frequency, or rate of vibration, used to be stated in cycles per second, abbreviated as cps. The unit most commonly used now means the same thing. It is the **hertz,** usually abbreviated **Hz,** defined as 1 cycle per second. So 1 cps is 1 Hz. One Hz is one complete back-and-forth vibration of the tuning fork and results in a compression, then a rarefaction, and finally a return to normal pressure (Fig. 9-1). If the tuning fork vibrates rapidly, it has a high rate of vibration, or a high frequency; if it vibrates slowly, it has a low frequency. The **wavelength** of a sine wave of pressure change is the distance over which a single cycle of air pressure change extends at a given instant. High-frequency, or rapid, vibrations result in short wavelengths. Low-frequency vibrations have long wavelengths. (The amplitude may remain the same for high- and low-frequency vibrations.) The relationship between frequency and wavelength is usually constant because sound waves travel at a fixed rate. In air, sound travels at 1,080 feet per second at sea level and 0° C. A compression and rarefaction wavelength of 1,080 feet could pass a given point once each second if the sound has a frequency of 1 Hz. If the wavelength were 108 feet, the sound wave would pass a given point ten times per second, for a frequency of 10 Hz (10 Hz × 108 feet = 1,080 feet per second). Frequency and wavelength can therefore be translated into one another. Frequency is usually the term used in sound. The ear detects differences in frequency as differences in **pitch.** In a denser medium than air (for example, water), sound travels at a higher rate since the molecules are closer together and need not travel so far to strike one another. As a result, wavelengths are shorter and frequencies are higher. For example, an outboard motor has a higher-pitched sound when one listens to it with his head under water. At high altitudes in air the molecules are farther apart and must travel farther to strike

one another. As a result, sound transmission is slower and apparent frequencies are lower. The rate at which sound moves in air can be appreciated by watching someone chop wood a half mile away. The sound will require more than 2 seconds to reach you after the axman swings—he may have raised the ax for a second stroke before you hear the sound of the first stroke.

Phase. A complete sound pressure wave goes from normal to compression to normal to rarefaction to normal again. The point reached by the alternating pressure wave at a given time and place can be specified in terms of 360 degrees as a complete cycle (Fig. 9-1). The beginning point could be taken as 0 degrees, with the first rarefaction peak as 90 degrees, normal as 180 degrees, compression as 270 degrees, and normal again as 360 degrees. If one sine wave is in compression while the other is in rarefaction, the first would be at 90 degrees in the cycle when the second is at 270 degrees. They would therefore be 270 minus 90 degrees, or 180 degrees, *out of phase* and exert opposite effects on air pressure at that instant.

Measurements of amplitude and loudness

Frequency is measured in hertz, and phase is measured in degrees. How, then, does one measure the amplitude of a sound wave? A complex average of the amount of pressure variation over each cycle is sometimes used by engineers, who integrate the square root of the mean square of pressure variation. This is done because a high-frequency tone has more rapid pressure variations and contains more energy than does a low-frequency tone of the same amplitude. However, most sound amplitude measurements are made to apply to human use. A physical intensity scale has therefore been developed that matches the characteristics of the human ear as closely as possible—the **decibel (db) scale.** The zero point of the scale approximates the absolute threshold of the human ear—an energy level of 0.0002

Table 9. Sound levels of some noises found in different environments
(intensities above 100 db may impair hearing)*

Overall level, db (re 0.0002 microbar)		Industrial and military	Community or outdoor	Home or indoor
130†		Armored personnel carrier (123 db)		
	Uncomfortably loud			
120		Oxygen torch (121 db) Scraper-loader (117 db) Compactor (116 db)		Rock band (108 to 114 db)
110		Riveting machine (110 db) Textile loom (106 db)	Jet flyover, 1,000 ft. (103 db)	
100	Very loud	Electric furnace area (100 db) Farm tractor (98 db) Newspaper press (97 db)	Power mower (96 db) Compressor, 20 ft. (94 db) Rock drill, 100 ft. (92 db)	Inside subway car, 35 mph (95 db) Cockpit—light aircraft (90 db)
90		Cockpit—propeller aircraft (88 db) Milling machine (85 db) Cotton spinning (83 db)	Motorcycles, 25 ft. (90 db) Propeller aircraft fly-over, 1,000 ft. (88 db)	Food blender (88 db) Garbage disposal (80 db) Clothes washer (78 db)
80	Moderately loud	Lathe (81 db)	Diesel truck, 40 mph, 50 ft. (84 db)	Living room music (76 db) Dishwasher (75 db)
70			Passenger car, 65 mph, 25 ft. (77 db) Near freeway, auto traffic (64 db)	TV—audio (70 db)
60			Air-conditioning unit, 20 ft. (60 db) Large transformer, 200 ft. (53 db)	Conversation (60 db)
50	Quiet		Light traffic, 100 ft. (50 db)	
40				
30	Very quiet			
20				
10	Just audible Threshold of hearing			
0	(1000 to 4000Hz)			

*From Cohen, A., Anticaglia, J. R., and Jones, H. H.: Noise-induced hearing loss, Arch. Environ. Health **20:**614-623, 1970.
†Unless otherwise specified, listed sound levels are measured at typical operator-listener distances from source.

dyne/cm² for a 1000-cycle tone. (A dyne is the amount of energy required to accelerate 1 gram at 1 cm/sec². The zero point is only 10 db above the point at which one would "hear" the random motion of molecules caused by heat!) Decibels of increase in intensity are on a scale based on the bel scale. The bel scale is chosen because it is a logarithmic scale in which the physical units increase in size at higher intensities. The human ear requires a larger increase in sound intensity for the same loudness difference, with more intense stimuli. If zero bels is 0.0002 dyne/cm², 1 bel is 10^1 (or 10) × 0.0002 dyne/cm² and 2 bels is 10^2 (or 100) × 0.0002 dyne/cm², and so on. However, a smaller unit is required to match the difference threshold of the human ear; therefore the decibel, or "tenth" of a bel, is used. To be technical, the number of decibels between two sound intensities, I_1 and I_2, is 10 log I_1/I_2. The decibel intensities of certain common sounds are given in Table 9. (In Table 9, the 0.0002 dyne/cm² reference is in terms of the minimum audible field (MAF), the pressure change in the air where the subject is located (in a theoretically echo-free open space). Sometimes sound stimuli are delivered by earphones so that the pressure delivered to the eardrum can be calibrated as the sound pressure level (SPL), giving lower threshold measurements.

Types of sound waves

The major characteristics of sound waves have been explained so far in terms of air pressure changes from a simple vibrating body that produces a simple **sine wave** of pressure variation with time or distance. The change is *simple* and *periodic* and results in a **simple tone** (Fig. 9-1). A complex body may vibrate with more than one frequency, and the pressure waves of sound that result may be periodic or aperiodic. If the complex vibrating body has many parts, each with its own characteristic frequency and amplitude of vibration, several sine waves of pressure variation may be produced at once (Fig. 9-2). As

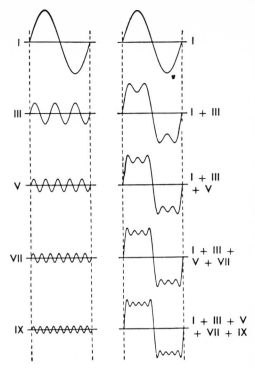

Fig. 9-2. Components of a complex sound wave. As sine waves shown on *left* are added to fundamental wave at *top*, increasingly complex periodic waves shown at *right* result. (From Newman, E. B.: Hearing. In Boring, E. G., Langfeld, H. S., and Weld, H. B., editors: Foundations of psychology, New York, 1948, John Wiley & Sons, Inc.)

these sine waves come in and out of phase because of their differing frequencies of vibration, they will alternately reinforce and cancel each other, as far as air pressure changes are concerned. A complex but repeated wave pattern will result—a **complex periodic wave** that is heard as a **complex tone.** However, if the component parts of the vibrating body begin and end vibrating at different times, the complex wave will not repeat itself; it will be **aperiodic.** Aperiodic complex vibrations constitute **noise,** especially when many high-frequency (high-pitched) components are in the complex. As a result, noise is harsh sounding and variable in character.

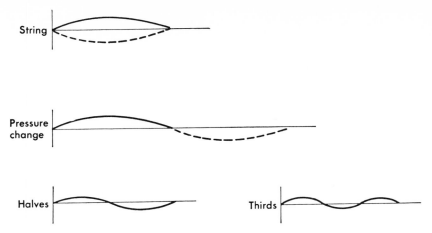

Fig. 9-3. Vibrations of violin string. String vibrates at a fundamental frequency whose corresponding wave length is twice the string's length. Overtones occur when the string also vibrates in halves, thirds, and so on.

Frequency analysis. Frequency analysis consists of analyzing a complex periodic tone to show its component sine waves of pressure change (Fig. 9-2). These sine waves have frequencies that are related to one another in a lawful way. The physical basis for the frequency analysis is best understood in terms of a simple example, such as the sound produced by plucking a violin string.

Harmonics

If a violin string is plucked, it will vibrate up and down, alternately compressing and rarefying the air molecules. The sine wave of pressure change that results will have a wavelength of twice the length of the violin string (Fig. 9-3). The length of the string can represent only the compression or the rarefaction half of the cycle of pressure change at any given moment as it vibrates back and forth. This simple vibration represents the largest movement of the string, and the resulting frequency is called the **fundamental,** or **first harmonic,** frequency. However, the string also has a smaller "double vibration"—it vibrates in halves (Fig. 9-3). The double vibration will produce a sine wave of half the wavelength and twice the frequency of the fundamental tone. The double vibration is the **first**

overtone, or **second harmonic.** The string also vibrates in thirds to produce the second overtone, or third harmonic, and so on. The frequencies of these sine waves are a function of their wavelengths. If the fundamental, or first, harmonic has a frequency of n, then the first overtone, or second harmonic, has a frequency of $2n$, the second overtone, or third harmonic, has a frequency of $3n$, and so on. This relationship between the fundamental frequency and the overtone frequencies is called **Fourier's law.** (The application of Fourier's law to sound waves is sometimes called Ohm's acoustic law to distinguish this application from the same law applied to other periodic phenomena such as heat, with which Fourier originally developed the principle.) Of course these simple sine waves combine into a complex periodic wave in the manner shown in Fig. 9-2.

Resonance

If a violin string is stretched between two points in open air, the amplitude of the fundamental frequency and the amplitude of the overtones would bear a simple relation to one another. The first overtone would be greater than the second, the second greater than the third, and so on; the complex periodic wave of pressure change would be formed accordingly. However, the string is stretched across the body of a "sound box," or resonance chamber—the violin. Each part of the violin has a frequency with which it naturally vibrates when struck. The size of the air chamber in the violin also reinforces sound waves—those whose wavelength is a multiple of the length of the sound chamber. When the parts of a violin are struck with air molecules at their natural frequency, they vibrate, or **resonate,** to amplify that frequency; thus the amplitude of certain overtone frequencies is increased. Although the fundamental frequency will be the largest component of the complex wave, various overtones will be increased in size in a pattern unique to the violin. The relative size of various overtones will be different for the same fundamental note played on a trumpet, for example. This variation in overtone pattern is recognized by the human ear as a difference in **timbre.** The violin has more parts that resonate with lower overtones; the trumpet has more parts that resonate with higher overtones. Their air chambers differ in a similar way. As a result the overtone pattern of the violin has a louder pattern of low overtones than does the trumpet. This is why the same note played on the two instruments "sounds different" in timbre.

ANATOMY

Analysis of the air pressure variations that form sound has shown the complexity of this form of stimulus. What kind of receptor apparatus can transduce differences in sound frequency, amplitude, and overtone patterns into nerve impulses in such a way that the brain can detect the corresponding differences in pitch, loudness, and timbre? As a receptor the auditory apparatus changes air pressure vibrations into vibrations of a fluid medium. The fluid vibrations in turn set off nerve impulses by acting on the hair cells of the organ of Corti, a modified "touch receptor." The timing and spatial distribution of the nerve impulses provide the brain with the cues to pitch, loudness, and

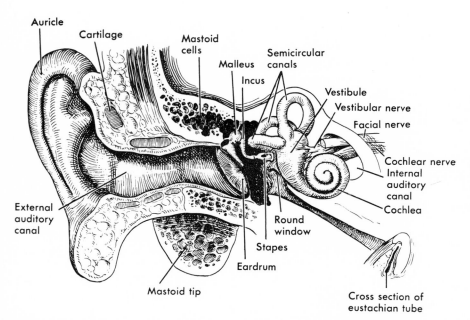

Fig. 9-4. Semidiagrammatic drawing of ear. (From Davis, H., and Silverman, S. R., editors: Hearing and deafness, New York, 1960, Holt, Rinehart & Winston, Inc.)

timbre. Further understanding of how all this is accomplished depends on knowing the parts of the auditory apparatus and how they relate to one another.

Outer ear

The **outer ear** consists of the **pinna** (auricle), **external auditory meatus** (canal), and **tympanum,** or eardrum (Figs. 9-4 and 9-5). The pinna is what you probably refer to as your ear—the convoluted flap that extends from the side of the head. It functions to collect air vibrations and funnel them into the external auditory meatus. Humans have lost most of the muscular control of the pinna (except for "wiggling" the ears as a parlor trick), but lower animals such as dogs and donkeys move the pinna in orienting themselves toward the source of sound—they "prick up" their ears. The external auditory meatus is the canal that curves through the mastoid bone of the skull to conduct vibrations to the tympanum which seals off its inner end. The tympanum is a membrane that vibrates in response to the pressure waves of sound. It is cone-shaped like a loudspeaker and pivots on a fold at its lower rim.

Middle ear

The **middle ear** contains the three bony **ossicles** that are vibrated mechanically by the rapid movements of the tympanum. The ossicles conduct vibrations to the fluid-filled inner ear. The **malleus,** or hammer, is connected to the eardrum. It moves the **incus** (anvil), which in turn moves the **stapes** (stirrup). The three bones are firmly connected by ligaments and vibrate almost as a unit. The stapes fits into the **oval window** of the fluid-filled inner ear and is sealed in place by a membrane. The lever system of the ossicles has little mechanical advantage, but the smaller area of the oval window and stapes, as compared to the eardrum, provides a good impedance match between air and the more resistant fluid medium of the inner ear. The small variations in air pressure, distributed over the larger eardrum, are concentrated on the smaller oval win-

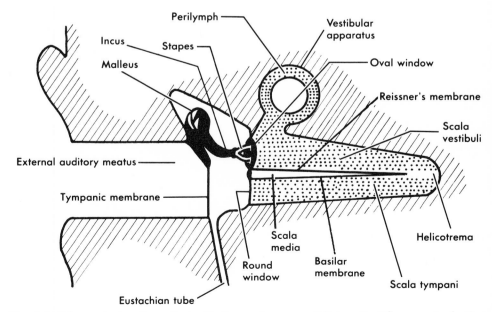

Fig. 9-5. Schematic drawing of ear. (Redrawn from von Békésy, G.: Pflueger. Arch. Ges. Physiol. **236:**58-76, 1935.)

dow to vibrate the fluid of the inner ear, because fluid is more resistant to movement than is air. To prevent this sensitive mechanism from being "overdriven" by loud sounds of low frequency, two muscles act to limit the motion of the ossicles. The **tensor tympani** pulls on the malleus to tighten the tympanum, and the **stapedius** pulls on the stapes to limit its motion at the oval window in response to loud sounds. These muscles, especially the stapedius, contract in a reflex reaction to loud sounds at frequencies below 1,000 Hz, where the amplitude of motion is greatest. The reflex may reduce sound intensity by as much as 20 db. As a chamber the middle ear is sealed off from the outside changes in atmospheric pressure. The **eustachian tube** connects with the rear of the oral cavity (mouth) and is opened to equalized pressure with the outside air in the act of swallowing or yawning. Any pressure difference is felt in the eardrums, which explains why they seem to "pop" if you swallow or yawn after a change in altitude. Outside air pressure changes with altitude, but middle ear pressure cannot change unless the eustachian tube is opened.

Inner ear

The **inner ear** contains the **cochlea,** which is coiled (2¾ turns) like a snail shell. There are three chambers in the cochlea (Figs. 9-5 and 9-6). The **scala vestibuli** begins at the oval window and is the "upper" chamber. It communicates with the "lower" **scala tympani** at the apex of the cochlea coil via a small opening, the **helicotrema.** The membrane-covered **round window** is found at the other end of the scala tympani. Both the scala vestibuli and scala tympani are filled with fluid **perilymph.** The third chamber of the cochlea is the **scala media,** or **cochlear**

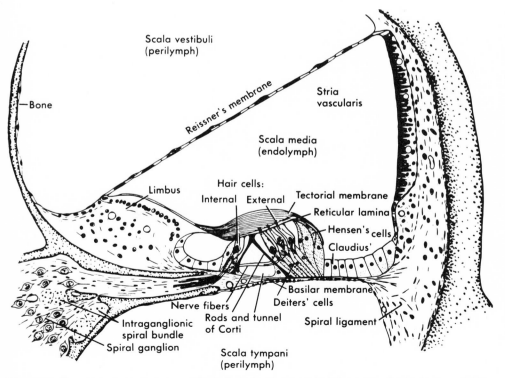

Fig. 9-6. Cross section of the cochlear duct (guinea pig). (From Davis, H. R., et al.: J. Acoust. Soc. Am. **25:**1180, 1953.)

duct. It is filled with fluid **endolymph** and does not communicate with the other two scalae. The scala media is triangular in cross section (Fig. 9-6), with **Reissner's membrane** separating it from the scala vestibuli as a "roof." The bony **spiral osseous lamina** forms part of the "floor" of the scala media, and the membranous **basilar membrane** completes the division from the scala tympani. The function of these parts of the cochlea is best appreciated in a schematic diagram such as Fig. 9-5. Air vibrations (sound) are transmitted from the eardrum to the stapes through the other ossicles. The footplate of the stapes vibrates in and out of the oval window. Pressure changes in the perilymph of the scala vestibuli result. The pressure changes are transferred to the endolymph of the scala media through the flexible Reissner's membrane. The pressure changes in the scala media affect the scala tympani through the basilar membrane. Since fluid is incompressible, pressure changes in the scala tympani cause the membrane over the round window to bulge in and out. There is little movement of fluid through the helicotrema caused by pressure changes in the perilymph, except in response to sound of very low frequency.

Organ of Corti. The **organ of Corti** is the receptor structure that rests on the basilar membrane (Fig. 9-6). It transduces vibrations of the basilar membrane into nerve impulses when the **hair cells** are bent by the motions of the basilar membrane. The hairs of the hair cells are bent because they are thrust into an overlying **tectorial membrane.** The organ of Corti extends along the basilar membrane from its base to its apex. It is organized in a **tonotopic** fashion, with hair cells near the base of the basilar membrane (near the round and oval windows) being more affected by tones of high frequency and hair cells near the apex (toward the helicotrema) being more affected by tones of low frequency. The reasons for this organization will be explained later. One feature of anatomy that contributes to tonotopic or-

ganization should be mentioned now, however. Although the cross section of the cochlea narrows from base to apex of its coil, the width of the spiral lamina narrows faster than the width of the whole cochlear duct. As a result, the basilar membrane *widens* as one traces it from the base to the apex of the cochlea. Neurons from the hair cells leave the organ of Corti all along the basilar membrane, from base to apex. Some neurons from near the base of the basilar membrane respond more readily to high-pitched tones; some from near the apex respond more readily to low-pitched tones.

Nervous connections of the ear

The nerve cells that invade the hair cells of the organ of Corti form the acoustic branch of the eighth, or **statoacoustic, nerve.** The first-order neurons reach the **dorsal** and **ventral cochlear nuclei** of the medulla on either side of the brain stem (Fig. 9-7). Second-order neurons from the dorsal nucleus cross the floor of the fourth ventricle (a band of fibers seen as the acoustic striae). Second-order neurons from the ventral nucleus either ascend without crossing or cross (and sometimes synapse) in the trapezoid body that forms a bulge across the ventral hind brain behind the pons. Other important connections are made to a nucleus of the medulla, called the **olive.** The ascending fibers form the **lateral lemniscus.** Synapses for reflex movements (such as turning the head in response to sound) are made in the **inferior colliculus** as well as in ascending and descending pathways going to the cranial and spinal nerves. The lateral lemniscus ends in the **medial geniculate body,** near the thalamus. From here, neurons reach the **auditory projection area** (area 41) on the temporal lobe. Input from the cochlea of each ear reaches the projection area of both hemispheres. However, the tonotopic organization of the cochlea is preserved at the cortex, with high, middle, and low tones stimulating different parts of the projection area.

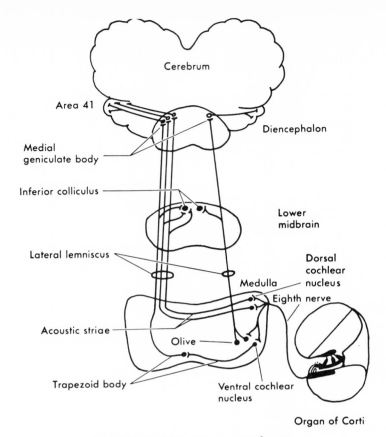

Fig. 9-7. Auditory nervous pathways.

PHYSIOLOGY OF THE COCHLEA
Tonotopic organization

It has already been stated that high-pitched tones stimulate the organ of Corti most near the base of the cochlea, and low-pitched tones stimulate most nearer the apex of the cochlea. There are three factors responsible for this relationship: (1) the laws of fluid motion, (2) traveling waves in the basilar membrane, and (3) the relative width and compliance of the basilar membrane.

Fluid motion. In a fluid medium, low-frequency (long-wavelength) vibrations reach maximum amplitude farther from the source than do high-frequency vibrations. One may illustrate this by vibrating one end of a heavy water-filled balloon with a tuning fork while the forearm is resting along its length. The lower the frequency of the tuning fork, the farther away from the tuning fork will maximum vibrations be felt on the skin. In the cochlea the lower the frequency of vibration of the stapes against the oval window, the farther away from the base of the cochlea will fluid displacement of the basilar membrane be at a maximum.

Traveling waves. The basilar membrane is under no tension and is of a limp and "leathery" consistency. However, it is stiffer near the base where the membrane is narrow than it is at the broader and more resilient apex. Because of this, the traveling waves will always move from base to apex, even if the vibrations are applied to parts of the cochlea other than their normal source at the oval window at the base of the cochlea. (This explains why bone-conducted sounds seem natural, even though the vibrations are conducted all over the cochlea. A tuning fork vibrated against the mastoid bone behind the ear does not change pitch and the bone-conducted vibrations of your own voice sound natural even though the timbre is different from listening to a recording of your voice.) Low-frequency vibrations cause maximum movement farther from the source of the vibrations (oval window); high-frequency vibrations, or fast movements, are maximum nearer the source of the movement.

Width of the basilar membrane. As previously described, the basilar membrane *widens* from base to apex of the cochlea. As a result the mass of the basilar membrane is least near the base of the cochlea and is less resistant there to rapid, high-frequency motion. Near the apex it is wider, has greater mass, and is therefore less resistant only to low-frequency motion. The resistance to motion of the basilar membrane changes by a factor of 100 from base to apex.

Pitch mechanisms

The location of maximum displacement of the basilar membrane is more precise for high frequencies than for low; below 50 Hz, for example, the whole basilar membrane vibrates almost as a unit. Yet pitch discrimination is excellent at low frequencies. It is now believed that the efferent fibers to the organ of Corti sharpen the tonotopic input, inhibiting input from areas along the length of the organ of Corti that do not receive maximum stimulation. Single cell recordings show that the efferent fibers respond to tones of over 40 db in loudness. The fibers that fire are inhibitory fibers going to the *region* of the organ of Corti that receives maximum stimulation at a given pitch. This should assure a sharp "cut-off" of the input from sensory fibers near the place along the length of the organ of Corti where maximum stimulation occurs. Localization

of the point of maximum stimulation along the organ of Corti would be thereby improved. Pitch discrimination could still, then, depend on tonotopic organization of the organ of Corti even at low frequencies.

A second factor accounts for better pitch discrimination at low frequencies than at high frequencies—the **volley principle** of pitch discrimination. It was once believed that individual nerve cells could fire at the same frequency as the sound stimulating them to carry pitch information to the brain (telephone theory). This idea came up against the absolute refractory period of nerve cells, which is at least one millisecond (1 msec, or 1/1000 second). As a result, nerve cells could fire no more than 1,000 times per second, yet we can detect frequencies of up to 20,000 Hz! At the lower frequency ranges—up to about 5,000 Hz—the volley principle can explain the contradiction. A small group of nerve cells can fire in "relays" to carry the overall frequency information. By analogy, four riflemen who can each load and fire every four seconds can fire one round per second as a "volley." (Eight riflemen would have a two-round volley.) Frequency following of this sort has been found in groups of individual cells of the auditory nerve in the squirrel monkey for frequencies of up to 5,000 Hz.

Loudness mechanisms

The detection of loudness differences depends on more hair cells firing more neurons as a result of an increase in the motion of the basilar membrane. This chain of events must occur irrespective of the location of the displacement along the basilar membrane and organ of Corti. Evoked potential measurements show that the relationship between intensity of sound stimulation and frequency of firing in individual nerve cells remains remarkably constant for the inferior colliculus, medial geniculate body, white matter of the cortex, and the cortex itself. The intensity mechanism seems to be governed by a part of the organ of Corti.

The organ of Corti includes two "rows" of hair cells (Fig. 9-6). The inner row has a single column of hair cells, and the outer row has three columns of hair cells. The outer row appears to be a loudness detection mechanism that responds to minimum intensity levels. There are two reasons for this supposition. (1) The outer row of hair cells is farthest from the "pivot points" of the basilar membrane and tectorial membrane (Fig. 9-6); as the basilar membrane and tectorial membrane "flap" up and down, they bend the hair cells in a lateral direction to fire nerve impulses. The outer-row hair cells are bent more by this motion than are the inner-row hair cells. (2) Several hair cells are innervated by each neuron going to the outer row, and an outer-row hair cell may be supplied by many nerve endings. This constitutes a *summation* mechanism; the generator potentials of several bending hair cells add their effects in order to fire a single neuron.

Differences in the innervation of the inner- and outer-row hair cells also support the idea that they function as pitch and loudness detectors, respectively. Studies with the electron microscope reveal two types of nerve cell endings that "contact" the hair cells. The small ones (type 1) are believed to be the efferent inhibitory fibers referred to in the preceding section. The larger endings (type 2) are the sensory endings. The inner-row hair cells show more large sensory endings than small inhibitory endings, in keeping with their role as detectors of the place of maximum stimulation along the basilar membrane. The outer-row hair cells show more variety in the ratio of large to small endings, corresponding to their more variable thresholds as loudness detectors.

Pitch and the hair cells

The inner row of hair cells seems designed to respond to the *place* along the length of the organ of Corti that is most displaced by sound. There are three reasons for this assumption. (1) The "traveling waves" of displacement have a maximum area of motion along the basilar membrane that depends on wavelength and therefore on frequency. (2) The inner-row hair cells seem to have a higher threshold than do the outer-row cells. As a result, they would respond only to the area of *maximum* displacement of the basilar membrane. As noted above, this location depends critically on pitch. (3) Each inner hair cell has 10 to 20 nerve fiber endings, and each fiber supplies 10 to 20 hair cells, providing for an overlapping "one-to-one" system. Each hair cell has a more or less "private" line in the auditory pathway to enable the brain to detect where the stimulation came from along the length of the organ of Corti. This improves discrimination by the central nervous system of which hair cells are firing neurons—and therefore where the organ of Corti was most stimulated along its length.

Cochlear microphonic

The individual hair cells bend in response to sound in a manner already described. The bending of the hair cells produces a change in a current that is continually flowing through them. This *change* in current flow probably constitutes a "generator potential" that fires the sensory neurons going to the hair cells. As originally recorded from the surface of the cochlea, such electrical changes are known as the **cochlear microphonic** because they differ from nerve impulses in certain important respects: (1) they are not "all-or-none" in character (Chapter 3) but increase in size as the stimulus increases in intensity (by contrast, a nerve cell fires or does not fire with a *rate* that depends on stimulus intensity) and (2) the electrical changes faithfully reproduce the *form* as well as the frequency of the sound wave stimulus. Nerve cell firing is an electrical change that is unlike the wave form of the stimulus. The cochlear microphonic potentials act like the electrical changes produced in a microphone by sound—they can be amplified to reproduce the sound through a loudspeaker. Microelectrode recording has shown that the cochlear microphonic originates at the cuticular ("skin") surface of the hair cells. (3) The wave forms of the cochlear microphonic "follow" frequencies as high as 16,000 Hz, where nerve cell firing cannot follow the higher frequencies.

Cochlear duct potential. There is a potential difference between the scala media and the other two scalae or any other indifferent point of the body fluids. The potential difference is technically known as the endolymphatic potential—a "resting" potential in which the scala media is 50 to 80 mV positive with respect to other tissue. (The potential appears to exist because the scala media has a much higher potassium [K^+] content and only a slightly lower sodium [Na^+] content than do the other body fluids.)

Origin of nerve impulse. Absence of hair cells abolishes auditory nerve responses as well as the cochlear microphonic, so that hair cell movement in response to basilar membrane movement (the "traveling wave") seems essential to hearing. Mechanical theories propose that bending or vibration of the hair cells originates both the cochlear microphonic and nerve impulses. Chemical theories invoke a neural transmitter such as acetylcholine because of the time delays measured in neural response to sound. The most widely accepted cochlear microphonic hypothesis states that the cochlear microphonic provides the generator potential for firing nerve impulses. In this view, bending of the hair cells changes the current flow that results from the endolymphatic or cochlear duct potential (see above). The *change* in current flow stimulates the nerve cells. Changes in the cochlear microphonic correspond well to threshold measurements for hearing. The three approaches are not mutually exclusive, and all three could be involved in the chain of events that initiates the impulse in nerve fibers.

Auditory defects

Defects in any part of the auditory mechanism, from external ear to cerebral cortex, may impair hearing, although cortical damage is often more perceptual than sensory in its effects. Sensory impairment may be too subtle to detect under ordinary circumstances. As a result, some persons are partially deaf without being aware of it. They are unable to compare their own hearing with the hearing of others, unless the defect is so striking as to make it obvious that they do not hear what others do. The nature of a sensory impairment must often be detected by **audiometry,** in which the auditory threshold is tested at selected points over a range of frequencies.

Outer ear defects. Defects in parts of the outer ear affect all frequencies fairly evenly. The external auditory meatus may become clogged with wax, which impairs conduction of sound waves to the eardrum. The eardrum may become infected, which impairs its flexibility. Punctures of the eardrum can result in some loss of its movement in response to sound waves. Infections of the eustachian tube of the middle ear can also impair the eardrum's movement, as when an air-pressure difference builds up between the middle ear and the outer ear across the eardrum because of the infection. The infection prevents opening of the eustachian tube to equalize the pressure difference.

Middle ear defects. Apart from eustachian tube infection, defects of the middle ear result in a greater loss of sensitivity to the lower frequencies. This is because such defects affect the ossicles that transmit mechanical motion from the eardrum to the fluid of the inner ear. The *extent* of motion of the ossicles is usually greater for low frequencies than for high frequencies; impairment of the ossicles limits their motion and therefore their ability to respond to low frequencies. The ligaments holding the ossicles together may lose elasticity. More commonly, the membrane that seals the footplate of the stapes into the oval window may harden (otosclerosis), limiting the motion of the stapes. These examples of **transmission deafness** often accompany old age. In extreme cases surgery may free the junction of stapes and oval window. Another treatment consists of cutting a new window and covering it with a tiny flap of skin (fenestration). Two types of hearing aids are used to overcome these defects. One amplifies sound waves; its "loudspeaker" is placed in the external auditory meatus (air conduction). The other transmits sound vibrations to the mastoid bone behind the pinna so that vibrations reach the cochlea by bone conduction.

Inner ear defects. Inner ear defects usually arise from nerve damage or damage to the hair cells. This damage is called **nerve deafness;** it is usually localized so that it affects high frequencies more than low frequencies. Nerve deafness is the most common hearing defect of old age. Such defects can also result from exposure to very intense sound—**exposure deafness.** The basilar membrane is overdriven by intense sound of a specific frequency range. This sound damages the hair cells in a specific region along the length of the organ of Corti, where the traveling wave of motion of the basilar membrane is at a maximum. The deafness is more or less limited to the band of frequencies produced by the exposure. High frequencies produce more damage at lower intensities because their sound waves contain more energy.

PSYCHOPHYSICS OF HEARING
Intensity thresholds

The absolute threshold of the human ear is so low that the sound source must be calibrated at intensities well above threshold. (Recent measurements on the cat eardrum with laser light interference techniques indicate threshold vibration amplitudes of the eardrum as small as 10^{-10} to 10^{-11} cm for 1,000 to 5,000 Hz tones!) Depending on the method used to determine threshold and the stimulus frequency, the absolute threshold may be as low as 80 db below 1 dyne/cm². The lever system of the ossicles in the middle ear has resonant frequencies of 1,200 and 800 Hz, and the external ear canal (meatus) resonates at 3,000 Hz; these features largely

determine the threshold curve for hearing, which is lowest in the 1,000 to 5,000 Hz range. The threshold increases less rapidly for lower than for higher frequencies outside this range. The terminal threshold for loudness is much less dependent on pitch. The terminal threshold is usually set by the beginning of somesthetic sensations from the ear—the so-called threshold of feeling. The chief attribute of these sensations is pain, although tickling and itching are sensed as well. Besides being masked by somesthesia, further increments of sensed loudness require stimulus intensities that can permanently damage the organ of Corti. At low intensities the ear is most sensitive to tones in the 1,000 to 5,000 Hz range for the reasons given above. This means that a high- or low-pitched tone that sounds just as loud as a 1,000 to 5,000 Hz tone must be of greater physical intensity.

Intensity discrimination

The difference threshold, or **difference limen** (DL), for intensity varies little with changes in frequency when the base intensity is below 30 db. At higher intensities the difference limen is minimal at 2,500 Hz. As intensity is increased, however, the amount of further increase that one can just detect grows even faster, especially for frequencies below 2,500 Hz.

Frequency thresholds and frequency discrimination

The limits—absolute and terminal thresholds—for pitch in human hearing are usually taken as 20 to 20,000 Hz. Below 20 Hz a "chugging" or a "fluttering" sound is heard. This sound acquires tonal character between 15 and 25 Hz, depending on the complexity and intensity of the tone. Above 20,000 Hz the most acute ear hears nothing, although unpleasant somesthetic "tickling" is sometimes experienced at high intensities. As noted before, little usually happens to sensitivity for lower frequencies with age, but upper-frequency limits are progressively reduced during and after middle age.

The difference threshold for pitch changes with loudness. In the first place, the difference limen for pitch increases with decreasing stimulus intensity—if you are off pitch, sing softly and others cannot tell the difference. The difference limen for pitch changes with frequency mostly between 500 and 4,000 Hz, and the increase is most rapid between 2,000 and 4,000 Hz. This overall frequency range includes most voice fundamentals. This means that an off-pitch bass would be easier to detect than an off-pitch soprano.

Localization

Many complex factors may affect the localization of sound: head movements to vary the sound entering the two ears, visual clues from objects that make common sounds, such as a telephone, the complexity of the sound wave, echoes, and so on. When pure tones or "click" stimuli are used, the head is held still, and the subject is blindfolded, certain cues emerge that may be important to the initial localization of a strange sound—intensity difference and time difference. These cues are caused by the difference in sensations from the two ears when the sound source is to one side of the head or the other.

Intensity difference to the two ears occurs because the head casts a "sound shadow" if the sound comes from one side. The sound will be louder to the ear nearer the source, especially if it is a sine-wave tone above 1,000 Hz. Long-wave (lower-frequency and lower-pitched) sounds "bend" around the head more readily and do not sound so different in intensity to the two ears as do higher-pitched, shorter-wave sounds.

Time difference is also important if the sound has a sharp onset, as a "click" stimulus does. The sound reaches one ear before it reaches the other. Sound travels at 1,080 feet per second, but human ears can detect a difference in sound onset of little more than half a millisecond (0.65 msec), which is sufficient to detect which ear was stimulated first.

More complex tones, like those of music, have localization characteristics that are complicated by their overtones. Generally speaking, lower-pitched tones are less accurately localized than are high-pitched tones. This is why "stereo" (stereophonic, or binaural) systems depend on overtones and higher frequencies to give the sensed difference in sound from the two loudspeaker systems.

SUMMARY

The discussion of audition included the physical energy of sound, the anatomy of the auditory mechanism, the physiology of hearing, the psychophysics of hearing, and complex auditory phenomena, in that order. Physically, sound is the alternate compression and rarefaction of air molecules caused by a vibrating body. The simplest vibrating bodies, such as a tuning fork, produce periodic variations in air pressure that can be plotted as a sine wave of pressure change over distance, depicting a simple tone. The graph in Fig. 9-1 shows simple characteristics of amplitude and wavelength. Amplitude is the amount of air pressure change interpreted by the ear as loudness. Since sound travels at a uniform rate of 1,080 feet per second, wavelength translates readily into frequency. Frequency is interpreted as pitch by the ear. Various points along the complete normal to compression to normal to rarefaction to normal sine wave can be indexed in terms of phase, the points mentioned being 0, 90, 180, 270, and 360 degrees, respectively. If one sine wave is in compression while the other is in rarefaction, they are 270 minus 90 degrees, or 180 degrees, out of phase.

The amplitude of a sound wave is measured on a log scale of pressure change constructed to match the absolute and difference thresholds of the human ear and is called the decibel scale. The zero point is an energy level of 0.0002 dyne/cm², and there are 10 db in a bel, the exponent to the base 10 multiplied by the zero point. Threshold measures are either minimum audible field or minimal audible pressure.

In addition to simple periodic sine-wave tones, sound includes complex periodic tones and complex aperiodic tones. Complex periodic tones are produced by bodies such as musical instruments that vibrate with more than one frequency to produce a complex repeated wave of pressure changes made up of several sine waves. The dominant and lowest frequency is the fundamental, or first harmonic; the other frequencies are overtones, or higher harmonics, that are simple multiples of the fundamental, according to Fourier's law. The overtones are caused by the resonance of parts of the instrument and its air chambers. Differences in the relative amplitude of various overtones in different instruments are interpreted by the ear as differences in timbre. When the sine waves produced by a vibrating body are not repeated in a regular pattern, they are aperiodic and heard as noise, especially if many high-frequency components are present.

The auditory mechanism transduces air pressure changes into fluid vibrations that cause the hair cells of the organ of Corti to fire nerve impulses. The outer ear funnels air pressure changes gathered by the pinna into the external auditory meatus, where they vibrate the tympanum like a drum. In the middle ear three bony ossicles, the malleus, incus, and stapes, transfer this motion to the fluid-filled inner ear; the stapes footplate is smaller than the tympanum, thus providing an impedance match between air and fluid. The motion of the ossicles resulting from loud sounds can be dampened by reflex contractions of the stapedius and tensor tympani muscles. The eustachian tube, from the middle ear to the oral cavity, equalizes middle ear pressure with the atmosphere. The coiled cochlea of the inner ear has three fluid-filled chambers. The scala vestibuli and scala tympani are filled with perilymph and communicate via the helicotrema at the cochlear apex. The scala media, or cochlear duct, is filled with endolymph. Vibrations by the stapes at the oval window

cause perilymph vibrations in the scala vestibuli, and these vibrations are transmitted across Reissner's membrane to the endolymph of the scala media. The vibrations are further transmitted across the basilar membrane, which is attached to the bony shelf of the spiral osseous lamina to form part of the "floor" of the scala media. The resulting pressure variations in the scala tympani cause the round-window membrane to bulge in and out.

The organ of Corti lies along the length of the basilar membrane. Its hair cells are thrust into an overlying tectorial membrane, so that as the basilar membrane moves, the hairs are bent. In response the hair cells generate firing in the nerve cells that innervate them. The hair cells are organized in a tonotopic fashion, those nearer the base of the cochlea firing more often in response to high-pitched tones and those near the apex responding to low-pitched tones. There are three reasons for this phenomenon: (1) high-frequency waves in fluid reach their maximum amplitude nearer the source than do low-frequency waves, (2) traveling waves of motion in the basilar membrane act in the same fashion, and (3) the basilar membrane widens from base to apex of the cochlea. Volley theory accounts for frequency following by groups of nerve cells up to 5,000 Hz as another pitch detector. The outer row of hair cells serves as a loudness mechanism. Several outer-row hair cells are innervated by each neuron; therefore they summate. The inner-row hair cells have high thresholds and overlapping single nerve cell innervation. Therefore they serve pitch by signaling the location of the maximum stimulus along the length of the basilar membrane. The central nervous system sharpens this tonotopic input by means of efferent pathways that inhibit input from areas not receiving maximum stimulation. Hair cells are responsible for the cochlear microphonic, which is an electrical change in the cochlea with sound, and for the firing of nerve impulses. There are mechanical, chemical, and electrical theories of impulse initiation. A potential difference between the scala media and the other scalae may provide the current flow changed by the cochlear microphonic, or there may be a separate generator potential.

The nerve cell axons form the acoustical branch of the statoacoustic nerve. This nerve reaches the dorsal and ventral cochlear nuclei. Fibers connecting here, both crossed and uncrossed, make up the lateral lemniscus, with synapses in its nucleus and in the olive. Collaterals reach the inferior colliculus and the path relays in the medial geniculate before reaching the auditory area in the cerebral cortex.

The effect of defects in the auditory mechanism depends on where they occur. Cortical damage is more perceptual than sensory in effect. Outer ear defects such as clogging of the meatus or eustachian tube (middle ear) or a ruptured eardrum affect all frequencies. Ossification of middle ear bones that limits their motion or hardens the stapes to the oval window affects low frequencies most. Inner ear damage to nerves or hair cells affects high frequencies most. These symptoms may be detected by audiometry and plotted on an audiogram. Exposure damage is frequency-specific.

The absolute loudness threshold is a function of pitch, being lowest in the 1,000 to 5,000 Hz range. The terminal threshold is fixed by the onset of somesthetic sensations at 100 to 120 db, where hair cell damage can occur. Below 30 db the loudness DL varies little with pitch; at higher intensities it is minimal at 2,500 Hz. The frequency limits for hearing are about 20 to 20,000 Hz. The DL for pitch improves as loudness increases and is smallest for lower frequencies below 4,000 Hz. Auditory localization is binaural and depends on intensity differences and time differences.

READINGS

Alpern, M., Lawrence, M., and Wolsk, D.: Sensory processes, Belmont, Calif., 1967, Brooks/Cole Publishing Company.

Beranek, L. L.: Noise, Sci. Am. **215:**66-74, Dec. 1966 (W. H. Freeman Reprint No. 306).

Mueller, C. G.: Sensory psychology, Englewood Cliffs, N.J., 1965, Prentice-Hall, Inc.

Rosensweig, M. R.: Auditory localization, Sci. Am. **205:**132-142, Oct. 1961 (W. H. Freeman Reprint No. 501).

Stevens, S. S., and Newman, E. B.: The localization of actual sources of sound, Am. J. Psychol. **48:**297-306, 1936 (Bobbs-Merrill Reprint No. P-335).

van Bergeijk, W. A., Pierce, J. R., and David, E. E.: Waves and the ear, Garden City, N.Y., 1960, Doubleday & Company, Inc.

von Békésy, G.: The ear, Sci. Am. **197:**66-78, Aug. 1957 (W. H. Freeman Reprint No. 44).

von Békésy, G.: Similarities between hearing and skin sensations, Psychol. Rev. **66:**1-22, 1959 (Bobbs-Merrill Reprint No. P-31).

von Buddenbrock, W.: The senses, Ann Arbor, 1958, University of Michigan Press.

Wightman, F. L., and Green, D. M.: The perception of pitch, Am. Scientist **62:**208-215, 1974.

CHAPTER **10**

Vision: how we see

OVERVIEW

The topic of vision, like audition, can be considered from three points of view: (1) the anatomy and physiology of the eye and its nervous connections, (2) the physical energy that provides the stimulus, and (3) the physiology of interaction between the stimulus and the visual mechanism that provides a sensation. The anatomy and physiology of the eye will be discussed before covering the nature of light because many aspects of the stimulus energy are easier to understand after one learns how the eye reacts to stimuli and sends signals to the brain. A simplified explanation of the physical nature of light follows.

Light interacts with visual anatomy as explained in the section on visual physiology, providing explanations for day and night vision, chemical reactions of the receptors, and the electrical responses of parts of the visual system that result in sensations of hue and brightness. Finally, various visual phenomena will be described and their basis in visual physiology given when it is known. In vision, the way in which light reaches the eye determines the colors that are seen. Newton's laws of color and the visual dimensions of hue, brightness, and saturation explain the basis of color. The visual phenomena discussed include adaptation, after sensations, acuity, cues to depth and distance, and color vision defects.

ANATOMY OF THE EYE

The eye is a sense organ and therefore an organization of different kinds of tissue; each tissue has a role to play in the eye's response to light. The tissues are organized into parts of the eye, each of which contributes to vision in unique ways. The various parts of the eye will be discussed first and the function of each part noted. Then the interaction of these parts in accommodation, convergence, and the pupillary reflexes will be described.

Extrinsic muscles

There are six muscles that originate in the bony orbit, or eye socket, and insert on the eyeball. Their function is to move the eyeball—to "point" it in various directions. The **extrinsic** eye muscles train the eye on objects in reflex and in learned responses to light, movement, and the input from other senses. The extrinsic eye muscles are named by contrast with the **intrinsic** muscles inside the eyeball that control the lens and the pupil.

Layers or coats

One way to understand some parts of the eye is to consider the eyeball as consisting of three layers—the sclerotic coat, the choroid coat, and the retina (Fig. 10-1). The **sclerotic coat,** or **sclera,** is the tough opaque outer fibrous tissue that forms the "white" of the eye. It serves a protective

150

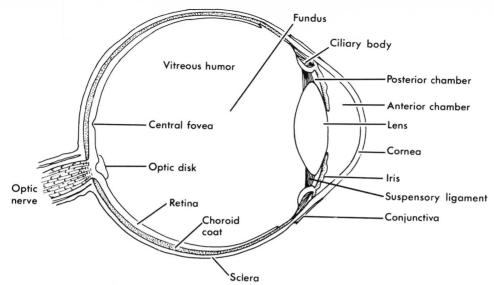

Vitreous humor
Fundus
Ciliary body
Posterior chamber
Anterior chamber
Central fovea
Lens
Cornea
Optic disk
Iris
Optic nerve
Suspensory ligament
Retina
Conjunctiva
Choroid coat
Sclera

Fig. 10-1. Cross section of the eye in diagrammatic form, as seen from above.

and binding function and to some extent prevents light from entering the eye except by way of the pupil. The sclera is continuous with the **cornea** at the front of the eye. Light first enters the interior of the eye through the transparent cornea. The cornea begins the focusing job that the **lens** completes by bringing light rays into focus on the retina.

The **choroid coat** is the middle layer of the eyeball. It contains many blood vessels that nourish the other tissues of the eye. It is pigmented, or dark colored, on its inner surface to minimize the scattering of light by reflection inside the eyeball. The choroid coat is continuous with the **ciliary body,** or **ciliary ring,** a ring of smooth muscle that is attached to the **lens** by the **suspensory ligament.** Contraction of the ciliary ring relieves tension on the syspensory ligament and causes the lens to *thicken* by its own elasticity. Thickening the lens focuses light from nearby objects on the retina. The ciliary body is also continuous with the **iris,** another smooth muscle structure; the iris determines the color of the eye and surrounds the pupil. It also con-

tains circular muscle fibers that contract to constrict the **pupil** and radial muscles that contract to open the pupil.

The **retina** covers only a part of the interior surface of the eyeball—the back portion. The retina contains the light-sensitive receptor cells as well as several kinds of nerve cells. It develops as an extension of the cerebral cortex of the brain and grows out from the brain on two large "stalks," the optic nerves, to invade the developing eyeballs. The retina therefore contains nerve cells and synapses in well-defined layers, as does the cerebral cortex. Much of its fine structure has recently been defined by the electron microscope.

The retina is arranged "inside out"; that is, the receptors lie nearest to the choroid coat, and light must pass through several layers of connecting nerve cells to reach the receptors (Fig. 10-2). The receptors, called **rods** and **cones,** form a distinct layer in the retina. The most distinct of the other layers of the retina are the **bipolar cell layer** and the **ganglion cell layer.** The rods and cones pass excitation to the bipolar cells when stimulated by light. The

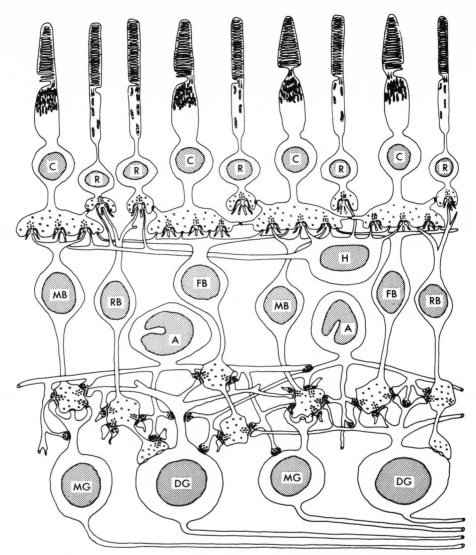

Fig. 10-2. Diagram of receptors and connecting nerve cells of retina. *R*, rod; *C*, cone; *MB*, midget bipolar; *RB*, rod bipolar; *FB*, flat bipolar; *H*, horizontal cell; *A*, amacrine cell; *MG*, midget ganglion cell; *DG*, diffuse ganglion cell. Light reaches the retina from the bottom of the diagram. (From Dowling, J. E., and Boycott, B. B. In Proc. R. Soc. Lond. (Biol.) **166:**80-111, 1969.)

bipolar cells, in turn, pass excitation on to the ganglion cells. The axons of the ganglion cells form the optic nerve, the nerve that carries excitation from the eye to visual centers in the brain. In the retina itself there are interconnections between the re-

ceptors via **horizontal cells; amacrine cells** interconnect the bipolar cells. Excitation and inhibition can thereby spread from one point to surrounding areas of the retina. This mechanism will become important later, when its function in sharpening

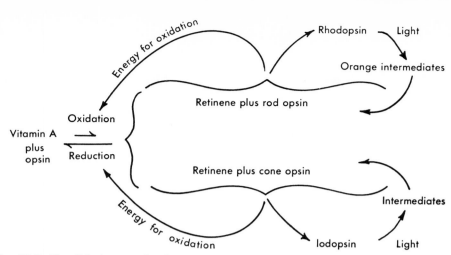

Fig. 10-3. Simplified synopsis of some of the major photochemical reactions in rod and cone vision.

visual input is discussed. Finally, there are *efferent* fibers reaching the retina from the brain. These fibers probably synapse with amacrine and ganglion cells; their function appears to be inhibitory. The efferent fibers may act to sharpen vision by blocking off extraneous input from other parts of the retina, or they may reduce visual input generally, but this is still speculation. (Efferent inhibitory fibers were found in the somesthetic and auditory systems as well.)

The **fovea** is a pit, or depression, in the retina that is in line with the pupil of the eye when the eye is directed toward an object (Fig. 10-1). The fovea is the point of clearest vision and is densely packed with receptors. The receptors are arranged radially around the pit, with connecting bipolar and ganglion cells radially connected to them. Therefore light does not have to pass through the ganglion and bipolar cells to reach the receptors in the fovea. Only cones are found in the fovea, but they are packed so densely together that they take on the elongated shape of rods. Since light reaches foveal cones directly and since they are so numerous, foveal vision is clearer than peripheral vision from other parts of the retina. Light rays from objects are fo-

cused by the lens on the fovea in visual accommodation.

The cones are the hue-sensitive receptor cells of the retina. Stimulation of cones results in sensations of hue as well as brightness. Cones are most numerous in the fovea, but they rapidly become scarcer as one moves toward the periphery of the retina. So few cones are found in the peripheral part of the retina (beyond about 20 degrees from the fovea) that they have no known function in peripheral vision. The cone input has a relatively high threshold—cone vision is daylight vision. Light stimulates the cones by breaking down a chemical pigment called **iodopsin,** as well as related chemicals, into intermediate compounds; light further causes the intermediate compounds to break down into vitamin A and cone opsin (Fig. 10-3). Iodopsin is found in the sensory end of the cone, next to the pigmented epithelium of the choroid coat, which furnishes the vitamin A. Studies with the electron microscope show that the light-sensitive ends of both rods and cones have the appearance of a "stack of disks," like stacked poker chips (Fig. 10-2). This appearance is caused by a regular infolding of the cell membrane. The probable function of the membrane's infolding is to increase the area of the membrane. Because this membrane contains the light-sensitive pigment, a larger supply of pigment is thereby ensured.

The rods are sensitive only to brightness and give sensations of varied shades of gray. Thus one does not have sensations of hue under conditions of night vision, when rod response predominates. At night there is often not enough light to stimulate cones. Instead of iodopsin the rods contain **rhodopsin.** Light breaks down rhodopsin into intermediate compounds, which stimulate rods; the intermediate compounds may further break down into rod opsin and vitamin A (Fig. 10-3).

Since visual response depends as much on the nature of the retinal pathways as on the receptors themselves, it is appropriate at this point to compare the rod system and the cone system. The threshold of the rod system is lower than the threshold of the cone system for three reasons: (1) cone pigments regenerate faster than rod pigments after exposure to light and therefore are better suited to continue stimulating sensory input under conditions of high illumination, when the rod pigments are for the most part broken down; (2) there is more convergence from a number of receptor cells onto a single optic nerve cell in the rod system than in the cone system, and thus the rod system is capable of more summation; and (3) the excitation of cones stimulates neural pathways that inhibit input at synapses of the rod system. Recent research suggests that the rods and cones themselves are of approximately equal sensitivity.

Rods and cones excite bipolar cells, which in turn stimulate ganglion cells. It is the ganglion cell axons that leave the eye to form the optic nerve. At the point where the axons leave the eye there are no receptors; this point (the optic disc) is called the blind spot because it is insensitive to light. The blind spot lies on the nasal (nose) side of the retina; since light travels in a straight line, there is a blind spot in the temporal (toward the temples) visual field in peripheral vision. One is ordinarily not aware of this small area of blindness. To demonstrate its presence, one can close the left eye, hold up a left finger at arm's length and focus on it with the right eye, and bring an upright right finger in from the periphery. When the right finger crosses the blind spot in the visual field, the right fingertip will seem to disappear.

Cavities and fluids of the eye (Fig. 10-1)

The **anterior chamber** of the eye lies between the cornea and the iris of the eye and communicates with the **posterior chamber** of the eye via the pupil. The posterior chamber lies between the iris on one hand and the ciliary ring, suspensory ligament, and lens on the other. Both anterior and posterior chambers are filled with **aqueous humor,** a watery fluid resembling the extracellular and lymph fluids of other parts of the body. Neither chamber communicates with the **fundus,** the large interior cavity of the eye, at least not directly. The fundus contains a jelly-like substance, the **vitreous humor,** that is much more viscous than the aqueous humor. Both fluids absorb some light rays and scatter others, as do the lens and cornea. Despite its pigment coating, the interior of the eyeball scatters some light, and still more light leaks through the opaque outer covering (sclera) of the eyeball. Considering all these facts, it is a matter of some wonder that we see as well as we do.

Mechanisms of accommodation

Light rays that reach the eye from objects more than 15 to 20 feet away are parallel, as compared to light rays from nearby objects that *diverge* noticeably in reaching the eye. The normal eye is arranged so that the parallel rays from distant objects are bent just enough by the cornea and lens to be focused on the retina (Fig. 10-4). Light rays travel in a straight line except as they are bent by the cornea and lens. The image focused on the retina

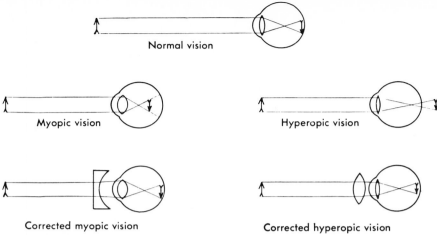

Fig. 10-4. Focus of light rays in normal, myopic, and hyperopic vision.

is therefore upside down and reversed. (Rays from the lower half of the visual field stimulate the upper part of the retina, and vice versa; rays from the left visual field stimulate the right half of the retina, and vice versa.) If the object is closer than 15 to 20 feet away, light rays from it *diverge* noticeably on their way to the eye. Such diverging rays must be bent more than parallel rays to be focused on the retina. This is accomplished by *thickening* the lens, a process called **accommodation.** The ciliary muscle contracts to constrict the ciliary ring, drawing it forward and decreasing its diameter. This relieves tension on the suspensory ligament holding the lens. Under decreased tension the lens, because of its own elasticity, bulges to become thicker, causing increased bending of diverging light rays as an object is brought closer to the eye.

A **myopic,** or nearsighted, person has a lens that is too thick or an eyeball that is too "long" in the front-to-back dimension. Parallel rays of light from distant objects are therefore bent too much and are brought into focus before they reach the retina, where the receptors are found (Fig. 10-4). Rays reaching the retina are therefore scattered again and "blurred," and the myopic person cannot see distant objects

clearly. Nearby objects can be brought into focus because their light rays diverge and require either a thickened lens or an elongated eyeball in order to be focused on the retina. Because the myopic individual must focus on objects closer to his eyes than an individual with normal vision, the myopic person without glasses holds things "close to his nose." The condition is corrected by *concave* lenses, which make parallel light rays diverge and thus compensate for the tendency of the myopic eye to bend light rays too much; parallel rays become diverging rays that can be focused on the retina of the myopic individual.

A **hyperopic,** or farsighted, person, has an eyeball that is too short or a lens that is too thin. In either case parallel rays of light from distant objects are not bent enough to be in focus when they reach the retina; these rays would focus "behind" the fovea if that were possible (Fig. 10-4). The hyperopic person can focus parallel rays of light from distant objects by thickening his lens in accommodation—the same response the normal eye makes to the diverging rays of nearby objects. The hyperopic eye is therefore accommodating all the time, whereas the normal eye accommodates only to nearby objects. Further, there is "disagreement" between the reflexes that converge ("cross") the eyes to focus on nearby objects and the reflexes that thicken the lens. Abnormal stresses in the extrinsic muscles that "point" the eyes can result in fatigue and headaches. The hyperopic person is unable to thicken his lens enough to focus on objects held close to his eyes; to read, he must hold a book at arm's length. The condition is corrected by convex lenses that partly bend the parallel rays from distant objects before the rays reach the lens. The lens completes the job of bringing the light into focus on the fovea.

Convergence and accommodation

The ciliary muscles of each eye contract to close the ciliary ring, allowing the lens to thicken because of its own elasticity and thus bringing diverging rays of light from nearby objects into focus on the retina, as explained previously. Ciliary contraction also serves as a cue to the distance of nearby objects, since the nearer the object, the greater is the ciliary contraction and the stronger is the sensation of muscle strain. One may experience these sensations by closing one eye, focusing on a fingertip held about a foot away, and then slowly bringing the finger as close to the eye as possible while keeping it in focus. If both eyes are used in this exercise, another set of muscle strain sensations will be experienced. In addition to the sensatons from the *intrinsic* ciliary muscles, sensations from the *extrinsic* muscles that "point" the eyeballs will be felt. The closer the object, the more "cross-eyed" one must look at it to keep the fovea of each eye "pointed" in visual **convergence.** These two sets of muscle sensations serve as *cues* to the distance of objects up to several feet away. In the normal eye the two sets of reflexes are linked so that the correct amount of convergence of both eyes accompanies the correct amount of thickening of the lens of each eye. In the myopic or hyperopic individual, correct focus does not accompany correct convergence, because the lens or cornea of one eye or both is abnormal. In the hyperopic person, especially, one eye

sees a blurred image because it is out of focus, or double images are seen because the eyes are not converged properly. As a result the brain learns to suppress the input from one eye and depend on the input from the other, a condition called **amblyopia.** It is especially common in children with undetected visual defects. If it is not discovered early enough, the input from one eye may be permanently suppressed, causing irreversible partial blindness in that eye. If amblyopia is detected early, the impaired eye's function can be restored by forcing its use, which is accomplished by partly or completely blindfolding the other eye for part of each day.

Pupillary reflexes

The pupil, the opening by which light reaches the interior of the eye, is surrounded by the colored iris. The contraction of intrinsic muscle fibers in the iris determines the size of the pupil and therefore the amount of light that reaches the retina. Contraction of the **radial fibers** of the iris opens the pupil to admit more light in dim illumination. Contraction of **circular fibers** of the iris constricts the pupil to admit less light under conditions of bright illumination. These *reflex* reactions to light are mediated by the autonomic nervous system. They help explain how the eye can react to very small amounts of light and yet function under brightnesses of hundreds of candlepower without damage.

NERVOUS CONNECTIONS OF THE EYE

As already noted, the retina itself is an extension of the brain, and many interconnections between nerve cells are made there. The axons of ganglion cells of the innermost layer of the retina converge on the optic disc, or blind spot, and emerge from the eyeball as the **optic nerve** (Figs. 10-1 and 10-5). The optic nerves from the two eyeballs are really *tracts*, since they are part of the central rather than the peripheral nervous system. However, for convenience the ganglion cell axons are called

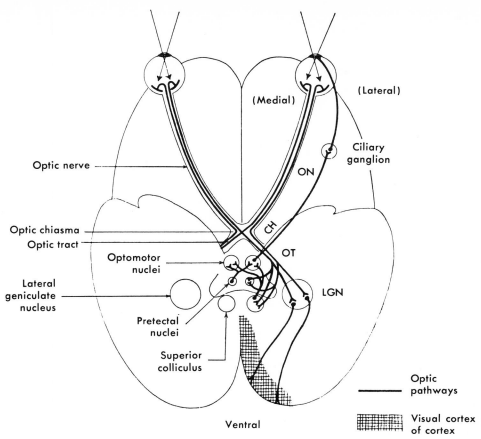

(Medial)

(Lateral)

Optic nerve

Ciliary ganglion

ON

Optic chiasma

Optic tract

CH

OT

Optomotor nuclei

Lateral geniculate nucleus

LGN

Pretectal nuclei

Superior colliculus

Optic pathways

Ventral

Visual cortex of cortex

Fig. 10-5. Optic pathways as viewed from beneath brain.

the optic nerve before they reach the **optic chiasma** and are called the **optic tract** after they leave it, as can be seen in Fig. 10-5. When the ganglion cell axons reach the optic chiasma, a hemidecussation, or "half crossing," occurs in the ganglion cells (in higher mammals). Fibers from the *nasal*, or medial, halves of each retina cross, whereas fibers from the *temporal* (toward the temple) halves of each retina do not cross. As a result the crossing fibers from the nasal halves of the retina of each eye send excitation to the *opposite* cerebral hemispheres, whereas fibers from the temporal half of each retina, which do not cross, send excitation to the cerebral hemisphere of the *same* side. The right optic *tract*, for example, would contain fibers from the nasal half of the left retina and

the temporal half of the right retina. Thus the nasal half of the left retina and the temporal half of the right retina "see" the *left* half of the visual *field*. Damage to the right optic tract would therefore impair vision in the left visual field. By contrast, cutting the right optic nerve would merely blind the right eye. Damage to the crossing fibers of the chiasma (as sometimes occurs from pituitary gland tumors) would destroy fibers from the nasal halves of both retinas, impairing peripheral vision from the temporal halves of both visual fields (tunnel vision).

The optic tract of each side terminates in the **lateral geniculate body,** or lateral geniculate nucleus (LGN). Like the sensory nuclei of the closely related thalamus, the lateral geniculate nucleus serves mainly as a relay station for the cortex and is topographically organized. The optic tract also sends fibers to the **superior colliculi** and **pretectal nuclei.** The superior colliculi mediate reflex movements of the eyeball in convergence and in other eye movements. These responses are handled by connections with the **optomotor nuclei** of the third, fourth, and sixth cranial nerves. The pretectal nuclei, on the other hand, are concerned with the intrinsic muscles of the eye, the ciliary muscles of lens accommodation, and the reflex regulation of the pupil by the iris. Intrinsic eye muscle reactions are controlled via the parasympathetic fibers of the third nerve and via sympathetic fibers that relay excitation from the spinal cord.

The major function of the lateral geniculate nucleus is to supply the **striate cortex,** the primary visual projection area in occipital lobes. This is the area called visual I, and it corresponds with Brodmann's area 17. (The lateral geniculate nucleus also sends fibers to the association nuclei of the thalamus.) Visual I is *topographically organized.* That is, each point on the retina that is excited by light causes excitation of a corresponding point in area I. (The same kind of organization was encountered in pressure sensitivity and audition.) The cerebral cortex has a visual II in the prestriate area (areas 18 and 19) and a visual III in parietal and temporal areas. The topographical organization of visual II is the mirror image of the organization of visual I. Visual II and visual III have been located mainly by recording from the cortex of anesthetized animals while the eye was stimulated with light. The exact anatomy of these pathways is not known. They are presumed to include the association nuclei of the thalamus (diffuse thalamic projection system) and the brain stem reticular formation (ascending reticular activating system).

Some of the functions of the three visual areas have been worked out in careful ablation experiments with monkeys. Removal of area I reduces visual function to brightness alone. Discrimination experiments show that the visual system is able to detect only the total amount of light entering the eye, like a photo cell. No form or pattern perception remains. When area I is intact but areas II and III are removed, a different sort of visual impairment follows. Visual pattern and form recognition are normal, but the monkey makes errors in spatial judgment and is confused by moving objects.

PHYSICS OF LIGHT

One should understand at least in elementary fashion the physics of the light energy that stimulates the retina before undertaking the study of the physiology and psychophysics of vision. Light is a complex form of energy that is part of the **electromagnetic spectrum** of energy. This spectrum is a different form of energy from the air pressure changes perceived as sound; unlike sound, electromagnetic energy travels readily through a vacuum and travels at a rate much higher than sound (the speed of light is about 186,272 miles per second). Light consists of individual particles of matter, each of which demonstrates the property of wavelike motion at a specific frequency. The "particles" are quanta, a quantum being the least measurable part of radiant energy. The wavelengths form a spectrum of wavelengths that are part of the more extensive electromagnetic spectrum (Fig. 10-6). The electromagnetic spectrum includes radio waves (18 miles to 1-inch wavelengths), infrared waves (1 inch to 32 millionths of an inch), light (32 millionths to 16 millionths of an inch), and x rays and gamma rays (down to 4 ten-trillionths of an inch). One can see that visible light forms a small part of the electromagnetic spectrum and that its wavelengths are very short. The wavelengths are measured in **nanometers** (nm, millionths of a millimeter, billionths of a meter, or 10^{-9} meters). The term **lambda** (λ) is sometimes used as a symbol to designate wavelengths. The upper atmosphere acts like a filter in reducing the

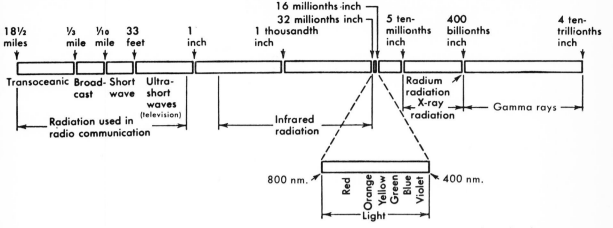

Fig. 10-6. Electromagnetic spectrum, showing range of wavelengths that stimulate visual receptors (light). (Modified from Dimmick, F. L. In Boring, E. G., Langfeld, H. S., and Weld, H. P., editors: Foundations of psychology, New York, 1948, John Wiley & Sons, Inc.)

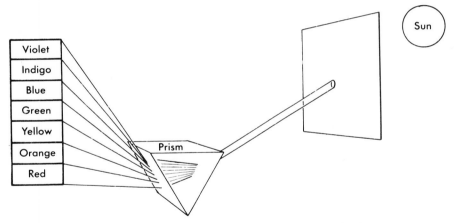

Fig. 10-7. Spectrum, as revealed through use of prism.

energy spectrum of electromagnetic radiation from the sun to a range of λ300 to λ760 nm. Our visual receptors have evolved to be most sensitive to this approximate range of frequencies.

Light reaching the eye from the sun is a mixture of all the visible wavelengths. If a small beam of sunlight from a point source is passed through a *prism,* the light will be bent, or refracted. A prism is a wedge-shaped block of glass that bends light rays as a function of their wavelengths. The longer wavelengths of light are bent less than the shorter wavelengths, so that an orderly array of wavelengths is produced by the prism (Fig. 10-7). The resulting **visible spectrum** will be seen as bands of different **hues,** from violet through blue, green, yellow, orange, and red, as shorter to longer wavelengths are separated. Any single wavelength is spectrally pure and fairly **saturated,** that is, distinct in hue.

(Some mixtures of wavelengths produce gray-looking hues, or colors low in saturation.) Single wavelengths are **homogeneous;** mixtures of wavelengths are **heterogeneous.** Increasing the *amplitude* of either a single wavelength of light or any mixture of wavelengths produces increases in **brightness.**

Light, then, varies in wavelengths, intensity (amplitude), and heterogeneity (wavelength mixture). Changes in wavelength are perceived by the eye as changes in hue; changes in amplitude, or intensity, are perceived as changes in brightness; changes in the homogeneity of light can result in saturation differences.

Light stimuli

Light reaching the eye from any point or surface varies in intensity, wavelength, and heterogeneity of wavelengths. The resulting sensation appears to vary in brightness, hue, and saturation, respectively. Light reaching the eye from the sun is uniform in brightness; sunlight lacks hue and saturation because it is a heterogeneous mixture of all visible wavelengths. Light reaching the eye from other objects has undergone changes in intensity and component wavelengths; therefore it is changed in brightness, hue, and saturation.

A physical object may **transmit, reflect, absorb, refract,** or **radiate** light. In each case it is the light reaching the eye that determines the hue, saturation, or brightness that is sensed. A color filter may be placed between the source and an observer; the filter will absorb some wavelengths and transmit others. For example, it may transmit only the longest wavelengths, resulting in a red hue. The mixture of wavelengths transmitted determines saturation, whereas the amount of light transmitted determines brightness. A prism, on the other hand, refracts, or bends, the light it transmits, resulting in a spectrum of wavelengths, as already pointed out. A surface such as a painted wall may absorb some wavelengths and reflect others. The wavelengths that are reflected to the eye determine the hue and saturation; those that are absorbed are not seen. The amount of light of any wavelength that is reflected would determine brightness. An object may also radiate light of certain wavelengths because of heat (incandescence) or chemical reactions (luminescence). Short-wave radiation causes fluorescent materials to glow during activation and luminescent materials (like the painted numbers on a watch face) to continue glowing after activation (phosphoresce). In all cases of light radiation, the wavelengths emitted are determined by the chemical properties of the object. Electricity passing through an ordinary light bulb heats a tungsten filament and causes it to give off more "yellow" wavelengths than others as a result. The hue of the luminescence of a "neon" light will depend on the type of gas used in it—different gases produce different wavelengths of light by chemical reactions. This property is often used in "neon" advertising signs.

VISUAL PHYSIOLOGY

Now that the anatomy of the eye, the visual pathways, and the physics of the stimulus have been discussed, the topic of visual physiology may be undertaken. Beginning with the reactions of the rods and cones to light, the known effects of visual stimulation can be traced to the highest parts of the brain.

Duplicity

The initial assumption made about the way in which rod and cone systems work assigns them different intensity ranges and reactions to hue. The rod system is supposed to be **achromatic,** or **scotopic;** that is, it has inputs that do not give sensations of hue and has very low thresholds for functioning in low illumination (night vision). The cone system is supposed to be **chromatic,** or **photopic;** it has a relatively high threshold (about 10 microlamberts) and functions under conditions of daylight vision. The evidence behind these statements can be summarized as follows:

1. Two different visual pigments in the eye, iodopsin and rhodopsin, have been discovered.

2. Relative sensitivity to indvidual wavelengths differs under high illumination as compared to low illumination; the cones seem most sensitive in the yellow-green region of the spectrum (555 nm), whereas the rods seem most sensitive in the green region of the spectrum (511 nm).

3. The curves for spectral sensitivity, or sensitivity to different wavelengths of light for rods and cones, look like curves measuring the amount of light of the same wavelengths that is absorbed by rhodopsin and iodopsin, respectively. Presumably, the more a given wavelength is absorbed to break down rhodopsin, for example, the more sensitive the rhodopsin-containing rod would be to that wavelength.

4. The central part of the retina—the fovea, which contains only cones—provides the most acute vision in high illumination; the periphery of the retina (peripheral vision), contains nearly all rods and is most sensitive in the dark-adapted eye.

5. When one is looking at a gray field, hues are seen only in the central part of the visual field, where the cones respond; spots of color in the periphery, where the rods respond, are seen as gray.

6. Adaptation to darkness from daylight seems to occur in two stages. For approximately the first five minutes the eyes become more sensitive at a diminishing rate as more iodopsin is built up in the cones, but there is not enough light to break it all down. Later, enough rhodopsin begins to be built up in the rods so that they begin responding. Since rod input is more sensitive than cone input, the eyes against start increasing in sensitivity at a rapid rate, reaching maximum sensitivity after a half hour or so.

There is other evidence supporting the duplicity theory, but these points seem to be the main ones. The theory needs restatement, however. For instance, new evidence shows that there are three kinds of cones that respond differently to different hues, and perhaps another kind of cone, or a mixed reaction of the retina, that responds to brightness alone.

Color vision theory

Over the last hundred years theories of color vision have been based on either a three-color or a four-color response of the eye. Three-color theorists (such as Young and Helmholz) have been impressed by the fact that three hues can be selected that mix to give white or gray; mixing these hues two at a time can reproduce all other hues. They proposed that the eye works the same way, having three kinds of cones that respond maximally to three different "primary" hues—a mixed response would signal other colors. Four-color theorists (such as Hering) were impressed by the unitary nature of red, green, yellow, and blue. When other hues are mixed to give red, green, yellow, or blue, their presence cannot be detected. By contrast, red and yellow can be detected in an orange, or blue and green in an aqua. Four-color theorists also note that color-blind individuals are usually deficient in red *and* green vision, or blue *and* yellow vision, not other combinations. Since the red and green in question mix to give gray or white, as do the yellow and blue, they proposed a red-green (R-G) cone and a blue-yellow (B-Y) cone. Red light would polarize the R-G cone oppositely to green light; the same kind of reaction would occur in the B-Y cone to blue and yellow light. In this manner two kinds of cones could signal four primary visual responses to the brain.

Modern research suggests that both sets of theorists may have been right. To oversimplify the findings that will be reported, it appears that there are three kinds of cones: a "blue" receptor with maximum sensitivity near 450 nm, a "green" receptor with maximum sensitivity near 525 nm, and a "red" receptor with maximum sensitivity near 555 nm. On the other hand, recordings from the connecting cells of the retina suggest positive electrical reactions to red and yellow and negative reactions to green and blue. There is still another negative reaction of the retina in signaling the amount of light of any wavelength (brightness). It appears that the cones may react on a three-color basis, but the retina transforms the input into a four-color signal to the ganglion cells that lead to the brain. Such notions will become clearer as some of the experiments giving rise to them are explained.

Absorption spectrum of single rods and cones

The rods are stimulated when the rhodopsin they contain is affected by light; the cones are stimulated when their iodopsin is changed by light. However, neither rhodopsin nor iodopsin is equally sensitive to all wavelengths of light. It is reasonable to assume that rods in the dark-adapted eye would absorb more of the wavelengths that break down rhodopsin most readily; cones in the light-adapted eye should absorb more of the wavelengths that affect iodopsin most. In a general way experiments have shown this theory to be correct. The rhodopsin and iodopsin used were chemical extracts of the retina, however, and the tests of visual sensitivity involved the whole eye. Newer optical techniques permit the stimulation of *single* rods and cones in the freshly removed living human retina by using exactly controlled wavelengths. The proportion of light absorbed at each wavelength can be measured over the whole visible spectrum for each single rod or cone. Presumably the more a given wavelength is absorbed by a rod or cone, the more sensitive the receptor is to light of that wavelength. In Fig. 10-8 there is a diagram of some of the results obtained by this method under conditions given in the legend. Only a single kind of rod was found, and its absorption spectrum agrees rather well with sensitivity to various wavelengths in night vision; maximum absorption was at 505 nm, whereas night vision is most sensitive at 511 nm. The difference

can probably be accounted for by the wavelengths absorbed by the fluids in the cavities of the normal eye, as well as light scattering, and so on, in normal vision. (The excised retina was stimulated directly.) The cone data are of greatest interest, however. Three kinds of cones were found, as predicted by the three-color theorists: a blue cone with an absorption peak at 450 nm, a green cone with an absorption peak at 525 nm, and a red cone with an absorption peak at 555 nm.

Retinal responses

So far there appear to be three kinds of cones affected differently by different wavelengths. What happens when these cones stimulate the bipolar and ganglion cells of the retina to send nerve impulses to the brain? Briefly, it appears that the cones cause the bipolar (and horizontal and amacrine) connecting cells to increase or decrease their polarity without firing; the change in polarity changes the rate of firing of the ganglion cells going to the brain in the optic nerve. In this manner it appears that three-color cone signals are changed into four-color signals in the ganglion cells—a red-green signal and a blue-yellow signal. In addition, another signal depends on brightness rather than on wavelength alone. Some of the color-coded cells fire when the visual stimulus is turned "on," representing excitation, and some fire when the stimulus is turned "off," representing inhibition (perhaps a "rebound effect" of firing that follows inhibition). Positive and negative responses of the retina to various hues may be represented by "on" and "off" types of responses that signal excitation and inhibition.

Graded potentials

As previously reported, excitation of the rods and cones sets up *graded* potentials of increased or decreased polarization in the cells that transfer excitation from rods and cones to ganglion cells. It was formerly believed that these potentials came from glial cells—the supporting cells of the retina. It

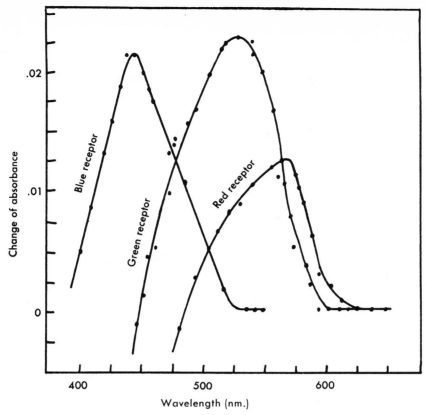

Fig. 10-8. Absorption spectrum of single cones. Freshly excised human retina, including the fovea, was placed in small container and axially exposed to light the width of a single cell from a recording spectrophotometer; absorption spectrum was measured while the cells were under ×2000 microscopically projected observation. Wavelengths were varied from 650 to 380 nm and back again, with recordings being taken after dark adaptation and after bleaching of receptors by exposure to a flashbulb. Curves are averages of the conditions. (Redrawn from Brown, P. K., and Wald, G.: Science **144:**46, copyright 1964 by the American Association for the Advancement of Science.)

now appears more probable that horizontal cells produce the potentials. Under conditions of dark adaptation the decay from maximum of the graded potential is more rapid in response to intense stimuli than it is to near-threshold stimuli. This may indicate a difference in the response of the horizontal cells to cone stimulation as compared to rod stimulation. In any case, the cells show generator potentials that have been called S potentials (slow potentials). Their resting potentials are reduced in the dark (dark adaptation), and

their response is of two main types, depending on the effect of the hue of the light. The type L (luminosity) response is the same depolarization of cells for all wavelengths of light. Only the *degree* of depolarization varies with wavelength in a way much like the sensitivity curve for brightness varies at different wavelengths (Fig. 10-9). This response may signal *brightness.* The type C (chromatic or hue) response, on the other hand, is a depolarization or a hyperpolarization of a cell that depends on wavelength. Type C responses

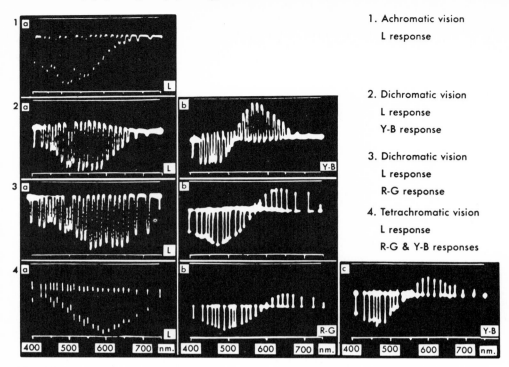

1. Achromatic vision

   L response

2. Dichromatic vision

   L response

   Y-B response

3. Dichromatic vision

   L response

   R-G response

4. Tetrachromatic vision

   L response

   R-G & Y-B responses

Fig. 10-9. Graded slow potentials recorded from retina as a function of wavelength of stimulus. (From Svaetichin, G., and MacNichol, E. F.: Ann. N. Y. Acad. Sci. **74**:388, 1958.)

seem coded to either yellow and blue or red and green wavelengths rather than to other combinations of wavelengths—a four-color signal. (Positive potentials in a single cell represent a depolarization effect and negative potentials a hyperpolarization effect because the electrode is *inside* the cell.) You will recall from Chapter 3 that the inside of the cell is normally negative with respect to the outside of the cell. If the inside of the cell becomes more positive, the cell is therefore less polarized in a positive to negative sense. If depolarization is excitatory, it may initiate an on response, and if hyperpolarization inhibits ganglion cells, it may initiate an off response. However, the experiments measure only the degree of response of each cell to each of the visible wavelengths.

Sometimes an attempt is made to adapt the eye to a band of wavelengths to see if adaptation changes the response of a cell. The subjects have usually been fish of various kinds believed to have color vision, but similar results have been found for the cat; the results can probably be generalized for many vertebrates. Three types of responses have been found: (1) an L (luminosity) response, (2) an R-G (red-green) response, and (3) a Y-B (yellow-blue) response. The L response is a change in cell polarization that depends on wavelength. It does not seem to be color-coded, however, since adaptation to specific wavelengths does not change the shape of the curve of polarization in a way that depends on wavelength; that is, if the cell becomes less sensitive to one wavelength stimulus, it adapts to all of them. The L response may signal brightness to the ganglion cells; its curve is strikingly like that of sensitivity of the light-adapted eye to various wavelengths. The R-G and Y-B responses *are* color-coded and may signal hue to the brain. In each case the response at the shorter end of the spectrum (G or B) is negative, and the response at the longer end of the spectrum (R or Y) is positive.

(Recall again that a positive response inside the cell means cell depolarization.) The G or B response will disappear after the eye selectively adapts to green or blue light; the R or Y response can be eliminated with red or yellow light. Different processes must therefore be involved; fatiguing the red process, for example, reduces the positive polarization response in the cells. If the positive (depolarization) Y or R responses are excitatory, they should cause "on" firing in ganglion cells, whereas the negative (polarization) G or B responses could cause "off" response in the ganglion cells. In this manner four-color signals could be sent to the brain.

As a practical matter, the student may ask how "off" firing to signal hue is possible when color-coded cells are polarized or inhibited and cannot fire until the stimulus is removed so that they can depolarize—the "rebound" effect. The answer may lie in the constant small (saccadic) movements of the eye that result in frequent stimulation and stimulus change for every point in the retina. Stimulus onset and stimulus removal (change) would be equally frequent under these conditions, allowing for as much "off" firing as "on" firing. Change in retinal stimulation appears necessary for retinal function. If a contact lens with a small mirror on the cornea to one side of the pupil is placed over the eye so as to reflect a tiny beam of light to a gray field, it will always stimulate the same small area of the retina; each time the eye moves, the spot in the visual field will move in a corresponding way. Under these conditions the image of the light spot will disappear in three to six seconds because of retinal adaptation. Eye movements are therefore necessary for the perception of both brightness (L, or luminosity response) and the on-off firing of color-coded cells.

Response of cerebral cortex to visual information

Recall that the primary visual projection area of the cerebral cortex (area I) is topographially organized (each point in visual space excites a corresponding point on the cortex). It is surrounded by two visual association areas, one that is topographically organized (area II) and one that is not topographically organized (area III). Cells in all three visual areas respond most readily to slits, edges, and lines—linear visual stimuli. The cells surrounding the linear receptive field of excited cells are inhibited, or else the excited cells are separated from inhibited cells along a linear margin. Furthermore, the linear stimulus must have a specific orientation to excite the cells—either vertical, horizontal, or oblique in specific cases. Moving lines are a more effective stimulus than stationary lines. Simple, complex, and hypercomplex neurons have been found in the information-processing complex of the visual cortex. Simple cells respond as just described only when the linear stimulus is in the part of the visual field that directly excites them. They are found in area I. Complex neurons in area I respond to linear stimulation of specific orientation anywhere in a broad visual field. Their response forms a broad uniform pattern of excitation and inhibition rather than the simple linear opposition of excitation and inhibition. Complex neurons seem to represent the first stage of abstracting the information from simple neurons for form perception. Hypercomplex neurons are found in areas II and III. Their response is similar to that of some simple neurons, except that they respond only to lines of a specified *length*. This appears to represent a further step in the process of form perception. The importance of these studies cannot be overemphasized—they represent our first reliable information on how the central nervous system processes sensory information to form complex perceptions. Geometrical angles and lines that our brain sees as three-dimensional squares, rectangles, and objects that become smaller with distance may be based on this kind of information processing by the brain.

VISUAL PHENOMENA

This section is a consideration of the phenomenology of vision, that is, the way in which hue, saturation, and brightness appear to interact in laboratory tests of color mxing, visual adaptation, after-sensations, acuity, the cues to depth and distance, and color blindness. Wherever possible, each visual phenomenon will be related to visual physiology on the one hand and everyday experience on the other.

Newton's laws of color

Many years ago Sir Isaac Newton produced a visible spectrum of hues by separating the wavelengths of light coming from the sun. Using a narrow beam of sunlight coming through a pinhole, he interposed a prism that bent, or refracted, the beam of light. Light refraction depends on wavelength; the shorter wavelengths were bent more than the longer wavelengths, producing an array of wavelengths—the visible spectrum. Different wavelengths are perceived by the eye as different hues, so that bands of different hues were seen from violet through blue, green, yellow, orange, and red, with shorter to longer wavelengths over the 400 to 750 nm visible spectrum (Figs. 10-6 and 10-7). Any single wavelength is fairly saturated, that is, distinct in hue, and the spectrum produced in this manner is of intermediate brightness. Having separated the wavelengths to produce the hues of the spectrum, Newton recombined individual hues, a process often called "color mixing." His experiments led to Newton's three laws of color, which can be rephrased as follows:

1. **Law of complements.** For each hue there is another hue that will mix with it in some proportion to cancel both hues and give a gray or white color. (Whether gray or white is obtained depends on brightness.)

2. **Law of supplements.** Noncomplementary hues will mix to give a hue that lies between them on the spectrum. For example, a chartreuse (yellow-green) and an orange will mix to give a yellow. Hues from the ends of the spectrum—violets and reds—mix to give purples, which are not spectral hues.

3. **Law of resultants.** The same hue may be produced by several mixtures. Mixing two similar hues produced in different ways alters nothing; mixtures that match one another mix without change in hue. For example, a green could be obtained with a single wavelength or by mixing yellow-green and orange-red. If the two greens matched, their apparent hue would not change when they were combined.

Visual response

The eye perceives changes in the physical amplitude—the rate of flow (flux) of light—as a change in brightness, from black to gray to white, for example. Changes in the wavelength of light are perceived as changes in hue—reds, greens, blues and yellows, for instance. But colors that are of the same hue and brightness may differ in saturation—a green may appear as green as it can be or it may be a grayish green—equally bright, of the same basic hue, but "not as colored." The last statement is a bit misleading since gray, black, and white are colors, although they lack hue or saturation. *Saturation is the amount by which a hue differs from the total lack of hue perceived in a gray of equal brightness.* A further complication arises because brightness and saturation *interact.* The hue, saturation, and brightness interactions of human visual response are diagrammed in the double pyramid of Fig. 10-10. (The dimensions are not psychophysically accurate.) The vertical dimension of the figure represents brightness differences and the horizontal dimensions represent saturation differences, with the outside surfaces at all vertical levels representing the maximum saturation response at a given brightness. The figure tells us that maximum saturation of any hue is possible only at intermediate levels of brightness. Thus a sky blue can never be as saturated as a blue or an indigo, but a blue

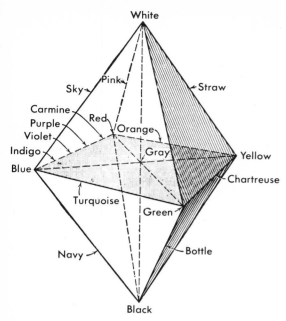

Fig. 10-10. Color pyramid. (From Dimmick, F. L.: Color. In Boring, E. G., Langfeld, H. S., and Weld, H. P.: Foundations of psychology, New York, 1948, John Wiley & Sons, Inc.)

can be desaturated (moved toward gray at the center) until it is no more saturated than the brighter sky blue of maximum saturation. The corners of the figure are labeled blue, red, yellow, green, white, and black, with gray at the center, since these seem to be unique colors (see below). This is why hues seem more saturated near sunset—in "bright" daylight, they seem "washed out," and as dusk approaches they seem "too dark" to be appreciated. Although black represents absence of stimulation, it is not a true sensation. The retina never ceases signaling the brain and a kind of "brain gray" results—the dark gray sensation you have when you close your eyes.

Unique colors

It has been estimated that there can be about 7,295,000 discriminable colors (including grays), although industry uses only about 5,000 in the National Bureau of Standards compilation. A careful study of

Chapanis (1965) suggests that the number of color names actually used by human subjects is 52 to 55. Some of these color names represent differences in brightness, others, differences in saturation, and still others, differences in hue. It is not necessary to have even this many color names, however, because colors can be classified by their resemblance to seven colors that are unique (in the Munsell system). A **unique color** is one that can be psychologically described only in terms of itself. This is true because the component colors making up a unique color cannot be perceived when the unique color is viewed. By this definition the seven unique colors are red, green, yellow, blue, white, black, and gray. A neutral gray may be composed of a mixture of black and white, but neither black nor white can be perceived by looking at gray. A green may be a mixture of a yellow-green and a blue-green, but neither the yellow nor the blue can be perceived in the green. By contrast, a non-unique hue, such as orange, recognizably contains red and yellow. A whole series of oranges can be described by reference to the relative amount of unique red or yellow they appear to contain. The same can be said for the blue and green in aqua, the red and blue in purple, or the yellow and green in chartreuse. The three achromatic unique colors—black, white, and gray—represent differences in brightness. The four chromatic unique colors—red, green, blue, and yellow—represent differences in hue. Mixing gray with any of the four unique hues reduces saturation. The seven unique colors are the seven **primary qualities** of vision, *the irreducible elements making up differences in visual hue, brightness, and saturation.*

Color mixing

The four **unique hues** (red, green, yellow, and blue) can be used, two at a time, to reproduce any other hue. Just as unique red and green or unique yellow and blue mix to give gray (complementary colors), all four unique hues mix to give gray.

These facts are in agreement with the four-color coding that the retina appears to use in signaling the brain. There are, however, only three kinds of hue-sensitive cones in the retina—a blue cone, a green cone, and a red cone; if all three were stimulated at once at the proper intensity, their response would probably "mix" to produce a visual sensation that *lacks* hue. It is therefore not surprising that three hues can be selected that are **primary hues** in the sense that (1) all three mix to give gray and (2) by mixing any two of these hues, any other hue can be produced. There are a large number of trios of primary hues. When one selects any hue made of any mixture, one has determined the composition of the other two hues that will mix with it to cancel hue response, leaving a gray or white. The three hues, thus determined, can be used two at a time to produce all the other hue responses. The relative brightness and saturation of each of the three components will have to be adjusted to obtain a gray. Reproducing some hues that lie between two of the primaries will also require adjustment of relative brightness and saturation. Within these limits, however, there are many sets of three primary hues, or primary colors, as they are often called.

Purkinje shift

According to the duplicity theory (see the discussion of visual physiology, above) the cones are chromatic, photopic receptors in a system that has a relatively high threshold. The rods are achromatic, scotopic receptors in a system that has a very low threshold. The absolute threshold of either system depends on wavelength. The rods "see only gray," but they are maximally sensitive at about 511 nm (green region) and are less sensitive to other wavelengths. For example, they do not react to red wavelengths (above 680 nm). The cones react to all wavelengths of the visible spectrum to some extent, but they are most sensitive at near 555 nm (yellow-green region). The change in the relative bright-

ness of various wavelengths in passing from photopic (daylight) to scotopic (night) vision and vice versa is called the **Purkinje** (poor'kin-yay) **shift.** For example, objects known to be green (such as grass) would appear as a brighter gray at night than objects known to be blue (such as a lake). For this reason, movie directors can shoot black and white moonlight scenes in the daytime by using a blue filter. The blue filter shifts the relative brightness of objects to the blue and green areas of the spectrum and produces the relative brightness one is used to seeing at night.

Adaptation

In common with other receptors the rods and cones of the eye become less sensitive with continued stimulation. The adaptation of rods differs from the adaptation of cones, however, because of differences in the brightness threshold of each system and in the *range* of brightness to which each responds.

Dark adaptation. During normal daylight vision few rods are responding. Their rhodopsin has been bleached into vitamin A by light, and there are few rods with enough rhodopsin left for light to affect. The cones are firing at intermediate sensitivity; their iodopsin is broken down by light to fire nerve impulses and is reconstituted in a continuous cycle. If the subject goes into a dark environment, both rods and cones increase their sensitivity by building up more visual pigment. The cones increase their sensitivity first by building up iodopsin in the absence of light—the more iodopsin that is built up, the more sensitive are the cones. The cone system reaches maximum sensitivity in five to ten minutes of darkness. It takes this long for the more sensitive rod system to build up enough rhodopsin from vitamin A so that it can begin to respond to light. As it begins to function, the threshold drops again, diminishing further over 20 minutes or so as rod vision increases in sensitivity. As a result there is a "break" in the threshold curve for dark adaptation;

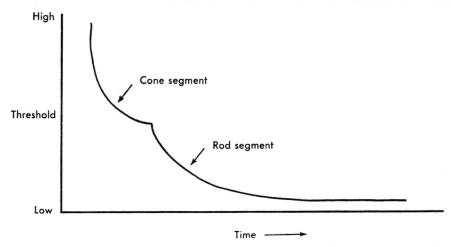

Fig. 10-11. Curve of dark adaptation. Two segments of the curve show first the adaptation of cones and then the adaptation of rods.

the first segment represents increased cone sensitivity to a limiting point; the second segment represents increasing rod sensitivity (Fig. 10-11). After a half hour in the dark, the retina's sensitivity increases one million times!

Light adaptation. Under conditions of darkness or dim illumination the cones are not stimulated; thus they build up a maximum supply of iodopsin because there is insufficient light to break it down. The rods may have a moderate supply of rhodopsin since it is being reconstituted as fast as it can be broken down by dim light. When a person suddenly comes into bright light, the threshold of most of the rods and cones is exceeded and most of the receptors of the retina fire, causing a "blinding" sensation of light. The pupil constricts in order to reduce the amount of light entering the eye and to protect the receptors from overstimulation. The rods cease to respond because all of their rhodopsin is broken down into vitamin A and because they are inhibited by the cone system. The cones reconstitute their iodopsin faster, however, and since their iodopsin continues to be broken down and reconstituted, these cells continue to respond with light sensations. Light adaptation, as measured in various ways, requires 20 to 30 minutes.

Hue adaptation. Continuous stimulation by a given hue appears to reduce the sensitivity of cones responding to that hue. The result is a decrease in the apparent saturation of the hue—the color appears grayer. Adaptation is the basis for visual aftersensations.

Aftersensations

Aftersensations are sensations that are caused by a stimulus, but they begin after the stimulus is removed. Visual aftersensations may be positive or negative. After stimulation ceases, the eye may continue to react with the same sensation for a time—a **positive aftersensation.** Or the eye may react with a quality or an intensity opposite to that caused by the stimulus after the stimulus is removed—a **negative aftersensation.** Examples will be given below for aftersensations of brightness (intensity) and hue (quality). Meanwhile, a good rule to remember is that *brief, intense* stimulation usually causes positive aftersensations, whereas *prolonged, moderate* stimulation usually causes negative aftersensations.

Brightness aftersensations. Stare at the filament of an electric light bulb for a few seconds and then look at the wall. You will continue to see the filament for a time as a positive aftersensation. The receptors continue to respond for a time after they have been intensely stimulated. Prolonged moderate light stimulation raises the brightness threshold because of light adaptation, however (see above). As a result a room looks darker after coming in from the sunlight than it will later—a negative aftersensation of brightness.

Hue aftersensations. Aftersensations of hue are usually negative. If one stares at a patch of color for a minute and then looks at a neutral gray wall, a patch of color will appear that is the *complement* of the stimulus patch. This is a negative aftersensation. There appears to be a balance among the color receptors that has been upset by adaptation to the stimulus hue; a hue of opposite quality results when stimulation ceases. For example, one sees a patch of yellow on a gray surface after staring at blue. As a technical point, negative hue aftersensations are not exactly complementary to the stimulus. Hues near the ends of the color spectrum have aftersensations displaced farther toward the other end of the spectrum than expected.

Brightness thresholds

The absolute threshold for light reaching the rods has been calculated in careful experiments to be 5 to 14 quanta; if a single quantum excites each rod, only one molecule of rhodopsin has excited each rod! This *is* visual sensitivity. However, the rod system is poorly organized to detect *differences* in brightness, because its brightness *range* is not great. The threshold of the cone system is 10,000 times greater than the threshold of the rod system, but it has 500 JNDs (just noticeable differences) of intensity difference compared to 30 for the rod system. Furthermore, the difference threshold decreases for the cone system as brightness increases; that is, the brighter the light, the smaller is the increase in brightness that can be detected.

Visual acuity

Visual acuity is just a special sort of intensity discrimination for which the cone system is better organized than is the rod system. Under daylight conditions it is the ability to distinguish the contours of an object from its background. Obviously the more the object and background differ in brightness, the easier this is to do. Given an equal brightness difference, smaller objects are more difficult to see than are larger ones, and larger objects may be seen at a greater distance than may smaller ones. With good brightness contrast, the only way to standardize a measure of acuity is in terms of the angle subtended by the light rays as they reach the eye from the object. A large object at a great distance may form the same **visual angle** at the cornea of the eye as a small object a short distance away. Technically, acuity is usually defined as the reciprocal (upside down fraction) of the angle separating two just distinguishable contours. "Normal" acuity is the ability to discern 1′ (1 minute or 1/60 of a degree) of arc for a score of 1, but some individuals score as high as 3 (1/3 of 1′). Scores also vary widely with the method of measurement used from the Snellen test (see below) to the minimum separable angle (space between two lines), minimum visible angle (narrowest line seen), stereoscopic (depth) acuity, line movement, and so forth. The minimum separable angle is used in a rough fashion in the most common test of visual acuity, the **Snellen test.** This test uses rows of letters of diminishing size, displayed from a distance of 20 feet. The horizontal bars of the large **E** found at the top of the chart form a separable angle, for example. When the test is scored, the distance at which a normal eye sees a given row of letters forms the denominator of a fraction; the distance in feet at which the subject must stand to see the same letters forms the numerator. Thus 20/20 eyes are normal, 20/40 indicates subnormal acuity, and 20/10 is superior acuity. The Snellen test is far from the best test of visual acuity, but it is the one most commonly used. Almost anyone who has had a general physical examination or who has consulted an eye specialist has seen a Snellen chart.

Cues to depth and distance

The perception of the distance of an object from the observer, or depth perception, depends on a number of sensations from the eyes, some of them visual and some kinesthetic. Two kinesthetic cues of muscle sensation have already been mentioned in this chapter—convergence and accommodation. Convergence is a **binocular cue,** since sensations from the extrinsic muscles of both eyes must be compared to judge how much the eyes are "crossed" in training them on a nearby object. Accommodation is a **monocular cue,** since it depends on sensations of intrinsic muscle strain that are the same for each eye when the lens is thickened to focus on nearby objects.

Binocular cues. Convergence depends on strain sensations from the extrinsic muscles of the eyes when the eyes are "crossed" to focus nearby objects on corresponding points in the foveae of the two eyes. The closer the object, the greater is the sensation. The geometry of seeing is such that the strain is perceived only within a very few feet. Since the eyes are only about 2½ inches apart in the head, muscular convergence of the visual axes of the eyes is noticeable only when the object is close to the eyes. The visual geometry of binocular vision is called **binocular parallax,** and it has consequences in visual as well as in kinesthetic sensations. Since the eyes are about 2½ inches apart, the visual angle, or angle of regard of an object, will differ for the left eye as compared to the right eye. Thus the left eye will see more of the left side of a three-dimensional object, and the right eye will see more of the right side of the object. The difference between the image formed on the right retina and the image formed on the left retina is called **retinal disparity.** The closer the object, the greater the difference in what the two eyes see—the greater the retinal disparity. You can demonstrate this phenomenon for yourself by holding up an index finger about 6 inches from your nose, closing one eye, and then opening it and closing the other; observe how much the finger appears to "jump" back and forth against the background. Then repeat the experiment with the finger at arm's length; it will appear to move less because the retinal disparity is less. The principle of retinal disparity is used to lend an illusion of depth in the **stereoscope.** Two pictures are taken at once: the two cameras (or twin lenses) are about as far apart as the two eyes. The resulting pictures are presented in a stereoscope, which presents the left picture to the left eye and the right picture to the right eye. A startling illusion of a single three-dimensional, or stereoscopic, photograph is obtained.

Monocular cues. Monocular cues to depth and distance are those that do not depend on the displacement of the eyes in the head; they are as useful to a one-eyed person as to one with two eyes. Monocular depth perception is not nearly so accurate as binocular depth perception within 15 to 25 feet, as can be rapidly discovered by trying to park a car with one eye closed. Beyond this distance one relies on monocular cues exclusively, since no convergence is needed to focus on distant objects and since the images formed in the two eyes are essentially identical. The most important monocular distance cue is *size.* The farther an object from the observer, the smaller is the visual angle subtended at the eye and the smaller is the image on the retina. Since it is assumed that objects remain constant in size, the smaller the object looks, the more distant it is judged to be.

Defects of color vision

Color blindness may be in the form of **protanopia, deuteranopia,** or **tritanopia,** depending on whether the first (red), second (green), or third (blue) inputs are absent as hue inputs. (Less severe hue deficiencies are known as protanomaly, or protanomalopia, for red weakness and deuteranomaly, or deuteranomalopia, for green weakness.) The defects in hue perception are not attributable to lack of receptors, because normal visual acuity is retained; there is no loss of detail vision aside from the hue deficiency. However, a case can be made for impairment of red, green, or blue perception on the following basis: both red and green receptors span most of the spectrum (Fig. 10-8). As a result, both protanopes and deuteranopes are deficient in detecting reds from greens, although the blue receptor covers the blues and yellows. Tritanopia could result from abnormal functioning of the blue input, with resulting confusion of blues and yellows. This disorder is quite rare. Both protanopia and deuteranopia are inherited as sex-linked recessive characteristics (Chapter 2) carried only by the female X chromosome. Therefore the defects are present to some degree in 8% of the male population but are found in only 0.5% of the female population.

Monochromatism is complete hue blindness. All hues appear as gray to the subject, and he cannot distinguish between any hue and a gray of equal subjective brightness. All colors that he sees lack hue and saturation because he responds only to differences in brightness. The disorder is rare and is sometimes caused by complete lack of cone vision, with the resulting foveal blindness and poor adaptation to daylight conditions that are the consequences of total dependence on rod vision.

SUMMARY

The eye, as a visual sense organ, is controlled or "pointed" by extrinsic muscles and is made up of specialized tissue in three layers—an outer sclerotic coat, an intermediate choroid coat, and an inner retina. The sclera is continuous with the cornea, and the choroid coat is continuous with the intrinsic muscles of the iris and the ciliary body, which holds the lens by the suspensory ligament. The retina contains several layers of nerve cells as well as the receptors (rods and cones) since it is an extension of the brain. Light must pass through the ganglion cell layer and the bipolar cell layer before reaching the rods and cones, except in the fovea. Horizontal and amacrine cells interconnect retinal areas; ganglion cells form the optic nerve as they leave the eyeball at the blind spot. After a hemidecussation the optic nerve forms the optic tract. Only the hue-sensitive, photopic, high-threshold cone system is found in the fovea; its photosensitive pigment is iodopsin. The more peripheral low-threshold rod system is scotopic and has rhodopsin for visual pigment. The anterior and posterior chambers of the eye contain aqueous humor; the fundus contains vitreous humor. In the normal eye parallel rays of light from distant objects are focused on the fovea by the cornea and lens; diverging rays from nearby objects are focused by thickening the lens in accommodation. The myopic eye has a lens that is too thick or an eyeball that is too long, errors that are corrected by concave lenses; the hyperopic eye has an abnormally thin lens or a short eyeball, requiring a convex correcting lens. Convergence and accommodation may become disassociated, causing amblyopia. Pupillary reflexes regulate pupil size in response to the amount of light reaching the eye.

Because of the hemidecussation that forms the optic tracts at the chiasma, damage to either tract causes loss of the opposite visual field, whereas damage to the crossing fibers causes "tunnel vision." The optic tracts terminate in the lateral geniculate nuclei (LGN), which send topographically organized fibers to cortical area 17, visual area I. Areas I and II are topographically organized. The optic tract also sends fibers to the superior colliculi for reflex eye movement, to the pretectal nuclei for the intrinsic eye muscles, ciliary muscles, and iris reflexes, and to the optomotor nuclei controlling eye movements. Other fibers reach visual areas II and III via association nuclei of the thalamus and brain stem reticular formation. Ablation of area I leaves only brightness discrimination; ablation of areas II and III impairs spatial judgment.

Light energy consists of wavelengths from 400 to 750 nm on the electromagnetic spectrum. Changes in wavelength cause perceived hue changes, mixtures of wavelength cause saturation changes, and amplitude differences change brightness. A physical object may transmit, reflect, absorb, refract, or radiate light; in each case light reaching the eye determines hue, saturation, and brightness.

The duplicity theory states that the rod system is a low-threshold achromatic scotopic system for night vision and that the cone system is a high-threshold chromatic photopic system for day vision. The theory is based on differences between rods and cones in visual pigments, wavelength sensitivity, absorption spectra, foveal and peripheral sensitivity, and color zones, as well as the break in the dark adaptation curve.

Some color vision theory has assumed three color responses of the cones because sets of three primaries can be used to match all hues. Other theories assume opposing red-green and blue-yellow processes because of the psychologically primary nature of these four hues, their paired opposition as complementary colors, and the usual red-green or blue-yellow color blindness. Research now suggests that there are three kinds of cones, but that their interactions in the retina result in a four-color signal to the brain.

Measurements of the absorption spectra of single rods and cones support the duplicity theory and the concept of blue-, green- and red-sensitive cones. The three types of human color cones may be coupled in a red-green and blue-yellow manner. Microelectrode recordings from horizontal cells reveal slow potentials from light stimulation: (1) a luminosity response (L response) of partial depolarization, which is like the cone sensitivity curve and is not color-coded; (2) a red-green (R-G) response; and (3) a blue-yellow (B-Y) response. The last two responses are negative at the short end of the spectrum (G or B) and positive at the long end (R or Y); they are color-coded because either the positive or negative response can be abolished by selective adaptation. The responses probably come from horizontal cells in the retina. The R and G responses seem excitatory to the ganglion cells and the B and Y responses seem inhibitory. They may be related to the excitatory "on" responses of firing ganglion cells that accompany the onset of visual stimulation and to the "off" responses of other ganglion cells that occur when stimulation ceases. Some of these cells are color coded, and the on response always has a lower threshold than the off response. In area I of the cerebral cortex there are simple and complex cells that respond to lines in the visual field with a pattern of excitation and inhibition; hypercomplex cells of areas II and III respond to the length of the line.

Most visual phenomena agree with what is known of visual physiology. Newton's laws of color include (1) the law of complements, (2) the law of supplements, and (3) the law of resultants. These laws govern complementary colors, supplementary colors, and color mixing as far as hue is concerned. The dimensions of brightness and saturation must be added in addition to the psychologically unique hues—red, green, yellow, and blue. Seven visual primary colors result: black and white for brightness, gray for saturation, and red, green, yellow, and blue for hue. However, brightness and saturation interact in that maximum saturation may occur only at intermediate brightness. Any hue may be reproduced by the mixture of two of any set of three primary hues that will combine as a trio of complements (brightness and saturation must be adjusted). The Purkinje shift involves a change in sensitivity to wavelengths, daylight (cone) sensitivity is maximum at 555 nm (yellow-green), whereas night (rod) sensitivity is maximum at 511 nm (green). Dark adaptation involves increasing sensitivity of the cones for about ten minutes as iodopsin is built up until the cones reach their minimum threshold to light; then the beginning and continued increase in rod sensitivity as rhodopsin is built up; the resulting threshold curve has cone and rod system segments. Light adaptation first involves incapacitating the rods as all their rhodopsin is bleached by light. The cone threshold is exceeded also, and the pupil constricts to limit light input to the range of optimum cone acuity. Adaptation to brightness or hue results in aftersensations that are positive if the same brightness or hue is seen, or negative if the opposite brightness, or complementary hue, is seen. The cone system is more sensitive than the rod system to brightness differences, increasingly so with greater brightness. Visual acuity is measured in terms of the angle subtended by the light as it reaches the eye from a just distinguishable object in various ways. One test of acuity is the Snellen test, scored as a ratio between the distances letters can be read by the subject and the normal eye.

Cues to depth and distance are binocular within 15 to 20 feet and monocular at any distance. Convergence and the retinal disparity that results from binocular parallax are binocular cues.

Color vision defects affect both hue and brightness sensitivity. Monochromats are completely color-blind and may have only rod vision. Dichromats include red-green blind protanopes and deuteranopes.

READINGS

Alpern, M., Lawrence, M., and Wolsk, D.: Sensory processes, Belmont, Calif., 1967, Brooks/Cole Publishing Company.

Begbie, G. H.: Seeing and the eye, Garden City, N.Y., 1973, Anchor Books.

Botelho, S. Y.: Tears and the lacrimal gland, Sci. Am. **211**:78-86, Oct. 1964 (W. H. Freeman Reprint No. 194).

Brindley, G. S.: Afterimages, Sci. Am. **209**:84-91, Oct. 1963.

Case, J.: Sensory mechanisms, New York, 1966, Macmillan Publishing Co., Inc.

Dowling, J. E.: Night blindness, Sci. Am. **215**:78-84, Oct. 1966 (W. H. Freeman Reprint No. 1053).

Epstein, J. P., and Casey, A.: The current status of the size-distance hypothesis. Psychol. Bull. **58**:491-514, 1961 (Bobbs-Merrill Reprint No. P-437).

Fatechand, R.: The cells that organize vision, New Scientist **24**:726-728, 1966.

Favrcau, O. F., and Corballis, M. C.: Negative aftereffects in visual perception, Sci. Am. **235**:42-48, 1976.

Granit, R.: Receptors and sensory perception, New Haven, Conn., 1955, Yale University Press.

Hubbard, R., and Kropf, A.: Molecular isomers in vision, Sci. Am. **216**:64-76, June 1967 (W. H. Freeman Reprint No. 1075).

Hubel, D. H.: The visual cortex of the brain. Sci. Am. **209**:54-62, Nov. 1963 (W. H. Freeman Reprint No. 168).

Kennedy, D.: Inhibition in visual systems, Sci. Am. **209**:122-130, July 1963 (W. H. Freeman Reprint No. 162).

MacNichol, E. F.: Three-pigment color vision, Sci. Am. **211**:48-56, Dec. 1964 (W. H. Freeman Reprint No. 197).

Michael, C. R.: Retinal processing of visual images, Sci. Am. **220**:105-114, Feb. 1969 (W. H. Freeman Reprint No. 1143).

Mueller, C. G.: Sensory psychology, Englewood Cliffs, N.J., 1965, Prentice-Hall, Inc.

Neisser, U.: The processes of vision, Sci. Am. **219**:204-214, Sept. 1968 (W. H. Freeman Reprint No. 519).

Pettigrew, J. P.: The neurophysiology of binocular vision, Sci. Am. **231**:84-95, Sept. 1974.

Pritchard, R. M.: Stabilized images on the retina, Sci. Am. **204**:72-78, June 1961 (W. H. Freeman Reprint No. 466).

Rodiech, R. W.: The vertebrate retina: principles of structure and function, San Francisco, W. H. Freeman & Company Publishers.

Rushton, W. A.: Visual pigments in man, Sci. Am. **207**:120-132, Nov. 1962 (W. H. Freeman Reprint No. 139).

Rushton, W. A.: Visual pigments and color blindness, Sci. Am. **232**:17-39, March 1975 (W. H. Freeman Reprint No. 1317).

Teeven, R. C., and Birney, R. C.: Color vision, Princeton, N.J., 1961, D. Van Nostrand Co., Inc.

Thomas, E. L.: Movements of the eye, Sci. Am. **219**:88-95. Aug. 1968 (W. H. Freeman Reprint No. 516).

von Buddenbrock, W.: The senses, Ann Arbor, 1958, University of Michigan Press.

Wald, G.: Eye and camera, Sci. Am. **184**:32-41, Aug. 1950 (W. H. Freeman Reprint No. 46).

Wald, G.: Life and light, Sci. Am. **201**:92-108, Oct. 1959 (W. H. Freeman Reprint No. 61).

Young, R. W.: Visual cells, Sci. Am. **223**:80-91, Oct. 1970 (W. H. Freeman Reprint No. 1201).

CHAPTER 11

Consciousness: sleep, dreaming, arousal, and other states

OVERVIEW

States of consciousness may be defined by physiological (objective) as well as psychological, or subjective, methods, at least in extent or intensity. Alert attention, resting wakefulness, dreaming sleep, and dreamless sleep will be treated as well as meditation and other states of awareness.

The sleep and arousal topic begins with Kleitman's evolutionary theory of sleep. The theory distinguishes between the wakefulness of necessity seen in human children and lower animals when they are hungry, thirsty, or uncomfortable and the wakefulness of choice found in adult humans and some adult animals. Wakefulness of choice involves a single sleep period and a single waking period during each day and is less dependent on the need state of the animal. Kleitman's ideas about the neural mechanisms underlying sleep and wakefulness are followed by modern theories and experiments on centers in the brain controlling sleep, wakefulness, attention, and arousal. Evidence has been obtained by using the EEG ("brain waves") and eye-movement recordings about the nature of human sleep patterns. Four stages of sleep are defined by the EEG patterns. A sleep stage that is often accompanied by rapid eye movements (REM) is associated with dream recall. The course of human sleep during the night is traced. Then certain phenomena of sleep distur-

bance that result from sleep deprivation are considered, as well as the effects on sleep of sedatives, biochemicals, alcoholism, and addiction. Chemical and hormone influences and methods of inducing sleep are included. The chapter closes with the topics of meditation and cerebral dominance.

PHYSIOLOGICAL AND PSYCHOLOGICAL STATES

Psychological states of awareness (or the lack of awareness) result from physiological changes in the brain. This point of view takes no position on whether any particular state of awareness is necessary to the behavior or lack of behavior that follows or whether the psychological state is just a "byproduct" of brain changes that govern behavior. In either case, research has shown that we can learn much about the state of awareness of the individual subject by recording the electrical and chemical changes going on in the brain.

States of awareness

Most of what we know about brain activity and states of awareness comes from monitoring EEG records in human subjects. Animal subjects cannot report states of awareness to compare with brain waves going on at the time. Clues provided by human research have, however, led to important animal experiments. These experiments concern biochemical changes at

175

specific places in the brain that appear to govern states of awareness because they result in the same EEG changes found in man.

Changes in brain waves and the biochemical changes that underlie them tell us about the intensity or extent of awareness but do not reveal conscious content. We can determine whether the subject is alert and attentive or daydreaming, whether he is asleep, and whether he is probably dreaming. A beginning has been made on finding out how brain activity may differ in the states of meditation practiced by eastern philosophies (Zen, yoga, and transcendental meditation, for example). The utility of an alert and vigilant state to behavior is obvious when conditions demand it. The role of other states of awareness and the changes in the brain that underlie them are less obvious. We can assume that sleep and dreaming are necessary to brain function and play a role in behavior because they occur regularly in all normal subjects. The utility of these states of the brain for brain function and behavior is the subject of several interesting theories but a general theory of the role of states of brain awareness has not yet emerged.

SLEEP, ACTIVATION, AND ATTENTION

A motivated animal is not asleep. The more motivated an animal, the more *activated* he seems, as the high level of CNS activity is accompanied by much restless behavior. In this sense, sleep was once believed to be the lowest point on a scale of CNS activation that extends through waking activity to extreme arousal. Sleep is now known to be more complex. It is a biochemically different state of the brain, as compared to the waking state, and it differs from the waking state in qualitative as well as quantitative ways.

A certain amount of sleep is required for normal CNS functioning. Sleep deprivation studies show that short mental tasks, such as arithmetic, do not suffer from loss

of sleep if the subject is well motivated; however, long-term alertness does suffer, and bodily discomfort is felt. Animal studies have revealed that forced and long-continued wakefulness results in death—thus sleep is required (a need) for existence, as is food or water. In this vein, investigators sought for years to find out why we sleep. Kleitman, on the other hand, learned much about sleep by asking the opposite question: Why do we stay awake?

Kleitman's evolutionary theory

In primitive animals and in children, sleep seems to be more a "natural," or homeostatic, state than waking activity. Infants and many lower animals sleep most of the time, unless they are aroused by bodily needs such as thirst, hunger, or discomfort. A human baby, for example, sleeps most of the day and night, waking at intervals when hunger or the discomfort of a wet diaper serves as a motivating stimulus to wakefulness. The wakefulness that results was called **wakefulness of necessity** by Kleitman, since it was necessary for the infant to awaken to satisfy his hunger or to remove the source of the discomfort. Wakefulness of necessity is **polyphasic,** that is, it occurs in several phases, or cycles, during the course of a 24-hour day. The infant awakens because of the stimulus of a bodily need and returns to a contented state of natural sleep soon after his needs are satisfied. With growth and development, however, the child sleeps for longer periods without waking and stays awake for still longer periods. When even the afternoon nap is abandoned, the youngster sleeps for a continuous eight- to ten-hour period at night and remains awake for a continuous daylight period, during which most of his bodily needs are satisfied. Kleitman called such a sleep cycle **monophasic,** since it consists of a single sleep and waking cycle each day. The continuous waking period he called **wakefulness of choice,** since it did not depend on the stimulus of an immediate need. He suggested that wakefulness of necessity depends on a primitive center in the diencephalon stimulated directly by bodily needs. With evolution the cerebral cortex developed, allowing an increase in learning ability that varied from species to species. Need satisfaction became associated with daylight (except for nocturnal animals), and there were more stimuli to arouse the animal during daylight hours. The cortex began to control the center governing sleep. Cortical activity as well as bodily needs stimulated the primitive "sleep center" (really a waking center). The animal *learned* to remain awake during daylight hours, when the cortex was stimulated by environmental events. With re-

duced stimulation at night the cortex ceased to arouse the "sleep center" (or, rather, the waking center), and the center failed to drive the cortex and other parts of the brain to keep the animal awake.

Neural mechanisms

Kleitman suspected the existence of a sleep center because of the symptoms shown by victims of sleeping sickness (encephalitis lethargica), when the disease damaged the diencephalon. (In parts of Africa, sleeping sickness is common; the spirochete is carried by the tsetse fly.) Victims of one variety of the disorder seemed to show only the primitive wakefulness of necessity, and Kleitman suggested that

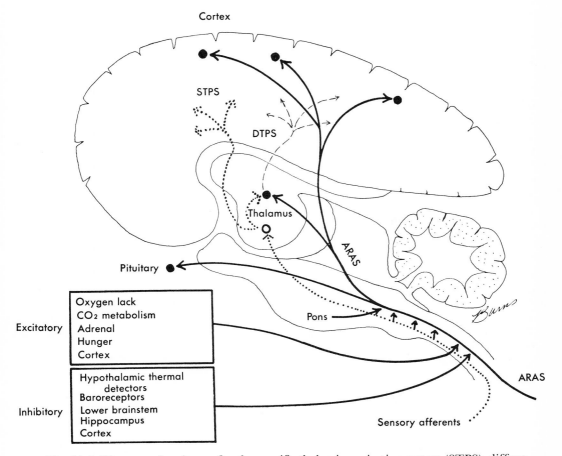

Fig. 11-1. Diagram of pathways for the specific thalamic projection system (STPS), diffuse thalamic projection system (DTAS), and ascending reticular arousal system (ARAS).

their "sleep center" (waking center) had been destroyed. The center was not aroused by cortical activity during daylight hours. As a result, the cortex, rather than the sleep center, "kept the brain awake," but only when it was directly stimulated by strong stimuli such as bodily discomfort, hunger, thirst, or other intense inputs. Dogs show a relatively monophasic sleep pattern in adulthood. If decorticated, however, they revert to the polyphasic sleep cycle of puppyhood. Wakefulness of necessity in this case is maintained by the subcortical center instead of the cortex.

Consciousness and the reticular formation

Kleitman's central idea concerned a brain "center" that can be stimulated by sensory input and conditioned by events to "keep the brain awake," principally waking the cerebral cortex. Increased cortical activity is associated with wakefulness; further increases in brain activity lead to states of aroused attention and vigilance. In modern terms the brain is aroused by a more diffuse *system,* the **ascending reticular arousal system (ARAS).** The ARAS is found in a part of the brain called the **brain stem reticular formation (BSRF).** The BSRF is the central gray core of the brain stem, largely short interconnecting nerve cells with many branches, surrounded by the white matter of sensory and motor tracts (Fig. 11-1). The sensory tracts (STPS in Fig. 11-1) give off branches to the BSRF, and ascending pathways through which many of the diffuse neurons of the BSRF form an ARAS that arouses higher centers (especially the cortex) to increased activity in a widespread fashion due to sensory stimulation. This leads to a conscious state of wakefulness with increasing ARAS activity resulting in states of arousal and vigilance. The ARAS is subject to other excitatory influences that lead to heightened awareness such as need states of the body from lack of oxygen to hunger (Fig. 11-1). Other influences

signaling quiescent states of the body can inhibit the ARAS and reduce conscious awareness. Increased activity in the BSRF can increase muscle tone, as pointed out in Chapter 4. Increased muscle contraction all over the body results in more sensory input from that source to the ARAS and cortex. This is referred to as a **descending reticular activating system (DRAS),** which is not separately identified in Fig. 11-1. Perhaps you have noted that your neck muscles ache or your leg muscles are tired after a period of alert, concentrated study, even though you have been seated in a comfortable chair for the entire time.

Attention

Sensory information for somesthesia and proprioception is carried in the white matter of tracts surrounding the BSRF (Chapters 6 and 7); other sensory inputs were described in Chapters 9 and 10. Because most of this input reaches the cortex by way of the thalamus and related (geniculate) nuclei, the sensory input is referred to as the **specific thalamic projection system (STPS).** The sensory information is carried to the cortical sensory projection area for each of the senses. (The sensory projection areas of the cortex were described in Chapter 3; see Fig. 3-12.) The sensory projection areas for vision, hearing, and proprioception have cortical association areas nearby (18 and 19, 42, and 5 respectively, in the Brodmann system), whose activity is associated with attention to that particular sensory input. These particular association areas are, then, somewhat specific to each sensory modality. They are excited by more diffuse nuclei of the thalamus than are the thalamic nuclei that form part of the STPS. Activity in a sensory pathway of the STPS can arouse part of the **diffuse thalamic projection system (DTPS)** for that sensory modality. The DTPS appears to be an older set of sensory pathways in evolutionary history. Their present function seems to involve information processing for each of the sensory inputs.

Arousal

The importance of the ARAS to states of alertness and attention can be seen in several ways. For instance, electrodes can be permanently implanted in the ARAS of a cat and used to stimulate the ARAS electrically. Such a stimulus will immediately rouse a sleeping cat to a state of alert attention. A similar stimulus delivered to areas located elsewhere in the brain has no such effect. When the ARAS is stimulated, the EEG of the sleeping cat is transformed immediately, from the high-voltage slow waves characteristic of sleep into the desynchronized low-voltage activity typical of alert attention. The ARAS seems much more important to attention and wakefulness than the sensory pathways of STPS. The pathways of the STPS are carried in the laterally placed white matter of the brain stem, whereas the ARAS occupies the central core of the brain stem. Cutting the lateral sensory (somesthetic and auditory) pathways in the midbrain of a cat has no obvious effect on behavior, surprisingly enough. The sleeping cat is aroused as readily as before by a sound stimulus, although the STPS is not carrying the sensory information to the cortex. Perhaps the ARAS serves in its stead. In any case the cat remains as alert as before, and the EEG shows the normal wakeful pattern. If the central core of the midbrain is severed, however, a different result follows, even when the lateral STPS pathways are left intact. The operation abolishes normal waking behavior (at least for a few days) and the desynchronized EEG pattern that accompanies it. The cat shows the slow-wave EEG pattern typical of sleep, and the most intense stimuli fail to wake it. Evidently the ARAS is necessary to wakefulness, although the part of the ARAS located in the posterior hypothalamus (waking center) may play a vital role in waking behavior and brain activity.

Selective attention

Sensory gating, habituation, and attention. It is evident that attention to one sensory modality often requires inattention to another. When a student is reading (attending to a complex visual input), he may have to be called several times before an auditory input shifts his attention. It is as if the auditory input were turned off, and some of the evidence from animal experiments supports this interpretation. On the other hand, a repeated, monotonous auditory stimulus such as a dripping faucet may arouse attention at first as a novel sound, and then no longer be "heard" if one is attending to other things.

Experiments with animals who have electrodes implanted in auditory or visual projection areas show large evoked potentials to a novel auditory or visual stimulus. As the stimulus grows repetitive and the animal appears to turn its attention elsewhere, the evoked potentials become smaller—*habituation* has occurred. One neural mechanism believed to be responsible for this phenomenon is the *efferent control of afferent input.*

Efferent pathways that go to the cochlea and can inhibit auditory input have been discovered (the olivocochlear tract of Rasmussen; see Chapter 9). Similar efferent inhibitory pathways have been found for vision and somesthesia. (In somesthesia, input is blocked at the gracile and cuneate nuclei; visual input is altered at the retina.) The efferent pathways to the receptors probably serve to "tune" the "local sign" of these topographical senses—to improve pitch discrimination in hearing, contrast in vision, and localization for touch. All the "local signs" depend on neurons firing in a given location and a lack of firing in adjacent neurons. However, efferent excitatory and inhibitory pathways to higher-level "relay" centers can serve habituation— they can reduce the input from one sensory modality and increase the input from another. Efferent pathways to sensory input are not all inhibitory—the "gate" may be opened wider instead of being closed. There are both excitatory and inhibitory efferent pathways to the thalamus and geniculate bodies to affect the STPS and the DTPS. Efferent pathways from higher levels can more diffusely excite, sensitize, or inhibit the ARAS, as has already been seen. The general principle of *efferent control of afferent impulses* is important to general arousal and specific attention as well as to habituation. By blocking or sensitizing specific sensory inputs in the STPS and DTPS, the CNS can pay attention to one or two sensory modalities while minimizing the input of others. At the same time the general arousal of the CNS may be increased by excitation of the ARAS from higher centers, creating a state of **vigilance.** Higher centers not only *select* the sensory input attended to; they also excite themselves by stimulating increased input from the ARAS. Repetitive stimuli, on the other hand, result in at least partial inhibition of their sensory channel and may reduce activity in the ARAS as well.

EEG during sleep and wakefulness

The **electroencephalogram (EEG)** is a recording made by cementing small electrodes to the scalp and by picking up and amplifying gross electrical changes in potential from the surface of the cortex through the skull. If the recording was taken from the surface of the cortex (**electrocorticogram,** or **ECG**), these potential changes would amount to about 1 mV (1/1000 volt). As measured at the surface of the skull, the electrical changes are as small as 1 μV (1/1,000,000 volt). The changes in potential are amplified and used to drive an ink-writing oscillograph. These changes wax and wane in a rhythmic fashion and may represent the moment-to-moment state of partial depolarization of nerve cells or the firing of dendrites in the more superficial layers of the cortex. In either case the more depolarized the cells, the more rapidly their axons are firing and, roughly speaking, the more "active" is the cortex. In states of extreme arousal the EEG is desynchronized; many of the cells are partly depolarized (negative), and they fire their axons at a rapid rate. As the cortex becomes less ex-

cited, the cells appear to wax and wane in potential in a synchronous fashion, producing regular brain waves of voltage change. Generally speaking, the less excited the cortex, the lower is the frequency of the brain waves and the greater is their amplitude. In other words, a less excited cortex features brain cells whose potentials change at a slower and rhythmic rate with greater amplitude. These and other predictable changes occur in the EEG pattern with reduced excitation of the cortex, from aroused excitation through a state of resting wakefulness, dozing, and sleep. The brain waves during sleep can be compared to how much stimulation is required to wake the subject, and a scale of EEG changes with sleep has been constructed. The most widely used scale of this kind was published by Dement and Kleitman. It has been extended and standardized by others (Table 10).

In the scale, four stages of sleep are added to the patterns that distinguish the aroused state from the resting but alert state. In the aroused state, as indicated above, the cortex is desynchronized, so that few regular rhythmic brain waves are seen. The **alpha rhythm** is dominant in the resting state of wakefulness of most human subjects. The alpha rhythm is a 10 to 14 Hz pattern of low and slightly irregular amplitude. This pattern shows its greatest amplitude from electrodes in the occipital region. Some subjects show a slightly faster low-amplitude beta rhythm. As the subject goes to sleep, differences in the EEG pattern occur. Four stages of sleep can be distinguished in the EEG pattern. Stage 1 occurs when the subject is dozing and can be easily aroused. Its EEG pattern is dominated by a low-voltage, mixed-frequency pattern, mostly in the 2 to 7 Hz range. Sleep spindles and K complexes are absent. (Sleep spindles are brief bursts of 12 to 14 Hz activity; K complexes consist of a single sharp negative wave followed by a positive component.) Slow eye movements are present, but rapid eye movements (REMs, see below) are absent. Stage 2 sleep

Table 10. Scoring criteria for the EEG*

Stage	
Stage W (wakefulness)	EEG containing alpha activity and/or low-voltage, mixed-frequency activity
Movement time (MT)	Scoring epoch during which polygraph record is obscured by movements of subject
Stage 1	Relatively low-voltage, mixed-frequency activity without rapid eye movements (REM)
Stage 2	Sleep spindles of 12 to 14 Hz and K complexes on a background of relatively low-voltage, mixed-frequency EEG activity
Stage 3	Moderate amounts of high-amplitude, slow-wave activity
Stage 4	Large amounts of high-amplitude, slow-wave activity
Stage NREM (non-REM)	Stages 1, 2, 3, and 4 combined
Stage REM	Relatively low-voltage, mixed-frequency EEG in conjunction with episodic REMs and low-amplitude electromyogram (EMG)

*Based on data from Rechtschaffen, A., and Kales, A., editors: A manual of standardized terminology, techniques, and scoring system for sleep stages of human subjects, Bethesda, Md., 1968, National Institutes of Health, Pub. no. 204, U.S. Department of Health, Education, and Welfare.

is defined by the presence of sleep spindles and K complexes. During stage 1 or 2, rapid eye movements (REM) are sometimes seen. Stage 3 is defined by the presence of waves of 2 to 7 Hz or slower in 20% to 50% of the record. Slow high-amplitude waves are called **delta waves** when their frequency is 2 to 7 Hz. Stage 4 is defined by the presence of delta waves in over 50% of the record. A distinction between slow-wave sleep (stages 3 and 4, or SWS) and light sleep (stage 1) is sufficient for most investigations, however.

During the night the amount of time spent in each sleep varies with the subject. For example, some people never demonstrate stage 4 sleep. However, all subjects show *phasic* cycles in stages of sleep during the night, shifting back and forth from SWS stage 3 or 4 to REM and stage 1 or 2. Slow-wave sleep and REM sleep cycles total 90 to 100 minutes in length. When averaged out over the course of a night's sleep, the typical subject spends more time in slow-wave sleep stages than in stage 1 during the first two or three hours of sleep. In the last two or three hours of sleep, increasing amounts of time are spent in stage 1, and REMs are more frequent. However, if one prevents slow-wave sleep for a night or two by waking the subject each time he shows a stage 3 or 4 sleep pattern, the subject will spend a greater part of his sleep period in slow-wave sleep on the subsequent night.

Dreaming is often accompanied by rapid eye movements. If the subject is awakened during REM sleep, he is more likely to recall that he had been dreaming than if he had been awakened during non-REM sleep. If an electrode is placed near the "corner" of each eye, and another is placed at an indifferent point, such as the earlobe, eye movements will be detected as a change in the potential between the electrodes (because the eye is polarized between the front and back of the eyeball). In slow-wave sleep, the eyes are motionless or move slowly. As REM sleep begins, the eyes often begin to move rapidly, largely in a back-and-forth scanning motion. The recording of REMs is accompanied by a change in the EEG from other stages to stage 1. The change from other stages to stage 1 has been called an E-1, or emergent stage 1.

If REM and E-1 are taken as signs of dreaming, there is evidence that dreams can last as long as an hour. Nearly all subjects have three or four dreams during the night, whether they remember the dreams or not. Subjects have been prevented from dreaming by waking them every time they showed the E-1 and REM pattern, for three or four nights. Compared with subjects who were awakened equally often during slow-wave sleep, the REM-deprived subjects were reported to be more irritable and anxious during their waking hours. If REM-deprived subjects are permitted un-interrupted sleep on subsequent nights, they will dream more (by REM criteria) for a night or two. These observations have led some to speculate that REM sleep is a symptom of some metabolic activity of the brain that is necessary for its proper development or functioning during sleep. Infants spend more time in REM sleep than do adults (up to one-half of sleep periods); as the polyphasic sleep cycle gives way progressively to the monophasic cycle, less time is spent in REM sleep. Observers have speculated that longer periods of REM sleep are necessary for the infant, who sleeps more than the adult and whose brain would not otherwise be active enough of the time for proper development.

Paradoxically, it is harder to wake a cat from REM sleep than from deeper stages of sleep. Cats showing REM sleep are harder to wake, even by ARAS stimulation. This is not the case for humans, who seem to be more alert after being awakened from REM sleep than from non-REM sleep. The brain of the cat seems to be more under the control of a center in the pons during REM sleep than subject to outside stimulation. In the BSRF of the rostral pons there is a nucleus (nucleus pontis caudalis) whose destruction abolishes REM sleep in cats. These cats show the other normal stages of sleep at first, but their condition progresses to insomnia and finally death. On the other hand, a decorticate cat shows nothing but slow-wave sleep; thus perhaps the cortex is necessary for REM sleep. (Normal cats do not display slow-wave sleep.)

Brain centers for the states of sleep

Studies by Jouvet on cats have pointed to chemical differences in the brain between light (dreamless?) sleep and REM sleep and have helped identify nerve centers that may be responsible for each state. In cats, the neck muscles are completely re-laxed during paradoxical sleep (REM sleep), and the cat is harder to waken; yet the EEG shows E-1 stage activity and the cat shows movements (dreaming?). In non-REM (stage 2) sleep, the cat's neck muscles show some tension and the cat is easily awakened. Certain midline nuclei in the brain stem (raphe nuclei) produce serotonin, a hormonelike substance found throughout the brain. If most of these nuclei are destroyed, the cat becomes sleep-less (less than 10% of the time spent in sleep compared to 66% in the normal cat). On the other hand, certain nuclei of the pons (locus ceruleus, output portion of the nucleus pontis caudalis—see preceding paragraph) produce epinephrine. When these nuclei are destroyed, paradoxical E-1 (REM) sleep is abolished. In the cat, then, serotonin produced by the raphe nuclei may stimulate non-REM sleep, whereas epinephrine produced by nuclei of the pons may result in REM sleep. It is in-teresting to note, however, that the slow-wave stages (3 and 4) of sleep in humans (who sleep much less) are not reported for the cat. Jouvet has also found that inhibit-ing the production of serotonin causes re-versible insomnia, whereas destruction of the raphe nucleus leads to fatal insomnia (inability to sleep). In an important theory he proposes that production of serotonin by the raphe nuclei initiates stage 2 sleep. (In humans, slow-wave sleep always occurs during the first part of the night, except in children.) The serotonin stimulates the locus ceruleus to produce epinephrine. Epinephrine production results in par-adoxical sleep; then the whole cycle begins again. Jouvet finds that rat brain serotonin is increased during the day, the period of time when these animals normally sleep; however, serotonin is reduced in the brains of rats who have been deprived of REM sleep.

More recently, another nucleus in the pons has been implicated in the "control-ling role" for paradoxical sleep in the cat, called desynchronized sleep by McCarley and Hobson (1975). This group of giant cells is in the tegmentum ("floor") of the fourth ventricle and is called the "gigantocellular tegmental field," abbreviated FTG. The cells of this group, as compared to the locus ceruleus and other pontine cell groups, seem the most important in controlling desynchronized sleep (DS). They show (1) activity rates most related to DS, (2) the longest discharge anticipating DS, and (3) the most bursts of activity associated with rapid eye movements. Chemical studies show that they are stimulated by acetylcholine (ACh) as a transmitter chemical and they release ACh to stimulate other cells. An anti-ACh chemical (carbachol) suppresses activity in the FTG more than the locus ceruleus (LC). Finally, in comparing FTG and LC cells, McCarley and Hobson found that the LC cells fire more during synchronized sleep (non-REM or SWS) and less during desynchronized (paradoxical or REM) sleep. The FTG cells are active during REM sleep and the LC cells are not. In contrast to Jouvet's theory, they propose that the FTG and LC cells interact to control each other in a reciprocal way, LC activity leads to REM ("dreaming") sleep but stimulates FTG activity and suppresses LC firing; non-REM sleep results, and the cycle is repeated.

Sleep phenomena

It is evident that sleep involves more than one biochemical state of the brain. An examination of some normal and abnormal phenomena of sleep may aid our understanding of the way in which these states relate to one another and the way in which they interact with the waking state.

Sleep deprivation. Studies of sleep deprivation have generally been of three types: (1) total sleep deprivation, (2) deprivation of REM sleep, and (3) deprivation of slow-wave sleep.

Total sleep deprivation studies are typified by one experiment in which four men were kept awake for 205 hours. The subjects experienced a gradual increase in fatigue, as well as a decline in perceptual,

cognitive, and psychomotor abilities, as shown by appropriate tests. After the fifth day they appeared to obtain a "second wind"; that is, their performances returned to normal after they were sufficiently aroused. Episodes of brief disorientation and of brief hallucinations were experienced by the subjects—one even went briefly berserk at 200 hours—but no evidence of psychosis was seen. Follow-up studies of the men after several months showed no evidence that the experience had had any permanent effects on them.

Experiments that deprive the subject of either REM sleep or slow-wave sleep have also been carried out. (As previously noted, REM sleep is associated with dream recall and epinephrine activity in a nucleus of the pons; slow-wave sleep has been associated with serotonin activity in the raphe nuclei or acetylcholine from FTG cells.) The usual procedure is to wake the subject every time his EEG record shows evidence of REM sleep or every time the record shows slow (delta) wave activity. (Although the subject's sleep is interrupted, it is of normal duration.) In the REM-deprivation studies, REM "attempts" increase over as many as seven successive nights. On recovery nights of uninterrupted sleep the incidence of REM sleep increases by as much as 30% over normal in a "rebound" effect that suggests that a "need" for REM sleep has been built up by the deprivation. Deprivation of stage 4 sleep for two nights also leads to a "rebound" of 60%, suggesting that stage 4 sleep may be more important to the brain than REM sleep. This data is further supported by the results from experiments in which subjects are restricted to three hours of sleep per night. Their sleep profile of early slow-wave sleep and of REM sleep, which occurs later in the sleep period, does not change. As a result, they "lose" more REM sleep than slow-wave sleep. Despite this, stage 4 sleep dominates their EEG record on recovery nights, when they sleep as long as they wish.

A review of the sleep literature suggests that poor sleepers—those who awake often during the night—show records that are deficient in REM sleep. This is often true of people who work night shifts and sleep in the daytime. On the other hand, elderly people are frequently poor sleepers, and their records show deficiencies in stage 4 sleep. This is also true of many middle-aged people. Within limits the distribution of sleep between REM sleep and slow-wave sleep seems more important than sleep duration.

Body temperature. There also appears to be a relationship between sleep stages and body temperature. For most of us who sleep from 11 or 12 PM until 7 or 8 AM, there is a regular daily cycle of body temperature change. Body temperature is low early in the morning, rises to a plateau during the afternoon, rises still higher in the evening, and falls during the night. Daytime nap records show more REM sleep, and evening nap records show a greater incidence of delta waves. Thus REM sleep accompanies a lower body temperature than does slow-wave sleep, and "slow" delta waves are found when the body temperature is higher. During normal sleeping hours more delta waves are found in the early hours of the night, when body temperature is high. More REM sleep is found later in the night, when body temperature is falling. Thus persons who travel by jet from one time zone to another often experience sleep disturbances. Their "biological clocks" of daily body temperature and sleep cycles have been set to the daily cycle of the time zone in which they live. They must readjust their circadian rhythms to a time that may be six or eight hours different. If they use sedatives to get to sleep at a new hour, they may experience REM deprivation (see below). Further evidence that body temperature and sleep are related is found in an experiment using cats. A diathermy machine, similar to those which create heat in the deeper layers of muscles to relieve cramps, was employed. Diathermic warming of the pre-

optic and anterior hypothalamic areas induced relaxation and normal sleep in these animals. The areas thus warmed are important "centers" for the regulation of both body temperature and sleep.

Another relationship between REM sleep and body temperature has been found by Glotzbach and Heller (1975). They used kangaroo rats as subjects because their body temperature is more dependent on the temperature of the hypothalamus and less dependent on reactions to temperature change like shivering or sweating than is true for most species. As a result, they could measure the effect of cooling or warming the hypothalamus on the body's metabolic rate in a direct fashion. During slow-wave sleep, metabolic rate increased to produce body heat when the hypothalamic temperature was lowered and the metabolic rate decreased to relieve the heat load when the hypothalamus was warmed. By contrast, these reactions did *not* occur during paradoxical sleep—"dreams can't keep you warm!" Studies on cats and rats show that at low room temperatures they spend more time in slow-wave sleep and less in paradoxical sleep in an apparent attempt to keep warm. Evidently the hypothalamus loses body temperature control during paradoxical or REM sleep.

The evolutionary development of REM sleep. REM sleep is absent in fish, probably absent in reptiles, present (but of brief duration) in birds, and present in all mammals studied, including the opossum, the elephant, and humans. This suggests that the development of REM sleep parallels the development of the cerebral cortex in evolutionary history. Fish and reptiles have no cortex. The cortex in birds is limited to a small area that serves vision. Mammals, on the other hand, all have a complete cerebral cortex, although the extent of its development varies from species to species.

Autonomic activity and sleep. During non-REM (NREM, or slow-wave) sleep, the electromyograph (EMG) activity is suppressed, indicating muscle relaxation in humans (muscle relaxation in the cat occurs during REM or paradoxical sleep). Reflexes are also suppressed, which would seem to indicate a less active nervous system. However, the autonomic nervous system shows more activity during sleep than it does in a relaxed waking state. Changes in heart rate, blood pressure, skin resistance (indicating sweat gland activity), and respiration are seen. The onset of autonomic activity is usually signaled by the spontaneous (unpredictable) appearance of K complexes in stage 2 sleep. Skin resistance fluctuations ("GSR storms") increase if the subject's sleep pattern then changes to SWS.

Drugs and REM deprivation. Barbiturates and most other sedatives suppress REM sleep. They appear to act by suppressing the activity of the brain and preventing the occurrence of the light sleep stage (stage 1) that always accompanies REM sleep. Alcohol also depresses neural activity, but it has different effects on sleep. Alcoholics frequently suffer night terrors and insomnia (inability to sleep). Both slow-wave sleep and REM sleep are reduced, but REM sleep is decreased the most. Most prescription "sleeping pills" are barbiturates and suppress REM sleep. An amino acid (L-tryptophan) has recently been discovered by Dr. Althea Wagman and her colleagues that induces sleep in insomniacs without resulting in REM deprivation.

Sleep disorders. The most common sleep disorders are enuresis (bed wetting), somnambulism (sleepwalking), night terrors (waking suddenly in a frightened state), and nightmares (bad dreams, technically called incubus). All four are commonly assumed to be caused or accompanied by dreaming as in the usual association of nightmares with bad dreams. EEG and eye movement recordings have now shown this assumption to be false (Broughton, 1968). All four disorders occur during rapid arousal from slow-wave sleep. Any REM sleep (dreaming) that occurs follows the

end of the sleep-disorder episode. The response of bed wetting may trigger a dream; then if the subject wakes he may have incorporated bed wetting into the content of his dream. Sleepwalking occurs during slow-wave sleep; the subject is hard to wake during the episode and then seldom reports a coherent dream. The sleep terror (pavor nocturnus) is common in children and not unusual in adults—the child sits up screaming, emotional, and staring wide-eyed at something he imagines; dream recall is rare and fragmented. The nightmare (incubus and succubus) is more common in adults. All the signs of anxiety like sweating, trembling, and heavy breathing are present and the subject may cry out. If wakened, he reports a terrifying situation like being suffocated or crushed, rather than a sequence of events in a narrative dream. (This is not to deny terrifying dreams that occur during REM sleep but cause no respiratory symptoms of the sort described.) The subject seldom recalls the attack the following morning. The four disorders are classified together because the first three are more common in children, two or all three of the first three disorders may occur in the same subject, and one or more of the three often shows up in the subject's family history. Since all four result during rapid arousal from slow-wave sleep, they could be more properly termed *disorders of arousal,* although the question of what triggers the disorders remains unanswered.

Dement and his colleagues have a clinic at Stanford for the diagnosis and experimental treatment of sleep disorders. The disorders of the preceding paragraph are called dysomnias, for sleep behavior that disturbs others; the more treatable other categories involve too much sleep (narcolepsy) or too little (insomnia). Insomnia often seems imagined, and those who complain of it are frequently found to sleep normally when objectively observed. When barbiturates or alcohol are used for insomnia, tolerance, increased dosage levels, addiction, and loss of REM sleep often result. Behavior modification techniques that forbid any bedroom activity except sleep and that reward each recorded shift toward normal sleep habits are often effective. Many insomniacs snore; the snoring episodes seem caused by a complete failure of breathing (apnea), which causes snoring as breathing is forced and also arouses the subject to wakefulness. Experiments with cats show that the transition from wakefulness to sleep depresses the respiratory mechanisms of the nervous system. In extreme cases, an opening in the throat below the larynx ("voice box") relieves apnea during sleep. Other insomniacs are awakened by involuntary squirming movements and muscle twitching in the legs (nocturnal myoclonus).

Narcolepsy, excessive sleepiness, is usually accompanied by sleepiness as a "sleep attack," sudden muscle weakness (cataplexy), hallucinations just before and after sleep, and sleep paralysis. The patient may go to sleep in midsentence while talking, and EEG recordings show that they go directly into REM sleep (as children often do) without the usual SWS period of 90 minutes or so first. Tricyclic antidepressant drugs (which block REM sleep) combat catalepsy and hallucinations, and about three short naps a day relieve the sleep attacks in many cases.

A sleep chemical? The search for a hormone or a natural hypnogenic chemical that induces sleep is an old one, with little in the way of reliable results until recently. Newer methods of separating brain chemicals according to their molecular weight (gel filtration) have renewed interest in research of this kind in Europe. Stimulation of a specific area in the thalamus of the rabbit induces continuous slow-wave sleep. A fraction of tissue fluid of defined chemical properties from the sleeping rabbits was injected continuously into the ventricles of the brain of normal rabbits for a period of about a half hour. Progressively over the first few minutes of this period, the recorded delta-wave activity nearly doubles; during the last part of the period,

the animal shows all the behavioral signs of sleep. Control animals that were treated in a similar way with other chemical fractions from the sleeping rabbits showed none of these effects. Some chemical seems to accumulate in the cerebrospinal fluid (CSF) of sleep-deprived animals; however, Pappenheimer and his colleagues at Harvard have succeeded in permanently implanting a "guide tube" to the fourth ventricle of goats (as a result of the shape of the skull of this species). A needle can be used to withdraw CSF without disturbing the animal. The goat is deprived of sleep for 48 hours before CSF is withdrawn. Rats are normally nocturnal (awake at night) but 0.1 ml of the goat CSF injected into rat CSF will reduce their nocturnal activity by 63%. The sleep induced in the rats is not continuous, but there is an increase in the frequency and duration of sleep episodes. Further, the size and duration of the delta waves typical of slow-wave sleep are greater in induced sleep than in normal sleep. The sleep changes in the rats follow injection by about three hours, presumably the time required for the sleep factor to reach its site of action in the brain. Filtration studies show that the factor has a molecular weight of between 350 and 500, but further chemical isolation is difficult. Withdrawal of the CSF from goats is a slow process. A similar sleep factor has been extracted from the brain stems of 1,000 sleep-deprived rats by Uchizons at the University of Tokyo, but their yield is one millionth of a gram per 100 g of brain! The object of all of this is, of course, to chemically analyze and then synthesize this mysterious chemical. Not only might the "perfect sleeping pill" result, but a powerful chemical tool for investigating the chemical and neural mechanisms would be at hand.

Sleep and the endocrine glands. In Chapter 2, endocrine glands and their hormones were defined; the endocrine glands and their functions were given in Table 3. Endocrine glands release hormones into the bloodstream to be carried all over the body. Specific hormones have given effects on selected specialized tissues in a way that is determined by their chemical structure—they are chemically "coded" to affect their "target" tissues. Three of these hormones have been related to sleep. The output of prolactin (lactogenic hormone) and testosterone (a male androgen, or sex hormone) is increased during sleep and decreased during wakefulness. It may be that prolactin from the anterior pituitary gland stimulates the gonads to produce testosterone. During sleep, the anterior pituitary increases its output of growth hormone during REM sleep and decreases it during slow-wave sleep. The meaning of these fluctuations is not yet clear. They should be mentioned, however, because they may play a role in sleep cycles.

Electrosleep. It has been known since the turn of the century that passing a low-voltage intermittent current through an animal's brain induces a state resembling sleep, although the brain structures affected by this treatment remain a mystery. During the last 20 years, the phenomenon has been intensely investigated in Russia; little work has been done outside of eastern Europe, although the equipment is commercially available here. Electrodes are placed over the eyes and behind the ears and a low-voltage intermittent direct current is used (pulse duration 0.1 to 1 msec, frequency 5 to 100 per second, intensity 0.4 to 8 milliamps, treatment duration 30 to 60 minutes, five to ten daily treatments). The patients report a tingling sensation but no discomfort. Sleep may or may not occur, depending on the current used, so electrosleep may be a misnomer. The treatment has received little experimental evaluation; the Russian studies are largely clinical reports of therapeutic effects in the treatment of sleep disorders, anxiety, brain disease, and a variety of symptoms from asthma to hypertension (high blood pressure).

MEDITATION

Research in several laboratories concerns whether there is a state of consciousness not previously studied from a physio-logical point of view. As organized in this chapter, we have defined four states of consciousness: (1) aroused attention, (2) quiet waking, (3) slow-wave sleep (or stages 3 and 4 NREM sleep—stage 2 may be transitional), and (4) REM sleep. The state in question involves a combination of psychological reports of awareness and physiological measures that do not appear to occur at the same time in the above four states of awareness. These are (1) reports of heightened awareness similar to aroused attention but not directed toward an arousing stimulus, (2) presence of a regular alpha rhythm of greater amplitude and regularity than is seen in quiet wakefulness, and (3) lowered metabolic activity and muscle relaxation similar to sleep stages that are not accompanied by increases in movement or autonomic activity.

Interest in the phenomenon began with EEG studies of meditation as practiced by devotees of the Indian philosophy of yoga. With the introduction and widespread popularity of transcendental meditation (TM), physiological study has shifted to meditation as practiced by this group. Two questions appear to arise: (1) Is there a state of brain function and awareness not previously defined? (2) Is this state beneficial in the relief of anxiety and symptoms of anxiety such as high blood pressure? Although the initial studies look promising, questions remain. For example: (1) Are the various forms of meditation practiced—Zen, yoga, TM, and so on—similar in their physiological and psychological attributes despite differences in the technique of meditation? (2) If the phenomenon is valid, can all subjects be taught to attain this state, or are there large individual differences in ability? (3) Are any benefits achieved from the practice of meditation transitory or lasting and do all subjects realize them to the same degree?

Some of the most discouraging evidence concerning meditation as a unique conscious state is the finding in one study (Pagano and co-workers, 1976) that five experienced meditators spent an average of 40% of their meditation time over ten sessions in slow-wave sleep according to EEG criteria! Although this does not show that meditation and napping are identical, it does indicate that meditation is not a "single, unique, hypometabolic state," according to the authors.

Biofeedback, conscious states, and the EEG

Biofeedback is a learning technique that will be explained more completely in Chapter 13. A brief explanation is in order here, however, because of attempts to create a quasimeditational state of consciousness by learned control of EEG patterns. To oversimplify, human and animal subjects are reported to have learned control over formerly "involuntary" responses (e.g., heart rate, digestive responses, EEG patterns) by being rewarded for each occurrence of the response. For human subjects, a signal that they have succeeded is reward enough—beginning with any occurrence of response and an increased strength or duration of response being required as training continues.

As noted, meditators are reported to have an alpha rhythm of greater amplitude and regularity than is normally seen in quiet wakefulness. This raised the question of creating a quasimeditational state by biofeedback training that enhances the alpha rhythm. Encouraging early reports of an "alpha experience" (Brown, 1970; Hart, 1968; Nowlis and Kamija, 1968; and Kimaya, 1970) have resulted in widespread advertisements in the popular press for alpha-training devices that signal the subject when alpha is enhanced. Later reports (Plotkin, et al., 1976) find no relationship between subjective reports of a quasimeditational alpha experience and alpha enhancement.

TWO MINDS IN ONE BRAIN?

Another topic that receives more extensive treatment in Chapter 13 deserves mention here because of its implications for consciousness: hemispheric specialization. Although we have known for 100 years that language function was localized in the cerebral cortex of the left hemisphere only in nearly all cases, the application of sophisticated learning techniques has shown that the two hemispheres of the brain differ in other important ways. The discovery began with tests of epileptic patients who had the corpus callosum, which interconnects the hemispheres of the brain, severed to prevent the spread of seizures ("epileptic fits") from one hemisphere to the other. Later it was found that information input could be restricted to one hemisphere of the brain by the use of sophisticated techniques for presenting stimuli. The results all show, as expected, that the right hemisphere is illiterate—without language function. Further results suggest other functions for the right hemisphere—form perception, including the recognition of faces, music, recognition, visual and body imagery, sexual arousal, and emotionality. Left hemisphere functions extend beyond language to mathematics, logic, abstraction, and analysis. The left hemisphere was originally called the dominant hemisphere because it controlled the right hand, and most of us are right-handed. It appears also to be dominant in the control of the conscious processes during waking behavior. There is some evidence that the right nonverbal hemisphere is more active in sleep, especially REM ("dreaming") sleep. Unity in conscious awareness appears to be provided by the corpus callosum.

SUMMARY

A position defining states of consciousness physiologically as well as psychologically began the chapter and promised to treat the topics of aroused alertness, resting wakefulness, "dreamless" and "dreaming" sleep, meditation, and cerebral dominance. In treating sleep and wakefulness together, Kleitman's evolutionary theory came first. To Kleitman, sleep seemed a more homeostatically normal state than wakefulness, and therefore his theory attempted to explain wakefulness. In Kleitman's theory, wakefulness of necessity in lower animals and children results from bodily needs or other discomforts and causes a polyphasic sleep cycle. As need satisfaction becomes conditioned to daylight, wakefulness of choice and a monophasic sleep cycle ensue. He postulated that a sleep center (really a waking center) in the diencephalon aroused the whole brain to wakefulness upon stimulation. The theory was supported by the somnambulance and wakefulness of necessity shown by some encephalitis victims with brain damage in that area. The sleep center in normal adults could be stimulated by the cortex during daylight hours to cause wakefulness of choice. In modern terms, the central gray core of the brain stem, the brain stem reticular formation (BSRF), contains an ascending reticular arousal system (ARAS) that arouses the rest of the brain when the ARAS is stimulated by collaterals from the sensory pathways (specific thalamic projection system or STPS). More diffuse thalamic sensory pathways to association areas related to specific sensory projection areas form the diffuse thalamic projection system (DTPS) that is involved in attention to that sensory input. Stimulation of the ARAS by implanted electrodes in the cat arouses the sleeping animal to alert attention and changes the EEG from a sleeping to a waking pattern. Transecting the STPS pathways in the brain stem has no gross effect on the animal, but cutting the ARAS pathways makes it somnambulant. Efferent inhibitory output to nuclei of the STPS from higher centers reduces or blocks sensory input in habituation; efferent excitatory output sensitizes these channels. Both types of output, known as sensory gating, provide efferent control of afferent input in states of attention. The ARAS and DTPS are under similar control.

Changes in the EEG parallel states of arousal from deep sleep to vigilance. EEG waves are believed to be synchronous changes in the depolarization of cortical cells that reflect the rate of firing in their fibers or else firing of cortical dendrites. During arousal the cells are largely depolarized and fire rapidly, producing a desynchronized EEG. With increasing quiescence and sleep, brain waves generally become synchronized and of lower frequency.

When brain wave patterns are used as a measure, four stages of sleep can be distinguished, each with its characteristic EEG pattern, whereas the alpha rhythm is often characteristic of the relaxed waking state. Sleeping subjects show cyclic shifts between the sleep stages every 30 to 90 minutes during the night but generally spend more time in the slow-wave stages 3 or 4 during the second through the third or fourth and subsequent hours. If deprived of slow-wave stages by being awakened from them during one night, the subject will compensate with longer slow-wave periods the next night. Dreaming can be detected by emergence of the EEG from a sleeping pattern to stage 1 (E-1) and the appearance of rapid eye movements (REM). When deprived of E-1 and REM sleep by being awakened, subjects become irritable and anxious, and spend more time showing these patterns on the subsequent night. Infants and other polyphasic animals spend more time in REM sleep than do adults. It is harder to wake animal subjects from REM sleep than from deeper sleep stages. Slow-wave sleep is stimulated by serotonin production in the raphe nuclei, according to Jouvet. REM sleep results from epinephrine production by nuclei of the pons. McCarley and Hobson attribute paradoxical (desynchronized) sleep to another nucleus of the pons (FTG cells), slow-wave sleep to LC cells, and sleep cycles to interactions between them.

Sleep deprivation affects orientation and efficiency but does not cause psychosis. Deprivation of either REM or slow-wave sleep will cause an increase in the deprived pattern on recovery nights. Slow-wave sleep "rebounds" more then REM sleep, and REM sleep accompanies a lower body temperature than does slow-wave sleep.

Hypothalamic control of body temperature is disrupted during REM sleep. Only mammals show much REM sleep and have a developed cortex. Autonomic changes often accompany stage 2 sleep when K complexes are seen. Most sedatives depress REM sleep. The sleep disorders of enuresis, somnambulism, night terrors, and nightmare are disorders of arousal from slow-wave sleep. Narcolepsy and insomnia can be treated with drugs and training.

There may be a hypnogenic chemical because extracts of CSF from sleep-deprived animals causes sleep in normal animals. Prolactin and testosterone output are increased during REM sleep. Electrosleep can be induced by passing a DC current through the brain.

Reports of enhanced alpha and a single unique hypometabolic conscious state during transcendental meditation conflict with EEG records of alpha training and sleep records during meditation. Studies of hemispheric specialization attribute language, logic, mathematics, and analysis to the dominant left hemisphere and form perception, music, imagery, and emotionality to the right hemisphere; the corpus callosum preserves unity in conscious awareness.

READINGS

Allison, T., and van Tuyver, H.: The evolution of sleep, Nat. History **79:**56-75, Feb. 1970. Also in Leukel, F.: Issues in physiological psychology, St. Louis, 1974, The C. V. Mosby Co.

Bakan, P.:The right brain is the dreamer, Psychol. Today **10:**66-68, Nov. 1976.

Berger, R. J.: Morpheus descending, Psychol. Today **4:**33-35, 70, June 1970.

Broughton, R. J.: Sleep disorders: disorders of arousal? Science **159:**1070-1078, 1968. Also in Leukel, F.: Issues in physiological psychology, St. Louis, 1974, The C. V. Mosby Co.

Dement, W., and Kleitman, N.: The relation of eye movements during sleep to dream activity: an objective method for the study of dreaming, J. Exp. Psychol. **53:**339-346, 1957 (Bobbs-Merrill Reprint No. P-87).

Johnson, L.: Are stages of sleep related to waking behavior? Am. Scientist **61:**326-338, 1973.

Jouvet, M.: The states of sleep, Sci. Am. **216:**62-72, Feb. 1967 (W. H. Freeman Reprint No. 504).

Jouvet, M.: Biogenic amines and the states of sleep, Science **163:**32-41, 1969. Also in Leukel, F.: Issues in physiological psychology, St. Louis, 1974, The C. V. Mosby Co.

Kleitman, N.: Sleep, Sci. Am. **187:**34-38, Nov. 1952 (W. H. Freeman Reprint No. 431).

Kleitman, N.: Patterns of dreaming, Sci. Am. **203:**82-88, Nov. 1960 (W. H. Freeman Reprint No. 460).

Kripper, S., and Hughes, W.: Genius at work, Psychol. Today **4:**40-43, June 1970.

Malmo, R. S.: Activation: a neuropsychological dimension, Psychol. Rev. **66:**367-386, 1959 (Bobbs-Merrill Reprint No. P-507).

Mittler, M., Guelleminault, J., Zarcose, V., and Dement, W.: Sleeplessness, sleep attacks, and things that go wrong in the night, Psychol. Today **9:**45-50, Dec. 1975.

Oswald, J.: Sleep, Baltimore, 1966, Penguin Books, Inc.

Pappenheimer, J.: The sleep factor, Sci. Am. **225:**24-29, Aug. 1976.

Sharpless, S., and Jasper, H.: Habituation of the arousal reaction, Brain **79:**655-680, 1956 (Bobbs-Merrill Reprint No. P-558).

Snyder, F.: The physiology of dreaming. In Kramer, M., editor: Dream psychology and the new biology of dreaming, Springfield, Ill., 1969, Charles C Thomas, Publisher. Also in Leukel, F.: Issues in physiological psychology, St. Louis, 1974, The C. V. Mosby Co.

Tune, G. S.: The human sleep debt, Sci. J. **21:**67-71, Dec. 1968.

van de Castle, R. L.: His, hers, and the children's, Psychol. Today **4:**37-40, June 1970.

Wallace, R., and Benson, H.: The physiology of meditation, Sci. Am. **228:**84-90, Feb. 1972. (W. H. Freeman Co. Reprint No. 1242).

Webb, W. B.: Sleep: an experimental approach, New York, 1968, Macmillan Publishing Co., Inc.

CHAPTER **12**

Motivation: behavior in response to need

OVERVIEW

This chapter treats the way the nervous system translates the needs of the body into behavior—the topic of motivation. When the behavior that results does not lead to need satisfaction (a state of "frustration"), increased arousal or nervous activity and behavior follows, and we call the resulting state an emotion. So it makes sense to find out first in this chapter about motivation and then take up the more extreme case of emotion in Chapter 13. Our discussion of motivation begins with some definitions and a conceptual framework. The terms used in the study of motivation often have varied meanings for the reader; thus a single meaning for each must be decided on before proceeding. Terms are defined in a conceptual framework that distinguishes between what is going on in the animal and what is going on in the environment. The definitions distinguish between changes in the external environment that stimulate the animal and the resulting behavior that follows from the altered body conditions in the internal environment. The distinctions assist in understanding the characteristics of drives and motives—hunger, thirst, and sex are used as examples. The roles of more or less *local states* that accompany these motives are considered first—the dryness of the mouth in thirst or the sensations of

stomach contractions in hunger, for example. When these states prove inadequate to explain motivated behavior, the *self-regulatory* characteristics of motives are added; for example, central factors control eating and drinking behavior so that we eat and drink enough, but not too much, in maintaining the consistency of the internal environment. These behaviors are controlled by *multiple factors,* no one of which dominates behavior. The role of the *hypothalamus* is central to motivated behavior, however. The specific mechanisms governing the thirst, hunger, and sex drives are then taken up in detail. Some central neural mechanisms of reward and punishment are surveyed. Centers in the brain have been found whose stimulation is so "rewarding" that the animal (or human) will work to stimulate himself. Conversely, others have been found whose stimulation the animal will avoid even though it takes considerable work to do so.

SPECIFIC MOTIVES

The neural mechanisms of specific motives will be discussed in this chapter—thirst, hunger, and sex motivation serving as the primary examples. Before these topics are discussed, there must be agreement on the terms to be used in describing stimulus events preceding motivated behavior, the resulting events in the internal envi-

191

ronment of the animal, and the consequent observed behavior. Much of the difficulty experienced in early studies of motivation came from confusion in regard to terminology. In using the term "need," for example, some would be referring to a lack, or absence, in the external environment, whereas others would be referring to a change in the animal's (internal) *state.* The statement that "the dog needs water" could refer to an empty water dish or be an inference about the animal's internal condition when it was panting in hot weather and probably dehydrated. In other instances an attempt would be made to explain behavior by merely naming it. "The dog inherits a 'water need' (internal state)." How does one know? "He drinks water every day (external behavior)." Similar difficulties led to the controversy over instincts, or complex motivation, which was presumed to be inherited. Women were assumed to inherit a "maternal instinct" defined as behavior involving child care. "Women inherit a love for children." How does one know this? "They love children." All these statements ignore the complex of internal conditions, external stimuli, and rewarding or punishing effects of the resulting behavior.

Terminology

In the definitions and the schema to be used here, an attempt will be made to *predict* behavior as a *consequence* of predetermined external stimulus events and known internal conditions of the organism. External stimulus events interact with pre-existing conditions in the internal environment of the organism; external stimulus events also result in further changes in the internal environment. From this interaction of external and internal events, behavior results. The behavior changes the external stimulus conditions and the internal state of the animal, which results in further behavior.

Both external and internal stimuli result in behavior, whether or not the stimuli are "known" to the organism and whether or not the stimuli can be seen by an outside observer. The organism may respond to an external stimulus that is not evident to another observer, as when a dog barks in response to a high-pitched whistle that is outside the frequency limits audible to a human observer. (The observer, of course, may use instruments to detect the sound and eventually discover that it is usually followed by a barking response.) The animal may react to some change in his internal environment that results from lack of water, an aspect that affects some center or system in the CNS. Only tedious and ingenious research can detect (1) what changes in the internal environment result from lack of water, (2) which of these changes affect the CNS, (3) how and where they affect the CNS, and (4) what kind of CNS activity leads to the behavior that usually follows lack of water.

Table 11 summarizes the order of events in motivated behavior and the terms to be used in the remainder of the chapter. A **need condition** is any state of affairs in the *external environment* that disturbs equilibrium, or homeostasis, in the internal environment. Thus a condition of adequate water would be required for the individual to survive, or the presence of the opposite sex would be needed for the species to survive. A need condition leads to a **need state,** the complex of resulting *inherent* or *acquired* changes in *internal* equilibrium. A **sensitizing stimulus** is the aspect of a need state that sets off a drive mechanism in the CNS. A **drive** is a CNS mechanism for arousing and sustaining behavior when the need state has a sensitizing stimulus. The lack of water (need condition), for example, causes many changes in the tissues (need state). The CNS is sensitive to some of these changes (sensitizing stimuli), and parts of the CNS (drive) arouse and sustain behavior. Not all inherent need states have sensitizing stimuli, however. Vitamin B_1 is required for survival, and a lack of this vitamin severely disturbs internal equilibrium. Yet aroused behavior does *not* result directly from vitamin B_1 deficiency (al-

Table 11. Schema for motivated behavior

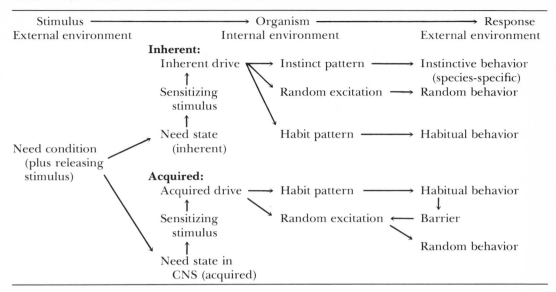

Stimulus ⟶	Organism ⟶	Response
External environment	Internal environment	External environment

though an animal can *learn* to choose foods rich in B_1 because of the rewarding effects on his internal condition).

A drive arouses and sustains behavior; it does not direct, or channel, behavior. Behavior appropriate to the drive occurs only in the presence of a **releasing stimulus** that is somehow related to the **incentive.** The incentive is the external stimulus that changes the need condition and therefore the need state, drive, and sensitizing stimulus. Water, for example, would be the incentive for the thirst drive. It is also a releasing stimulus for thirst since it releases behavior appropriate to the drive, that is, drinking. Other stimuli that serve as *cues* to the presence of water are also releasing stimuli for behavior appropriate to thirst. For a thirsty man a water fountain leads to complex behavior that is appropriate to thirst; the water fountain is a releasing stimulus but not the incentive per se, because a water fountain cannot relieve thirst. The water fountain leads to thirst-related behavior only as a result of learning.

Inherent need states and inherent drives arouse behavior. In the case of some lower animals, behavior appropriate to the drive is "built into" the nervous system, and this behavior is the same for all members of the species (species-specific). In this case one speaks of an **instinct,** consisting of an inherent drive and inherited CNS systems for complex behavior. The behavior may or may not require releasing stimuli. For example, nest building is an instinct in many species. For certain wasps the only need condition required is absence of a nest; the wasp produces its own nest-building material and will usually build a nest whenever a nest is lacking. The rat, however, builds a nest only in the presence of nest-building materials (releasing stimuli) *and* certain internal conditions (sensitizing stimuli) such as cold or the hormonal changes of pregnancy.

The primates, including humans, do not seem to inherit CNS patterns for complex organized behavior in response to inherent drives. Primates appear to lack instincts. Drive arousal results in random behavior until the incentive is reached. Behavior becomes less random and variable with learning, and the animal develops a **habit**—behavior patterns appropriate to the drive under the conditions in which he lives. The existence of a drive *and* a habit is referred to as a **motive.** Organized and learned behavior follows an aroused hunger drive in adult humans, so that the adult has a hunger motive. An infant responds to the hunger drive with random behavior since he has no hunger motive prior to learning how to obtain food. If hunger-motivated behavior does not lead to food, however, it will become more variable and random until new and successful habits have been learned. Finally, there are certain habits that lead to changes in the internal environment and thus cause **addiction.** The habitual use of certain drugs can change the internal equilibrium of the body so that the CNS no longer functions well in the absence of the drug. Strong need states and sensitizing stimuli result from withdrawal of the drug, and the CNS reacts as it does to an inherent drive.

It should be stressed at this point that no explanation of motivated behavior has been given so far. Definitions of terms have been made explicit to avoid confusion later on. The schema in Table 11 is not explanatory because it is essentially "circular"—a need condition leading to a need state, drive, motive or instinct, behavior related to an incentive, and removal of the need condition. The explanation of drives and motives will require proof of what conditions terminate motivated behavior as well as what conditions initiate it. Nearly all references to thirst, hunger, and sexual behavior will refer to inherent needs and drives. The terms "need" and "drive" will refer to inherent needs and drives unless otherwise specified. The role of learning in behavior will be taken up in Chapter 14.

Characteristics of drives and motives: local states

Early approaches to the thirst, hunger, and sex drives were made with the assumption that humans were *aware* of their sensitizing stimuli. In this view, need states in the body resulted in consciously perceived stimuli that were restricted to local sensory areas of the body—hence the term "local states." In thirst one is aware of dryness of the mouth and throat. When one is extremely hungry, powerful stomach contractions may be perceived as "hunger pangs." In the male it was assumed that accumulation of seminal fluid in the vesicles made the penis more sensitive to stimulation, arousing the sex drive. All these stimulus sites are "peripheral" to most of the internal environment, although the stimulation *results* from changes in the internal environment. Local-state drive theories have been called "peripheral theories" for that reason, in contrast to theories about the direct effect of internal changes on the brain. To prove that "local states" are the sensitizing stimuli for drives, they must be shown to be both *necessary* and *sufficient* to the arousal of appropriate motivated behavior.

Thirst. When the body is dehydrated, or low on water, salivation is reduced as one way of reducing loss of water in the tissues. This results in the dry mouth sensations one experiences when thirsty. Cannon (1963) suggested that dryness of the mouth and throat arouses and sustains thirst-drive behavior when an animal is thirsty. This means that mouth and throat dryness is the sensitizing stimulus for the thirst drive. Is mouth and throat dryness a necessary and sufficient condition to arouse and sustain the thirst drive? The evidence suggests that it is not. In the first place, the first swallow of water when one is thirsty abolishes these sensations; yet drinking behavior continues for some time before one is satiated. Dryness of the mouth and throat could therefore arouse the first swallow, but what sustains subsequent drinking behavior? Experimenters have tied off the ducts of salivary glands in animals to make them permanently "dry mouthed." Such animals drink more frequently, but they do not consume more water in the course of the day than do normal animals. The same has been found true of humans born without functional salivary glands. It is evident that mouth and throat dryness has something to do with the *initiation* of drinking behavior, but it has little to do with the *regulation* of how long drinking behavior is sustained or the amount of water drunk. The evidence does not show that mouth and throat dryness is *necessary* to the initiation of drinking behavior, although the sensation may contribute to initiation of drinking.

Hunger. Another local stimulus that could arouse a drive comes from stomach contractions that may accompany hunger and are sensed by the subject as hunger pangs. Sensations of stomach distention usually accompany satiation and could terminate eating behavior. A low blood glucose level induced by insulin injections can cause stomach contractions, but whether blood glucose gets that low during ordinary hunger is not clear. Cannon suggested that hunger was caused by stomach contractions after he performed an experiment in which he abstained from food for several days and then swallowed a balloon that was connected by a tube to a pressure-measuring device. When the stomach contracted, it squeezed the balloon, and increased pressure was indicated. Without seeing the pressure measurements, he signaled when he sensed a hunger pang. The sensations corresponded with stomach contractions. Subsequent studies have cast some doubt on this famous experiment. It has been shown that the presence of the balloon in the stomach stimulates stomach contractions, for example. However, powerful stomach contractions and hunger pangs do occur during starvation, although they are reported to last for only three to five days. None of this tells us whether stomach contractions, as a sensitizing stimulus, are necessary and sufficient to arouse and sustain the hunger drive. Other evidence suggests that stomach contractions are unnecessary to the hunger drive, although they may contribute to the aroused and sustained behavior for a time. (Certainly the starving man is still hungry for days after the contractions cease!)

Some of the evidence comes from operations performed on people with stomach ulcers. In some cases nerves leading to the stomach were cut to block parasympathetic facilitation of automatic stomach contractions and stop the stimulation of acid secretion by the stomach. Denervating the stomach also cuts sensory nerves and eliminates sensations caused by stomach contractions. It does not alter the arousal or regulation of eating behavior in these patients. In other ulcer operations all or part of the stomach is removed without interference with eating behavior, except that less can be eaten at one time (until the small intestine enlarges to store food as the stomach once did). Although these patients eat less, they eat more frequently, and food intake is thus regulated as before. Removing the stomach of animals produces the same general effects. Animals without a stomach show aroused and sustained behavior when deprived of food, and they will learn complex habits to obtain a food reward. Therefore stomach contractions as a sensitizing stimulus are neither necessary nor sufficient to arouse or sustain the hunger drive, although they may contribute to the regulation of normal food intake.

Sex. In the mature male, semen is stored in the seminal vesicles after being produced by the gonads. If the accumulation is not drawn off by intercourse, nocturnal emissions occur at fairly regular intervals. In the absence of regular copulation and ejaculation, the accumulation of unspent semen in the vesicles might act as a sensitizing stimulus that arouses the sex drive in males. No similar mechanism was proposed for females. Research on the function of the endocrine glands has now shown that both the sex drive and the production of germ plasm are under the control of the sex hormones of the endocrine glands in vertebrate species. In humans the sex drive becomes dominated by learning, and sensitizing stimuli are more a function of past experience than hormone levels. As a result the female sex drive becomes largely independent of the regular monthly changes in hormone level caused by the estrus cycle, and sexual behavior continues after germ plasm and sex hormone production ceases in both sexes with aging. This is not to say that the strength of the sex drive or the frequency of intercourse is independent of sex hormone level in the human. However, sex hormones are neither necessary nor sufficient to arouse and sustain sexual behavior, at least in the human adult with past sexual experience.

Characteristics of drives and motives: self-regulation

In general, motivated behavior is organized to maintain the consistency of the internal environment. Evidence will be presented to show that animals, including humans, can estimate their need for food or water very closely after a given amount of deprivation. Experiments show that normal animals drink or eat the amount necessary to replace a loss from deprivation, and very little more or less. The time required to replace the lost food or water is not enough to enable the body to restore internal equilibrium. An animal will drink enough to restore body water level (within 0.5% of body weight) within a few minutes and *stop,* even though the body has not had time to distribute the water to most of the tissues. This means that there must be shut-off stimuli to signal satiation as well as sensitizing stimuli to signal need. Furthermore, behavior that satisfies one need of the body can create others. For example, perspiring to keep the body temperature down in hot weather results in dehydration and consequent thirst. Continuous adjustment is necessary to keep the body's needs in balance. There are, however, inherent drives, or "appetites," that seem independent of the body's needs. They are externally controlled by releasing stimuli instead of being initiated by internal changes (for example, in animals and children, the taste for nonnutritive sweet substances such as saccharin). On the other

hand, there are need states that threaten survival but appear to have no sensitizing stimuli because they do not arouse and sustain behavior. Certain vitamin deficiencies are examples.

Hierarchy of need states. The need states of the body are not independent of one another. They compete or cooperate for behavior priority when their drives are aroused by need conditions in the environment and need states in the body. In general the priority of a need state that arouses a drive depends on how long that internal imbalance can be tolerated by the body. For example, needs for breathing, heat regulation, thirst, and hunger coexist in that order of priority in the body. Breathing must be regulated from moment to moment because the body stores little oxygen. Yet breathing may be interrupted momentarily to permit the swallowing of water. Heat regulation has more "inertia" of gain or loss—errors may be corrected over periods of many minutes without an undue change in body temperature. Body heat is continuously lost in breathing, whatever the body temperature. A change in body temperature has more immediate effects than water loss; therefore water may be sacrificed for cooling (as in a perspiring man or panting dog), since a water deficit can be tolderated for two or three days. Food intake and energy output can be out of balance for even longer, and a thirsty animal eats little because water is required for digestion and waste elimination. The behavior that results from drives and regulates drives depends on other drives and the effect of the behavior on the internal environment.

Satiation. Experiments have shown over and over again that deprived animals are able to estimate their food and water deficiencies quite accurately. A dog will begin to drink when it has lost only 0.5% of its body weight in water. If deprived of water for a period of time, the amount of water it drinks will correct the deficit it has undergone. Furthermore, it will drink this amount within five minutes. Five minutes is almost surely too short a time for water to be absorbed from the stomach and change the dehydrated state of the other tissues of the internal environment. The state of the tissues that initiated the thirst drive has not changed—the sensitizing stimulus is still there. Therefore, one must look for satiation, or stop, stimuli that halt drinking behavior when enough has been ingested to eventually restore internal balance (even though the balance has not yet been restored).

Hunger seems to act in much the same way. Animals seem to estimate their caloric needs and respond accordingly. Animals, including humans (not always!), maintain their weight at a constant level by varying their intake according to the caloric value of a changing diet; less will be eaten of high-calorie than low-calorie foods to maintain body weight within narrow limits. An animal will stop eating when it has "had enough," even though the food it has eaten is not utilized until after digestion has taken place. Since animals eat at intervals, some state of the body arouses eating behavior and serves as a sensitizing stimulus. But animals stop eating before digestion has taken place; therefore, satiating stimuli must be found that tell the organism when enough calories have been ingested. If the customary diet of a dog or a rat is "diluted" with a nonnutritive bland substance, the animal will increase its intake accordingly, up to the limit of stomach capacity. If offered diluted alcohol, rats (like some people!) will prefer a certain amount of alcohol to pure water. They will, however, reduce their caloric intake of food enough to compensate for the calories gained from the alcohol. Most convincing of all is the fact that rats will restore their normal body weight by reduced caloric intake after having been artificially fattened.

Insulin is required in certain amounts to utilize the blood glucose obtained from food. If too much insulin is present, the animal either must eat more or suffer insulin shock—fainting and possible death—because the blood glucose has been used up by other tissues and does not reach the brain, where a constant supply is necessary for brain function. Injections of insulin will cause an animal to eat more to keep up blood glucose supplies to the brain. The extra calories form fat deposits, and the animal gains weight and becomes obese. As soon as the injections are stopped, however, the rat will reduce its caloric intake for 20 days or so, losing weight until its normal body weight is reached. When the rat is overweight, either the sensitizing stimulus loses potency, or (more probably) satiation stimuli are more readily aroused.

Drives controlled by releasing stimuli: "appetites" and palatability. Both the initiation and the cessation of eating or drinking behavior are influenced by the palatability of the substances ingested, although not beyond the bounds of keeping water and food intake in balance with each other and with the need states of the body. If water or food is made bitter with quinine, it is avoided by the animal when other sources of water or food are available. If not, the animal will eat or drink just enough of most quinine concentrations to maintain itself. On the other hand, it will prefer water sweetened with saccharin to natural water, even though saccharin has no nutritive value. Here is a case of an 'appetite"—a drive controlled by the releasing stimulus in the absence of an internal sensitizing stimulus. Rats prefer the taste of saccharin to many nutritive solutions, even when they are deprived of food, and will choose saccharin-flavored water over pure water when satiated for food.

Inherent need states without sensitizing stimuli or drive mechanisms. In some instances, need states of the body that imperil survival have no apparent way of arousing and sustaining behavior. The body requires minimum amounts of vitamins A and D for survival, but the complete absence of either or both will not arouse and sustain behavior. Breathing is almost completely regulated by the CO_2 level of the blood. In a closed room a lack of oxygen is accompanied by an increased

CO_2 level. But a lack of O_2 not accompanied by increased CO_2 (as at high altitudes) causes no aroused and sustained behavior and no symptoms of suffocation (though some intoxication may result). Other need states of the body without effective sensitizing stimuli to the CNS could be cited.

Multiple-factor control of motivated behavior. Both external (releasing) and internal (sensitizing) stimuli control the arousal of motivated behavior in a complex fashion. There may be several releasing stimuli for thirst, hunger, or sexual behavior because the cues vary from one situation to another. As a result, even instinctive behavior, such as sexual behavior in the rat, is complex and variable rather than stereotyped and falls under the control of a variety of releasing stimuli. Smell, taste, touch, visual, and other stimuli combine to release sexual behavior in the rat. Experiments that eliminate these sensory inputs, singly or in combination, show that several sensory channels must be lost before the sexual response of the male rat to the female is eliminated. Furthermore, the number of sensory inputs that must be eliminated to abolish sexual behavior depends on the internal level of sex hormones. The higher the hormone level, the more sensory inputs must be eliminated to abolish male sexual behavior. Since the sex hormones act as sensitizing stimuli for sexual behavior in the male, it is evident that the effectiveness of releasing stimuli depends on the level of sensitizing stimuli. (Sexual behavior in the female is harder to eliminate by depriving her of sensory input, but the responses required of the female are less complex and less subject to varied stimulus control.) Thirst and hunger behavior are also jointly under the control of sensitizing and releasing stimuli. The effectiveness of cues (releasing stimuli) in a learning situation to a food or water reward depends on how deprived the animal is. Up to a point, greater deprivation means stronger sensitizing stimulation, higher drive level, more effective releasing stimuli, and more rapid learning.

Hypothalamic centers

The hypothalamus contains important "centers" that arouse drives. The hypothalamus receives nervous input from higher centers that regulate its activity (particularly the limbic system), but it is also aroused by the ARAS and forms a part of it. The discussion of sleep (Chapter 11) emphasized the role of the posterior hypothalamus in mobilizing the brain's activity in states of alertness and attention—states that are important to drive-aroused and sustained behavior. Many pathways for sensory input pass near and possibly stimulate the hypothalamus on the way to the thalamus and cerebral cortex. The sensory input is aroused by sensations from taste, smell, and eating or drinking behavior, as well as from the stomach and intestines, which react to their contents. On the motor side the hypothalamus governs the activity of the sympathetic and parasympathetic nervous systems. Sympathetic activity is increased when the animal mobilizes to meet the threat of deprivation. The parasympathetic system is more active in states of quiescence and satiation. Finally, cell groups in the hypothalamus are *directly sensitive* to conditions in the internal environment (extracellular tissue fluid). The internal changes that accompany thirst, hunger, sexual deprivation, and possibly loss of sleep affect different centers in the hypothalamus. As a result, behavior is aroused and sustained. In some cases (for example, thirst) we know which tissue fluid changes affect which centers in the hypothalamus. In other cases we only suspect that the centers exist because removing the areas where they are believed to be located abolishes the drive in question, and stimulating these areas initiates specific motivated behavior. Therefore, these areas are termed "excitatory" hunger, thirst, or sexual centers. In some drives (for example, hunger and possibly sleep) *inhibitory* centers have been found. Stimulating these centers *abolishes* the motivated behavior. The inhibitory area may respond to sensory input from the nervous system or to changes in the internal environment to tell the animal when it has "had enough." Therefore, the inhibitory area for a given drive may act as a satiation, or stop, center. The excitatory area would respond to sensitizing stimuli as the "start" center for motivated behavior. In other cases, destroying part of the hypothalamus may involve the destruction of nearby pathways carrying sensory input that signals behavior (for example, eating) and the consequences of that behavior in sensations of "fullness" of the stomach—the hypothalamus may not be directly involved at all.

Some authors (Valenstein, Cox, and Kakolewski, for example) put less emphasis on the hypothalamic "centers" that seem to arouse motivated behavior, and more emphasis on the role of the releasing stimuli that elicit motivated behavior. They point out that electrical stimulation of hypothalamic "centers" that elicits eating in the presence of food will also elicit drinking in the presence of water, or gnawing, if there is something to gnaw on. They propose that the hypothalamus or nearby sensory pathways can arouse several overlapping behavior patterns that are "stimulus-bound," that are specific to a given stimulus, and that involve many other areas of the brain. For example, object carrying in the rat does not require learning, and it serves several motivated behaviors, such as hoarding or retrieving pups. In their view the simple carrying out of the response is rewarding to the animal.

Regulation of thirst, hunger, and sex drives

In studying the thirst, hunger, and sex drives, one needs to know (1) what internal sensitizing stimuli are necessary to arouse the behavior, (2) how these stimuli act on the hypothalamus or other parts of the brain, (3) what stimuli terminate motivated behavior, that is, what is satiation, and (4) how these stimuli act on the brain. Evidence in regard to thirst, hunger and sexual behavior will be discussed.

Regulation of the thirst drive. As pointed out previously, the body is continually losing water through (1) respiration, (2) per-

spiration, and (3) formation of urine. The body has little control over water loss from breathing or sweating; neither process can be interrupted long enough to prevent significant water loss. However, the kidney can reabsorb about one-third of the water it uses to flush wastes from the blood. The kidney acts to reabsorb water when it is stimulated to do so by the antidiuretic effect of vasopressin (ADH, or antidiuretic hormone, effect) of the posterior pituitary gland (Table 3). The posterior pituitary releases ADH in response to excitation from nerve fibers that originate in the anterior hypothalamus (supraoptic nucleus). What stimulates the anterior hypothalamus to begin this chain of events when the water supply of the body is low? One factor is the change in osmotic pressure (viscosity) of the blood that normally occurs when the fluid level of the body falls. Most of the solid particles in the blood and tissue fluids (except for wastes) are retained by the kidney; therefore, as the water level is reduced, the blood and tissue fluids become more concentrated. As a result, fluid is drawn from the cells, including cells in the anterior hypothalamus (osmotic thirst). In response the hypothalamic cells seem to stimulate the posterior pituitary to release ADH. A minute amount of salt deposited in the anterior pituitary by an implanted tube will cause water-satiated goats to drink. (Not enough salt is used to affect other areas of the brain.) Therefore dehydration of these cells can initiate drinking behavior as well as kidney regulation; the behavior is probably initiated by connections between the hypothalamus and other parts of the brain.

A more important factor in regulating thirst is the volume of extracellular fluid, that is, fluid outside of the cells. Because of the reduced (extracellular) fluid volume, this is called hypovolemic thirst, or, more accurately, hypovolia. Although some cells in the lateral and anterior hypothalamus are sensitive to dehydration, other anterior cells are sensitive to a hormone that is activated by the kidney when the blood pressure falls. When fluid volume of the body

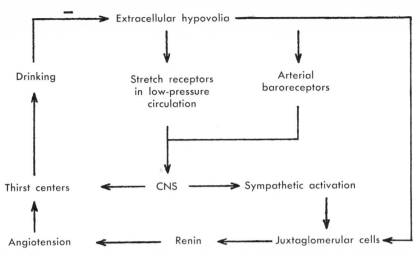

Fig. 12-1. Proposed mechanism for drinking caused by extracellular dehydration. Reduced blood pressure attributable to reduced blood volume stimulates the kidney (juxtaglomerular cells) both directly and indirectly by way of pressure receptors in the arteries and veins (the low-pressure circulation of the veins returning blood to the heart is more sensitive to changes in blood pressure than the high-pressure circulation of arteries). Input from the pressure receptors to the CNS reflexly stimulates the thirst centers and the kidney. The juxtaglomerular cells react by producing renin. Renin activates blood plasma angiotensinogen into a form that stimulates thirst centers in the hypothalamus (see text). There is also a delayed increase in sodium appetite not shown in the figure. (From Fitzsimons, J. T.: The renin-angiotensinogen system in the control of drinking. In Martini, L., Motta, M., and Fraschini, F., editors: The hypothalamus, New York, 1970, Academic Press Inc.)

is decreased because of dehydration, so is the amount of circulating blood. Reduced blood volume results in reduced blood pressure. Reduced blood pressure affects pressure receptors in the arteries and veins (see Fig. 12-1). The pressure receptors affect the hypothalamic thirst centers in two ways: (1) directly by way of the CNS and (2) indirectly by sympathetic fibers to the kidney. The kidney itself also responds to low blood pressure. In reaction to both sympathetic stimulation and to low blood pressure, certain kidney cells (juxtaglomerular cells, Fig. 12-1) release an enzyme called **renin.** The renin converts one of the normal blood proteins **(angiotensinogen)** into a form (angiotensinogen II) that stimulates thirst centers in the hypothalamus. Both the antidiuretic effect of vasopressin release and drinking behavior are aroused.

Satiation stimuli. All this says something about the sensitizing stimuli for thirst but nothing about satiation stimuli. How does the CNS know when the animal has had enough water? In the first place, water intake is dependent on food intake, because water is required to digest food. A second factor appears to be the act of drinking itself—consummatory behavior. In dogs the esophagus can be cut and the upper and lower ends brought to the surface. When the animal drinks, the water passes through the throat and out the upper end of the esophagus, never reaching the stomach ("sham drinking"). A thirsty dog, prepared in this way, will drink enough water to replace the deficit in about five minutes and then stop, almost as if it had a water meter in its throat or had been counting the swallows. If the water balance is not restored, however, the dog will go back and drink again in a few minutes; thus consummatory behavior is not the only factor regulating the thirst drive. If water is placed in the lower end of the esophagus, the thirsty dog can be "preloaded" with water and released to see if it will drink. If released immediately, it will sham drink as before. If 15 minutes elapse after "preloading," it will not drink at all. This period of time is probably enough for water to reach the tissues via the stomach and intestinal walls and reduce stimulation to cells in the hypothalamus. This older work by Bellows and others on dogs has recently been challenged by Blass and co-workers. They find that sham drinking in water-deprived rats is four times greater than normal drinking in response to the same deprivation. Perhaps there are species differences.

Regulation of drinking by water that reaches the stomach may be more precise. Rats can be prepared with tubes inserted into the stomach so that all water intake bypasses the mouth and throat and enters the stomach directly. Rats prepared in this fashion can be trained to press a lever to receive a squirt of water directly into the stomach. After initial training they can regulate their water intake solely by this means over a long period of time, and they do it about as well as normal animals do, although their body weight is reduced.

Although animals can be taught to press a lever in order to have food delivered directly into the stomach by a tube, experiments have shown that *both* an oral stimulus (for example, saccharin) and intragastric injections are necessary to maintain the response. Humans can be trained to press a lever that causes liquid diet food to be injected directly into the stomach by a tube. When either one meal (Stellar) or all three (Jordan) were consumed in this fashion, the subjects regulated their caloric intake rather well. However, when they fed themselves, both orally and intragastrically at the same time, they tended to overeat. Obviously, both oral and gastric factors are involved in the control of food intake.

Regulation of the hunger drive. As in the case of the thirst drive, food intake depends on water intake. It will be seen that regulation of hunger as well as thirst is determined by several factors. However, regulation of the hunger drive is more complex, and more factors are involved. In thirst, arousal of the drive has little to do with oral factors such as dryness of the mouth and throat—hypothalamic cells govern arousal. In hunger, sensitizing stimuli probably act to arouse activity, but the oral releasing stimuli of taste (and smell) are more important in determining whether the animal will eat. Water is water, but there are many tastes to food. Oral factors also determine *what* foods are eaten according to the animal's dietary needs, but that is a subject for a later section. Here the interest is in whether the animal eats and how much. Thirst satiation can be regulated by oral factors in sham drinking, but an animal can also learn to control the amount of water directly delivered to his stomach, so that both oral and gastric cues *can* be used. (Of course, animals without a stomach can control both food and water intake.) In hunger, many factors can influence satiation, although they seem to act through a mechanism that "counts calories." Earlier it was seen that animals could regulate their intake according to the caloric value of the diet available and their caloric needs—forced exercise such as swimming to exhaustion will cause rats to increase their caloric intake to meet the demand.

Sham feeding. One way of determining the importance of oral factors in arousal and satiation is sham feeding. A dog with the esophagus severed and stitched to the surface will eat, but the food never reaches the stomach. Experimenters agree that a hungry animal prepared in this way will work to obtain food that passes only through the mouth; thus oral taste (and smell) stimuli serve as effective releasing stimuli. There is disagreement about whether oral factors—taste and the act of eating and swallowing—have anything to do with satiation. It has been reported that a hungry animal will sham feed to exhaustion, an indication that oral stimuli are not a major factor in satiation. However, milk taken by mouth (that reaches the stomach) reduces intake more than direct gastric (stomach) injection does, indicating that oral factors may have an influence in satiation. Gastric factors seem more important, however. Just as in thirst, rats can be prepared with tubes leading directly to the stomach and can learn to feed themselves through these tubes by pressing a lever than controls injections of liquid food directly into the stomach. The animals can maintain their normal weight for a long time with this apparatus. Furthermore, they will regulate the amount they feed themselves according to how much the diet is diluted with tap water. Quinine added to the diet in concentrations that caused normal animals to reduce their intake had no effect on intragastric feeding because oral factors of taste were not involved. All this control of the diet by intragastric factors is puzzling in view of the fact that animals (and humans) *without* stomachs can regulate their food intake. However, since food absorption takes place in the intestine, perhaps the control site lies there; liquid food reaches the intestine quite rapidly.

There are two recent experiments that bear on the question of stomach cues versus intestinal cues in satiation. An inflatable cuff may be surgically placed around the pyloric sphincter of rats to stop food in the stomach from reaching the small intestine (Deutsch and Wang, 1977). Fluids can also be directly injected into the stomach of these animals by a surgically placed tube. The rats were food-deprived and given their choice of drinking either of two non-nutritive fluids with distinctive tastes. When milk was injected as they drank one fluid, they learned to prefer that fluid over the taste of the other fluid when drinking the other fluid led to stomach injections of saline. Neither milk nor saline

reached the intestine; the stomach evidently "told the brain" which fluid taste resulted in nutrition.

In the other experiment, food "signals" from the small intestine were tested (Koopmans, 1975). The digestive systems of pairs of rats were connected so that food passed through the stomach and small intestine of one rat, then to the small intestine of a second rat (bypassing its stomach), and was returned to the intestine of the first rat. When the first rat ate, the second rat only received food in its small intestine (where most nutrition is absorbed). The first rat ate normally and up to 60 minutes were allowed for the second rat to absorb the food as it passed through its intestine. Despite this, the second rat ate a normal-sized meal. It appears that messages by the nervous system or hormones from the small intestine cannot produce satiation by themselves. This is puzzling, because there is a hormone produced by the small intestine called CCK (cholecystokinin) whose injection causes satiation in either normal or sham-fed rats (Antin and co-workers, 1975).

Glucostatic theory. One theory, the **glucostatic theory,** proposed that the level of blood glucose affects cells of the hypothalamus that arouse eating when the blood glucose level is low. This view has been largely abandoned for a number of reasons, chiefly the lack of evidence of a relationship between normal fluctuations in blood glucose and the hunger drive. This leaves us with the suspicion that some change or changes in the tissue fluids, osmotic or otherwise, affect hunger and satiation centers in the hypothalamus, but this conclusion does not tell us what the changes are or how they are affected by food or lack of food.

Lipostatic theory. There is also a hypothesis that the level of fatty acids in the blood can serve as an arousal or a satiation stimulus for hunger mechanisms. This idea encounters the same difficulties as did the glucostatic theory, in that there is little evidence that normal fluctuations in the fatty acid content of the blood and tissue fluid affect eating behavior.

Plasma amino acids. Since neither carbohydrate level (glucostatic theory) nor fat level (lipostatic theory) can clearly be shown to govern eating behavior, other investigators (Leung and Rogers, 1969) have turned to protein. Their interest was aroused by the fact that animals who were given a surplus of all but one of the amino acids on a low-protein diet showed a depression of their food intake in 5 to 12 hours. They tube-fed rats through the carotid artery (an artery going to the brain) with a surplus of all of the amino acids except a growth-limiting one (either threonine or isoleucine). Other rats ate the same diet in a normal way. Both groups showed a 40% to 50% reduction of food intake, thus proving that oral factors were not responsible for the lack of appetite. Restoring the missing amino acid led to a normal food intake. The data suggest that a food intake regulation mechanism somewhere in the brain is sensitive to the amount of amino acids in the blood.

Hypothalamus and the hunger drive. Many parts of the brain are involved in the hunger drive. However, certain focal centers in the hypothalamus seemed to have the most to do with hunger drive arousal and with satiation. Two centers seemed to be involved. The first center is the **ventromedial nucleus** of the hypothalamus. This nucleus appeared to function as a **satiation,** or **satiety, center,** reacting to changes in the tissue fluid that signal when the body has had enough food. The second center is made up of a pair of nuclei, located in the lateral hypothalamus on both sides and overlapping with centers controlling thirst behavior. These nuclei are more scattered than is the ventromedial nucleus, but their location is well known. The **lateral hypothalamic nuclei** appeared to react to sensitizing stimuli—changes in the tissue fluid that occur when the animal's food reserves are low. For this reason they have often

been called the **feeding center.** Their activity was assumed to set off the widespread CNS and behavior changes of the aroused hunger drive. Experiments suggest that lesions of the ventromedial hypothalamus (VMH) damage nearby pathways leading to the forebrain, especially to the limbic system from the brain stem sensory nuclei (chiefly trigeminal). The brain stem nuclei receive fibers from the mouth, pharynx, stomach, and intestine that pass input from eating behavior and the presence of food in the stomach and gut. These pathways are adrenergic—norepinephrine is probably the transmitter substance for the cells involved. Lateral hypothalamic (LH) lesions appear to damage descending pathways from the anteror (preoptic) thirst centers and ascending pathways from the mouth, pharynx, stomach, and so on. These pathways seem to be cholinergic, utilizing acetylcholine as a synaptic transmitter. There are several reasons for this point of view. In the first place, lesions adequate to produce either overeating or starvation must be large enough to damage nerve tracts passing through nearby areas of the hypothalamus; lesions strictly confined to these nuclei do not seem to produce significant changes in eating or drinking behavior. When chemical stimulation is used (Grossman), carbachoi (which mimics acetylcholine) produces drinking, not eating, whereas norepinephrine produces eating and not drinking. Finally, lesions and chemical stimulation of several limbic areas reproduce some of the symptoms of lesions and stimulation of the ventromedial hypothalamus and lateral hypothalamus.

Hypothalamic hyperphagia. Lesions in various parts of the limbic system will cause rats to overeat and become quite obese. Lesions near the ventromedial hypothalamus seem most effective in this regard. After the area is destroyed, the animals double or triple their normal food intake within a few days and continue eating at this rate until their weight is two or three times normal. Then their intake drops to the amount necessary to maintain their obese condition and remains at that level. The syndrome is called **hypothalamic hyperphagia.** The most reasonable explanation is that pathways involved in the shut-off mechanism for hunger have been destroyed.

Several lines of evidence support this view. In the first place, hyperphagic rats that are fed a liquid diet of low bulk eat no more often while they are gaining weight than do normal rats. They just eat for longer periods of time. Second, hyperphagic rats are more sensitive to the palatability of their food than are normal rats—they seem more finicky about what they eat. Normal rats will tolerate considerable 'bitterness" (caused by adulterating the food with quinine) without reducing their food intake; small amounts of quinine will reduce the hyperphagic rats' intake drastically. Third, normal rats will eat more when the caloric value of their food is reduced by mixing it with nonnutritive kaolin (clay) or cellulose; hyperphagic rats will not. Since hyperphagic rats are more finicky about their food than are normal rats, their overeating cannot be caused by increased avidity. They just stop eating less readily. If required to press a bar to obtain food, they will not work so hard or so long as normal rats; if required to cross a shocking grid to obtain food, they will not tolerate as much shock as will a normal animal. Because their metabolism is otherwise normal, it is reasoned that they are less sensitive to bodily changes that result from overeating; because an essential part of the stop mechanism has been removed, they have a *higher threshold* of satiation.

Hyperphagics regulate their weight just as do normal animals, by reducing their food intake *after* they have become obese; they just maintain their weight at a higher level, being less sensitive to the internal changes that accompany obesity and excess fat storage. It seems to make no difference whether the animal is made obese before or after the operation—it will still level off at the same weight. As previously noted, normal rats can be made obese by injecting them with insulin since they must eat more to keep the brain supplied with blood glucose. Normal rats fattened in this manner become almost as obese as hyperphagic rats. If they are operated on *after* being fattened in this way, they will increase their food intake only enough to reach the same weight as that of the control animals, who are already hyperphagic. The hyperphagic rat, then, just has a higher threshold to the bodily changes that accompany overeating or obesity. Whatever these changes are, they seem to be present in the hyperphagic as much as in the normal rat.

Stimulation. If the ventromedial area contains satiation pathways, one would expect a feeding animal to stop eating when it is stimulated, and this is just what happens. Furthermore, there is a rebound effect, and the animal resumes eating more rapidly after the stimulus ceases, or if the animal was not eating before the stimulus, it often begins to eat. Animals that have learned a response to obtain food will not perform the response during stimulation; they will not cross a shocking grid to obtain food during stimulation but will do so either before or after stimulation. Of course electrical stimulation of the hypothalamus may be aversive or may inhibit all behavior. But if cannulas (tubes) are implanted in the ventromedial area, the same results can be obtained with chemical stimuli. Anesthetics injected into the same area act like ventromedial lesions by causing overeating until the anesthetic wears off.

One investigator (Schacter) has made a number of interesting comparisons between hyperphagic rats and obese people. It is his contention that both kinds of subjects are less sensitive to the cues that accompany satiation than are their leaner counterparts. In the case of humans it may be that they have insensitive satiation receptors or that they do not associate these stimuli or more local stimuli, such as stomach distention, with satiation. In other words, they do not know when they have "had enough." Their eating behavior seems to be determined by the external cues of palatable food, whereas that of normal subjects appears to be determined more by internal cues of satiation. In comparing hyperphagic rats and obese humans to their normal counterparts in a series of experiments, it was found that both obese rats and obese humans were more finicky about the taste of food, were less active, ate fewer but larger meals, ate more rapidly, were more emotional, ate less when food was difficult to obtain, and reacted less to distant stimuli as opposed to more prominent stimuli. In view of the external control of eating behavior in the obese, it may be that environmental control would do more to help them lose weight than would dieting—the cues to eating, as well as the food itself, could be removed, less palatable food could be eaten, and the like.

Lateral hypothalamic syndrome. If the ventromedial pathways signal satiation, hunger-arousal pathways should be found at a different location in the hypothalamus. Hunger-arousal input should respond to changes in the internal environment (sensitizing stimuli) caused by lack of food intake by arousing hunger drive behavior. If the hunger-arousal fibers are destroyed, the animal should be insensitive to body changes in hunger, and **aphagia** (lack of appetite) should result. These areas have been found on both sides of the *lateral hypothalamus* in the rat; destruction results in sudden and continued refusal to eat, and the animal starves to death. The aphagia is accompanied by **adipsia;** the rat refuses liquids as well as food. There are three probable reasons for the lateral hypothalamic symptoms: (1) There is a metabolic association of food and water intake. A food-deprived animal drinks less and a water-deprived animal eats less. Presumably, disruption of a hunger-arousal system would impair drinking behavior and vice versa. (2) Descending pathways from the previously described anterior hypothalamic nuclei that are involved with

water regulation have been interrupted. The anterior control nuclei have lost pathways exerting control over behavior. (3) Ascending pathways from brain stem sensory nuclei to the thalamus have been severed. These inputs along these pathways carry sensations from the mouth (taste, eating, and drinking behavior), pharynx (smell), and stomach. Teitelbaum notes a lack of response to touch of the snout or smell that he calls *sensory inattention.* Poor motor control of eating during recovery results in much spilled food.

Certain methods of reintroducing food and water can result in recovery from the effects of lateral hypothalamic lesions. There are four definite steps in the recovery process, which are described as the **lateral hypothalamic syndrome.** In the first stage the animals refuse food and water and must be tube-fed; they are aphagic and adipsic. After several days the animals will eat moist and palatable food but will continue to refuse water. In the second stage they still will not eat enough to maintain body weight, and supplemental tube feedings are required. In the third stage the animals regulate their own food intake normally (even on dry foods) if fluid intake is artificially maintained; they will not drink "pure" water, however, and if they become dehydrated, their food intake drops below maintenance level. They will drink water only if it is sweetened with sugar or saccharin. The fourth stage constitutes recovery—the animals maintain themselves on dry food and "pure" water. They are still finicky about their food, however. Like hyperphagic rats, they will not tolerate as much "bitter" quinine in their food as will normal rats.

Recovery by stages suggests relief from the effects of the lesions, relief that is attributable to the recovery of a few undamaged cells. The symptoms also suggest that the hunger and thirst mechanisms overlap anatomically. One can make satiated animals eat by stimulating the lateral hypothalamus electrically or with local injections of the neuron transmitter chemical epinephrine. Thirst arousal pathways, by contrast, appear to use acetylcholine as a transmitter. At least stimulation with cholinergic chemicals arouses drinking behavior. It is interesting to note that the lateral hypothalamic feeding areas are among the ones whose stimulation is rewarding to the rat—at least the animal will work hard to obtain electrical stimulation in the lateral hypothalamus. (The reward areas will be discussed later.)

Regulation of sex drive

To make a long story short, sexual behavior seems to be under joint hormone and nervous control, and the major site of interaction of these factors is the hypothalamus and its connections with the pituitary gland. Hormonal factors (Chapter 2) will be briefly reviewed first. Then neural factors will be considered. A review of the effect of sensory input on the system will conclude this section.

Hormonal factors. In adolescence the increased output of gonadal hormones causes the appearance of secondary sexual characteristics. The sex hormone level also governs the sex drive in lower animals. The constant level of androgen output by the testes in most adult male species (except seasonal mating species) maintains the sex drive in males. The fluctuating estrogen level of the monthly cycle in females causes them to come into heat during ovulation, when the female egg, or ovum, is produced to be fertilized by copulation with the male. In lower species, removal of the gonads, either before or after puberty, often abolishes sexual behavior as soon as the hormone level drops enough. Normal sexual behavior in adult castrates of either sex can be restored by injections of sex hormones. Early puberty can be induced in humans or lower animals of either sex by injection of sex hormones before the gonads have begun to produce them. In lower animals the effects of senility on the sex drive (when the gonads cease producing hormones) can be overcome by injections of sex hormones. As the nervous sys-

tem develops in higher species, it becomes as important as the hormones to the sex drive in primates and more important than the hormones in man. The increased influence of the CNS on the sex drive is caused by the enormous effect of learning on sexual behavior. In subhuman primates castration before puberty prevents the appearance of most normal sexual behavior in both male and female (though fragments of sexual responses may survive). Castration before puberty may prevent adult sexual behavior in humans. If castration occurs after puberty and sexual experience, sexual behavior takes some time to disappear in lower species—longer than hormone levels would predict. The effect of castration, however, is more severe in the female than in the male. In higher primates, such as chimpanzees, sexual behavior may survive castration in the adult and may be unaffected in the male. In humans, adult castration has little effect on the male and a variable effect on the female. Both sexes seem to show little reduction in sexual behavior after sexual senility has abolished hormonal effects. The general picture is one of decreased importance of the hormones and increased importance of learning as the brain develops through evolution.

Important as they are, the gonadal hormones are governed by pituitary hormones, which are controlled in turn by the hypothalamus. The anterior pituitary controls the output of germ tissue (ova or sperm) by the gonads by its production of **follicle-stimulating hormone,** or FSH; it governs the output of sex hormones (and thus the onset of puberty) by its output of **leutinizing hormone,** or LH (see Table 3). The fluctuating sexual cycle and sex drive of females and the maintained sex drive of males of most species are governed by the output of anterior pituitary LH. LH production, in turn, is under the influence of the hypothalamus. Ablation of the pituitary may abolish sexual behavior, just as castration does (the production of sex hormones falls off because of loss of LH), but hormone injections restore the sex drive.

Neural factors. At the lowest levels of nervous organization, erection and ejaculation are spinal reflexes and can be elicited by genital stimulation, even in men who have a severed spinal cord. Erection is largely governed by the parasympathetic nervous system and ejaculation by the sympathetic nervous system. As such, these reflexes come under the control of the hypothalamus, which largely controls the autonomic nervous system. It is probable that the hypothalamus also governs the output of LH and FSH. The output of these hormones from the anteror pituitary seems controlled by nerve fibers from the hypothalamus to the posterior pituitary. These fibers release **neurohumors** that are carried by a portal system of blood vessels from the stalk of the posterior pituitary to the anterior pituitary, to affect hormone output there.

The hypothalamus is also sensitive to the level of sex hormones in the internal environment and regulates the sex drive accordingly. Studies show that estrogen crystals implanted in the hypothalamus of female rats do not dissolve for up to two months, and during all that time the female remains in heat. The sensitivity of the hypothalamus to hormone level may be destroyed when lesions are made in ventral and anterior areas of the hypothalamus. The gonads do not atrophy, and yet sexual behavior is abolished and not restored by hormone injections. The normal condition of the gonads suggests that they still receive normal LH and FSH stimulation from the pituitary and produce a normal supply of gonadal hormones. The damaged hypothalamus is just not sensitive to the hormones. On the other hand, destruction of the mamillary bodies of the hypothalamus probably abolishes its ability to stimulate the output of pituitary FSH and LH. As a result, the gonads atrophy, and sexual behavior is impaired—the gonads are not being stimulated to produce sex hormones. Injection of sex hormones re-

verses the condition and restores normal sexual behavior. Therefore, a feedback relationship seems to exist between the hypothalamus and the gonads. The hypothalamus stimulates sex hormone output by the gonads through pituitary LH, and the sex hormone level arouses the sex drive by stimulating the hypothalamus. More extensive neural structures are involved, of course, but the hypothalamus appears to play a pivotal role.

NEURAL MECHANISMS OF REWARD OR PUNISHMENT
Reward centers

Sites in the brain of the rat have been discovered where electrical stimulation by implanted electrodes has the effect of reward. A physiological psychologist (Olds) was investigating the effect of stimulating the brain stem ascending reticular arousal system (ARAS) in healthy and active rats with permanently implanted electrodes. One of the electrodes was misplaced, and he made the serendipitous discovery that the rat seemed to "like" being stimulated there—at least the animal would return often to that part of the table where he had received the brain stimulation. It was then discovered that the rat would learn a T maze for a reward of brain stimulation, or press a lever in a Skinner box when the lever was wired to the stimulator so that the rat could stimulate himself.

Systematic studies were made, and a variety of reward centers were discovered, some more effective than others. To receive brain stimulation in the most effective centers, rats would cross a shocking grid at currents they would not endure for food when hungry, water when thirsty, or copulation with another rat when stimulated by sex hormones. Reward areas have been found in the septal areas, cingulate gyrus, dorsal thalamus, tectum, anterior hypothalamus, and medial forebrain bundle. Some of these centers are related to other drives. For example, the lateral hypothalamic "feeding pathways" (see lateral hypothalamic syndrome) presumably arouse the hunger drive. It is an effective reward center, but it is more effective when the animal is hungry than when it is satiated by food or when the ventromedial satiety pathways are stimulated. Psychiatrists have tried implanting electrodes in reward areas in the brains of psychotic patients in an attempt to improve their condition by effectively rewarding more normal behavior. The reports of these patients on their sensations when stimulated are open to some question because of their disorganized condition, but more rational epileptics have been tested in a similar way. Some sites of stimulation resulted in vague sensations of "well-being" or "pleasure." Others gave rise to sexual fantasies.

"Punishment" centers

The work of several investigators (Olds, Delgado, Miller, and others) has led to the locating of punishment centers in the brain of the cat and rat. Stimulation of these brain centers will serve as a negative reinforcement in the learning of escape or avoidance habits, as does painful electric shock. Cats will learn to turn a wheel to end or avoid stimulation in these areas of the brain, or they will learn to escape a compartment where they had been stimulated previously. Some of these areas lie in the medial lemniscus and posteroventral nuclei of the thalamus and are part of the pain sensation pathways from pain receptors to the brain. Stimulation in these areas should affect the cat in the same way as does the stimulation of pain receptors. However, other areas of the posterior parts of the brain have elicited reactions in animals that look more like "fear" responses, and these negative reinforcement centers are also effective in teaching cats avoidance or escape habits. Implanted electrodes in human psychotics and epileptics have produced aversive sensations as well as pleasurable ones. Reports indicate fright, a feeling of being sick, or apprehension. A more extensive and intricate system than that of pain stimulation seems indicated.

Other investigators (Stein and Margules) have "mapped" the "reward" and "punishment" areas in the brain of rats in a clever series of experiments using chemical stimulation and analysis. Cannulas (small tubes) were implanted in known neural systems in the brain stem reticular formation and the limbic areas. During brain stimulation, chemicals were used to block conduction in either the ascending or descending systems; radioactive tracer chemicals were used to analyze the chemical transmitters normally utilized by the nerve

Medial forebrain bundle
(reward)

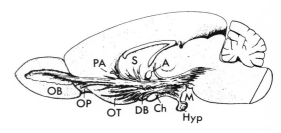

Periventricular system
(punishment)

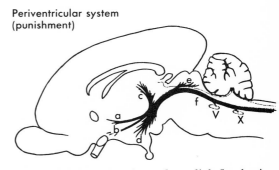

Fig. 12-2. Midline view of medial forebrain bundle (MFB), or reward system, and periventricular system (PVS) for punishment, in a generalized and primitive mammalian brain. **Upper:** *A*, Anterior commissure; *DB*, nucleus of the diagonal band; *M*, mammillary body; *OP*, olfactory peduncle; *PA*, paraolfactory area; *S*, septum. **Lower:** *a*, Periventricular nucleus; *b*, supraoptical nucleus; *c*, dorsomedial thalamus; *d*, posterior hypothalamus; *e*, tectum of midbrain; *f*, motor nuclei of cranial nerves. (From Le Gros Clark, W. E., et al.: The hypothalamus, Edinburgh, 1938, Oliver & Boyd, Ltd.)

cells involved. As a result of these experiments, two systems that control reinforcement in the brain have been proposed (Fig. 12-2). The median forebrain bundle (MFB) is believed to be the reward system, and the periventricular system (PVS) is thought to be the principal punishment system. The medial forebrain bundle is primarily an ascending system whose chemical transmitter is norepinephrine. The periventricular system is primarily a descending system whose chemical transmitter is acetylcholine. Interactions between the two systems are held to be largely a function of the limbic system at sites in the thalamus, hypothalamus, and amygdala. The principal site of interaction is held to be the amygdala, a behavior-suppressing part of the periventricular system that inhibits behavior in response to punishment (learning what not to do). Behavior is released from inhibition when the median forebrain bundle inhibits the behavior-suppressing amygdala to explain the reinforcing effect of reward (learning what to do). The theory is a complex one, but is shows considerable promise.

There has been considerable controversy over whether "reward" and "punishment" systems of the brain are involved in natural reinforcement events, or whether they are merely a laboratory curiosity. Some (for example, Trowill) hold that electrical stimulation of the brain (ESB) has the same properties as natural incentives. They hold that stimuli that *arouse* a drive cannot be rewarding. Others (for example, Valenstein and associates) challenge the view that discrete drive states are aroused by ESB, pointing to the "stimulus-bound" properties of behavior referred to earlier. Others (Wurtz and Olds) have found discrete sites in the amygdala where ESB elicits escape behavior and other sites where ESB elicits approach behavior. Roberts trained rats to push one of two pedals to turn ESB on or off in stimulating the hypothalamus. He found that the rats used the "on" pedal to maintain a series of stimuli of short duration and the "off" pedal to rid themselves of long duration stimuli all applied at the same "rewarding" location—apparently the rewarding stimulus turned aversive with time. The whole research area of ESB is in a state of rapid change, and no general theory of the relationship between ESB and drive states has been clearly stated.

SUMMARY

Precisely defined terminology is needed to distinguish between events in the environment and events in the organism before specific motives can be discussed. A need condition in the environment sets up a need state in the organism; some aspect of the need state may serve as a sensitizing stimulus to arouse a drive in the CNS. The drives discussed are inherent, but there are acquired need conditions, states, and drives. If the behavior that results from an inherent drive is caused by "built-in" nervous patterns, the whole is an instinct; a drive and learned behavior that lead to the incentive constitute a motive.

The incentive or the cues to its presence are releasing stimuli for motivated (goal-directed) behavior. Addiction results when drugs alter the CNS so that their absence causes a need state. Thirst, hunger, and sex deprivation cause local states such as mouth dryness, stomach contractions, and full seminal vesicles (in the male). These states are neither necessary nor sufficient to arouse drives. In the case of hunger and thirst, local states are abolished immediately by eating and drinking and therefore cannot tell the animal when it has had enough. In adult man the sex drive is more a function of learning than of local states or hormone levels. Furthermore, need states affect one another, one need state being increased to satisfy another. In general, a hierarchy is established, and the need state, or internal imbalance, that can be tolerated for the shortest time is given priority. Mechanisms for signaling satiation to the CNS must also be sought for each drive—an animal stops eating or drinking before the need state of its tissues has time to change, and an animal regulates its food and water intake accurately.

Some drives, however, are controlled by their releasing stimuli; these drives are called appetites or aversions. There are need states, such as those for certain vitamins, that do not arouse drives (have no sensitizing stimuli). Most motivated behavior is controlled by many factors that serve as releasing stimuli once the drive is aroused, and their effectiveness depends on the degree of drive arousal by sensitizing stimuli. Sensitizing stimuli to drives often act on the hypothalamus, which is sensitive to internal need states, carries need-related sensory input from the brain stem, is a part of the ARAS, and controls the autonomic nervous system. Stimulation and ablation studies have shown excitatory and inhibitory areas for several drives in the hypothalamus; these areas are responsive to sensitizing and satiation stimuli, respectively. However, the behavior aroused by electrical stimulation of some areas depends on the incentive stimuli that are present at the time.

In thirst the body conserves water by the release of antidiuretic vasopressin from the posterior pituitary gland, which has been excited by the hypothalamus. Intercellular dehydration appears to stimulate this process as well as to arouse the thirst drive. A more important mechanism for the thirst drive seems to be extracellular (hypovolemic) dehydration, which reduces blood pressure to stimulate anterior hypothalamic thirst cells by a blood pressure reflex and by kidney release of renin, activating an angiotensinogen to stimulate the hypothalamus.

The thirst and hunger drive cells in the hypothalamus differ chemically, the former being adrenergic and the latter cholinergic. Experiments in sham drinking show that consummatory behavior alone serves as a temporary satiation stimulus— the animal stops drinking for a few minutes after it has "replaced" the lost water,

even though none of it reaches the stomach. A rat can, however, learn to control its water balance by pressing a lever for intragastric injections of water.

Food intake depends on water intake, since water is required for digestion. Animals accurately regulate their caloric intake, but this ability depends more on gastrointestinal factors than on oral factors, since a hungry sham-fed animal eats to exhaustion. Animals that press a lever for intragastric squirts of food can regulate their intake according to their needs and the caloric value of the food. Stomach cues may control intake—rats learn to associate a taste with gastric injections of milk even though the milk does not reach the intestine. Conversely, if food passes only through the intestine of a hungry rat (where it is absorbed), the food does not curb the rat's appetite. Yet an intestinal hormone (CCK) can induce satiation.

The glucostatic theory proposes that blood glucose level controls the hypothalamically regulated hunger drive, but reliable relationships have not been found. The lipostatic theory holds that the hunger drive is controlled by the level of fatty acid in tissue fluid; another hypothesis cites certain essential amino acids as the controlling factor. The ventromedial area of the hypothalamus seems to carry pathways from the brain stem giving sensory information concerning satiation; its ablation causes hypothalamic hyperphagia, and chemical or electrical stimulation of this center stops eating behavior. Several lines of evidence show that hyperphagic rats are more finicky about their food than are normal rats, and therefore the hunger arousal mechanisms are not involved; rather, the satiation threshold is higher. Both hyperphagic rats and obese humans seem less sensitive to internal cues that signal satiation. The lateral hypothalamus seems to contain hunger pathways because ablation of these areas makes a rat aphagic. The animal shows adipsia as well, and four separate stages, called the lateral hypothalamic syndrome, are found in recovery. Recovery probably results from the restored function of injured cells in the lesion area. Electrical or epinephrine stimuli to the lateral hypothalamus cause eating behavior, whereas cholinergic chemicals cause drinking.

The sex drive, on the other hand, seems to be under both nervous and hormonal control. Male androgen and female estrogen output by the gonads is stimulated by anterior pituitary LH and FSH at puberty, and the anterior pituitary is stimulated by neurosecretions from hypothalamic fibers en route to the posterior pituitary. The maintained hormone level and sex drive of the male, as well as the estrous fluctuations of both in the female, are under the control of the anterior pituitary by FSH and LH. In higher animals the sex drive is controlled by learning, and the drive survives castration or senility in adults (more effectively in the male than in the female). In lower animals, ablation of the pituitary, like castration, abolishes most sexual behavior, but hormone injections restore it. Ventral and anterior hypothalamic lesions can abolish sex behavior without change in hormone levels; thus these lesions may indicate drive arousal areas. Mammillary body destruction probably destroys anterior pituitary output, since the gonads atrophy.

Reward centers have been found in the rat brain—stimulation of these centers serves as reinforcement for maze learning, and a rat will rapidly learn to stimulate itself with a Skinner box lever. Some of these centers seem related to those for hunger and sex. Punishment centers have been found in more posterior brain areas, some in the pain pathways, but others are found in areas that appear unrelated to pain. In both instances a complex and interrelated neural system is probably involved. The reward system appears to be organized as an adrenergic medial forebrain bundle and the punishment system as a cholinergic periventricular system. They interact at the amygdala, where the medial forebrain bundle inhibits behavior suppression by the periventricular system. There is considerable controversy over whether electrical stimulation of the brain acts like normal incentives.

READINGS

Andersson, B.: The effect of hypertonic NaCl solutions into different parts of the hypothalamus of goats, Acta. Physiol. Scand. **28:**188-201, 1953 (Bobbs-Merrill Reprint No. P-9).

Andersson, B.: Thirst—and brain control of water balance, Am. Scientist **59:**408-415, July-Aug. 1971.

Beach, F. A.: Evolutionary changes in the physiological control of mating behavior in mammals. Psychol. Rev. **54:**297-315, 1947 (Bobbs-Merrill Reprint No. P-27).

Bermant, G.: Copulation in rats, Psychol. Today **1:**53-60, July 1967.

Butler, R. A.: Curiosity in monkeys. Sci. Am. **190:**70-75, Feb. 1954 (W. H. Freeman Reprint No. 426).

Cannon, W. B.: The wisdom of the body, New York, 1963, W. W. Norton & Co., Inc.

Carlton, P. L.: Cholinergic mechanisms in the control of behavior by the brain, Psychol. Rev. **70:**19-39, 1963 (Bobbs-Merrill Reprint No. P-416).

Cicala, G. A.: Animal drives, Princeton, N.J., 1965, D. Van Nostrand Co., Inc.

Delgado, J.: ESB, Psychol. Today **3:**49-54, April 1970.

Deutsch, J.: Brain reward/ESB and ecstasy. Psychol. Today **7:**46-48, July 1972.

Deutsch, J. A., and Howarth, C. I.: Some tests of a theory of intracranial self-stimulation. Psychol. Rev. **70:**444-460, 1963 (Bobbs-Merrill Reprint No. P-427).

Fernston, J. D.: Nutrition and the brain, Sci. Am. **230:**84-91, Feb. 1974.

Fischer, A. E.: Maternal and sexual behavior induced by intracranial self-stimulation. Science **124:**228-229, 1956 (Bobbs-Merrill Reprint No. P-113).

Fischer, A. E.: Chemical stimulation of the brain, Sci. Am. **210:**60-68, June 1964 (W. H. Freeman Reprint No. 485).

Fleming, J. D.: Pursuit of intellectual orgasm, Psychol. Today **8:**68-77, March 1975.

Fuller, J. L.: Motivation: a biological perspective, New York, 1964, Random House, Inc.

Hebb, D. O.: Drives and the CNS (conceptual nervous system), Psychol. Rev. **62:**243-254, 1955 (Bobbs-Merrill Reprint No. P-151).

Hess, E. H.: Attitude and pupil size, Sci. Am. **212:**46-54, April 1965 (W. H. Freeman Reprint No. 493).

Holst, E. von, and Saint Paul, U. von: Electrically controlled behavior, Sci. Am. **206:**50-59, March 1962 (W. H. Freeman Reprint No. 464).

Keesy, R. E., and Powley, T. L.: Hypothalamic regulation of body weight, Am. Scientist **63:**558-565, 1975.

Levine, S.: Sex differences in the brain, Sci. Am. **214:**84-90, April 1966 (W. H. Freeman Reprint No. 498).

Margules, D. L., and Olds, J.: Identical feeding and rewarding systems in the hypothalamus of rats, Science **135:**374-377, 1962 (Bobbs-Merrill Reprint No. P-508).

Olds, J.: Pleasure centers in the brain, Sci. Am. **195:**105-116, Oct. 1956 (W. H. Freeman Reprint No. 30).

Olds, J.: Self-stimulation of the brain. Science **127:**315-324, 1958 (Bobbs-Merrill Reprint No. P-264).

Pribram, K. H., editor: Brain and behavior. I. Mood, states, and mind, Middlesex, England, 1969, Penguin Books, Ltd.

Richell, M.: Biological clocks, Psychol. Today **3:**33-60, May 1970.

Schacter, S.: Eat, eat, Psychol. Today **4:**45-50, April 1971.

Schacter, S.: Some extraordinary facts about obese humans and rats, Am. Psychol. **26:**129-144, 1970. Also in Leukel, F.: Issues in physiological psychology, St. Louis, 1974, The C. V. Mosby Co.

Stein, L.: The chemistry of reward and punishment. In Efron, D., Cole, J., Levine, J., and Wittenborn, J., editors: Psychopharmacology: a review of progress, 1957-67, USPHS Publication No. 1836, Washington, D.C., 1968, U.S. Government Printing Office, pp. 105-123. Also in Leukel, F.: Issues in physiological psychology, St. Louis, 1974, The C. V. Mosby Co.

Teevan, R. C., and Smith, B. D.: Motivation, New York, 1967, McGraw-Hill Book Company.

Thomas, D., and Meyer, J.: The search for the secret of fat, Psychol. Today **7:**74-79, Sept. 1973.

Zeigler, H. P.: The sensual feel of food, Psychol. Today **9:**62-66, Aug. 1975.

CHAPTER 13

Emotion: a special case of motivation

OVERVIEW

At first glance this chapter may seem to have been written in reverse. Although it begins with historical and definitional problems, it continues with theories of emotion, and examines the evidence only after the theories have been discussed. There are reasons for this approach. In the first place, definitions of emotion vary so widely that one must understand an investigator's theoretical approach before one can understand why he designed his experiment and what his results contribute to the understanding of emotion. Second, studies on the role of parts of the nervous system in emotion produce such variable and conflicting results that they can be understood only in terms of a widespread "nervous" circuit that governs emotional behavior—and proposing such a circuit involves theory. Thus the chapter begins with definitional problems in distinguishing emotion from other kinds of motivated behavior and experience. Then the criteria for useful theory in emotion are established. The phenomena to be explained are set forth—conscious states, behavior, and physiological events. The phenomena explained determine the position the theorist adopts and whether he believes that emotion organizes or disorganizes behavior. Theories of emotion, each contributing to the understanding of emotional

phenomena, are taken up in historical order so that they increase gradually in complexity and generality. When the known factors contributing to emotion are understood, the evidence can be studied in a meaningful context. Therefore neural mechanisms in emotion follow. The topic begins with the effect of somatic and visceral feedback on emotion and then proceeds to the role of the autonomic nervous system, the hypothalamus, and finally the limbic system. The uniquely human emotional area of sexual behavior forms the final section. Human sexual development and adult sexual behavior are considered.

APPROACHES TO EMOTION

The first problem encountered in the study of emotion results from habits of language and thought inherited from the seventeenth and eighteenth century rationalist philosophers. Especially as seen by Descartes and others, *reason* was *the* unique attribute responsible for man's artistic and scientific accomplishments. Man's intelligence governed his actions in a rational way only as long as emotion did not *interfere* with the process. Emotional arousal was seen as a regrettable feature of physical existence that disrupted intelligent behavior. When Darwin revolutionized scientific theory in biology by classifying man as only one of many species that evolved from other animals, he pointed out that emotion would not exist unless it was adaptive, that is, useful for the survival of humans as well as other animals. Rationalistic thought persisted, however, in treating emotion as a regrettable inheritance from "lower" animals that disrupted intelligent and rational behavior in humans. (This view will be encountered later on when the behavior disorganization theory of emotion is considered.) A change in approach has done as much toward understanding emotion as have improved methods for studying emotion. This approach recognizes *emotion as a special case of motivation.* Animals, including humans, are emotional when they are extremely motivated or aroused and when no adaptive habit or instinct can immediately solve the problem. Fear occurs when immediate escape is not assured; anger is aroused when mastery of the situation is not easy. Sexual arousal is a different case of extreme motivation to be treated later in this chapter, but frustration in this regard often leads to the further arousal of emotion.

An initial problem encountered in the study of emotion is definitional—what is being studied? Earlier writers on the topic were attempting to explain emotional *experience,* the conscious events accompanying the highly motivated states of anger, fear, joy, and so on. Others, both long ago and recently, have attempted to explain emotional *behavior*—why one snarls, runs, or laughs. Still other students of emotion have tried to understand the *physiological events* accompanying emotion, from the responses of the autonomic nervous system to activity in various centers of the brain. The nature of any investigation of emotion will depend on which of these phenomena the investigator is trying to "explain," and his theory, or explanation, will, for the most part, involve these limited phenomena. To assert a theory of emotion is to state what emotion *is* or what emotions are—conscious states, behavior, or physiological events. A theory should state the conditions that are both *necessary* and *sufficient* for the emotional state.

Definitions

What is an emotion? Although no two authorities seem to agree completely, an emotion may be characterized as a highly motivated state, usually accompanied by heightened awareness (in humans), often recognizable approach or withdrawal behavior, much autonomic activity, and widespread activation in the central nervous system. Consider the classic emotional states of fear, anger, and joy. All involve a high degree of motivation. Changes in conscious content are evident. Fear involves withdrawal behavior, whereas anger or joy implies approach, aggressive or peaceful. In all three states, increases in heart rate, rapid breathing, and "butterflies in the stomach" signal heightened autonomic activity. Finally, none of these conditions can be maintained without widespread increases in CNS activity.

Conscious states. Novelists, many philosophers, and early psychologists tried to classify emotion as a "conscious state." They believed that different kinds of awareness resulting from the perception of external events "caused" different conscious states. These conscious states *were* emotions, each in turn causing a different kind of emotional behavior. This position asserts that conscious events are *necessary* to emotional behavior and *sufficient* to cause emotional behavior. Because so much behavior (emotional or otherwise) is not accompanied by awareness, such assumptions seem unfounded. Much emotional behavior is "unconscious"; that is, the "cause" of the behavior cannot be verbalized. It is a common occurrence to encounter hostile behavior from persons who insist they are not angry; timidity and anxiety from persons with (objectively) nothing to fear; and exhilarant behavior for "no good reason," perceived or experienced. A given conscious state seems neither necessary nor sufficient for a given kind of emotional behavior. However, conscious states can serve as *clues* to the presence of emotion *if* one recognizes that these clues are not always reliable.

Behavior. Other writers have asserted

that emotion *is* behavior of one kind or another. Anger *is* aggressive behavior, fear *is* flight or withdrawal, joy *is* laughter, and so on. This approach ignores many instances when the defined overt behavior does *not* accompany conscious states nor physiological events that strongly indicate the presence of emotion. A well-controlled individual can avoid emotional behavior, exhibiting a "poker face" or calm and unhurried normal movements when he is angry, frightened, or happily excited. The internal physiological responses may be present—the pounding heart, and so forth—but an external observer can sense no change in his demeanor. This may be true only of humans, however. Some forms of emotional behavior, such as the rage-attack pattern in animals, seem to be controlled by some of the same CNS systems that govern autonomic arousal in emotion.

Physiological events. Emotional behavior and emotional awareness are accompanied by physiological events, many of which are mediated by the autonomic nervous system. In aroused emotion the heart beats faster, blood pressure may rise, blood may drain from the stomach, causing "butterflies," "goose pimples" form because of the erection of body hair, and so on. Both these events and somatic responses, such as striking out or running, are caused by physiological events in the central nervous system. The necessary and sufficient conditions for emotion may therefore be certain kinds of autonomic activity or events in certain brain systems that control *both* autonomic activity and behavior. Those who assert that autonomic arousal is the necessary and sufficient condition for emotion must explain different emotions by different patterns of autonomic arousal. In autonomic activity some differences have been found between rage and fear and between either of these emotions and "positive" emotions such as joy or sexual arousal (Arnold). As far as is known, however, there are not enough differences in the patterns of autonomic arousal to account for the variety of emotions experienced

and acted out by humans. Furthermore, simple exercise causes autonomic arousal. Most theorists would not call the bodily changes in exercise an "emotional state." On the other hand, centers or systems can be found in the central nervous systems that control *both* the patterns of autonomic response *and* the overt behavior in emotion. "Centers" have been found for rage, fear, and pleasure, by they exist in bewildering variety. More subtle emotions, moreover, seem to depend on learning and involve widespread CNS activity. A *system* interrelating emotional "centers" seems necessary if emotion is to be understood in terms of CNS activity. Such a system should include all brain centers whose stimulation or removal directly alters emotional behavior and (in humans) emotional experience. The interrelationships among these centers are far from understood, but some attempts have been made to systematize them as a "limbic system," to be discussed later.

Behavior organization and disorganization

Much of the early interest of psychologists in emotion came from the apparent effect of emotion on learning behavior in both humans and laboratory animals. The "goal-seeking" activity of a highly motivated rat in a maze became disorganized when the animal encountered a barrier in its accustomed path. Error behavior increased, and emotion was seen as a "disorganized" state that resulted from interference with highly motivated behavior. The behavior of a highly motivated student often becomes similarly disorganized when he encounters a question he cannot answer on an examination, and he then misses subsequent questions that he would otherwise have answered correctly. P. T. Young and others have proposed, therefore, that emotion is the disorganization that results from the blocking of highly motivated goal-oriented behavior. Later theorists (Duffy, Leeper, Webb, Bindra, and others) have taken issue with this point of view. In the first place, the disruption is necessary if "blocked" or unsuccessful behavior is to change so that adaptation may occur; if the behavior is highly motivated, extreme changes will occur that are not typical of less motivated behavior. They point out that autonomic emotional responses and the overt behavior patterns of rage, fear, and so on would not have developed in the course of evolution if such internal and external responses did not have survival value for the organism. It is further evident that autonomic responses in rage and fear are highly organized and support highly organized overt behavior. Darwin was the first to compare the expression of emotion in animals and humans to show that emotional expression was useful to survival—a biological adaptation. One example he used was the baring the teeth in rage that anticipates biting one's enemy. Cannon's emergency theory states that the sympathetic nervous system responses in rage and fear prepare an animal for fight or flight, and in a general way this seems to be the case. Fight and flight are both highly motivated and very organized responses, and sympathetic arousal helps prepare an animal for the exertion required in either case. Neither type of behavior, however, is appropriate for a rat learning a maze or a student taking an examination. But neither maze-running nor exam-taking was important to survival in the primitive world in which emotional behavior evolved; fighting and fleeing *were* important survival mechanisms. The conclusion follows that emotional responses, autonomic and somatic, are highly organized and serve as a primitive mechanism for *motivation,* arousing and sustaining behavior appropriate to a primitive emergency. The fact that such behavior is not appropriate to highly artificial situations such as maze-running for the rat or exam-taking for the student seems beside the point.

THEORIES OF EMOTION

As suggested earlier, attempts to explain emotion often differed widely because theorists were trying to explain different phenomena, each considered to *be* emotion. Attempts to explain the conscious events accompanying emotion will be quite different from attempts to explain observed emotional behavior, autonomic responses in emotion, or brain function in emotion. From this point of view, none of the theories to be considered is right or wrong, and each contributes something to the understanding of emotional phenomena. On the other hand, one can better examine which of these phenomena—conscious, behavioral, autonomic, of CNS activity—is a necessary and sufficient condition for emotion after one sees how each could theoretically control emotional states.

James and Lange theories

For William James, emotion was a *conscious state* that resulted from sensed emotional behavior and visceral reactions. He sought the causes of this conscious state in the reactions of the body to stimuli that called forth anger, fear, or joy. His famous dictum that we do not run because we are afraid, we are afraid because we run, summarizes his position. To James a perceived stimulus became a consciously emotional stimulus *after* reaction to the stimulus began. When a threatening stimulus resulted in flight, it also resulted in sensations of running and sensations from the visceral reactions of the autonomic nervous system. The somatic sensations of running and the sympathetically aroused sensations of rapid heartbeat, panting, "gooseflesh," and so on were *added to* the initial perception of the threatening stimulus. Adding the somatic sensations of running and visceral sensations from the autonomic reactions to a perception resulted in a perception of conscious fear. The stimulus was therefore feared after the reaction to it began. A simple example might be your own reaction to an emergency while driving an automobile at high speed. Another car pulls out in front of you, you react quickly to avoid it, and only after the incident is over do you begin to tremble, sweat, and feel frightened. Anger, as another emotion, would include some of the same and other sensations of autonomic arousal, but it would also include somatic sensations of overt or suppressed attack behavior. Joy would involve more parasympathetic arousal, perhaps, and sensations of approach reaction; sexual arousal would involve a different autonomic sensation pattern, feedback from copulation responses, and so on. (Lange proposed the same kind of theory, except that he restricted the sensations to those that come from the blood vessels.)

Behavioristic theory of emotion

Several decades ago the famous behaviorist John B. Watson rejected consciousness as a cause of behavior. He believed that stimuli caused behavior as a direct result of their action on the sense organs and nervous system, and consciousness did not belong in this sequence of events.

For Watson rage *was* attack, fear *was* flight, and lust *was* sexual behavior. He sought to determine which of these and other emotional responses were "inherited," in what form they began, and what stimuli controlled them. His experiments with six-month-old children convinced him that there were three inherited patterns of emotional behavior controlled by four stimuli. Pattern X, tentatively identified as "fear," consisted of withdrawal responses and wailing cries in response to either a loud noise or sudden loss of support when being held (falling). Pattern Y, assumed to be "rage," was aroused by restraining an infant's movements, which resulted in strident crying and a flushed face. Pattern Z, called "lust," resulted in the inhibition of active behavior and was accompanied by gurgling, smiling, and sometimes erection of the penis. The stimulus was stroking of the skin, especially near the genitals. To Watson the more complex emotional behavior of adults in response to more varied stimuli resulted from conditioning. If the child was frightened by a loud noise while he was petting a rabbit, he would "attach" the fear response to the rabbit. Furthermore, he would show the fear response to objects resembling the rabbit in any important way; he would *generalize* his fear, and contact with any furry object would result in the fear response. With learning, the fear response would also become more varied, and the withdrawal response would include running and other means of avoiding the feared stimulus. Although these notions may seem oversimplified today, physiologists have found "centers" in the brain that seem to control both visceral and somatic reactions of flight and attack. Other centers that control sexual behavior have been found. Certain responses, such as smiling, seem to have inherited neural mechanisms. In this sense, perhaps Watson was correct in his assumptions about the inheritance of mechanisms for emotional behavior.

Autonomic response theories of emotion

Many writers have identified autonomic nervous system responses with emotion. Most of them state that parasympathetic nervous system reactions, or PNS dominance, are necessary (at least at first) to positive, or pleasurable, emotions. Sympathetic nervous system reactions are necessary to rage or fear, with a different SNS pattern of response for rage, as compared to fear. Some assert a different autonomic pattern acquired through learning for each of the more subtle emotions. Others have said that different autonomic patterns are inherited as a few beginning emotional reactions—PNS dominance for elation or joy, SNS patterns for rage, fear, and perhaps a few others such as "disgust" or "apathy." In some cases it is suggested that the autonomic reaction *is* the emotion and is always necessary to it. Other writers believe it is necessary only at first; after learning has occurred, only activity in the brain systems that normally control the autonomic nervous system is necessary. Some have suggested inherited autonomic patterns that *are* simple emotional reactions such as lust, rage, and fear; the more subtle and varied emotions are one or more of these patterns plus varied somatic responses. Jealousy, for example, could be a mixture of rage and fear of a given degree, along with both approach and avoidance reactions. In any case all assert that the ANS reactions *are* emotion, at least at first.

Cannon-Bard theory of emotion

The Cannon-Bard theory originated as an attempt to explain the behavior of decorticate cats. After removal of the cerebral cortex the animals do not respond, except in a reflex fashion, to vision, audition, or smell. However, they are capable of reflex standing, and their response to sudden somesthetic input from the skin is attack. Stimuli such as pinching the skin or pulling the tail merely cause moving away in normal cats. In decorticates an immediate and integrated rage-attack behavior pattern results. The response was called **sham rage** because the animal lacked the sensory and nervous equipment to direct and maintain the attack behavior. The animal attacked in whatever direction it happened to be "pointed" at the moment, without attacking the source of the stimulation. Furthermore, the attack behavior stopped as soon as the stimulus was removed; rage behavior did not continue for a time, as in the normal animal. However, the rage response was integrated; both organized overt behavior *and* a generalized autonomic nervous system reaction were present. In further experiments more and more of the higher nervous system areas were removed. As long as the posterior third of the hypothalamus was intact, the sham rage pattern was present. When this area was removed, the sham rage behavior disintegrated into isolated "part responses" of somatic and visceral reactions. Snarling might occur, or some autonomic change, but the organized rage reaction had disappeared. The experimenters suggested, therefore, that centers in the posterior part of the hypothalamus organized *both* the ANS responses in rage *and* the behavior pattern in rage. (An early version of the theory placed these "centers" in the thalamus.) Extending this idea, others assumed that the hypothalamus contained centers responsible for behavior and autonomic reactions in each of the major emotional states. They also proposed that activity in the same centers stimulated the cerebral cortex to give rise to the "conscious state" appropriate to the emotion. Overt behavior, autonomic responses, and conscious states in emotion were assumed to be aroused by stimuli from the sense organs that reached appropriate centers in the hypothalmus. Other emotions could of course be added by learning—conditioning of the hypothalamic centers to new stimuli and elaboration of the response patterns initiated there.

Subsequent experiments on sham rage have shown that partial decortication that spares the cingulate gyrus, ventral paleocortex, or allocortex, makes cats *placid*, raising their rage threshold rather than lowering it. Yet either cingulate lesions or lesions in the ventral complex (amygdala, piriform cortex, and hippocampus) make these placid animals ferocious! It is evident that a more widespread neural "circuit" than the hypothalamus is involved in the control of rage and perhaps other emotions as well. There is little doubt that rage-attack behavior and autonomic responses are *organized* at a subcortical level. Posterior hypothalamic lesions produce somnambulant (sleeping) animals that are unemotional, and medial and ventromedial lesions of the hypothalamus make cats ferocious. With the rest of their nervous system intact, however, the ferocity of the lesioned cats is well directed and outlasts the stimulus—they are difficult and dangerous to handle. However well the hypothalamus organizes the rage-attack pattern and perhaps other emotional responses, more widespread areas of the nervous system are involved in its *control*. For example, selective lesions in the piriform areas, amygdala, or hippocampus make animals ferocious, beginning several weeks *after* the operation. Other investigators report placidity after lesions in some of these same areas. Stimulation of one part of the amygdala causes rage responses, whereas stimulation of another part causes fearlike responses; stimulation of the latter site can suppress rage behavior from hypothalamic stimulation. Lesions of the septal area lower the rage threshold, but removal of the amygdala reverses this effect, and so on. Even changing the stimulus parameters, such as voltage or frequency, can elicit fright behavior or rage behavior from the same stimulus site. Obviously, widespread systems *control* the expression of emotional responses, even if there is a focus of organization. Even the stimulation of still *lower* centers in the midbrain can suppress rage behavior that was brought on by hypothalamic stimulation; these sites are often more effective in suppressing rage behavior than are the higher centers. Others (Freeman and Arnold) have proposed that emotional behavior and experience are *initiated* by the cortex, and merely carried out by the hypothalamus and other subcortical centers.

Papez-MacLean theory

The Papez-MacLean theory is a gradually evolving set of notions about a system of nervous centers that perhaps *control*, rather than organize, emotional behavior (and perhaps emotional experience). The centers and pathways involved are shown in Fig. 13-1 as the limbic system. The septal area of the cortex, the cortical cingulate and entorhinal areas, the hippocampus, and most of the amygdaloid nuclei are involved. Papez suggested a circuit from the entorhinal cortex to the hippocampus, thence to the hypothalamus via the fornix, from there to the anterior thalamus, and finally to the cingulate gyrus. Most of these structures had been associated with smell

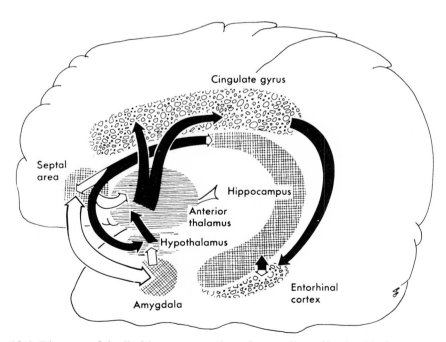

Fig. 13-1. Diagram of the limbic system, projected on outline of brain. *Black arrows,* neural pathways referred to by Papez as the limbic pathways. *White arrows,* connections discovered since that time. (Modified from McCleary, R. A., and Moore, R. Y.: Subcortical mechanisms of behavior, New York, 1965, Basic Books, Inc., Publishers.)

input, but Papez suggested that they were involved in emotional experience. Mac-Lean elaborated on Papez' ideas, and the additional circuits shown in Fig. 13-1 have been traced by subsequent work. Since then the work of many scientists has shown the involvement of many of these structures in emotional *behavior*, whereas stimulation of and surgery on human epileptics and psychotic patients have shown some of these structures to be involved in emotional *experience*. The "connections" of Fig. 13-1 are supposed to integrate perception by higher centers with emotional behavior that is organized by the diencephalon (chiefly the hypothalamus) and perhaps midbrain structures.

NEURAL MECHANISMS IN EMOTION
Somatic and visceral feedback

To what extent are somatic and visceral reactions essential to emotion as it has been defined? To what extent do visceral reactions vary for different emotions, and are they essential for emotional experiences? Rage and fear involve the diffuse reactions of the sympathetic nervous system as well as fight or flight behavior. In one early experiment Cannon removed the sympathetic chain ganglia and collateral ganglia from cats, which abolished most sympathetic responses. After recovery these cats appeared normal, except that their tolerance for cold and stress was reduced. Their reaction to a dog showed normal "emotionality," including the baring of teeth and claws, arched back, spitting, and hissing.

It could be argued that the brain centers controlling sympathetic response had already been conditioned to "emotional" stimuli and that these centers were intact and were sufficient for the emotional behavior now that learning had taken place. Yet it is evident that major sympathetic *reactions* are unnecessary to emotional behavior, at least in the adult animal. In humans, who can tell us about emotional experience, visceral sensations seem to have

more to do with emotional experience than emotional behavior. **Paraplegic** patients, with the spinal cord severed as high as at the neck level, have become a common casualty of war and traffic accidents. Some of these patients are paralyzed from the neck down, and facial expression is their only somatic expression of emotion aside from verbal responses. Diffuse sympathetic arousal cannot be organized by the brain. Furthermore, sensations from the body cannot reach the brain; thus any isolated autonomic reflexes that *do* occur cause no sensations. Of course, the extent to which paraplegic patients receive visceral sensations depends on the level at which the spinal cord is severed. At the neck level, no somatic or visceral sensations are possible save for facial expression (somatic) or oral (visceral) input. As the cut becomes as low as the level of the lowest attachment of the ribs, sensations of rapid heartbeat, "butterflies" in the stomach, and some lower somatic inputs become possible. Schacter reports a study by Hohman of changes in rated emotional feeling for 15 subjects before and after spinal lesions at various levels (Fig. 13-2). The higher the level of the break in the cord, the fewer the somatic and visceral sensations, and the less intense the reported emotional experience in the case of either anger or fear. However, the patients often *behave* in an appropriate way even though they may report only a "mental sort of anger." Except for the group with the lowest level of section (the group with the most somatic and visceral sensations) an increase in "sentimentality" as evinced by more frequent crying or tears in the eyes was reported.

Evidently, autonomic *reactions* are not *necessary to* emotional *behavior*. There is little doubt, on the other hand, that autonomic and somatic reactions *contribute to* emotional experience and behavior. An injection of epinephrine, which mimics the effect of mass sympathetic response, will cause the subject to experience a "cold emotion"—sensations such as a pounding heart, empty stomach, and so on. Unless

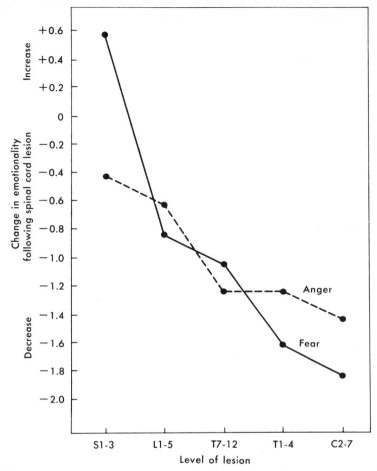

Fig. 13-2. Changes in rated emotional feeling after lesions of the spinal cord for patients with lesions at different levels. Compare this figure with Figs. 3-6 and 3-7 to clarify the level at which the spinal cord has been severed. (From Schacter, S.: Emotion, obesity, and crime, New York, 1971, Academic Press Inc. Adapted from the data of Hohman, G.: Psychophysiology **3:**143-156, 1966.)

the subject *perceives* these inputs as resulting from emotional upset, no emotional behavior will result. In one experiment by Schacter, subjects were given injections of epinephrine under another name or a placebo (fake drug) and were either informed of the effects of epinephrine or told the drug would have no side effects at all. (Epinephrine causes a rapid heartbeat, "butterflies" in the stomach, and other internal sensations usually associated with emotion.) Both groups of subjects believed

the experiment involved drug effects on a visual acuity test. While supposedly waiting in a room for the vision test, each subject was accompanied by a stooge of the experimenter acting like another waiting subject. Under one set of conditions—euphoria— the stooge began acting in an exuberant way by flying paper airplanes, dancing, and keeping up a happy patter while asking the subject to join him. The other set of conditions—anger—involved filling out an extremely personal and insulting questionnaire, which asked, for example, how many extramarital affairs the subject's mother had had. While filling out the same questionnaire, the stooge increasingly expressed rage and finally tore up the offending questionnaire and left in a huff. The experimenters observed the action through a one-way screen and systematically rated how much the subject's behavior resembled the stooge's behavior. After the stooges left, the experimenters, giving a plausible reason, had the subject fill out a standard rating scale to assess the intensity of anger or euphoria. Both the behavior observations and rating scales came out as expected. Subjects who had a placebo or who knew their inner sensations resulted from the drug were relatively indifferent to either kind of stooge and rated their emotions as neither angry or euphoric. Subjects who did not know the reason for their inner turmoil became angry or euphoric in both behavior and rating scale, depending on which stooge they were with.

In another experiment, injections of a tranquilizer that reduces autonomic activity also reduced the laughter and reported amusement to a slapstick movie, whereas epinephrine had the opposite effect when the subjects were not informed of the effects of the drugs. Although autonomic reactions may be *unnecessary* to emotional experience and behavior, they *can* initiate both, depending on how the subject interprets them.

ANS and emotion

According to Cannon's emergency theory, diffuse sympathetic discharge prepares an animal for fight or flight, both highly emotional responses. Both responses are highly organized and motivated, as already pointed out. Are different emotional behavior patterns, such as rage and fear, accompanied by different ANS reactions? Do the different ANS reactions influence typical emotional "experience" in humans? It appears that there *are* different autonomic response patterns for rage, fear, and sexual arousal and perhaps for other emotions, such as apathy. Studies of psychotic patients suggest that their predominant autonomic pattern strongly influences their reported "mood," as well as their behavior. As far as the more pleasant emotions are concerned, many of them appear to be accompanied by widespread but discrete parasympathetic responses, which are cholinergic and governed from the anterior and medial hypothalamus. Such parasympathetic reactions include sexual excitement and dilation of blood vessels supplying the viscera and the skin. Rage and fear, on the other hand, are accompanied by diffuse sympathetic discharge, reinforced by hormones from the adrenal medulla.

The adrenal gland produces two hormones: epinephrine and norepinephrine. Epinephrine is sympatheticomimetic (has the same effect as SNS discharge), whereas in some respects norepinephrine is not. Epinephrine raises the blood pressure by cardioacceleration (increasing the rate of beating of the heart). Norepinephrine raises the blood pressure by constricting blood vessels leading to the skin and viscera. It appears that more epinephrine is released in fear reactions, and that greater norepinephrine release accompanies anger. Parasympathetic stimulation would therefore lower the blood pressure more in fear than in anger because it slows the heart and combats the effect of epinephrine more directly. This can be tested by injecting a drug (methacholine [Mecholyl]) that mimics parasympathetic stimulation. The drug rapidly lowers the blood pressure of depressed psychotics or of normal people experiencing fright because it slows their rapid heartbeat. A smaller effect on blood pressure is typical of a high norepinephrine response in rage because the drug has no effect on constricted blood vessels that raises the blood pressure. This response is found in paranoid psychotics and normal subjects experiencing anger. The tests show that predatory animals such as lions have a higher norepinephrine level in the blood, whereas animals that survive by flight, such as the rabbit, produce more epinephrine. Funkenstein suggests that sympathetically aroused animals exhibit only rage and fear, but humans experience self-directed anger, which leads to depression. Depression, like anxiety or fear, is accompanied by a high epinephrine output. Since the visceral blood flow is not reduced in fear, the stomach is flushed, making a large hydrochloric acid output possible, which can cause ulcers. If physiological development parallels psychological development, one would expect the young child to demonstrate more anger than fear and produce more norepinephrine than epinephrine. With training—"development of a conscience"—more self-directed anger and anxiety should be accompanied by a higher epinephrine output. As far as the adrenal output is concerned, the ratio of norepinephrine to epinephrine *is* higher in infants than in older children.

Hypothalamus and emotion

Removal of the brain anterior to the posterior third of the hypothalamus leaves a cat able to display sham rage—integrated attack behavior, however brief, accompanied by the autonomic responses of typical rage. Subsequent removal of this area reduces the rage behavior to fragments of the original response. Posterior hypothalamic lesions of the rage area in an otherwise intact animal results in placidity and somnambulance. These observations led many researchers to conclude that the hypothalamus was the seat of integration of the somatic and visceral responses in rage and perhaps in other emotions as well. Subsequent studies with implanted electrodes seemed to confirm these conclusions, although the locations differ, since stimulation of the anterior hypothalamus and related areas (basal septal nuclei, preoptic area, lateral hypothalamus, basal medial thalamus) produces organized and lasting rage behavior. Furthermore, stimulation of the posterior hypothalamus produces fear-escape responses (Hess and Akart), and self-stimulation "reward" areas (Chapter 12) lie in the anterior medial hypothalamus. It appears that there are "centers" in the hypothalamus that are important to pathways for rage, fear, and pleasure whose stimulation produces both the autonomic and somatic reactions of these emotions.

A question remains: How dependent are these stimulus areas on the input of other centers at higher and lower levels, and to what extent do these cells dominate the activity of other parts of the brain at higher and lower levels? Stimulation of a hypothalamic area may be merely exciting a pathway to another part or parts of the brain where the somatic and visceral responses are actually integrated. And ablation of an area in the hypothalamus may be merely interrupting a major pathway going to a more important integrating center elsewhere in the brain. Important as the hypothalamus is to the integration of the somatic and visceral responses of emotion, it appears to be part of a larger system, involving higher and lower centers, that organizes emotional response and perhaps emotional experience as well.

Limbic system and emotion

In more primitive animals the cerebral cortex began as a set of centers for correlating smell input. As a result, many of the older cortical structures were classified along with the olfactory bulbs as **rhinencephalon** ("nose brain"). Papez, in a theory elaborated by MacLean, proposed that some of these cortical centers and certain subcortical structures serve to integrate perception by higher centers with emotional expression that originates in the diencephalon (primarily the hypothalamus). As previously explained, he proposed a "circuit" (Fig. 13-1) from the hippocampus and amygdala to the hypothalamus via the fornix and thence to the anterior thalamus and gyrus cinguli. Subsequent studies have added other pathways to the system as indicated in Fig. 13-1.

Pribram and Krüger, taking a phylogenetic approach to the development of cortical and associated subcortical structures, have traced the evolutionary development of cortical and subcortical centers from their origin in smell. They classify as "nose brain" the olfactory bulb connections with the prepiriform areas on the base of the brain and parts of the amygdaloid nuclei. Connections exist from these areas, but not from the olfactory bulb, to areas beneath the corpus callosum (subcallosal), the presubiculum, and the frontotemporal areas. Connections from here go to the third system of hippocampus and cingulate gyrus. In terms of the evolutionary age of the cortical parts of this system, the hippocampus, piriform lobe, and olfactory bulb are the oldest and constitute the **paleocortex.** The cingulate gyrus, presubiculum, and frontotemporal areas are intermediate, or **transitional, cortex.** The remainder of the cerebral cortex is the **neocortex** ("new cortex").

Papez' original speculations were fruitful ones, leading to experiments on what has been called the **Klüver-Bucy syndrome,** after its discoverers. They found that bilateral ("both sides") temporal lobe ablations made rhesus monkey docile, oral (mouthing things), indiscriminative (putting anything in their mouths), and hypersexed. The changes in emotional behavior were profound and obvious. The ablations involved included, along with the temporal lobes, the frontotemporal cortex, piriform lobe, amygdala, presubiculum, and hippocampus. These areas are involved in Papez' circuit and in the second and third systems, which Pribram and Krüger believe to have evolved from the olfactory brain. However, until the role of each part of the limbic system is known, as well as the manner in which it interacts and affects other parts of the brain, few conclusions are possible.

Cerebral cortex and emotion

Septal area. The septal area is a part of the transitional cortex that forms a part of the limbic circuit (Fig. 13-1). Lesions in this area produce the type of savageness in rats that results from stimulation of certain hypothalamic and amygdala nuclei that were previously described (Brady and Nauta). A striking difference is that the animals *can* be tamed, if handled, within a couple of weeks; recovery does not occur if the animals are isolated. An explanation of the phenomenon has not appeared. Presumably pathways involved in the inhibition of rage behavior have been destroyed, but other sources of inhibition are available.

Frontal lobes. A major output of the limbic system seems to project to the frontal areas of the cerebral cortex from the anterior nuclei of the thalamus. These cortical areas are anterior to the motor and premotor areas; so they are sometimes known as the **prefrontal lobes** (Fulton and Jacobsen). In studies on the ability of primates in a learning task involving a delay between stimulus presentation and discrimination, the effects of removing the prefrontal areas were tested. A side observation noted was that the animals were less "excited" (emotional) in response to errors and were more generally docile.

Psychosurgery

With all of the research involving the effects of brain stimulation and lesions on emotional behavior in animals, it should come as no surprise to find that these procedures have been attempted to relieve emotional disorders in man. The legal and ethical issues involved in perhaps changing permanently the emotional behavior of another human being are outside the scope of a simple textbook. It can be said that the effects are complex and profound and the procedures are susceptible to misuse, unless careful social control is exercised. Even then, the emotional behavior of humans is so much more complex than that of other animals—even other primates—that unpredictable results may follow the most careful diagnosis and surgery. The procedures have been used to relieve severe pain in terminal cancer, terrifying anxiety that is not relieved by psychotherapy, psychosis, and severe assaultive behavior. Some fear their use in controlling anger that has legitimate cause in social deprivation or in "socializing" criminals whose crimes have social rather than neurological causes. The debate can be left to relevant readings at the end of the chapter, should the student wish to pursue it.

Prefrontal lobectomy. Cases of prefrontal lobectomy result in most instances from accidental brain damage, although surgery to remove tumors may remove prefrontal areas. The consequences are similar to prefrontal lobotomy (see below) and are more severe if most of the prefrontal areas are removed.

Prefrontal lobotomy. Moniz perfected the prefrontal lobotomy in response to animal experiments reported by Jacobsen. The surgery involves severing some or all of the fibers connecting the anterior thalamus and prefrontal cortex (similar to standard lobotomy, Fig. 13-3). It is estimated that over 70,000 of these operations were performed between 1935 and the mid-1950s. The early operations were done primarily on institutionalized psychotics and extreme-anxiety neurotics (Freeman and Watts) where side effects beyond the relief of anxiety and fear were not obvious because their behavior was so abnormal to begin with. With more widespread use of the technique for anxiety, side effects like apathy, impulsiveness, possible loss of intelligence (not usually on standard tests), asocial behavior, and impaired judgment became more evident. (The operation was also used to relieve pain in cases of terminal cancer, with patients reporting that pain had lost its insistent quality—it did not bother them because they did not have to pay attention to it.) More careful and selected lesions of the prefrontal lobes were made in conjunction with a careful program of testing at Greystone Hospital by Columbia University scientists in the

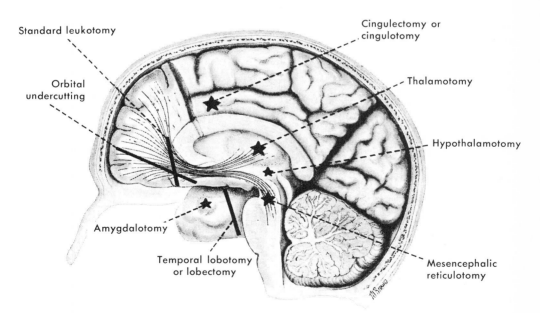

Fig. 13-3. Medial (cut down the center) view of human brain, showing different sites for destroying tissue in psychosurgery. *Bars,* Cutting tracts (lobotomy, orbital undercutting, temporal lobotomy) or removing a lobe (temporal lobectomy). *Stars,* Focal brain sites destroyed by current at the tip of a precisely placed electrode (stereotaxic surgery). (From Hitchcock, E.: Ann. Clin. Res. **3:**187-198, 1971.)

1950s with some degree of success in the treatment of anxiety, but the results were still quite variable (Mettler). The advent of tranquilizers and electroshock treatment led to near abandonment of the treatment by the 1960s.

Limbic operations. With the many animal experiments on changes in emotional behavior that result from lesions of the limbic system, attention turned to these areas of the brain. It was pointed out that interrupting excitation to and from the frontal lobes via the thalamus to the amygdala could be responsible for the behavior changes seen in prefrontal lobotomy. More recently, frontal and parietal areas have been found to receive fibers from the hypothalamus. Research of this kind raised hopes that precise lesions of the limbic system and related cortical areas could change emotional behavior in a desired way without undesirable side effects. The most carefully documented cases are those of Mark and Irwin (see readings); most of the literature, however, is based on subjective observations of small numbers of cases.

Mark and Irwin tried to reduce violent assaultive behavior that seemed associated with temporal lobe epilepsy in a number of cases and experienced a fair degree of success. They performed lesions (amygdalotomy, Fig. 13-3) in areas where abnormal seizure discharges were recorded with depth electrodes, hoping to obtain the "calming" effect demonstrated in animals, but only after noting that they could induce the initial symptoms of aggression by stimulating at these sites. The whole temporal lobe has been removed from one or both sides of the brain in tumor operations or to relieve epilepsy. Reports of a calming effect also reported disturbances of memory. Cingulate lesions have been performed for aggression and obsessive behavior. Orbital undercutting has been tried for anxiety and depression. Thalamic lesions were an attempt to destroy the source of the fibers involved in lobotomies (with less extensive damage). Lateral hypothalamic lesions are supposed to relieve anxiety, aggression, and so on. Most of the reports, as previously noted, are subjective reports of a small number of cases where the results are quite variable.

SEXUAL BEHAVIOR IN HUMANS

The hormones controlling the reproductive cycles of subprimate species were explained in Chapter 2. It was noted in Chapter 12 that primates, especially humans, were more strongly influenced by learning in the development, expression, and decline of sexual behavior than were other mammals. This results in a greater variety of sexual behavior, with more frequent occurrence of "deviant" sexual behavior. At the same time, sexual motivation in humans as in other animals is a highly motivated state subject to frustration and is therefore an emotion.

Fetal development

The **genetic sex** of the embryo is determined at fertilization, being female (XX) if both female chromosomes are joined or male (XY) if one male chromosome is inherited (see Chapter 2). In either case, the embryo has the pregenital structures to be either male (wolffian) or female (müllerian), as shown in Fig. 13-4, where male and female are identical. Although both hormones will be present in later life, the embryo will be male only if androgen is present in the embryo, otherwise the female structures develop. As seen in Fig. 13-4, when the female structures develop, the male structures degenerate, and vice versa. This process can be interfered with before birth by injection of androgens into the mother with a female (XX) embryo—a genetic female offspring will be born with a well-developed penis (but no testes, thus a pseudohermaphrodite). Normally, however, genetic sex determines the **gonadal sex** at birth—the appearance of the external genitals. Hormone imbalances in the mother may result in the birth of a **hermaphrodite,** with a genetic female looking like a male without testes or a genetic male having the external genitals of a female.

Development before puberty

At birth, the influence of learning begins to be evident, as the child is assigned a sex role according to the appearance of the external genitals. Male and female babies are assigned sex roles at birth, and children assigned sex roles usually behave accordingly even if the assigned gender role contradicts genetic, gonadal, or genital sex (Money and Ehrhardt).

Puberty

Somewhere between 12 and 15 years of age, the hypothalamus reacts to unknown influences to initiate the onset of puberty, as defined by the appearance of the **secondary sexual characteristics.** In the male, the voice takes a lower pitch, the muscles develop (especially in the chest), and facial and chest hair appears and darkens. In the female, a slight change in

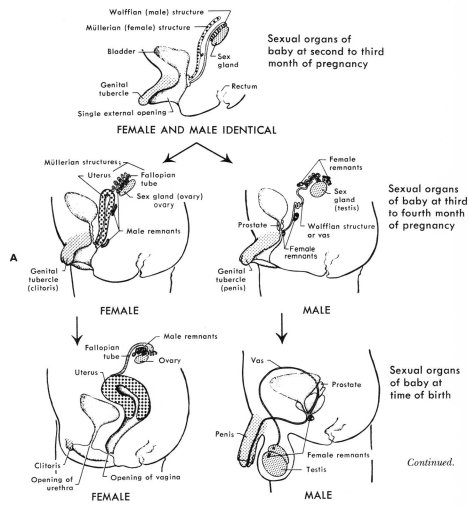

Fig. 13-4. Development of internal (**A**) and external (**B**) genitals in the human embryo and fetus. (From Money, J., Hampson, J. G., and Hampson, J. L.: Bull. Johns Hopkins Hosp. **97:**284-300, 1955. Reprinted by permission of The Johns Hopkins Medical Journal.)

voice quality results, and the hips, breasts, vulva, and vagina enlarge. In both sexes, underarm and pubic hair appear. As shown in Table 1, the hypothalamus stimulates the anterior pituitary gland to release luteinizing hormone (LH), which stimulates production of androgens by the male testes and estrogens by the female ovaries to cause the appearance of secondary sexual characteristics. At the same time, the hypothalamus stimulates anterior pituitary release of follicle stimulating hormone (FSH), resulting in the production of sperm in the male and ova in the female.

Adult sexual behavior

It was not until the pioneering survey work of the biologist Alfred C. Kinsey and his colleagues in the late 1940s and early

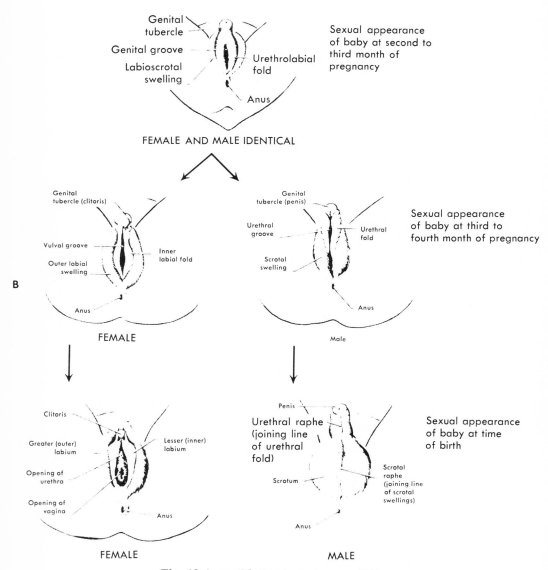

Fig. 13-4, cont'd. For legend see p. 227.

1950s that the variety of human sexual behavior became known in any scientific fashion. As social taboos in research with human sexual behavior gradually became less formidable, the research of William H. Masters and Virginia E. Johnson became possible. Out of their work on physiological responses during sexual intercourse, meaningful methods of treating sexual frustrations emerged in the Reproductive Biology Research Foundation in St. Louis. Others have taken up their approaches (Kaplan, for example), and courses on human sexuality are finding their way into the curriculum of many colleges and universities. The general picture that emerges is one of four stages of a normal sex cycle, important differences in recovery characteristics between the male and female, and methods for treating sexual dysfunction with a high degree of success. The treatment of these topics in this chapter can only be cursory at best; the student should consult the readings and references for a more extensive treatment.

Normal sexual behavior. Masters and Johnson define four phases in the sexual response cycle (before, during, and after sexual intercourse): (1) excitement, (2) plateau, (3) orgasm, and (4) resolution (see Fig. 13-5). In the male, the *excitement phase* is characterized by erection and enlargement of the penis caused by engorgement with blood because more blood flows into the organ than out of it as a result of a spinal reflex action. The early excitement phase of the female is the moistening of the vagina with a lubricating fluid and occurs within seconds of the onset of sexual excitement in the "sweating reaction" of the walls of the vagina, also caused by vascular engorgement—of the vagina in this case. The increase in local blood pressure causes a "seepage" of plasma from the engorged blood vessels into the vagina. As the excitement phase in the female continues, the clitoris (Fig. 13-4) enlarges, the nipples of the breasts swell, and later on the breasts themselves increase in size. (The nipple change occurs to a minor de-

gree in the male.) Then the inner and outer lips of the vagina swell and the vaginal "barrel" expands. There is an increase in heart rate and blood pressure in both sexes, and a flushing (vasodilation) of the skin that begins in the abdomen and spreads over the upper body. The excitement phase blends into the *plateau phase*. The male testes double in size and are pulled higher into the scrotum and the ridge at the base of the glans of the penis enlarges. In females, the swelling of the outer third of the vagina reduces its diameter by half and increases the frictional stimulation of the penis; the inner vagina enlarges and the clitoris becomes more erect, while a darkening of the inner lips of the vagina signals imminent orgasm. The *orgasm* in the female is distinguished by rhythmic muscular contractions (at intervals of four-fifths of a second) of the outer third of the vaginal barrel and surrounding tissues, usually 3 to 12 in number. The uterus also contracts in a rhythmic way. The male orgasm is also distinguished by a series of muscular contractions at the same intervals during which the semen is ejected. The semen has collected in the seminal vesicles and the connected bulblike ampullae. The latter contract to force their contents into the urethra (duct of the penis) while the prostate gland contracts to add its fluids. A bulb in the urethra near the base of the penis enlarges to receive these fluids, which produce the first sensations of ejaculation. Contractions of this bulb and the penis eject the semen with considerable force. In both sexes, muscles of the neck, abdomen, buttocks, and limbs contract, and vigorous grasping occurs. *Resolution* in females is first seen in return to normal of tissues around the nipples, disappearance of the sex flush, and widespread perspiration. In seconds, the clitoris relaxes, the outer vaginal barrel increases in diameter, the uterus shrinks, and the passage from vagina to uterus (cervix) enlarges, permitting easier entrance of sperm. Total resolution may require as long as a half hour. The male reso-

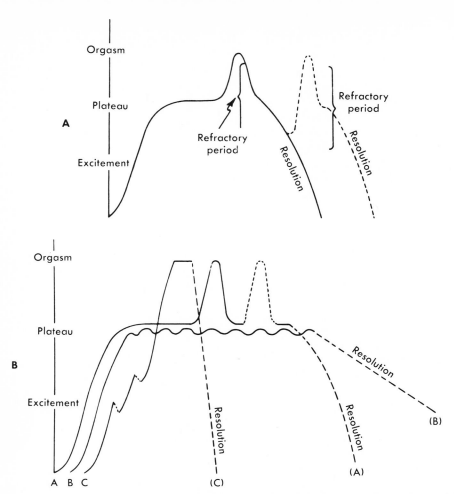

Fig. 13-5. Male, **A,** and female, **B,** sexual response cycles. Four successive phases during sexual intercourse are excitement, plateau, orgasm, and resolution. Note that only the male has a refractory period after orgasm when erection declines even though sexual excitement is otherwise present. Rearousal and a second orgasm is shown after a refractory period, *dotted line. Solid line,* Resolution without a second excitation and orgasm. **B,** Reactions of three females. Female *A* has a second orgasm after returning only to the plateau phase after the first orgasm. Female *B* does not reach orgasm; resolution occurs after a period spent in the plateau phase. Female *C,* with no plateau, reaches resolution after a single orgasm. (From Masters, W. H., and Johnson, V. E.: Human sexual response, Boston, 1966, Little, Brown & Co.)

lution is quickly seen in loss of erection of the penis and return to its normal size. The sex flush disappears and the testes descend. Breathing and heart rate return to normal in both sexes.

Males and females differ most in the "re-fractory period" that follows the male reso-lution but not the female resolution (Fig. 13-5). During this period, the male cannot be aroused to an erection. This period lasts several minutes in most men and increases in duration with age. By contrast, con-tinued sexual stimulation can result in a series of orgasms in females, during which their sexual excitement does not fall below the plateau phase.

Sexual dysfunction. Human sexual behavior is so variable that what is "normal" becomes difficult to define. Male homosexuality or female homosexuality (lesbianism) can apparently result from a difference between genetic sex and gonadal sex. This can result from hormone disturbances of the individual's mother during pregnancy (see previous discussion). There have been widely publicized cases where the gonads have been surgically altered to agree with the individual's desired sex role. I am not aware of any reliable large-sample studies of homosexuality that assess the relative influence of genetic sex, gonadal sex, development of secondary sex characteristics, or assigned gender role and experience. The majority of medical opinion seems to indicate that homosexuality results from sexual experience. The most common sorts of human sexual dysfunctions appear to be in the heterosexual area, where the individual desires a "normal" sex life.

SUMMARY

Language habits resulting from rationalistic philosophy treat emotion as disruptive when emotion should be considered as a special case of motivation that occurs when adaptive behavior is blocked. Students of emotion have also been variously concerned with emotional experience (conscious events), overt emotional behavior, or the internal physiological events accompanying emotion. Individual differences in emphasis determine the way emotion is defined and theoretically explained.

The most useful definition includes all three aspects of emotion and how they are organized by the CNS. Theories emphasizing conscious states fail because awareness is neither necessary nor sufficient for emotional behavior. Theories emphasizing emotional behavior ignore instances of physiological and conscious signs of emotion without evidence of overt emotional responses. Theories emphasizing autonomic response fail because ANS response does not differ for each emotion; furthermore, emotion occurs when the ANS response is blocked by drugs or surgery, and simple exercise causes ANS response changes without emotion. Because emotion disrupts complex learning behavior, it was once defined as a disorganized response; the evolutionary development of emotion suggests that it is a highly organized, primitive CNS mechanism for motivation in an emergency. James believed that conscious emotional events were sensations aroused by visceral and somatic emotional responses. For Watson, emotion *was* overt behavior—inherited fear, rage, and lust responses to specific stimuli; the responses were made more variable and the stimuli eliciting them increased through conditioning and generalization. ANS response has been identified with emotion by other writers who believe that the ANS responses are necessary to emotion, at least until some learning has occurred.

The Cannon-Bard theory of emotion originated as an attempt to explain the sham rage behavior of decorticate cats by assuming that centers in the hypothalamus organized overt and autonomic emotional responses on the one hand and caused the perception of emotions by higher centers on the other. However, more widespread areas in the CNS that control emotion have been discovered since the Cannon-Bard work. The Papez-MacLean theory proposed that a more widespread system formed a circuit in the rhinencephalon that included the entorhinal cortex, hippocampus, hypothalamus, anterior thalamus, and cingulate gyrus. Subsequent work has shown some of these areas to be involved in both emotional behavior and experience.

Somatic and visceral feedback contributes to emotion, but this feedback seems unessential to emotion in the adult animal because sympathectomized cats show emotional behavior and so do paraplegic humans, although the extent of human emotional "feelings" depends on the extent of their somatic and visceral input (level of spinal cord section). However, ANS responses can cause emotion. If human subjects are aware that the internal ANS responses they perceive are caused by a drug, they do not become emotional; if they are unaware of the cause of the internal upset, they often think they are emotional and behave accordingly. Although ANS responses are not varied enough to account for all emotions, pleasure seems to be accompanied by parasympathetic responses, whereas rage and fear involve widespread sympathetic response.

In fear the adrenal medulla produces mostly epinephrine, which raises the blood pressure by increasing the heart rate. In rage it produces more norepinephrine, which raises blood pressure by constricting the arteries supplying the viscera and skin. Humans are capable of learning the self-directed anger and depression that lead to epinephrine output just as fear responses do.

It seems that there are areas in the hypothalamus that are important to the autonomic reactions of rage, fear, and pleasure and that stimulation of these areas produces both the autonomic and somatic reactions of these emotions. Hypothalamic areas seem dependent on lower midbrain centers for rage behavior and dependent on rhinencephalic centers of the Papez-MacLean variety for emotional responses. For example, bitemporal lobectomies, including the amygdala and hippocampus, make monkeys docile, hypersexed, indiscriminative, and oral in their behavior (the Klüver-Bucy syndrome). The hypersexual symptom seems to be caused by piriform cortex lesions and the docility by loss of the amygdala. Pathways from the hypothalamus and other basal areas to the frontal and parietal cortex have been traced. Septal lesions cause savagery in rats, yet they can be tamed. Prefrontal lobectomy reduces emotionality in monkeys.

Psychosurgery is an attempt to relieve emotional disorders in humans and has variable results. Prefrontal lobectomy and lobotomy relieve intractable pain and reduce anxiety but often result in irresponsible behavior. Limbic surgery, especially of the amygdala, has some effectiveness in relieving assaultive behavior.

In humans genetic sex is determined by chromosomes, although embryonic androgen is necessary to produce a male. Endocrine disturbances in the mother can produce a hermaphrodite. Gonadal sex determines gender role after birth, and learning that largely determines future sexual behavior results. The hypothalamus stimulates the anterior pituitary to initiate changes in gonadal hormones that result in the secondary sex characteristics of puberty.

The early survey work by Kinsey and co-workers revealed the variety of human sexual behavior. Masters and Johnson defined the phases of excitement, plateau, orgasm, and resolution in sexual intercourse and described physiological changes that accompany each phase. Only the male has a refractory period after orgasm.

Human sexual dysfunction is difficult to define. Homosexuality in both sexes (called lesbianism in women) can be caused by disparate gonadal and genetic sex, but it is probably learned in most cases.

READINGS

Andrew, R. J.: The origins of facial expressions, Sci. Am. **213:**88-94, Oct. 1965 (W. H. Freeman Reprint No. 627).

Arnold, M. B., editor: The nature of emotion, Baltimore, 1968, Penguin Books, Inc.

Ax, A. F.: The physiological differentiation between anger and fear in humans, Psychosom. Med. **15:**433-442, 1953 (Bobbs-Merrill Reprint No. P-16).

Brady, J. V., and Nauta, W. J. H.: Subcortical mechanisms in emotional behavior: affective changes following septal forebrain lesions in the albino rat, J. Comp. Physiol. Psychol. **46:**339-346, 1953 (Bobbs-Merrill Reprint No. P-46).

Brecher, R., and Brecher, E., editors: An analysis of *Human sexual response,* Boston, 1966, Little, Brown and Company.

Candland, D. K., editor: Emotion: bodily change, New York, 1962, D. Van Nostrand Co., Inc.

Cannon, W. B.: Bodily changes in pain, hunger, fear and rage, New York, 1963, Harper & Row, Publishers.

Charover, S.: The pacification of the brain, Psychol. Today **7**:59-69, May 1974.

Darwin, C.: The expression of the emotions in man and animal, Chicago, 1965, The University of Chicago Press.

Denenberg, V. H., and Zarrow, M. X.: Rat pax, Psychol. Today **3**:45-68, April 1970.

Funkenstein, D. H.: The physiology of fear and anger, Sci. Am. **192**:74-80, May 1955 (W. H. Freeman Reprint No. 428).

Grastyán, E.: Towards a better understanding of human emotion, Impact of Science on Society **18**:187-205, 1968. Also in Leukel, F., editor: Issues in physiological psychology, St. Louis, 1974, The C. V. Mosby Co.

Heiman, J. R.: Woman's sexual arousal, Psychol. Today **8**:90-94, April 1975.

Kaplan, H.: No-nonsense therapy for six sexual malfunctions, Psychol. Today **8**:77-86, Oct. 1974.

Katchadorian, H.: Fundamentals of human sexuality: sense and nonsense, San Francisco, 1974, W. H. Freeman Co.

Klüver, H., and Bucy, P. C.: Preliminary analysis of functions of the temporal lobes in monkeys. In Isaacson, R. L., editor: Basic readings in neuropsychology, New York, 1964, Harper & Row, Publishers.

McCary, J.: Sexual myths and fallacies, New York, 1973, Schocken Books, Inc.

McCleary, R. A., Moore, R. Y.: Subcortical mechanism in behavior, New York, 1965, Basic Books, Inc., Publishers.

Malmo, R.: Emotions and muscle tension, Psychol. Today **3**:64-83, March 1970.

Mark, V.: A psychosurgeon's case for psychotherapy, Psychol. Today **8**:28-38, July 1974.

Mark, V., and Irwin, F.: Violence and the brain, New York, 1970, Harper & Row, Publishers.

Moyer, K.: The physiology of violence, Psychol. Today **7**:35-38, July 1973.

Pomeroy, W. B.: Dr. Kinsey and the Institute for sex research, New York, 1973, The New American Library, Inc.

Pribram, K.: The new neurology and biology of emotion: a structural approach, Am. Psychol. **22**:830-838, 1967. Also in Leukel, F., editor: Issues in physiological psychology, St. Louis, 1974, The C. V. Mosby Co.

Rosvold, H. E., Mirsky, A. F., and Pribram, K.: Influence of amygdaloidectomy on social behavior in monkeys, J. Comp. Physiol. Psychol. **47**:173-178, 1954 (Bobbs-Merrill Reprint No. P-296).

Schacter, S., and Singer, J. E.: Cognitive, social and physiological determinants of emotional state, Psychol. Rev. **69**:379-399, 1962 (Bobbs-Merrill Reprint No. P-553).

Watson, J. B., and Rayner, R.: Conditioned emotional reactions, J. Exp. Psychol. **3**:1-13, 1920 (Bobbs-Merrill Reprint No. P-360).

CHAPTER 14

Learning: the where, when, and how of changes in the brain

OVERVIEW

This chapter is divided into four sections. The first concerns where in the brain the anatomical changes that constitute learning occur. This search for the "engram"—the physical trace of learning—is one of the oldest problems in physiological psychology and leads to consideration of brain mechanisms in language and the specialization for different functions found in the two cerebral hemispheres. The second topic—the "when" of learning—leads to the conclusion that memory formation is a process that continues after formal practice is over. Then the "how" of learning is taken up—what changes occur at the "molar" level of synapses in learning and how at the "molecular" level the brain cells themselves are changed. The chapter closes with a brief section on biofeedback technique for learning voluntary control over involuntary responses.

WHERE DO CHANGES IN THE BRAIN OCCUR?
Historical background: search for the engram

Two principles seemed to guide early investigators who studied the physiological basis of learning and memory. The first principle was the "reflex model" of the nervous system. In this model, simple connections are made at synapses between incoming sensory neurons, association neurons, and outgoing motoneurons. Such connections in the brain are variable; thus responses to stimuli vary. An action would follow a sensory stimulus by chance, and the action would be rewarded. The rewarded response would be repeated when the stimulus appeared, and the synaptic connections between stimulus and response would be improved through *use* until the stimulus-response relation became automatic, like a reflex. The model does not say, however, how reward affects synaptic connections in the first place. This problem was encountered in Chapter 12 in terms of brain systems for rewards and punishment.

The second principle that seemed obvious to early researchers was **encephalization.** As newer parts of the brain developed through evolution, they came to dominate the activity of older parts of the brain. In mammals, such as man, the newest part of the brain is the cerebral cortex. The most distinctive feature of animals with complex brains like man is their superior ability to learn complex behavior. It was therefore assumed that the cerebral cortex had taken over the newest kind of complex brain function—the formation of new connections between stimulus and response at synapses. If these synaptic connections were to be found in the cerebral cortex, they would be found in the association areas rather than in the sensory projection areas for incoming stimuli or in the motor projection areas for outgoing responses; the synaptic connections of the association areas would link the sensory and motor projection areas.

The simple model of the early investigators explains why they sought the **engram**—the physical synaptic changes of learning—in the cerebral cortex. They used the method of **ablation,** taking out parts of the cortex and observing the effect on learning and memory. If removing a given part of the cortex impaired learning and memory, it was assumed that the stimulus-response connections for the habit being studied were ordinarily made in the part of the cortex that had been removed.

Cortical ablation effects on maze learning and retention. Lashley studied the effects of ablating cortical tissue in rats. He studied their ability to learn and remember mazes of three levels of difficulty (based on the number of blind alleys) by operating on them either before or after they had learned. The results of his pioneering experiments can be summarized, in an oversimplified way, by three conclusions:

1. Cortical ablation had more effect on retention of a given maze habit than on ability to learn mazes; that is, if the rat was operated on before it learned, its ability to learn was impaired in comparison with control rats. However, if it learned a maze, was operated on, and was then tested on the same maze, its retention was affected more than its ability to learn new mazes.

2. The more difficult the maze (that is, the more blind alleys), the greater was the effect of removing a given amount of cortex on *either* learning or retention. Removing 10% of the cortex would affect learning or memory for complex mazes more than for simple ones.

3. It did not seem to matter which areas of the cortex were damaged, but the *amount* of cortex removed was critical. Removing 10% of the frontal area had about

the same effect as removing 10% of the parietal area, but removing 50% of any area would have a greater effect on learning and memory. From these results Lashley evolved the principles of **mass action** and **equipotentiality,** each a corollary of the other. The principle of mass action states that the cortex acts *as a whole* in learning—that all areas of the cortex are involved at once. Equipotentiality therefore means that one cortical area is as good as another for learning the maze habit; if a rat has 75% of the cortex left, it does not matter where the 75% is located as far as the rat's ability to learn or retain the maze habit is concerned.

Cortical connections. It was originally assumed that learning consisted of establishing synaptic connections between (incoming) sensory projection areas and (outgoing) motor areas through the neurons of the association areas of the cortex. It was believed that perhaps these connections could be cut to affect learning and retention, even if they differed from one rat to another. However, thin cuts made in the cortex in such a way as to isolate small squares of cortex had no effect on learning or retention (Lashley). Even electrically insulating these squares from one another by the placement of small strips of mica in the cuts had no effect (Sperry). Cortical cells seem to conduct vertically rather than horizontally. On the other hand, cuts of this kind do not sever fibers that "loop" down through the interior white matter to connect one cortical area with another, nor do they sever the crossing fibers **(commissural fibers)** that connect corresponding areas of the two hemispheres. More will be explained later about the effects of cutting the fibers that connect the two hemispheres.

Subcortical centers. The cortex is "vertically organized"; that is, most cells connect with others above or below them, and one part of the cortex connects with another mostly by subcortical routes, including the thalamus. Accordingly, thalamic areas were damaged in rats (Gheselli and

Brown), with minimum cortical damage, by use of the stereotaxic instrument. The effects on learning and retention resembled mass action.

Lashley's paradox. The work of Lashley and others who attempted to locate the engram, or trace of memory, leads to a paradox. If memory is impaired by the destruction of nerve cells in many cortical and subcortical locations, it must mean that many millions of cortical and subcortical cells participate in the memory in some fashion and are altered by learning in some way. One conclusion that follows is that single individual cells must participate in each of the thousands of memories we accumulate in a lifetime! How can a single cell contain this much information? We will return to this question near the end of the chapter when we consider molecular biochemical changes in learning. However, considerations of this kind led Lashley to say in 1950: "I sometimes feel in reviewing the evidence on the localization of the memory trace, that the necessary conclusion is that learning is just not possible."

Extent of recorded brain changes in learning. In an attempt to simplify the problem of neural changes in learning, Olds has recorded changes in the response of cells of the auditory pathway while training rats to associate a tone with delivery of food to a food dish in their cage. He recorded cell activity to the tone at the following five "stations" along the auditory pathway: (1) cochlear nucleus, (2) nucleus of the lateral lemniscus, (3) inferior colliculus, (4) medial geniculate body, and (5) auditory cortex. Other electrodes recorded what was going on in other parts of the brain—the hypothalamus, reticular formation, extrapyramidal motor system, and cerebral cortex. In terms of behavior, the rats seemed to learn nothing at all during the first 10 to 20 trials, learned to go to the food box when the tone sounded during the next 10 trials, and learned to move more rapidly and smoothly during later trials. For each block of ten trials a "map" of cell response changes were made for each of the five

sensory stations in the auditory pathway and at the other brain locations. The sensory message initiated by the tone moved through the five stations of the sensory pathway at about two milliseconds per station, accelerating the firing of cells as it passed each location. With learning, the change in the pattern of firing was largest at the thalamus (medial geniculate body) and next largest at the inferior colliculus, but all stations changed their firing pattern. The surprising aspect of the changes is that they occurred at *every* station about ten milliseconds after the tone. However, the changes did not have a common source because changes at the inferior colliculus occurred at the beginning of training, whereas those at the medial geniculate body began after about 20 trials. Other recordings showed changes in the pattern of firing with learning. The hypothalamus "learned" during the first 20 trials when no behavioral changes were seen (drive mechanism?). The reticular formation learned during the next ten trials while the animal began to orient toward the source of the tone. The extrapyramidal system learned as the animal began to move toward the food in response to the tone. The sensory cortex learned as the movement became more coordinated, but the frontal cortex only after the movement became rapid and smooth. The reticular formation seemed important to the changes at other locations; large changes occurred here two milliseconds before they appeared in the auditory pathway.

Equipotentiality quantified. Although many cells in the brain participate in learning, some locations seem more important than others. E. Roy John and his associates, Bartlett, Hudspeth, and others, have recorded and computer-averaged evoked potentials from many parts of the brains of animals while the animals learn. The computer analysis enables them to determine the difference between evoked potentials attributable to simple sensory input ("exogenous") and those that occur only after the animals have learned ("endogenous").

With the "endogenous" changes being representative of brain changes during learning, the changes are found to be widely distributed throughout the brain. However, the greater the response of an area to the initial (exogenous) sensory input, the greater the change with learning. The relationship is a logarithmic one. This represents a compromise between a strict localization view of the engram and the ideas of mass action and equipotentiality.

Split-brain and spreading depression

Split-brain techniques. The two hemispheres of the brain, and therefore the cortex of those hemispheres, are connected by **commissural fibers,** particularly the **corpus callosum** (Chapter 3 and Fig. 3-9), although the anterior and posterior commissures participate as well. Neurosurgeons were puzzled for years by the absence of any gross behavioral or perceptual abnormalities in human patients after the corpus callosum had been severed. In some instances the operation was necessary to remove brain tumors in the third ventricle. When no apparent consequences were seen, one prominent investigator facetiously remarked that the only apparent function of the corpus callosum was mechanical—to keep the hemispheres from sagging apart! Another reason for the operation was to keep epileptic seizures from spreading from one hemisphere to the other, which prompted the remark that the function of the corpus callosum was to spread seizures! However, during subsequent careful investigation a technique was developed for confining visual and somesthetic input to one hemisphere of the brain and for separating one hemisphere of the brain from the other (Sperry). The initial experiments using the technique asked the following questions:

1. If sensory input is restricted to one hemisphere of the brain in training, will the other hemisphere learn too (with the two hemispheres still connected)?

2. If the sensory input requires the cerebral cortex for discrimination and if the connections between the two hemispheres are cut, can the training be restricted to one hemisphere?

Pattern discrimination requires the cerebral cortex. Each eye supplies both hemispheres, the left visual field (right half of both retinas) stimulating the right visual cortex and the right visual field (left half of both retinas) stimulating the left visual cortex (Fig. 10-5). Thus it is not surprising that a cat that has been taught a visual discrimination with the left eye blindfolded can perform the discrimination with the right eye blindfolded; both sides of the cortex receive information from each eye, and both sides learn the habit at once. If the crossing fibers of the optic chiasma are cut, however, only fibers from the temporal halves of the retina will survive (Fig. 10-5). The cat will have "tunnel" vision, and the right eye will supply only the visual cortex of the right hemisphere, whereas the left eye supplies only the left visual cortex. If such a cat is trained in a visual discrimination with the right eye only (left eye blindfolded) and then tested with the left eye only, he will perform perfectly. Obviously, the trace laid down in the right visual cortex has been transferred to the left visual cortex through the parts of the corpus callosum that connect them.

What happens if the corpus callosum and other commissural fibers are severed prior to training under the above conditions? If the corpus callosum and other commissural fibers are severed, the two hemispheres are no longer in communication. The operation severs the anterior and posterior commissures, thalamic connections, and midbrain tectum, so that no crossing fibers exist above the hind brain. If such cats are trained in a pattern discrimination with one eye only and then tested with the other eye only, they show no evidence of learning. The memory trace has been confined to the cortex of one hemisphere. To obtain food, split-brain cats can be taught to go to a door with a cross on it when one eye is blindfolded and to go to the adjoining door with a circle on it when the other eye is blindfolded. The two hemispheres have learned contradictory habits. Furthermore, contradictory training can occur on alternate trials by blindfolding one eye and then the other. Finally, polarized glasses can be fitted to these cats so that the left door has a cross and the right door a circle as seen by one eye, whereas the left has a circle and the right a cross as seen by the other eye. As training proceeds, one hemisphere learns to go to the cross and the other hemisphere learns to go to the circle on the same trials. The effect is not confined to vision. Roughness discrimination requires the somesthetic cortex, and the sensory input from one paw goes to somesthetic sensory projection areas in the opposite hemisphere (the fibers cross in the hind brain, below the split-brain section; Fig. 6-5). Split-brain cats cannot perform a roughness discrimination with the left paw if they are trained with the right, and vice versa; the memory trace has been confined to one hemisphere.

Spreading depression. According to Leao and Bures, animals without cortical convolutions (fissures, gyri, and sulci), such as the rat, are useful in a technique that depresses the activity of one hemisphere at a time. Potassium chloride (KCl) solution can be administered to the cortex of one hemisphere through a small hole in the skull. This causes a depression of electrical activity in the cortex that spreads over the entire hemisphere, "anesthetizing" it, so to speak. The spreading depression should not cross the fissure dividing the two hemispheres; thus the effect is confined to one hemisphere of the brain. Furthermore, because the cortex recovers after a period of time, the technique allows a reversible decortication of one hemisphere at a time. If a rat is trained in a visual pattern discrimination while one hemisphere is depressed, allowed to recover, and then tested while the other hemisphere is depressed, the untrained hemisphere will show no results of the training. Only one hemisphere learned when the other was inactive, and the inac-

tive hemisphere could not "copy" the trace. However, only a few trials are needed while both hemispheres are active for the untrained hemisphere to copy the trace; depressing the originally trained hemisphere will not impair performance thereafter.

More recently, doubts have been raised about the technique of spreading depression. The following points have been made: (1) hypoesthesia (loss of sensitivity) has been used as a criterion for spreading depression, although brain wave recordings show that hypoesthesia does not always result from spreading depression; (2) saline flushing of the cortex, used to abolish spreading depression, does not always do so; (3) KCl applied to one hemisphere sometimes causes spreading depression in both hemispheres; (4) KCl can cause irreversible cortical damage; and (5) the spreading depression that results from KCl is sometimes of shorter duration than expected. It appears from these findings that one should always monitor the spreading depression that results from the application of KCl by recording neural activity from several sites in the cortex, to ensure that cortical activity is being depressed in the expected manner. Allowance should also be made for cortical damage, and cortical tissue should be examined under a microscope after the experiment is over.

All these experiments suggest that rats and cats can learn as well with the cortex of the right hemisphere as with the cortex of the left hemisphere. Is the same true of man? In humans the left side of the brain controls the right hand and vice versa, and they exhibit right- or left-handedness far more frequently than do animals, especially where language skills such as writing are concerned. Many years of brain surgery have convinced Penfield that language habits are confined to the left ("dominant") hemisphere in most normal humans, and that the right hemisphere "specializes" in nonverbal memory and space perception. (Left-handed people sometimes have a right dominant hemisphere containing the speech areas.) Perhaps in this manner, humans have "doubled" their cranial capacity in a way not possible for other mammals, and this has enabled them to learn the immensely complex skills of language. Patients who have undergone split-brain surgery have difficulty in responding to verbal commands with their left hand. The right hemisphere controls the left hand, and it does not have access to verbal information stored in the left hemisphere. These patients also cannot recognize written words presented in their left visual field (input to the nonverbal right hemisphere). However, the right hemisphere is more skilled in nonverbal memory and space perception problems presented to the left visual field. Penfield believes that the speech areas of the dominant hemisphere are fully established by the age of about 12 years. In an aside to educators, he suggests that unless a child has learned a second language by that age, he never will be truly bilingual—as facile with one language as with the other.

Role of the corpus callosum. Doty proposes that for primates, the corpus callosum has two major roles in memory: (1) controlling the formation of memory traces so that they are laid down in only one hemisphere instead of both and (2) providing access by each hemisphere to memory traces stored in the other. He suggests that the anterior commissure, but not the corpus callosum, can transfer an engram from one hemisphere to the other. Finally, the posterior part of the corpus callosum (splenium) serves in a pathway from the visual system of one hemisphere to the amygdala of the other hemisphere. The amygdala, in this case, serves in an emotional role because its removal has a "taming" effect on the monkey. These conclusions are based on evidence from split-brain humans (see Bogen) that non-language spatial memories are stored in the right hemisphere and that visual pattern discrimination in the split-brain monkey is confined to one hemisphere (Gazza-

niga), and they are based on a series of Doty's experiments with an ingenious technique. The technique allows him to split the brain of a monkey without surgical aftereffects that would confuse the experimental results. Either the anterior commissure or the posterior corpus callosum is "ensnared" or surrounded by a ligature (length of surgical thread) that is led to a small hole in the bone flap (which allowed access to the brain during surgery) and left just below the skin. After recovery from the operation, the skin can be locally anesthetized and cut in a conscious monkey, and pulling the ligature splits the brain— the only reaction is a slight blink! In one experiment the optic tract of one hemisphere was cut to make it blind, the amygdala of the opposite hemisphere was removed, and the splenium was ensnared. After recover, as long as the hemisphere with sight was in communication with the amygdala of the other hemisphere, the monkey would flee at the approach of a human, when the human was "seen." When the snare was pulled to interrupt these connections, the monkey would not flee unless touched (nonvisual information for the blind hemisphere that has an amygdala). In another experiment the optic chiasma was cut (to restrict visual information from each eye to the hemisphere of the same side) and the splenium was snared. One hemisphere was taught a five-choice maze. The monkey could perform perfectly after that with either eye (hemisphere). The "naïve" hemisphere was getting its information from the trained hemisphere because the monkey could not perform with the naïve eye (and hemisphere) after the snare was pulled. These experiments were extended in teaching a monkey to press a lever for food in response to electrical stimulation of the visual cortex of one hemisphere or the other. As long as the splenium was intact, stimulation of the "untrained" hemisphere resulted in lever pressing; after the snare was pulled, the response was abolished permanently. If the splenium was cut *before* the training and the anterior commissure was snared, the untrained hemisphere could respond after the snare was pulled. The engram had been transferred from one hemisphere to the other by the anterior commissure. (The splenium ordinarily restricts visual training to one hemisphere, but it was cut in this experiment.) Doty suggests that "achievement of unilateral engrams with bihemispheric transcallosal access to them effectively doubles the mnemonic storage capacity of the brain" (Doty, 1973, p. 726).

Language and the brain

The study of brain functions in language is over 100 years old, and information has accumulated very slowly because humans are the only really useful subjects (see Geshwind, 1969, for a historical review). Until recently, most of the information has come from tumors that distort the brain to cause errors in locating the injury, from penetrating head wounds when there were few examinations after death to locate the injury, or from strokes (bursting blood vessels in the brain). The last source was the best because postmortem dissections were common, the "weak point" where the blood vessels burst was often near the cortical areas serving language in one hemisphere, and language behavior was often observed before death. Recently, however, the split-brain operation involving the corpus callosum and anterior commissure has become a practice for human epileptics so that brain seizure activity can be prevented from spreading from one hemisphere to the other in attempts to control epileptic "fits" that will not respond to other treatments. Careful testing of these subjects shows the extent of hemispheric specialization in man, as an extension of Doty's work on monkeys in the preceding section. Then we can examine the older work, showing typical organization of the language areas within one hemisphere.

Split brain in humans

The topic could have been reviewed in Chapter 11 on conscious awareness be-

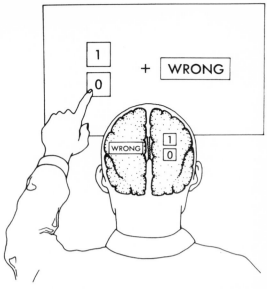

Fig. 14-1. Stimulus input for split-brain subjects learning a discrimination task. (From Gazzaniga, M.: One brain—two minds? Am. Sci. **60:**311-317, 1972. Reprinted by permission of American Scientist, journal of Sigma Xi, The Scientific Research Society of North America.)

cause the human split-brain subject has a disrupted unity of consciousness, with a verbally aware left hemisphere (usually) and a non-verbally-aware right hemisphere—in effect, two minds in one brain (Gazzaniga). However, both hemispheres normally receive the same sensory input; so the disunity can only be demonstrated by special testing techniques. Further, nonverbal learning procedures are necessary to communicate with the right hemisphere.

Special learning and testing techniques show that two different value systems can compete for the same response mechanisms (Gazzaniga). Information presented to the left visual field goes only to the right hemisphere and vice versa (Fig. 14-1). In the split-brain patient the information is not available to the unstimulated hemisphere through the corpus callosum and anterior commissure. If a discrimination between 0 and 1 is presented to the right hemisphere and reward or punishment—the word "right" or "wrong"—is presented to the left hemisphere, no learning occurs in over 30 trials (normals require one or two trials). If reprimanded for errors, however, quick learning occurred. The patient would respond to the reprimand with a sigh or exclamation or gesture of disgust, whereupon the other hemisphere would "catch on" to which symbol was incorrect (therefore which symbol was correct).

I should not leave the impression that the right (nonverbal) hemisphere is incapable of symbolic thought. Various tests show that it is. When the language areas of the left hemisphere are completely destroyed by a stroke, a patient can be taught a language based on cut-out paper symbols with concepts like "same" or "different" for other symbols. Sodium amobarbital (Amytal Sodium) can be injected into a major blood vessel (the carotid artery) going to one hemisphere or the other in tests (the Wada test) that involve anesthetizing of one hemisphere of the brain at a time. When the left (language) hemisphere of the brain is "asleep," the patient cannot speak or use language but will perceive a spoon placed in his left hand (sensory input to the right hemisphere, Chapter 6). After recovery, he cannot say what was placed in his left hand but will point out the spoon with his left hand from among a series of objects.

Hemispheric specialization in normal subjects

If a device (a tachistoscope) is used to flash visual information to one visual field fast enough, the input will go to only one hemisphere in the normal subject. If the information is verbal, the response will take longer if it is flashed to the right (nonverbal) hemisphere than to the left (verbal) hemisphere—communication through the corpus callosum requires several milliseconds. The right hemisphere is faster, however, in space-perception problems. Other tests have shown the right hemisphere to be superior in recognizing faces,

remembering music, and so on. EEG recordings of the normal resting alpha rhythm can be taken from each hemisphere to show that the rhythm is blocked when each hemisphere is active. The alpha rhythm of the left hemisphere is blocked when language, mathematical, or analytical problems are presented; the alpha waves of the right hemisphere are blocked for spatial and nonverbal inductive tasks. People tend to glance to the right (left hemisphere field) when solving verbal or math problems and to the left (right hemisphere field) when solving spatial recognition problems. The normal subject seems to have two specialized hemispheres, and unity in conscious awareness is contributed by the corpus callosum and commissures.

Language areas of the brain

There is evidence that the language areas are restricted to the left hemisphere in nearly all right-handed people and in the majority of those who are left-handed or ambidextrous. Using the sodium amobarbital Wada test and anesthetizing one hemisphere at a time on 95 right-handed subjects, researchers found only seven right-hemisphere and one bilateral speech areas. For 74 left-handed or ambidextrous people, there were 13 right hemisphere and 10 bilateral areas (Milner, Branch, and Rasmussen). Geshwind has examined over 100 normal brains and found one left-hemisphere language area (Wernicke's area, see Fig. 14-2) about one third larger than the corresponding area of the right hemisphere. Wada has found this to be true of human infants who died shortly after birth, so the left hemisphere language specialization would seem to be an inherent and inherited condition.

The term **aphasia** refers to disorders of language of several varieties that result from brain damage. These are not disorders of *speech* caused by lack of control over the muscles of speech but are disorders of *language,* because the verbal output is incorrect. The term includes disorders of verbal comprehension or understanding as well. The subject may be un-

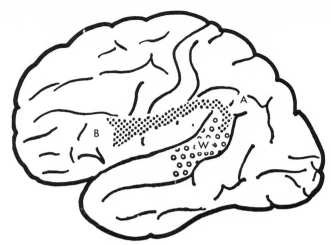

Fig. 14-2. Lateral surface of left hemisphere of human brain. *B (closed circles)*, Broca's area, which lies anterior to the lower end of the motor cortex. *W (open circles)*, Wernicke's area. *A*, Arcuate fasciculus, which connects Wernicke's to Broca's area. (From Geschwind, N.: Science **170:**940-944, copyright 1970 by The American Association for the Advancement of Science.

able to understand written or spoken language even though his vision and hearing are normal. Paul Broca was the first to relate difficulties of spoken language to specific areas of damage in the left hemisphere of the brain in the 1860s. Carl Wernicke in the 1870s extended this study to other areas of damage that result in impaired comprehension of language. He also related the functions of the two areas.

Broca's aphasia results from damage to a specific area of the left frontal lobe, just anterior to the lower end (face area) of the motor cortex (Fig. 14-2, *B*). These patients speak with great effort and poor articulation, omitting small grammatical words and endings. They cannot even repeat aloud a correct sentence that they read or that is spoken to them. Geschwind reports that if asked about the weather, a patient might say, "Overcast"; asked to produce a sentence, he might manage, "Weather . . . overcast."

Wernicke's aphasia results from damage to a different area of the left temporal lobe (Fig. 14-2, *W*). Since no motor or premotor areas are involved, speech is rapid and ef-

fortless, but remarkably free of meaningful information. Geschwind reports many errors in word usage like "spoot" for "spoon" or word substitutions such as "fork" for "spoon." He quotes a patient as saying: "I was over in the other one, and then after they had been in the department, I was in this one." The written output is of the same variety. In addition the patient does not understand written or spoken language, although he is free of sensory defects in vision or hearing.

Wernicke established that Broca's area contained the complex code for turning perceived language into speech. Broca's area lies just in front of the cortical motor areas controlling the tongue, lips, and vocal cords and is in close communication with these areas. Wernicke's area is next to the sensory projection area for hearing and is responsible for the complex code ruling the recognition of the patterns of spoken language. He showed that the two areas were connected by a band of fibers (the arcuate fasciculus, Fig. 14-2, *A*). Spoken language is learned first, and the complex code is established in Wernicke's area.

(Written language is learned in terms of perceived speech, so destruction of Wernicke's area impairs the perception of both.) The decoded perception is then transferred to Broca's area through the arcuate fasciculus. Broca's area then organizes the verbal response.

Brain stimulation and memory

Operations for brain tumors are often carried out under local anesthesia; the patient is conscious but experiences no pain. Under these conditions the surgeon can stimulate the brain electrically, and the patient can report the sensations he experiences as a result. (The procedure is done so that the surgeon can "map" the brain to avoid damaging sensory projection areas when removing a tumor, for example.) If the patient has a tumor in the temporal lobe, the temporal lobe will have a low threshold to brain stimulation and will give a large electrical response to stimulation. Vivid reenacted memories are reported by such patients during temporal lobe stimulation. They will "see" a friend walking across the room toward them or "hear" a familiar piece of music. This is of interest to the physiological psychology of learning because of the close connections of the temporal lobes with the limbic system via the amygdaloid nucleus and hippocampus.

THE WHEN OF LEARNING: PERSEVERATION AND CONSOLIDATION
Two-phase hypothesis

Another approach to events in the brain accompanying learning concerns the time course of these events, irrespective of their location. Activity in many brain centers, both cortical and subcortical, accompanies learning and memory. Experiments have shown that the brain activity accompanying learning lasts for a longer time than was previously suspected. It may outlast the practice experience by as much as a half hour or more. A **two-phase hypothesis** of learning and memory has gained wide acceptance. This hypothesis further

distinguishes between immediate memory and long-term memory. During the brain activity that occurs immediately after practice, the subject remembers perfectly; thus one may dial a telephone number without error just after having read it. However, unless the brain activity continues for a time without interruption, no "permanent" trace will be formed in the brain (memory). Brain activity that occurs after practice is called **perseveration,** and the consequent formation of a learning trace is called **consolidation.** Perseveration is believed to be the basis for immediate memory and and is perhaps necessary for consolidation of the memory trace. Whether ordinary environmental events can interrupt perseveration and thereby prevent consolidation is a moot question to be taken up later.

Development of the hypothesis. The two-stage, or perseveration-consolidation, hypothesis was invented to explain **retroactive inhibition** (Müller and Pilzecker). It was found that subjects could not remember a list of nonsense syllables well if they had learned a subsequent list. It was proposed that learning the second list interrupted perseveration of the first list before consolidation of a permanent trace of the first list was complete. Later experiments showed, however, that most of the forgetting was caused by confusion between the syllables of the two similar lists. In the same way one might have difficulty remembering two telephone numbers that were very much alike—digits from one phone number might appear in one's attempt to recall the other. Furthermore, the second list was learned more than an hour after the first, and it is doubtful that perseveration of the first list would last that long. More recently, another writer (Hebb) was speculating about perceptual learning. He proposed that the stimuli of learning initiated activity in reverberating circuits of the associative cortex, self-reexciting "loop circuits" of nerve cells. This activity constitutes the basis for immediate memory and could last for up to an hour. The activity spreads to **cell assemblies,** whose synapses are changed by their activity; therefore they are more likely to excite each other the next time. When a series of cell assemblies is excited in order in a perception, such as when the corners of a triangle are viewed successively, a **phase sequence** is built up, with the cells that unite the cell assemblies being the basis for the permanent memory of the perception.

Interruption of consolidation

At about the same time the above hypothesis was proposed, another investigator (Duncan) was studying the effects of **electroconvulsive shock (ECS)** on learning and memory in rats. ECS is a strong electrical current stimulus to the brain, usually delivered by electrodes attached to the head. The massive brain stimulation that results causes a convulsion that resembles an epileptic seizure or the seizures that result from insulin shock or overdoses of stimulating drugs. ECS, insulin, and drugs have been used to induce seizures as a form of treatment for mental patients. Side effects on memory were noted that were the same as those occurring after other trauma or damage to the brain—retroactive amnesia. Memory of events that occurred immediately before the treatment was impaired more than were older memories.

In the investigation of retroactive amnesia at short time intervals, the amnesia effect in rats for a just-practiced habit was profound, even though a simple habit was used. (Retroactive amnesia for complex habits, such as a maze, can occur, even when treatments follow practice by several hours.) In Duncan's pioneering study, rats were trained to jump a barrier to avoid electric shock. If they jumped from the black side of a box to the white side of the box within ten seconds after being placed in the apparatus, they avoided shock to the feet. If ECS occurred after each trial by 20 seconds, 40 seconds, 4 minutes, or 15 minutes, the rats learned more slowly than did **those** given no ECS. ECS given 2 to 14

hours after each trial did not affect learning of this simple response; therefore brain trauma could not have been the reason for the impairment (as may be the case for ECS effects on more complex habits, such as maze learning). The amount of brain trauma would not depend on the interval between practice and ECS, yet the shorter this time interval, the more poorly the animals performed. The rats could have hesitated to jump the barrier if the ECS treatment that followed was painful. (The effect of punishment on learning the response was checked with control groups. It was found that punishment [foot shock with the ECS apparatus] had to be given within two minutes after each trial to impair performance, whereas ECS was effective at much longer intervals.) Duncan reasoned that the massive brain stimulation of ECS caused a convulsive "storm" of neural activity in the brain, which interrupted the perseveration of the habit in the brain after each trial if ECS was given while perseveration was still going on. The longer that perseveration was allowed to go on after each trial before interruption of it with ECS, the greater was the consolidation of the memory trace and the better was the performance on subsequent trials.

Since this pioneering study, it has been found that less traumatic treatments can be used to interrupt perseveration and thereby impair consolidation. For example, anesthetizing rats (thiopental sodium [Pentothal]) within five minutes after each trial in a maze slows learning. Furthermore, both anesthesia and convulsions impair one-trial learning of a conditioned avoidance response (CAR) if given within a few minutes of the trial. The animal was shocked while bar pressing in a Skinner box for water and then was given a convulsive or drug treatment to interrupt subsequent consolidation of the experience. If it did not learn, it would continue to bar-press for water the next day. This proved to be the case for many of the treated animals. If the treatment had been punishing, the animals would have avoided bar pressing because they would have anticipated shock for doing so, as well as a painful treatment afterward. Other agents have proved useful in interrupting the consolidation process—hypoxia in rats through simulated altitude or carbon dioxide or heat narcosis in goldfish, for example. Finally, human patients under deep surgical anesthesia often report retroactive amnesia for the events just preceding onset of anesthesia.

Stimulating consolidation

Another group of experiments (McGaugh and others) has shown that brain stimulants (such as strychnine) administered within a few minutes *after* each practice trial has ended, can improve the rate of maze acquisition in rats. Presumably, the neural processes underlying consolidation are more effective when the brain is most active. A variety of stimulants have been used (pentylenetetrazol [Metrazol], caffeine, picrotoxin, 1757 I.S., and so forth), so that the effect is not specific to any one drug. The treatment is more effective for rats bred to be poor maze learners (maze-dull rats) than for maze-bright rats. Other experiments seem to show that the maze-bright rats consolidate faster after each trial than do the maze-dull rats. Consolidation can be interrupted, or at least learning is impaired, when ECS is administered at a longer interval after each trial for the maze-dull rats than for the maze-bright rats. The "bright" rats appear to finish consolidation within 45 minutes, but the "dull" rats do not. These experiments are exciting because of their implications for improving the learning rate in subnormal people.

A moot point remains. Even if drugs or ECS can affect consolidation to improve or impair learning, these are extreme conditions. There is no clear evidence that everyday experiences interfere with consolidation. The superior recall that occurs when sleep rather than waking activity follows learning or when practice trials follow each other by hours rather than by min-

utes has been cited as an example of improved learning caused by less stimulus interference with consolidation. Interference explanations that depend on confusion at the time of recall, caused by stimulus similarity, are also offered. Similar events can become confused because they occurred one after the other rather than because one event interfered with consolidation of a previous one. On the other hand, differences in sleep *stages* seem to affect memory. In Chapter 11, slow-wave sleep stages were distinguished from rapid eye-movement (REM) sleep, called paradoxical sleep in animals. Reports of dreaming frequently accompany REM sleep awakenings. It may be that the neural activity that accompanies REM and paradoxical sleep has something to do with rearousing perseveration and thereby improving consolidation. Rats and mice can be deprived of paradoxical sleep by forcing them to sleep on a pedestal above a pool of water; if the muscles relax, as they do in paradoxical (but not slow-wave) sleep, the animal falls off the pedestal into the water (this was called the "flower pot" technique in some experiments because upside-down flower pots were used as pedestals!). In passive-avoidance tasks, Y mazes, brightness discriminations, and other experiments, depriving the animal of paradoxical sleep by this technique impairs memory.

Short- and long-term memory and the hippocampus

It has already been reported that stimulation of the temporal lobes causes vivid reenacted memories in patients being operated on for brain tumors. The same investigator (Penfield) has reported two cases of penetrating brain injury that damaged the temporal lobes and underlying parts of the hippocampus in both hemispheres. These patients seemed unable to form new memories, even though their recall for events prior to their accidents seemed normal for brain-damaged individuals. Yet they were not able to recall anything new over an interval longer than ten minutes. Perhaps some of the connections between the hippocampus and temporal cortex that were destroyed in these patients are essential to the process of forming permanent memories—the process called consolidation. As an overstatement, the patients seemed able to operate on perseverating neural traces only, but the perseveration left no permanent traces, or "memory." Upon meeting someone new, for example, they could converse with him and use his name. If the person left for an hour and returned, they were unable to recall ever having met him.

Memory storage processes

As work of the nature described in this section continues, theories of the relationship between memory storage and retrieval begin to emerge. One of the most prominent theorists in the field is James L. McGaugh. After extensively reviewing the literature, he concludes that consolidation is a "time-dependent" process that is essential to the formation of long-term memory. Although the evidence is indirect, he suggests that "immediate memory" depends on neural activity, whereas the formation of long-term memory depends on a slower process that probably involves protein synthesis. As will be seen in a later section, protein synthesis is involved in memory phenomena. His ingenious hypotheses and those of others are summarized in Fig. 14-3. Incoming sensory information is "held" in a sensory buffer. This is to prevent our being overwhelmed by sensory information; feedback to the inputs allows selection or rejection of inputs for immediate action (like dialing a telephone number) and those for later storage. One example of the action of such a perceptual buffer can be seen when you are a part of one of two conversational groups of friends. You are paying attention only to your own group until your name is mentioned in the other conversation. This commands your attention and you find out that you can immediately recall not only the mention of your name, but several preceding words from the other conversation that were being "held" in the sensory buffer. Once items are selected from the sensory buffer, they enter short-term memory for action and/or storage. Short-term memory is immediate memory and is believed to be based on the neural activity of perseveration. Feedback from short-term memory to the sensory input continues to select items for attention from the sensory buffer. Reverberating items from short-term memory may be acted on and forgotten, or perseveration can last long enough

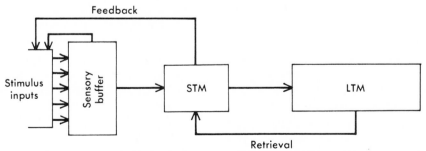

Fig. 14-3. Model for information selection, storage, and retrieval. A number of stimulus inputs that do not exceed the information-processing capacity of the organism are selected by feedback from a sensory buffer that determines the selection process. Selected inputs reach short-term memory, *STM,* for immediate action, changes of attention by feedback, or continuing activity that leads to long-term memory, *LTM.* Remembering (retrieval) is a process of rearousing some part of the original STM by LTM patterns.

so that the information enters long-term memory. Long-term memory is believed to be based on some protein change in the nerve cells, as will be seen later on. When you "remember" the information later on ("retrieval"), the changed nerve cells initiate a version of the perseverating activity that initiated short-term memory.

Old and new memories

Although many variables control how well one remembers things, an old memory is frequently recalled with more clarity than a recent event. When an event becomes a part of the array of memories that can be recalled on demand, an older memory can often be recalled more readily than a newer one. Some suggest that this is because it has been recalled more often. In line with such an idea, one writer (Russell) has suggested that the underlying trace of a memory in the nervous system is a pattern of excitation that is more readily aroused by random activity than is a new pattern. If so, a pattern would have been stimulated more often by random brain activity the longer it had existed—there would have been a series of many perseverations and consolidations. Perhaps for this reason, old memories are less susceptible than newer memories to the brain trauma of ECS, strokes, concussions, and so on. Their neural traces have been activated more often, have become more numerous and fixed, and thus are less susceptible to severe disruption.

Whatever the cause, older memories are less subject to disruption than newer ones, and this effect is an orderly one over a very long time period. Dr. Larry Squire of the Veteran's Administration Hospital in San Diego has developed tests of memory for events and for radio and television programs that most subjects would normally recall. The tests are designed to sample various periods of time. For example, one test involves recognizing the names of television programs that were on the air for only one season between 1957 and 1972. He administered these tests to patients be-

fore, during, and six months after a course of ECS therapy. The more recent the memory, the more susceptible it was to loss due to the ECS. He showed for the first time that retroactive amnesia can be accurately predicted over a period of years.

"Poisoned bait response"

To look at the other end of the time scale in learning and memory, it has always been assumed that reward or punishment must rapidly follow a response if the response is to be learned or eliminated. In "housebreaking" a dog, for example, one does not wait for hours after it has wet the floor before punishing the act or learning will not occur. It is assumed that memory for the act must still be perseverating in the CNS if the punishment is to form a part of the same memory. Yet it has been observed that wild animals will avoid a food that has made them ill even though the illness occurred hours after eating the food. This can be systematically demonstrated in the laboratory. For example, a rat will avoid a novel flavor if he is made ill by radiation some hours later. Associating a light or a buzzer with subsequent illness is more difficult for the rat and is confined to about a half-hour interval. A flavor aversion is more readily learned if the taste is a novel one. Flavor aversions have been found in humans to result from later radiation treatment for cancer that nauseated the patient. The response is obviously adaptive if the individual is to survive in the course of encountering novel foods, and it is probably an old ability in evolution. The response has been found in monkeys, rats, reptiles, fish, snails, and slugs. The brain areas involved may be different from those active in other kinds of learning. In some animals the aversions are still formed if the forebrain is removed between the time the taste cue is presented and the onset of the illness. The cortex may be depressed chemically (spreading depression) during the learning or the illness may occur under anesthesia and the aversion will still appear.

Improving capacity for verbal learning and memory

Nootropyl (Piracetam UCB 6215, 2-pyrrolidone acetamide) has been reported to facilitate learning in animals, improve coordination in deteriorated alcoholic humans, and improve learning and memory in cases of senility. Doses of 400 mg per day were given to normal volunteer human subjects for two weeks. They learned three lists of words—one list before taking the drug and others at one- and two-week intervals. There was no difference between subjects taking the drug or a placebo on the first two tests, but the drug group showed superior verbal learning on the third test (Dimond and Brouwers, 1976). Perhaps a "smart pill" has at last been found!

THE HOW OF LEARNING: CHANGES IN THE BRAIN
Molar biochemical changes

Learning involves a change in response to stimuli. Many writers believe that memory is caused by some physical change, or "memory trace," in the nervous system that results from learning. Whatever parts of the brain are involved in learning, any physical changes should logically occur at synapses—the anatomical sites where one neuron excites another neuron. Synapses appear to be the only places in the central nervous system where pathways between stimulus and response can be changed, however complex the pathways. This section concerns the nature of the change at synapses during learning, without regard to where the synapses are located.

Biochemical and anatomical changes in the rat brain. Synapses in which one neuron stimulates another by the release of **acetylcholine (ACh)** have been demonstrated in autonomic ganglia, the spinal cord, and some centers of the brain. The ACh acts only briefly because it is hydrolized (chemically removed), a reaction speeded by the enzyme **acetylcholine esterase (AChE),** which is present at all cholinergic synapses. Such cholinergic synapses may be involved in learning. Repeated synaptic "use" during learning could increase the efficiency of synapses by leading to the release of more ACh. The difference between fast and slow learners could be caused by a biochemical difference in the ACh/AChE ratio rather than by anatomical differences in their brains. Either high ACh or low AChE could make synapses more excitable.

Such speculations have led to a fascinating series of experiments under the direction of Rosensweig, Krech, and Bennett. The earlier studies in the series demonstrated chemical differences in the brains of rats selectively bred to be maze-bright or maze-dull, according to their ability to learn a complex maze. The maze-bright rats had a greater brain AChE content than did the maze-dull rats. Later studies showed that this difference was largely confined to the cortex and that in different strains of rats it was the ACh/AChE *ratio* that seemed most closely related to learning ability. ACh and AChE content appeared to be independently determined, genetically. Breeding for AChE content in the brain, for example, can lead to high-AChE, maze-dull animals and low-AChE, maze-bright animals, provided that the ACh content varies only randomly.

Having established that hereditary differences in brain chemistry could affect learning ability, this Berkeley group asked whether environmental stimulation could affect brain chemistry and, perhaps, the anatomy of the brain as well. In those experiments one group of rats was raised in solitary confinement (isolated controls, or IC rats). Their litter mates were raised in groups and given training in several tasks as well as having frequently changed toys in their cages (ladders, wheels, and so forth) for stimulation (environmental complexity and training, or ECT). Animals given ECT for 30 days after weaning were compared with those suffering IC for a similar period. In over seven strains that were tested, the ECT animals had less cortical and more subcortical AChE in their brains than did the IC rats when sacrificed. In other experiments the ECT animals were found to have thicker and heavier cortical tissue, better blood supply to the brain, and biochemical changes (in proteins, hexokinase, and serotonin) expected of a more active brain. In more recent experiments, it has been shown that as little as two hours a day of ECT protects rats from some degenerative changes in the brain that result from isolation. Finally, it has been found that rats in a seminatural environment showed greater brain development than did the ECT rats. Despite generations of laboratory conditions, the natural conditions under which rats have evolved proved to the be the most enriching of all.

The effects do not seem restricted to early growth and development; similar results have been obtained when the difference in treatment began at 105 days of age (young adult rats). Considering the attention being given today to human mental deficiency and to "head start" preschool programs for environmentally deprived children, the Berkeley experiments may have far-reaching implications. Biochemical and anatomical differences in the brain may be effected in humans in the same general way as in the rat—by differences in environmental stimulation.

Molecular biochemical changes

As explained in Chapter 2, the cell reproduces itself and repairs its parts according to patterns contained in the DNA molecules of the chromosomes in its nucleus. In cell reproduction by cell division each DNA molecule is reproduced in the nucleus of each of the two daughter cells. In repairing parts of the cell, sections of the DNA molecules assemble simpler RNA molecules, with the form of the DNA section serving as a pattern. The messenger RNA, so assembled, migrates from the nucleus to the cytoplasm of the cell. There it assembles transfer RNA by a similar process. The transfer RNA, in turn, assembles enzymes to speed the needed chemical

reactions of cell metabolism. Some theorists believe that changes in the DNA molecules, the RNA molecules, or the enzymes they form produce changes in nerve cell excitability that accompany learning. DNA, RNA, or enzymes could change the structure of a nerve cell. Changes in the structure of the nerve cell membrane could make the cell more excitable or cause it to release more transmitter substance at synapses. It is pointed out that nerve cells in mammals do not reproduce themselves. Perhaps part of the DNA-RNA mechanism involved in cell repair and cell reproduction is used for learning instead. (Such changes would not be passed on to the animal's progeny—inheritance of acquired characteristics—because the reproductive cells in the gonads would not be affected. Only the nerve cells would change, and these would die with the animal.) If the DNA mechanism can store the blueprint for assembling an entire organism in cell reproduction, it certainly should have enough information capacity to store the memories of a lifetime, especially if relieved of the reproductive task. This theory could explain Lashley's paradox that was cited earlier, explaining how single cells could participate in each of the thousands of memories we accumulate in a lifetime.

Most of the evidence for this view comes from experiments by McConnell, of the University of Michigan, with flatworms **(planarians),** small primitive invertebrates with a "nerve net" nervous system, a primitive ganglion type of "brain" in the head end, and visual receptors in the head. Unlike vertebrates, they reproduce asexually as well as sexually and can reproduce missing parts after amputation, *including nervous tissue,* to the extent that two complete planarians are regenerated if one is cut in two. The head end grows a new tail, and the tail end grows a new head. McConnell and his colleagues wondered if changes in the nerve cells caused by learning would be passed on to new nerve cells as the new nerve cells were formed to regenerate amputated parts of the worm. The DNA-RNA-enzyme mechanism is involved in cell reproduction. Any change in nerve cells caused by learning might involve the same mechanism. If so, the change resulting from learning would be reproduced when new nerve cells were "copied" from old ones in cell division. To test these notions, flatworms were trained, cut in two, and tested after regeneration. Flatworms respond to electric shock by curling into an S shape. The response was conditioned to a flash of light. The worms were then cut in two, and the head ends grew new tails, and the tails grew new heads. Both groups of regenerated flatworms learned the habit faster than did the "naïve" worms.

The next question concerned the role of the nerve ganglion in the head, which serves as a flatworm's brain. If the head is split so that the ganglion is cut in half longitudinally, each half of the head creates a matching half, and a two-headed worm results. The two-headed worm learns the CR faster than does a normal worm. Two heads seem better than one, at least for this purpose, and the head ganglion seems to dominate the nervous system of the flatworm. A further test of the head dominance hypothesis was made in the following way. An enzyme, RNAase, interferes with the regeneration process and would presumably interfere with learning patterns being passed on to regenerating tissue. After learning the conditioned response, the worms were cut in two, and their missing parts were regenerated in RNAase solution. The trained heads were thus prevented, at least partly, from passing on the learning change and developed "naïve" tails; the trained tails developed "naïve" heads. If the head dominates, the worms with experienced heads should show the results of training, whereas those with "naïve" heads should not. In a general way this is what happened.

These experiments have been extended at the University of California at Los Angeles by Jacobson. The general plan of his experiments involves teaching rats a simple habit, such as lever pressing in a Skinner box or a simple discrimination. The rat's brain is then removed and the RNA is extracted from it. The extract is then injected (intraperitoneally) into a second "naïve" rat, which is then taught the same habit. The learning of the second rat is compared with the learning of rats that have been injected with RNA extracts from rats that have had no learning experience. Jacobson's results indicate that rats that have received extract from "experienced" rat brains learn faster than rats that have received extract from "naïve" rat brains. These "memory transfer" experiments have led to much controversy, and many attempts have been made to replicate Jacobson's results. Both failures and successes have been reported. Some investigators suggest that RNA is too large a molecule to cross the blood-brain barrier and therefore cannot reach the brain from the blood. The RNA extraction procedure is a complex ones, and mistakes in the procedure could account for differing results.

Ungar, of Baylor University, has recently reported a series of even more controversial experiments. Rats are normally nocturnal—they prefer a dark compartment to a lighted one. The Baylor scientists taught over 4,000 rats to avoid the darkest of three compartments by shocking them if they entered it. A peptide composed of 14 amino acids was extracted from the brains of these rats and injected directly into the brains of 3,000 "naïve" rats. Before the injections, these rats had spent most of their time in the dark compartment. After the injections, they spent only a few seconds there, and many of them would not enter the dark compartment. Most recently, Ungar has reported synthesizing all of the amino acids in correct sequence for the extracted peptide. He reports that brain injections of the synthetic molecule have the same kind of "fear of the dark" effect as did the extract (called scotophobin for fear of darkness). Results of this kind are mind boggling for most scientists and will generate much debate and experimentation before they can be validated.

Another line of evidence for the DNA-RNA-enzyme-protein synthesis idea comes from the effects of the drug puromycin. Puromycin inhibits protein synthesis in the cell. It must be injected directly into the brain to affect learning because it does not pass the blood-brain barrier. Strangely enough, the injection must follow learning (a Y maze) in the rat by three to six days to be effective. Under these conditions it blots out the habit, leaving intact the responses learned before or after this period.

BIOFEEDBACK

Biofeedback is a term that has come to mean learning "voluntary" control over what was previously an "involuntary" response. The approach assumes that voluntary control becomes possible when the subject receives information or "feedback" about the biological response. Learning to control the rate of one's heartbeat becomes possible when the subject knows when it changes in the desired way—information not ordinarily available to the subject. In experiments with human subjects the only reward necessary to learn the response is knowledge of success. In animal experiments, other kinds of reinforcements are used in conditioning techniques.

Types of conditioning

A technique called "bell shock" conditioning can be described. A bell (conditioned stimulus) is sounded, followed by a shock to the paw (unconditioned stimulus), which forces leg flexion. After a number of trials, the bell alone will elicit a leg withdrawal—a conditioned response has been formed. This is an example of a type of conditioning often called *classical conditioning*. Reward as well as punishment can be used to force the response. For example, food may be used to condition salivation to a conditioned stimulus. Much everyday learning takes place in a different way, however. In a trial-and-error learning situation the subject hits on the correct (or

incorrect) response by accident and is immediately rewarded (or punished). In this situation the subject, rather than the experimenter, is in control of the behavior. This is an example of *operant conditioning*. The question then arises, How do you induce the subject to make the response that you wish to reward? The most effective method lies in a technique called **shaping.** Any movement approximating the desired response is rewarded. Then closer and closer approximations to the desired responses are required for subsequent rewards until the desired response emerges. Escape from punishment can be used as a reinforcement in the same way.

Somatic versus visceral and glandular learning

For many years it has been the conventional wisdom in psychology that visceral and glandular responses are capable of classical conditioning only, and that only somatic responses can be operantly conditioned. Visceral and glandular responses were believed to be "involuntary"—not under the control of the subject, as are somatic responses. The experimenter would therefore have to "force" the response he wished to reward with a reflex stimulus before he could reward it. Many theorists held that classical and instrumental conditioning are different kinds of learning, rather than merely different learning procedures. However, in a series of important experiments, Neal Miller and his associates at Rockefeller University have shown that the so-called involuntary visceral and glandular responses can be operantly conditioned. The consequences of their findings will be noted after a survey of some of the experiments involved.

Visceral and glandular conditioning

The initial study involved conditioned salivation for a water reward in thirsty dogs. (Water has no effect on bursts of spontaneous salivation.) One group of dogs was conditioned through shaping techniques to increase salivation frequency, and the other group was taught to decrease salivation frequency. This procedure eliminated the possibility of the water's forcing either salivation or lack of salivation. The group conditioned to increase salivation seemed more active than the other group; thus the possibility that somatic motor activity resulted in salivation had to be eliminated. Because curare, used to paralyze the animals, resulted in increased salivation, another response was chosen. (Curare blocks the junction between nerves and somatic muscles, necessitating artificial respiration; curare has no effect on visceral muscles, so it cannot affect the heart rate.) Because it is difficult to reward paralyzed animals in the usual manner, rewarding brain stimulation was used. Rats were conditioned to either increase their heart rate or decrease it. Furthermore, a discrimination response was conditioned—a light indicated when reward was available, and the rats learned to increase or decrease their heart rates only when the light was on. Memory for the training survived a three-month retention interval. Heart rate conditioning could be shaped to avoidance of a punishing shock as well, when heart rate change in the first ten seconds after the light turned on prevented a shock to the tail. Heart rate conditioning that was carried on in the curarized state appeared in the normal state, and no differences in activity were seen between rats trained to increase heart rate and those trained to decrease heart rate. Choosing a response less related to activity than heart rate, the investigators trained curarized rats to either increase or decrease the frequency of intestinal contractions (recorded by a balloon inserted in the anus) for a rewarding brain stimulation. Heart rate did not change significantly in either group. Catheterized rats (a tube to the bladder) have been trained to either increase or decrease their rate of urine formation. Tests showed that the rats changed their blood flow through the kidney to control the response. Both vasoconstriction (constriction of blood vessels) and

vasodilation in the tail have been conditioned, and rats have been trained to show these responses in one ear and not in the other. Finally, the investigators showed that operant control of visceral responses could be initiated by the animal to balance an abnormal homeostatic condition. Rats "preloaded" with water learned to choose the arm of a Y maze that led to a saline injection rather than one that led to an injection of antidiuretic hormone (ADH results in water retention by the kidney).

There has been some recent difficulty in repeating these careful experiments in other laboratories. Whether the conflicting results are caused by technical problems or by some artifact in the procedures used, only time and much work will tell. However, the basic principles of visceral conditioning and biofeedback seem to be established.

Implications for humans

Evidence for the instrumental, or operant, learning of visceral responses has profound implications for so-called "psychosomatic" disorders in humans. Many disorders, such as asthma, stomach ulcers, piles, and hives, may occur as a result of psychological stress, in the absence of disease or other trauma. However, the particular symptom that results may depend as much on learning as on any "weakness" in the organ itself. As Miller points out in an example, a child may fear going to school to face an examination for which he is unprepared, and this fear can result in a variety of fluctuating autonomic symptoms, including perhaps pallor and faintness, as well as stomach upset. The mother may decide the child is sick and must stay at home. If she makes her decision on the basis of the faintness, she is rewarding one symptom, and if she makes it on the basis of the stomach upset, she is rewarding another symptom.

On the more positive side, operant conditioning of visceral responses in humans may be used to control, if not cure, a variety of disorders. Patients with high blood pressure could be taught to control their heart rate. Similar benefits could occur for spastic colitis, asthma, acid stomach, and so on.

EEG experiments have shown that some subjects can learn to control the appearance of their own alpha rhythms. All that seems to be required is a reliable signal that tells the subject when he is displaying alpha rhythms—a light or a buzzer will suffice. The signal is always on when the subject's EEG is displaying alpha waves and never on when the EEG does not contain alpha waves. Some subjects learn to control alpha waves more readily than do others, but none of the subjects are able to report how they do it. Interest in the technique arises because the subject must be in a relaxed state in order to display alpha waves. Thus if a subject can be conditioned to display alpha waves, he is being conditioned to relax. The phenomenon has obvious applications in cases of hypertension (high blood pressure) and anxiety. Interest among less scientific circles has been aroused by the finding that yogis show extremely stable alpha rhythms while meditating. This has led some enthusiasts to learn how to control their own alpha rhythms as a shortcut to learning how to meditate, although there is no proof that alpha control is the only element in meditation. The appearance of alpha-signaling electronic devices on the open market has been one result.

SUMMARY

Using a reflex model and assuming encephalization, early investigators sought to locate the "trace" left in the brain by learning. They removed parts of the cortex of rats and observed the effect on learning and memory for mazes of differing difficulty. The lesions had more effect on memory than on new learning, and impaired performance in difficult mazes the most; the effects depended on the size rather than on the locus of the lesion. The latter finding led to the mass action and equipotentiality principles. Cortical con-

nections made in learning seem to be vertically organized interactions with subcortical centers because thin cuts that isolate sections of rat cortex from one another impair neither learning nor memory. Damage to the thalamus affects learning, but again the size rather than the locus of the lesion determines the effect. This leads to Lashley's paradox: When many cells are involved in each memory trace, each *single* cell must carry many memory traces. Recordings show electrical changes at several "stations" along the acoustic pathway when rats learn an avoidance response to a tone; different parts of the brain also "learn" at a different rate. Some changes are more important than others, as revealed by computer-averaged EEGs, with areas that show greater response showing more change as well. If evoked potentials are averaged in animals, exogenous changes attributable to sensory input can be distinguished from endogenous changes attributable to learning.

If the commissural fibers connecting the two cerebral hemispheres are cut, little difference is seen in human behavior. Animal experiments show, however, that visual input from one eye can be restricted to the hemisphere of the same side if the crossing fibers of the optic chiasma are cut, as seen in split-brain cats and monkeys. Somesthetic input and motor control are restricted to the opposite hemisphere in split-brain animals. The traces of visual or somesthetic learning can be restricted to the one hemisphere by the split-brain technique, and contradictory habits can be taught to the two hemispheres. "Temporary decortication" of one hemisphere in rats can be caused by a spreading depression of neural activity that follows application of potassium chloride to that hemisphere. (This technique appears to be valid only when the brain waves are monitored so that one can be certain that depression has actually occurred.) Discrimination learning in rats can be confined to one hemisphere in this manner. Only a few trials are necessary after recovery for the untrained hemisphere to "copy" the trace in the trained hemisphere. In humans, however, language habits seem restricted to the dominant hemisphere (the left hemisphere in right-handed people). The other hemisphere appears to be more specialized for nonverbal memory and space perception. The corpus callosum in primates appears to permit the formation of memory traces in one hemisphere only. Only the anterior commissure can transfer the trace from one hemisphere to another. The testing of split-brain humans reveals that they have two minds in one brain: a verbally aware left hemisphere and a nonverbal right hemisphere that can form different value systems and compete for the same response mechanism. The language areas in the left hemisphere are Broca's area that contains the code for articulating language and Wernicke's area for perceiving language; damage to these and related areas result in aphasias of various kinds.

Brain stimulation during brain surgery in humans causes vivid memories to occur to the patient when the temporal lobe is stimulated. It appears that neural activity that outlasts practice (perseveration) is necessary to the formation of a "permanent" memory trace (consolidation). Perseverative activity may link cell assemblies into a "phase sequence" in a perceptual task such as successively viewing the corners of a triangle. This two-phase hypothesis of learning and memory is supported by experiments that show that the longer posttrial perseveration is permitted to go on before interruption by ECS, the faster an avoidance habit is learned by the rat. Drugs can also be used to interrupt perseveration, with similar effects on maze learning or on a one-trial conditioned avoidance response (CAR). Stimulating drugs seem to potentiate perseveration and consolidation to improve learning when administered *after* practice in a maze. The effect is greater for maze-dull than for maze-bright animals. The latter appear to consolidate faster because ECS given 45 minutes after practice does not impair

their learning, but it does affect the maze-dull rats. Deprivation of paradoxical sleep seems to impair consolidation. It is still not known whether everyday stimuli can interrupt the consolidation process.

Human patients with bilateral damage to the temporal lobes, amygdala, and hippocampus have normal memories but seem unable to learn anything new. It appears that a sensory buffer selects stimuli for action by short-term memory; short-term memory may be stored in long-term memory for recall. Over longer periods of time older memories seem less susceptible to trauma than newer memories, perhaps because they have been recalled more often, thereby becoming more fixed and less subject to impairment. It does appear that consolidation is necessary for the formation of long-term memory. ECS studies on human patients also show that the treatment impairs memories in inverse relation to their age. At the other end of the time scale for memory formation, animals and humans can learn to avoid novel flavors even if the punishing effect occurs hours after the taste. The "poisoned-bait response" is probably mediated by lower brain centers than those involved in other kinds of learning. The capacity for verbal learning is enhanced by the drug Nootropyl.

Wherever learning occurs, changes in the excitability of nerve cells at synapses may be involved. Such changes may involve the chemical transmitter, ACh, or the enzyme that speeds its removal, AChE. Rats selectively bred to be maze-bright have a higher ACh/AChE ratio in their cortex than do rats bred to be maze-dull; ACh and AChE are under separate genetic control in different strains of rats. Rats isolated for 30 days after weaning (isolated control, or IC, group) were compared with their litter mates raised in groups with maximum "play" and learning opportunities (environmental complexity and training, or ECT, group). The ECT rats had less cortical and more subcortical AChE, thicker cortical tissues, and superior cortical circulation and biochemical activity. The results are the same if the experiment is done with young adult rats. ECT for only two hours a day helps to prevent IC changes in the brain. A semi-natural environment results in more brain improvement than does the ECT condition.

The nerve cell changes in learning may also be molecular, involving the DNA-RNA-protein-enzyme mechanism, for cell repair and alteration. DNA and RNA are involved in cell reproduction (including nerve cells) in flatworms that have the ability to regenerate missing parts. A simple flexion response to shock is conditioned to a light stimulus in these animals. After learning the conditioned response (CR), flatworms were cut in two and they regenerated. The regenerated subjects "relearned" the CR faster than did "naïve" worms. The conclusion that the head ganglion dominates the CR was arrived at after experimentation showed that (1) two-headed flatworms (produced by regeneration) learn the CR faster than do normal planarians and (2) trained flatworms, cut in two and regenerated in RNAase (which interferes with DNA-RNA processes in cell reproduction), retain the habit only if the tail end (not the head) is the regenerated part. The RNA aspect has been extended to rats in memory-transfer experiments in which RNA extract from the brain of trained rats has been injected into "naïve" rats. A peptide has been extracted from the brains of rats who had been taught to fear the dark; when it was injected into the brains of "naïve" rats, they too feared the dark. The compound has been synthesized from amino acids. Puromycin, which interferes with protein synthesis, may be injected into the brain to affect retention of the learning of a Y maze in rats. The effect appears only if the habit is three to six days old.

Biofeedback experiments show that animals and humans can learn voluntary control over involuntary responses if reinforcement informs them when they are successful. In contradiction to former beliefs, it has been shown that operant, as well as classical, conditioning is possible with visceral and glandular responses. Rewarding brain stimulation and shaping techniques have been used with paralyzed and normal animals to teach control of salivation, heart rate, intestinal contractions, and urine output. Humans can learn to control their own alpha rhythms if they are given a signal when alpha waves are present in their EEGs. Human control of psychosomatic symptoms therefore appears possible.

READINGS

Agranoff, B. W.: Memory and protein synthesis, Sci. Am. **216:**115-122, June 1967 (W. H. Freeman Reprint No. 1077).

Bakam, P.: The eyes have it, Psychol. Today **4:**64-96, April 1971.

Bennett, E. L., Diamon, M. C., Krech, D., and Rosensweig, M. R.: Chemical and anatomical plasticity of brain, Science **146:**610-619, 1964 (Bobbs-Merrill Reprint No. P-400).

Best, J. G.: Protopsychology, Sci. Am. **208:**54-62, Feb. 1963 (W. H. Freeman Reprint No. 149).

Bitterman, M. E.: The evolution of intelligence, Sci. Am. **212:**92-100, Jan. 1965 (W. H. Freeman Reprint No. 490).

Breen, R. A., and McGaugh, J. L.: Facilitation of maze learning with post-trial injections of picrotoxin, J. Comp. Physiol. Psychol. **54:**498-501, 1961 (Bobbs-Merrill Reprint No. P-591).

Bures, J., and Buresova, O.: The use of Leao's spreading depression in the study of interhemispheric transfer of memory traces, J. Comp. Physiol. Psychol. **53:**558-563, 1961 (Bobbs-Merrill Reprint No. P-412).

Butter, C. M.: Neuropsychology: the study of brain and behavior, Belmont, Calif., 1968, Brooks/Cole Publishing Company.

Chauchard, P.: The brain, New York, 1962, Grove Press, Inc.

Deutsch, J. A.: Neural basis of memory, Psychol. Today **2:**56-61, May 1968.

DiCara, L. V.: Learning in the autonomic nervous system, Sci. Am. **122:**31-39, Jan. 1970.

Dyal, J.: Transfer of behavioral bias and learning enhancement: a critique of specificity experiments. In Adam, G., editor: Biology of memory, Budapest, 1971, Akadémiai Kiadó. Also in Leukel, F., editor: Issues in physiological psychology, St. Louis, 1974, The C. V. Mosby Co.

Gazzaniga, M. S.: The bisected brain, New York, 1970, Appleton-Century-Crofts.

Gerard, R. W.: What is memory? Sci. Am. **189:**118-126, Sept. 1953 (W. H. Freeman Reprint No. 11).

Glickman, S. E.: Perseverative neural processes and consolidation of the memory trace. Psychol. Bull. **58:**218-233, 1961 (Bobbs-Merrill Reprint No. P-459).

Golub, A., Masiarz, F., Villars, T., and McConnell, J.: Incubation effects in behavior induction in rats, Science **168:**392-395, 1970. Also in Leukel, F., editor: Issues in physiological psychology, St. Louis, 1974, The C. V. Mosby Co.

Gurowitz, E. M.: The molecular basis of memory, Englewood Cliffs, N.J., 1969, Prentice-Hall, Inc.

Halstead, W. C., and Rucker, W. B.: Memory: a molecular maze, Psychol. Today **2:**38-41; 66-67, May 1968.

Hudspeth, W. J., McGaugh, J. L., and Thompson, C. W.: Aversive and amnesic effects of electroconvulsive shock, J. Comp. Physiol. Psychol. **57:**61-64, 1964 (Bobbs-Merrill Reprint No. P-591).

Hyden, H.: Satellite cells in the nervous system, Sci. Am. **205:**62-70, Dec. 1961 (W. H. Freeman Reprint No. 134).

Kandel, E. R.: Nerve cells and behavior, Sci. Am. **223:**57-67, July 1970.

Kimble, D. P., editor: The anatomy of memory, vol. 1, Palo Alto, Calif., 1965, Science & Behavior Books, Inc.

Landauer, T. K.: Two hypotheses concerning the biochemical basis of memory, Psychol. Rev. **71:**167-179, 1964 (Bobbs-Merrill Reprint No. P-499).

Lang, P. J.: Learning to play the internal organs, Psychol. Today **4:**37-41; 86, Oct. 1970.

Lashley, K. S.: Brain mechanisms and intelligence, New York, 1963, Dover Publications, Inc.

Learning and memory. In Gross, C. G., and Zeigler, H. P., editors: Readings in physiological psychology, New York, 1969, Harper & Row, Publishers.

Louttit, R. T., editor: Advancing psychological science, vol. 4, Belmont, Calif., 1965, Wadsworth Publishing Co., Inc.

McConnell, J. V.: Confessions of a scientific humorist, Impact Sci. Soc. **19:**241-252, 1969. Also in Leukel, F., editor: Issues in physiological psychology, St. Louis, 1974, The C. V. Mosby Co.

McConnell, J. V., Jacobson, A. L., and Kimble, D. P.: The effects of regeneration upon retention of a conditioned response in the planarian, J. Comp.

Physiol. Psychol. **52:**1-5, 1959 (Bobbs-Merrill Reprint No. P-222).

McGaugh, J.: Facilitation of memory storage processes. In The future of the brain sciences, New York, 1969, Plenum Publishing Corp. Also in Leukel, F., editor: Issues in physiological psychology, St. Louis, 1974, The C. V. Mosby Co.

Miller, N.: Learning of visceral and glandular responses, Science **163:**434-455, 1969. Also in Leukel, F., editor: Issues in physiological psychology, St. Louis, 1974, The C. V. Mosby Co.

Milner, P. M., and Glickman, S. E., editors: Cognitive processes and the brain, Princeton, N.J., 1965, D. Van Nostrand Co., Inc.

Olds, J.: Ten milliseconds into the brain, Psychol. Today **8:**45-48, 1975.

Peterson, L. R.: Short-term memory, Sci. Am. **215:**90-95, July 1966 (W. H. Freeman Reprint No. 499).

Pfeiffer, J.: The human brain, New York, 1965, Pyramid Publications, Inc.

Pribram, K. H.: The brain, Psychol. Today **5:**44-48, 88-90, Sept. 1971.

Pribram, K. H.: The neurophysiology of remembering, Sci. Am. **220:**73-85, Jan. 1969 (W. H. Freeman Reprint No. 520).

Pribram, K. H., editor: On the biology of learning, New York, 1969, Harcourt Brace Jovanovich, Inc.

Schwartz, G.: Biofeedback, self-regulation, and the patterning of physiological processes, Am. Scientist **63:**314-324, May-June 1975.

Skinner, B. F.: How to teach animals, Sci. Am. **185:**26-29, Dec. 1951 (W. H. Freeman Reprint No. 423).

Sperry, R. W.: The great cerebral commissure, Sci. Am. **210:**42-52, Jan. 1964 (W. H. Freeman Reprint No. 174).

Talland, G.: Amnesia: a world without continuity, Psychol. Today **1:**43-50, May 1967.

Ungar, G.: Molecular approaches to neural coding, Int. J. Neuroscience **3:**193-199, 1972. Also in Leukel, F., editor: Issues in physiological psychology, St. Louis, 1974, The C. V. Mosby Co.

Warden, C.: Animal intelligence, Sci. Am. **84:**64-68, June 1951 (W. H. Freeman Reprint No. 424).

Willows, A. O. D.: Giant brain cells in mollusks, Sci. Am. **224:**68-76, Feb. 1971.

CHAPTER 15

Stress: normal and abnormal reactions

OVERVIEW

This chapter is concerned with the effects of stress on the human organism. The stresses discussed range from those common to everyone and easily tolerated to those that result in metabolic disorders, disease, abnormalities of personality, drug addiction, neuroses, psychoses, and mental retardation. Much of the evidence comes from clinical studies of individual cases; therefore the information is not so reliable as information from well-controlled experiments. A book on physiological psychology should not end, however, without an attempt to survey the effects of stress on humans.

The chapter opens by considering the relationships between stress, conscious states such as anxiety, and physical symptoms. Individual differences in tolerance for stress and the syndrome (set of symptoms) that follows stress that has gone beyond tolerance limits are considered. The balance of the chapter is in four parts: (1) normal stressors and metabolic activity, (2) abnormal stressors and functional disorders, (3) brain injury, and (4) mental deficiency. These categories overlap, but they seem as effective a way as any to organize the material.

The "normal" stress conditions that are met every day include variations in diet, exercise, hypoxia, aging, and sleep. Adjustments to small variations are consid-

ered, and the effects on behavior of extreme stresses resulting from greater variations are outlined. "Abnormal" stressors—those that often result in functional disorders of brain activity and behavior—are then discussed. Isolation, drugs, and epilepsy, as well as neurosis and psychosis, are included. Some physical therapies for psychosis are discussed. Brain injury effects are considered next. The results of traumatic injury, diseases, and senility on brain activity and behavior organization are included. Finally, the causes and consequences of mental deficiency are briefly discussed. The chapter concludes with some general observations on how the kind of stress that causes lasting impairment may be avoided.

STRESS AND THE MIND-BODY PROBLEM

According to many philosophers of science, conscious events are not legitimate scientific data because conscious events are *directly* observed by only one person. The content of his conscious experience can be reported by that individual, but the accuracy of his report cannot be verified by the *direct* observation of others; others cannot "look into his head," so to speak. However the presence or absence of conscious activity and its "intensity" *can* be verified by publicly observed means. The presence of conscious activity in humans is accompanied by activity in certain parts of the brain, notably the brain stem reticular formation (ARAS areas) and cerebral cortex. Activity in the cerebral cortex that accompanies various levels of conscious awareness—from sleep to aroused vigilance—can be publicly monitored with the electroencephalograph. Experts observing the EEG can agree on whether a subject is asleep or awake, whether his sleep is light or deep, whether he is "daydreaming" or in a state of aroused vigilance, and so on. From one point of view conscious events can be considered as a *symptom* or "byproduct" of certain levels of cortical activity that are measurable. From this point of view consciousness is not a cause of behavior but a symptom of activity in the cerebral cortex, activity that is necessary to some kinds of complex behavior. Other varieties of complex behavior may not be accompanied by conscious events or corresponding EEG changes at all.

Psychosomatic disorders

The term **psychosomatic** originates with the notion that certain mental, or psychic, states can cause somatic, or bodily, disorders, as in the case of continuous anxiety that results in stomach ulcers. The term is too well embedded in the literature to discard, although the premise implied seems to be a false one. Environmental stress that results in a physical symptom is not always accompanied by conscious (that is, reportable) anxiety. The individual may not be aware of being under stress and may not feel anxious, whatever physical symptoms he shows—irritability, muscle tension, and so on. It *can* be shown that enough environmental stress will reliably produce physical disorders—psychosomatic disorders, if you will. It *cannot* be reliably shown that psychic states, such as sensed anxiety, always produce physical disorders. It is therefore well to look for the conditions underlying psychosomatic disorders among environmental stresses and to use reports of psychic states such as anxiety only as clues to the possible existence of stress.

Stress

Stress can be defined as any stimulus, internal or external, that disturbs the dynamic equilibrium (changing balance) of the systems of the body (homeostasis, Chapter 2). In these terms any stimulus is a **stressor,** but it is considered to cause stress only to the degree and for the time that homeostasis is disturbed. The body is continually encountering stressful stimuli, or stressors, as a condition of life and of adjusting to a variety of environmental changes—heat or cold, the consequences of exercise, food deprivation, and so on. Stressors also include impediments to, or frustrations of, highly motivated behavior of very complex varieties in man. Frustration in attempts to perform well in an executive position can disturb the body's equilibrium as much as exposure to severe cold. Stress is more or less severe, depending on how successful the body is in restoring homeostasis, or the internal equilibrium necessary to sustain life over a long period. Restoration of equilibrium will depend on the severity of the stress, on the stress tolerance or the adaptability of the individual, and on the period of time the stress is continued.

Stress tolerance. Individuals differ in their ability to resist or adjust to many varieties of stress—temperature change, disease organisms, strenuous physical exercise, or the work and social demands of a complex society. An individual may have a high **stress tolerance** for one variety of stress and a low stress tolerance for another variety, depending on age, physical conditioning, learned behavior adjustments, and many other factors. The tolerance for some kinds of stress can be increased by physical conditioning or the learning of more effective modes of behavior. These statements may seem self-evident, but one must keep them in mind in evaluating the complex consequences of stress.

Stress syndrome. If the severity of a stressor is well within an individual's stress tolerance, he can adjust to the stress over a long period of time. The more a particular

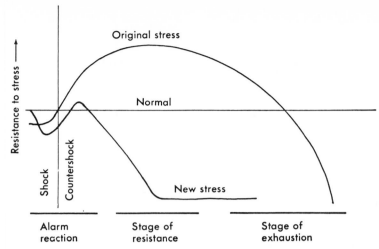

Fig. 15-1. General adaptation syndrome. Under prolonged stress, initial shock and countershock reactions may be followed by a stage of resistance and then a stage of exhaustion that culminates in death. Adding a new stress to the original stress will accelerate the process. (From Selye, H.: The physiology and pathology of exposure to stress, Montreal, 1950, Acta, Inc.)

type of stress exceeds an individual's stress tolerance, the shorter will be the period before the resources of the body are exhausted and physical deterioration sets in. The sequence of events is a predictable one (Selye). The shock of the initial stress is followed by initial countershock response in the *alarm reaction;* then a *period of adjustment* and apparent tolerance of the stress will be followed by a period of disorganization, physical disorders, a *stage of exhaustion,* and finally, death (Fig. 15-1). The adjustments of rats to stress and their eventual failure can be seen in rats kept in freezing temperatures. Their metabolism will increase to produce body heat with the aid of enlarged pituitary, thyroid, and adrenal glands during the period of adjustment. As the resources of the body are exhausted, however, physical deficiencies such as loss of weight, decreased activity, and stomach ulcers will result. Finally, the loss of homeostasis will exceed the limits that support life, and death will ensue. This sequence of events is remarkably similar when rats are intolerably stressed by means of varying from daily swimming to exhaustion to continued exposure to un-

predictable electric shocks. Presumably, the same things happen to humans who are exposed to intense stress of many varieties.

NORMAL STRESSORS AND METABOLIC ACTIVITY

Normal stressors are those that fall within the range of conditions to which the body adjusts easily—those conditions encountered in everyday life. Changes in diet, exercise, hypoxia, aging, and sleep are included as examples. The effects of these changes are most easily understood in terms of the "metabolic equation" of Chapter 2—the balance between the intake of food and oxygen on one hand and the output of work, carbon dioxide, and waste on the other. The effect of extreme deficiencies or excesses in any factors is considered only to illustrate the more normal variations. Those effects on the CNS that influence behavior will be emphasized.

Diet

The body requires carbohydrates, fats, and proteins, although the first can be manufactured from the other two. In addition, certain vitamins, traces of certain minerals, and several essential fatty acids and amino acids that the body cannot reconstruct from fats and proteins, respectively, are required. The diet, or food intake, may therefore be deficient or excessive in either a quantitative or a qualitative fashion. An individual on a balanced diet—one containing all the essentials just mentioned—may eat too much or too little. The diet would then contain too many or too few calories of food intake for that individual's work output. On the other hand, the diet may contain adequate calories but an oversupply or an undersupply of one of the essentials previously listed. Quantitatively, excess intake of calories results in excess fat deposits in the body, but fat acts as a stressor only because of the excess load put on the heart and circulatory system in supplying the excess tissue. The efficiency of the nervous system seems unimpaired, and a fat man is as intelligent as a thin man, even if getting fat seems to be a stupid thing to do. Qualitative excesses usually have little effect; the body rids itself of excess vitamins, amino acids, and minerals (excess quantities of some fat-soluble vitamins can be harmful). Starvation, however, puts greater stress on the nervous system than does obesity whether the starvation is selective or general.

General starvation. Insufficient caloric intake may or may not be accompanied by vitamin or mineral deficiencies or by inadequate protein or fat. In most areas of the world where malnutrition is common, general starvation is accompanied by selective starvation, particularly for vitamins and protein. So far as general starvation is concerned, however, there is no clear evidence that postnatal (after birth) malnutrition affects the nervous system, although it may have severe and lasting effects on other systems of the body. Metabolism seems organized to supply the CNS at the expense of the other tissues of the body when there are not enough dietary essen-

tials to go around. Prolonged infant or adult malnutrition does not appear to affect intelligence, provided that certain amino acids and vitamins do not drop below critical levels (see below). Motivational effects are profound, however, and many may impair test performance. Starving individuals are motivated by little but food, show extreme lassitude, and sleep much of the time to conserve energy.

Selective starvation. Severe deprivation of vitamin B_1 in infancy or lack of certain amino acids (lysine, cystine) at any age impairs learning ability. Diets deficient in iodine lower the metabolic rate, and those deficient in calcium or magnesium may cause CNS irritability and seizures. If any of these elements are available, however, the nervous system seems to be supplied at the expense of other tissues.

Exercise

Physical exercise increases the metabolic rate and consumes blood glucose stored in the liver and muscles as glycogen. These stores are replaced by increased food intake or by the conversion of stored fat into glucose for consumption by the cells. In reacting to the stress of vigorous regular exercise, the heart and circulatory system become more efficient, the contractile efficiency of muscle tissue is improved, the lung capacity is increased, and the body becomes able to tolerate increased exercise for longer periods. Regular exercise has also been found to prevent artificially induced ulcers in animals. On the other hand, continuous or repeated exercise to exhaustion may permanently impair these systems.

Fatigue

Physiological fatigue results from an insufficient oxygen supply to the muscles, when they consume oxygen faster than the lungs, heart, and circulatory system can provide it. An **oxygen debt** of the amount of oxygen needed to restore equilibrium accumulates. At the same time the waste products of muscle metabolism—CO_2 and lactic acid—accumulate faster than the circulatory system can remove them. Accumulated lactic acid can result in cramps, or contractures of the muscles (contractions without nerve cell excitation), and nerve endings for pain are stimulated. **Impairment** of the muscles' ability to do work results, and a **work decrement** follows. The CNS, however, seems immune to oxygen debt under most conditions. Work decrement resulting from long periods of mental work can usually be ascribed to boredom or conflict of motives. An office worker, for example, would show no physical impairment at the end of a long day, despite reports of fatigue. Factory workers seldom show impairment, either. Studies of their output often show an end spurt of increased output near the end of each work period, before a coffee break, lunch, or the end of the day. Their output increases at the end of a work period, at a time when one would expect more fatigue and a work decrement. Such end spurts probably reflect increased motivation at the prospect of stopping a monotonous task. Their increased level of performance "spills over" into increased work output.

Hypoxia

Hypoxia is a condition in which the tissues are not receiving enough oxygen from the lungs through the circulatory system to sustain metabolic activity. The tissues therefore accumulate an oxygen debt. Sensations of suffocation and hard breathing result only if carbon dioxide accumulates in the tissues at the same time; the nervous system is sensitive to increases in carbon dioxide but does not respond in many ways to decreases in oxygen. As already explained, hypoxia can result from physiological fatigue. It can also result from impairment of the lungs or circulatory system, as in cases of emphysema (a lung disorder) or reduced cardiac output (heart failure). **Anemia,** or lack of enough red blood corpuscles to carry oxygen from the lungs to the tissues, can cause hypoxia. In all these cases, capacity for physical work is reduced (impairment), an oxygen debt is acquired with less work, and sensations of suffocation and fatigue result. Hypoxia can result from reduced air pressure at high altitudes. The increased air pressure experienced in diving has opposite effects, which raise their own problems for the body.

Altitude effects. Air consists of a mixture of about 20% oxygen and 80% nitrogen. Air pressure is the amount of these gases per cubic foot of air. With increases in altitude there is less air per cubic foot, and, whereas the *proportion* of oxygen in the air remains constant, its *partial pressure* (20% of the total pressure) decreases along with the total air pressure. Oxygen diffuses into the blood from the lungs because the partial pressure of oxygen in the air of the lungs is greater than the partial pressure of oxygen in the blood returned by the heart from the tissues. As the partial pressure of oxygen falls, there is less difference between the concentration of lung oxygen and the concentration of blood oxygen. As a result, less oxygen diffuses from the lungs into the blood for distribution to the tissues. The outside pressure can be so low that one can breathe pure oxygen at that pressure and still not absorb enough oxygen for the tissues. Aircraft or manned satellites at high altitudes must be pressurized at about 0.9 kg (5 pounds) per 6.25 cm² of oxygen pressure to provide for enough absorption of oxygen by the blood (sea level air pressure is about 6.75 kg [15 pounds] per 6.25 cm²). Alternatively, a pressure suit and helmet may be worn. When the lungs are exposed to a vacuum, the blood "boils" as all its absorbed gases come out of solution, and immediate and total anoxia (loss of all oxygen) results, accompanied by widespread tissue damage (explosive decompression). When the blood oxygen drops sufficiently at high altitudes, the cerebral cortex ceases functioning, and sleepiness, followed by unconsciousness, results. Continued oxygen lack results in brain damage, coma, and death. No sensations of suffocation result because carbon dioxide is readily diffused and does not accumulate to stimulate the CNS.

Diving effects. In deep-sea diving, air must be delivered to the lungs at a pressure equal to the outside water pressure, or else the diver is unable to expand his chest to inflate his lungs. In a diving bell or diving suit, air is delivered to the diver from the surface by a hose until enough air has accumulated to equal the outside water pressure. In scuba diving (self-contained underwater breathing apparatus), a valve from tanks attached to the diver's back senses the water pressure and delivers air at the same pressure to a mouthpiece in the diver's mouth. In either case, water weighs much more than air, the pressure on the diver's chest increases as he descends, and air must be delivered to him at increasing pressures. More and more air (oxygen and nitrogen gases) is forced into solution in the blood. Much more nitrogen (80%) than oxygen (20%) goes into solution in the blood. At great depths enough dissolved nitrogen accumulates to cause nitrogen narcosis of the CNS, sometimes romantically called the "rapture of the deep." Disorientation, euphoria, disturbances in judgment, bizarre behavior, coma, and death may result. In returning to the surface—decompression—another difficulty is encountered. The deeper a diver has been and the longer he has been down, the more nitrogen gas is dissolved in his body tissues and blood. If he returns toward the surface too rapidly, water pressure and the competing air pressure are reduced too fast. The lungs cannot rid the body of dissolved nitrogen fast enough, and bubbles of nitrogen gas come out of solution in the bloodstream. These bubbles cause intense pain (the bends) when they accumulate at body joints. They burst capillaries in the brain, causing permanent brain damage. The only cure is rapid return to high air pressures (recompression) in a tank or beneath the water. The only prevention seems to be slow decompression if normal air is breathed, giving the lungs time to rid the body of accumulated nitrogen. Strangely enough, helium gas, as inert as nitrogen, does not cause narcosis and comes out of solution in the body much more readily than nitrogen. Experts have been experimenting with mixtures of oxygen and helium to avoid nitrogen narcosis and reduce decompression time.

Sleep

Sleep was discussed extensively in Chapter 11. Sleep is a bodily need, like hunger or thirst; if special brain operations or continuous stimulation keeps an animal awake for several days, the result is death. The role of sleep is an unknown one in the metabolic equation of food and air intake, energy, carbon dioxide, and waste disposal. The usual diet contains enough calories to sustain 24-hour waking activity. Yet sleep is a known requirement that seems especially essential to the CNS. In humans those functions most related to higher CNS activity—alertness, problem-solving, and so forth—demonstrate most clearly the effects of loss of sleep. Yet experiments on the effect of prolonged wakefulness in humans show no evident tissue damage, and complex mental tasks *can* be performed normally if the subject is sufficiently motivated and aroused.

Aging

As progress is made in the prevention and control of fatal diseases in modern society, more and more people are living longer. As the elderly population has increased, interest in the study of the aging process has resulted in expanded research in the science of **gerontology** (sometimes called **geriatrics**). The object of this research is to understand the aging process well enough to retard aging and to increase the life span, vigor, and health of the aged.

Some theories of aging propose that the reason for aging lies in the DNA-RNA-enzyme process that is the basis of cell reproduction (Chapter 2). According to this view, cells can divide only so often before the DNA "templates" that control all normal cell division and all the chemical reactions of life "wear out." Others suggest that this is what happens to the pattern controlling the frequency of cell division to cause the uncontrolled growth in number of cancerous cells. One consequence of this theory would be that we would all die of cancer if we lived long enough. A recent suggestion expands on the idea that mechanisms in the hypothalamus like those controlling the endocrine gland changes in the day and night cycle also are "programmed" to limit the life span. However, some theorists believe that aging has no specific cause and that hormones and numerous other factors play decisive roles.

Nonetheless, the physiological changes of aging reduce the body's resistance to many kinds of stress and are themselves stressful to the individual. The reduced efficiency of the heart and circulatory system impairs physical adjustment to exercise. As the arteries of the brain harden and blood pressure rises, blood vessels burst in the brain (stroke) and neural tissue is damaged, particularly in the cerebral cortex. Other degenerative changes that occur with aging impair CNS function. The most common result is disturbance of recent memory—the retroactive amnesia discussed in Chapter 14. Sensory mechanisms deteriorate, particularly vision and hearing. Finally, motor degeneration is seen in tremor and occasionally, in paralysis.

ABNORMAL STRESSORS AND FUNCTIONAL DISORDERS

Stress imposed on the nervous system by a variety of factors, such as isolation or persistent conflict, can cause disorders of the *functioning* of the CNS—**functional disorders.** Long-continued functional disorders of the CNS can damage the *structure* of various organs of the body whose activities are controlled by the CNS. Damage to body organs caused by functional disorders of the nervous system *are* the psychosomatic symptoms already discussed. Many psychosomatic symptoms can result from

functional disorders as well as from diseases or allergies—asthma, hives, stomach ulcers, colitis (irritation of the colon), and piles (hemorrhoids) are a few examples. More specific agents such as drugs and toxic agents can likewise disturb the functioning of the CNS; they can also damage nerve tissue, which cannot be replaced in humans.

Isolation

The brain seems to require a minimum level of sensory input to maintain normal functioning. Human subjects, deprived of sensory stimulation, develop bizarre hallucinations ("seeing things" or "hearing things") after a period of time. The length of time required for the effects depends on the extent of the **sensory deprivation.** In extreme cases the subject may be blindfolded (visual deprivation), have his ears plugged (auditory deprivation), and be lowered into a bath of tepid water (deprivation of temperature sensations and kinesthetic input from the muscles stretched by gravity). An initial period of sleep ensues, followed by disembodied *feelings;* then bizarre hallucinations develop within 24 to 48 hours. Some have speculated that sensory input is so necessary to organization of the brain's activities that the brain hallucinates sensations when they are not provided by the sense organs. Some of the symptoms resemble those of psychosis, and psychiatrists have subjected themselves to sensory deprivation in an attempt to understand the experiences of psychotics.

Drug effects

As would be expected from its high rate of metabolism, the CNS is more sensitive to drugs than are other cells of the body. The specific effects of various drugs on the CNS vary widely, however, and neither the site of their action nor how they affect nerve cells is known in many cases. Some drugs may *stimulate* activity in the CNS, preventing sleep when they affect the cortex either directly or through the ARAS. Other drugs may *depress* the cortex or

Table 12. Classification of some major drugs*

Drug class	Group	Example	Trade or common name	Natural or synthetic	Usage	How taken	First used	Evidence of addiction
Psychotherapeutics These drugs typical of many used in treatment of psychological and psychiatric disorders								
Antipsychotic drugs used primarily to treat major psychoses such as schizophrenia and manic-depressive and senile psychoses	Antipsychotic Rauwolfia alkaloids	Reserpine	Serpasil	Nat.	Greatly diminished	Injected	1949	No
	Phenothiazines	Chlorpromazine	Thorazine	Syn.	Widespread	Ingested	1950	No
Antianxiety drugs used to combat insomnia, induce muscle relaxation, treat neurotic conditions, and reduce psychological stress	Antianxiety Propanediols	Meprobamate	Miltown	Syn.	Widespread	Ingested	1954	Yes
	Benzodiazepines	Chlordiazepoxide	Librium	Syn.	Widespread	Ingested	1933	Yes
	Barbiturates	Phenobarbital	See *Sedatives, below*					
Antidepressant drugs effective in treatment of psychiatric depression and phobic-anxiety states	Antidepressant MAO inhibitors	Tranylcypromine	Parnate	Syn.	Diminished	Ingested	1958	No
	Dibenzazepines	Imipramine	Tofranil	Syn.	Widespread	Ingested Injected	1948	No
Stimulants (see *Stimulants, below*)	Stimulant	Amphetamine	See *Stimulants, below*					
Psychogenics These drugs produce changes in mood, thinking, and behavior; resultant drug state may resemble a psychotic state, with delusions, hallucinations, and distorted perceptions; little therapeutic value	Ergot derivative	Lysergic acid diethylamide	LSD, lysergide	Syn.	Widespread?	Ingested	1943	No
	Cannabis sativa	Marijuana	Hemp, hashish	Nat.	Widespread	Smoked	?	No
	Lophophora williamsii	Mescaline	Peyote button	Nat.	Localized	Ingested	?	No
	Psilocybe mexicana	Psilocybin		Nat.	Rare	Ingested	?	No
Stimulants These drugs elevate mood, increase confidence and alertness, and prevent fatigue; analeptics stimulate central nervous system and can reverse depressant effects	Sympathomimetics Analeptics	Amphetamine Pentylenetetrazol	Benzedrine Metrazol	Syn. Syn.	Widespread Rare	Ingested Injected	1935 1935	Yes No
	Psychotogenics	Lysergic acid diethylamide	See *Psychotogenics, above*			Ingested Injected		

Description	Class	Drug	Other name	Nat./Syn.	Use	Administration	Year	Addictive
Caffeine and nicotine, found in beverages and tobacco, are mild stimulants	Nicotinics	Nicotine		Nat.	Widespread	Smoked / Ingested	?	Yes
	Xanthines	Caffeine		Nat.	Widespread	Ingested	?	Yes
Sedatives and hypnotics Most of these drugs produce general depression (sedation) in low doses and sleep (hypnosis) in larger doses; used to treat mental stress, insomnia, and anxiety	Bromides	Potassium bromide		Syn.	Widespread	Ingested	1857	No
	Barbiturates	Phenobarbital	Luminal	Syn.	Widespread	Ingested / Injected	1912	Yes
	Chloral derivatives	Chloral hydrate		Syn.	Rare	Ingested	1875	Yes
	General	Alcohol		Nat.	Widespread	Ingested	?	Yes
Anesthetics, analgesics, and paralytics These drugs are widely used in field of medicine								
General anesthetics act centrally to cause a loss in consciousness	General anesthetics	Nitrous oxide	"Laughing gas"	Syn.	Rare	Inhaled	1799	No
		Diethyl ether		Syn.	Greatly diminished	Inhaled	1846	No
		Chloroform		Syn.	Rare	Inhaled	1831	No
Local anesthetics act only at or near site of application	Local anesthetics	Cocaine	Coca	Nat.	Widespread	Applied / Ingested	?	Yes
		Procaine	Novocain	Syn.	Widespread	Injected	1905	No
Analgesic drugs, many of them addicting, typically produce euphoria and stupor; effective pain relievers	Analgesics	Opium derivatives	Morphine, heroin	Nat.	Widespread	Injected / Smoked	?	Yes
Paralytic drugs act primarily at neuromuscular junction to produce motor (muscular) paralysis; commonly used by anesthesiologists	Paralytics	d-Tubocurarine	Curare	Nat.	Widespread	Injected	?	No
Neurohumors (neurotransmitters) Adrenergic and cholinergic compounds known to be synaptic transmitters in nervous system; other natural compounds (e.g., 5-HT, aminobutyric acid, substance P) may also be neurotransmitters	Cholinergic	Acetylcholine		Nat. / Syn.	Laboratory	Injected	1926	No
	Adrenergic	Norepinephrine		Nat. / Syn.	Laboratory	Injected	1946	No
	Others (?)	5-Hydroxytryptamine	5-HT, serotonin	Nat. / Syn.	Laboratory	Injected	1948	No

*From Jarvik, M. E.: The psychopharmacological revolution, Psychol. Today **1**:51-59, 1967.

ARAS, causing drowsiness, unconsciousness, or coma. Still other drugs are *selective* in their effects for largely unknown reasons, interfering with the perception of pain or with sympathetic nervous system arousal, for example. Some drugs *disorganize* CNS activity, causing distorted perceptions or hallucinations. Finally, some drugs may alter the functioning of the CNS, if they are taken habitually over a period of time, so that the CNS cannot function normally in their absence—this is **addiction.** Table 12 gives a classification of some of the major drugs and their properties and indicates which drugs appear to be addicting. A drug may be found in more than one category when it seems to have more than one kind of effect. For example, lysergic acid diethylamide (LSD) is a stimulant but also a psychotogenic drug (one that produces delusions and hallucinations, like a psychosis). Only drugs that are likely to be of greatest interest to the student will be discussed. The psychotherapeutic drugs will be considered in a later section on physical treatments for psychosis.

Stimulants. Stimulants increase the metabolic rate of cells of the CNS and increase their excitability. Some stimulants affect the whole CNS, whereas others have their greatest effect at selected sites in the brain. Some act directly on the ARAS or cortex; others excite sympathetic nervous system arousal by their influence on the hypothalamus. A few stimulants reset the "thermostats" regulating the level of SNS arousal, presumably in the hypothalamus or ARAS. The body adapts to the latter drugs, so that their removal results in a lower than normal level of CNS activity. A craving for, or an addiction to, these drugs results because the CNS is no longer able to function normally without them.

Caffeine is an example of a mildly addicting cortical stimulant present in coffee, tea, cocoa, and some soft drinks. The effect on the user depends on the *tolerance* he may or may not have for the drug. Tolerance is increased by habitual usage. Small doses of caffeine seem to improve performance in psychomotor tasks such as typing. However, doses that exceed individual tolerance levels can result in indigestion, nervousness, and inability to sleep.

Nicotine is not the only drug in tobacco, and the action of all the various drugs taken by smoking is not understood. Tobacco smoking acts as a selective stimulant, leading to increased SNS activity. This results in increased heart rate, peripheral vasoconstriction, release of blood glucose from the liver and muscles, and so on. The extent and intensity of these effects depend on how much tolerance the individual has developed through habitual smoking and how much he inhales. (Inhaling enables the drugs in tobacco smoke to reach the bloodstream rapidly through the lungs.) In addition to drugs that cause the above effects, such as nicotine and pyridine, tobacco smoke contains **carcinogens**—agents such as "tars" that irritate tissue and seem thereby to predispose the tissue to **cancer.** Cigarette smokers are probably predisposed to cancer of the lungs and pipe smokers to cancer of the mouth. For reasons not clearly understood, cigarette smokers seem to be predisposed to circulatory disorders, including heart disease. Habitual tobacco smoking is addicting for most persons, altering physiological equilibrium so that abnormal sensations and irritability occur after withdrawal. Most of these people need one to three weeks of abstinence before the physiological withdrawal symptoms disappear. Some studies suggest that adjustment to exercise is impaired for about a half hour after smoking; other studies detect no effect.

Benzedrine is the trade name and a common term for **amphetamine,** a kind of drug that mimics some of the SNS arousal effects such as peripheral vasoconstriction. For this reason it was introduced into nasal inhalers as a decongestant; it shrinks the mucous tissue by constricting its blood vessels to increase the size of the nasal passages for freer breathing when they are clogged by a head cold. It is also a cerebral stimulant that combats sensations of drowsiness and fatigue and may lead to feelings of euphoria in larger doses. It has been widely used by military personnel, truck drivers who are driving at night, and students cramming for examinations, but toxic side effects have led to deafness and nervous disorders, and its use has been restricted. Because it raises the metabolic rate and diminishes appetite for food, it is employed as an aid to losing weight by reducing food intake while "burning up" stored fat deposits at a more rapid rate. As a stimulant, amphetamine and its derivatives have been used to combat psychotic depression or the low metabolic rate caused by thyroid insufficiency. In large doses, amphetamine has been used to elicit or intensify the symptoms of schizophrenia in research on psychosis. In an attempt to reduce undesirable side effects, researchers have developed drugs that are derived from or are similar to amphetamine, such as Dexedrine and Dexamyl. Amphetamines probably are addicting, and "bennies" are often taken among potential drug addicts for "kicks" (euphoria from large doses). Large doses are called "speed" by addicts.

Cocaine is a drug obtained from the leaves of the coca shrub of South America. Peruvian Indians chew coca leaves to alleviate symptoms of hunger and fatigue from hard work at high altitudes (where some hypoxia is inevitable). Cocaine is used medically as a local anesthetic for mucous tissue. Addicts take cocaine through the mucous tissue of the nose by sniffing it in the same way as tobacco was commonly taken as snuff long ago. Cocaine is a powerful CNS stimulant that causes "mood swings" from euphoria to depression, epinephrine-like effects on the CNS, insomnia, weight loss, and sensory hallucinations of "bugs" crawling on the skin. There is conflicting evidence on whether cocaine is addicting.

Psychotogenic drugs are also called hallucinogens because they distort perception and cause hallucinations. Overdoses of several drugs (bromides, cocaine, and so forth) can have this effect. The major hallucinogens, however, cause hallucinations at any effective dosage and are called **psychotomimetic,** or psychotogenic, drugs because they mimic the effect of psychosis in producing hallucinations. They are also called **psychedelic** (Gr., "mind-revealing") drugs. Marijuana, LSD-25 (lysergic acid diethylamide), and mescaline (peyote) are examples. Peyote is used in some American Indian religious ceremonies.

Depressing drugs. Drugs that depress the activity of the CNS may act in several ways. Sedatives and hypnotics produce a general lowering of CNS activity for general depression and sleep, respectively. The general anesthetics such as ether reach the brain almost directly by the bloodstream as they are inhaled. The resulting coma leaves the individual insensitive to pain so that surgery can be performed. Local anesthetics work only at their site of application for local surgery. Analgesic drugs relieve more general pain without causing unconsciousness. Little is known of their mode of selective action on pain. Analgesics range from aspirin (acetylsalicylic acid) to the opium derivatives such as heroin and morphine and include any depressing drug in a dosage that relieves pain without causing unconsciousness. Unfortunately, many of them are addicting (aspirin is not). Paralytic drugs do not act on the CNS at all; they merely block neuromuscular transmission, producing complete relaxation of all the muscles of the body. Some of the depressing drugs are of interest because they are used socially (alcohol), as sleeping pills (barbiturates), as anesthetics (ether), or as addicting drugs (opium). An initial sensation of euphoria may be experienced after taking these drugs as the CNS combats their effects with overexcitation, but the result of increased dosage in every case is unconsciousness. Intake of enough of any depressing drug disorganizes coordination and abstract thinking because depressing drugs usually affect the highest centers of the brain first.

Ethyl **alcohol** is contained in beer, wine, and whiskey. It is usually produced by the effects of living organisms in yeast on the sugars contained in grapes or grain (fermentation). The alcohol content of beer and wine is measured in percentage of total volume, being 3% to 6% in most beer and up to 12% in naturally fermented wine. Some wines, principally ports and sherries, which may contain up to 20% alcohol, are fortified by the addition of ethyl alcohol obtained by distillation. Whiskeys, by contrast, are all distilled. After natural fermentation their alcohol content is increased by boiling; the alcohol boils first and is condensed, and water is left behind. The alcohol content of whiskey is measured in *proof*—200 proof is pure ethyl alcohol. A 100-proof bourbon is therefore half alcohol, and 86-proof scotch is 43% alcohol.

The effects of alcohol on the CNS depend on the concentration of alcohol in the blood and tissue fluid. As little as 0.1% to 0.2% alcohol impairs reaction time and complex behavior such as driving an automobile, as well as impairing most accurate tests of judgment and depth perception. About 0.5% results in coma. Blood alcohol content depends, in turn, on (1) rate of intake, (2) rate of elimination, and (3) size of the individual (since the human body is 96% fluid, larger individuals must ingest more alcohol to reach a given fluid percentage of alcohol). Rate of intake depends on the percentage of alcohol content of drinks, the rate of consumption, and, at first, stomach contents (alcohol is absorbed through the stomach wall like water, and the presence of food, especially greasy food, retards this process). The rate of elimination depends largely on metabolic rate, especially as it is increased by exercise, since alcohol is converted into blood glucose, which is used up in metabolism. Coffee and most other common stimulants do not "sober" a drunk very much because they do not increase the metabolic rate enough. Stimulants do more toward combating the depressing effects of alcohol on the CNS so that the drunk is a wide-awake drunk rather than a sleepy drunk! Aside from body size and its effects on

the percentage of alcohol content, some persons appear to "hold their liquor" better than others. In large measure the reason is that learned reactions such as habits of speech, walk, and self-arousal compensate superficially for the effects of alcohol on behavior. Alcohol does not seem to be addicting, as addiction has been defined, unless it is used consistently over a period of years. Some studies report that alcoholics seem less able to tolerate anxiety than nonalcoholics can and depend on the relief from anxiety that alcohol gives them. In addition, alcohol taken for the symptoms of a hangover can result in continuous drinking, whose cumulative effects on the CNS can eventually result in hallucinations known as delirium tremens (the "dt's"). Alcoholism often results in dietary deficiencies (especially vitamin B_1), since it reduces appetite by providing immediately available blood glucose without providing needed fats, proteins, and vitamins. Alcohol affects the highest levels of the CNS first, impairing cortical functions while the vital functions of the medulla (breathing, heart rate, and so forth) remain unimpaired, even after the individual has "passed out." Continuous overindulgence in alcohol for many years can cause cortical damage leading to psychotic symptoms (Korsakoff's syndrome).

Recent research has revealed a possible mechanism of the addiction that results from the long-term use of alcohol. One of the compounds that results from the breakdown of alcohol into blood glucose by the liver is acetaldehyde. This compound also results from the destruction of dopamine—one of the neural transmitters of the brain. When an excessive amount of acetaldehyde is present, dopamine destruction is incomplete. The incompletely destroyed dopamine combines with the acetaldehyde to form a compound with the awesome name of tetrahydropapaveroline (THP). THP is one of the central ingredients in morphine, a highly addicting narcotic drug. Thus it may be that alcoholism and morphine addiction have something in common. There is evidence, however that morphine also affects other transmitters. An additional side effect of alcohol is that it reduces REM sleep (Chapter 11). Perhaps that is why alcoholics sleep poorly.

Opium (heroin is a close relative), extract of the opium poppy, is one of a class of alkaloids whose active ingredient is **morphine.** The action of the drug is narcotic, whether smoked as opium or injected as heroin or morphine. With daily usage addiction results within three weeks, secondary to the development of increasing tolerance for the drug. Its use as an analgesic is therefore limited. Withdrawal symptoms for the addict are severe, including vomiting, incessant yawning, sweating, and sometimes collapse and death.

Psychotogenic drugs. **LSD** is a synthesized drug that is effective in minute doses. It produces bizarre perceptions, hallucinations, and a state that often resembles catatonic schizophrenia, a psychosis. For this reason it has been used experimentally to study psychotic disorders. Research is underway on its effects on alcoholism and drug addiction. There are indications that some forms of LSD may cause brain damage. Its effects seem to depend on the personality of the user; there have been reports of individuals becoming actively psychotic and not recovering after taking LSD. There are also reports of delayed effects, in which symptoms have returned after weeks or months.

Marijuana, on the other hand, barely qualifies as a psychotogenic drug because its chief effects are mild distortions of perception, particularly time perception. It comes from the leaves of a plant (Indian hemp) that grows wild over most of the country. The leaves are dried, crumpled, and made into cigarettes by users in the same way that tobacco leaves are made into cigarettes. Inhaling the smoke from one or two marijuana cigarettes is enough to make the user "high." The initial sensations are usually those of euphoria and feelings of "floating," and events seem to

occur very slowly. Feelings of depression frequently follow. The effects of marijuana depend on the concentration of its most active ingredient, Δ^1-3,4-*trans*-tetrahydrocannabinol, or THC. The upper leaves of the plant are "stronger" in this regard and exude a yellow sap that is even more concentrated. THC concentration varies with the climate and soil where the plant is grown. As a result, the illegal marijuana sold on the street varies widely in its effects.

Research on whether marijuana is addicting and has harmful side effects is still ongoing, and opinions vary widely in the absence of sufficient facts. However, tests made on users while they were under its influence reveal disordered time perception and disturbances of recent memory. Chemical tests show that the body does not clear itself completely of the drug for as long as eight days. Perhaps it is for this reason that habitual users receive more of a "high" from the drug than do novices. Research has not continued long enough to reveal any long-term effects from habitual use of the drug, except for reports that long-term male users develop female breast characteristics. There are clinical reports that habitual users "drop out," become listless, disoriented, and unable to concentrate. However, because there were no control groups, such reports do not prove that these effects were caused by the drug rather than by personality problems.

Epilepsy

Epilepsy is considered here because it is a disorder in the functioning of the brain and therefore an abnormal stress caused by a functional disorder. It may have an organic cause in a brain tumor, or it may be caused by an unknown and widespread overexcitability of the brain cells, with no structural abnormality than can be detected. Epilepsy does not usually result in brain damage, nor does it cause psychotic symptoms. Epileptic symptoms are the result of abnormally increased brain cell excitability, detectable by a peculiar spike and slow-wave pattern in the EEG of the victim. Epileptic seizures vary from momentary loss of awareness (petit mal) to convulsions of the whole body (grand mal). Grand mal is caused by massive excitation of most of the brain cells, which causes a rigid extension of the body (tonic phase), followed by convulsive movements (clonic phase), and then coma. The seizures are similar to those caused by electroconvulsive shock (ECS), pentylenetetrazol (Metrazol) injections, or the extremely low blood glucose caused by insulin injections—all treatments that massively stimulate brain cells. Seizures induced by the latter methods are used in treating mental patients; however, they cause greater tissue damage and disturbances of memory than epilepsy does because the seizures are usually induced daily or every other day—epileptics seldom have more than one seizure a month. Epilepsy that is caused by a brain tumor can often be cured by surgical removal of the tumor. Epilepsy of all varieties can usually be controlled by small doses of drugs that reduce brain activity (anticonvulsive drugs) and thus prevent the seizures. In extreme cases, the fibers connecting the two cerebral hemispheres are severed to prevent the spread of seizure activity from one hemisphere to the other (see split-brain techniques, Chapter 14).

Neurosis

The term **neurosis** has become a catchall category for persistent maladaptive behavior, accompanied by reports of anxiety and physical symptoms of muscle tension, digestive disorders, "fatigue," and lassitude, as well as other psychosomatic symptoms. The origins of the maladjustive behavior of the neurotic seem to lie in stress beyond the individual's tolerance, and in early and highly developed learning of inadequate behavioral adjustments to stressful situations. No physical damage can be found in the nervous system, but the persistent autonomic arousal that accompanies constant anxiety leads to stomach ulcers, colitis (irritation of the lower intestine), hemor-

rhoids (piles), allergies, and many other physical disorders. The physical disorders are no less debilitating because they have functional rather than organic (disease or brain damage) causes. In general, neuroses and some psychoses are termed "functional" for two reasons: (1) they have no known organic causes and (2) they are relieved by psychotherapy or improve without treatment (spontaneous remission).

Psychoses

A **psychotic** individual is one who suffers from unrealistic and illogical **delusions** (false beliefs) and bizarre hallucinations, and whose behavior is so disorganized that he is unable to care for himself in society, although there are many borderline cases who manage, especially in low-stress occupations. These disorders seem to differ in a qualitative way from neuroses, since organic causal factors seem involved even in the so-called functional psychoses and since the psychotic individual shows symptoms that the neurotic person does not have—delusions, hallucinations, and frequent lack of response to the "outside world." The psychotic in a low-stress situation may be free of these symptoms much of the time, but they often recur in an unpredictable way. "Organic" psychosis can result from brain damage, but many psychotics are termed "functional" because even an autopsy reveals no abnormalities in the brain.

If a hereditary predisposition to a specific psychosis moves the disorder from the functional to the organic category, schizophrenia and manic-depressive psychoses might be termed "organic." A higher proportion of these psychoses appears among offspring and siblings of those with the same disorder than appears in the normal population. Schizophrenics appear to beget schizophrenics, and manic-depressives pass their susceptibility to the disorder on to their offspring. Furthermore, protein metabolism in schizophrenics appears to differ from that in the normal population; the output of adrenal steroids in response to stress is subnormal, and the autonomic balance is abnormal. Which among these factors underlie the disorder and which *result* from it, is difficult to say. However metabolic factors may underlie both schizophrenia and manic-depressive psychosis, and the most promising research leads may be found in the study of brain metabolism. Schizophrenia and manic-depressive psychosis do differ clearly from one another and seem to offer the most promising categories for research of this kind. Varied symptoms accompany schizophrenia, but the most prominent are delusions, hallucinations, withdrawal, and apparent lack of affect (feeling tone). By contrast, manic-depressive psychosis involves, besides delusions and hallucinations, alternating periods of extreme euphoria and depression that may last days, weeks, or months. There are other kinds of psychosis and many other symptom patterns, but no one has come up with a classification system on which the majority of psychologists and psychiatrists can agree. Some experts believe that all psychosis has an organic basis, probably in disorders of brain metabolism. Other experts suggest that rejection and traumatic childhood experiences can result in functional psychoses—the so-called psychogenic theory of psychosis. As is usual in the area of behavior disorders, the specialists disagree.

Therapies

Various forms of psychotherapy are the most common treatment for neuroses. Most psychologists and psychiatrists agree that neurotic behavior disorders are *learned,* and some kind of learning experience—psychotherapy—is therefore required to rid the patient of his anxiety and other symptoms. Disagreement is found on the nature of the most effective kind of psychotherapy. Psychoses, on the other hand, are usually treated with physical therapies of one kind or another, although psychotherapy may be used as well. Physical therapies seem to be the treatment of choice for psychoses because many believe they have an organic basis and because physical therapies can alter the withdrawn or violent behavior of the psychotic, making him accessible to psychotherapy. Physical therapies include drug treatments, brain operations, induced seizures, and so on. Evaluating the effectiveness of the various therapies is difficult because an unknown number of patients recover without treatment (spontaneous remission). Untreated groups are often not compared with treated groups, and a before-and-after comparison does not allow for spontaneous remission. In addition, treatment effects are seldom systematically compared by disorders.

Drug therapies. Tranquilizers are used to calm neurotics and psychotics who show extreme anxiety, and "energizers" (stimulants) are used to arouse patients who evince depression and withdrawal. The tranquilizers appear to relieve anxiety and to make psychotic patients easier to manage, although wide individual differences in reaction occur. Drug therapies are reported to be most successful when combined with psychotherapy, but, again, systematic and well-controlled studies are few. Some of the psychotherapeutic drugs are shown in Table 12. Reserpine and chlorpromazine were the original drugs used to calm neurotic anxiety reactions and psychotic agitation. Both were therefore classified as tranquilizers, and they replaced the restraints and straitjackets that were used to keep agitated mental patients from injuring themselves or others. Many new tranquilizers with fewer side effects have been synthesized in recent years. The tranquilizing drugs have made it possible for a large proportion of these patients to be treated at home, rather than in mental hospitals. The action of these drugs on the CNS is far from being understood; the drugs seem to reduce the level of sympathetic arousal without depressing the CNS in general, at least not as much as do sedatives and hypnotics. The antianxiety drugs (Table 12) are most often used as tranquilizers for neurotic patients and others undergoing temporary stresses such as bereavement or illness. Antidepressant drugs are better understood than are the tranquilizers. One theory holds that feelings of well-being depend on adrenergic stimulation of brain receptors by catecholamines such as norepinephrine or dopamine. A compound called monoamine oxidase (MAO) destroys catecholamines. Therefore anything that inhibits MAO (MAO inhibitors) increases the supply of norepinephrine and produces feelings of well-being. Anything that depletes the supply of brain catecholamines would induce a state of depression. Reserpine, one of the antipsychotic tranquilizers, is believed to have this effect, and its use has been limited as a result. The theory has not been thoroughly tested, but it seems to be holding up well so far.

More recently, organic theories of psychosis have resulted from biochemical treatments that have proved to be effective in a large percentage of cases involving mania and depression. According to one theory, mood depends in part on the balance between serotonin and epinephrine in the brain—the same two neurotransmitters that control non-REM and REM sleep, respectively. (This is an extension of the theory cited in the preceding paragraph.) As a matter of fact, the early cues that mania and depression might result from imbalances in brain biochemistry came from studies of sleep abnormalities in these two psychoses. The basic strategy is based on the hypothesis that brain biochemistry is unbalanced in favor of serotonin in depression and in favor of epinephrine in mania. A large percentage of mania sufferers are helped by large doses of lithium, which is believed to alter the serotonin-norepinephrine balance in favor of serotonin. MAO inhibitors and tricyclic antidepressants are believed to have the opposite effect and have been used with success in a large pecentage of depressive cases. In a related strategy, sleep deprivation has been used in treating depressed

psychotics with some reports of success.

One of the greatest difficulties in developing an organic theory of schizophrenia comes in diagnosis—the disorder has many bewildering symptoms so that experts disagree whether it is a distinct entity or a conglomeration of disorders. More agreement is found in "classic" schizophrenia as defined by Bleuler: (1) a particular thought disorder, (2) a disturbance of emotional or affective responses to the environment, and (3) autism, a withdrawal from interactions with other people. He felt that hallucinations and delusions were secondary symptoms not always present. If neural transmitters are involved in mania and depression, they may be involved in schizophrenia as well. A strategy evolved by Snyder and his colleagues at Johns Hopkins University consists of examining the effect on neural transmitters of drugs that (1) alleviate the three basic symptoms of schizophrenia, (2) elicit "model" psychosis in normal people, and (3) intensify the symptoms of schizophrenia. Following this strategy, they have found that the phenothiazines and butyrophenone tranquilizers are the most effective in relieving schizophrenic symptoms and that the amphetamines are more effective (in large doses) than LSD in eliciting a model psychosis in normal subjects. In small doses, amphetamines intensify the symptoms of schizophrenic patients. The chief effect of the phenothiazines and butyrophenone drugs is the blocking of dopamine receptors in the brain—an antidopamine action that sometimes has side effects resembling Parkinson's disease. Amphetamines seem to increase the brain's dopamine supply, and amphetamine psychosis responds well to the phenothiazines and butyrophenones. Overactivity in pathways of the brain that use dopamine as a transmitter looks like a promising lead in attempts to discover the cause and cure of schizophrenia. A recent report from Seeman and Lee at the University of Toronto finds an abnormal number of dopamine receptors in the brains of deceased schizophrenics. Tranquilizers (used to quiet anxiety) compete with dopamine for access to receptor sites on the membrane of nerve cells. A tranquilizer (haloperidol) was made radioactive, mixed with the brain tissue, and then filtered. Only the tranquilizer that had adhered to receptor sites remained after filtration, and the number of receptor sites could be estimated by the radioactivity of the tissue. By comparison with normal brains, schizophrenic brains had many more dopamine receptors only in the limbic and caudate regions. (The caudate region is involved in Parkinson's disease, and the limbic area is involved in emotion.)

A recent study of brain endorphins offers another promising lead in the study of schizophrenia (Bloom, Segal, Ling, and Guillemin, 1976). Brain endorphins are peptides found in minute amounts in the hypothalamus and pituitary gland and were mentioned in our discussion of pain (Chapter 6). One of the four varieties found (B-endorphin) produces muscular rigidity and immobility in rats when injected into the cerebrospinal fluid. The response lasts for hours and resembles the catatonic rigidity often seen in schizophrenics. All four endorphins at appropriate dosages cause "wet dog shakes" in rats—behavior that resembles that caused by withdrawal symptoms resulting from opiate addiction. The shakes and the catatonic state are counteracted by naloxone, an opiate antagonist. Beta-endorphin has been administered to a few schizophrenic and depressed patients with promising results. A more recent approach to the role of endorphins in schizophrenia involves cleansing the blood of schizophrenics with an artificial kidney (dialysis). In research at the University of Florida, Cade and Wagemaker gave 16 weekly dialysis treatments to 21 schizophrenics; 18 of them became symptom free. Palmour, of the University of California at Berkeley, analyzed the first and sixteenth samples of dialysis fluid and found a difference of 100 times in the amount of leuendorphins

(for leucine endorphins) as well as a smaller decrease in a precursor (tryptophan) of the neural transmitter serotonin. When injected into animals, leuendorphin causes convulsive changes in brain wave patterns.

Psychosurgery. In extreme cases, especially in cases of psychotics with debilitating anxiety, the fibers connecting the anterior part of the frontal lobes with lower brain centers may be cut surgically. Individual reaction to the operation differs widely, but reduced anxiety is common. Personality changes also occur, however, including irresponsibility, indifference to consequences, disturbances in attention, and possible impairment of abstract intelligence. More restricted topectomy (ablation) of selected cortical areas in the frontal lobes seem to relieve anxiety with fewer side effects in personality changes. The use of tranquilizers has largely replaced these procedures. More recently, stereotaxic lesions of sites in the limbic system have been tried to calm assaultive behavior as they do in animal experiments. The results have been quite variable and need further evaluation.

Shock therapies. Various treatments massively stimulate the brain to cause a convulsive seizure that resembles an epileptic convulsion. A stimulant drug such as pentylenetetrazol may be used (Metrazol shock), the blood glucose may be reduced with insulin (insulin shock), or an electrical current may be passed briefly through the brain from electrodes on the temples (electroconvulsive shock, or ECS). A series of 25 treatments or more may be given daily or on alternate days. Disturbances of memory follow, retroactive amnesia (RA) being greatest for recent events. Theorists have proposed that the amnesia (forgetting) of stressful events precipitating the disorder may account for any beneficial effects of the treatment. Hypertrophy of the pituitary and adrenal glands occurs in the pattern previously described as part of the stress syndrome. Some claim that this mobilization of the body in response to the stress of the treatment is useful to the patient in combating psychological stress or recovering from apathy and depression. As usual, the shock therapies have had widespread use with little systematic evaluation.

Electrosleep. Over the past 20 years, a technique known as **electrosleep** has been developed in Russia; it has been little used in other parts of the world. Two electrodes are placed over the eyes and two just behind the ears. A low-intensity alternating current (100 Hz) is passed between the two sets, with the intensity level set below the level of discomfort for the patient. The treatment lasts 30 to 60 minutes, and five to ten daily treatments are given. (The term electrosleep is a misnomer—some patients never lose consciousness.) Initial clinical trials outside Russia have been promising with patients who have chronic anxiety, depressive symptoms, and associated insomnia (inability to sleep). The treatments appear to be relaxing, and insomnia and other symptoms are relieved. However, because few controlled and systematic studies of the technique have been published, it is difficult to evaluate its effect on specific disorders.

BRAIN INJURY

Brain injury can result in derangement of any or all the brain functions described in Chapter 3, in addition to the more complex disorders resulting from the impairment of the interaction of parts of the brain with different functions. Damage to the motor projection areas, to premotor areas of the cortex, or to subcortical motor centers results in paralysis, spasticity, tremors, and incoordination (sometimes called cerebral palsy). Damage to the sensory projection areas or to the subcortical thalamic and related nuclei that project to them produces sensory impairment. Damage to parietal, occipital, and temporal cortex impairs memory and learning ability and causes language disorders (aphasia, agnosia, and aphrasia). Damage to the frontal lobes results in widespread personality changes and impaired abstract behavior. Finally, damage to the limbic system can cause irritability or rage behavior or extreme apathy. Temporal lobe damage can result in docility as well as memory disorders. Any or all of these symptoms can be seen singly or in combination, depending on the location and extent of the brain damage. Reeducation in cases of motor impairment and some sensory impairment is possible, healthy cortical areas substituting for the damaged ones. Focal lesions are often more easily compensated for than are widespread and diffuse ones. If the damage is sufficiently widespread, the whole functional organization of the brain is upset, and psychosis may result.

Traumatic brain injury

Damage to the brain can result from tumors, blows to the head, hypoxia, and long-standing alcoholism. The symptoms that result depend on the extent of the brain damage or on its location if it is focal. Tumors, for example, cause focal lesions. Subcortically, therefore, they may cause sensory or motor disorders or disturbances of emotional behavior. A cortical tumor can cause a specific impairment that depends on its location. In addition, cortical tumors frequently serve as an irritative stimulus to brain tissue, resulting in focal epilepsy. Penetrating injuries to the brain made by a blow from a sharp object that penetrated the skull will cause localized damage, with effects similar to those of a tumor, and may cause focal epilepsy.

More diffuse and widespread damage to the brain is caused by blows to the head that slam the brain against the skull despite its surrounding liquid cushion. Frequent blow to the head that occur in body contact sports such as boxing, football, or ice hockey often kill widespread brain cells by mechanical damage or by bursting small blood vessels to cause hemorrhage. An event of this kind is called a **concussion.** A large number of concussions result in symptoms that are commonly seen in the person described as "punch drunk," which indicates sensory impairment, motor incoordination, loss of intelligence, and psychotic irrationality, the symptoms of extreme drunkenness. Brain hemorrhages result from the bursting of blood vessels in the brain, a so-called "stroke." Strokes can result from high blood pressure in the small capillaries in the brain. They burst from the pressure, and the cells they nurture die. The damage is most likely to be cumulative and widespread, with the resulting symptoms increasing over a period of time, but focal damage can occur. Sometimes many little strokes occur over weeks and months, but a recognizable stroke means more massive damage. Sometimes the damage is confined to one hemisphere of the brain, resulting in paralysis of one side of the body. The symptoms of brain damage that result from anoxia differ from those just described in that the cells of the cortex succumb first, and the damage is total and extensive. If anoxia is severe enough, the individual never recovers from coma. The cortical cells are largely destroyed, whereas the lower centers survive to maintain the automatic (homeostatic) activities of the body. Patients of this sort may "live" for years in a coma with or without the support of devices that supply the bloodstream with nutrition and eliminate body waste. One consequence is recent legal controversy over the definition of death as lack of "vital signs" such as heart action or permanent coma by brain-wave criteria. Alcoholism of long standing diffusely impairs the brain, although some symptoms can be reversed after withdrawal and improved diet. Korsakoff's syndrome includes amnesia, irresponsibility, impaired intellect, delusions, and euphoria.

Disease

Certain disease organisms attack the brain directly, whereas others impair its circulatory and protective structures. In either case the effects on behavior can be profound. For example, syphilis begins to attack brain tissue within five years of the original primary infection. It seems to impair frontal lobe function more than the functions of other parts of the brain. The symptoms therefore include listlessness, irritability, lack of social concern, indifference to consequences, and, eventually, delusions.

Cerebrospinal meningitis, as the name implies, attacks the meninges, or covering tissue, of the brain and spinal cord. Unless it is arrested, neurological symptoms follow. Cord damage results, of course, in crippling and in somesthetic sensory impairment. The damage to higher centers shows up in impairment of memory, concentration, and emotional stability.

Encephalitis often has more focal effects. This disorder was discussed in Chapter 11 because one form of the disorder damages brain centers that seem to control activation of other parts of the brain. Encephalitis, literally speaking, means only "brain inflammation." But encephalitis lethargica, or sleeping sickness, results from an organism carried by flies and was common at one time in Africa. This form of the disease attacks centers in the diencephalon that form part of the ARAS, and the victim sleeps much of the time. Inflammation of the hypothalamus, in another form of the disorder, results in emotionality, restlessness, irritability, and sometimes seizures. The victim is subject to extreme mood changes, from euphoria to depression, and to some indifference to the consequences of his behavior. There are also occasional movement disorders. Children seem especially susceptible to various kinds of encephalitis. **Rheumatic fever,** a variety of the disorder, is more common among children than adults and can leave behind the symptoms noted above.

Senile psychosis

Sooner or later, degenerative changes in the brain seem to occur with old age in the majority of the population. Whether these changes result in personality disorders seems to depend on how extensive they are and whether circulatory disorders (principally arteriosclerosis) are a complicating factor. Losses in brain weight and volume that are not accompanied by arteriosclerosis are common findings in postmortem examinations of the elderly. These changes are related to varied and diffuse symptoms, the most common being disturbances of recent memory (RA), emotional apathy, and lapses of attention. (The symptoms are difficult to distinguish from changes in morale and motivation that are often seen in the elderly, as they react to their diminishing physical ability to cope with the world around them.) Mild incoordination and tremors are usual. Arteriosclerosis and the strokes that result cause more specific symptoms as more specific brain areas are damaged.

MENTAL DEFICIENCY

Severe mental deficiency can often be detected at birth or in early childhood, suggesting that prenatal or hereditary factors are involved in various kinds of mental deficiency. In some cases the factors responsible are known, and in other cases sets of well-known symptoms have been classified. Many mentally deficient children are born, however, to normal parents after apparently normal prenatal development.

Prenatal factors

Any of a number of factors may cause failure of the brain to develop normally and result in a mentally deficient child. Although the nervous system seems less susceptible to damage before birth than later, it is subject to trauma despite its protected environment and early stage of development. Food and waste material are exchanged between the blood of the mother and the embryo in the placenta; extreme malnutrition of the mother, toxins (poisons), or drugs in the mother's blood may therefore affect the developing nervous system of the embryo. Disease organisms may reach the embryo by the same route if they are not effectively neutralized by the leukocytes of the mother. One common example is measles. Excessive use of roentgen rays (x rays) may cause genetic changes in the cell nuclei of the infant (mutations), resulting in abnormalities of nervous system development.

Mechanical damage

Mechanical damage to the brain of the fetus usually occurs at birth, although the mother may suffer internal injuries caused by accidents that can damage the unborn child's brain. When instruments are required to help the mother expel the fetus at birth, they may damage the brain of the infant because the physician cannot always see to place them accurately, or he may have to apply too much pressure to the soft skull of the infant. Hemorrhage or mechanical damage to the brain may result. During a long and difficult delivery, the umbilical cord may become twisted, or the infant may not begin to breathe soon enough after birth, depriving the brain of oxygen for a period long enough to asphyxiate brain cells. All these factors affect the brain more than they affect other tissue, and brain cells cannot replace themselves to overcome the effects of impairment.

Hereditary factors

Hereditary factors certainly underlie much mental deficiency. **Mongolism,** a type of mental deficiency named for the mongoloid facial features of these children, is caused by an excess chromosome in the germ tissue of one parent, a chromosome that has been identified. Less specifically classified mental deficiency may also be caused by hereditary factors. Many studies show that mentally deficient parents produce mentally deficient children at a high rate of probability.

Specific disorders

Mongolism has already been identified. **Phenylpyruvic oligophrenia** is a metabolic disorder that impairs brain development and often results in mental deficiency. It is caused by the individual's inability to metabolize a specific amino acid (phenylpyruvic acid).

A **microcephalic** child, as the term implies, is born with an undersized brain and head and is usually mentally deficient. **Hydrocephalus** (water on the brain) is caused by an imbalance in the production and drainage of cerebrospinal fluid. Excess cerebrospinal fluid collects in the ventricles and beneath the meninges of the brain. The resulting fluid pressure can cause mechanical damage to the brain, which results in mental deficiency if the pressure is not relieved in time. Since the sutures, or "joints," between the cranial bones of the infant have not yet hardened, the skull becomes large and domelike as it expands under this pressure. On the other hand, premature hardening of the cranial sutures can cause pressure on the developing brain of the infant, retarding his development and causing mental retardation.

Cretinism results from thyroid deficiency or lack of stimulation of the thyroid gland by the anterior pituitary. Unless the disorder is diagnosed early and treated with thyroxin or some other drug that will raise the metabolic rate, mental deficiency follows.

Infantile autism is a disorder that has received increased attention in recent years. There is some controversy over whether it is a variety of mental retardation or a defect in mechanisms of attention and sensory processing, but the outcome is the same. It has been found that the blood platelets of these children contain abnormally large amounts of 5-hydroxytryptamine (5-HT), one of the catecholamines believed to be a synaptic transmitter.

SUMMARY

Since one can be under stress without being aware of it and since the level of awareness can be objectively measured by the EEG, it appears that stress, rather than conscious events such as anxiety, should be investigated as the origin of psychosomatic disorders. Any stimulus can upset homeostasis, and therefore any stimulus can be a stressor, but only to the degree and for the time that it creates internal imbalance. Individuals differ in their tolerance of various kinds of physical and psychological stress; tolerance may be improved by physical and psychological exposure to stress within tolerance limits. Exposure beyond those limits leads to the stress syndrome, which includes the alarm reaction (shock and countershock), a period of adjustment with glandular and other changes, a stage of exhaustion, and death. Neither quantitative nor qualitative excesses in diet seem to affect the brain unduly, nor does starvation affect it if certain dietary essentials are provided. Deprivation of vitamin B_1 in infancy or of certain amino acids, calcium, or magnesium impairs brain function. Exercise within tolerance limits improves tolerance for exercise; beyond these limits physical impairment results. Physiological fatigue results from an oxygen debt in the muscles, but a work decrement can follow motivational changes as well. Hypoxia can result from impairment to the lungs, heart, or circulatory system (including anemia), or from reduced air pressure at high altitudes, when the partial pressure of oxygen is insufficient for diffusion from the lungs to blood in the capillaries. In the near vacuum of space the blood boils as the gases of air come out of solution. The increased air pressure required for diving can put enough nitrogen from the air into the blood to cause nitrogen narcosis. Decompression must be slow, or else the nitrogen will form bubbles in the blood.

Sleep seems to be a necessity for CNS functioning. Sleep results from the absence of arousal and is part of the day-night cycle in humans and some adult animals but not in infants.

Study of the effects of aging is called gerontology, or geriatrics. Such study aims to relieve the stressful effects of aging, as well as to prolong human life.

Functional disorders of the nervous system cause no observable damage to the brain, but they may cause psychosomatic damage to many organs of the body that malfunction as a result. The sensory deprivation resulting from isolation disorganizes brain function, as shown by the hallucinations that follow this treatment. The CNS is susceptible to stimulating, depressing, and disorganizing drugs. Caffeine is a mild and nonaddicting stimulant. The drugs in tobacco are addicting and some of them can irritate tissue enough for cancer to result. Benzedrine is an addicting cortical stimulant used for wakefulness and to raise the metabolic rate. Cocaine is a stimulant that causes extreme mood swings. Ethyl alcohol is a depressant, measured in proof or in percentage, whose effects depend on intake rate, body size, and elimination rate through exercise. It is not addicting unless it is used regularly for a long time. The addictive effects of alcoholism may have something in common with morphine because they both increase THP in the brain. REM sleep deprivation also results from alcoholism. Marijuana is intoxicating but not addicting. Opium and its derivatives (heroin and morphine) are addicting narcotics. Analgesics such as aspirin relieve pain without causing sleep. Tranquilizers such as chlorpromazine or reserpine affect ARAS or SNS activity more selectively, to relieve anxiety and reduce muscle tension. Hallucinogens, psychotomimetics, or psychedelic drugs such as LSD and peyote cause distorted perceptions and hallucinations in small doses.

Epilepsy is caused by a focal tumor or injury or by widespread brain excitability, is detectable by means of the EEG, and results in seizures similar to those produced by stimulant drugs or ECS. The seizures are too infrequent to cause brain damage and can usually be controlled with anticonvulsant drugs.

Neurosis is a vague term that refers to anxiety and persistent maladaptive behavior. Neuroses have no known organic causes, seem to be functional disorders resulting from stresses, and are relieved by psychotherapy or spontaneous remission. Psychoses may be functional or organic, are manifested by delusions and hallucinations, and usually require institutional care. Schizophrenia and manic-depressive psychosis have hereditary components.

Neurosis and psychosis have been treated by various therapies. The evidence favors physical therapies for psychosis, particularly drug therapy. The tranquilizers seem particularly effective in calming agitated psychotics. The antidepressant drugs may act by controlling the level of brain catecholamines. Depression and mania can be treated with drugs that alter the balance between serotonin and norepinephrine in the brain. Schizophrenia seems to respond to drugs in a way that suggests overactivity in brain pathways that use dopamine as a transmitter. Brain endorphins found in the hypothalamus and pituitary gland cause symptoms of catatonia (and opiate withdrawal) in rats as a clue to the causes of schizophrenia. Other physical therapies include prefrontal lobotomy, topectomy, or limbic lesions, shock therapies, and electrosleep therapy, but little systematic evaluation of the effects of these therapies has been made.

Brain injury can cause sensory or motor disorders, disturbances of emotion or memory, or even psychosis, depending on the site or extent of the injury. Focal tumors and penetrating injuries often cause epilepsy. Repeated concussions can result in a "punch-drunk" syndrome that includes mild psychosis. Strokes (hemorrhage) can be focal or widespread in effect. Long-standing alcoholism damages the brain, and psychosis results.

Disease organisms cause syphilis and cerebrospinal meningitis by attacking the brain; psychotic symptoms often follow. One form of encephalitis attacks the ARAS, causing stupor, and another the hypothalamus, causing emotional symptoms. Senile psychosis results from changes in the brain with age, including shrinkage and, sometimes, arteriosclerosis.

Defects in recent memory and attention follow, together with a state of apathy.

Mental deficiency can result from hereditary, prenatal, or traumatic causes. Prenatal malnutrition, toxins, and disease are included. The use of instruments at birth can cause mechanical damage to the brain. Mongolism, caused by an abnormal chromosome, is hereditary. Less specific mental deficiency can also be hereditary. Phenylpyruvic oligophrenia is the result of a metabolic disorder. The causes of microcephaly are not known, but hydrocephalus results from excess cerebrospinal fluid. Cretinism is caused by subnormal thyroid output. Infantile autism may be a disorder of sensory or attentional mechanisms. It is accompanied by excessive 5-HT in the blood platelets.

READINGS

Arehart-Treichel, J.: The mind-body link, Sci. News **108**:394-395, Dec. 1975.

Arehart-Treichel, J.: Brain peptides and psychopharmacology, Sci. News **110**:202-206, Sept. 1976.

Arehart-Treichel, J.: Probing the aging process, Sci. News **111**:26-27, Jan. 1977.

Barron, F., Jarvik, M. E., and Bunnell, S.: The hallucinogenic drugs, Sci. Am. **210**:38-49, April 1964 (W. H. Freeman Reprint No. 483).

Chapman, C. B., and Mitchell, J. H.: The physiology of exercise, Sci. Am. **212**:88-96, May 1965 (W. H. Freeman Reprint No. 1011).

Clark, W. H., and Funkhouser, G. R.: Physicians and researchers disagree on psychedelic drugs, Psychol. Today **3**:48-73, April 1970.

Collier, H. O.: Aspirin, Sci. Am. **209**:96-108, Nov. 1963 (W. H. Freeman Reprint No. 169).

De Ropp, R. S.: Drugs and the mind, New York, 1957, Grove Press, Inc.

Ebin, D., editor: The drug experience, New York, 1961, Grove Press, Inc.

Gates, M.: Analgesic drugs, Sci. Am. **215**:131-136, Nov. 1966.

Goldstein, K.: Prefrontal lobotomy: analysis and warning, Sci. Am. **182**:44-47, Feb. 1950 (W. H. Freeman Reprint No. 445).

Gray, G. W.: Cortisone and ACTH, Sci. Am. **182**:30-36, March 1950 (W. H. Freeman Reprint No. 14).

Hammond, E. C.: The effects of smoking, Sci. Am. **207**:39-51, July 1962 (W. H. Freeman Reprint No. 126).

Heron, W.: The pathology of boredom, Sci. Am. **196**:52-56, Jan. 1957 (W. H. Freeman Reprint No. 430).

Himvich, H. E.: The new psychiatric drugs, Sci. Am. **193**:80-86, Oct. 1955 (W. H. Freeman Reprint No. 446).

Isaacson, R. L.: When brains are damaged, Psychol. Today **4**:38-42, Jan. 1970.

Jackson, D. D.: Schizophrenia, Sci. Am. **207**:65-74, Aug. 1962 (W. H. Freeman Reprint No. 468).

Jaffe, J.: Whatever turns you off, Psychol. Today **3**:43-62, April 1970.

Jarvik, M. E.: The psychopharmacological revolution, Psychol. Today **1**:51-59, May 1967.

Levine, S.: Stress and behavior, Sci. Am. **224**:26-31, Jan. 1971.

Lewin, R.: Starved brains, Psychol. Today **9**:29-33, Sept. 1975.

Mark, V. H., and Ervin, F. R.: Violence and the brain, New York, 1970, Harper & Row, Publishers.

Melzack, R., and Thompson, W. R.: Early environment, Sci. Am. **194**:38-42, Jan. 1956 (W. H. Freeman Reprint No. 469).

Nichols, J. R.: How opiates change behavior, Sci. Am. **212**:80-88, Feb. 1965 (W. H. Freeman Reprint No. 491).

Roueche, B.: Alcohol, New York, 1960, Grove Press, Inc.

Selye, H.: The stress of life, New York, 1956, McGraw-Hill Book Company.

Selye, H.: It's a G.A.S., Psychol. Today **3**:24-26, Sept. 1969.

Selye, H.: Stress without distress, New York, 1974, J. B. Lippincott Company.

Stewart, M. A.: Hyperactive children, Sci. Am. **222**:94-98, April 1970.

Suedfeld, P.: The benefits of boredom: sensory deprivation reconsidered, Am. Scientist **63**:60-69, 1975.

Trotter, R. J.: Stress: confusion and controversy, Sci. News **108**:356-359, May 1975.

Weeks, J. R.: Experimental narcotic addiction, Sci. Am. **210**:46-52, March 1964 (W. H. Freeman Reprint No. 178).

Weil, A. T.: Cannabis, Sci. J. **5A**:36-42, Sept. 1969.

Windle, W. F.: Brain damage by asphyxia at birth, Sci. Am. **216**:79-84, March 1967 (W. H. Freeman Reprint No. 1158).

Glossary

ablation removal of part of the brain or part of the body by surgical means.

absolute threshold minimum physical energy that stimulates a receptor 50% of the time; a statistical average of receptor sensitivity.

accommodation process of thickening the lens of the eye to focus diverging rays of light from nearby objects on the fovea of the retina; visual focusing on nearby objects.

acetylcholine (ACh) a chemical transmitter substance released at synapses by the synaptic knobs of one neuron to excite other neurons.

acetylcholine esterase (AChE) an enzyme that speeds the destruction of acetylcholine (ACh) after ACh release at the synapse. The presence of acetylcholine esterase limits the response of a neuron to the chemical transmitter released at synapses.

ACh acetylcholine.

adaptation decrease in the response of a receptor and in the perceived intensity of a stimulus resulting from a constant rate of stimulation; loss of receptor sensitivity caused by stimulation.

addiction physiological dependence on a drug.

adequate stimulus an energy change that activates a receptor and is the form of energy to which the receptor is most sensitive, such as light for the eye or sound for the ear.

afferent carrying impulses toward a center, as when sensory nerves carry nerve impulses toward the brain or spinal cord.

afterimages sensations that occur after stimulation has ended. The sensation to the stimulus may continue or change.

agonist muscles muscles that perform a given movement.

alcohol a depressant drug contained in wine, beer, and whiskey.

allocortex in evolutionary terms, the oldest areas of the cerebral cortex, originally devoted to smell.

all-or-none law the statement that the nerve cell responds with the maximum polarization change that its electrical and chemical conditions permit, if it responds at all.

alpha rhythm a 10- to 14-hertz rhythm often seen in the EEG of a resting but awake subject.

amblyopia impaired vision that does not result from detectable defects in the eye; often caused by suppression of the input from one eye by the brain to avoid double vision caused by conflicting images from the two eyes.

amino acid type of organic acid that is the major ingredient of protein molecules, which are an essential part of the structure of the cell.

ampere a measure of the rate of flow of current (electrons). A potential difference of 1 volt will cause a flow of 1 ampere of current through 1 ohm of resistance in a conductor.

amphetamine a nonaddicting type of drug that stimulates the SNS, causes peripheral vasoconstriction, and promotes wakefulness and arousal.

amplitude in physics, the difference between extreme limits of an oscillation or vibration, such as limits of the air pressure change in a sound wave.

ampulla a bulblike swelling on the end of each semicircular canal, where it contacts the utriculus; contains the crista, a receptor that responds to head movements.

analgesic any drug that relieves pain without causing unconsciousness; also, an area of the body that does not respond to pain stimuli.

anastomosis in neurology, a network of interlaced nerves and nerve fibers.

anemia lack of red blood corpuscles.

angiotensinogen a normal blood protein that is converted during thirst by renin from the kidney into angiotensinogen II, which stimulates thirst centers in the hypothalamus to release vasopressin for an antidiuretic effect (ADH) and arouse drinking behavior.

anion a negatively charged ion (element or molecule in solution) that is attracted to the positively charged anode.

anode a positively charged electrode, that is, one that lacks electrons.

anosmia lack of smell sensitivity; smell blindness.

ANS autonomic nervous system.

antagonist muscles muscles that would oppose a given movement if not relaxed; for example, the extensor muscles of the arm are the antagonist muscles for arm flexion.

anterior chamber cavity of the eyeball that lies between the cornea and the iris.

aperiodic pertaining to a change that does not repeat itself, such as the aperiodic air pressure changes of noise.

aphasia impairment in language skills, usually caused by brain damage; inability to recognize words by sight (word blindness) or by sound (word deafness), for example.

aqueous humor fluid that fills the anterior and posterior chambers of the eyeball.

ARAS ascending reticular activating system.

archicerebellum in terms of evolution, the oldest part of the cerebellum. See flocculonodular lobe.

arcuate nucleus that part of the ventrolateral nucleus of the thalamus where second-order neurons excited by sensory nerves from the tongue and face terminate; a part of the nerve pathways serving taste and somesthesia.

ascending reticular activating system (ARAS) a system of many short fibers of the central gray matter of the brain stem that is excited by collaterals of the afferent spinothalamic system and that activates or arouses activity in the whole brain, particularly the cortex.

association neuron a nerve cell of the CNS that is neither sensory nor motor in function.

auditory projection area area 41 of the temporal lobe of the cerebrum, where fibers of the classic auditory pathway terminate; the sensory projection area of the cortex for audition.

autonomic nervous system (ANS) motor nerve supply to the viscera; the efferent fibers of the peripheral nervous system that supply the viscera with a dual innervation of two divisions, the sympathetic and parasympathetic.

axoaxonic synapses synapses between the axon terminals (end feet) of one axon and the axon filaments of another.

axodendritic synapses synapses between the axon terminals (end feet) of one axon and the dendrites and cell body of another.

basal ganglia certain subcortical nuclei of the endbrain, including the putamen, caudate nucleus, and globus pallidus.

basilar membrane the membrane forming part of the division between the scala media and scala tympani of the cochlea. The organ of Corti rests on the basilar membrane, which is part of the auditory apparatus.

Benzedrine amphetamine.

bipolar cell layer a layer of cells in the retina that transfer excitation from the rods and cones to the ganglion cells of the optic nerve.

blood-brain barrier a physiological mechanism that filters the extracellular fluid of the brain from blood in a manner that makes it chemically different from other extracellular fluids of the body.

brain (encephalon) a large soft mass of nervous and supporting tissue contained within the skull.

brain stem all of the brain except the cerebral and cerebellar hemispheres.

brain stem reticular formation (BSRF) mass of gray matter of the brain stem made up chiefly of short, branching Golgi type II cells. The BSRF arouses the brain to activity and stimulates or inhibits extensor motoneurons.

brightness visual sensation that results from light intensity.

Brodmann system a system for identifying different areas of the cerebral cortex by the relative thickness of the six cortical layers, assigning each such area an arbitrary number.

BSRF brain stem reticular formation.

caffeine a mild but addicting cortical stimulant present in coffee, tea, and some soft drinks.

cancer an abnormal tissue growth (tumor) caused by uncontrolled cell multiplication.

carbohydrates sugars and starches of various kinds from which the body derives glucose, the essential food of specialized cells.

carcinogen an agent that can cause cancer.

cardiac muscle the muscle that forms the heart; intermediate in structural and functional characteristics between striated and smooth muscle.

carrier in genetics, an individual whose germ tissue contains genes for a given physical characteristic, whether or not that individual has the characteristic.

cathode a negatively charged electrode, that is, one that has surplus electrons.

cathode-ray oscilloscope a device for measuring rapid voltage changes using a glowing trace left on the face of an evacuated tube by the rapid elevation of a stream of electrons that sweeps across the tube face at a known rate.

cation a positively charged ion (element or molecule in solution) that is attracted to the negatively charged cathode.

cell a protoplasmic body that is the unit of life. A cell can be an independent living organism or a specialized unit of a complex many-celled organism.

cell assemblies groups of interconnected cortical cells supposed to excite one another over and over again. Cell assemblies are involved in the phase sequence hypothesis of perceptual learning.

cell body the part of the nerve cell that contains its nucleus.

cell membrane the membrane that separates the cytoplasm of a cell from the environment of the cell.

cell metabolism chemical reactions of a cell that are required for life.

center a group of nerve cell bodies where many synapses are found. See nucleus.

central nervous system (CNS) brain and spinal cord.

central sulcus the sulcus that divides each cerebral hemisphere into an anterior one-third and posterior two-thirds; it separates the somesthetic sensory and motor projection areas.

cerebellar hemisphere cerebellum.

cerebellar system all proprioceptive and cortical input to the cerebellum and all cerebellar output to cortical and subcortical centers involved in movement.

cerebellum a large paired suprasegmental structure of the hindbrain, consisting of two hemispheres connected by a central vermis and mediating postural responses to input from the vestibular senses, muscle spindles, and cerebral cortex.

cerebral aqueduct tubular passage inside the midbrain that connects the third and fourth ventricles.

cerebral cortex gray matter covering the cerebral hemispheres.

cerebral hemispheres large twin suprasegmental masses of the brain of higher mammals that develop embryologically from the endbrain and overlie most lower parts of the brain.

cerebrospinal fluid tissue fluid surrounding the brain and spinal cord and filling the ventricles.

cerebrospinal meningitis a disease that attacks the meninges (covering) of the brain tissue and causes brain damage.

cerebrum cerebral hemispheres.

chorea (St. Vitus' dance) a disorder characterized by spasmodic involuntary movements of the limbs or facial muscles or both.

choroid coat vascular pigmented middle layer of eye tissue that lies beneath the sclerotic coat.

chromosomes microscopic rod-shaped bodies in the cell nucleus. Chromosomes contain the DNA molecules that govern hereditary characteristics, cell specialization, and cell function.

ciliary body a ring of muscle tissues that surrounds the lens of the eye, is attached to the lens by the suspensory ligament, and contracts in accommodation to thicken the lens for focus on nearby objects.

ciliary ring ciliary body.

circular fibers smooth muscle fibers that circle a visceral tube or the pupil and that constrict when contracted.

cocaine a powerful stimulant drug usually absorbed through the mucous membranes.

cochlea coiled, fluid-filled structure of the inner ear. The cochlea contains the structures that transduce sound vibrations into nerve impulses in hearing.

cochlear duct scala media.

cochlear microphonic an electrical response to sound of the organ of Corti. It follows the form of the sound wave as does a microphone.

collateral ganglia ganglia of the SNS found in the body cavity and neck; formed by cell bodies and synapses of postganglionic sympathetic neurons.

commissural fibers fibers connecting the cerebral hemispheres, such as those of the corpus callosum and anterior and posterior commissures.

common chemical sense pain sensitivity of the mucous membranes, particularly of the eyes, nose, and mouth, when stimulated by substances in solution.

compensation lack of sensation caused by the simultaneous stimulation of different (opposed) qualities.

complex periodic wave graph of a complex change that repeats itself, such as the pressure changes of a complex tone.

complex tone a tone made up of several simple tones produced by a complex vibrating body.

concentration gradient difference in concentration of an element or molecule in a solution, taken between two points in the solution or on each side of a membrane dividing the solution.

concussion a blow on the head that damages brain cells or impairs their function.

conduction property of a cell membrane that involves transmitting excitation from one part of the cell to another.

cones high-threshold chromatic visual receptors containing iodopsin and found in the central area of the retina; most active in daylight.

consolidation according to the two-phase hypothesis, the process of laying down a permanent memory trace that is caused by perseveration of neural activity after practice.

contraction ability of a cell to change shape; a property especially developed in muscle cells.

contrast in sensory psychology, when stimulation by one sensory quality enhances sensitivity to another sensory quality.

convergence in vision, extent to which the two eyes are crossed so as to focus a nearby object on the fovea of each eye.

coordination divergence of many (motor) outputs from a single center or group of centers in the nervous system.

cornea transparent outer tissue in the front of the eyeball that light first encounters when entering the eye.

corpus callosum sickle-shaped band of crossing nerve fibers that connect the cerebral hemispheres.

corpus striatum striped bodies; subcortical centers within the cerebral hemispheres, consisting of alternating layers of gray and white matter.

correlation convergence of many inputs on a single area of the nervous system.

cortically originating extrapyramidal system (COEPS) neurons of the extrapyramidal system that originate in the cortex and descend the brain stem and spinal cord to the motoneurons.

corticobulbar tract fibers that run from the motor projection area and excite the cranial motoneurons.

corticopontocerebellar tract a tract running from the premotor cortex to the pons and thence to the cerebellar hemispheres (neocerebellum).

cranial nerves the 12 pairs (in humans) of nerves that connect the brain directly with the receptors and effectors of the head.

cretinism a variety of mental deficiency caused by hypothyroidism (insufficient thyroid secretion) in childhood.

crista a ridge of sensory cells inside the ampulla that

thrust hair endings into the cupula. The cells respond to rotary acceleration and deceleration of the head.

cross-extension reflex extension of a limb caused by pain stimulation of the contralateral (opposite) limb.

cuneate nucleus a nucleus of the medulla containing synapses between first- and second-order neurons serving kinesthesis and pressure impulses ascending from the spinal cord. See gracile nucleus.

cupula gelatinous mass that crowns the crista; a part of the receptor mechanism for head movement.

cutaneous pertaining to the skin.

cytoplasm protoplasm of the cell external to the nucleus.

decerebrate rigidity a posture of rigid extension of the limbs (in a four-legged animal) caused by release of the BSRF and vestibular nuclei from cortical inhibition by removal of cortex or cerebrum.

decibel scale a physical scale of sound intensity designed to match the response characteristics of the human ear. The zero point is a pressure energy of 0.0002 dyne/cm². Each unit is an exponent to the base 10, multiplied by the zero point; thus 15 decibels would be $10^{1.5} \times 0.0002$ dyne/cm², and so on.

delusions false beliefs.

dendrites extensions of the cell body of a nerve cell that receive excitation or inhibition from other nerve cells.

dentate nucleus output nucleus of the cerebellar hemisphere (neocerebellum).

dentatorubrothalamic tract a tract from the dentate nucleus of the cerebellar hemispheres to the red nucleus, thalamus, and motor projection area.

dermatone an area, especially on the skin, that sends somesthetic input in a single dorsal spinal root.

descending reticular activating system (DRAS) outflow from the BSRF that increases muscle tone and thereby increases the sensory feedback that mobilizes the brain in an aroused state.

deuteranopia red-green hue blindness in which reds and greens are confused with bluish and yellowish grays.

difference threshold least difference between two stimuli in a given direction that can be detected 50% of the time.

differential limen (DL) difference threshold.

diffuse thalamic projection system (DTPS) sensory projection to the cortex via the nonspecific association nuclei of the thalamus, excited by collaterals of the sensory pathways (STPS).

DNA (deoxyribonucleic acid) complex helical molecule found in the chromosomes of all cells. The sequence of amino acids in these molecules determines the inherited characteristics (genes) of the individual and regulates the metabolism of each cell.

dominant in heredity, pertaining to a gene that determines a physical characteristic of the individual, whether or not a paired recessive gene is present.

dorsal toward the back.

dorsal cochlear nucleus one of the two sensory nuclei of the acoustical branch of the statoacoustical nerve. See ventral cochlear nucleus.

dorsal columns the dorsal funiculus (of both sides of the cord) that carries kinesthetic and pressure input from the spinal cord to the brain.

DRAS descending reticular activating system.

drive a CNS mechanism for arousing and sustaining behavior in the presence of a need state.

DTPS diffuse thalamic projection system.

ECS electroconvulsive shock.

EEG electroencephalogram.

effector a muscle or gland; any organ of response.

efferent carrying impulses away from a center, as when motor nerves carry nerve impulses from the brain and spinal cord to an effector.

electroconvulsive shock (ECS) an electrical current stimulus to the brain that results in massive stimulation and an epileptic form of convulsion.

electrocorticogram (ECG) a recording of the electrical activity of the cerebral cortex, taken from electrodes placed directly on the cortex.

electrode any conductor carrying an electrical charge that is used to transfer that charge to a solution or to animal tissue.

electroencephalogram (EEG) a recording of the electrical activity of the brain, particularly the cortex, taken from electrodes placed on the scalp.

electro-olfactogram (EOG) an electrical recording taken from the olfactory epithelium in studying smell.

electrolyte a molecule that breaks up in a water solution into positively and negatively charged ions.

electromagnetic spectrum energy spectrum that includes radio waves, light, roentgen rays, and so on.

electron a negative particle in an atom of matter.

electron microscope a device for magnifying the image of submicroscopic structures by passing electrons through them and focusing the electrons with electromagnets.

electrosleep electrical stimulation of the brain through electrodes placed on the head at an intensity level that does not cause convulsions and does not cause discomfort.

encephalitis literally, "brain inflammation"; usually refers to encephalitis lethargica (sleeping sickness), an infectious disease that destroys the arousal centers of the brain; the patient sleeps much of the time unless outside stimuli arouse him.

encephalization concept that phylogenetically newer and more complex parts of the brain take over, or dominate, the functioning of older parts of the brain.

endocrine glands glands that deposit their secretions into the bloodstream through the extracellular fluid and capillaries.

endolymph fluid contained in part of the membranous labyrinth of the inner ear; fluid of the semicircular canals and sacs and the scala media of the cochlea.

endorphins a class of four peptides, probably neurotransmitters, found in the third ventricle near the hypothalamus and in the pituitary gland. Endorphin effects include morphinelike relief of pain or symptoms resembling schizophrenia.

epilepsy seizures caused by an abnormal amount of activity in brain cells.

equipotentiality the principle that any part of the cortex can serve as well as any other part in learning. See mass action.

ergotropic having to do with drive or arousal, such as the centers controlling the sympathetic nervous system in the hypothalamus.

eustachian tube the tube that connects the middle ear with the throat.

evoked potential a recording of the electrical response of some part of the nervous system to a controlled stimulus.

exposure deafness an auditory defect for certain frequency ranges that is caused by overstimulation of the auditory mechanism by loud sounds at those frequencies.

extensor thrust reflex reflex extension of a limb in response to either pressure on the sole of the foot or spreading of the digits.

extent the sensed size of a sensation caused by the extent of the perceptual field for the sensation aroused by the stimulus.

external auditory meatus opening leading from the pinna to the tympanum (eardrum) in the ear. The pressure waves of sound reach the eardrum through this passage.

exteroceptors receptors located at or near the surface of the body that respond to physical events in the environment.

extrapyramidal system a system of many short branching cells connecting the premotor area of the cortex with subcortical nuclei and with the motoneurons.

extrinsic outside of, particularly with reference to the muscles attached to the eye that move the eyeball.

fat a compound made up of a glycerol and a fatty acid. Fats, along with proteins and carbohydrates, are essential for life.

fatty acid an acid compound that forms the basis of fats.

feeding center centers in the hypothalamus whose stimulation by internal changes of hunger arouse the CNS in a hunger drive.

final common path motoneurons to a given reflex response whatever stimulus is used to elicit the response.

first harmonic fundamental.

first overtone the sine-wave component of a complex tone that is twice the frequency of the fundamental.

first-order neuron a sensory neuron that runs from receptors to the CNS.

flaccid paralysis lack of motor control accompanied by muscle relaxation, usually caused by damage in the pyramidal system.

flexion reflex the reflex flexion of a limb in response to pain stimulation of that limb.

flocculonodular lobe the two flocculi (sing., flocculus) and the nodule of the cerebellum. These structures receive input from the vestibular senses.

Fourier's law in any complex tone with a fundamental frequency, n, the overtone frequencies are $2n$, $3n$, and so on.

fourth ventricle the ventricle (central cavity) of the hindbrain.

fovea point of clearest vision in the retina, formed by a depression that is in line with the pupil of the eye when vision is directed toward an object.

frequency number of times an event happens per second, such as the number of air pressure variations per second in a tone of a given frequency.

frontal lobe that part of each cerebral hemisphere anterior to the central sulcus.

functional disorders disturbances in the functioning of the CNS, resulting from stress, that cause physical symptoms and behavior abnormalities.

fundamental lowest frequency of the sine wave components of a complex tone; the component having greatest amplitude that determines the pitch of a complex tone.

fundus large interior cavity of the eyeball that extends from the lens and ciliary ring to the retina.

fusion sensation that results when two different sensory qualities fuse to give a third quality, such as the fusion of red and yellow into orange.

ganglia (sing. ganglion) collection of nerve cell bodies that lies outside the brain and spinal cord (whether or not synapses occur).

ganglion cell type of cell making up the optic nerve.

ganglion cell layer the layer of cells in the retina that receive excitation from the bipolar neurons and whose axons make up the optic nerve.

gas chromatograph theory in the study of smell, a theory that states the receptor surface responds to different odorous molecules to provide a pattern of nerve impulses in space and time as a code for odor detection and discrimination.

general senses sensory receptors found at locations over the entire body.

generator potential partially depolarized state of a receptor that results from receptor excitation and fires sensory nerve impulses.

genetic sex the sex of the individual as determined at conception by the presence of an XX chromosome pair (female) or an XY chromosome pair (male).

geriatrics gerontology.

gerontology the study of aging in animals, including humans.

glomeruli complex synapses in the olfactory bulbs where the sensory nerve fibers from olfactory receptors end.

glucose the form of foodstuff best utilized by the specialized cells of the body; colloquially "blood sugar."

glucostatic theory the theory that the level of blood glucose affects hypothalamic cells to arouse eating behavior when the blood glucose level is low.

glycogen compound into which blood glucose is transformed for storage in the liver and muscles.

gonadal sex the sex of the individual as determined by the appearance of the external genitals at birth.

gonads structures (male or female) containing endocrine cells or reproductive tissue that produces sex hormones and cells (sperm or ova) necessary for reproduction.

gracile nucleus a nucleus of the medulla containing synapses between first- and second-order neurons serving kinesthesis and pressure impulses ascending from the spinal cord. See cuneate nucleus.

gyrus the surface area between two sulci (sing. sulcus) in the cerebral cortex.

habit a learned pattern of behavior.

habituation loss of attention to a stimulus caused by repetition or lack of novelty.

hair cells receptor cells ending in hairlike processes, such as those of the organ of Corti, vestibular senses, or olfactory epithelium.

helicotrema opening at the apex of the cochlea that connects the scala vestibuli with the scala tympani.

hermaphrodite a genetic female with a penis but no testes or a genetic male with the external genitals of a female.

hertz (Hz) cycles per second.

heterogeneous containing varied components.

homeostasis maintenance of a dynamic equilibrium (changing balance) of the internal environment of the body, keeping the environment of the cells within the physical and chemical limits that support life.

homogeneous containing only one type of component.

hormones secretions of the ductless, or endocrine, glands carried by the circulation to affect metabolic reactions in selected target tissue over the entire body.

hue response of the eye to the wavelength of light.

hyperopia an eye condition in which the lens is too thin or the eyeball too "short" (in an anteroposterior dimension). The patient cannot focus distant objects on the retina without accommodation.

hypothalamic hyperphagia a syndrome of overeating, obesity, and ferocity that results from destruction of the ventromedial nucleus of the hypothalamus.

hypothalamus an area of the brain in the walls and floor of the third ventricle that controls reactions of the hypophysis and ANS and is sensitive to internal changes in the body (need state).

hypoxia a condition in which the tissues are not receiving enough oxygen from the lungs, the circulatory system, or both to sustain their metabolic activity. The condition usually results from insufficient oxygenation of the blood by the lungs.

Hz hertz.

impairment impaired function of a tissue, usually caused by the oxygen debt that accompanies fatigue.

inadequate stimulus an energy change that activates a receptor but is not the form of energy for which the receptor is specialized to respond.

incentive a reward. More technically, the external stimulus that changes the need condition and therefore reduces the need state, drive, and sensitizing stimulus in motivated behavior.

inclusions an approximate and inclusive term for the many specialized structures found in the cell's cytoplasm.

incus the ossicle that conducts sound vibrations from the malleus to the stages in the middle ear.

infantile autism a disorder of attention in young children that has the effect of making them mentally retarded.

inferior colliculi (sing. colliculus) a pair of auditory reflex centers found in the tectum (roof) of the midbrain.

inhibition prevention of a response. Use of the term ranges from nerve conduction at the synapse to observable behavior.

inner ear cochlea and the vestibular senses.

innervate to supply with nerve fibers or to stimulate excitation through those nerve fibers.

instinct a drive plus inherited patterns in the CNS that arouse behavior appropriate to that drive, such as nest-building behavior in the rat as a response to low temperatures.

intensity change in sensation that results from an increase in stimulation.

intention tremor trembling of a limb that occurs only when movement is attempted.

intermediary metabolism chemical reactions that go on outside the cells, supply the cells with glucose and oxygen, and eliminate carbon dioxide and waste.

internal environment chemical, physical, and other conditions inside the body, surrounding the individual cells.

interoceptors receptors located in the viscera that respond to physical events inside the body.

intrinsic included wholly within an organ.

introspection observation of conscious events and reporting on them.

iodopsin the photochemical visual pigment of the cones.

irritability excitability. See stimulus.

kinesthesis sensations of position and movement from the limbs, neck, and body trunk.

kinesthetic senses receptors in the joints, tendons, and muscles that give rise to sensations of limb and body position and movement.

Klüver-Bucy syndrome Docile, oral, undiscriminative, and hypersexed behavior in monkeys that results from bilateral removal of the temporal lobes of the brain.

labyrinth membranous sensory structures for both audition and proprioception in the inner ear.

lambda (λ) a term and symbol (from the Greek letter) used as a prefix to designate wavelengths, especially in light measurements.

lateral corticospinal tract a crossed motor tract of the lateral funiculus of the spinal cord. The tract originates in the motor projection area, and the axons terminate near the motoneurons of the cord.

lateral fissure the fissure between the temporal and parietal lobes of each cerebral hemisphere.

lateral geniculate body (LGN) the terminus of ganglion cell axons from the eye and the origin of fibers going to the visual projection area of the cerebral cortex.

lateral hypothalamic nuclei paired nuclei in the hypothalamus that appear to act as a feeding center.

lateral lemniscus the auditory pathway that ascends the brain stem to the medial geniculate body.

lateral spinothalamic tract fibers that originate in neuronal synapses and that carry pain and temperature input to the cord. They ascend the lateral funiculus of the cord and join the medial lemniscus to end the thalamus.

lateral ventricles ventricles of the cerebral hemispheres.

law of complements for each hue there is another hue that will mix with it to give gray, white, or black.

law of resultants mixed hues that match will mix without changing hue, irrespective of their components.

law of specific nerve energies the generalization that chemical and electrical characteristics of the nerve impulse do not depend on the receptor or nerve stimulated; all nerve impulses have the same general characteristics.

law of supplements noncomplementary hues mix to give an intermediate hue.

lens the crystalline structure behind the pupil of the eye that focuses light rays on the retina.

longitudinal fissure the fissure that divides the right and left cerebral hemispheres.

loudness sensation that results from changes in the intensity of sound.

macula patch of sensory tissue, including otoliths, hair cells, and gelatinous mass inside the sacs of the inner ear. The cells respond to linear acceleration and deceleration and to head position.

macula sacculi macula of the sacculus, which is one of the two structures containing a macula.

macula utricula macula of the utriculus, which is one of the two sensory structures containing a macula.

main sensory nucleus of fifth nerve nucleus of termination for the sensory fibers of cranial nerves serving pressure.

malleus one of a chain of three bones that conduct sound vibrations from the eardrum to the cochlea. The bony ossicle is connected to the tympanum, which conducts sound vibrations to the incus.

marijuana a nonaddicting depressant drug from the leaves of a common plant; it is usually smoked like tobacco.

mass action a principle that asserts that all parts of the cortex act as a whole in learning. See equipotentiality.

medial geniculate body a nucleus of the auditory nervous pathways; the terminus of the auditory fibers of the lateral lemniscus that relays excitation to the cortex.

medial lemniscus a tract of the brain stem serving the somesthetic senses of pressure, pain, and temperature. It terminates in the posteroventral nucleus of the thalamus, which relays excitation to the cerebral cortex.

medulla the posterior part of the hindbrain.

mesencephalic nucleus of fifth nerve the nucleus of termination for the sensory fibers of cranial nerves serving kinesthesis.

metabolism chemical reactions of life that change foodstuff into energy and waste.

microcephalic a feebleminded child born with an abnormally small head and brain.

microelectrode an electrode of 0.5 to 5 μm in diameter, usually made by stretching a heated glass tube until it breaks, leaving a fine point, and then filling it with a potassium chloride solution.

midbrain the middle of the three primitive enlargements of the developing brain in the embryo.

mitotic division normal cell reproduction by cell division or mitosis.

mixing olfactometer a device for mixing odorous vapors of known concentrations to test the sensations that result.

mongolism a type of hereditary feeblemindedness caused by an excess chromosome in the germinal material.

monochromatism complete hue-blindness.

monophasic having only one change of condition. In sleep, a cycle consisting of a single waking period and a single sleeping period each 24-hour day.

morphine a powerful, addicting, narcotic drug.

motive a drive plus a habit appropriate to that drive, such as hunger accompanied by learned behavior leading to satiation.

motoneuron a single nerve cell connecting the CNS with an effector.

motor nerve a bundle of independently conducting nerve fibers connecting the central nervous system with the effectors (muscles and glands).

motor projection areas those parts of the cerebral cortex where nerve pathways to the striated muscles originate.

motor unit a single motor, or efferent, neuron and the several striated muscle cells it innervates (excites to contraction).

muscle action potential polarization reversal of the muscle cell sarcolemma (membrane) that excites contraction of the cell.

muscular pertaining to the striated muscles.

myelin sheath a fatty covering of axons believed to be secreted by the neurolemma (Schwann cell) in the peripheral nervous system and by the glial cells in the CNS.

myopia an eye condition in which the lens is too thick or the eyeball too "long" in an anteroposterior dimension. The patient cannot focus the image of distant objects on the retina.

nanometer (nm) a billionth of a meter (10^{-9} meter).

nasal septum the cartilage, covered with mucous membrane, that divides the two nostrils and nasal passages from one another.

nasopharynx nasal passages, mouth, and upper throat.

need a change in the internal environment that disturbs homeostasis, the internal balance of condition necessary for survival.

need condition any state of affairs in the external environment that disturbs equilibrium in the internal environment.

need state the disturbance in the equilibrium of the internal environment caused by a need condition.

negative afterimage a visual sensation of opposite hue or brightness that follows prolonged visual sensation of a given hue or brightness.

negative aftersensation appearance of an opposite sensation after a continuous stimulus ceases to act. See negative afterimage.

neocerebellum in evolutionary terms, the newest part of the cerebellum, the cerebellar hemispheres, which are in two-way communication with the cerebral cortex.

neocortex the phylogenetically newest part of the cerebral cortex, including all but the cortex lining the fissure between the hemispheres, the cortex covering ventral parts of the hemispheres, and the hippocampus.

nerve deafness auditory defects resulting from damage to the hair cells or to the sensory nerve cells that innervate them.

nerve impulse action potential.

nerves bundles of independently conducting nerve fibers that make up the peripheral nervous system.

neurolemma (Schwann cell) a multinuclear supporting cell that covers axons of the peripheral nervous system and sometimes secretes a myelin sheath that covers the axon.

neuron a nerve cell.

neurosecretion a transmitter substance released by neurons at synapses and at junctions with muscle and gland cells.

neurosis persistent maladaptive behavior accompanied by reports of anxiety and psychosomatic symptoms.

nicotine a drug found in tobacco that is an SNS stimulant.

nodes of Ranvier regular interruptions in the myelin sheath covering an axon.

nodule a centrally located cerebellar structure that receives input from the vestibular senses. See flocculus.

noise sounds made up of aperiodic air pressure changes with many high-frequency components.

norepinephrine a hormone secreted by the adrenal medulla, whose affects mimic sympathetic nervous system arousal and cause peripheral vasoconstriction; also a transmitter substance at postganglionic endings of the SNS. See epinephrine.

nucleus the central body within a cell that contains the basic mechanisms for cell growth, repair, and reproduction; also a collection of nerve cells where many synapses are made.

occipital lobe the part of each cerebral hemisphere that is posterior to the parietal lobe; the most posterior lobe of the cerebral hemisphere.

ohm a unit of electrical resistance in a conductor. One volt of potential difference will result in 1 ampere of current if the resistance of the conductor is 1 ohm.

olfactory bulbs enlargements of the ends of the olfactory tracts on the base of the brain, where the olfactory neurons terminate.

olfactory cleft olfactory epithelium.

olfactory epithelium smell-sensitive area on the roof of the nasal passages to both sides of the nasal septum.

olfactory tracts extensions on the base of the brain formed by tracts that run between the olfactory bulbs and the prepiriform area.

olive an important nucleus of the auditory pathway in the medulla and an accessory nucleus to the cerebellum.

opium a variety of morphine that is smoked by addicts; an addicting drug.

optic chiasma the hemidecussation (half-crossing) of the ganglion cells from the retina of the eye in the diencephalon.

optic nerve the visual ganglion cell axons that run from the eyeball to the optic chiasma.

optic tract ganglion cell axons that run between the optic chiasma and the lateral geniculate bodies.

optomotor nuclei nuclei of the third, fourth, and sixth cranial nerves that regulate eye movements.

organ an organization of differently specialized cells (tissues) that are arranged in a cooperative way to perform a function; for example, the stomach is an organ of muscular, connective, glandular, and other tissue for digesting food.

organ of Corti auditory receptor structure of the inner ear that rests on the basilar membrane and transduces fluid movements in the cochlea of the inner ear into nerve impulses.

organic compounds a class of compounds made up of carbon atoms to which oxygen, hydrogen, nitrogen, or sulfur is chemically linked. Living organisms are made of organic compounds.

organic senses receptors in the viscera for pressure, cold, warmth, and pain.

ossicles the three bony levers in the middle ear that connect the tympanum with the oval window of the inner ear; the ossicles conduct sound vibrations from the tympanum to the oval window.

otoliths particles of calcium carbonate that are embedded in the gelatinous material of the macula.

outer ear pinna, tympanum, and external auditory meatus.

oval window the membrane-covered opening to the fluid-filled inner ear; sound vibrations are carried by the ossicles to the oval window, which communicates with the scala vestibuli.

ovaries female gonads or reproductive organs.

ovum female reproductive egg cell.

oxygen debt the amount of oxygen necessary to restore a tissue to equilibrium after its metabolic need for oxygen has exceeded the available supply.

paleocerebellum a phylogenetically older part of the cerebellum that consists of the anterior and posterior lobe, receives input from muscle spindles, and regulates postural extensor tone.

paleocortex allocortex.

paraplegic an individual whose spinal cord has been severed. Parts of the body below the separation are paralyzed and anesthetic as a result.

parasympathetic division a division of the autonomic nervous system (ANS); an efferent nerve supply that innervates the viscera and discretely stimulates digestive functions as well as forming part of certain reflexes of the smooth muscles.

parasympathetic ganglia collectors of cell bodies of the postganglionic PNS nerve fibers. The ganglia lie near the smooth muscles and glands, which the postganglionic fibers innervate.

parasympathetic nervous system (PNS) parasympathetic division.

parietal lobe that part of each cerebral hemisphere that lies between the occipital lobe and the central sulcus.

Parkinson's disease a disorder characterized by tremors at rest, muscle rigidity, and lack of facial expression, all caused by damage of the basal ganglia.

perilymph the fluid of the labyrinth that surrounds it. It is also contained in the scala vestibuli and scala tympani of the cochlea.

peripheral nervous system nerves that lie outside the brain and spinal cord and connect the latter with receptors and effectors.

peripheral somatic nervous system (PSNS) the peripheral nervous system, exclusive of the autonomic nervous system, that connects the CNS with receptors and striated muscles.

perseveration brain activity that follows practice, is the basis for immediate memory, and lays down the permanent memory trace (consolidation) in the two-phase hypothesis of learning and memory.

phase sequence a number of cell assemblies, repeatedly excited in order by a perceptual act, such as in successive viewing of the corners of a triangle.

phenylpyruvic oligophrenia an inability to metabolize an essential amino acid that results in feeble-mindedness.

physiological fatigue the oxygen debt incurred by muscles when they are exercised beyond the capacity of the body to supply them with oxygen.

physiological psychology study of the relationships between physiology and behavior.

physiological zero the range of skin temperatures at which neither warmth nor cold is sensed.

pinna the "ear"; the convoluted structure on each side of the head that channels the pressure waves of sound to the external auditory meatus.

pitch the single quality of hearing; the sensation that changes with changes in the frequency of a tone as in the musical scale.

planarian small primitive invertebrate with a nerve net nervous system and the ability to regenerate missing parts; used in experiments on the role of DNA and RNA in learning.

PNS parasympathetic division.

polarized condition a difference in voltage across a poor conductor, such as the difference in charge, positive to negative, on the outside and inside of the cell membrane.

polyphasic pertaining to many alterations between two states, usually refers to a sleep cycle consisting of several periods of sleep and several periods of wakefulness each day.

pons the ventral surface enlargement on the anterior part of the hindbrain formed by crossing tracts from higher parts of the brain en route to the cerebellum.

positive afterimage a visual sensation that continues after the stimulus initiating it ceases to act.

positive aftersensation continuance of a sensation after the stimulus initiating it ceases to act. See positive afterimage.

postcentral gyrus the gyrus of the cerebral cortex just posterior to the central sulcus.

posterior chamber the cavity of the eyeball that lies between the iris and the lens.

posteroventral nucleus a nucleus of the thalamus that receives input from somesthesia and projects this input to the cerebral cortex.

postganglionic refers to neurons of the ANS that run from ganglia that are outside the CNS to effectors.

postsynaptic inhibition direct inhibition such as occurs when Renshaw cells hyperpolarize a neuron.

precentral gyrus the gyrus of the cerebral cortex that lies just anterior to the central sulcus.

prefrontal lobe area of the cerebral hemispheres that is anterior to the premotor area.

prefrontal lobotomy severing of the fibers connecting the thalamus with the prefrontal areas of the cerebral cortex.

preganglionic pertaining to neurons of the ANS that run from the CNS to ganglia, where they synapse with postganglionic neurons going to the effectors.

premotor area area 6 of the cerebral cortex in the Brodmann system; the original of most cortical fibers participating in the extrapyramidal system regulation of background movements and the origin of fibers going to the cerebellum.

prepiriform area the projection area for smell located at the base of the brain; terminus of the olfactory tracts.

presynaptic inhibition direct inhibition by axoaxonic synapses that blocks effective excitation of presynaptic endings.

pretectal nuclei visual reflex centers of the diencephalon that regulate the iris and ciliary body.

primary qualities irreducible attributes of a sensory modality such as primary hues in vision or primary tastes; sensory qualities whose component sensations cannot be detected.

proprioceptors the general kinesthetic receptors of the joints and muscles and the special vestibular senses of the inner ear, both of which give rise to sensations of position and movement.

protanopia red-green hue blindness with a shortened visible spectrum at the red end.

protein a large organic compound that is primarily composed of amino acids; it is both an essential food and an essential part of the structure of cells.

PSNS peripheral somatic nervous system.

psychedelic drugs psychotomimetic drugs.

psychosomatic stress-induced malfunction of the organs of the body.

psychotic an individual who has unrealistic and illogical delusion, bizarre hallucinations, and disorganized behavior.

psychotomimetic drugs drugs that mimic the effect of psychosis by producing hallucinations and bizarre sensations.

pupil opening in the iris of the eye through which light enters.

pyramidal system fibers that run from the motor projection area to the level of the motoneurons and are carried in the pyramids of the brain and pyramidal tracts of the spinal cord.

pyramidal tract pyramidal system.

quality the attribute that distinguishes one sensory modality from another and that distinguishes sensation differences within a modality that are not caused by intensity, extent, or duration.

radial fibers smooth muscle fibers that radiate from an opening such as the pupil; their contraction increases the size of the opening.

receptors structures specialized for irritability in response to various forms of energy, such as light, heat, cold, sound, or mechanical deformation.

recessive in heredity, pertaining to a gene that will not determine a physical characteristic of the individual unless paired with another recessive gene for the same characteristic.

reciprocal innervation excitation arrangements in the CNS that inhibit an antagonist muscle when the paired agonist muscle contracts.

reflex preparation an animal whose brain or spinal cord has been severed to isolate a reflex for study from nerve impulses that originate above the level of the cut.

Reissner's membrane the membrane between the scala vestibuli and the scala media in the cochlea of the inner ear.

releasing stimulus an incentive, or a cue to an incentive, that releases behavior appropriate to an active drive such as hunger or thirst.

REM rapid eye movement.

renin a substance released by the kidney in thirst that converts angiotensinogen into a form that stimulates the hypothalamus to initiate drinking behavior and release vasopressin for an antidiuretic effect on the kidney.

Renshaw cells short Golgi type II neurons that release GABA at synapses to hyperpolarize and thereby inhibit other neurons.

reproduction the production of two cells from one in cell mitosis or the production of a new cell by the joining of egg and sperm cells to form a multicellular organism.

resonance the tendency of an object to vibrate at a characteristic frequency. In a complex instrument of several parts, this produces overtones as well as a fundamental frequency.

resonate resonance.

resting potential the difference in charge, positive to negative, across the membranes of cells when they are not stimulated.

retina an extension of the brain that contains the visual receptors found in the posterior part of the fundus of the eyeball.

retroactive inhibition forgetting of an event because of the occurrence of an intervening event.

rheumatic fever inflammation of joints caused by bacteria that sometimes destroy tissue in the brain and spinal cord.

rhinencephalon hippocampus, amygdala, cingulate gyrus, and piriform area; brain structures once believed to be integrating centers for smell.

rhodopsin photochemical visual pigment of the rods that is chemically changed by light to stimulate optic nerve impulses.

RNA ribonucleic acid. A molecule that participated in cell metabolism in a fashion determined by the DNA molecule.

rods low-threshold achromatic visual receptors containing rhodopsin, found in the periphery of the retina; night vision receptors.

round window the membrane-covered window that relieves the pressure changes of cochlear fluid caused by sound vibrations.

sacculus a sensory apparatus of the inner ear that responds to head position and linear acceleration. See utriculus.

sacs sacculus and utriculus.

satiation center satiety center.

satiety center a center in the hypothalamus, probably the ventromedial nucleus, whose stimulation by the internal changes that result from feeding stops eating behavior.

saturated pertaining to colors that contain maximum hue (contain little gray).

scala media the middle chamber of the cochlea that lies between the scala vestibuli and scala tympani and contains the organ of Corti.

scala tympani the fluid-filled lower chamber of the cochlea that receives sound vibration from the scala media through the basilar membrane; pressure changes are relieved by the round window.

scala vestibuli the fluid-filled upper chamber of the cochlea that receives vibrations from the oval window through the ossicles.

sclera sclerotic coat.

sclerotic coat tough opaque white outer fibrous tissue that forms the white of the eyeball.

second harmonic first overtone.

secondary qualities mixtures of primary qualities within a sensory modality to produce a different sensation, such as, in vision, the mixture of red and yellow for an orange sensation.

secondary sexual characteristics the physical changes that occur at puberty in body characteristics (pubic hair, breast development, voice changes, etc.).

second-order neuron the neuron that runs from the first-order neuron (sensory neuron) to a subcortical center such as the thalamus.

secretion ability of a cell to manufacture a needed substance and supply it to the cell itself or to other cells; especially developed in endocrine glands and exocrine glands.

semicircular canals the three semicircular membranous structures of the nonauditory labyrinth of each inner ear; a sensory apparatus for detecting rotary movements of the head.

sensitizing stimulus any aspect of a need state that arouses a drive in the CNS.

sensory appropriation alteration of a cell into a specialized receptor cell because of its invasion by a sensory nerve fiber.

sensory deprivation severe reduction in sensory input by experimental techniques.

sensory nerve a bundle of independently conducting nerve fibers connecting receptors with the central nervous system.

sensory neuron a single nerve cell connecting a receptor with the CNS.

sham rage violent but brief attack responses in decor-ticate animals that are caused by the release of hypothalamic rage centers from cortical inhibition.

shaping the rewarding of increasingly accurate approximation to the desired response in an operant conditioning situation. Escape from punishment can be used in a similar manner.

simple tone a tone whose pressure variations can be graphed as a sine wave.

simultaneous contrast increase in the perceived intensity of a sensation of one quality caused by the simultaneous stimulation of another quality.

sine wave a function, similar to a horizontal S, that describes periodic phenomena such as the air pressure changes produced by a simple tone.

smooth muscle the muscle that lines the walls of all hollow viscera (except the heart), the arteries, intestines, stomach, and so on.

Snellen's test a test of visual acuity that determines the subject's ability to read letters of diminishing size at a distance of 20 feet.

SNS sympathetic division.

somatic muscle striated muscle.

somesthetic projection area area of the cerebral cortex that is the terminus of the nerve pathways for skin sensations.

spastic spastic paralysis.

spastic paralysis loss of motor control accompanied by exaggerated extensor tone; usually caused by damage to the extrapyramidal system.

special senses receptors found only in the head.

specific thalamic projection system (STPS) classical and anatomically distinct sensory pathways for vision, hearing, and somesthesia.

sperm male reproductive cells.

spike potential explosive polarization reversal that carries the nerve impulse down the axon of the nerve cell.

spinal cord ovoid mass of soft nervous and supporting tissue contained within the vertebral canal.

spinal nerves nerves that originate in the spinal cord.

spinal nucleus of fifth nerve the nucleus of termination for sensory fibers of the cranial nerves serving temperature and pain.

spinal shock a syndrome (set of symptoms) that ensues when the spinal cord is severed; for example, all muscles receiving innervation from below the lesion lose tone and become flaccid because of lack of excitation from higher centers.

spinocerebellar tracts tracts that run from the spinal cord to the cerebellum.

spiral osseous lamina a bony shelf in the cochlea of the inner ear that forms part of the division between the scala media and scala tympani.

stapedius a muscle that pulls on the stapes, limiting the response of the middle ear bones to loud sounds in a reflex that prevents damage to the auditory apparatus.

stapes the ossicle of the chain of middle ear bones that conducts sound vibrations from the incus to the oval window.

statoacoustic nerve the cranial nerve serving the organ of Corti and the vestibular senses for hearing and balance respectively.

stereochemical theory a theory about the effects of molecular shape; in olfaction, the theory that primary odor qualities depend on the shape or charge of the odorous molecules.

stimulation activation of sense organs or nervous tissue by any form of physical energy—mechanical, chemical, acoustical, photic, or electrical.

stimulus any physical energy change that activates a receptor.

stress any stimulus, internal or external, that disturbs the dynamic equilibrium of the systems of the body.

stress syndrome sequence of events that follows application of severe stress to an organism.

stress tolerance individual ability to withstand stress without disability.

stressor a stimulus that causes stress.

stretch reflex reflex contraction of a muscle to stretch of that muscle; a monosynaptic reflex.

striated muscles muscles that move the body and limbs.

successive contrast increase in the perceived intensity of a quality caused by the prior stimulation of an opposite quality, such as increased sensitivity to a red hue after prolonged exposure to greeen.

sulcus (pl. sulci) surface folds that are found in the cerebral cortex.

superior colliculi (sing. colliculus) a pair of visual reflex centers found in the tectum (roof) of the midbrain.

suspensory ligament the structure that attaches the ciliary body to the lens in the eye.

sympathetic chain ganglia interconnected ganglia that lie on the bony vertebral column and receive excitation from the spinal nerves, send excitation to the viscera, and form part of the sympathetic division of the ANS.

sympathetic division a division of the autonomic nervous system (ANS) that innervates the viscera and diffusely prepares it for vigorous body arousal in emotional states.

sympathetic nervous system (SNS) sympathetic division.

synapse where the terminal arborization of one neuron meets the dendrites and cell body of another to transfer excitation from one nerve cell to another.

synaptic vesicles small globules in the synaptic knobs of axon filaments at synapses; they are believed to release a chemical transmitter in synaptic condition of excitation between nerve cells.

system a number of organs, anatomically and functionally arranged for the performance of generalized function, such as the organs of the digestive system—stomach, intestines, and so on.

target tissue similarly specialized cells that are affected in a specific way by hormones of the endocrine glands.

taste bud a "moat and island" structure on the tongue that contains receptor cells for taste.

tectorial membrane the overlying membrane in which the hair cell endings of the organ of Corti are embedded.

temporal lobe the part of each cerebral hemisphere that lies below the lateral fissure.

tendon jerk a rapid muscle contraction (caused by the stretch reflex response) in response to a blow to the muscle's tendon.

tensor tympani a muscle that pulls on the malleus to tighten the tympanum in a protective reflex that limits the response of the middle ear bones to loud sounds.

terminal threshold the intensity of receptor stimulation in which the increase of stimulus intensity results in a change in sensation only 50% of the time; a statistical measure of the maximum response of a receptor, or sense organ.

testes male gonads that produce reproductive cells and sex hormones.

thalamus a pair of egg-shaped masses of nuclei on the walls of the diencephalon; an integrating center that relays excitation to the sensory projection areas of the cerebral cortex.

third ventricle ventricle of the diencephalon.

third-order neuron any neuron that runs from subcortical centers such as the thalamus to a sensory projection area, usually in the cortex.

threshold the least change in physical energy that will on the average affect the response of a receptor. Without a modifier, it usually refers to the absolute threshold.

timbre (pronounced tam'ber) complex of overtones in a complex tone that enables the listener to recognize the source, such as the difference between a trumpet and a violin playing the same fundamental tone.

tissue a collection of cells specialized for a common function, such as nervous tissue or muscle tissue.

tonotopic tonotopic organization.

tonotopic organization the organization of various nuclei of the auditory pathway; points along the length of the organ of Corti respond to tones of different pitch and are spatially represented in an organized way.

topographical organization in neuroanatomy, an arrangement whereby stimulus inputs from different parts of the body arrive at corresponding points in brain centers, such as the cerebral cortex.

tract a bundle of axons carrying excitation from one part of the CNS to another.

tractus solitarius a tract of the brain stem that carries first-order neurons from the receptors serving taste.

transitional cortex areas of the cerebral cortex in the longitudinal fissure and elsewhere that are phylogenetically younger than allocortex but older than neocortex.

transmission deafness defects in hearing caused by failure of the middle ear bones to accurately conduct to the cochlea the vibrations of the eardrum in response to sound.

tritanopia an absence of perception of yellow and green hues.

trophotropic pertaining to functions having to do with digestion, satiation, cell maintenance, and so on, controlled largely by the PNS centers of the hypothalamus.

turbinate bones baffle-shaped formations in the nasal passages that cause eddy currents in inspired air.

two-phase hypothesis the hypothesis that learning occurs in two stages, such that immediate memory depends on perseveration of neural activity that lays down a permanent engram (consolidation).

two-point threshold the closest together two points may be placed on the skin and still be distinguished by a subject as separate; used as an indicator of receptor density in the skin when sensitivity to pressure is being tested.

tympanum the eardrum; the membrane that closes off the inner end of the external auditory meatus and vibrates in response to the air pressure variations of sound.

unique color one whose components cannot be visually detected (red, green, yellow, blue, black, white, or gray).

utriculus a sensory apparatus of the inner ear that responds to head position and linear acceleration. See sacculus.

ventral in humans, toward the front, or "belly" side.

ventral cochlear nucleus one of two sensory nuclei of the acoustic branch of the statoacoustic nerve. See dorsal cochlear nucleus.

ventral corticospinal tract a tract of the ventral funiculus of the spinal cord that originates in the motor projection area and terminates near the motoneurons of the cord.

ventral spinothalamic tract fibers that originate in the spinal cord form synapses with sensory fibers serving pressure, ascend the cord in the ventral funiculus, and join the medial lemniscus to end in the thalamus.

ventricle a large hollow area inside the brain.

ventromedial nucleus a pair of nuclei in the hypothalamus that acts as satiety centers to reduce eating behavior; destruction of these nuclei results in hypothalamic hyperphagia.

vestibulospinal tract a tract of the spinal cord that originates in the vestibular nuclei and ends on the extensor motoneurons of the cord.

viscera stomach, intestines, heart, bladder, arteries, and so on; the internal organs.

visceral pertaining to the viscera.

visceral muscles muscles that line the walls of the viscera.

visible spectrum light; the visible part of the electromagnetic spectrum composed of seven colors.

vision stimulation of the eye by light.

visual angle the angle subtended by the eye by light rays coming from an object.

visual projection area area of the cerebral cortex that is the terminus of the nerve pathways for vision.

vitreous humor the jellylike substance that fills the fundus of the eyeball.

volley principle a statement that the frequency of auditory nerve impulses follows the frequency of sound waves by means of nerve cells firing in alternation.

volt amount of electrical charge (potential difference) that will result in a current of 1 ampere passing through a conductor with a resistance of 1 ohm.

wakefulness of choice the wakefulness of a monophasic sleep cycle that results from conditioning; a single waking period each day.

wakefulness of necessity wakefulness resulting from bodily need or discomfort.

wavelength the measured length of a complete cycle of change in a periodic (repeated) phenomenon, such as the wavelength of the pressure variation of a tone or of the electromagnetic spectrum of a given light frequency.

work decrement reduction in work output.

References

References are given by chapter heading to original sources or to secondary sources in which references to the original literature may be found. Such references include review articles, individually authored chapters in edited books, and books useful only in narrow areas of physiological psychology. Originally articles appear when they are of particular importance or are not mentioned in secondary sources.

GENERAL REFERENCE

Leukel, F.: Introduction to physiological psychology, ed. 3, St. Louis, 1976, The C. V. Mosby Co.

Chapter 1

Bures, J., Petrán, M., and Zachar, J.: Electrophysiological methods in biological research, ed. 3, New York, 1967, Academic Press, Inc.

Sidowski, J. B.: Experimental methods and instrumentation in psychology, New York, 1956, McGraw-Hill Book Company.

Suckling, E. E.: Bioelectricity, New York, 1961, McGraw-Hill Book Company.

Chapter 2

Barrai, I.: Human genetics and public health, WHO Chron. **24:**1-7, 1968.

Claude, A.: The coming of age of the cell, Science **189:**433-435, 1975.

Diassi, P. A., and Horwitz, Z. P.: Endocrine hormones, Annu. Rev. Pharmacol. **10:**219-236, 1970.

Ling, G. N.: A new model for the living cell: a summary of the theory and recent experimental evidence in its support, Int. Rev. Cytol. **26:**1-61, 1969.

Martini, L.: Action of hormones on the central nervous system, Gen. Comp. Endocrinol. (suppl. 2), pp. 214-226, 1969.

Oppenheimer, J. M.: Cells and organizers, Am. Zool. **10:**75-88, 1970.

Phillips, A. P.: Unwinding models for double-helical DNA during its replication and transcription, J. Theor. Biol. **24:**273-278, 1969.

Sinsheimer, R. L.: The prospect for designed genetic change, Am. Sci. **57:**134-142, 1969.

Temin, H.: The DNA provirus hypothesis, Science **192:**1075-1080, 1976.

Tomkins, G.: The metabolic code, Science **189:**760-763, 1975.

Turner, C. D., and Bagnara, J. T.: General endocrinology, ed. 5, Philadelphia, 1971, W. B. Saunders Company.

Chapter 3

Brazier, M. A.: The growth of concepts relating to brain mechanisms, J. Hist. Behav. Sci. **1:**218-234, 1965.

Brazier, M. A.: The electrical activity of the nervous system, ed. 2, London, 1960, Pitman Medical Publishing Co., Ltd.

Cook, W. A., and Cangiano, A.: Presynaptic inhibition of spinal motoneurons, Brain Res. **24:**521-524, 1970.

Curtis, B. A., Jacobson, S., and Marcus, E. M.: An introduction to the neurosciences, Philadelphia, 1972, W. B. Saunders Company.

Eccles, J. C.: Neuron physiology: introduction. In Field, J., editor: Handbook of physiology, vol. 1, Baltimore, 1960, The Williams & Wilkins Company.

Eccles, J. C.: Ionic mechanism of postsynaptic inhibition, Science **145:**1140-1147, 1964.

Eccles, J. C.: The physiology of synapses, New York, 1964, Academic Press, Inc.

Hochwald, G. M., Wallenstein, M. C., and Mathews, E. S.: Exchange of proteins between blood and spinal subarachnoid fluid, Am. J. Physiol. **217:**348-353, 1969.

Hodgkin, A. L.: The ionic basis of nervous conduction, Science **145:**1148-1154, 1964.

Hodgkin, A. L.: The conduction of the nervous impulse, Springfield, Ill., 1964, Charles C Thomas, Publisher.

Isaacson, R. L.: The limbic system, New York, 1974, Plenum Press.

Katz, B.: Quantal mechanism of neutral transmitter release, Science **173:**123-126, 1971.

Levin, E., and Scicli, G.: Brain barrier phenomena, Brain Res. **13:**1-12, March 1969.

Lindsley, D. B.: Attention, consciousness, sleep and wakefulness. In Field, J., editor: Handbook of physiology, vol. 3, Baltimore, 1960, The Williams & Wilkins Company.

McCleary, R. A., and Moore, R. Y.: Subcortical mechanisms of behavior, New York, 1965, Basic Books, Inc., Publishers.

McLennan, H.: Synaptic transmission, ed. 2, Philadelphia, 1970, W. B. Saunders Company.

Magoun, H. W.: The waking brain, ed. 2, Springfield, Ill., 1963, Charles C Thomas, Publisher.

Papez, J. W.: Comparative neurology, New York, 1929, Hafner Publishing Co.

Patton, H. D.: Spinal reflexes and synaptic transmission. In Ruch, T. C., Patton, H. D., Woodbury, J. W., and Towe, A. L., editors: Neurophysiology, ed. 2, Philadelphia, 1965, W. B. Saunders Company.

Quarton, G. C., Melnechuk, T., and Schmitt, F. O., editors: The neurosciences: a study program, New York, 1967, Rockefeller University Press.

Roberts, E. D., Salganikoff, L., Zeiher, L. M., and Araiz, G. R.: Acetylcholine and cholinacetylase content of synaptic vesicles, Science **140:**300-301, 1963.

Roberts, E. D.: Molecular biology of synaptic receptors, Science **171:**963-971, 1971.

Schmitt, F. O., editor: The neurosciences: second study program, New York, 1970, Rockefeller University Press.

Stevens, C. F.: Neurophysiology: a primer, New York, 1966, John Wiley & Sons, Inc.

Suckling, E. E.: Bioelectricity, New York, 1961, McGraw-Hill Book Company.

von Bonin, G.: Essay on the cerebral cortex, Springfield, Ill., 1950, Charles C Thomas, Publisher.

Chapter 4

Coyle, J. T., and Snyder, S. H.: Antiparkinsonian drugs: inhibition of dopamine uptake in the corpus striatum as a possible mechanism of action, Science **166:**899-901, 1969.

Eccles, J. C.: The development of the cerebellum in relation to the control of movement, Naturwissenschaften **56:**525-534, 1969.

Fuxe, K., Goldstein, M., and Ljungdahl, A.: Antiparkinsonian drugs and central dopamine neurons, Life Sci. **9:**811-824, 1970.

Gottlieb, G. L., Agarwal, G. C., and Stark, L.: Interaction between voluntary and postural mechanisms of the human motor system, J. Neurophysiol. **33:**365-381, 1970.

Grillner, S., Hongo, T., and Lund, S.: Descending monosynaptic and reflex control of gamma motoneurons, Acta Physiol. Scand. **75:**592-613, 1969.

Huxley, H. E.: The mechanism of muscular contraction, Science **164:**1356-1366, 1969.

Katz, B.: Quantal mechanism of neutral transmitter release, Science **173:**123-126, 1971.

Krieg, W. J. S.: Functional neuroanatomy, ed. 2, New York, 1953, Blackiston Co.

Lawrence, D. G., and Henricus, D. G.: Pyramidal and nonpyramidal pathways in monkeys: anatomical and functional correlation, Science **148:**973-975, 1965.

Patton, H. D.: Spinal reflexes and synaptic transmission. In Ruch, T. C., Patton, H. D., Woodbury, J. W., and Towe, A. L., editors: Neurophysiology, ed. 2, Philadelphia, 1965, W. B. Saunders Company.

Patton, H. D.: Reflex regulation of movement and posture. In Ruch, T. C., Patton, H. D., Woodbury, J. W., and Towe, A. L., editors: Neurophysiology, ed. 2, Philadelphia, 1965, W. B. Saunders Company.

Ruch, T. C.: Basal ganglia and cerebellum. In Ruch, T. C., Patton, H. D., Woodbury, J. W., and Towe, A. L., editors: Neurophysiology, ed. 2, Philadelphia, 1965, W. B. Saunders Company.

Ruch, T. C.: The cerebral cortex: its structure and motor functions. In Ruch, T. C., Patton, H. D., Woodbury, J. W., and Towe, A. L., editors: Neurophysiology, ed. 2, Philadelphia, 1965, W. B. Saunders Company.

Ruch, T. C.: Pontobulbar control of posture and orientation in space. In Ruch, T. C., Patton, H. D., Woodbury, J. W., and Towe, A. L., editors: Neurophysiology, ed. 2, Philadelphia, 1965, W. B. Saunders Company.

Woodbury, W. J., and Ruch, T. C.: Muscle. In Ruch, T. C., Patton, H. D., Woodbury, J. W., and Towe, A. L., editors: Neurophysiology, ed. 2, Philadelphia, 1965, W. B. Saunders Company.

Chapter 5

Broadbent, D. E.: Information processing in the nervous system, Science **150:**457-462, 1965.

Held, R., and Freedman, S. J.: Plasticity in human sensorimotor control, Science **142:**455-462, 1963.

Johnson, L. C.: Psychophysiological research: aims and methods, Int. J. Psychiatr. **5:**565-573, 1974.

Nihm, S. D.: Polynomial law sensation, Am. Psychol. **31:**808-809, 1976.

Stevens, S. S.: Mathematics, measurement, and psychophysics. In Stevens, S. S., editor: Handbook of experimental psychology, New York, 1951, John Wiley & Sons, Inc.

Stevens, S. S.: Neural events and the psychophysical law, Science **170:**1043-1050, 1970.

Stevens, S. S.: The surprising simplicity of sensory metrics, Am. Psychol. **17:**29-39, 1962.

von Békésy, G.: Similarities of inhibition in the different sense organs, Am. Psychol. **24:**707-719, 1969.

von Békésy, G.: Inhibition as an important part of sensory perception, Laryngoscope **69:**1366-1386, 1969.

Woodworth, R. S., and Schlosberg, H.: Experimental

psychology, rev. ed., New York, 1954, Henry Holt & Co., Inc.

Chapter 6

Able-Fessard, D.: Organization of central somatic projections. In Neff, W. D., editor: Contributions to sensory physiology, vol. 2, New York, 1967, Academic Press, Inc.

Akil, H., Mayer, D. J., and Liebskind, J. C.: Antagonism of stimulation—produced analgesia by naloxone, a narcotic antagonist, Science **191:**961-962, 1976.

Barber, T. H.: Toward a theory of pain, Psychol. Bull. **56:**430-460, 1959.

Becker, D. P., Gluck, H., Nelsen, F. E., and Jane, J. A.: An inquiry into the neurophysiological basis for pain, J. Neurosurg. **30:**1-13, Jan. 1969.

Corkin, S., Milner, B., and Rasmussen, T.: Somatosensory thresholds, Arch. Neurol. **23:**41-58, 1970.

Dubuisson, D., and Melzack, R.: Classification of clinical pain descriptions by multiple-group discriminant analysis, Exp. Neurol. **51:**480-487, 1976.

Fox, E., and Melzack, R.: Transcutanious electrical stimulation and acupuncture: comparison of treatment for low back pain, Pain **2:**141-148, 1976.

Geldard, F. A.: Cutaneous channels of communication. In Rosenblith, W. A., editor: Symposium on principles of sensory communication, Cambridge, Mass., 1961, The Technology Press of the Massachusetts Institute of Technology.

Harrington, T., and Marzenich, M. M.: Neural coding in the sense of touch: human sensations of skin indentation compared with the responses of slowly adapting mechano-receptive afferents innervating the hairy skin of monkeys, Brain Res. **10:**251-264, 1970.

Kane, K., and Taub, A.: A history of local electrical analgesia, Pain **1:**125-136, 1975.

Lim, R. S.: Pain mechanisms, Anesthesiology **28:**106-111, 1967.

Lindbom, U., and Meyerson, B. A.: Influence on touch, vibrations and cutaneous pain of dorsal column stimulation in man, Pain **1:**257-270, 1975.

Long, D. M., and Hagfors, N.: Electrical stimulation in the nervous system: the current status of electrical stimulation of the nervous system for relief of pain, Pain **1:**109-123, 1975.

Mayer, D. L., and Liebskind, J. C.: Pain reduction by focal electrical stimulation of the brain: an anatomical and behavioral analysis, Brain Res. **68:**73-93, 1974.

Manfredi, M.: Modulation of sensory projections in anterolateral column of cat spinal cord by peripheral afferents of different size, Arch. Ital. Biol. **108:**72-105, 1970.

Mellon, D.: The physiology of sense organs, San Francisco, 1968, W. H. Freeman & Co., Publishers.

Melzack, R.: Effects of early experience on behavior: experimental and conceptual considerations. In

Psychopathology of perception, New York, 1965, Grune & Stratton, Inc.

Melzack, R.: Prolonged relief of pain by brief, intense transcutaneous stimulation, Pain **1:**357-373, 1975.

Melzack, R.: The Brompton mixture: effects on pain in cancer patients, CMA Journal **115:**125-129, 1976.

Melzack, R.: The McGill pain questionnaire: major properties and scoring methods, Pain **1:**277-299, 1975.

Melzack, R., and Schecter, B.: Itch and vibration, Science **147:**1047-1048, 1965.

Melzack, R., and Wall, P.: Pain mechanism: a new theory, Science **150:**971-979, 1965.

Mountcastle, V. B.: Physiology of sensory receptors: introduction to sensory processes. In Mountcastle, V. B., editor: Medical physiology, ed. 13, St. Louis, 1974, The C. V. Mosby Co.

Mountcastle, V. B., and Darian-Smith, I.: Neural mechanisms in somesthesia. In Mountcastle, V. B., editor: Medical physiology, ed. 13, St. Louis, 1974, The C. V. Mosby Co.

Price D. D., and Wagman, I. H.: Physiological roles of A and C fiber inputs to the spinal dorsal horn of *Macaca mulatta*, Exp. Neurol. **29:**383-399, 1970.

Rose, J. E., and Mountcastle, V. B.: Touch and kinesthesis. In Field, J., editor: Handbook of physiology, vol. 1, Baltimore, 1960, The Williams & Wilkins Co.

Ruch, T. C.: Neural basis of somatic sensation. In Ruch, T. C., Patton, H. D., Woodbury, J. W., and Towe, A. L., editors: Neurophysiology, ed. 2, Philadelphia, 1965, W. B. Saunders Company.

Rushmer, R. F., Buettner, K. J., Short, J. M., and Odland, G. F.: The skin, Science **154:**343-348, 1966.

Simmel, M. L., and Shapiro, A.: The localization of nontactile thermal sensations, Psychophysiology **5:**415-425, 1969.

Sternbach, R. A.: Pain: a psychophysiological analysis, New York, 1968, Academic Press, Inc.

Straile, W. E.: Vertical cutaneous organization, J. Theor. Biol. **24:**203-215, 1969.

Sweet, W. H.: Pain. In Field, J., editor: Handbook of physiology, vol. 1, Baltimore, 1960, The Williams & Wilkins Co.

Wall, P. D., and Sweet, W. H.: Temporary abolition of pain in man, Science **155:**108-109, 1967.

Zotterman, Y.: Thermal sensations. In Field, J., editor: Handbook of physiology, vol. 1, Baltimore, 1960, The Williams & Wilkins Co.

Chapter 7

Bard, P.: Postural coordination and locomotion and their central control. In Mountcastle, V. B., editor: Medical physiology, ed. 13, St. Louis, 1974, The C. V. Mosby Co.

Curtis, B.: Vestibular and auditory systems. In Curtis, B., Jacobson, S., and Marcus, E., editors: An introduction to the neurosciences, Philadelphia, 1972, W. B. Saunders Company.

Gernandt, B. E.: Vestibular mechanisms. In Field, J.,

editor: Handbook of physiology, vol. 1, Baltimore, 1960, The Williams & Wilkins Co.

Gottlieb, G. L., and Agarwal, G. C.: The role of the myotatic reflex in the voluntary control of movements, Brain Res. **40:**139-143, 1972.

Grillner, S., Hongo, T., and Lund, S.: Descending monosynaptic and reflex control of gamma motoneurons, Acta Physiol. Scand. **75:**592-613, 1969.

Guedry, F. E.: Psychophysiological studies of vestibular function. In Neff, W. D.: Contributions to sensory physiology, vol. 1, New York, 1965, Academic Press, Inc.

Henneman, E.: Peripheral mechanisms involved in the control of muscles. In Mountcastle, V. B., editor: Medical physiology, ed. 13, St. Louis, 1974, The C. V. Mosby Co.

Ruch, T. C.: Pontobulbar control of posture and orientation in space. In Ruch, T. C., Patton, H. D., Woodbury, J. W., and Towe, A. L., editors: Neurophysiology, Philadelphia, 1965, W. B. Saunders Company.

Wersall, J., and Flock, A.: Functional anatomy of the vestibular and lateral line organs. In Neff, W. D., editor: Contributions to sensory physiology, vol. 1, New York, 1965, Academic Press, Inc.

Chapter 8

Adey, W. R.: The sense of smell. In Field, J., editor: Handbook of physiology, vol. 1, Baltimore, 1960, The Williams & Wilkins Co.

Amoore, J. E.: Current status of the stereochemical theory of odor, Ann. N. Y. Acad. Sci. **116:**457-476, 1964.

de Lorenzo, A. J. D.: The chemical senses: taste and olfaction. In Mountcastle, V. B., editor: Medical physiology, ed. 13, St. Louis, 1974, The C. V. Mosby Co.

Doetsch, G. S., and Erickson, R. P.: Synaptic processing of taste-quality information in the nucleus tractus solitarius of the rat, J. Neurophysiol. **33:**490-507, 1970.

Frank, M., and Pfaffman, C.: Taste nerve fibers: a random distribution of sensitivities to four tastes, Science **164:**1183-1185, 1969.

Gorman, W.: Flavor, taste, and the psychology of smell, Springfield, Ill., 1964, Charles C Thomas, Publisher.

Moncreiff, R. W.: The chemical senses, Cleveland, 1967, Chemical Rubber Co.

Mozell, M. M.: Evidence for a chromatographic model of olfaction, J. Gen. Physiol. **55:**46-73, 1970.

Patton, H. D.: Taste, olfaction, and visceral sensation. In Ruch, T. C., Patton, H. D., Woodbury, J. W., and Towe, A. L., editors: Neurophysiology, ed. 2, Philadelphia, 1975, W. B. Saunders Company.

Pfaffman, C.: DeGustibus, Am. Psychol. **20:**21-33, 1965.

Sato, M.: Gustatory response as a temperature-dependent process. In Neff, W. D., editor: Contributions to sensory physiology, vol. 2, New York, 1967, Academic Press, Inc.

Tucker, D., and Smith, J. C.: The chemical senses, Annu. Rev. Psychol. **20:**129-158, 1969.

Wang, M. B., and Bernard, R. A.: Adaptation of neural taste responses in cat, Brain Res. **20:**277-282, 1970.

Chapter 9

Ades, H. W.: Central auditory mechanisms. In Field, J., editor: Handbook of physiology, vol. 1, Baltimore, 1960, The Williams & Wilkins Co.

Cassady, J. H., and Neff, W. D.: Localization of pure tones, J. Acoust. Soc. Am. **54:**365-372, 1973.

Clopton, B. M., Winfield, J. A., and Flammio, F. J.: Tonotopic organization: review and analysis, Brain Res. **24:**1-20, 1974.

Davis, H.: Excitation of auditory receptors. In Field, J., editor: Handbook of physiology, vol. 1, Baltimore, 1960, The Williams & Wilkins Co.

Davis, H., and Silverman, S. R., editors: Hearing and deafness, rev. ed., New York, 1962, Holt, Rinehart & Winston, Inc.

Eldredge, D. E., and Miller, J. D.: Physiology of hearing, Annu. Rev. Physiol. **33:**281-310, 1971.

Goldstein, M. H.: The auditory periphery. In Mountcastle, V. B., editor: Medical physiology, ed. 13, St. Louis, 1974, The C. V. Mosby Co.

Green, D. M.: Audition, Annu. Rev. Psychol. **20:**105-128, 1969.

Harris, J. D., editor: Forty germinal papers in human hearing, J. Aud. Res., 1969.

Harrison, J. M., and Irving, R.: Visual and nonvisual auditory systems in mammals, Science **154:**738-743, 1966.

Jeffers, L. A.: Detection and lateralization of binaural signals, Audiology **10:**77-84, 1971.

Lipscomb, D. M.: The increase in prevalence of high-frequency hearing impairment among college students, Audiology **11:**231-237, 1972.

Marsh, J. T., Wordon, F. G., and Smith, J. C.: Auditory frequency-following response: neural or artifact? Science **169:**1222-1223, 1970.

Mountcastle, V. B.: Central neural mechanisms in hearing. In Mountcastle, V. B., editor: Medical physiology, ed. 13, St. Louis, 1974, The C. V. Mosby Co.

Plomp, R.: Auditory psychophysics. In Rosenzweig, M. R., and Porter, L. W.: Am. Rev. Psychol. **26:**233-262, 1975.

Rose, J. E., Brugge, J. F., Anderson, D. J., and Hind, J. E.: Phase-locked response to low-frequency tones in single auditory nerve fibers of the squirrel monkey, J. Neurophysiol. **30:**769-793, 1967.

Towe, A. L.: Audition and the auditory receptors. In Ruch, T. C., Patton, H. D., Woodbury, J. W., and Towe, A. L., editors: Neurophysiology, ed. 2, Philadelphia, 1965, W. B. Saunders Company.

von Békésy, G.: Traveling waves as frequency analyzers in the cochlea, Nature **225:**1207-1209, 1970.

Chapter 10

Arden, G. B.: Receptor potentials, Br. Med. Bull. **26:**125-129, May 1970.

Bartley, S. H.: Central mechanisms of vision. In Field, J., editor: Handbook of physiology, vol. 1, Baltimore, 1960, The Williams & Wilkins Co.

Bishop, P. O., and Henry, G. H.: Striate neurons: receptive field concepts, Invest. Ophthalmol. **11:**346-354, 1972.

Brown, K. T.: Physiology of the retina. In Mountcastle, V. B., editor: Medical physiology, ed. 13, St. Louis, 1974, The C. V. Mosby Co.

Brown, P. K., and Wald, G.: Visual pigments in single rods and cones of the human retina, Science **155:**273-279, 1967.

Chapanis, A.: Color names for color space, Am. Sci. **53:**327-346, 1965.

DeValois, R. L.: Behavioral and electrophysiological studies of primate vision. In Neff, W. D.: Contributions to sensory physiology, vol. 1, New York, 1965, Academic Press, Inc.

DeValois, R. L.: Processing of intensity and wavelength information by the visual system, Invest. Ophthalmol. **11:**417-427, 1972.

Dimmik, F. L.: Color specification based on just noticeable differences of hue, Vision Res. **5:**679-694, 1965.

Dowling, J. E.: The site of visual adaptation, Science **155:**273-279, 1967.

Fatehchand, R., Laufer, M., and Svaetichin, G.: Retinal receptor potentials and their linear relationship to light intensity. Science **137:**666-667, 1962.

Fisher, K. D., Carr, J. E., and Huber, T. E.: Dark adaptation and night vision, Fed. Proc. **29:**1605-1638, 1970.

Glickstein, M.: Organization of the visual pathways, Science **164:**917-926, 1969.

Gouras, P.: Color opponency from fovea to striate cortex, Invest. Ophthalmol. **11:**427-432, 1972.

Gouras, P.: Electroretinography: Some basic principles, Invest. Ophthalmol. **9:**557-569, 1970.

Hartline, H. K.: Vision-introduction. In Field, J., editor: Handbook of physiology, vol. 1, Baltimore, 1960, The Williams & Wilkins Co.

Hartline, H. K.: Visual receptors and retinal interaction, Science **164:**270-278, 1969.

Henry, G. H., and Bishop, P. O.: Striate neurons: receptive field organization, Invest. Ophthalmol. **11:**354-368, 1972.

Ingling, C. R.: A tetrachromatic hypothesis for human color vision, Vision Res. **9:**1131-1148, 1969.

Lakowski, R.: Theory and practice of color vision testing, Br. J. Ind. Med. **26:**173-189, 1969.

Marks, W. B., Dobelle, W. H., and MacNichol, E. F.: Visual pigments in single primate cones, Science **143:**1181-1183, 1964.

Poggio, G. F.: Central nervous mechanisms in vision. In Mountcastle, V. B., editor: Medical physiology, ed. 13, St. Louis, 1974, The C. V. Mosby Co.

Riggs, L. A.: Human vision: some objective explorations, Am. Psychol. **31:**125-134, 1976.

Rodrieck, R. W., and Rushton, W. A. H.: Cancellation of red signals by cones and cone signals by rods in the cat retina, J. Physiol. **254:**775-785, 1976.

Ruch, T. C.: Vision. In Ruch, T. C., Patton, H. D., Woodbury, J. W., and Towe, A. L., editors: Neurophysiology, ed. 2, Philadelphia, 1965, W. B. Saunders Company.

Rypps, H.: Color vision, Annu. Rev. Psychol. **20:**193-215, 1969.

Schneider, G. E.: Two visual systems, Science **163:**895-902, 1969.

Steinberg, R. H.: Rod and cone distributions to S-potentials from the cat retina, Vision Res. **9:**1319-1329, 1969.

Steinberg, R. H.: Rod-cone interactions in S-potentials from the cat retina, Vision Res. **9:**1331-1344, 1969.

Steinberg, R. H., and Schmidt, R.: Identification of horizontal cells as S-potential generators in the cat retina by intracellular dye injection, Vision Res. **10:**817-820, 1970.

Svaetichin, G., and MacNichol, E. F.: Retinal mechanisms for chromatic and achromatic vision, Ann. N. Y. Acad. Sci. **74:**385-404, 1958.

Svaetichin, G., Negishi, K., and Fatehchand, R.: Cellular mechanisms of a Young-Hering visual system. In Wolstenholme, G. E., and Knight, J., editors: Ciba Foundation Symposium on physiology and psychology of color vision, London, 1965, J. & A. Churchill, Ltd.

Svaetichin, G., Negishi, K., Fatehchand, R., Drujan, B. D., and DeTesta, A. S.: Nervous function based on interaction between neuronal and nonneuronal elements. In DeRobertis, E. D. P., and Carrea, R., editors: Progress in brain research, vol. 15, New York, 1965, American Elsevier Publishing Co., Inc.

Wald, G.: The photoreceptor process. In Field, J., editor: Handbook of physiology, vol. 1, Baltimore, 1960, The Williams & Wilkins Co.

Wald, G.: The receptors of human color vision, Science **144:**1007-1016, 1964.

Wald, G.: Molecular basis of visual excitation, Science **162:**230-240, 1968.

Westheimer, G.: The eye. In Mountcastle, V. B., editor: Medical physiology, ed. 13, St. Louis, 1974, The C. V. Mosby Co.

Weymouth, F. W.: The eye as an optical instrument. In Ruch, T. C., Patton, H. D., Woodbury, J. W., and Towe, A. L., editors: Neurophysiology, ed. 2, Philadelphia, 1965, W. B. Saunders Company.

Chapter 11

Amatruda, T., Black, D., McKenna, T., McCarley, R., and Hobson, J.: Sleep cycle control and cholinergic mechanisms: differential effects of cabachol injections at pontine brain stem sites, Brain Res. **98:**501-515, 1975.

Aserinsky, E.: Drugs and dreams, a synthesis, Exp. Med. Surg. **25**:131-138, 1967.

Bakan, P.: Dreaming, REM sleep, and the right hemisphere: a theoretical integration, Proc. 2nd Int. Cong. Sleep Res., 1975.

Banquet, J. P.: Spectral analysis of the EEG in meditation, Electroencephalogr. Clin. Neurophysiol. **35**:143-151, 1973.

Broughton, R. J.: Sleep disorders: disorders of arousal? Science **159**:1070-1078, 1968.

Brown, B.: Recognition of aspects of consciousness through associates with EEG activity represented by a light signal, Psychophysiol. **6**:442-452, 1970.

Cedarbaum, J., and Aghayanian, G.: Norodrenergic neurons of the locus ceruleus: inhibition by epinephrine and activation by the α antagonist piperoxane, Brain Res. **112**:413-419, 1976.

Dement, W., Holman, R., and Guilleminault, C.: Neurochemical and neuropharmacological foundations of the sleep disorders, Psychopharmacol. Comm. **2**:77-90, 1976.

Drucker-Colin, R., Spanis, C., Hunyadi, J., Sassin, J., and McGaugh, J.: Growth hormone effects on sleep and wakefulness in the rat, Neuroendocrinol. **18**:1-8, 1975.

Glotzback, S., and Heller, S.: Central nervous regulation of body temperature during sleep, Science **194**:537-539, 1976.

Hart, J.: Autocontrol of EEG alpha, Psychophysiol. **4**:506, 1976, (abstract).

Hösli, L.: Dialysis of sleep and waking factors in blood of the rabbit, Science **146**:796-798, 1964.

Johnson, L. C.: Psychophysiological research: aims and methods, Int. J. Psychiatry Med. **5**:565-573, 1974.

Johnson, L. C.: A psychophysiology for all states, Psychophysiology **6**:501-516, 1970.

Johnson, L. C., Burdick, J. A., and Smith, J.: Sleep during alcohol intake and withdrawal in the chronic alcoholic, Arch. Gen. Psychiatry **22**:406-418, 1970.

Jouvet, M.: Neurophysiology of the states of sleep, Physiol. Rev. **47**:117-177, 1967.

Jouvet, M.: Biogenic amines and the states of sleep, Science **163**:32-41, 1969.

Karczmar, A. G., Longo, V. G., and de Carolis, A. S.: A pharmacological model of paradoxical sleep: the role of cholinergic and monoamine systems, Physiol. Behav. **5**:175-182, 1970.

Kleitman, N.: Sleep and wakefulness, Chicago, 1963, University of Chicago Press.

Kollar, E. J., Pasnau, R. O., Rubin, R. T., Naitoh, P., Slater, G. G., and Kales, A.: Psychological, psychophysiological, and biochemical correlates of prolonged sleep deprivation, Am. J. Psychiatry **126**:488-497, 1969.

Kovacevic, R., and Radulovacki, M.: Monoamine changes in the brain of cats during slow wave sleep, Science **193**:1025-1027, 1976.

Malmo, R. B.: Activation: a neuropsychological dimension, Psychol. Rev. **66**:367-386, 1959.

Mandell, A. J., and Mandell, M. P.: Peripheral hormonal and metabolic correlates of rapid eye movement sleep, Exp. Med. Surg. **27**:224-236, 1969.

McCarley, R., and Hobson, J.: Discharge patterns of cat pontine brain stem neurons during desynchronized sleep, J. Neurophysiol. **38**:751-766, 1975.

McCarley, R., and Hobson, J.: Neuronal excitability modulation over the sleep cycle: a structural and mathematical model, Science **189**:58-60, 1975.

McCarley, R., Hobson, J., and Wyzinski, P.: Sleep cycle oscillation: reciprocal discharge by two brain stem neuronal groups, Science **185**:55-58, 1975.

Monnier, M., Hatt, A., Cueni, L., and Schoenenberger, G.: Humoral transmission of sleep, Pfluegers Arch. **331**:257-265, 1972.

Murray, E. J.: Sleep, dreams and arousal, New York, 1965, Appleton-Century-Crofts.

Nowles. D., and Kamija, J.: The control of electroencepholgraphic alpha rhythms through auditory feedback and the associated mental activity, Psychophysiol. **6**:476-484, 1970.

Orme-Johnson, D.: Autonomic stability and transcendental meditation, Psychosom. Med. **35**:341-349, 1973.

Pagano, R., Rose, R., and Warrenburg, S.: Sleep during transcendental meditation, Science **191**:308-310, 1976.

Pappenheimer, J.: The sleep factor, Sci. Am. **235**:24-29, Aug. 1976.

Pasnau, R. O., Naitoh, P., Stier, S., and Kollar, E. J.: The psychological effects of 205 hours of sleep deprivation, Arch. Gen. Psychiatry **18**:496-505, 1968.

Pivik, T., and Dement, W. C.: Phasic changes in muscular and reflex activity during non-REM sleep, Exp. Neurol. **27**:115-124, 1970.

Plotkin, W.: On the self-regulation of the occipital alpha rhythm: control strategies, states of consciousness, and the role of physiological feedback, J. Exp. Psychol. (Gen.) **105**:109-121, 1976.

Plotkin, W., Mazer, C., and Loewy, D.: Alpha enhancement and the likelihood of an alpha experience, Psychophysiol. **13**:466-471, 1976.

Roberts, W. W., and Robinson, T. C.: Relaxation and sleep induced by warming of preoptic region and anterior hypothalamus in cats, Exp. Neurol. **25**:282-293, 1969.

Rubin, R., and Poland, R.: Synchronies between sleep and endocrine rhythms in man and their statistical evaluation, Psychoneuroendocrinol. **1**:281-290, 1976.

Schwartz, G., Davidson, R. J., and Maer, F.: Right-hemisphere lateralization for emotion in the human brain: interactions with cognition, Science **190**:286-288, 1975.

Siegel, P. V., Gerathewohl, S. J., and Mohler, S. R.: Time-zone effects, Science **164**:1249-1255, 1969.

Vanderlaan, W., Parker, D., Rossman, L., and Vanderlaan, E.: Implications of growth hormone release in sleep, Metabolism **19**:891-897, 1970.

Wallace, R. K.: Physiological effects of transcendental meditation, Science **167:**1751-1754, 1970.

Wallace, R., Benson, H., and Wilson, A.: A wakeful hypometabolic physiologic state, Am. J. Physiol. **221:**795-799, 1971.

Williams, H. L.: The new biology of sleep, J. Psychiatr. Res. **8:**445-478, 1971.

Chapter 12

Albert, D. J., Storlien, L. H., Wood, D. J., and Ehman, G.: Further evidence for a complex system controlling feeding behavior, Physiol. Behav. **5:**1075-1082, 1970.

Antin, J., Gibbs, H., Holt, J., Young, R., and Smith, G.: Cholecystokinin elicits the complete behavioral sequence of satiety in rats, J. Comp. Physiol. Psychol. **89:**784-790, 1975.

Blass, E., Jobaris, R., and Hall, W.: Oropharyngeal control of drinking in rats, J. Comp. Physiol. Psychol. **90:**909-916, 1976.

Blatt, B., and Lyon, M.: The interrelationship of forebrain and midbrain structures involved in feeding behavior, Acta Neurol. Scand. **44:**576-595, 1968.

Buggy, J., and Fisher, A.: Anteroventral third ventricle site of action for angiotensin induced thirst, Pharmacol. Biochem. Behav. **4:**651-660, 1976.

Cannon, W. B.: The wisdom of the body, New York, 1963, W. W. Norton & Co., Inc.

Deutsch, A., and Wang, M.: The stomach as a site for rapid nutrient reinforcement centers, Science **195:**89-90, 1977.

Epstein, A., Kissileff, H., and Stellar, E., editors: The neuropsychology of thirst, New York, 1973, Halsted Press, John Wiley & Sons, Inc.

Eriksson, L., and Fyhrquist, F.: Plasma renin activity following central infusion of angiotensin II and altered CSF sodium concentration in the conscious goat, Acta Physiol. Scand. **98:**209-216, 1976.

Heath, R. G.: Electrical self-stimulation of the brain in man, Am. J. Psychiatry **120:**571-577, 1963.

Hetherington, A. W., and Ranson, S. W.: Hypothalamic lesions and adiposity in the rat. In Isaacson, R. L., editor: Basic readings in neuropsychology, New York, 1964, Harper & Row, Publishers.

Hoebel, B.: Feeding: neural control of intake, Annu. Rev. Psychol. **33:**533-568, 1971.

Holman, G. L.: Intragastric reinforcement effect, J. Comp. Physiol. Psychol. **69:**432-441, 1969.

Jordan, H. A.: Voluntary intragastric feeding: oral and gastric contributions to food intake and hunger in man, J. Comp. Physiol. Psychol. **68:**498-506, 1969.

Koopmans, H.: Jejunal signals in hunger satiety, Behav. Biol. **14:**309-324, 1975.

Leibowitz, S.: Pattern of drinking and feeding produced by hypothalamic norepinephrine injection in the satiated rat, Physiol. Behav. **14:**731-742, 1975.

Leibowitz, S.: Ingestion in the satiated rat: role of alpha and beta receptors in the mediating effects of hypothalamic adrenergic stimulation, Physiol. Behav. **14:**743-754, 1975.

Leung, P. M., and Rogers, Q. R.: Food intake: regulation by plasma amino acid pattern, Life Sci. **8:**1-9, 1969.

Margules, D. L.: Noradrenergic basis of inhibition between reward and punishment in amygdala, J. Comp. Physiol. Psychol. **66:**329-334, 1968.

Margules, D. L.: L-Norepinephrine: a possible synaptic transmitter for the suppression of feeding behavior by satiety. Proceedings of the seventy-seventh American Psychological Association Convention, pp. 205-206, 1969.

Margules, D. L., and Steir, L.: Cholinergic synapses of a perventricular punishment system in the lateral hypothalamus, Am. J. Physiol. **217:**475-480, 1969.

Miller, N. E.: Chemical coding of behavior in the brain, Science **148:**328-338, 1965.

Olds, J., and Milner, P.: Positive reinforcement produced by electrical stimulation of septal area and other regions of rat brain. In Isaacson, R. L., editor: Neuropsychology, New York, 1964, Harper & Row, Publishers.

Olds, J., Travis, R. P., and Schwing, R. C.: Topographical organization of self-stimulation functions, J. Comp. Physiol. Psychol. **53:**23-32, 1960.

Saint-Laurent, J., and Beaugrand, J.: Brain stimulation, reinforcement, and behavior, Rev. Can. Biol. **31**(supp.):193-213, 1972.

Schacter, S.: Obese humans and rats, New York, 1974, Halsted Press, John Wiley & Sons, Inc.

Schacter, S.: Some extraordinary facts about obese humans and rats, Am. Psychol. **26:**129-143, 1970.

Stein, L.: The chemistry of reward and punishment. In Efron, D., Cole, J., Levine, J., and Wittenborn, J., editors: Psychopharmacology: a review of progress, 1957-1967, USPHS Publication No. 1836, Washington, D.C., 1968, U.S. Government Printing Office, pp. 105-123. Also in Leukel, F.: Issues in physiological psychology, St. Louis, 1974, The C. V. Mosby Co.

Stellar, E.: Hunger in man: comparative and physiological studies, Am. Psychol. **22:**105-117, 1967.

Teitelbaum, P., Cheng, M., and Rozin, P.: Development of feeding parallels its recovery after hypothalamic damage, J. Comp. Physiol. Psychol. **67:**430-441, 1969.

Teitelbaum, P., and Cytawa, J.: Spreading depression and recovery from lateral hypothalamic damage, Science **147:**61-63, 1965.

Teitelbaum, P., and Epstein, A.: The lateral hypothalamic syndrome, Psychol. Rev. **69:**74-90, 1962.

Tralor, R. A., and Blackburn, J. G.: Effects of temperature on the electrical activity of hypothalamic feeding centers, Exp. Neurol. **23:**91-101, 1969.

Trowill, J. A., Panksepp, J., and Gandelman, R.: An incentive model of rewarding brain stimulation, Psychol. Rev. **76:**264-281, 1969.

Valenstein, E. S., Cox, V. C., and Kakolewski, J. W.: Reexamination of the role of the hypothalamus in motivation, Psychol. Rev. **77:**16-31, 1970.

Chapter 13

Aprison, M. H., Hingtgen, J. N., and McBride, W. J.: Serotonergic and cholinergic mechanisms during disruption of approach and avoidance behavior, Fed. Proc. **34:**1813-1822, 1975.

Arnold, M. B.: The nature of emotion: selected readings, Baltimore, 1968, Penguin Books, Ltd.

Arnold, M. B.: Emotion, motivation, and the limbic system, Ann. N. Y. Acad. Sci. **159:**1041-1058, 1969.

Bard, P., and Mountcastle, V. B.: Some forebrain mechanisms involved in expression of rage with special reference to suppression of angry behavior. In Isaacson, R. L., editor: Neuropsychology, New York, 1964, Harper & Row, Publishers.

Bindra, D.: A unified interpretation of emotion and motivation, Ann. N. Y. Acad. Sci. **159:**1071-1083, 1969.

Brady, J. V., and Nauta, W. J. H.: Subcortical mechanisms in emotional behavior: affective changes following septal forebrain lesions in the albino rat, J. Comp. Physiol. Psychol. **46:**339-346, 1953 (Bobbs-Merrill Reprint No. P-46).

Cannon, W. B.: Bodily changes in pain, hunger, fear and rage, New York, 1963, Harper & Row, Publishers.

Colpaert, F. C.: The ventromedial hypothalamus and the control of avoidance behavior and aggression: fear hypothesis versus response-suppression theory of limbic system function, Behav. Biol. **15:**27-44, 1975.

Fehr, F. S., and Stern, J. A.: Peripheral physiological variables and emotion: the James-Lange theory revisited, Psychol. Bull. **74:**411-424, 1970.

Freeman, W., and Watts, J.: Psychosurgery, Springfield, Ill., 1942, Charles C Thomas, Publishers.

Fulton, J., and Jacobsen, C.: The functions of the frontal lobes: a comparative study in monkeys, chimpanzees, and man, Adv. Mod. Biol. **4:**113-123, 1935.

Gellhorn, E.: The neurophysiological basis of anxiety: a hypothesis, Perspect. Biol. Med. **8:**488-515, 1965.

Goddard, G. V.: Functions of the amygdala, Psychol. Bull. **62:**89-109, 1964.

Goldstein, M. L.: Physiological theories of emotion: a critical historical review from the standpoint of behavior theory, Psychol. Bull. **69:**23-40, 1968.

Grastyán, E.: Towards a better understanding of human emotion, Impact Sci. Soc. **18:**187-204, 1968.

Hess, W., and Akart, K.: Experimental data on the role of the hypothalamus in mechanisms of emotional behavior, Arch. Neurol. Psychiatry **73:**127-129, 1955.

Hohman, G.: Some effects of spinal cord lesions on experienced emotional feelings, Psychophysiology, **3:**143-156, 1966.

Isaacson, R.: Hippocampal destruction in man and other animals, Neuropsychologia **10:**47-64, 1972.

Isaacson, R. L.: The limbic system, New York, 1974, Plenum Press.

Kaplan, H.: The new sex therapy, New York, 1974, Bruner/Mazel, Inc.

Kievet, J., and Kuypers, H.: Basal forebrain and hypothalamic connection to frontal and parietal cortex in the Rhesus monkey, Science **187:**660-662, 1975.

Kinsey, A., Pomeroy, W., and Martin, C.: Sexual behavior in the male, Philadelphia, 1948, W. B. Saunders Company.

Kinsey, A., Pomeroy, W., Martin, C., and Gebhard, P.: Sexual behavior in the female, Philadelphia, 1953, W. B. Saunders Company.

Kiser, R. S., and Lebovitz, R. M.: Monoaminergic mechanisms in aversive brain stimulation, Physiol. Behav. **15:**47-53, 1975.

McCleary, R. A.: Response-modulating functions of the limbic system: initiation and suppression. In Stellar, E., and Sprague, J. M., editors: Progress in physiological psychology, vol. 1, New York, 1966, Academic Press, Inc.

MacLean, P. D.: Psychosomatic disease and the visceral brain: recent developments bearing on the Papez theory of emotion. In Isaacson, R. L., editor: Neuropsychology, New York, 1964, Harper & Row, Publishers.

Masters, W., and Johnson, V.: Human sexual response, Boston, 1966, Little, Brown & Co.

Melzack, R.: The role of early experience in emotional arousal, Ann. N. Y. Acad. Sci. **159:**721-730, 1969.

Mettler, F. A., editor: Psychosurgical problems, New York, 1952, The Blakiston Co.

Money, J., and Ehrhardt, A.: Man and woman, boy and girl, Baltimore, 1972, Johns Hopkins University Press.

Moyer, K. E.: The psychobiology of aggression, New York, 1976, Harper & Row, Publishers.

Olds, J.: Emotional centers in the brain, Science **156:**87-92, 1967.

Papez, J. W.: A proposed mechanism of emotion. In Isaacson, R. L., editor: Neuropsychology, New York, 1964, Harper & Row, Publishers.

Pribram, K. H.: The new neurology and the biology of emotion: a structural approach, Am. Psychol. 22:830-838, 1967.

Pribram, K. H., and Krüger, L.: Functions of the olfactory brain. In Isaacson, R. L., editor: Neuropsychology, New York, 1964, Harper & Row, Publishers.

Pribram, K. H.: Languages of the brain, Englewood Cliffs, N.J., 1971, Prentice-Hall, Inc.

Reis, D., and Lars-Magnus, G.: Brain catecholamines: relation to the defense reaction evoked by amygdaloid stimulation in cat, Science **149:**450-451, 1965.

Ruch, T. C.: Neurophysiology of emotion. In Ruch, T. C., Patton, H. D., Woodbury, J. W., and Towe, A. L., editors: Neurophysiology, ed. 2, Philadelphia, 1965, W. B. Saunders Company.

Rule, B. G., and Nesdale, A. R.: Emotional arousal and aggressive behavior, Psychol. Bull. **83:**851-863, 1976.

Schacter, S., and Singer, J. E.: Cognitive, social and

physiological determinants of emotional state, Psychol. Rev. **69:**379-399, 1962 (Bobbs-Merrill Reprint No. P-553).

Schreiner, L., and Kling, A.: Behavioral changes following rhinencephalic injury in the cat. In Isaacson, R. L., editor: Neuropsychology, New York, 1964, Harper & Row, Publishers.

Simon, A., Herbert, C. C., and Strauss, R., editors: The physiology of emotions, Springfield, Ill., 1961, Charles C Thomas, Publisher.

Terzian, H., and Ore, G.: Syndrome of Klüver and Bucy reproduced in man by bilateral removal of the temporal lobes, Neurology **5:**373-380, 1955.

Webb, W. B.: A motivational theory of emotions, Psychol. Rev. **55:**329-335, 1948.

Wenger, M. A.: Emotion as visceral activation: an extension of Lange's theory. In Reymert, M. L., editor: Feelings and emotions: The Moosehart symposium, New York, 1950, McGraw-Hill Book Company.

Chapter 14

Bartlett, F., and John, E.: Equipotentiality quantified: the anatomical distribution of the engram, Science **181:**764-767, 1973.

Bennett, E. L., Diamond, M. C., Krech, D., and Rosensweig, M. R.: Chemical and anatomical plasticity of brain, Science **146:**610-619, 1964.

Bogoch, S.: The biochemistry of memory, New York, 1968, Oxford University Press, Inc.

Briggs, M. H., and Kitto, G. B.: The molecular basis of learning and memory, Psychol. Rev. **69:**537-541, 1962.

Byrne, W. L.: Molecular approaches to learning and memory, New York, 1970, Academic Press, Inc.

Carew, T. J., Crow, T. J., and Petrinovich, L. F.: Some problems with the technique of cortical spreading depression. Paper presented at the 1970 Western Psychological Association Convention, Los Angeles, Calif., Dec. 30, 1970.

Deutsch, J. A.: The physiological basis of memory, Annu. Rev. Psychol. **20:**85-104, 1969.

Deutsch, J. A., Hamburg, M. D., and Dahl, H.: Acetylcholinesterase-induced amnesia and its temporal aspects, Science **151:**221-223, 1966.

Dimond, S. J., and Brouwers, E. Y.: Increase in the power of human memory in normal man through the use of drugs, Psychopharmacol. **49:**307-309, 1976.

Doty, R., Negras, N., and Yamaga, K.: The unilateral engram, Acta Neurobiol. Exp. **33:**711-728, 1973.

Duncan, C. P.: The retroactive effects of shock on learning, J. Comp. Physiol. Psychol. **42:**32-34, 1949.

Fishbein, W.: Interference with conversion from short-term to long-term storage by partial sleep deprivation, Comp. Behav. Biol. **5:**171-175, 1970.

Fishbein, W., McGaugh, J. L., and Swarz, J. R.: Retrograde amnesia: electroconvulsive shock effects after termination of rapid eye movement sleep deprivation, Science **172:**80-82, 1971.

Gaito, J.: A biochemical approach to learning and memory, Psychol. Rev. **68:**285-292, 1961.

Gaito, J.: DNA and RNA as memory molecules, Psychol. Rev. **70:**471-480, 1963.

Gaito, J., editor: Macromolecules and behavior, New York, 1966, Appleton-Century-Crofts.

Gaito, J., and Zavala, A.: Neurochemistry and learning, Psychol. Bull. **61:**45-61, 1964.

Gazzaniga, M. S.: The bisected brain, New York, 1970, Appleton-Century-Crofts.

Geschwin, N.: The organization of language and the brain, Science **170:**940-944, 1969.

Glickman, S. E.: Perseverative neural processes and consolidation of the memory trace, Psychol. Bull. **58:**218-233, 1961.

Glickstein, M.: Neurophysiology of learning and memory. In Ruch, T. C., Patton, H. D., Woodbury, J. W., and Towe, A. L., editors: Neurophysiology, ed. 2, Philadelphia, 1965, W. B. Saunders Company.

Greenburn, R., and Pearlman, C.: Cutting the REM nerve: an approach to the adaptive role of REM sleep, Perspect. Biol. Med. **17:**513-521, 1974.

Guirgea, C.: The pharmacology of paracetem [UCB6215]: a nootropic drug. Report UCB-Pharm. Division DRDM, rue Berkendael 58, Brussels, Belgium, 1971.

Hebb, D. O.: The organization of behavior, New York, 1961, Science Editions, Inc.

Hostetter, G.: Hippocampal lesions in rats weaken the retrograde amnesic effect of ECS, J. Comp. Physiol. Psychol. **66:**349-353, 1968.

Hudspeth, W. J., and Gerbrandt, L. K.: Electroconvulsive shock: conflict, consolidation, and neuroanatomical functions, Psychol. Bull. **63:**377-383, 1965.

Hudspeth, W. J., McGaugh, J. L., and Thompson, C. W.: Aversive and amnesic effects of electroconvulsive shock, J. Comp. Physiol. Psychol. **57:**61-64, 1964.

Hutt, L. D., and Elliot, L.: Chemical transfer of learned fear: failure to replicate Ungar, Psychosom. Sci. **18:**57-59, 1970.

Jacobson, A., Babich, F., Bubash, S., and Jacobson, A.: Differential approach tendencies produced by injection of ribonucleic acid from trained rats, Science **150:**636-637, 1965.

Kimble, D. P.: The anatomy of memory, Palo Alto, Calif., 1965, Science & Behavior Books, Inc.

Lashley, K.: In search of the engram, Symp. Soc. Exp. Biol. **4:**425-482, 1950.

Luttges, M., Johnson, T., Buck, C., Holland, J., and McGaugh, J.: An examination of "transfer of learning" by nucleic acid, Science **151:**834-837, 1966.

McConnell, J. V., Jacobson, A. L., and Kimble, D. P.: The effects of regeneration upon retention of a conditioned response in the planarian, J. Comp. Physiol. Psychol. **52:**1-5, 1959 (Bobbs-Merrill Reprint No. P-222).

McGaugh, J. L.: Time-dependent processes in memory storage, Science **153:**1351-1358, 1966.

McGaugh, J. L.: Analysis of memory transfer and enhancement, Proc. Am. Philosoph. Soc. **111:**347-351, 1967.

McGaugh, J. L.: Drug facilitation of learning and memory. In Effron, D. H., editor: Proceedings of the Sixth Annual Meeting of the American College of Neuropsychopharmacology, Dec. 12-15, 1967.

McGaugh, J. L.: A multi-trace view of memory storage processes, Atti Accad. Naz. Lincei Rend. **109:**13-24, 1968.

McGaugh, J. L., and Dawson, R. G.: Modification of memory storage processes, Behav. Sci. **16:**45-63, 1971.

Miller, N. E.: Learning of visceral and glandular responses, Science **163:**434-445, 1969.

Miller, R. R., Small, D., and Berk, A. M.: Informational content of rat acotophobin, Behav. Biol. **15:**463-472, 1975.

Milner, B.: Visual recognition and recall after right temporal-lobe excision in man, Neuropsychologia **6:**191-209, 1968.

Milner, B. V., Branch, C., and Rasmussen, T.: Evidence for bilateral speech representation in some non-right-handers, Trans. Am. Neurol. Assoc. **91:**306-308, 1966.

Olds, J.: Ten milliseconds into the brain, Princeton, N.J., 1965, D. Van Nostrand Co., Inc.

Pearlman, C., and Becker, M.: Brief posttrial REM sleep deprivation impairs discrimination learning in rats, Physiol. Psychol. **1:**373-376, 1973.

Potts, A., and Bitterman, M. E.: Puromycin and retention in goldfish, Science **158:**1594-1596, 1967.

Robbins, K., and McAdam, D.: Interhemispheric alpha symmetry and imagery mode, Brain and Language **1:**189-193, 1974.

Rosensweig, M. R.: Environmental complexity, cerebral change and behavior, Am. Psychol. **21:**321-332, 1966.

Rosensweig, M. R., Krech, D., and Bennett, E. L.: A search for relations between brain chemistry and behavior, Psychol. Bull. **57:**476-492, 1960.

Rosensweig, M. R., Love, W., and Bennett, E. L.: Effects of a few hours a day of enriched experience on brain chemistry and brain weights, Physiol. Behav. **3:**819-825, 1968.

Russell, W. R.: Brain, memory, learning, Oxford, England, 1959, The Clarendon Press.

Schacter, S.: Some extraordinary facts about obese humans and rats, Am. Psychol. **26:**129-144, 1970. Also in Leukel, F.: Issues in physiological psychology, St. Louis, 1974, The C. V. Mosby Co.

Schiffrin, R. M., and Atkinson, R. C.: Storage and retrieval processes in long-term memory, Psychol. Rev. **76:**179-193, 1969.

Schmitt, F. O.: Molecules and memory, New Scientist **23:**643-645, 1965.

Selnes, O.: The corpus callosum: some anatomical and functional considerations with special reference to language, Brain and Language **1:**111-139, 1974.

Smith, D. D.: Mammalian learning and behavior, Philadelphia, 1965, W. B. Saunders Company.

Sperry, R. W.: Cerebral organization and behavior, Science **133:**1749-1757, 1961.

Stegnick, A. J.: The clinical use of piracetam: a new nootropic drug. The treatment of symptoms of senile involution. Arzneimittel-Forsch and Drug. Res. **22:**975-977, 1972.

Thompson, R. F.: The search for the engram, Am. Psychol. **31:**209-227, 1976.

Ungar, G.: Chemical transfer of learned behavior, Agent Action **1:**155-163, 1970.

Ungar, G., Gelson, L., and Clark, R. H.: Chemical transfer of learned fear, Nature **217:**1259-1261, 1968.

Wallace, P.: Animal behavior: the puzzle of flavor aversion, Science **193:**989-991, 1976.

Wechroth, J., and Mikkonen, H.: On the effect of UCB6215 on certain intellectual, perceptual, and psychomotor performance traits and traits of subjectively rated mental state. Communications of the 30th International Congress on Alcoholism and Drug Dependence, Sept. 1972, Amsterdam, The Netherlands.

Chapter 15

Ax, A. F., Bamfors, J. L., Beckett, P. G. S., Domino, E. F., and Gottleib, J. S.: Autonomic response patterning of chronic schizophrenics, Psychosom. Med. **31:**353-364, 1969.

Benerová, O.: Neurophysiological and biochemical aspects in the action of antidepressant drugs, Active. Nerv. Sup. **12:**222-234, 1970.

Berger, ,F. M.: Mental disease and the drugs affecting it, Prospect. Biol. Med. **13:**31-44, 1969.

Berry, H. K.: Hereditary disorders of amino acid metabolism associated with mental deficiency, Ann. N. Y. Acad. Sci. **166:**66-73, 1969.

Bliss, E. L., and Ailion, J.: The effect of lithium on brain monoamines, Brain Res. **24:**305-310, 1970.

Bloom, F., Segal, D., Ling, N., and Guilleman, R.: Endorphins: profound behavioral effects in rats suggest new etiological factors in mental illness, Science **194:**630-632, 1976.

Boakes, R. J., Bradley, P. B., Briggs, I., and Dray, A.: Antagonism of 5-hydroxytryptamine by LSD 25 in the central nervous system: a possible neuronal basis for the actions of LSD 25, Br. Med. J. Pharmacol. **40:**202-218, 1970.

Boullin, D. J., Coleman, M., O'Brien, R. A., and Rimland, B.: Laboratory predictions of infantile autism based on 5-hydroxytryptamine efflux from blood platelets and their correlation with the Rimland E-2 score, J. Autism Childh. Schizophrenia **1:**63-71, 1971.

Brady, R. O.: Inherited metabolic diseases of the nervous system, Science **193:**733-739, 1976.

Calloway, N. O.: The concept of biological half-life in relation to senescence, J. Am. Geriatr. Soc. **17:**974-978, 1969.

Clancy, H., and McBride, G.: The autistic process and its treatment, J. Child Psychol. Psychiat. **10**:233-244, 1970.

Cochin, J.: Possible mechanisms in the development of tolerance, Fed. Proc. **29**:19-27, 1970.

Cohen, G., and Collins, M.: Alkaloids from catecholamines in adrenal tissue: possible role in alcoholism, Science **167**:1749-1751, 1970.

Comfort, A.: Biological theories of aging, Hum. Dev. **13**:127-139, 1970.

Davis, B. D.: Prospects for genetic intervention in man, Science **170**:1279-1283, 1970.

Dole, V. P.: Biochemistry of addiction, Annu. Rev. Biochem. **39**:821-840, 1970.

Dietrich, R. A.: Biochemical aspects of alcoholism, Psychoneuroendocrinol. **1**:325-346, 1976.

Eiduson, S., Geller, E., Yuwiler, A., and Eiduson, B. T.: Biochemistry and behavior, Princeton, N.J., 1964, D. Van Nostrand Co., Inc.

Farnsworth, N. R.: Hallucinogenic plants, Science **162**:1086-1092, 1968.

Fuller, J. L.: Experimental deprivation and later behavior, Science **158**:1645-1652, 1967.

Gershon, S.: Lithium in mania, Clin. Pharmacol. Ther. **11**:168-187, 1970.

Goel, N. S., and Yoas, M.: The error catastrophe hypothesis with reference to aging and the evolution of the protein synthesizing machinery, J. Theoret. Biol. **55**:245-282, 1975.

Hartman, E.: Pharmacological studies of sleep and dreaming: chemical and clinical relationships, Biol. Psychiatry **1**:243-258, 1969.

Heston, L. L.: The genetics of schizophrenic and schizoid disease, Science **167**:249-256, 1970.

Himwich, H. E., and Alpers, H. S.: Psychopharmacology, Annu. Rev. Pharmacol. **10**:313-334, 1970.

Hollister, L. E.: Marijuana in man: three years later, Science **172**:21-29, 1971.

Johnson, F. G.: LSD in the treatment of alcoholism, Am. J. Psychiatry **126**:481-487, 1969.

Johnson, L. C., Burdick, J. A., and Smith, J.: Sleep during alcohol intake and withdrawal in the chronic alcoholic, Arch. Gen. Psychiatry **22**:406-418, 1970.

Larsen, J. R., Lindberg, M. L., and Skovgaard, B.: Sleep deprivation as a treatment for endogenous depression, Acta. Psychiatry Scand. **54**:167,173, 1976.

Loew, D. M., and Taeschler, M.: Profiles of activity of psychotropic drugs: a way to predict therapeutic effects, Int. Pharmacopsychiatry **1**:1-20, 1968.

Matthysse, S. W., and Kidd, K. K.: Estimating the genetic contribution to schizophrenia, Am. J. Psychiatry **133**:185-191, 1976.

Meier-Ruge, W.: Experimental pathology and pharmacology in brain research and aging, Life Sciences **17**:1627-1636, 1976.

Mechoulam, R.: Marijuana chemistry, Science **168**:1159-1166, 1970.

Mirsky, A. F.: Neurophysiological bases of schizophrenia, Annu. Rev. Psychol. **20**:321-348, 1969.

Pauling, L.: Orthomolecular psychiatry, Science **160**:265-271, 1968.

Pollin, W., Martin, G. A., Hoffer, A., Stabenau, J. E., and Hrubec, Z.: Psychopathology in 15,909 pairs of veteran twins: evidence for a genetic factor in the pathogenesis of schizophrenia and its relative absence in psychoneurosis, Am. J. Psychiatry **126**:43-56, 1969.

Praag, H. M.: Monoamines and depression, pharmakopsychiat. Neuro-Pharm. **2**:151-160, 1969.

Rabkin, J. G., and Struening, E. L.: Life events, stress, and illness, Science **194**:1013-1020, 1976.

Ritvo, E. R., Yuwiler, A., Geller, E., Ornitz, E. M., Saeger, K., and Plotkin, S.: Increased blood serotonin and platelets in early infantile autism, Arch. Gen. Psychiatry **23**:566-572, 1970.

Rosenthal, S. H., and Wulfson, N. L.: Electrosleep: a preliminary communication, J. Nerv. Ment. Dis. **151**:146-151, 1970.

Schwartz, A. S., and Eidelberg, E.: Role of biogenic amines in morphine dependence, Life Sci. **9**:613-624, 1970.

Selye, H.: The physiology and pathology of exposure to stress, Montreal, 1960, Acta, Inc.

Selye, H.: Adaptive steroids: retrospect and prospect, Prospect. Biol. Med. **13**:343-363, 1970.

Selye, H.: Stress and aging, J. Am. Geriatr. Soc. **18**:669-680, 1970.

Skalickova, O., Dejmal, V., and Pavlovski, P.: A study of the families of schizophrenics from the genetic aspect, Acta Univ. Carol. (Med.) **15**:343-363, 1969.

Snyder, S., Banerjeer, S., Yamamura, H., and Greenberg, D.: Drugs, neurotransmitters, and schizophrenia, Science **184**:1243-1253, 1974.

Stein, L., and Wise, C. D.: Possible etiology of schizophrenia: progressive damage to the noradrenergic reward system by 6-hydroxydopamine, Science **171**:1032-1036, 1971.

Svendsen, K.: Sleep deprivation therapy in depression, Acta. Psychiatr. Scand. **54**:184-192, 1976.

Towbin, A.: Mental retardation due to germinal matrix infarction, Science **164**:156-162, 1969.

Weil, A. T., Zinberg, N. E., and Nelsen, J. M.: Clinical and psychological effects of marijuana in man, Science **162**:1234-1242, 1968.

Winokur, G.: Genetic findings and methodological considerations in manic-depressive disease, Br. J. Psychiatry **117**:267-274, 1970.

Wynder, E. L., and Hoffman, D.: Experimental tobacco carcinogenesis, Science **162**:862-871, 1968.

Zigler, E.: Familial mental retardation: a continuing dilemma, Science **155**:292-298, 1967.

Zubek, J. P.: Sensory deprivation: fifteen years of research, New York, 1969, Appleton-Century-Crofts.

Index